PROCEEDINGS OF THE

BRITISH ACADEMY

VOLUME LXVII

1981

LONDON

PUBLISHED FOR THE BRITISH ACADEMY

BY THE OXFORD UNIVERSITY PRESS

1982

The papers contained in this volume are issued as separate booklets and can be obtained from the British Academy, 20–21 Cornwall Terrace, Regent's Park, London NW1 4QP. Many off-prints from earlier volumes are also available from the same address; and photocopies can normally be supplied of items for which printed stock is no longer held.

Published in the United States by
Oxford University Press, New York

**British Library Cataloguing
in Publication Data**

British Academy
    The proceedings of the British Academy.—
    Vol. 67 (1981) 1. Humanities—Periodicals
    I. Title
    001.3'05   AS121
    ISBN 0 19 726015 2

*Printed in Great Britain
at the University Press, Oxford
by Eric Buckley
Printer to the University*

CONTENTS

CONTENTS

LIST OF ILLUSTRATIONS

OFFICERS AND COUNCIL
1981-2

President
THE REVD PROFESSOR W. O. CHADWICK, KBE

Vice-Presidents
PROFESSOR E. ULLENDORFF
PROFESSOR H. W. R. WADE, QC

Council
[81] PROFESSOR G. W. S. BARROW
[79] THE REVD PROFESSOR G. B. CAIRD
[80] PROFESSOR R. DAHRENDORF
[79] PROFESSOR R. H. C. DAVIS
[81] PROFESSOR E. A. GELLNER
[80] PROFESSOR J. R. HALE
[79] PROFESSOR M. B. HESSE
[81] DR D. M. LEWIS
[79] PROFESSOR F. G. B. MILLAR
[81] PROFESSOR F. R. PALMER
[80] PROFESSOR J. K. S. ST. JOSEPH, CBE
[81] PROFESSOR F. M. L. THOMPSON
[80] DR A. W. TYSON
[79] PROFESSOR E. ULLENDORFF
[81] PROFESSOR H. W. R. WADE, QC

Treasurer
PROFESSOR P. MATHIAS

Foreign Secretary
PROFESSOR E. W. HANDLEY

Publications Secretary
PROFESSOR G. R. ELTON

Secretary
MR J. P. CARSWELL, CB

[79] Elected 1979   [80] Elected 1980   [81] Elected 1981

PROCEEDINGS OF THE

BRITISH ACADEMY

1981

REPORT OF COUNCIL 1980–1981

THIS Report covers the year between the Annual General Meetings of July 1980 and July 1981. Part I gives a brief summary of the main events during the year, and Parts II and III describe the Academy's activities in greater detail.

PART I

OFFICERS

1. The Academy's honorary officers for the year were: President, Sir Kenneth Dover; Treasurer, Professor P. Mathias; Foreign Secretary, Professor E. W. Handley; Publications Officer, Professor J. M. Wallace-Hadrill. The Revd Professor W. O. Chadwick and Professor E. Ullendorff were nominated Vice-Presidents.

THE FELLOWSHIP

2. During the year the Academy lost ten Ordinary and eighteen Corresponding Fellows by death. The Ordinary Fellows were Professor J. A. W. Bennett, Sir Rupert Cross, Professor W. K. C. Guthrie, the Revd Professor G. W. H. Lampe, Professor R. Pascal, Professor E. J. W. Simon, Professor E. T. Stokes, Mr S. Strelcyn, Dame Lucy Sutherland, and Mr J. B. Ward-Perkins; and the Corresponding Fellows were Professor A. Alföldi, Professor L. Bieler, Professor J. Filip, the Very Revd Dr G. Florovsky, Professor F. L. Ganshof, Professor A. Gerschenkron, Professor R. T. Hallock, Professor W. Jaffé, the Revd Professor Dr H. Jedin, Professor W. K. Jordan, Professor W. Kunkel, Professor J. F. Lemarignier, Professor Dr A. Lesky, Professor A. J. Marder, Professor Dr K. Michalowski, Professor A. Parrot, Professor T. Parsons, and Professor Dr L. Raiser.

3. Twenty-one Ordinary and seven Corresponding Fellows, and two Honorary Fellows, were elected in July 1981. The Ordinary Fellows were Professor J. L. Ackrill, Dr F. R. Allchin, Professor J. A. Barnes, Professor Averil Cameron, Professor A. C. Graham, Professor F. H. Hinsley, Professor J. P. Kenyon, Dr E. Miller, Professor M. Morishima, Professor D. M. Nicol, Professor S. S. Prawer, Dr J. R. Rea, Professor A. L. F. Rivet, Mr B. W. Robinson, Professor J. D. Sargan, Professor M. A. Screech, Professor Q. R. D. Skinner, Dr B. H. I. H. Stewart, Professor Lord Wedderburn of Charlton, the Revd Professor M. R. Wiles, and Dr D. M. Wilson; the Corresponding Fellows were Professor I. B. Cohen, Professor D. H. Davidson, Professor P. Lemerle, Professor M. Rodinson, Professor T. Scitovsky, Mr H. M. Seervai, and Professor E. T. Vermeule; and the Honorary Fellows were the Rt. Hon. Harold Macmillan and Sir Peter Medawar.

4. On 2 July 1981, with the new elections, the Fellowship stood at 433 Ordinary Fellows (of whom 132 were Senior Fellows), 267 Corresponding Fellows, and nine Honorary Fellows.

5. The Annual Dinner was held in the Middle Temple Hall on 2 July 1981, following the Annual General Meeting. The guest speech was given by Lord Todd, OM, FRS.

FINANCE

6. The statement of accounts for the year ending 31 March 1981 appears as an appendix to this report. Comparison with the figures under main heads for earlier years shows that the upward trend of research expenditure as a proportion of the Academy's expenditure has now ceased, and has stabilized at about 28.5 per cent. The proportion of expenditure claimed by Schools and Institutes, though still more than half the total, eased further, largely because of political conditions in Iran and Afghanistan. On the other hand, expenditure on overseas exchange programmes increased to 6.4 per cent of the total, in response to the operation of additional agreements with overseas organizations.

7. Administrative costs were stable at under 9 per cent of total expenditure, despite substantial salary awards which fell to be met during the year. Since full loadings at more senior levels of the secretariat have now been reached, the marginal administrative cost of further expansion of the Academy's work would be relatively high. The impending occupation of new premises, which will probably be completed by the time this report appears, will require a rearrangement of our accounts which up to now have shown the occupation costs of our present rent-free premises as part of our administrative charges. The rent and other outgoings on our new premises, which will be recognized by an addition to our grant, will in future be shown under a separate premises head.

8. Publication expenditure rose, reflecting higher costs and an increased number of titles published. Sales income also rose substantially, but for the second year in succession it was necessary to draw on reserves. Energetic steps are being taken to contain costs by the adoption of new methods of production. Only then can the Academy in future sustain its large publishing commitments without encroaching upon the support it gives elsewhere.

9. The following summary shows the comparison with 1979/80.

TABLE I: INCOME

	1981 £	1980 £
Government Grant received	2,172,410	(1,803,000)
Other Income (excluding publication income)	48,140	(31,636)
	2,220,550	(1,834,636)

TABLE II: EXPENDITURE

	1981 £	1980 £
Schools and Institutes	1,185,560	(1,021,000)
Research	639,519	(527,984)
Overseas work of the Academy	143,772	(114,288)
Publication (net of sales)	77,526*	(27,637)
Administration and General Expenses	196,523	(150,655)
Exchange of delegation with Chinese Academy	1,618	(11,000)
	2,244,518	(1,852,564)

   * After a decrease of £29,801 in provision for future publications (£43,247 in the previous year).

10. It may be of interest to repeat the comparison over two years, which was last made in the report for 1978-9. The earlier comparison showed an increase of trial expenditure over the previous two years of £599,000 or 58 per cent. Between 1978-9 and 1980-1 the increase was not much more in money terms (£609,000) and in percentage terms was substantially less (37 per cent).

ACCOMMODATION

11. Detailed conditions were settled for the lease of 20-2 Cornwall Terrace, and work on converting the premises for the Academy began. The accommodation, besides adequate office space, will include a Council Room, two other committee rooms, and a Fellows' Library which will house the Academy's growing collection of books. There will also be a lecture theatre of approximately the same capacity as our present one, with very much better acoustics.

PUBLICATIONS

12. Apart from the annual *Proceedings*, eleven titles were published during the year, in addition to off-prints of lectures and memoirs. They were: Classical and Medieval Logic Texts, Volume III, *Al-Farabi's Commentary and Short Treatise on Aristotle's 'De Interpretatione'*; Corpus Vasorum Antiquorum, Canada: *Royal Ontario Museum, Ontario*; *Dictionary of Medieval Latin from British Sources, Fascicule II, C*; Early English Church Music, Volume 24, *Christopher Tye: II: Masses*; *The Emergence of Man* (a joint publication with the Royal Society); *The Index to the Proceedings of the British Academy, Volumes I-LXIII*; Oriental Documents, Volume III, *The Archive of Yogyakarta* (Volume I); *Revised Medieval Latin Word-List from British and Irish Sources with Supplement*; Sylloge of Coins of the British Isles, Volume 26, *Museums in East Anglia*, Volume 28, *Index to Volumes I-XX*; Sylloge Nummorum

Graecorum, *Ashmolean Museum, Oxford* (Volume V), *Paconia–Thessaly* (Part 4).

LECTURES

13. The lectures delivered at the Academy during the year have been published in the appropriate volumes of the *Proceedings* and separately.

1981 MEDALS AND PRIZES

14. The Burkitt Medal for Biblical Studies was awarded to Professor G. B. Caird; the Derek Allen Prize (for achievements, on this occasion, in numismatics) to M. Jean-Baptiste Colbert de Beaulieu; the Sir Israel Gollancz Prize (in English Studies) to Mr A. J. Aitken; the Kenyon Medal (for Classical Studies) to Professor A. D. Momigliano; the Rose Mary Crawshay Prize (for English Literature) to Dr Helen Peters for her edition of Donne's *Paradoxes and Problems*; and the Serena Medal (for Italian Studies) to Professor Giulio Einaudi.

OVERSEAS SCHOOLS AND INSTITUTES; SPONSORED SOCIETIES

15. Grants-in-aid to a number of British research institutes overseas have been administered through the Academy since 1952. The Standing ˋCommittee on the Schools and Institutes advises Council and governing bodies on financial and other matters. It allocates grants-in-aid—listed on p. 30—to the nine autonomous Schools and Institutes (at Amman, Ankara, Athens, Baghdad, Jerusalem, Kabul, Nairobi, Rome, and Tehran), to the Institute at Singapore, which is under direct Academy control, and to the four Sponsored Societies (the Council for British Archaeology, the English Place-Name Society, the Egypt Exploration Society, and the Society for Libyan Studies).

The Standing Committee, chaired by the President, consisted of the Academy's officers, the Chairman of its Archaeology Section, Lord Brimelow, Lord Roll, and Sir Toby Weaver. During the year Sir Donald Barron replaced Lord Roll, whose term ended in August.

As will be seen from its report, the newly established Institute at Amman has flourished since it was given full autonomy in March 1980. Reports by this and the other thirteen bodies are to be found on pp. 30–49.

OVERSEAS RELATIONS

16. In addition to making grants in support of private research overseas, the Academy enjoys a wide range of contacts with foreign institutions, including formal Exchange Agreements with nine overseas Academies. During the year two new Agreements came into effect. The first was with the Academy of Sciences of the GDR and a number of visits took place successfully in each direction. The second, signed jointly on the British side by the Academy and the Social Science Research Council, was with the Chinese Academy of Social Sciences in Peking. During the

course of the year approval was given for twenty-five visits to China under the exchange programme and nominations were made. On the Chinese side there was some initial delay in making nominations, but towards the end of the year under review four nominations were received. Not all British nominations were accepted by the Chinese Academy and discussions proceeded on the kinds of facilities that could be made available for British scholars engaged in work on China. There was an hiatus in relations with the Academy of Sciences of the USSR following the rejection without explanation of two British nominations. It was eventually agreed to receive a delegation from the Soviet Academy to discuss the difficulties that had been experienced in operating the Agreement, and the discussions concluded in agreement to resume exchange relations.

LEVERHULME VISITING PROFESSORSHIPS AND FELLOWSHIPS

17. Two 1980/1 Leverhulme Visiting Professorships were awarded during the year under the new scheme of awards generously funded by the Leverhulme Trust. The Professorships are designed to support, for a period of up to three months, senior scholars who wish to pursue their research in overseas countries (other than China and the countries of Eastern Europe with which the Academy has formal Exchange Agreements).

WOLFSON FELLOWSHIPS

18. Fifteen Fellowships were awarded in 1980/1 from funds made available by the Wolfson Foundation for research in the fields of history, law, economics, and political studies. The Fellowships, tenable for periods of between three and nine months, are designed for younger British and continental scholars. The 1980/1 awards were made to four British, one German, one Finnish, one Swedish, and eight Italian scholars. The British Academy gratefully acknowledges the generous support provided by the Wolfson Foundation for this programme over the past six years. Funds remain to permit awards for one more year.

THANK-OFFERING TO BRITAIN FUND EUROPEAN RESEARCH FELLOWSHIPS

19. This Fund was given to the Academy in 1965 by refugees from Nazi oppression as a token of gratitude to Britain. Applications for Fellowships tenable during 1978/9 were restricted to scholars of forty years of age or under, whose subject of research was within the humanities or social sciences. The Fellowships were tenable in any European country apart from the UK. At its meeting in June 1979 the Committee decided that from 1980 Fellowships should be open to scholars of any age, and tenable in the UK as well. Preference would be given to projects of contemporary importance.

In 1980/1 two Fellowships were awarded:

Dr D. McMahon: A biography of Eamon de Valera, 1882 to 1975.

Ms J. Seaton: Broadcasting and political change in Britain during the Second World War.

UNION ACADÉMIQUE INTERNATIONALE

20. The Annual Meeting was held in Budapest from 14 to 20 June 1981. The Academy was represented by Professor C. H. Wilson and the Secretary. The Academy continued to collaborate in the nine UAI projects listed in the 1978/9 report.

EUROPEAN SCIENCE FOUNDATION

21. Professor C. H. Wilson succeeded Professor Sir Eric Turner as the Academy's representative on the Standing Committee for the Humanities; Professor J. Lyons continued to serve as the Academy's representative on the Standing Committee for the Social Sciences. As in previous years, the Academy supported the ESF Additional Activities in Byzantine Studies, the Tsao Tang Scriptures, and the Chinese Theory of the State.

PART II

AWARDS MADE UNDER THE ACADEMY'S SCHEMES FOR THE SUPPORT OF RESEARCH

1. *From Government grant and general funds: for the subvention of research in the humanities by individual scholars*

Mr D. A. Andrews: Excavation and research at Breno, Italy

Dr P. Andrews: A survey of princely tents in India

Dr P. Ashdown: Marcus Garvey and the politics of Belize

Mr A. Aspinall: Study of medieval ceramics by traditional methods

Dr P. G. Bahn: The economic prehistory of the Spanish Pyrenees

Dr G. J. Bamber: The effects of technical change on management/employee relations in retailing in Britain and Sweden

Dr A. M. Birrell: Courtly love poetry in early medieval China

Mr H. M. Blake: Medieval and modern pottery found in Assisi

Dr P. H. Blyth: Persian and Scythian arrows, 530–460 BC

Professor J. Boardman and D. C. Kurtz: A third year of work at completing a bibliography and basic descriptions from publications of Athenian figure decorated vases

Mr R. J. Bradley: A fifth season of re-excavation at South Lodge Camp, Wiltshire

Dr J. A. Brand: The development of Andalusian consciousness

Dr S. Bruce: A sociological study of British Fundamentalism

Dr R. Canzio: Tibetan liturgies in the Bonpo community

Dr R. J. Carwardine: Protestant evangelism and politics in the United States in the 1840s

Dr W. G. Cavanagh and Dr R. R. Laxton: Accurate measured surveys of five Late Minoan Corbel-Vaulted Tombs

Mr R. A. Chambers: Romano-British burial practices

Mr J. D. Charmley: British policy towards General de Gaulle

Dr C. P. Courtney: The correspondence of Benjamin Constant

Dr R. L. S. Cowley: To publish a monograph on Hogarth's 'Marriage à la Mode'

Professor J. E. Cross: The sources of *The Old English Martyrology*

Professor B. W. Cunliffe (1): A twelfth season of excavation at Danebury, Hampshire

Professor B. W. Cunliffe (2): A third season of excavation at Hengistbury Head, Dorset

Dr C. A. Curwen: A bibliography of Western language materials relating to the Taiping Rebellion in China

Miss B. De Cardi: A survey in the southern enclave of Ras al-Khaimah, United Arab Emirates

Dr M. A. Di Gregorio: Cataloguing of Charles Darwin's library

Professor C. R. Dodwell: Provision of colour plates for a book on Anglo-Saxon art

Mr M. K. Durkin: To establish the provenance of building stones at Knossos

Mrs E. S. Eames: Continued work on the Census of Medieval Tiles

Dr R. Eatwell: Poujadism in France in the 1950s

Mrs M. Edwards: Medieval cross-bearing grave slabs of Lancashire and Cumbria

Mr J. R. Fairbrother: Preparation of the final report on the excavation of the late Saxon and medieval manor of Faccombe, Hampshire

Mr A. M. Fleming: Continued investigation of the prehistoric land boundaries of Dartmoor

Dr J. M. Fletcher: The internal accounts of Merton College, Oxford

Dr G. Fowden: Late Roman paganism

Dr J. D. M. Freeberne: Tang settlements in China and Hong Kong

Dr M. G. Fulford: Further excavations at the Forum-Basilica, Silchester

Professor J. Gardner: Papal and cardinals' tombs and cardinals' seals in France

Mr E. Garrison: An edition of the handwritten files of the Garrison Collection of early medieval manuscript painting in Italy

Dr M. T. Gibson: The manuscripts of Boethius

Mr C. G. Gilbert: Georgian vernacular furniture

Dr J. Gooch: Army and state in Italy, 1870 to 1915

Dr P. Gordon: The papers of the fifth Earl Spencer, 1835 to 1910

Mr J. M. Gray: Tennyson's *Idylls of the King*

Dr H. S. Green: Palaeolithic settlements in Wales

Professor N. G. L. Hammond: The history of Macedonia

Dr R. J. Harrison: A second season of excavation at Moncin, Borja, northern Spain

Dr M. Henig: Roman engraved gems

Dr A. K. Henry: A study of watermarks in the *Biblia Pauperum*

Dr N. J. Higham: The excavation and publication of Tatton township

Professor R. Hinton Thomas: Nietzsche and Weimar Germany

Dr R. A. Hodges: Further excavation of the early medieval monastic site at San Vincenzo al Volturno, Italy

Professor J. C. Holt: Continued work on an edition of the 'acta' of Henry II and Richard I and members of their family

Mr M. S. F. Hood: Mason's marks in ancient Crete

Dr J. Hook: The Sienese ruling élite, 1525 to 1560

Mr J. C. Irwin: Origins of monumental art in India

Professor G. D. B. Jones: Further investigation of the pre-Hadrianic Solway Frontier

Dr R. F. J. Jones: A third season's investigation of ancient settlement on the coastal plain of Ampurdan, north-east Spain

Professor E. M. Jope: Defensive works of the eleventh century in Britain

Dr G. Kay: Urbanisation in Zimbabwe

Mr H. R. Kedward: The French Maquis

Dr J. P. C. Kent: Preparation for publication of the late D. F. Allen's catalogue of Continental Celtic coins

Mr J. R. Kenyon: Fortifications in Ireland

Mr A. Killick: Excavation at Udruh, southern Jordan

Dr R. K. Kindersley: Russian perceptions of the French Revolution

Dr R. C. Lane: Nineteenth century Russian Catholics in France

Mrs H. Lawrence: The life and work of John Speed, 1552 to 1629

Mr R. G. Lawson: A survey of archaeological collections for the study of early music

Mr J. A. Lloyd: Further excavation at the Matrice Roman villa, Molise, Italy

Mr F. I. Lowe and Mrs L. Murdin: Horrocks and 17th century astronomy before Newton

Dr M. G. Lyttelton: To continue investigation of the complex of Roman buildings at Le Mura di S. Stefano, Anguillara

Miss J. E. Mann: Preparation of a report on objects from Flaxengate, Lincoln

Mrs S. Markham: John Loveday, scholar and antiquary, 1711 to 1789

Dr V. A. Maxfield: Excavation at Camelon Roman Forts, Stirlingshire

Dr C. E. Meek: The role of Paolo Guinigi in Lucca 1400 to 1430

Mr A. H. S. Megaw: Resumption of excavation of a Byzantine Crusader castle at Paphos

Dr J. H. Musgrave: Archaeological bone studies in Greece

Mr H. C. Mytum: A second season of investigation of three Iron Age farmsteads in south-west Wales

Dr P. R. Newman: Agriculture in the Ainsty of York, 1500 to 1900

Dr D. G. Nicholls: The Syrian, Lebanese and Palestinian communities in the Caribbean

Dr D. J. Nicholls: Religion and peasant movements in Normandy during the early Reformation

Dr A. J. Parker: Survey and excavation of a Roman shipwreck in south-east Sicily

Mr P. J. Parr: Further excavations at Tell Nebi Mend (Qadesh), Syria

Dr M. L. Parry: Settlement frontier history and climatic variability

Dr M. Pegg: German Reformation tracts in Switzerland

Dr E. J. Peltenburg: Study of excavated material from Lemba

Mr I. G. Philip: Foreign users of the Bodleian Library, 1602 to 1750

Dr A. P. Phillips: Middle Neolithic sites in southern France

Dr S. Radcliffe: The nineteenth century novelist Wilhelm Raabe

Professor P. A. Rahtz: Preparation for publication of excavated material from Bordesley Abbey

Dr R. M. Reece: Coins from the Roman forum at Bath

Dr D. N. Riley: Archaeological air surveying methods

Dr R. H. Roberts: Karl Barth

Professor J. C. G. Röhl, A biography of Kaiser Wilhelm II

Dr N. J. Seeley: Natural inorganic materials in antiquity

Professor J. Seznec: Diderot's *Salons*

Dr M. Shackley: To extend the programme of field survey in the central Namib Desert, south-west Africa, into a previously unexplored region

Mr G. de G. Sieveking: Flint sickles

Dr D. E. Simpson: British and American English 1776 to 1850

Dr S. Smith: The collected letters of Charles Darwin

Mr T. Snoddy: A Dictionary of 20th century Irish artists

Professor J. K. St. Joseph: Roman military remains in Scotland

Dr C. Storey: A critical bibliography of *La Vie de Saint Alexis*

Dr G. Storey: The *Letters of Charles Dickens*

Mr D. Sturdy: Artefacts and illustrations of American Indians in Europe, 1497-1720

Dr G. R. Swain: The Profintern

Dr H. M. Taylor: An archaeological survey of the general history of Repton

Professor M. Todd: Excavation and environmental research at Hembury, Devon

Professor R. A. Tomlinson: Excavation in the upper area of Perachora, near Corinth

Miss R. Torrence: Bronze Age stone tools in Greece

Mr R. Truby and Mr B. Ife: Spanish keyboard music of the sixteenth to eighteenth centuries

Sir Edgar Vaughan: Joseph Lancaster in Caracas 1824-27, and his relations with Simón Bolívar

Dr J. Walvin: Abolition of slavery

Dr K. A. Wardle: Preparation for publication of a study of the excavated material from Assiros

Dr R. C. Webb: Genet and his Critics

Mrs B. L. Wedgwood: The life and works of Frances Julia Wedgwood

Miss J. Weinberg: An edition of a manuscript in Italian on the Syriac Gospels

Mr A. D. P. Wells-Cole: The influence of Jan Vredeman de Vries on architecture and decoration in England

Dr A. Whitehead: Socio-economic differentiation in northern Ghana

Dr R. D. Whitehouse: A third season of excavation at Botromagno, Gravina, south-east Italy

Mr J. W. M. Willett: Development of the arts in the Soviet Union, 1917 to 1939

Dr A. R. Williams: The manufacture of armour in Europe

Dr C. Wilson: An architectural study of stone fragments from excavations at York Minster

Dr T. Wishart: The development of computer programmes to achieve transformation between complex sounds in music

Dr P. C. Woodman: To excavate in the Glencoy, County Antrim

Dr A. R. Woolley: Jade from Alpine prehistoric axe factories

Mr D. F. Wright: The manuscripts of St. Augustine's *Tractatus in Evangelium Iohannis*

Dr C. E. Yeldham: The *Monthly Repository* in the 1830s

2. *From Government grant and general funds: for the subvention of research in the humanities by groups of scholars*

Berlioz Edition Editorial Committee, New: Continued work on a complete edition of Berlioz's musical works

Bristol City Museum and Art Gallery: The archaeological and scientific examination of an Egyptian mummy

British Archaeological Association: Publication of *Medieval Art and Architecture at Wells Cathedral*

British Record Society: Publication of an index to the 'Probate Records of the Bishop and Archdeacon of Oxford 1516 to 1732', Vol. I

Brixworth Archaeological Research Committee: A sixth season of research at the Anglo-Saxon church of Brixworth

Buckinghamshire Record Society: Publication of an Index to Wills proved in the Archdeaconry of Buckinghamshire 1483–1660

Calendars of Papal Registers: To continue the preparation and editing of Volume XVI of the Calendars of Papal Registers

Cambridge/Bradford Boeotian Expedition: The third season of an inter-disciplinary survey of Boeotia

Cambridge University Library: To continue compilation of a catalogue of the Rabbinic fragments in the New Series of the Taylor–Schechter Genizah collection

Comité Permanent du Château-Gaillard: To publish papers delivered at conferences held at Basle and Durham

Derbyshire Record Society: To publish the third and final part of the Diary of James Clegg of Chapel en le Frith, 1705 to 1755

Devon and Cornwall Record Society: Publication of Volume II of 'The Fabric Accounts of Exeter Cathedral, 1279 to 1353'

Dictionary of British Arms: Preparation and publication of the medieval section of the Dictionary

Hayling Island Project: Completion of excavation at Hayling Island of the Iron Age and Roman temples

Ice-House Hunt: To investigate ice-houses in Britain

Institute of Classical Studies: To continue up-dating the archive of photo-graphs of monuments illustrating New Comedy and to publish in two volumes a revised and enlarged version of the catalogue by T. B. L. Webster

International Institute of Philosophy: To assist with the administrative expenses of the Institute

Journal of Theological Studies: To produce the third cumulative Index of the New Series Volumes I to XXX

Lancashire Parish Register Society: Publication of the Parish Register of Hollinfare

Musica Britannica: To reprint Richard Dering's 'The Country Cries' and 'The City Cries'

Norfolk Archaeological Unit: Study, interpretation and publication of a second millennium occupation complex in Hockwold-cum-Wilton parish

Oxford Archaeological Unit: Continued research into Iron Age and Romano-British settlement in the Upper Thames

Palestine Exploration Fund: Continued work on the conservation of the Fund's archives

Portsmouth Record Series: To publish 'University Adult Education in Portsmouth, 1886 to 1938', Vol. V

Purcell Society: Publication of parts for performance of Purcell's Ten Sonatas of IV parts in conjunction with the new edition of the sonatas to be published by the Society as Volume 7 of the complete works of Purcell   (loan)

Richard III Society: To compile a critical index to the edition of BL Harleian MS 433

Scottish Dictionaries Joint Council: Continued work on the 'Dictionary of the Older Scottish Tongue'

Scottish Field School of Archaeology: Continued excavation at Strageath

Sette Finestre Committee: A sixth season of excavation and survey at Sette Finestre

Society for the Study of Medieval Languages: To publish a cumulative Index supplement to *Medium Aevum*

Suffolk Record Society: Publication of the Cartulary of Blythburgh Priory, Part II

Survey of English Usage: Continued work on the survey

Thesaurus Linguae Latinae: Continued work on the Thesaurus

Wakefield Court Rolls: Publication of the Rolls, 1348 to 1350

Wessex Archaeological Committee: A programme of hillwash related fieldwork as part of the Stonehenge Environs Project

Wiltshire Record Society: Publication of a collection of abstracts of Wiltshire coroners' bills covering the late eighteenth century

York Archaeological Trust: Further excavations at Coppergate, York

York Minster Archaeological Advisory Committee: Preparation for publication of Volumes 2 and 3 of the Report on the excavations beneath and around York Minster, 1966 to 1977

Yr Academi Gymreig: Preparing an English/Welsh Dictionary

3. *Awards from Special Funds*

(i) From the Andrew Browning Historical Fund: to provide for the promotion of historical studies, particularly in the area of modern history.

Dr A. H. Smith: Continued work on the papers of Nathaniel Bacon of Stiffkey

(ii) From the Albert Reckitt Archaeological Fund: 'for the exploration and excavation of ancient sites in any part of the world with a view to increasing knowledge of early civilisations and the history of mankind; and for the preservation and exhibition of objects discovered by such exploration and the publication of the results thereof'.

Mr P. J. Banks: A third season of excavation at Gormaz castle, Soria, Spain

Mr J. C. Bonsall: Continued investigation of Mesolithic sites at Eskmeals, Cumbria

Dr J. F. Cherry: A survey of the Cycladic island of Keos

Dr E. A. F. Kendall: Continued investigation at Cusichaca, Peru

Mr D. L. Kennedy: Examination of two major Roman roads in north-east Jordan

Dr D. Price Williams: Continued archaeological excavation in north-west Swaziland

Mr C. J. Scarre: Study and excavation at Poitou and Bourgon, France

Dr I. M. Stead: Further excavation at the La Tène cemeteries, Champagne, France

(iii) From the Caton-Thompson Fund for Archaeological Research: 'for the furtherance of archaeological research, whether in the field or in publication, by scholars selected preferably but not necessarily from the Fellows of the British Academy'.

Professor D. Oates: A fourth season of excavation at Tell Brak, north-east Syria

4. *Small Grants Research Fund in the Humanities 1980–1*

Dr S. L. Adams (University of Strathclyde): Anglo-Palatine relations, 1560 to 1620

Dr J. J. Anderson (University of Manchester): Drama, music and public ceremony in Newcastle upon Tyne

Dr J. L. Anderson (University of Oxford): Giovanni Morelli and the connoisseurship of Italian painting

Mr R. Austin (New University of Ulster): Educational and youth policies of the Vichy government

Dr W. Baker (West Midlands College of Higher Education): Studies in the work of G. H. Lewes and George Eliot

Mr M. Banham (University of Leeds): Manuscripts of Pinero

Dr T. Barnard (University of London): Industrial ventures in Restoration Ireland

Mr J. Batchelor (University of Oxford): Ruskin as literary critic

Dr R. M. Beaton (University of London): Modern Greek oral narrative poetry

Dr D. Bellos (University of Edinburgh): Leo Spitzer's essays on French literature

Dr G. R. Berridge (University of Leicester): The Union-Castle Line since 1945

Mr J. H. Betts (University of Bristol): Late Bronze Age sealstones of the Aegean area

Ms B. G. Birtwhistle (University of Southampton): The sonnets of G. G. Belli

Dr E. O. Blake (University of Southampton): Political and social formations in late medieval Germany

Dr A. W. Bower (University of Hull): The Ravenscroft-Stephen family papers

Dr P. T. Bradley (University of Newcastle upon Tyne): Defence in the Viceroyalty of Peru

Professor K. Branigan (University of Sheffield): Post-Minoan metalwork from Knossos

Dr F. G. T. Bridgham (University of Leeds): Mozart and his relation to the literature of his day

Dr C. W. Brooks (University of Durham): The lower branch of the legal profession, 1550 to 1640

Dr N. Bryson (University of Cambridge): Ingres and Delacroix

Dr J. B. Bullen (University of Reading): The literary response to the Post-Impressionist painters

Dr R. Byron (Queen's University, Belfast): Swedish fishing communities

Dr T. B. Caldwell (University of Leeds): A history of adult education in France

Dr J. P. Canning (University College of North Wales): Medieval political thought

Mr R. D. Catani (University College of Cardiff): The polemics of astrology

Dr M. Cave (Brunel University): The French planning system, 1981-5

Dr J. C. R. Childs (University of Leeds): The Anglo-Dutch Brigade in the seventeenth and eighteenth centuries

Dr D. S. Clark (University College of Swansea): Demonological beliefs and writings in early modern Europe

Professor I. F. Clarke (University of Strathclyde): The iconography of the future

Dr C. H. Clough (University of Liverpool): The palaces of Urbino and Gubbio

Mr H. M. Colvin (University of Oxford): Preparation for publication of a book on unbuilt Oxford

Professor G. E. Connell-Smith (University of Hull): United States policy towards Latin America

Professor R. A. Crossland (University of Sheffield): Hittite texts

Dr B. P. Crossley (University of Manchester): Late Gothic architecture in the Rhineland and in Bavaria and Swabia

Mr A. Cruttenden (University of Manchester): Intonation in children

Dr I. M. Cumpston (University of London): British and Australian economic relations in the 1930s

Dr R. L. Curtis (University of London): The manuscripts of *Prose Tristan*

Dr W. Davies (University of London): Nineteenth-century cadastral material in Brittany

Dr F. K. Dawson (University of Nottingham): A bibliography of tragedies and tragi-comedies from 1590 to 1635

J. Day (University of Leicester): A history of the African nationalist movement in Zimbabwe from 1955 to 1980

Dr D. C. Derbyshire (University of London): South American linguistics

A. P. Dobson (University College of Wales, Swansea): The politics of Anglo-American international economic relations from 1941 to 1945

Dr R. Domb (University of Cambridge): The Arab in Hebrew prose from 1948 to the present date

Dr J. Dunkerley (University of London): The Bolivian Revolution of 1952

Dr J. Dunkley (University of Aberdeen): Gambling in the French provinces in the eighteenth century

Mr J. Eadie (University College of North Wales): Lollard texts

Dr V. Edwards (Bulmershe College of Higher Education): Speech events in the Gujarati community in Britain

Dr J. P. England (University of Sheffield): The works of Don Juan Manuel

Mr E. C. Fernie (University of East Anglia): Romanesque monuments relevant to the architectural history of Norwich Cathedral

Dr C. J. Fischer (University of Edinburgh): Political patronage under the Nazis

Professor D. J. Fletcher (University of Durham): (i) A critical edition of Voltaire's *Epître sur la calomnie*; (ii) Bolingbroke and France

Dr R. Foot (University of Sussex): The American appraisal of Sino-Soviet relations, 1950–3

Dr T. Gallagher (University of Bradford): Protestants and Catholics in Scotland, 1880 to 1980

Dr D. Gareth Walters (University of Glasgow): The poetry of Quevedo

Dr G. Gargett (New University of Ulster at Coleraine): Voltaire and the Sirven affair

Dr P. Garside (University College of Wales, Cardiff): The manuscripts of Walter Scott

Mr P. J. Godman (University of Oxford): Alcuin and Carolingian poetry

Dr J. Goodman (University of Essex) and Dr K. Honeyman (University of Leeds): Sir Isaac Holden and the French worsted industry

Mr W. Gould (University of London): The Coole edition of the works of Yeats

Dr A. Gransden (University of Nottingham): The abbey of Bury St. Edmunds

Dr E. G. Grant (Middlesex Polytechnic): Neolithic territorial patterns on the Isle of Arran

Professor J. R. Gray (School of Oriental and African Studies): The Vatican and the Atlantic slave-trade

Professor D. H. Green (University of Cambridge): The *Willehalm* manuscript

Mr T. A. Greenan (University of Liverpool): The life and works of Sukhanov

Professor J. Grenville (University of Birmingham): Propaganda in Hamburg, 1936-45

Dr J. F. Haldon (University of Birmingham): Political and social history of the Byzantine State

Professor K. H. D. Haley (University of Sheffield): Sir William Temple and Anglo-Dutch relations

Dr A. F. Harding (University of Durham): Henge monuments of the British Isles

Mr N. Harding (University College of Wales, Swansea): The theory and practice of the dictatorship of the proletariat in Russia

Professor U. R. Q. Henriques (University College of Wales, Cardiff): Sir Moses Montefiore and the British Foreign Office, 1830 to 1875

Professor L. J. Herrmann (University of Leicester): Turner's *Liber Studiorum*

Dr J. W. Hiden (University of Bradford): Historical writing on the Third Reich

Mr J. C. Higgitt (University of Edinburgh): Anglo-Saxon illuminated manuscripts with a Scottish provenance

Dr R. A. Higham (University of Exeter): Landscape in Powys

Ms P. J. Hilden (University of Cambridge): Socialist feminism in France, 1880 to 1914

Dr R. Hillenbrand (University of Edinburgh): Early Islamic art

Dr P. Honan (University of Birmingham): Jane Austen

Dr N. Hope (University of Glasgow): German and Scandinavian Protestantism

Mrs P. M. Huby (University of Liverpool): Fragments of Theophrastus

Dr P. B. Humfrey (University of St. Andrews): The paintings of Cima da Conegliano

Mr A. C. Hutchinson and Mr J. N. Wakefield (University of Newcastle): Writings on legal theory

Professor J. C. Ireson (University of Hull): French Romanticism

Dr G. R. Jackson (North London Polytechnic): Wordsworth's sonnet sequences and itinerary poems

Mr H. James (University of Cambridge): German banking and financial policy between 1924 and 1933

Dr A. Johnston (University of London): Greek archaic and classical storage amphorae

Mr J. B. Jones (UWIST) and Dr M. J. Keating (University of Strathclyde): The Labour Party and the British State

Dr M. C. E. Jones (University of Nottingham): The language of treason in later medieval France

Dr S. Jones (University of Glasgow): William Hazlitt

Dr S. E. Jones (University of London): The Abbé Du Bos

Dr W. J. Jones (University of London): Middle High German Studies

Professor E. M. Jope (Queen's University of Belfast): Medieval pottery in the Southern Midlands

Mr J. A. Jowitt (University of Leeds): The rise and decline of two textile communities in Yorkshire and Massachusetts

Mr B. Keith-Smith (University of Bristol): The literary works of Lothar Schreyer

Dr J. S. Kelly (University of Oxford): The letters of Yeats

Dr A. J. Kennedy (University of Glasgow): Christine de Pisan

Dr A. P. Kerr (University of Reading): The correspondence of de Tocqueville

Mrs P. Kirkham (Leicester Polytechnic): Harry H. Peach and design in British industry

Dr E. H. Klein (University of Newcastle upon Tyne): English syntax

Professor W. G. Lambert (University of Birmingham): Cuneiform tablets in the British Museum

Mr E. Lauterpacht (University of Cambridge), and Dr A. V. Lowe (University of Manchester), and Dr M. Shaw (Liverpool Polytechnic): British practice in international law, 1945 to 1980

Dr J. E. Law (University College, Swansea): Rome, the Papal States and the Kingdom of Naples, 1380 to 1530

Dr M. A. Leahy (University of Birmingham): Historical inscriptions of the twenty-sixth dynasty

Professor F. W. Leakey (University of London): The poems of Baudelaire

Mr E. D. Lilley (University of Bristol): The life and works of La Font de Saint-Yenne

Mr C. H. Lloyd (Ashmolean Museum, Oxford): Working methods of Impressionist painters

Mrs S. J. Loach (University of Oxford): English religious writings in the sixteenth century

Dr C. A. Lodder (University of St. Andrews): Russian Constructivism 1913 to 1933

Mr E. A. Lovatt and Mr R.-J. Herail (University of Leeds): A dictionary of modern colloquial French

Mr D. S. Low (University College of Wales, Aberystwyth): Arthur Schnitzler and George Saiko

Dr N. Luker (University of Nottingham): Mikhail Artsybashev 1878 to 1927

Professor C. E. Luscombe (University of Sheffield): Sententiae Abaelardi

Professor F. Lyall (University of Aberdeen): Legal problems arising from telecommunications by satellite

Professor J. D. McClean (University of Sheffield) and Professor K. W. Patchett (University of Wales): The Recognition of Judgments in the Commonwealth

Professor J. J. McEvoy (Queen's University, Belfast): Robert Grosseteste

Professor P. V. McGrath (University of Bristol): The Catholic 'underground' in the reigns of Elizabeth I and the early Stuarts

Mr J. S. H. Major (University of Hull): The United States and Panama from 1903 to 1955

Mr J. A. C. Mantle (University of Cambridge): East Lothian colliery communities

Dr G. M. Martin (Portsmouth Polytechnic): Andean indigenist literature

Dr G. T. Martin (University of London): Tomb reliefs of the eighteenth and nineteenth Egyptian dynasties

Mrs J. Mawby (University of East Anglia): The Norwegian writer Jens Bjørneboe

Dr G. I. Meirion-Jones (City of London Polytechnic): The vernacular architecture of Brittany

Mr P. Merchant (University of Warwick): The plays of Thomas Heywood

Dr E. A. Millar (University of Glasgow): The life and work of Ignazio Silone

Dr E. A. Moignard (University of Glasgow): Orientalizing pottery from Knossos

Dr P. J. Morgan (University of Hull): The Italian PNF in the 1930s

Professor A. J. A. Morris (Northern Ireland Polytechnic): Studies in the Anglo-German problem in the early twentieth century

Dr D. Nash (University of Oxford): Roman coins from Bath

Dr L. A. Newson (University of London): The Indian in sixteenth-century Ecuador

Dr J. A. North (University of London): Studies in the history and religion of Rome

Dr C. O'Baoill and Dr C. O'Dochartaigh (University of Aberdeen): The Irish metrical form, *Trí Rainn agus Amhrán*

Dr M. Palmer (University of Loughborough): The first Marquis of Hastings

Mr H. Pálsson (University of Edinburgh): Classical and medieval *sententiae* in Icelandic sagas

Dr J. Parkin (University of Bristol): Medieval French folklore in Rabelais

Dr S. Parkinson (University of Aberdeen): Old Portuguese non-literary documents, 1200 to 1550

Professor A. E. Pennington (University of Oxford): A catalogue of Slavonic Medieval Manuscripts in Britain

Dr G. Pontiero (University of Manchester): The life and times of Eleonora Duse

Mr D. Powell (Nene College of Higher Education): The poems of John Clare

Dr S. Powell (University of Manchester): Middle English sermons in the Harley/Royal collections

Mr D. Punter (University of East Anglia): Blake, Hegel and dialectic

Dr R. Reece (Institute of Archaeology, London University): Roman coins

Dr A. Reid (Research Fellow, Gonville and Caius College, Cambridge): Woodworking machinery in Britain and the United States, 1850 to 1900

Dr J. H. Reid (University of Nottingham): German literature in the 1970s

Professor H. S. Reiss (University of Bristol): Carl Sternheim's conception of art and the artist

Professor K. Richards (University of Manchester): Aspects of late-nineteenth- and early twentieth-century drama

Dr L. Richards (University of Salford): The theatre of Pirandello

Dr C. E. Richardson (University of Oxford): Hellenistic Dress

Professor J. Richmond (University of Lancaster): Theologians of the *Aufklärung*

Mr P. J. Riden (University College of Wales, Cardiff): The Derbyshire Collections of Samuel Pegge

Dr D. W. R. Ridgway (University of Edinburgh): Archaeological studies in southern Italy

Professor J. P. C. Roach (University of Sheffield): The history of secondary education in England and Wales, 1815 to 1870

Dr E. Rosenhaft (King's College, Cambridge): The history of the German Communist Party

Dr C. C. Rutter (University of Warwick): Elizabethan playhouse documents

Mr G. J. S. Sanderson (University of Oxford): Abhinavaguptan Śaivism

Dr A. M. Saunders (University of Aberdeen): The sixteenth-century French emblem book

Professor P. H. Sawyer (University of Leeds): Viking-age Scandinavia

Dr R. Schofield (University of Nottingham): Architecture in Lombardy, 1450 to 1550

Dr A. Seal (University of Cambridge): The transfer of power and the partition of India

Miss D. R. Shanzer (University of Manchester): Alan of Lille's *Anticlaudianus*

Mr R. W. Sharples (University of London): Fragments of Theophrastus

Dr F. Shaw (University of Bristol): Manuscripts of Heinrich von München's *Weltchronik*

Professor G. Singh (Queen's University, Belfast): The papers of Dr F. R. and Mrs Q. D. Leavis

Dr M. Slater (University of London): Dickens and Women

Dr F. M. Snowden (University of London): The peasant movement in Apulia from 1880 to 1922

Mr E. M. Spiers (University of Leeds): The radical general, Sir George de Lacy Evans

Professor R. W. Steel (University College of Wales, Swansea): A study of geography in the twentieth century

Dr F. W. Sternfeld (University of Oxford): Poetry and music in the Renaissance

Dr R. L. Stirrat (University of Sussex): Roman Catholicism in Sri Lanka

Dr R. A. Stradling (University College, Cardiff): Spanish policy and power in maritime affairs, 1570 to 1670

Dr J. Sutherland (University of London): Victorian novelists and publishers

Dr J. S. Symmons (University of Essex): Art patronage in late-eighteenth-century Spain

Mr G. W. Taylor (University of Manchester): Victorian acting

Dr P. M. Taylor (University of Leeds): British propaganda during the First World War

Dr D. Thomson (University of East Anglia): Architectural drawings in Stockholm

Dr H. M. Tomlinson (University College at Buckingham): The poetry of Victor Brodeau

Dr A. J. Tooke (University of London): A critical edition of *Par les champs et par les grèves* by Flaubert and Maxime Du Camp

Mr T. F. S. Turville-Petre (University of Nottingham): The Middle English poem *The Wars of Alexander*

The Revd Canon D. Walker (University College of Wales, Swansea): Crown and episcopacy, 1066 to 1216

Dr K. Walker (University of London): Rochester's poems

Dr R. E. A. Waller (University of Liverpool): The Académie des Inscriptions et Belles Lettres

Professor W. R. Ward (University of Durham): Protestant religious revivals in Germany and Austria in the eighteenth century

Mr I. R. Warner (University of Sheffield): Reactions to the execution of Fermín Galán

Dr T. Watkins (University of Edinburgh): Metal objects from the Ur 'Royal Cemetery'

Dr G. B. Waywell (University of London): Greek and Roman sculptures at Port Sunlight

Dr T. G. West (University of East Anglia): Literary and scientific writings, 1850 to 1900

Dr C. H. Williams (North Staffordshire Polytechnic): Welsh language and culture in the twentieth century

Dr H. Willmer (University of Leeds): Christian social thinking in south India

Dr T. J. Winnifrith (University of Warwick): Poems of Charlotte and Branwell Brontë

Mrs J. E. Wright (University of Nottingham): Panel paintings of Antonello da Messina

Dr D. M. Wood (University of Birmingham): Benjamin Constant and Isabelle de Charrière

Dr F. A. Woodman (University of East Anglia): The architectural history of King's College Chapel, Cambridge

Mrs E. M. Yearling (University of Glasgow): James Shirley's *The Cardinal*

5. *Overseas Exchanges and Special Programmes*

(i) LEVERHULME VISITING PROFESSORSHIPS

Held in 1980/1 (the first under the new scheme):

Sir Alec Cairncross, KCMG, FBA, visited India for two months, spending one month at the Institute of Social and Economic Change in Bangalore, one month at the Institute of Economic Growth in Delhi, and a week in Bombay, for discussions with economists.

(ii) ACADEMY VISITING PROFESSORSHIPS

Held in 1980/1:

Professor M. Fernandez Alvarez, of the University of Salamanca, Spain, visited Britain to meet British scholars working on Spanish history of the early modern period.

Professor A. Das Gupta, Professor of History at Visva-Bharati, Santiniketan, West Bengal, visited Britain to work on the effects of the breakup of the Mughal Empire and the spread of the European East India Companies on Asian merchants and indigenous trading networks.

Professor J. R. Green, of the University of Sydney, Australia, visited Britain to work on a catalogue of Greek dramatic monuments.

Professor H. W. Pleket, Professor of Ancient History in the University of Leiden, visited Britain to meet British colleagues concerned with the economic history of the ancient world.

Professor J. Pouilloux, of the Centre National de la Recherche Scientifique, Paris, visited Britain to meet British colleagues.

The Academy also offered support, to a more limited extent, to the following scholars:

Professor D. Del Corno, of the Institute of Papyrology of the University of Milan, visited Britain to lecture and meet British papyrologists.

Professor S. Kili, of Bogaziçi University, Istanbul, visited Britain to consult British colleagues working on modern Turkish history.

Dr C. Krikonis, of the Faculty of Theology in the University of Thessalonika, visited Britain to forward his research on the theological works of the emperor Theodore II Laskaris.

Professor B. Rutkowski, Professor of Classical Archaeology in the University of Warsaw, and a Member of the Polish Academy of Sciences, visited Britain to further his work on Minoan and Mycenean religion.

Mrs A. Stohler-Zimmermann, a conservationist from Zürich, visited Britain to demonstrate her techniques for the dismounting of three-dimensional pieces of mummy cartilage.

Professor E. Winter, of the University of Trier, visited Britain to deliver lectures and meet British scholars working on late Egyptian papyrology.

Professor E. Zürcher, Professor of Chinese History in the University of Leiden, visited Britain to meet British colleagues working on Chinese history.

(iii) EXCHANGES WITH WEST EUROPE

Maison des Sciences de l'Homme

Six scholars visited France under the terms of the Exchange Agreement with the Maison des Sciences de l'Homme:

Dr G. J. Crossick, Lecturer in History, University of Essex; for work on the *petite bourgeoisie* in nineteenth-century Europe.

Dr N. M. Horsfall, Lecturer in Greek and Latin, University College London; for work on a miniature Hellenistic narrative relief in the Cabinet des Médailles at the Bibliothèque Nationale.

Professor J. V. S. Megaw, Professor of Archaeology, University of Leicester; to consult French colleagues on a re-publication of the Basse-Yutz, Moselle, find in the British Museum.

Mr B. T. Rothwell, Lecturer in English, The Queen's University of Belfast; for work in the August Rondel collection in the Arsenal Library in connection with his research on Strindberg.

Mr L. H. Sawkins, Senior Lecturer in Music, Roehampton Institute; to continue research on the *grands motets* of Lalande.

Dr G. Williams, Lecturer in Sociology, University College of North Wales, Bangor; for work on texts relating to the status of minority languages in Europe.

Fonds National Suisse de la Recherche Scientifique

Seven scholars visited the Fondation Hardt in Geneva under the terms of the Agreement with the FNRS:

Mrs E. M. Craik, Lecturer in Greek, University of St. Andrews; for work on an essay on *Marriage and Property in Ancient Greece*.

Ms J. D. Harries, Lecturer in Ancient History, University of St. Andrews; for work on the position of upper-class women in the Later Roman Empire, with particular reference to a group influenced by St. Jerome.

Mr J. C. B. Lowe, Lecturer in Latin, Bedford College, London; for work on plays of Plautus and Terrence.

Dr R. O. A. M. Lyne, University Lecturer in Classics and Fellow of Balliol College, Oxford; for work on the diction of Virgil's *Aeneid*.

Professor R. M. Ogilvie, FBA; for work on the evidence for Early Roman history, and on Paganism and Christianity.

Dr M. J. Osborne, Senior Lecturer in Ancient History, University of Lancaster; for work on the Attic portion of the Lexicon of Greek Personal Names and on materials for a prosopography of Athens in the Imperial Period.

Mr S. F. Ryle, Lecturer in Latin, University of Liverpool; for work on the *Apologia* of Apuleius.

In addition, the Revd Professor Henry Chadwick, FBA, visited the Bodmer Library, Geneva, to study an Isaac Newton manuscript, *History of the Church*. The Bodmer Library had invited a British scholar to work on this manuscript.

(iv) EXCHANGES WITH EAST EUROPE

The following scholars visited East Europe under the terms of the British Academy's Exchange Agreement with:

Bulgarian Academy of Sciences

Dr T. J. Cadoux: Graeco-Roman sites in Bulgaria.

Hungarian Academy of Sciences

Dr I. Gershevitch, FBA: to meet Hungarian colleagues and attend an international colloquium on Central Asian Pre-Islamic history.

Polish Academy of Sciences

Mr J. M. Kolankiewicz: the changing class structure of Polish society and its impact on socio-political activity.

Romanian Academy of Social and Political Sciences

Dr J. D. Leslie: history of Austria-Hungary, 1867–1918.

Professor G. H. N. Seton-Watson, FBA: work on the correspondence and papers of R. W. Seton-Watson.

Dr F. Shaw: medieval German manuscripts in Transylvania.

Academy of Sciences of the USSR

Mr A. H. Brown: recent Soviet writing on political science; and writings on S. E. Desnitsky and I. A. Tretyakov.

Dr P. Dukes: seventeenth- and eighteenth-century Russian history with special reference to Scottish connections.

Professor E. Lampert: late-nineteenth-century and early twentieth-century Russian intellectual history.

Dr M. J. B. McAuley: socio-political study of Leningrad since 1917.

(These exchanges took place in the financial year 1980/1.)

(v) EXCHANGES WITH COUNTRIES OUTSIDE EUROPE

The following scholars visited countries outside Europe under the terms of the Academy's Exchange Agreements with:

Newberry Library (Special American Programme)

Dr N. G. Parker: for work on the W. B. Greenlee Collection, on the Portuguese overseas empire, and the E. Ayer Collection, on European exploration, in connection with research on Europe and the outside world, 1100–1756.

Israel Academy of Sciences and Humanities

Professor E. Ullendorff, FBA: visited Tel Aviv, Jerusalem, and Haifa for work on aspects of Semitic syntax.

Japan Academy

Dr L. E. R. Picken, FBA: visited Japan for work on historical musicology and aspects of Japanese language.

Japan Society for the Promotion of Science

Dr D. L. McMullen: visited Japan for work on state and scholarship in T'ang China, and on the T'ang officer and writer Yüan Chieh, 719–772.

(The Israel and Japan visits took place during the financial year 1980/1.)

(vi) BRITISH CONFERENCE GRANTS

The Academy supported the following conferences held in Britain:

Annual Conference of the Society for Caribbean Studies, in Hoddesdon, Hertfordshire

Archaeoastronomy Symposium, in Oxford

Commonwealth Conference on Labour History, centred on working life in Britain, Canada, and Australasia, in Coventry

Conference on Bulgaria 81: Archaeology and History, in Nottingham

Conference in honour of Professor Tom Burns, on Economy and Society in the Twentieth Century, in Edinburgh

Conference on Common Denominators in Art and Science, in Edinburgh

Conference on New Perspectives in the History of Technology, in Manchester

Conference on Space, Time, and Causality, in Keele

Conference on Victims of Sexual Assault, in Middlesbrough

Conference on Literature and Society in Southern Africa, in York

Conference on Semantic Anthropology: the Linguistic in the Social, in Durham

Cumberland Lodge Conference of Senior Historians, at Cumberland Lodge, Windsor

Dostoevsky Conference, in Nottingham

Fourth Battle Conference in Anglo-Norman Studies, in Battle, Sussex

Fourth International Conference in Archaeozoology: the Contribution of Faunal Analysis to the Study of Man, in London

Joint Conference of the Hegel Society of Great Britain and the Hegel Society of America, in Oxford

Linguistics Association of Great Britain Spring Meeting, in Manchester

Prehistoric Society Conference: European Societies in the First Millenium BC, in London

St. Andrews–Umea Workshop and Conference on Criminality and Social Deviance, in Edinburgh and St. Andrews

Sixteenth Spring Symposium of Byzantine Studies: The Byzantine Aristocracy, in Edinburgh

Society for Mediterranean Studies: Conference on Bread and Circuses: Problems of Control and Order in Mediterranean Cities, in Coventry

T. H. Green: A Commemorative Conference, in Oxford

Third British Colloquium in Ecclesiastical History, in Durham

(vii) OVERSEAS CONFERENCE GRANTS

The British Academy awarded one hundred and twenty Overseas Conference Grants during the year 1980/1.

(viii) CHINA

The Exchange Agreement between the Chinese Academy of Social Sciences and the British Academy/Social Science Research Council had been signed in spring 1980. The first of the three British scholars to go to China during the 1980/1 period arrived early in 1981.

On the Chinese side, difficulties were met in identifying suitable scholars for visits to Britain. No visitors were received from China during the period.

6. *Grants to Learned Journals in 1980–1*

Grants totalling £26,130 were made to the following journals:

> Aerial Archaeology
> Africa
> Annual Bulletin of Historical Literature
> Anthropological Index
> Antiquity
> Archaeologia Cambrensis
> Architectural History
> Bibliography of Philosophy
> Board of Celtic Studies Publications
> Book List for the Society of Old Testament Studies
> British Journal for Eighteenth Century Studies
> British Numismatic Journal
> Bulletin of Hispanic Studies
> Cambridge Medieval Celtic Studies
> English Goethe Society Publications
> Fort
> French Studies
> Irish Economic and Social History
> Italian Studies
> Journal of the Gypsy Lore Society
> Journal of Hellenic Studies
> Journal of the Royal Asiatic Society
> Journal of Semitic Studies
> Journal of Theological Studies
> Journal of the Warburg and Courtauld Institutes
> Landscape History
> London Journal
> Medieval Archaeology
> Northern History
> Oxford Slavonic Papers
> Palestine Exploration Quarterly
> Proceedings of the Cambridge Antiquarian Society
> Proceedings of the Prehistoric Society
> Publications of the Society for the Promotion of
>   Roman Studies
> Royal Musical Association Research Chronicle
> Scottish Historical Review
> Studies in Church History
> Transactions of the Architectural and Archaeological
>   Society of Durham and Northumberland

PART III

REPORTS OF OVERSEAS SCHOOLS AND INSTITUTES, SPONSORED SOCIETIES, BRITISH NATIONAL COMMITTEES, AND COLLECTIVE RESEARCH PROJECTS

(a) GRANTS AWARDED IN 1980/1 TO BRITISH SCHOOLS AND
INSTITUTES OVERSEAS AND TO SPONSORED SOCIETIES

	£
British Institute at Amman for Archaeology and History	42,000*
British Institute for Afghan Studies	5,000
British Institute for Archaeology at Ankara	137,000
British School at Athens	176,000
British Institute in Eastern Africa	105,000
British Institute in South-East Asia	55,000
British School of Archaeology in Iraq	90,000
British School of Archaeology in Jerusalem	83,000
British School of Persian Studies	72,000
British School at Rome	248,000
Egypt Exploration Society	40,000
Society for Libyan Studies	18,000
Council for British Archaeology	87,000
	£1,158,000

* Excluding £12,000 grant brought forward from 1979/80 for basement conversion.

Three of the bodies listed above also received grants totalling £21,000 as compensation for overseas inflation and adverse exchange rates during 1979/80.

BRITISH INSTITUTE IN AMMAN FOR ARCHAEOLOGY
AND HISTORY

The year under review saw encouraging consolidation of this new Institute, formally launched on 1 April 1980.

The overstretched Director, Mrs C. M. Bennett, OBE, was in sole charge of the Institute, its research programme, and its hostel, with only domestic and part-time secretarial help, until in June an Administrative Assistant was dispatched from England, pending the hoped-for appointment of an Assistant Director in April 1982.

The Institute's well-sited premises were greatly improved, thanks to an Academy grant, by converting the large basement into a well-equipped working area with four desks, ample table-space and shelving, central heating, and good lighting. A theodolite, plane-table, projector, and screen were acquired. The Institute is now equipped for basic surveying and photography, and work began on a small laboratory. Its Library was built up to 752 volumes but still needs much reinforcement. Hostel accommodation just sufficed for the Director, her assistant, scholars, and visitors from sundry countries, who numbered ninety-one during the period under review.

The Director completed in the summer of 1980 a final season of excavations at Buseirah, which further confirmed the importance in the eighth/seventh centuries BC of this focal point on the ancient King's Highway from Damascus to Aqaba. She also did preliminary work on the intended survey of sites in the Wadi Araba, continued her lectures and seminars in Amman University, carried out in March/April 1981 with Directors of other Institutes a lecture tour of northern British universities, and gave the Institute's annual lecture in London in October 1980. Her 1981 season of excavation at Tawilan in south Jordan (where she had taken extensive soundings some years ago) had to be deferred because of ill health. In May 1981 she received a welcome visit from the Secretary of the Academy.

Apart from allocations to the Director's own programme, research awards were made to Mr Alistair Killick for his survey of Udruh, a site in south-central Jordan which promises to be of great importance; to Mr C. Philips to enable him to join Mr Parr's excavation at Tell Nebi Mend in Syria; and to Miss H. Dodge to continue her survey of Roman sites in Jordan. The Institute also provided facilities for Mr Alistair Northedge in the preparations for his doctoral thesis on the Amman Citadel (excavated by the Director from 1975 to 1979).

The Institute's excellent rapport with the Jordanian authorities, notably Crown Prince Hassan and the Directorate of Antiquities, were a testimony to the Director's attention to public relations. The degree of collaboration with the growing number of archaeological schools and missions in Jordan was also gratifying.

The results of an initial drive for membership were disappointing. Together with the fifty-four recruited by Mrs Bennett in Jordan the modest total at the end of the period was ninety-two. A further drive was planned. Membership of the Council, which held four meetings, remained as initially appointed, save for a change of Treasurer because of ill health.

The Institute succeeded in establishing itself during the period under review as a lively and widely respected feature of the archaeological scene in Jordan.

H. G. BALFOUR-PAUL
Chairman

BRITISH INSTITUTE OF AFGHAN STUDIES

During 1980/1 the Society devoted most of its efforts to the task of preparing for publication the results of the excavations at Old Kandahar since 1974. Dr Svend Helms, who has directed the excavations in recent years, worked full time on this as Senior Research Fellow in London. The Society has an excellent photographic record in London of most of the key finds, plans, and sections. As editor of the volume Dr Helms will be co-ordinating the contributions from a number of specialists and will himself be making the major contribution in respect of stratigraphy and architecture, small finds, and general conclusions.

Mr P. W. M. Wright was reappointed Research Fellow in Kabul for a second year in 1980/1. Unable to make a special pottery study, because it has been impossible for him to travel to Kandahar, he has been able to make a series of special studies on arts and crafts. He has completed a study of brick-making—the production of bricks in the Kabul region in the 1970s, of the Nadalaf—the fluffing of cotton stuffings for pillows and quilts, of bow drilling and wire drawing. Perhaps the most interesting work that he has been able to do has been the development of the techniques of bazaar studies—the recording and study of some 200 objects that passed through the bazaars of Kabul during the year.

Because of the difficulties of travel, there have been few visitors to the Institute in Kabul. Mr W. Ball completed the basic work for the index of archaeological sites in Afghanistan. This is now being put into card form and copies of the card index will be available for consultation in London and in the Institute in Kabul and the Afghan Directorate of Archaeology. The Committee made a small additional grant to Mr Ball during the year to help him complete a gazetteer of archaeological sites in Afghanistan in a form that can be published by the Centre des Recherches Scientifiques in Paris during 1982. Mr Ball has now been appointed Senior Research Fellow of the Institute in Kabul for 1981/2. He hopes to complete his study of the Institute's collection of survey pottery collected in 1974 in Kandahar Province, and Casal's survey material from 1951.

In London the Society has continued with its regular programme of meetings. Dr Helms lectured on a 'Review of Kandahar Excavations 1976 to 1978' at the Annual General Meeting in December, Mr Richard Blurton lectured on 'The Stupa and Vihara of Kandahar in October', and Mr John Irwin lectured on 'Buddhism and the Cosmic Pillar, a Background for the Minar-i-Chakri'. During the year Volume 2 of *Afghan Studies* was published, with a wide variety of articles reflecting the range and scope of interests at the Institute: 'The Old Kandahar Excavations 1976', by S. Helms; 'The Greek Inscriptions from Kandahar', by P. M. Fraser; 'Linguistic Stratification', by G. Morgenstierne; 'Linguistic Studies', by D. Elphenbein; 'Nokonzok's Well', by I. Gerschevitch; 'Archival Resources in Afghanistan', by Miss L. Hall; and 'Pre-Islamic Coins in Herat Museum', by D. W. MacDowall and M. Ibrahim.

D. W. MacDowall
Hon. Secretary

BRITISH INSTITUTE OF ARCHAEOLOGY AT ANKARA

During 1980 and 1981 there were two excavation seasons at Tille Hüyük on the Euphrates, conducted by the Director, Dr D. H. French. In the first season the excavation of the late Roman bath house beside the modern road was continued, and finds included a much larger sample of Roman pottery than before, as well as more stamped tiles. On the mound itself part of the upper Islamic levels was cleared, and a step trench cut to ascertain the nature of the earlier periods. This revealed occupation during the third millenium, the second millenium, and the first half of the first millenium, as well as the medieval period. To judge from the pottery the early first-millenium deposits seem particularly promising, and the third-millenium buildings appear to have been very substantial. There may also be Hellenistic settlement on the mound, but then and in the Roman period the main occupation was elsewhere. In 1981 the upper of the two Islamic levels was completely cleared in eight 10 × 10 trenches. The walls have rough stone foundations and are faced with roughly squared limestone blocks. There are traces of small-scale industrial activity, including copper smelting, as well as domestic occupation, and the buildings apparently belong to the eleventh century AD. Beneath it there is a second Islamic level, with notably good masonry, which should be uncovered by the end of 1981.

After a two-year interval Mr Alan Hall returned to Oenoanda. Professor Smith recorded two substantial new fragments of the Diogenes inscription and corrected and improved earlier readings; Dr Coulton completed his work on the city's aqueduct, water-line, and system of water distribution; and Mr Hall concentrated on the mausoleum of Licinnia Flavilla and its genealogical inscription. The survey of the site, within the limits imposed by current Turkish regulations, is now essentially complete, and any further work will have to be carried out with a different type of permit.

The RECAM epigraphic project received considerable attention. Mr Hall and Miss H. C. van Bremen worked on the collections in the Konya and Burdur Museums, and Dr Stephen Mitchell completed the manuscript for the volume covering North Galatia, which is due to appear late in 1981 or early in 1982. The Director's survey of Roman roads and milestones also continued, with particular emphasis on the north of Anatolia, from Bithynia to the *limes*. As a result most earlier conjectures about the course of roads in this area will have to be revised, and some notable new results were obtained in the north-east, between Trabzon and the upper Euphrates basin.

Apart from work on finds from the excavation at Tille the prehistoric period received less attention this year, but the balance of the Institute's activities was maintained by the appointment to the Assistant Directorship of Miss Ann Murray, who has begun her doctoral research on the Hittite period.

In April 1981 Mr John Carswell, the Academy Secretary, visited Ankara. During three days Mr Carswell met representatives from the TTK, universities, the Museums Service, the Ministry of Culture, the British Council, and the Embassy, and was given a full picture of the running of the Institute and its place in the Turkish archaeological scene. His report was received by the Institute in June.

In London the Institute sponsored a series of lectures, including Miss Joyce Reynolds on the 'Inscriptions from Aphrodisias', Mr David Hawkins on the 'Origins of the Lycians', Professor Martin Harrison on 'Lycia in Late Antiquity', and Sir Steven Runciman on 'Great Families of Byzantine Anatolia'. The Director, with the heads of other British

Schools and Institutes abroad, also addressed audiences in Manchester and Sheffield on the Institute's current work. Arising from the excavation at Tille and current interest in the Roman frontier in Turkey, a colloquium, under the auspices of the Institute, was organized in Swansea by Dr Stephen Mitchell, in which the delegates, including participants from the USA, Germany, and Turkey, heard sixteen papers on 'Armies and Frontiers in Roman and Byzantine Anatolia'. A volume on this theme is now in preparation.

Volume XXX of *Anatolian Studies* was a Festschrift for Professor Oliver Gurney, edited by Mr J. G. MacQueen, and the contents, naturally enough, are mainly concerned with the Hittites and their contemporaries in the Near East, reflecting Professor Gurney's own scholarly interests. A handsomely bound copy was presented to him at the Annual General Meeting as an expression of the esteem and affection in which he is held by all members of the Institute. The year also saw the appearance of the first three titles in a series of Institute monographs, published by British Archaeological Reports in their International Series: Stephen Mitchel, *Asvan Kale I. The Hellenistic, Roman and Islamic Sites* (1980); H. F. Russell, *Pre-Classical Pottery of Eastern Anatolia; based on a survey by Charles Burney of sites along the Euphrates and Lake Van* (1980); and David French, *Roman Roads and Milestones in Asia Minor I. The Pilgrim's Road* (1981).

STEPHEN MITCHELL
Acting Hon. Secretary

BRITISH SCHOOL AT ATHENS

The 1980/1 session proved to be an eventful one. The School was in constant use throughout and a large number of students were able to take advantage of the facilities both in Athens and at Knossos. In all some 130 Full Students were admitted during the session and 110 Associates, of whom 64 participated in excavations or survey projects sponsored by the School.

The School's excavations at Knossos continued for a fourth season under the direction of the Chairman, Professor P. M. Warren. Substantial architectural remains were uncovered, together with a large number of vases, fragments of decorated fresco, and several interesting small finds. An account of the excavation is published in the current issue of *Archaeological Reports*, no. 27, 1980/1, 'Knossos: Stratigraphical Museum Excavations 1978–80', Part 1.

At the Menelaion, Sparta, the Director, Dr H. W. Catling, continued his excavations on the south side of the Aetos Hill where a substantial building, possibly of megaron type, was revealed.

The joint Greek–British excavation at Lefkandi 'Toumba' under the direction of M. R. Popham and L. H. Sackett (for the School) was able to resume. The apsidal building, partially destroyed by illegal bulldozing, contained two well-preserved Dark Age burials, of a warrior and of four horses. Other rich finds came to light in the adjacent cemetery. The text volume of *Lefkandi I: The Iron Age: The Settlement: The Cemeteries* (Popham, Sackett *et al.*) was published during 1980.

Work was also resumed at the site of the lead-ore washery of the Athenian silver mine at Agrileza in Attica, enabling J. Ellis Jones to complete the plan of this extensive complex.

At Assiros Toumba in central Macedonia, K. A. Wardle continued the study of finds from previous seasons excavations and undertook some cleaning work on the site, necessitated by the 1978 Thessalonika earthquake.

A joint team from the Universities of Cambridge and Southampton resumed their study of the palaeolithic sequence in Epirus and the Hon. Mrs C. Ridley continued the classification of the late Neolithic pottery from her excavations at Servia. At Mycenae and Agios Stephanos study of material from earlier excavations also continued.

A first season's survey work was successfully completed by a joint team from the Universities of Sheffield and Swansea in an area to the south of modern Megalopolis, currently threatened by industrial development. A number of sites were recorded ranging in date from prehistoric to post-classical.

Professor Cadogan continued his study of the finds from Pyrgos, Crete, and undertook some conservation work on the site.

At Saranda Kolones, Paphos (Cyprus), A. H. S. Megaw directed a further season of excavation on the site of this important castle and was able to confirm a Byzantine date for the basic structure. A remarkable find was a well-preserved glass flask belonging to the later, Crusader, phase of the building.

In April a second course for Teachers of Classics in Schools was held in Athens under the joint sponsorship of the School and the Department of Education and Science. The theme was 'Athens: The Development of the City-State'. Twenty-one teachers participated in the two-week course.

In September the School's annual course for undergraduates on 'The Archaeology and Topography of Ancient Greece' took place, with twenty-five students participating.

As in previous years, a number of public lectures were held in the School during the session, as well as several informal seminars in which members of the American School of Classical Studies were invited to participate.

The Library continued to be well used throughout the session and the number of outside readers rose to sixty-one. The School was fortunate to receive further donations of books, papers, and photographs, both for the library in Athens and at Knossos. During the course of the year an updating of the Union Catalogue of periodicals held by foreign schools in Athens was completed.

The Fitch Laboratory, which now includes a petrological section, was in constant use and new equipment, for which the School is indebted to the Corinth Excavations, includes a Hewlett Packard 85 computer and dual disc drive. The main pottery project in hand is the chemical analysis of certain decorated wares from known Byzantine production centres in Greece, Cyprus, and Constantinople. In January the Fitch Laboratory organized a one-day meeting, attended by some seventy Greek and foreign archaeologists, at which papers were delivered by archaeological scientists, highlighting recent developments in their fields and demonstrations of work currently in progress in the Laboratory were given. Finally, a magnometer survey of the Byzantine town site of Khrysoupolis in Macedonia was carried out as part of a current reconnaissance of the site.

Late in February two severe earth tremors were felt in Athens but happily the School premises sustained only slight damage and later in the same week the Visiting Fellow, Mr M. S. F. Hood, was able to deliver his open lecture, 'Knossos through the Ages' to a large audience in the School.

P. M. WARREN
Chairman

BRITISH INSTITUTE IN EASTERN AFRICA

During the past year the Institute undertook field-work in the southern Sudan, in south-west Kenya, and in Somalia. The two-month expedition (January/March 1981) to the southern Sudan, led by the Assistant Director, Dr P. Robertshaw, was multi-disciplinary and included an anthropologist and a linguist. Among its members were representatives from the National Museum of Helsinki and Aalborg University, Denmark. Six pastoralist mound sites on the edge of the seasonally flooded grasslands in Lakes Province proved to be of the Iron Age and to date back to the first millenium AD. Oral traditions about these sites, of pre-Dinka origin, were collected. In the summer the Director, Dr H. N. Chittick, carried out test excavations in the centre of Mogadishu, capital of Somalia. Finds confirmed literary and epigraphic evidence that the city reached its peak in the thirteenth and fourteenth centuries and is unlikely to have been a place of significance before the twelfth century AD. In south-west Kenya the Assistant Director continued the archaeological survey begun last year. Shell mounds on the shore of Lake Victoria were excavated and numerous pastoralist Neolithic and Iron Age sites were investigated in Norok District.

In December 1980 an international seminar, jointly organized with the School of Oriental and African Studies, was held at the School on the archaeology and ethno-history of the southern Sudan. Papers read will be published as a Research Memoir of the Institute.

Dr Richard Pankhurst's Senior Research Fellowship was extended for a further year, to enable him to complete the second volume of his medieval history of Ethiopian towns. Seven Research Grants and loans of equipment were made. With the aid of a generous grant from the British Academy, the Institute's Library in Nairobi has been re-organized and re-indexed and facilities improved, including the photographic collection. The Library, of over 2,300 volumes and 230 periodicals, is much used by students and staff of the University and by visiting scholars. The Institute's staff continued to contribute to the University's teaching programme.

Plans were made during the year to begin excavations in 1981/2 at the large, early urban site of Soba East in the Sudan, on the Blue Nile south of Khartoum. Major archaeological work in Somalia, requested by the Somali Government, will have to be postponed because of conditions arising from the Ogaden War. Meanwhile the Institute has undertaken to advise the Somali Government on measures to preserve and schedule sites and monuments. The archaeological survey of south-west Kenya will continue.

L. P. KIRWAN
President

BRITISH INSTITUTE IN SOUTH-EAST ASIA

The year was marked by a modest but steady expansion and diversification of the Institute's activities, made possible in large measure by an increase of over 30 per cent in its grant from the British Academy, which more than compensated for risen costs.

The number of scholars who visited the Institute on their way through Singapore during the year increased to more than 100, indicating that the Institute is becoming more widely known internationally. This is no doubt due as much to the publication of the quarterly *South-East Asian Studies Newsletter* as to the extensive programme of travel carried out by the Director.

The *Newsletter* began publication in September 1980 and has met with a very good response from scholars and academic institutions throughout the world. It now has a mailing list of some 650 names, which include university departments and libraries from Aberdeen to Otago and Kyoto to California as well as individual scholars from more than twenty countries. A number of exchanges of material have also been started with the publishers of other newsletter and information bulletins.

The first symposium to be held under the auspices of the Institute took place in Singapore in January 1981. Five Indonesian, four Malaysian, and three Filipino historians came together to read papers and hold discussions over three days on the general theme of 'South-East Asian Responses to European Intrusions'. The papers presented at this symposium have now been accepted for publication under the Director's editorship. A second symposium along similar lines, in which it is hoped scholars from mainland South-East Asia will also participate, is planned for January 1982 in Manila.

Grants from the Institute's funds were made to assist the following to attend international conferences and present papers: Dr Andrew Forbes and Dr Michael Madha (Conference on Thai Studies, New Delhi, February 1981); Mr C. W. Watson (Symposium on Minangkabau, Amsterdam, April 1981); and Dr David Reeve (IIIrd Colloquium on Malay and Indonesian Studies, Naples, June 1981).

The Institute also awarded a grant to Dr J. L. Bay-Petersen to enable her to spend three months continuing her work on the excavation of Masbate, Philippines, which she began in 1978.

In November 1980 the Director gave a series of three lectures at the University of the Philippines on 'The Portuguese in the Indonesian Archipelago and the China Seas in the Sixteenth Century', and in June 1981 he conducted a seminar on 'Portuguese Malacca and Spanish Manila: Two Concepts of Empire' at Universiti Sains Malaysia, Penang. In August 1980 he attended the VIIIth Conference of the International Association of Historians of Asia in Kuala Lumpur, where he presented a paper on 'Trade and Society in the Banda Islands in the Sixteenth Century'. In October 1980 he went to Lisbon for the IInd International Seminar of Indo-Portuguese History where he presented a paper on 'The Sandalwood Trade and the First Portuguese Settlements in the Lesser Sunda Islands'. He also delivered a paper on 'The Jesuits in Moro 1546-1571' at the IInd Seminar on Halmahera and Raja Empat in Jakarta in June 1981.

At the Institute of Southeast Asian Studies in Singapore, the Director conducted two seminars during the year. The first, in January 1981, was on 'The Historical and Religious Significance of Borobudur', and the second, in March 1981, on 'The *Ramayana* in Indonesia'.

During 1980 the British Academy published the first volume of *The Archive of Yogyakarta* by Dr P. B. R. Carey, who was the Academy's first Travelling Fellow in South-East Asia. The Director went to Jakarta in February 1981 to present a copy of this publication to the Sultan of Yogyakarta.

Arrangements were set in train with the assistance of Professor Andrew Strathern for the addition of Papua New Guinea to the countries in the region with which the Institute might maintain scholarly links, particularly in the field of anthropology.

The Institute's reference collection of books and periodicals continued to develop and the target of 1,000 volumes by the end of 1980 was reached.

Mr Michael Evans, Assistant Secretary at the British Academy, visited Singapore in January 1981 to attend the Institute's symposium and discuss with Professor K. S. Sandhu at the Institute of Southeast Asian Studies the detailed arrangements for the award of the Leverhulme Fellowship in South-East Asian Studies which is to be tenable at

ISEAS. In April 1981 Professor Eugene Kamenka, Secretary of the Australian Academy of the Humanities, Canberra, which contributes to the Institute's funds, also paid a visit to Singapore and called on the Director.

JOHN VILLIERS
Director

BRITISH SCHOOL OF ARCHAEOLOGY IN IRAQ

This year in Iraq, the beginning of the autumn season was overshadowed by the outbreak of the Iraq-Iran war. Fortunately, the effects of hostilities have not been seriously felt in Baghdad. In the country generally travel for unescorted individuals has been restricted but archaeological teams with their government representatives have been able to move comparatively freely. Excavation permits were not forthcoming in the autumn either for Abu Salabikh or for the 'Ana island rescue project. The Director, Mr Postgate, was able to put in a period of study and preparation at Abu Salabikh, and he and the Assistant Director, Dr Roaf, were able to visit 'Ana and plan the mosque of Al-Meshhed and make preparations for excavations.

In the spring Mr Postgate excavated at Abu Salabikh for a ten-week season beginning 7 March. Areas to the south of areas E and A were subjected to surface clearance with a view to excavation. In the former area a building was then excavated, of which a coherent plan was recovered, belonging probably to Early Dynastic II. On the east side, the continued clearance of the Early Dynastic III ash tip yielded further sealings, miniature vessels, and figurines. Further graves were cleared, which provided interesting grave goods.

For 'Ana no permit was received for the spring season and the commencement of excavations was deferred to the following autumn.

Mr R. G. Killick was appointed Secretary-Librarian in the British Archaeological Expedition to Iraq and arrived in Baghdad in November to take up his appointment along with his fiancée Jane Moon, a former holder of the post.

Mr Postgate visited Toronto in December to act as one of the academic referees for the Royal Inscriptions of Mesopotamia project. Dr Roaf, during a spring visit to Britain, lectured at the universities of Manchester, Sheffield, and Oxford.

The uncertainties of the year and the restrictions on travel and work in the Iraq Museum resulted in fewer visits than usual to our Baghdad establishment by lecturers, grant holders, and others. Visitors included: Mr John Warren, an architect who had visited the mosque of Al-Meshhed with the Director and written a report for the State Organization for Antiquities and Heritage; Miss Deborah Downs, to complete her study on the human skeletal remains from Abu Salabikh, to be published in the Director's report on the graves, and from Tells

Madhhur and Rubeidheh, to be published in the Hamrin report of the Iraqi State Organization for Antiquities and Heritage; Mr Anthony Green (Fellow) to work on apotropaic foundation figurines; Mr Charles Burney (University of Manchester) to prepare for a projected Manchester University expedition to participate in the Eski Mosul Dam rescue project.

The Annual General Meeting was held on 2 December 1980. The new British Ambassador in Baghdad, Mr S. L. Egerton, CMG, was elected Vice-President in succession to the outgoing Ambassador, Mr A. J. D. Stirling, CMG, to whom thanks are due for his period of service. The Hon. Treasurer, Mr J. F. C. Springford, CBE, resigned his office and Mr G. J. Warren, General Manager of the Ottoman Bank, was elected to take his place. Mr Springford was elected to serve on the Council as were also Mr A. R. Millard (University of Liverpool), Miss M. J. Munn Rankin (University of Cambridge), and Dr J. E. Curtis (British Museum). Among the nominated members, Miss L. H. Jeffrey was succeeded by Miss E. Mackenzie (Lady Margaret Hall) and Mr P. Hulin by Professor James Barr, FBA (Board of Oriental Studies, University of Oxford).

Following the Annual General Meeting, the Vice-Chairman, Professor David Oates, gave the lecture entitled 'The Excavations at Tell Brak, 1980' in which he reported the successful results of the third post-war season at the site, conducted from March to May 1980, with the support of this School.

On 2 June 1981 Dr P. R. S. Moorey, FBA, gave the fourth Bonham Carter Memorial Lecture entitled 'Was There a Neo-Sumerian Cemetery at Ur?'

The School has changed its financial year from 1 June–31 May to 1 April–31 March in order to conform with the financial year of the British Academy.

We are very grateful to the State Organization for Antiquities and Heritage in Iraq and its President Dr Mu'ayyad Damerji, for their assistance and co-operation in what could have been a difficult year.

J. D. HAWKINS
Hon. Secretary

BRITISH SCHOOL OF ARCHAEOLOGY IN JERUSALEM

The principal field projects of the School continued to be the Architectural Survey of Mamluk and Ayyubid monuments in Jerusalem and the Survey of Ecclesiastical Buildings of the Latin Kingdom of Jerusalem.

The Head of Survey, Dr Michael Burgoyne, was assisted for four and a half months by the architect Mr R. Brotherton, for eight months by Mr Mark Potter, and for lesser periods by three students. During this period the survey of all the Mamluk buildings on the west of the Haram al-Sharif between Suq al-Qattanin and Tariq Bab al-Hadid was completed. Plans and sections of two buildings near the Bab al-Nazir were also carried through; one, the Ribat of Ala al-Din al-Basir, consists of two Crusader Halls converted to a Mamluk pilgrims' hospice in AD 1267-8 by adding ranges of cells; the other, the Hasaniyya Madrasa, is a small but beautifully decorated school of the fifteenth century.

Regular discussions have taken place with the Awqaf administration, which continued to facilitate the work of the survey.

The field survey part of the Crusader project also got under way with the arrival of Mr Peter Leach to assist Dr Pringle. In the course of the year Dr Pringle extended his catalogue and bibliography of churches within the area of the twelfth- to thirteenth-century Latin Kingdom. The list covers some 300 buildings, remains of 140 of which exist. The interim results are impressive and the final results, incorporating the evidence of contemporary records, will make a considerable contribution to the study of this period. Dr Pringle extended his activities in this period by preparing for publication medieval pottery found at Acre, 'Athlit, Caesarea, and St. Mary de Carmelo, near Haifa. He published an article on Crusader masons' marks in *Levant* XIII.

Dr Pringle also saw his book on *The Defence of Byzantine Africa, from Justinian to the Arab Conquest* (BAR, Oxford, 1981), through the press.

The Director, Canon John Wilkinson, worked on the origins of Palestinian church plans. His researches included work on a number of Byzantine church sites on both sides of the Jordan; and also on H. C. Butler's archive which he studied at Princeton University. He has also worked on the city plan of Jerusalem in the Byzantine period from the Madaba mosaic map.

He has lectured on these topics both to the AGM in London in January, in Manchester and Norwich, and also in Jerusalem, Jordan, and Minnesota. His article on 'Architectural Procedures in Byzantine Palestine' appeared in *Levant* XIII.

The Chairman visited the School in March and gave a lecture and a seminar to Old Testament scholars. Other lectures were given in the School by Dr Zehava Jacoby on the 'Crusader Portal of the Church of the Annunciation at Nazareth' and by Dr Hector Williams and Dr Caroline Williams on their work at Anamur (Turkey), and on Roman columned streets.

The hostel was well used in the course of the year by about thirty members in addition to staff of the architectural Survey and visiting students.

The Senior Scholarship for 1979/80 was awarded to Mr Richard Brotherton to study the stone muqarnas of medieval Syria. He spent nine months during 1980 engaged on this study, recording the muqarnas of seventy portals and thirty domes, making new plans of fourteen buildings, taking numerous elevations and photographs and contributing both to the Bilad al-Sham conference and to the International Mission for the Preservation of Damascus.

The Senior Scholarship for 1980/1 was awarded to Miss Shefali Rovik to work on Templar history and in particular the Order's use of the buildings in the Haram al-Sharif and elsewhere. She arrived in Jerusalem in February 1981.

Grants were also given to a number of students and to research projects. The latter included the excavations at Tell Nebi Mend (Syria), Buseirah (Jordan), and Lemba (Cyprus). Grants were made to Dr Carolyn Elliott for her catalogue of Chalcolithic ground stone objects from Cyprus; Miss A. Betts for her survey of Neolithic sites in Transjordan; Mr A. Killick for his survey of the Roman fortress at Udruh in Jordan, and to Miss G. Bentley to participate in underwater excavation at Haifa (Israel). Several of these students made use of the School's library or its hostel as a base for studying comparative collections in Museums.

Work on the publication of the Kenyon excavations at Jerusalem and Jericho continued. The publication of *Jericho* III was, however, subject to various delays and will, it is hoped, appear at last in the next report.

Dr Kay Prag
Hon. Secretary

BRITISH INSTITUTE OF PERSIAN STUDIES

The political situation in Iran remained unsettled throughout the year and brought the Institute's activities there to a virtual standstill except for the limited use made of the library. Travel outside Tehran was circumscribed and no foreign archaeological expeditions were authorized by the Iranian authorities, although a small number of students were permitted to make brief study visits, staying at the Institute.

Deterioration of the political situation caused the withdrawal of the Embassy staff in September when the Swedish Government became the Protecting Power. The Assistant Director, Martin Charlesworth, though encouraged to leave at the same time, preferred to remain in Tehran. He and his Iranian wife lived at the Institute throughout the year and were thus able to look after the premises, supervise repairs, and rearrange the library as well as catalogue new books posted from the UK which have arrived regularly. Despite shortages of petrol and heating fuel and a restricted social life, Mr Charlesworth's morale remained high; he also performed useful work by keeping close and friendly touch with the various Iranian authorities of concern to the Institute. His contract as Assistant Director was renewed for a further year.

Because of the situation within Iran it was decided to make Fellowship and Bursary awards available for candidates wishing to complete work on research and field-work already undertaken. Two Fellows, Miss Vanessa Martin and Mr Robert Wells, had their grants extended for a further year and two Bursaries were awarded, one to Mr Stephen Evans, to continue his work at Tehran University (later transferred to St. Antony's College, Oxford) and one to Mr Robert Bewley to study material from Houmian collected by the late Professor Charles McBurney.

With a view to maintaining and stimulating interest in Persian studies at this difficult time Council encouraged and organized lectures at a number of universities, museums, and school sixth forms. Some sixteen such lectures on a wide variety of topics were given by members of Council.

Council also attached particular importance to publications. The continued production of the journal *Iran* to a very high standard is to the credit of editors and printers. In July the first of the Siraf Report fascicules, *Siraf III: The Congregational Mosque*, was published.

The annual Summer Lecture and tea party was held at the British Academy on 2 July 1980 when Dr Michael Rogers spoke on 'A Renaissance of the Islamic Arts; Nineteenth Century Khiva'.

The Eighteenth Annual General Meeting took place on 12 November 1980. Following the meeting Professor David Stronach delivered the Annual Lecture on 'Twenty Years of Iranian Archaeology', a comprehensive survey not only of his own discoveries, but also of those of others working in Iran during this period. Large attendances at both lectures testified to the continued interest of members in Persian studies.

DENIS WRIGHT
President

BRITISH SCHOOL AT ROME

HRH Prince Philip, Chairman of the Royal Commission for the Exhibition of 1851 (which supports the Rome Scholarships in Architecture, Painting, Printmaking, and Sculpture) visited the School in October.

In September we welcomed Miss Amanda Claridge, BA, who works in the field of classical sculpture, as Assistant Director. Mrs Monique Bildesheim (Assistant Librarian) resigned during the session, following her husband's retirement. Miss Valerie Scott, BA, was appointed in her place.

The School enjoyed a busy year. Fourteen Scholars were in residence, there were 150 visitors, and the number of outside readers in the Library increased by nearly 50 per cent.

The Balsdon Senior Fellow, Professor G. D. B. Jones of Manchester University, devoted his tenure to preparing publications on the prehistoric and Roman archaeology of Apulia.

In March and April we joined the British Council in sponsoring a series of lectures by British and Italian scholars on poetry and drama in the fourteenth century. We arranged five other public lectures: 'Aspetti dell'iconografia dei vasi apuli', by Professor A. D. Trendall; 'Modern Latinity', by Dr David Greenwood; 'Il tavoliere romano' and 'The UNESCO Libyan Valleys Survey', by Professor Jones; and 'Gli scavi di Anguillara e di Farfa', by the Director. Professor Jones gave a series of seminars on Roman provincial archaeology.

The School's programme of archaeological research was dominated by the third season of excavation at Anguillara and Farfa Abbey. At Anguillara excavation revealed a group of buildings clustered round the ninth- or tenth-century church, while at Farfa work continued in the area between the Carolingian church and the Torrione, a massive tower, possibly bounded by a corridor or portico, beyond which was a large rectangular room and a chapel. It is tempting to regard at least the portico as the work of Abbot Siccard (830–42). The School also undertook an exploratory excavation at Tortoreto and a study season concerned with material from Otranto, excavated in 1977–8.

The annual Exhibition of work by Scholars in the Fine Arts took place in June, as did an exhibition of sculpture and drawings by Sarah Lee, a former Gulbenkian Rome Scholar.

In July we organized an undergraduate Summer School in Roman history and archaeology, directed by Dr David Shotter of Lancaster University. Shortly afterwards, a group of students from the School of Architecture, Manchester University stayed at the School while surveying the medieval atrium of S. Clemente. We also welcomed a group of sixth-formers from Rugby School.

In addition to routine maintenance of the building, work began on a thorough overhaul of the Lutyens façade. The portico was completed in the autumn of 1980 and a contract has been placed for work on the wings in the summer of 1981. A mezzanine was constructed in the print-making studio to provide a 'clean' working area and new lighting was installed throughout the studio corridor. A new dark-room was made. Finally, the electrical wiring in the Library was inspected and partly renewed.

DAVID WHITEHOUSE
Director

EGYPT EXPLORATION SOCIETY

For several reasons the Society was unable to mount all the expeditions planned for the 1980–1 season. Work was continued, however, in the Temple Town area of North Saqqara, in the New Kingdom necropolis at South Saqqara, and in the Workmen's Village at Akhenaten's capital of El-Amarna. In addition to these three projects, the Society resumed its pre-war work in the North City at El-Amarna, and undertook overall responsibility for a photographic mission to the Cairo Museum, led by Dr R. Coles and Dr H. Maehler, concerned with recording the Cairo Zenon papyri, documents found by Grenfell and Hunt, and texts discovered in the recent seasons at Qasr Ibrim.

Work at North Saqqara, under the direction of Professor H. S. Smith (University College London), continued from October to December 1980. There was considerable progress on the final Anubieion report: chapters were written on the stratigraphy and architecture of the temple and settlement sites; publication drawings, survey maps, and diagrams were completed. The expedition also did investigations at Mitrahina, in preparation for the survey and rescue work at Memphis the Society hopes to launch in celebration of its centenary year in 1982.

In the New Kingdom necropolis Dr G. T. Martin (University College London) led a combined team from the EES and the Leiden Museum. The season, from January to March 1981, explored an area west of the tomb of Horemheb. Two Ramesside tombs were discovered. One belongs to Paser, Overseer of Builders, and his wife Pepwy; three stelae were found, and there is a fourth, apparently from this tomb, in the British Museum. The other tomb was owned by Raia, Chief Singer of Ptah. On one wall Raia is shown as a blind harpist; on the opposite wall he has normal eyesight.

The expedition at El-Amarna was under the leadership of Mr Barry Kemp (University of Cambridge) and lasted from January to March 1981. An extra-mural area south of the Workmen's Village produced a series of T-shaped basins embedded in a flat terrace; and in another sector a complex stratigraphy was revealed suggesting at least three building levels, which may have far-reaching significance for the chronology of El-Amarna. The North City work was supervised by Michael Jones, the principal aim being to complete the Society's pre-war records for publication in the City of Akhenaten series. Two main areas were investigated: the grounds of a large estate with a set of circular granary bins; and a sector in front of the great gateway of the North Riverside Palace.

The Society produced three significant volumes during the year: its fiftieth Excavation Memoir appeared in the form of G. T. Martin's *The Sacred Animal Necropolis at North Saqqara*, incorporating some of the late Professor Emery's work; a commemorative book, *Papyri Edited in Honour of E. G. Turner*, was made possible by the collaboration of fifty-three scholars from thirteen different countries, and was produced to mark the occasion of Sir Eric's seventieth birthday; and Volume 66 of *The Journal of Egyptian Archaeology* was published towards the end of 1980. A considerable body of research has been carried out during the year towards the production of further memoirs.

R. D. ANDERSON
Hon. Secretary

SOCIETY FOR LIBYAN STUDIES

During the past twelve months the Society has held four lectures in London. At the Annual General Meeting, on 2 December 1980, Dr

Graeme Barker gave an account of the recently completed second successful season of the UNESCO Libyan Valleys Survey which had been sponsored by the Society and which has greatly enlarged our knowledge of prehistoric, Roman, and Islamic settlement in the Tripolitanian hinterland. In April 1981 Dr P. M. Kenrick lectured to the Society on 'Roman Cities of North Africa' and, during May 1981, Dr J. A. Riley spoke on 'Economic Activity in Cyrenaica during the Hellenistic and Roman Periods'. In June 1981 members were addressed by Professor Donald White of the University Museum of Pennsylvania who gave a résumé of the early history of Cyrene in the light of recent archaeological discoveries.

The Society is pleased to report that a further successful season has been completed at Medinat Sultan and it is expected that work on the full publication of this site will be undertaken during 1982. A third season of field-work has taken place in the Tripolitanian Valleys where a UNESCO-backed team led by Dr Barker and Professor Jones has continued to produce much new evidence pertaining to settlement sites and their relationship to water resources during ancient times.

Financial assistance has been given to a number of projects during the year. Two grants were made to Dr Allan, the first to assist with the expenses of his conference on 'Economic and Social Development in Libya During the Late Nineteenth and Twentieth Centuries' and the second to support his work on the application of Remote Sensing techniques to the study of Libyan agriculture. Dr Riley also received a grant to assist with the costs of his project concerned with the sectioning of Cyrenaican pottery.

The first volume of the major report on the excavations at Sidi Khrebish (Benghazi) has now been published and is available from the Secretary of the Society. Volume II is at press.

The Library of the Society, which is housed in the School of Oriental and African Studies, University of London, continues to expand and a number of important purchases have been made during the last twelve months. The Society has been particularly pleased to obtain a copy of the first English edition of Leo Africanus, *A Geographical Historie of Africa*.

Membership has remained steady despite a recent increase in subscription charges and the number of Libyan members has continued to increase.

SHELAGH LEWIS
Secretary

COUNCIL FOR BRITISH ARCHAEOLOGY

A number of meetings were organized during the year, the most important of which was the symposium on the impact of aerial reconnaissance on archaeology, held at the University of Nottingham in December. Several contributions were made by archaeologists from overseas to a well-balanced programme; the proceedings are to be published by the Council in 1982. The Archaeological Science Committee organized a seminar on the characterization of structureless organic materials from archaeological contexts, also in December, and played a major role in the conference on quantitative methods in archaeology, in March. The Urban Research Committee arranged a two-day meeting in Oxford in May to discuss recent developments in urban archaeology in Britain: a volume containing short reports on recent work in over 100 towns was published to coincide with this meeting. A seminar on the reconstruction of timber buildings from archaeological evidence, arranged by the Historic Buildings Committee, was held at West Dean in May. Professor Maurice Barley (President 1964-7) delivered the 5th Beatrice de Cardi Lecture on 'Houses and History' at Canterbury in December: the full text appears in the CBA's Annual Report No. 31.

The Research Board began preparations for the compilation, with the assistance of the specialist committees that report to it, of a statement of research priorities in British archaeology over the next decade. This important policy statement, a successor to the famous *Survey and Policy* of 1947, will be published in 1982. The Churches Committee extended its work in two ways: it took active steps to encourage greater provision for church archaeology in Scotland, and it set up a working party on non-conformist places of worship, with the intention of formulating proposals for an advisory system. The Industrial Archaeology Committee continued its work on the preparation of a manual for the recording of industrial monuments. The work of the Countryside Committee was concentrated on the establishment of closer links and the formulation of joint projects with outside bodies such as the Countryside Commission, the National Farmers' Union, and the National Trust.

The Council's work in the field of education continued on a broad front. The British Universities Archaeology Committee was preoccupied with problems of graduate careers, vocational training in university courses, and links between universities and schools. The newly reconstituted Adult Education Committee initiated a survey of current provision for archaeology teaching in adult education. The Council was awarded a three-year grant by the Leverhulme Trust to fund a research project for the teaching of archaeology in secondary schools.

A working relationship has been developed with French archaeologists. The Council collaborated with the Délégation Générale à la Recherche Scientifique et Technique in placing young French archaeologists with professional units in London and Oxford for practical training, and also administered a DGRST Fellowships scheme to enable senior British archaeologists to carry out research in France.

The flow of CBA publications continued at a high rate. In addition to the periodical publications (*Newsletter and Calendar*, *British Archaeological Abstracts*, *Archaeology in Britain*, and *Archaeological Bibliography*), the Council published three Research Reports on archaeology in Essex,

excavations in Hereford, and coinage in Britain and Gaul, two fascicules of *The Archaeology of Lincoln* and three of *The Archaeology of York*,
and three shorter booklets, on archaeology in the Ordnance Survey,
survey by prismatic compass, and recording old houses. Grants totalling £4,500 were made to thirteen member societies to assist them
in the publication of research papers.

HENRY CLEERE
Director

ENGLISH PLACE-NAME SOCIETY

The present year saw the publication only of *Journal* 13, though the first
two of the three volumes of *Cheshire V* have gone through proof stage and
are promised by the press before the end of 1981. The final part is not yet
ready. The cost of publication of these two volumes, however, shows
such a steep rise that it is clear that after the completion of the Cheshire
survey a new method of printing will have to be devised in order to cut
these costs drastically.

Good progress continues on *Durham* (Mr V. E. Watts), *Kent* (Mr
J. McN. Dodgson), *Norfolk* (Dr K. I. Sandred), and *Shropshire* (Dr
Margaret Gelling). Meanwhile, after having had to spend considerable time on the new *Old English Dictionary* project, Dr Barrie Cox
has resumed work on *Rutland* which he is preparing with Mr John Field.
The appointment of Mr Field as Editorial Assistant on *Lincolnshire*
has also proved so successful that the first volume, dealing with the
County of the City of Lincoln, may be complete by the end of the
summer of 1982.

Again I thank our Secretary, Mrs M. D. Pattison, for her stalwart
work, without which I could not continue as Honorary Director. Our
Research Assistant, Miss K. Coutts, has settled into her post most
successfully, and is to be congratulated for the excellence of her
transcriptions and for the sensitive way in which she has provided
editors with helpful pieces of additional information.

I have already touched upon the support I have received from Mr
John Field, now our Editorial Assistant. I have long claimed that only
with the help of such a person could the Society ever hope to catch up
with publications. Already this appointment means that I can hope to
complete the first volume of the Lincolnshire survey by late summer
1982, at least two years earlier than I could have done on my own. If we
succeed in finding a cheaper way in which to print this volume the salary
involved will have been more than repaid.

The Society continues to enjoy considerable material support
from the University of Nottingham. Our grateful thanks are due to
the Vice-Chancellor, and to my colleagues, through Professor James
Kinsley, for all their sympathetic support. Similarly, we have to thank
the Provost and Professor Randolph Quirk for continuing to allow

our Research Assistant the use of a room in University College London.

KENNETH CAMERON
Honorary Director

(*b*) GRANTS TO BRITISH NATIONAL COMMITTEES

	£
British National Committee for the Association Internationale d'Études du Sud-Est Européen	500
British National Committee of the International Congress of Historical Sciences	2,000
British National Committee for the History of the Second World War	4,250
British National Committee for Logic, Methodology, and Philosophy of Science	750
British National Committee for Geography	1,000
British National Committee for Linguistics	1,000
	£9,500

BRITISH NATIONAL COMMITTEE OF THE ASSOCIATION INTERNATIONALE D'ÉTUDES DU SUD-EST EUROPÉEN (Chairman: The Hon. Sir Stephen Runciman)

The Committee sponsored two open meetings of specialists in the field of South-East European Studies in British universities. The purpose of the meetings was to discuss how best these studies might be protected in the current financial crisis affecting the universities and to make suggestions for greater co-operation between universities in this area of study. One outcome of the discussions was the decision to institute a South-East European studies newsletter, subsidized by the Committee. The Committee also made grants in connection with the conference on Ancient Bulgaria held at the University of Nottingham in September 1981; the Committee of Honour created in connection with the 1300th anniversary of the foundation of the Bulgarian State; and the conference on 'Greece in the 1980s', held at King's College in January 1981 to mark the accession of Greece as the tenth member of the EEC.

The third Anglo-Romanian historical colloquium took place under the joint auspices of the British and Romanian National Committees of AIESEE at the AD Xenopol Institute of History and Archaeology, Jassy. Seven British scholars took part and the proceedings are in the course of publication.

R. R. M. CLOGG
Secretary

BRITISH NATIONAL COMMITTEE OF THE INTERNATIONAL
CONGRESS OF HISTORICAL SCIENCES (Chairman: Professor
T. S. Barker)

The British National Committee, with financial help from the British
Council, organized the third Anglo-Polish Conference of Historians,
which was held in London between 22 and 24 September 1981. The
following papers were discussed: Dr I. N. R. Davies, 'British Attitudes to
Poland, 1772-1832'; Dr Jerzy Jedlicki, 'Polish Images of England,
1764-1900'; Professor Antoni Mączak, 'Rural Society in Poland in the
16th and 17th Centuries'; Dr I. Joan Thirsk, 'The Exchange of Agricultural Knowledge in Europe, 1500-1700'; Professor F. M. L. Thompson, 'The Effects of Agricultural Depression in Britain, 1870- 1914'; and
Professor Andrzej Jezierski, 'British-Polish Trade in the 19th Century,
1815-1914'. The lively discussions led to an additional, informal session
at which the current situation in Poland was freely talked about. The
British Academy gave a dinner in honour of the visiting delegation.

The Chairman, Professor Barker, attended a meeting of the Bureau of
CISH which was held in Andorra from 21 to 23 September, and was
therefore unable to be present at the Anglo-Polish Conference. At its
meeting the Bureau had its first discussion of plans for the XVIth International Congress, which will be held in Stuttgart in August or early
September 1985.

BRITISH NATIONAL COMMITTEE FOR THE HISTORY OF THE
SECOND WORLD WAR (Chairman: Sir William Deakin)

The grant given this year has gone towards a joint Conference with the
American Committee, details of which can be found in the 1979/80
Annual Report.

BRITISH NATIONAL COMMITTEE FOR LOGIC, METHODOLOGY,
AND PHILOSOPHY OF SCIENCE (Chairman: Professor S. Korner)

The Committee is affiliated to the General Assembly of the International Union for History and Philosophy of Science (Division of
LMPS).

(c) ACADEMY COLLECTIVE RESEARCH PROJECTS

1. *Lexicons, Dictionaries, Bibliographies, and Maps*

ICONOGRAPHICAL LEXICON OF CLASSICAL MYTHOLOGY
COMMITTEE (Chairman: Professor J. Boardman)

The Committee was created in 1972 to oversee the British contribution
to an international project sponsored by the Union Académique Internationale and UNESCO and supervised by a Foundation established

under Swiss Law in Basel. It is the aim of the project, of which the British Academy is a founder member, to publish a major Lexicon devoted to the iconography of scenes and figures of myth in Greek and Roman art in the form of five double volumes. The publication is in the hand of Artemis Verlag, Zurich. The editorial and documentation centre is in Basel.

The first double volume has been printed; and the text and plates of the second volume are being prepared for the press.

British Documentation. Work continues in the British Museum (Mrs Woodford) and with objects on the London market (Dr Johnson). Most other British collections have already been carded. Professor Boardman attended editorial and Foundation Council meetings in Basel, Paris, and Athens.

LEXICON OF GREEK PERSONAL NAMES COMMITTEE (Chairman: Mr P. M. Fraser)

The project, adopted by the Academy in 1972, aims to record all Greek personal names and names in Greek from the earliest Greek period to the Islamic conquests of the Near East in the middle of the seventh century, with the purpose of producing a new onomastic lexicon to replace the standard current lexicon, published in 1862.

Slipping of material for the Lexicon is now nearly complete for the mainland of Greece, and should be completed by the end of 1982. The principal task is now to edit and computerize this material, combined with work on font and format for final printing. The work promised by contributors for Part I has now largely been received; for Part II (especially Palestine and Syria) slipping will continue for some time, as originally envisaged.

It has been agreed that, instead of holding the whole material on file, before submitting it for photographic printing by the Oxford University Press, publication should be on the basis of regional volumes, to enable the work to be available to scholars interested in particular areas. A final volume will combine addenda with various computerized indexes. The aim is to have one volume—the Greek Islands and Cyrenaica—ready for the Press by the end of 1982, and thereafter the work should proceed according to the completion of the individual regions.

LIDDELL AND SCOTT SUPPLEMENT COMMITTEE (Chairman: Professor M. L. West)

This is a new Committee, established in 1981 with the aim of producing in about ten years a second Supplement to Liddell and Scott's *Greek-English Lexicon* (to replace the first Supplement of 1968). It is envisaged that interim Bulletins will be published at intervals.

An agreement has been concluded with the Oxford University Press by which the Press provides office space and clerical support for the editor, and undertakes to publish the Supplement when complete.

Mr P. G. W. Glare has been appointed as editor, and an office has been set up in the Clarendon Building, Oxford. Contacts have been established with the *Diccionario griego-español* in Madrid and the *Thesaurus Linguae Graecae* at Irvine.

MEDIEVAL LATIN DICTIONARY COMMITTEE (Chairman Dr M. Winterbottom)

The first Academy Committee for this project was formed in 1924. The present Committee, formed in 1963, works in close association with the Public Record Office. The aim of the project is to produce, from British sources, a Dictionary of Medieval Latin.

Fascicule II (C) was published on 14 May 1981. D–E will form Fascicule III. D-*emanare* is already stored on magnetic tape at the Cambridge Literary and Linguistic Computer Centre. Prepared text may reach the end of E by December 1982, a year ahead of schedule.

PROSOPOGRAPHY OF THE LATER ROMAN EMPIRE (Chairman: Professor Philip Grierson)

The project was adopted by the Academy in 1970, following the death of Professor A. H. M. Jones. Its aim is to undertake and complete research on a compilation of the Later Roman Empire, down to the death of Heraclius in 641.

Since the publication of Volume II of the Prosopography (a. 359–527) in the autumn of 1980, work has continued steadily on the preparation of Volume III, the final volume, with the reading of further sources and the collection of more material. A visit by Dr John Nesbitt, an authority on Byzantine lead seals from Dumbarton Oaks, provided much valuable information and fresh material. At the same time work on composing preliminary drafts and compiling lists of office holders went ahead. A number of draft entries was circulated among various Committee members for comment and criticism.

During the year the second set of *Addenda et Corrigenda* to Volume I (a. 260–395) was published in *Historia*. (Volume I was published in 1971, and reprinted in 1975; the first set of *Addenda et Corrigenda* appeared in *Historia* in 1974.)

TABULA IMPERII ROMANI COMMITTEE (Chairman: Professor A. L. F. Rivet)

This international project has since 1957 been the responsibility of the UAI. Its aim is the publication of maps covering the whole of the Roman Empire. The British Committee is responsible for the preparation of Sheet M30 (Londinium–Lutetia) and has taken on responsibility for Sheet J36 (Ancyra–Iconium).

Principally owing to the prolonged illness and subsequent death of the Chairman, Mr J. B. Ward-Perkins, no meetings were held during the year. Work on both Sheets J36 and M30, however, progressed satisfactorily and the latter is on the point of being submitted for publication.

2. Archaeology, Numismatics, and Art History

CARTHAGE COMMITTEE (Chairman: Professor B. W. Cunliffe) In 1973 the Academy agreed to establish a Committee to administer a grant made by the Ministry of Overseas Development to the Save Carthage Project; in 1979 it was agreed to keep the Committee in being when ODM funds were exhausted, and grants from Academy funds in this and subsequent years were approved. The Academy has accepted a commitment to publish six volumes of report, two each for the three sites excavated by the British Mission. For each site one volume will cover both the excavation and the finds other than pottery (edited by the field Director, Mr Henry Hurst), and the second will cover the pottery (edited by the Director of the Ceramics Unit, Dr David Peacock).

The Committee's activities were overshadowed by the death in June of the Chairman, Mr J. B. Ward-Perkins. He has been succeeded by Professor B. W. Cunliffe.

The Committee reports that Parts I and II of the Committee's six-part series on Excavations at Carthage, covering the Avenue Habib Bourguiba Salammbô (Part I site report; Part II ceramic studies), were submitted for publication in March. Work is currently well advanced on the report of the second of the Committee's three sites, the north site of the Circular Harbour. Major progress was also made with the presentation of the site remains on the Îlot de l'Amirauté.

CORPUS OF ANGLO-SAXON STONE SCULPTURE COMMITTEE (Chairman: Professor G. Zarnecki) The Committee was established in 1972 with the purpose of supervising the production of an illustrated catalogue of Anglo-Saxon Stone Sculpture in Britain, arranged by areas and estimated to extend to six volumes. During 1980 it was established that the University of Durham is very glad to provide a home for the project.

Work of the Committee concentrated on getting the first volume ready for publication and this has been achieved. An experienced outside editor was employed to read the text before it was submitted to the Publications Committee. A part-time research assistant, Mr Eric Cambridge, has been appointed through the University. The Durham meeting enabled the Committee to meet all the authors who reported on the progress of the work. The next volume which will cover Cumbria and Yorkshire is well advanced.

CORPUS INSCRIPTIONUM IRANICARUM COMMITTEE (Chairman: Sir Harold Bailey)

The Corpus Inscriptionum Iranicarum was founded in 1951 with the purpose of publishing complete collections of inscriptions (with fac-similes and commentaries) in Iranian and other historically related languages, bearing on Iranian civilization taken in its broadest sense. This international project was adopted by the UAI in 1973 and the Committee supervising the British Contribution was formally con-stituted an Academy Committee in 1978.

The work of J. Greenfield and B. Porten, *The Bisitun Inscription of Darius the Great: Aramaic Version*, is now in proof, and the return of the marked sheets is being awaited. The typescript and photographs for Dr A. R. Shahbazi's portfolio *Old Persian Inscriptions of the Persepolis Platform* have now been received. Several supplementary photographs are to be ordered from museums, and the printer's estimate is being obtained. Typescript for the first volume of Dr F. Vallat's edition of the Achaemenid Elamite inscription is expected in March 1982. This will be a substantial work, ultimately to consist of two volumes, the second of which will contain a grammar and glossary of Achaemenid Elamite. Dr M. Shokoohy has offered a portfolio of Persian inscriptions of the Sultanate period in Rajastan, which would represent the first contribu-tion to the Committee's long-projected plan for a collection of the Persian inscriptions of India. The Committee is to review the material offered in March 1982. If suitable, it will be included in the programme for 1983. A volume with illustrations and texts on the Persian inscrip-tions of Azarbaijan has been offered by Dr Gerd Gropp of Hamburg. This now requires a small supplement of additional material, which the contributor is being invited to add.

CORPUS SIGNORUM IMPERII ROMANI COMMITTEE (Chairman: Professor J. M. C. Toynbee)

The project was adopted by the Academy in 1974 with the purpose of preparing for publication the Romano-British fascicules of the inter-national series Corpus Signorum Imperii Romani.

The Committee reports that it has suffered two grievous set-backs during the year: the first was the death of Mr J. B. Ward-Perkins and the second, the early retirement of Mr E. J. Phillips, whose first fascicule, on the eastern sector of Hadrian's Wall, published in 1977, was a model for the series. Mr Phillips's second fascicule (on the western sector of Hadrian's Wall) was at an advanced stage when he became ill and he has consigned his unfinished manuscript to the Committee together with his work to date on the third fascicule, that on the hinterland of Hadrian's Wall.

The fascicule on Bath and the rest of Wessex, by B. W. Cunliffe and M. Fulford, is with the printers. There have been editorial delays on the Yorkshire fascicule, by R. S. Tufi, but this is virtually finished. Good progress has been made on the fascicule for Scotland, by L. Keppie, who expects to be in a position to submit it by early summer 1982. A start has been made on the fascicule for Wales, by G. C. Boon.

CORPUS VASORUM ANTIQUORUM COMMITTEE (Chairman: Professor J. Boardman)

The Committee was created by the Academy in 1962 to supervise the British contribution to an international project sponsored by the Union Académique Internationale, whose intention is to publish all public and private collections of Greek pottery.

Volume I of the Toronto, Royal Ontario Museum series (ed. J. Hayes) was published in January 1981, jointly with the Museum and with the help of a grant from the Social Sciences and Humanities Research Council of Canada.

Work is proceeding to prepare Volume II of the New Zealand series for publication (ed. J. R. Green).

BIBLIOGRAPHY OF ILLUSTRATIONS OF ATHENIAN VASES

This project, funded for three years by means of Academy Research Grants, was accepted by Council in 1981 as an Academy Research Project, to be managed by the Corpus Vasorum Antiquorum Committee. It is based on the Beazley Archive in Oxford.

Its aims are (a) To bring up to date the bibliography of the vases attributed by Sir John Beazley and listed in his publications. This should be published, with further publications of supplementary material, at regular intervals of four or five years. (b) To create descriptive and bibliographical entries for vases not in Beazley's lists. These are kept in the Oxford computer, and are not for publication, but various relevant combinations of information and indexes can be supplied to scholars on request.

Progress on (a) has been such that it is nearly complete to date. The Committee propose to put the information on to the Oxford computer so that it can be both processed for publication via Lasercomp, and stored to be updated with fresh data for future publications. Work on (b) has resulted in taping over 6,000 cards covering the last fifteen years of publications. Experiments to determine the most useful method of handling the material are in hand and some indexes have already been produced.

CORPUS VITREARUM MEDII AEVI COMMITTEE (Chairman: Dr A. R. Dufty)

The Corpus Vitrearum Medii Aevi Committee was set up in 1956 to supervise the British contribution to the international Corpus Vitrearum, sponsored by the Union Académique Internationale and the Comité International d'Histoire d'Art. Its primary aim is to publish illustrated catalogues of the medieval stained and painted glass in Britain. It is also concerned to monitor and assist with current restoration and to sponsor the establishment of research archives.

The second British volume, *The Windows of Christ Church Cathedral, Canterbury* by Madeline Caviness, was published in October 1981 (372 pages of text, with 963 black-and-white and 18 colour illustrations).

During the year negotiations with the Royal Commission on Historical Monuments (England) for the establishment of a CVMA archive at the National Monuments Record were successfully concluded. Work began in November 1981 with the appointment of a Research Worker, Mr M. Michael, to compile a topographical and iconographical index of the existing photographic coverage. The establishment of the archive will not only make the material collected under its auspices available to scholars and the general public, but will also bring the British organization into line with its continental partners.

Because of the length of time and the expense involved in the production of volumes, the British Corpus authors are now directing their efforts to completing their work in fascicules and monographs. Work on the following fascicules and monographs is near completion: Lincoln (Mr N. J. Morgan); City of Oxford (Miss J. Kerr and Dr P. A. Newton); York Minster West Wall (Mr T. French and Mr D. O'Connor). Work is in progress on Norwich (Mr D. J. King); and Kent (Mr N. J. Morgan).

SYLLOGE OF COINS OF THE BRITISH ISLES COMMITTEE (Chairman: Professor H. R. Loyn)

The project was adopted by the Academy in 1956 with the aim of publishing a detailed account of the British coinage. Twenty-eight volumes have so far been published.

Two volumes have appeared during the year: Volume 27, *Lincolnshire Collections*, by A. Gunstone, and Volume 28, *Cumulative Index of Volumes 1–20*, by Mrs V. S. Smart. Work is in progress on several other volumes: *Merseyside County Museums*, by Mrs M. Warhurst, and *American Collections*, by J. D. Brady are in proof. It is hoped that *British Museum I* and the *J. G. Brooker Collection of Coins of Charles I* will be ready for the printer in 1982.

A Co-ordinating Committee for Celtic Coins has been set up and referred to the Sylloge Committee as an extension of its general remit. The Co-ordinating Committee, under Professor B. W. Cunliffe will act as a loosely associated subcommittee of the Sylloge.

The Academy has agreed to participate in the proposed publication of the collection of Medieval European Coins deposited by Professor Philip Grierson, FBA, in the Fitzwilliam Museum, Cambridge, and has extended the terms of reference to the Committee to include this enterprise. The full publication is expected to comprise thirteen fascicules and is estimated to take about seven years to complete. It is hoped to appoint a Research Assistant to work with Professor Grierson on the Collection.

SYLLOGE NUMMORUM GRAECORUM COMMITTEE (Chairman: Dr C. H. V. Sutherland)

The project was established in 1931 and adopted by the Academy as a Major Project in 1967. Its aim is the publication of a series of volumes describing and illustrating collections of Greek coins in the British Isles. Five volumes have been published, all in several parts.

SNG V (Oxford), iv (Paeonia–Thessaly) was published in March 1981. Mr K. Sugden is continuing his work on *SNG* Blackburn as is Mr J. Healey on *SNG* Manchester. The next part to be received for publication is likely to be the second and final part of *SNG* VI, Lewis Collection Corpus Christi College, Cambridge.

3. *Texts (classical, medieval, and modern)*

ANGLO-SAXON CHARTERS COMMITTEE (Chairman: Professor G. W. S. Barrow)

The Committee, which consists of representatives of the Academy and of the Royal Historical Society, was formed in 1966 to plan and oversee the publication of a new corpus of Anglo-Saxon Charters. Two fascicules have so far appeared.

The Committee has proposed no change in this project since the last report. Professor C. R. Cheney's request to resign was reluctantly accepted and the Committee has recommended the Academy to appoint Dr Simon Keynes of Trinity College, Cambridge, as an additional member.

Two fascicules are nearing completion; the charters of Sherborne by Miss O'Donovan and those of Selsey by Mr Roper. Both are being revised in the light of comments made by members of the Committee.

BENTHAM COMMITTEE (Chairman: Professor H. L. A. Hart)

The project was established in 1959 with the aim of preparing and publishing a comprehensive edition of the works and correspondence of Jeremy Bentham. It was adopted by the Academy in 1969. In November 1979, the status of the Committee was changed. It was formally reconstituted as a committee of the Council of University College London, and this included a provision that two members of the Committee should be nominated by the Academy.

Dr J. R. Dinwiddy continued as part-time General Editor, and Dr C. F. Bahmueller took up his post as Assistant General Editor (financed by University College and the British Academy) on 1 July 1981.

The Correspondence, Volumes IV and V, were published in November 1981. *Constitutional Code*, vol. i, and *Deontology, together with a Table of the Springs of Action and the Article on Utilitarianism*, are in process of production. The volume on *Chrestomathia* was delivered to OUP in July 1981.

CLASSICAL AND MEDIEVAL LOGIC TEXTS (Chairman: Professor P. T. Geach)

The project was adopted by the Academy in 1966 with the aim of publishing new editions and translations of philosophical works. Its present aim is the preparation in about twenty fascicules of an *en face* edition, with notes, of Paul of Venice's *Logica Magna* from the Venice printed text, corrected by reference to the Vatican Manuscript. The Committee has decided not to occupy itself with any other schemes falling within its terms of reference for the foreseeable future.

During the past year two volumes have appeared, the third and fourth in the series: F. W. Zimmermann's *Al Farabi's Commentary and Short Treatise on Aristotle's 'De Interpretatione'*, and Miss Patricia Clarke's fascicule of *Paul of Venice, 'Logica Magna, Prima Pars, Tractatus de Scire et Dubitare'*.

This year the Committee has had the good luck to secure the co-operation of Professor George Hughes of the Victoria University of Wellington, New Zealand; his edition and translation of some of Buridan's *Sophismata* will shortly be forthcoming from Cambridge University Press and he has already begun work on a fascicule of Paul of Venice.

Professor Eileen Serene of Yale University has finished transcribing her fascicule (dealing with modal logic); Dr D. P. Henry's half-fascicule is complete and in the hands of his collaborator Dr T. C. Potts; Dr C. Williams's work is also well advanced; and Dr L. M. de Rijk has provided a Latin text for Professor Geach's fascicule.

CORPUS OF BRITISH MEDIEVAL LIBRARY CATALOGUES COMMITTEE (Chairman: Mr N. R. Ker)

The project was established in 1981 with the aim of editing (*a*) the two medieval union catalogues, the Franciscan *Registrum Librorum Angliae* and the *Catalogus Scriptorum* of the Benedictine Henry of Kirkstede, and (*b*) the pre-Dissolution book catalogues of religious and other institutions in Britain.

Dr Gibson's work on the Christ Church, Canterbury, catalogue and also Professor and Mrs Rouse's work on their edition of the *Registrum Librorum Angliae* should be complete early in 1983. Dr Bruce Barker-Benfield has begun transcribing the catalogue of St. Augustine's, Canterbury. Dr Watson is working on the two Augustinian catalogues, Lanthony and Leicester. Dr Kenneth Humphreys expects to start work on the catalogue of the York Austin Friars this year and Mr Alan Piper, Dr Elaine Drage, and Dr Katherine Waller are to edit the Durham, Exeter, and Rochester catalogues respectively.

CRITICAL EDITION OF THE GREEK NEW TESTAMENT COM-
MITTEE (Chairman: The Revd Professor J. M. Plumley)

The aim of the project is to compile a comprehensive critical apparatus to the Greek text of the Gospel of Luke using the evidence of all the Greek uncial manuscripts and 126 selected Greek minuscule manuscripts, and the significant variants in the early version in ten languages, as well as in the biblical texts quoted by the Greek, Latin, and Syriac Fathers. This will be the essential foundation for the establishment of any new critical edition and for studies on the subsequent history of the text.

In March 1977 Council decided, and the Committee agreed, that no further application for Academy funds should be considered until after the delivery of the second fascicule of the Third Gospel, as required by the terms of the agreement with the Oxford University Press.

This condition has now been fulfilled since copy for chapters 6-10, together with chapters 1-5, was handed over to the Oxford University Press on 29 April 1981. The Press now intends to publish, not in fascicules, but in two volumes; Volume I to contain chapters 1-10 and Volume II the rest of the Gospel. Chapters 11 and 12 will receive their final revision by the end of November 1981. Chapter 13 is at an advanced stage of readiness. Chapters 14 and 15 lack only the Latin Fathers and three small items. If the recent rate of progress is maintained (seven chapters in 1979-81 during the Editorship of Dr J. K. Elliott), the Gospel will be completed in 1986.

Dr C. Lash ceased work on the Ethiopic collation, and Dr Josef Hofmann, of West Germany, has supplied the Ethiopic evidence for chapters 7-24. Dr Birdsall has given up his last connection with the Committee, viz. the Irenaeus material, which Mr Pattie is working on.

EPISCOPAL ACTA COMMITTEE (Chairman: Professor C. R. Cheney)

The Committee, comprising Fellows of the Academy together with representatives of the Canterbury and York Society and of the University of York, was established in 1973 to supervise the editing and publication of English medieval episcopal acta. It has the services of a salaried General Editor (part-time) in the person of Dr D. M. Smith, Director of the Borthwick Institute of Historical Research in the University of York. The Borthwick Institute is the headquarters of the project and houses an archive of photocopies and transcripts of episcopal acta.

On 18 June 1981 the Editor delivered to the Academy the final typescript of *Canterbury acta 1162-1205* (two volumes) prepared by C. R. Cheney. Volume IV (*Lincoln 1186-1235*), edited by Dr D. M. Smith, is likely to be submitted late in 1982. Work on *York 1070–1154* is being checked by the General Editor and this (with or without *York 1154–1212*) will probably be Volume V. Other volumes nearing completion are those for Canterbury 1070–1139 and for Durham, Norwich, and Worcester.

FONTES HISTORIAE AFRICANAE COMMITTEE (Chairman: Professor P. M. Holt)

The Committee was formed in 1973 to co-ordinate the British contribution to the Fontes Historiae Africanae project, sponsored by the Union Académique Internationale, and directed by Professor J. O. Hunwick. The Committee was reconstructed in 1979 and approved new terms of reference defining the scope of the project as follows: (i) to supervise, on behalf of the British Academy, the British contribution to the project organized by the Union Académique Internationale, the Fontes Historiae Africanae; (ii) to sponsor and encourage scholarly work on the preparation of editions and translations of texts of importance for the history of Africa, and to recommend to the Academy's Publications Committee works suitable for publication by the Academy in the international Fontes series; (iii) to give attention to texts in indigenous languages as well as Arabic relating to Africa south of the Sahara, and to works originally written or published in lesser-known European and other languages; (iv) to encourage scholarly work on African historical texts and publication of such texts under auspices other than those of the Academy; (v) to establish and maintain relation with scholars working on the project in other countries.

N. Cigar, *Al-Qādirī's Nashr al-Mathānī* was published during the year. The revised text of G. W. B. Huntingford, *Historical Geography of Ethiopia* will be prepared by Dr D. L. Appleyard on a typewriter with special keys, for photographic reproduction. Professor J. O. Hunwick is revising the text of *The Replies of al-Maghīlī*, and the delivery of his manuscript is expected in the coming year. During 1981–2 it is expected that Professors Birmingham and Oliver will assist the Committee to select for publication texts in European and African languages respectively.

MEDIEVAL TEXTS EDITORIAL COMMITTEE (Chairman: Sir Richard Southern)

The Committee was established by the Academy in 1959 to supervise the production of a series of medieval texts.

It has been agreed to concentrate activity for the immediate future on two main areas: (i) British scholastic works in the thirteenth century, with the works of Robert Grosseteste as a central part of the programme, supported by works of Alexander Nequam and (if possible) Robert Kilwardby; (ii) scientific works (including grammar, mathematics, and natural sciences) mainly of the eleventh and twelfth centuries, and the works of Adelard of Bath and Abbo of Fleury.

The Committee has suffered some delays and setbacks with regard to volumes authorized and in course of production. The following volumes are being prepared: Robert Grosseteste: *Hexaemeron*, ed. by R. C. Dales; the collected works of Gilbert Crispin, ed. by G. R. Evans; and the later letters of Peter of Blois, ed. E. Ravell.

With regard to methods of production, the Committee has been deeply concerned about the need for cheaper methods of publication, and it has attempted so far as possible to adjust its editorial and typing procedures to take advantage of the economies of computerized methods of production as they become available. Its appointment of Dr Evans as its secretary was partly prompted by her knowledge of this subject, and despite difficulties and disappointments in practice, it intends to persist in these efforts.

ŒUVRES COMPLÈTES DE VOLTAIRE COMMITTEE (Chairman: Professor R. Shackleton)

The Voltaire Foundation was established by the late Theodore Bester-man to continue the publication of the *Complete Works of Voltaire*. Following his death in November 1976, control of the Foundation passed to his Executors who have established two committees for the purpose, one of which advises on questions of publishing policy and academic content. In 1978 the project was adopted on the recommenda-tion of the Academy by the Union Académique Internationale, but receives no money from that body.

Sixty volumes, out of a proposed total of 137 plus index volumes, have been produced so far. Four volumes, 9, 14, 33, and 50, are being technically processed for publication, and should be published during the winter of 1981/2. Typescripts for two major works, each requiring several volumes, are expected during the coming year. Certain miscel-laneous volumes also now await only one or two minor contributions to be complete. Editorial work is in progress on all but a small minority of texts.

Publications of the Voltaire Foundation are now being 'printed' by computer-assisted photocomposition and offset lithography. Introduc-tion of these new techniques this year has inevitably caused some delay, but they will in future result in considerable savings in both time and publishing costs, without loss of quality of presentation.

ORIENTAL DOCUMENTS COMMITTEE (Chairman: Professor Edward Ullendorff)

The aim of the project, adopted by the Academy in 1972, is to promote and supervise the editing and publication of documents of historical and archival importance in oriental scripts, preserved in public collections in Britain, and to encourage the identification and listing of such documents.

Dr Wong's work on *Chinese Diplomatic Records in the PRO* has been completed and is currently in the press. The same applies to Mrs Ashtiany's work on *Arabic Material in Kuwait Agency Records* of which, the Director of the IOL reports, proofs are already available. Professor Anisuzzaman's *Catalogue of the Bengali Factory Records* has been published under the joint auspices of the Oriental Documents Committee and the India Office Library. Dr Hopkin's *Letters from Barbary* is being published by the Academy, and the first proofs of this work have already been inspected.

OXYRHYNCHUS PAPYRI COMMITTEE (Chairman Mr P. J. Parsons)

This long-term project was adopted by the Academy in 1966 with the purpose of transcribing, editing, and publishing the Oxyrhynchus papyri. The research is financed by the Academy; publication is the responsibility of the Egypt Exploration Society.

During the past year three complete boxes of papyri have been catalogued, and two of them photographed; photography of the third, and cataloguing of three more, are in hand. Further photographs of published papyri have been added to the photographic archive. Professor A. P. Mathias has refined his enzymic process for resolving flat cartonnage. Professor Maehler will publish texts obtained in the earlier experiments.

There were two publications during the year, *Papyri Edited in Honour of E. G. Turner* and *Oxyrhynchus Papyri XLVIII* (Menander, Herodotus; and an archive of the fourth century AD, the revealing papers of two understrappers). *Oxyrhynchus Papyri XLIX* (New Comedy, Dinarchus, Strabo, etc.) is in press, *L* in active preparation, and the editors have typescript for two or three further volumes.

RECORDS OF SOCIAL AND ECONOMIC HISTORY COMMITTEE (Chairman: Professor D. C. Coleman)

The Committee was reconstructed in 1970 after a lapse of many years to oversee the production of a new series of records of social and economic history. Three volumes in this series have been published.

Dr Gervers's edition of the *Cartulary of the Knights of St. John of Jerusalem*, which was sent to the printers last year, has experienced numerous delays. Dr Alcock's edition of the account book of Peter Temple and Thomas Heritage, *Warwickshire Grazier and London Skinner, 1532–55* and Dr Chibnall's volume *The Charters and Custumals of the Abbey of Holy Trinity, Caen,* have been approved by the Publications Committee and sent to the printers. Publication, as Volumes IV and V of the New Series, is expected in December 1981 and early 1982. It is hoped that Dr Gervers's volume will follow shortly thereafter.

4. Other

CENTRE OF SOUTH ASIAN STUDIES ARCHIVE PROJECT COM-
MITTEE (Chairman: Professor P. N. S. Mansergh)

The Academy adopted the project in 1980. Its purpose, which is
approaching completion, is to collect and catalogue archive material
relating to the memoirs of British people who served or lived in south
Asia under the Raj: (i) to supervise the final collecting and cataloguing
phase of the Centre's archive project, concerned with the records of
British India; (ii) to ensure that the work is completed in the three-year
period envisaged for Academy support; (iii) to submit to the Academy
annual progress reports and budgets.

During the year twenty-four written accessions to the archive and five
collections of films have been received. A total of fifty-seven tape-
recordings have now been made, and films were lent to BBC 2 for film
on British India. The Archivist collected material and made tape-
recordings in Sussex, Surrey, Jersey, Norfolk, Suffolk, Oxfordshire,
Kent, Bedfordshire, Wiltshire, Leicestershire, Shropshire, Suffolk,
Devon, Cornwall, Dorset, Hertfordshire, Somerset, and London.

EARLY ENGLISH CHURCH MUSIC COMMITTEE (Chairman:
Professor P. M. Doe)

This long-term undertaking was adopted by the Academy as a Major
Project in 1963. Its terms of reference are to prepare and publish a series
of editions of church music by British composers from the Norman
Conquest to the Commonwealth. In addition, it has published a
supplementary source-catalogue of church music with English text, and
will shortly be ready to publish a second. Two years ago the Academy
approved the Committee's further proposal that the somewhat fragmentary surviving manuscripts of fourteenth-century polyphony be
published in the form of a volume of photographic facsimiles.

Twenty-five volumes have been published (by Stainer and Bell), of
which two appeared during the year 1980/1: Volume 24, *Christopher
Tye II: Masses*, ed. Paul Doe. Published 15 November 1980; Volume 26,
Manuscripts of Fourteenth Century English Polyphony: Facsimiles, eds. Frank
Harrison and Roger Wibberley. Published 1 July 1981, including a
limited edition of 100 copies in de luxe binding.

Further volumes are planned to complete publication of the church
music of a number of major composers and also to publish the contents of
selected major sources.

BALANCE SHEET
AND ACCOUNTS

31 MARCH 1981

BALANCE SHEET, 31 MARCH 1981

1980 £		*Private Funds* £	*Public Funds* £	*Total* £
	ACCUMULATED FUNDS			
43,842	General Fund, Balance 1 April 1980	23,357	3,103	
546	*Less*: Loss on realization of investments	(564)		
(17,928)	*Less*: Excess of Expenditure over Income as per Income and Expenditure Account	518	23,450	
26,460		22,275	(20,347)	1,928
384,015	Special Funds (Schedule 1A)	381,162		381,162
82,853	Funds Administered (Schedule 1B)	103,598	1,282	104,880
	PROVISIONS FOR EXPENDITURE AUTHORIZED			
	(Schedule 3)			
155,903	Grants	17,279	177,293	194,572
123,836	Publications	2,210	91,825	94,035
16,043	Other Expenses	347	7,532	7,879
	CURRENT LIABILITIES			
—	The Linbury Trust Loan		20,000	20,000
2,098	Creditors	10	2,300	2,310
£791,208		£526,881	£279,885	£806,766

1980 £		Private Funds £	Public Funds £	Total £
	INVESTMENTS AT COST OR VALUATION			
	(Schedule 4)			
	(Market Value or Broker's valuation:			
	1980—£418,930			
327,900	1981—£499,895)	323,740		323,740
	CURRENT ASSETS			
18,741	Debtors—General	15,709	8,767	24,476
	Cash at Bank:			
154,167	Deposit Accounts	171,713		
30,400	Current Accounts	15,719	21,118	
260,000	Paymaster General Account		250,000	458,550
	(non-interest bearing)			

Notes: (1) In accordance with previous practice no amount has been included in the Balance Sheet for fixed assets.

(2) Stocks of publications are valued at the lower of cost and net realizable value. At 31 March 1981 the officials of the Academy estimated the value at £120,670 (1980—£98,388).

(3) There is a contingent liability of £3,500 not provided for in these accounts which may become payable to Pilgrim Trust from sales of Early English Church Music.

(4) The Linbury Trust Loan is non-interest bearing and is repayable not later than 31 December 1981.

| £791,208 | | £526,881 | £279,885 | £806,766 |

PETER MATHIAS
Honorary Treasurer

AUDITOR'S REPORT

We have audited the financial statements and attached schedules in accordance with approved Auditing Standards.

In our opinion the financial statements, which have been prepared under the historical cost convention, give a true and fair view of the state of the affairs of the British Academy at 31 March 1981 and of the excess of expenditure over income and source and application of funds for the year then ended.

PANNELL KERR FORSTER
Chartered Accountants

Lee House
London Wall
London EC2Y 5AL

GENERAL FUND

INCOME AND EXPENDITURE ACCOUNT FOR THE YEAR ENDED 31 MARCH 1981

EXPENDITURE

1980 £	£		£	£
		ADMINISTRATION AND MAINTENANCE		
97,702		Salaries, Pension, and Staff Insurances	121,604	
12,720		Heating, Lighting, Cleaning, and Rates	14,972	
12,478		Travelling Expenses	16,496	
30,854		General Expenses	35,668	
4,579		Office Furniture and Equipment	6,794	
158,333		*Less*: Contribution to administrative		
9,911	148,422	expenses from Schools and Institutes	11,219	184,315
		SUBSCRIPTIONS		
730		Union Académique Internationale	673	
380	1,110	European Science Foundation	304	977
		ACADEMIC PRINTING AND PUBLISHING		
18,018		Proceedings	39,828	
83,045		Monographs	102,343	
3,507		Papers	8,228	
2,938		Storage, Insurance, Publicity	5,266	
1,210		Distribution Centre Handling, charges	1,834	
—		Refund of Schweich Publication Reserve	2,500	
108,718			159,999	
37,834		*Less*: Sales of Publications	52,672	
70,884			107,327	
		Increase/(Decrease) in provision for		
(43,247)	27,637	future publications	(29,801)	77,526
		ALLOCATIONS		
1,663,195		Per Schedule 2	1,978,465	
1,200		Lecture Fees	1,000	
—		Senior Fellows' Fund	347	
		Exchange of delegations with Chinese		
11,000		Academy	1,618	
—	1,675,395	Medals	270	1,981,700
	£1,852,564			£2,244,518

INCOME

1980 £	£		£	£
	1,803,000	GOVERNMENT GRANT		2,172,410
		GENERAL INCOME		
2,931		Subscriptions and Entrance Fees	4,893	
689		Income Tax recoverable on Subscriptions under Covenant	784	
170		Contribution from Special Funds for Administration	170	
30		Hire of Rooms	—	
2,647		Donations and Contributions	18,147	
4,103	10,570	Refunds	7,707	31,701
		SMALL GRANTS FUND		
5,000		N. Ireland Department of Education	5,000	
2,500	7,500	Scottish Education Department	2,500	7,500
		INTEREST GROSS		
2,036		On Investments	2,113	
11,530	13,566	On Deposit	6,826	8,939
17,928		Excess of Expenditure over income per Balance Sheet		23,968

£1,852,564   £2,244,518

SPECIAL FUNDS
YEAR ENDED 31 MARCH 1981

	INCOME	EXPENDITURE			Excess of Income over Expenditure or of (Expenditure over Income)	Profit/(Loss) on Realization of Investments	Total Accumulated Fund 1 April 1980	Total Accumulated Fund 31 March 1981
FUND	Total Income £	Grants, Lectures, etc. £	Administration and Printing £	Total Expenditure £	£	£	£	£
Consolidated Investments (1)	20,109	7,376	1,836	9,212	10,897	(3,096)	109,615	117,416 (2)
Stein–Arnold	1,994	2,250	85	2,335	(341)	—	21,990	21,649
Albert Reckitt	10,568	7,060	1,156	8,216	2,352	—	33,290	35,642
Thank-Offering to Britain	16,670	16,800	1,388	18,188	(1,518)	(12,056)	114,799	101,225 (5)
Stenton	5,587	2,000	166	2,166	3,421	(35)	51,742	55,128 (3)
Webster	4,968	7,394	176	7,570	(2,602)	125	52,579	50,102
		£42,880 (4)					Total per Balance Sheet	£381,162

(1) Consolidated Investments Fund includes:
Leopold Schweich Fund, English Literature and Language Fund, Henriette Hertz Fund, Cromer Greek Prize Fund, Italian Lecture Fund, Raleigh Fund for History, Serena Medal Fund, Sir John Rhŷs Memorial Fund, Kenyon Medal Fund, William Hepburn Buckler Memorial Fund, Dawes Hicks Fund, Chatterton Lecture Trust Fund, Maccabaean Lecture Fund, Sarah Tryphena Phillips Lecture Fund, Caton–Thompson Fund, Radcliffe-Brown Fund, Browning Fund, and the Derek Allen Prize Fund.

(2) The Fund was increased during the year by £8,500 being capital of £6,000 donated to the English Literature and Language Fund and a transfer of £2,500 from the publications reserve to capital of the Leopold Schweich Fund.

(3) The accumulated Fund includes royalties totalling £9,960 of which £1,171 was added in the current year. £2,873 has been transferred during the year from Accumulated Income to Accumulated Capital.

(4) Grants, Lectures, etc., includes £32,660 for grants per Schedule 2, Lecture Fees of £1,800, Prizes and Medals of £1,026 and Representation Expenses of £7,394.

(5) The Fund was increased during the year by a donation of £200.

FUNDS ADMINISTERED BY OR FOR THE BRITISH ACADEMY

YEAR ENDED 31 MARCH 1981

COMMITTEE OR FUND	INCOME Total Income £	EXPENDITURE Salaries and Insurances £	Grants £	Travelling, Printing, and General £	Total £	Excess of Income over Expenditure or (Expenditure over Income) £	Accumulated Income 1 April 1980 £	Accumulated Income 31 March 1981 £
Corpus Vitrearum Medii Aevi	6,418	7,004		915	7,919	(1,501)	1,501	—
Early English Church Music	—			1,971	1,971	(1,971)	3,253	1,282
Hebrew Illuminated Manuscripts	1,300			966	966	334	119	453
Lexicon of Greek Personal Names	16,771	17,071		814	17,885	(1,114)	1,114	—
Leverhulme Trust (Professorships)	—		1,093	—	1,093	(1,093)	5,338	4,245
Leverhulme Trust (Chinese Studies)	6,625			—	—	6,625	—	6,625
Save Carthage Ceramic Unit	—			731	731	(731)	731	—
Medieval Latin Dictionary	26,816	25,897		1,029	26,926	(110)	110	—
Rose Mary Crawshay Prize	615			560	560	55	645	700
Save Carthage	10,000			10,188	10,188	(188)	188	—
Sylloge of Coins of the British Isles	—			231	231	(231)	1,000	769
Wolfson Fellowships	50,200		27,620	628	28,248	21,952	68,854	90,806
								£104,880
							Total per Balance Sheet	

GRANTS

MOVEMENTS ON FUNDS AVAILABLE FOR GRANTS

	Balance available at 1 April 1980	Provision at 1 April 1980	Receivable during year	Total Funds available	Grants paid and Administrative expenses	Provision for Expenditure authorized	Balance available at 31 March 1981
Schools and Institutes	—	2,863	1,185,560	1,188,423	1,180,991	7,432	—
Research Grants	—	69,625	421,268	490,893	426,024	64,869	—
Small Grants	5	35,444	218,251	253,700	193,721	59,979	—
Overseas Grants	—	17,886	103,687	121,573	95,114	26,459	—
Conference Grants	—	7,479	29,956	37,435	29,202	8,233	—
Publication Subsidies and Subventions	14,683	6,050	10,591	31,324	9,653	11,510	10,161
British National Committees	—	1,868	9,152	11,020	10,091	929	—
	£14,688	£141,215	£1,978,465	£2,134,368	£1,944,796	£179,411	£10,161
			As per I and E Account				
Special Funds	—	—	£32,660	—	£27,660	£5,000	—
			As per Note Schedule 1A			As per Schedule 3	

PROVISION FOR EXPENDITURE AUTHORIZED
Schedule 3

1980 £		£
	GRANTS (Schedule 2)	
141,215	Grants voted, not yet paid	179,411
14,688	Balance available for grants	10,161
—	Special Funds	5,000
£155,903	Total per Balance Sheet	£194,572
	PUBLICATIONS	
2,500	Printing and binding Schweich Lectures	—
2,302	Fontes Historiae Africanae	1,875
335	Lincolnshire Mint Signature Coins	335
158,869	Monographs reserve at 1 April 1980 £118,699	
	Plus Allocation out of grant for year ended	
25,000	31 March 1981 45,000	
183,869	163,699	
65,170	*Less*: Net Expenditure 71,874	
118,699		91,825
£123,836	Total per Balance Sheet	£94,035
	OTHER EXPENSES	
3,073	Exchange of delegations with the Chinese Academy	—
3,284	British Academy/Royal Society Symposium	—
9,686	Removal Expenses	7,532
—	Senior Fellows' Fund	347
£16,043	Total per Balance Sheet	£7,879

INVESTMENTS AT 31 MARCH 1981   Schedule 4

	Cost £	Market Value at 31 March 1981 £
Consolidated Investments	115,631	130,279
Albert Reckitt Archaeological Fund	22,139	164,668

Note: The investments of the Albert Reckitt Archaeological Fund are subject to certain restrictions as to disposal. A figure of £19,622 for Reckitt & Colman Ltd. Ordinary Shares represents the valuation at the date the Bequest was made.

	Cost £	Market Value at 31 March 1981 £
Stein–Arnold Exploration Fund	18,357	18,021
Thank-Offering to Britain Fund	78,246	88,058
Stenton Fund	48,332	48,142
Webster Fund	41,035	50,727
Total per Balance Sheet	£323,740	£499,895

STATEMENT OF SOURCE AND APPLICATION OF FUNDS

FOR THE YEAR ENDED 31 MARCH 1981

		1980/1 £	*1979/80* £
SOURCE OF FUNDS			
Profit on realization of Investments		—	546
FUNDS FROM OTHER SOURCES			
Proceeds from sale of Investments		97,324	57,108
Add: Loss (Less Profit) on realization of Investments transferred directly to Special and Administered Funds			
		97,324	57,654
APPLICATION OF FUNDS			
Excess of Expenditure over Income	23,968		17,928
Loss on realization of Investments	564		—
Purchase of Investments	108,790		58,170
Add: Profit (Less Loss) on realization of Investments transferred directly to Special and Administered Funds	(15,626)		2,964
		(117,696)	
(Decrease)/Increase in Funds		£(20,372)	£(21,408)
Represented by:			
(Decrease)/Increase in Debtors		5,735	(5,477)
(Decrease)/Increase in Cash and Bank Balances		13,983	(86,352)
(Increase)/Decrease in Creditors		(20,212)	(978)
Decrease/(Increase) in provisions for Expenditure authorized		(704)	93,729
(Increase) in Special and Administered Funds		(19,174)	(22,330)
		£(20,372)	£(21,408)

PRESIDENTIAL ADDRESS

By SIR KENNETH DOVER

2 July 1981

I HAVE been given the opportunity, with leave of my College, to spend three months early next year lecturing in America, Australia, Japan, and China. A convenient opportunity to accept long-standing invitations to so many different places within the compass of a single journey may not recur, and, since it did not seem to me right that a President should be absent for so long at a time of year which is busy and important for the Academy, I decided not to seek re-election for the year 1981/2. I must confess that my conscience on this matter might have been more flexible had there been a prospect of holding the January Reception in our new premises in Cornwall Terrace; but those premises will not in fact be ready until near the end of 1982. I must also confess that my appetite for office might have been less jaded if the conflicts of last summer had not swallowed up the greater part of the Long Vacation. It is the great good fortune of the Academy that the Revd Professor Owen Chadwick has acquiesced in the desire of Council to nominate him, as a man who combines pre-eminent scholarship with vision and practical wisdom, for election to the Presidency. I am glad to say that Professor Handley and Professor Mathias are willing to continue as Foreign Secretary and Treasurer respectively. Professor Wallace-Hadrill has resigned his office as Publications Secretary, in which he has skilfully guided the greatly increased publishing activity of the Academy; the past year has seen the appearance of eleven volumes and almost a doubling of our income from sales. I am glad to report that Professor Elton is willing to take over as Publications Secretary. I must not leave the subject of changes without paying a grateful tribute to our Accounts Officer, Miss Jean Saies, who retires in December; after thirteen years in charge of our accounts, she will be very greatly missed.

Much more information about events of the year now ending will be given in the Secretary's Report, but there are two categories of event on which I wish to comment. One is our foreign relations: we have signed an exchange agreement with the Consejo Superior de Investigaciones Científicas in Spain similar in scope to our existing agreement with the French CNRS; and after a period of coolness amounting to breakdown, our relations with the Soviet Union seem to be taking a turn for the better, this time on Soviet initiative. Secondly, the year has been marked by some acts of great generosity, for which we are deeply grateful. A covenanted donation from Dame Helen Gardner will eventually increase the resources available for subvention of publications by some £5,700. The late Miss Marguerite Gollancz gave £6,000 for support of the prize and lecture on English literature which are named after her father, our first Secretary. The Linbury Trust made the Publications Fund an interest-free loan of £20,000 towards the heavy initial expenditure required for the splendid volume on the stained glass of Canterbury. Under arrangements concluded with the Sir Ernest Cassel Educational Trust we shall in future be administering post-doctoral grants, amounting to some £3,000 a year, on behalf of the Trust. From the Senior Fellows Fund, which was established on the initiative of Professor Hayek and has attracted generous donations, a drawing of Lord Robbins was commissioned from Milein Cosman (Mrs Hans Keller); it is exhibited today in the Fellows' Room.

It was fifteen years ago, on the day of the Annual General Meeting, that Lord Robbins inaugurated the Thank-Offering to Britain series of lectures by giving a lecture on academic freedom. He was speaking at a time which witnessed a spectacular investment of our national resources in the enlargement and creation of universities, and it is not surprising that he had occasion to remind us of the old adage about the piper and the tune. Today, when universities are faced with retrenchment, I feel that my choice of topic is inexorably dictated by the situation which is being disclosed to Parliament this afternoon.

The Academy is not the spokesman of universities, and I think we have been right to decline involvement, whether as partisan or as assessor, in the evaluation of particular colleges, institutions, and departments, in London or elsewhere. None the less, our purpose is identical with part of the purpose of some part of all universities, and when they are handicapped in the realization of that purpose, consideration of alternative or supplementary means to the same end becomes our urgent business.

Summary reports published this morning indicate that measures of contraction and closure are not likely to fall as heavily on the humanities as some of us were inclined to fear. However, satisfaction that criteria of industrial and medical utility have not on this occasion been applied ruthlessly would be short-sighted.

Where capacity for research is at issue, the humanities and the sciences would be better advised to stand together—for reasons about which I will say more in a moment—than to rejoice each in the discomfiture of the other. The University Grants Committee, as our past dealings with it would have led me to expect, is very willing to hear what we have to say on this matter. I am not unduly disturbed by the fact that the Committee's consultations with the Research Councils earlier this year were not stretched so far as to include the Academy. In the context of the total national expenditure on research of all kinds, the cost of maintaining capacity for research in the humanities is small enough to be beautiful. But from year to year one can never be confident that this beauty will be seen by the eye of the official beholder.

Within the constraints of our present budget, we cannot do more for research in the humanities than we do already. Particularly in archaeology we have been faced this year with a choice: either to reduce the grants requested by undoubtedly valuable projects to a degree which may imperil their realization, or to starve research which is not archaeological. At the same time, the special funding which we have received for the establishment of British Academy Readerships has resulted in 135 applications for the first three readerships. The process of selection can hardly be completed before the end of this month, and it will be a striking illustration of an aspect of our work to which attention is seldom drawn: the time spent by the Research Fund Committee, the Overseas Policy Committee, and other committees, above all the Section Sub-Committees, on reading and assessing every year some six hundred applications for grants, quite apart from the new Readership applications. The agenda for the Research Fund Committee are not uncommonly an inch in depth, even after Section Sub-Committees have exercised their right to give an unqualified yes or no within certain categories.

Suppose, however, that we had much more money for many more grants; suppose that the work of assessment were spread more thinly over a much larger number of Fellows and supported by a proportionate increase in our administrative staff; in those circumstances it is not hard to show that if a severe reduction in secure appointments to universities were matched by an increase in temporary appointments at the bottom of the pay scale, the total capacity of our universities for research in the humanities could well be greater and cost the taxpayer less than is now the case. Under such a system anxious competitiveness among temporary lecturers and graduate students, already sharp, would become intense, and the ground would be littered with dashed hopes. More students would be taught, for more of the time, by inexperienced lecturers and tutors. None the less, if we are committed to the furtherance of knowledge, we must try to identify the direction in which that commitment would point if it were taken by itself, unencumbered by other social and educational considerations. I hope that during the coming year Fellows will put forward many alternative ideas about the ways in which our commitment to research in the humanities can best be met.

Problems of organization are not the only problems. The university lecturer in a subject which falls under the humanities is beset by an anxiety broader and deeper than his understandable fear that he will be put out of a job. He observes that some public criticism of our universities appears to be founded on misapprehensions about the structure and working of foreign universities; and if comparisons are in order, he may not see why reference should not be made to some German universities in which departments virtually untroubled by the presence of students are none the less lavishly funded because they are active in research, rather than to Italian universities in which the majority of students who matriculate do not attend courses (indeed, if they tried to, the available lecture-rooms and laboratories would not contain them) or to French universities whose destructive convulsions in recent years were caused, more than anything, by a staff/student ratio which precluded adequate contact between staff and students. The British lecturer is also aware that public opinion, even among people who are themselves graduates of universities, is not particularly well-disposed to research in humanities. Keep your ears open in the company of those concerned with administration, law, management, or finance, and you will hear much that is disquietingly jocular, patronizing, or contemptuous—in short, from our standpoint, philistine. The lecturer's anxiety is inevitably coloured with bitterness when he reflects that reduction of the universities' share of resources is closely related to an increase in the reward of all those involved, as workers, managers, entrepreneurs, or investors, in a process on which our type of civilization appears to depend: the design, production, and marketing of senseless junk.

To this gloomy generalization there is one intermittent strand of exceptions. Although the number of art-forms consistently and universally valued in our culture is restricted—I would include among them farce and interior decorating—quite a lot of people who never study the history of literature or of art may nevertheless enjoy reading books and looking at pictures, and the humanities profit from their association with the qualities possessed by some of the matter which, part of the time, they study. A confusion underlies this association, and precisely because it is a confusion, to some extent engendered and sustained by the idiosyncratic ways in which the application of the English words 'science', 'art', and 'arts' differs from the application of corresponding words in related languages, we should take some trouble not to exploit it.

Ever since that brisk and vehement war between the late Lord Snow and the late Professor Leavis on the subject of 'the Two Cultures' (an episode which reawakened in Lord Snow the deep suspicion that the humanities are, as I heard him put it on a comparatively informal occasion, 'an intellectual slum') the fact that there are three cultures has been consistently overlooked. The third culture embraces all those who create works of art, literature, and music—or rather, it embraces all of us to the extent to which we are artistically creative. The activity of creating something which will attract by reason of the relation between its form and its content, or by reason of its form alone, seems to me profoundly, totally different from the activity of posing and answering questions, whether in the sciences or in the humanities, about what is already there, attractive or not. A person of strong religious faith is unlikely to accept the view that his own beliefs are a 'Third Culture' phenomenon, but he can hardly deny that the majority of religious beliefs must belong there, since they are irreconcilable with his. The very essence of what is commonly called 'the artistic temperament' is an inclination to accept a view of the past or of the universe not because it can be sustained by evidence but because it evokes a welcome aesthetic or emotional response.

Dissociating the academic activity which we call 'humanities' or 'arts' from the imaginative activity which brings into being some of the subject-matter of the humanities does not in the least mean trying to disguise the humanities as science. It does mean recognizing how much the first two cultures have in common. For many reasons which are intelligible but ultimately inadequate, public opinion associates the sciences with enquiry, discovery, and communicable reasoning, the humanities with learning, the transmission of an inheritance, and intuitive, arbitrary, private judgement. I am no expert in public relations, but I have no doubt that by contrast with the sciences, the humanities have not succeeded in implanting in public opinion adequate recognition of the part which enquiry, discovery, and reasoning play in them. I recall, for example, the speck of straw on one page of the codex

Laurentianus 32.2 which, having masqueraded for centuries as an idiosyncratic punctuation-mark, on 3 June 1960, under the eyes of Professor Zuntz, came loose from the surface of the page and solved in an instant a central problem in the history of the text of Euripides. Anything affecting the history of the text of a Greek author necessarily affects our weighing of the evidence in deciding what he actually wrote in more than one passage, as well as our estimation of Byzantine scholarship; and both in turn have repercussions on our treatment of the texts of other authors. The unmasking of the speck of straw reminds us that the correct interpretation of the minutest datum may bear the same relation to a chain of statements on a historical topic as correctness or error in a single instrumental reading may bear to a chain of scientific experiments. What is more important, the movement of the speck was not an event, simultaneously lucky and embarrassing, which proved that all scholars had been wrong; it proved rather that a long-standing and growing body of scholarly opinion, founded upon convergent reasoning from several different categories of evidence, was right.

This kind of thing is very far away from the world of the creative arts. Many artists would find it repugnant; I hope that a scientist would not. The contrast between the humanities and what I have called 'the Third Culture' does not end there, for there is another, more material contrast. Many works of art at the present time change hands for prices which appear, even to people who care a great deal about art, insane. It may be, of course, that if a work of art is justly described as 'priceless', as some great works of art can be, no price is less sane than any other. But if I dare venture to expose a philistine streak in myself, I must admit to a measure of surprise at the price sometimes commanded by a specimen of a genre which is fairly well represented or by what appear to me to be trivial and ephemeral works by minor contemporary artists. When appeals are made for very large sums in order to retain a work of art in this country, I simply cannot help reflecting on what could be achieved by the contribution of money on that scale to scholarly publication, including, of course, publications in the history of art, of a kind which we as an Academy would be delighted to undertake. I do not think we should be too readily shamed into silent acquiescence in current values.

ROBERT AUTY MEMORIAL LECTURE
(Thank-Offering to Britain Fund)

LANGUAGE AND NATIONAL CONSCIOUSNESS

By HUGH SETON-WATSON

Read 12 March 1981

I AM deeply moved and honoured to be invited to give this lecture in memory of Robert Auty, a fine scholar and a good man, who was also my friend. As many of you know, he began his scholarly career as a Germanist, completed a doctor's degree at Münster University, got to know Germany and its people well, and played an active part in saving German scholars of Jewish faith from Hitlerian persecution. In the course of these activities he got to know Czechoslovakia, and the emphasis of his intellectual activities then moved from the Germanic to the Slav languages. He did not confine himself even to these, for during his post-war travels and studies he acquired a good knowledge not only of the relatively easily learned Romanian but also of the much more difficult Hungarian and Estonian.

I first met him, I think, in Prague just after the war, and common interests brought us together from time to time in his Cambridge years. In 1962 he was appointed Professor of Comparative Slavonic Philology at the School of Slavonic and East European Studies, thus becoming my immediate colleague. I am bound to say that I look back, as to my halcyon days, to the years when he was there, and if it is not presumptuous to say so, to a kind of intellectual partnership which developed between us, and which meant a great deal to me.

Let me just mention two occasions, both in 1966, after he had left the School. One was our joint participation in a conference held not far from Bratislava on the Slovak linguist and political leader Ludovit Štúr, and the other was at the celebration of the centenary of the Yugoslav Academy in Zagreb. On the first occasion he had to make a speech in Slovak, and on the second I in Croatian. His was certainly excellent.

However, good things come to an end. Already in 1965,

Robert Auty was appointed to the Chair of Slavonic Philology in Oxford. His years with us at the School turned out to be only a mid-way pause in a pilgrimage from his old university to mine, where he soon won the same admiration and affection as he enjoyed wherever he went.

My subject of today was of great importance to us both, to him as a professional linguist seriously interested in history, and to me as a historian who has long dabbled in languages. Auty stressed the connection between the two disciplines in his inaugural lecture in London in 1963. Let me quote his words: 'If language is the supremely characteristic human attribute and thus merits the attention of an independent branch of scientific study, languages are intimately bound up with human societies, in particular national societies, and cannot be studied in isolation from the history of those societies.'[1] This is also my own view. The history of language is not just a subject for philologists, but forms a very important part of social history, and one which seems to me to be relatively neglected by most historians. Specialist historians of language seem to keep to themselves, and their problems to be ignored by other historians—whether social, economic, political, demographic, cliometric, or any of the other numerous sub-disciplines into which they divide themselves. I may perhaps be exaggerating, but of this at least I am strongly convinced, that there ought to be closer and more frequent co-operation on the middle ground between language and history, more putting of questions from one side to the other, than there is today.

The expression 'national consciousness' requires some explanation. Others may prefer a different terminology, but these seem to me the best words to describe a collective state of mind, a belief by members of a community that they, and others like them, form a single nation. The community of the nationally conscious may at one stage be much smaller than the community to which they ascribe the quality of nation. It is one of the aims of the nationally conscious élite to spread their consciousness downwards among all those who possess the characteristics—cultural, political, territorial, or other—which in their view constitute the nation. This is a political task, to be pursued until the nationally conscious are co-extensive with the whole population concerned. The aim can only be achieved by the creation of a nationalist movement.

We thus have three different concepts: national consciousness, nation and nationalism, and it is important not to confuse them with each other. Nationalism is a movement designed to further

[1] Printed in *Slavonic and East European Review*, vol. 42, p. 272.

the interests of the nation, and also a doctrine about these interests. The nation is a community which either shares a national consciousness or accepts the political leadership of persons who have such consciousness. National consciousness is a state of mind. Not all members of the community, which the nationally conscious regard as a nation, need share this feeling; and not all nationally conscious persons need be nationalists. Whether they are or not will depend on the political and economic circumstances of the place and time.

The formation of national consciousness is a historical process, which may be protracted and unplanned, or short and artificial. Examples of both types abound. In those which I prefer to call the old continuous nations, a specific culture, way of life, sense of belonging to each other, grew gradually out of historical experience. No one took a decision to form these peoples into nations—though in periods of crisis or external danger appeals were made to their patriotism. The two most obvious examples of slow unplanned growth of national consciousness are the English and the French.

Sometimes a limited period of extreme danger and effort may transform an incipient national consciousness and push it in an unexpected direction. A specific national culture developed in the late Middle Ages in the Low Countries, but the religious divisions, the long struggle against Spain, the partition of the Netherlands by war, and the growth of the world-wide sea-borne trade and naval power of the northern provinces combined to create a Dutch nation, from which the southerners were excluded, and later excluded themselves.

However, in modern times the process of formation of national consciousness has been widespread, premeditated and much shorter. The proliferation of nationally conscious élites may in general terms be traced to the spread, in Central and Eastern Europe and then in other parts of the world, of the ideas of the European Enlightenment; and the French Revolution and Napoleonic era greatly stimulated the growth of national movements and doctrines.

Although we know a great deal about the history of nationalist movements, there is still plenty of confused thought, and I should like to hope that I could make some small contribution to clarifying it. First, a few words about the relation between nation and state. One of the main themes of late medieval and early modern history is, as we all well know, the rise of the sovereign state, whose ruler ignored the authority, at least nominally recognized in earlier times, of those two universal powers, the Emperor and the Pope. Unfortunately, in English-speaking countries the rise of the sovereign state is often erroneously and harmfully described as the rise of the nation state. The error is harmful because these two things are not the same, and to equate the one with the other can lead to serious obfuscation of political thinking.

Some sovereign states were indeed nation states, in the sense that national consciousness grew and spread together with the rise of the state. The two most conspicuous examples were France and England. Beyond the Rhine, the Alps, and the Pyrenees this was not the case. Sovereign states indeed arose, but either they were multi-national or they encompassed much less than a whole nation. In these lands a different pattern occurred. Comparatively small cultural élites began to think of themselves, and of larger communities which they identified with their aspirations, as nations; they spread this national consciousness to increasing numbers of their compatriots; they convinced themselves, and increasing numbers of their compatriots, that such sufferings and discontents as afflicted them were due to the fact that they were ruled by foreigners, and would disappear when the foreigners went; and created nationalist movements, which in most cases resulted in the creation of more and more sovereign states. Thus we have two different patterns: for the old nations the state came first, then national consciousness, and then the nation; for the newer nations first came national consciousness, then the nation and the nationalist movement, and last the state. My subject today is the nation, and national consciousness, not nationalism or nationalist movements—though from time to time I shall be obliged to refer to the last too.

During the earlier stages of the process, the nationally conscious are a small minority, but they consider themselves to be the nation. The question, how large must the minority be in order that one may say that a nation exists, is unanswerable. It would be convenient if these things could be quantified, if we could say for example that if ten per cent of the population feel themselves to be a nation, then that nation exists, but that if only five per cent feel that way, it does not. But in fact such statements would be meaningless. Even in long established nations large numbers may long remain unaffected by national consciousness. There certainly was a French nation already in the time of Richelieu; but in his brilliant book *Peasants into Frenchmen*[1] Eugene Weber gives massive

[1] Chatto and Windus, 1977.

evidence from local archives to show that as late as 1870 the word Frenchman was meaningless to hundreds of thousands of persons living south of the Loire. The French nation existed in the south, but it was confined to the towns: the peasants were béarnais or auvergnats or whatever.

Another question with no precise answer is: what are the objective differences between national consciousness and tribal, or other nondescript regional solidarity? My own reply would be that the difference is not objective but subjective. A nationally conscious élite consists of persons who claim that they are a nation, that their cultural identity and solidarity are above the tribal or regional level. But who can decide whether they are right or not? Perhaps the only real test is whether or not they are able to mobilize their compatriots into an effective nationalist movement.

I have not hitherto used the adjective ethnic or the noun ethnie, both much used by sociologists to describe cultural communities. I doubt whether these words are really very helpful. Ethnies usually turn out to be more precisely identifiable units, such as religious groups, language groups, persons with common folklore and customs or the like. Wouldn't it be simpler to call them such? But whatever terminology we use, the problem remains, both in history and in the present. How does it come about that some of these cultural communities produce from their midst a nationally conscious élite, while others do not?

This question I cannot answer in general terms. I can say only that there are certain characteristics which often play a part in the process, such as language, religion, history, geographical features, and economic interests. I propose to devote myself today to the operation of only one of these, to the connection between language and national consciousness. This is not because I wish to discount the other factors, but because it was in the study of this connection, and in the region in which it can best be studied—Central and Eastern Europe—that my intellectual interests came close to those of Robert Auty, whom we are remembering today. Central and Eastern Europe will be the starting point, and the subject of the main part, of what I have to say today.

First I must introduce one more concept which is of importance to the subject. This is what I call 'historical mythology', a mixture of truth and fantasy, a simplified version of a nation's historical past offered to children in the home and in the school. Every nation has such a mythology, even the old continuous nations whose professional historians have long been accustomed to go a good deal more deeply into historical evidence. To take a few examples, the English have King Alfred and the cakes, the Scots King Robert and the spider, the French St. Louis dispensing justice as he sat under the oak tree. To old nations, secure in their nationhood, their mythologies are not important; they are children's tales once learnt and then put out of mind. To new nations, recently emancipated and still threatened by powerful neighbours, they are very important, and they matter not just to intellectuals but to working men and women in factory and field.

Of the nations who live to the east of the Germans and Italians two may be described as old and continuous as regards national consciousness, though in both cases the continuity of their state was broken for long periods. These are the Poles and the Hungarians. In both, the bearers of national identity were the members of one legally defined class, the nobility, which in both cases formed, by comparison with West European societies, a rather large proportion of the population. In both cases also the national consciousness of the nobility was formed, as in Western Europe, over a long period, concomitant with the establishment of the medieval Polish and Hungarian states. During this process language too played its part, especially in Poland, where already in the sixteenth century there was a flourishing secular literature, and Polish culture attracted and absorbed many whose first language had been Ukrainian or Belorussian or Lithuanian. But in neither case can one say that language was the dominant factor. More important was religion. Both Poland and Hungary were Catholic countries, and in both Protestantism in its Calvinist form made rapid progress among the nobility. However, whereas the Counter-Reformation restored the Catholic faith among the nobility of Poland, with an almost complete absence of persecution, unique in Europe, the Hungarian nobility of Transylvania remained largely Calvinist, perhaps above all because Ottoman suzerainty obstructed the operation of the Counter-Reformation. Catholicism united the Poles in contrast to their Prussian and Russian neighbours, but Hungarians were divided by religion. After the partition of Hungary from 1526, and of Poland from 1795, there could be no doubt of the survival of both Hungarian and Polish national consciousness, but the development of nationalism, of the movement for independence and unity, raised new problems.

The history of five other peoples of the region contained periods of medieval independent kingdoms and flourishing culture, but had then been interrupted by conquest or by subjection to vassal status. In the process the former political class had been largely destroyed or assimilated, and the peasant majorities retained only semi-mythical folk memories. Thus not only continuity of the state (as in the case of Poles and Hungarians) but continuity of national consciousness was interrupted. These five were Czechs, Croats, Serbs, Romanians, and Bulgarians. When small nationally conscious élites began to appear among them from the mid-eighteenth century onwards, their main efforts were directed to developing language and rewriting history. Two other peoples had no substantial history at all as independent communities. These were the Slovaks and Slovenes, similar names but quite different peoples, the one inhabiting the southern slopes of the north-western Carpathians, the other living between the south-eastern Alps and the head of the Adriatic.

The decisive factor in what became known as the national revivals is the appearance of the new cultural élites. The rise of national consciousness is the result of a social process. The social and cultural processes cannot be neatly separated, whatever doctrinaires may wish.

The story really begins with the development of a modern school system in the Habsburg Monarchy under Maria Theresa and Joseph II. The first to gain from this were the Czechs. In the mid-eighteenth century, Czech, once the language of the rulers and nobility of Bohemia before 1620, was spoken by the peasants and was unknown to the majority of the nobility. The language of government, business, and of intellectual intercourse was German. With the growth of the school system, increasing numbers of Czech-speaking peasant children became educated, and began to be influenced by the ideas of the European Enlightenment, which of course reached them in German. To develop Czech so that it could express modern ideas, to make these ideas known to the people, and to serve their people, became the aim of these pupils of the Enlightenment. And their people meant those who spoke their language. The language-group was made the basis of the nation. In place of the old Bohemian nation of before 1620, which had had two languages, there now appeared two nations in Bohemia, distinguished from each other by language, the Czechs and the Germans. In this process the key figure is Josef Dobrovský (1753-1829) whose researches produced the first systematic Czech grammar, as well as a history of the Czech language and early literature. A second key figure was the historian František Palacký (1798-1876), who reinterpreted Bohemian history, and especially the Hussite wars, stressing the struggles of Slavs against Germans. It is a historical irony, not untypical of Habsburg culture, that both men—the founder of the modern Czech literary language and the creator of the Czech historical mythology—were enabled to achieve scholarly eminence thanks to material support received from German-speaking noble patrons.

The Slovaks were descended from the same distant ancestors as the Czechs, but for nine hundred years they had been ruled by Hungarian kings and landowners. In the late eighteenth century educated Slovaks were extremely few, confined to a section of the Catholic priesthood and a higher proportion of the less numerous Lutheran pastors. Slovak historians in recent times have been able, by studying the records of two societies with a few score members, one Catholic and one Protestant, and then of the Association of Lovers of Slovak Speech and Literature, founded in 1834, which had both Catholic and Protestant members, to trace fairly precisely the emergence of a Slovak intellectual élite. For these pioneers of national consciousness the language was far the most important issue. Some favoured the adoption of the language of the Czech Bible, others the dialect of the Vah valley in western Slovakia, and others the dialect of the central county of Turec. It was the third which prevailed, thanks to the efforts of the writer and schoolmaster Ludevit Štúr. On this basis a standardized literary Slovak language was formed, through the publication of books and especially of a periodical press whose readers grew steadily more numerous. It was defence of this language, and insistence on its use for public and private business in Slovakia first against the Hungarians in the last years of the Habsburg Monarchy, and then against the Czechs in the first Czechoslovak Republic, which formed the basis of modern Slovak nationalism.

Competition between different dialects was also a problem in the South Slav lands. There were three main dialects, known by the respective words used for the pronoun 'what'. The one man who more than any other single person deserves the credit for establishing one of these (the *štokavski* version) as the literary Serbo-Croatian language was Vuk Karadžić, who for many years studied popular speech and collected many of the epic poems, derived from the period of the Turkish conquest, which had been preserved by oral tradition. This Serbo-Croatian language was accepted and developed both within the Habsburg Monarchy and in the Kingdom of Serbia. However, though there was one language there were two historical mythologies, associated with the separate medieval kingdoms of Croatia and Serbia, the first

Catholic and the second Orthodox. Thus, though there was one language there were two nations, whose relations with each other in most of the nineteenth and still more the twentieth century were seldom good and sometimes murderous. As in the case of Anglo-Irish relations, the identifying mark of membership of either nation was religious, but the national conflicts were not, at least in modern times, mainly about religion.

The Serbo-Croat language was not accepted by the Slovenes of the Alpine valleys, who developed into a distinct nation. There again a grammarian and philologist was the key figure, Jernej Kopitar, active in the first decades of the nineteenth century. It was not until the middle of the century that there emerged, from competition between the dialects of Carniola, Carinthia and Styria, a standardized literary language.[1] The struggle for the assertion of Slovene national identity, in the next half century, was essentially fought out in the village church and village school, by priests and schoolmasters, against the claims for supremacy of the two great European languages of culture between whose territory the Slovenes were wedged—German and Italian.

In the early nineteenth century the pioneers of these languages were mostly inclined to the belief that there was one single language, one single nation, to which they all belonged, the Slav. In this view, there were a number of developed literary dialects, but there would eventually be one overarching Slav language. The reasons for this belief were not so much linguistic as political and psychological. Small nations, threatened by much bigger ones —Germans, Italians, Turks, Hungarians—needed a protector, and they imagined that they had found one in the most numerous nation of Slav speech and its powerful state—Russia. Panslavism was not a Russian but a west Slav invention. The small nations cast the Russians in the saviour role. The only large west Slav nation, the Poles, claimed the role for themselves and argued that the Russians were not Slavs at all but Tatars or Finns who had learnt a Slav tongue. Be that as it may, the history of the last 150 years has clearly shown that Panslavism is an illusion, and has shown the Russians to be rather different from the image created of them. The separate languages, and very distinct national cultures of Czechs, Poles, Slovaks, Croats, Slovenes, Serbs, and Bulgarians remain.

The combination of language and historical mythology may also be seen in the case of the Romanians. The Romanian

[1] See Robert Auty, 'The formation of the Slovene literary language against the background of the Slavonic national revival' in *SEER*, vol. 41, pp. 391–402.

language is Latin in structure and predominantly in vocabulary, though many Slav words have been brought into it—on a scale roughly comparable with the extent of French words in English—and some Greek, Hungarian and Turkish too. Since the earliest times for which concrete information is available, Romanians have formed a majority of the population in three principalities—Moldavia, Wallachia, and Transylvania. The first two were ruled by indigenous princes in the fifteenth century. Their successors became vassals of the Ottoman empire but remained sovereign in their territory until the eighteenth century, when Greeks were appointed to rule them. By this time Romanian national consciousness had grown very dim, and was confined to a very small number. The third principality, Transylvania, was ruled by Hungarians, first by the kings and after 1526 by princes who were vassals of the Sultan until 1699, after which Transylvania became a province of the Habsburg Monarchy. Romanians, unlike Hungarians and Germans, had no part in the representative institutions of Transylvania.

Modern Romanian nationalist doctrine was first formulated in Transylvania in the eighteenth century. The establishment by the Habsburg emperor Leopold I of a Uniate Church, into which the Romanian Orthodox church was officially merged, recognizing the authority of the Pope, made it possible for Romanians to have greater access to education. A Uniate bishop, Inocentiu Micu, who had studied in Rome, maintained that the Transylvanian Romanians were the direct descendants of the legions of the Roman Empire and the true indigenous people of the country. In the second half of the century a number of works on this subject were published. Transylvanian Romanians, being better educated than the Romanians of Moldavia and Wallachia, also made an important contribution to the school system of those lands. After the Greek rebellion of Ypsilanti in 1821, the Turks encouraged Romanian national feeling in opposition to Greek. Finally, as a result of the Crimean War, Moldavia and Wallachia became genuinely self-governing, were united with each other, and from 1866 were known as the Kingdom of Romania. In 1918, after the defeat and disintegration of Austria-Hungary, Transylvania and other territory to the west and south-west of it were united with Romania.

In the Romanian nationalist movement in the nineteenth century, and right up to the present, the historical mythology of descent from the Romans, and from the Dacians whom the Romans conquered, has played a central part, and it is firmly based on the fact of the Latin character of the language. Whether Latin-speaking people have remained continuously in the Romanian lands, or on the contrary as the Hungarians claim, only came there in the fourteenth century, cannot be proved or disproved, though it seems likely that there was an element of continuity, even if the biological origins of the modern Romanian nation certainly include Slav, Turkish, Hungarian, Greek, and other constituents. But whatever the truth of that period—which we shall never know—it remains certain that the development of Romanian national consciousness, and the nationalist movement to which it gave rise, was based on a historical mythology founded on language.

In the original formation of Hungarian national consciousness I argued that language played only a secondary role. However, at the turn of the eighteenth and nineteenth centuries the situation was transformed. This was a period of great achievement in the study and the expansion of the language and the flowering of literature. Here the lexicographer and philologist Nicholas Revai and the writer Francis Kazinczy (1759-1831) were the leading figures.[1] In the following years Hungarians insisted that the rejuvenated Hungarian language should replace Latin as the language of official business and this was achieved in the 1830s and 1840s. Imperceptibly the meaning of the concept of Hungarian nation changed. In place of the traditional definition by class—only members of the nobility being included in the nation—arose a new definition by language. The Hungarian nation, in the view of the democrats who were gaining ground, and who came to power briefly in the revolution of 1848, consisted of all persons, whatever their class, whose language was Hungarian and who called themselves Hungarian (Magyar). However, half the population consisted of persons of a language other than Hungarian, and among these people—mainly Romanians, Slovaks, Serbs, and Ukrainians—the number of the nationally conscious was steadily increasing. After 1867, when Hungary obtained a great measure of sovereignty over its internal affairs, it became the policy of Hungarian governments, both by inducements and career opportunities and by administrative pressure, to turn Romanians, Slovaks, and Serbs into Hungarians. This policy, known as Magyarization, was pursued especially in the schools; and the extremely restricted parliamentary franchise made it difficult for the non-Magyars to defend their interests. The

[1] See article by G. F. Cushing, 'The birth of national literature in Hungary', in *SEER*, vol. 38, no. 91 (June 1960).

policy had some success, because Magyar culture certainly had its attractions, but it brought diminishing returns. Romanian, Slovak and Serbian nationalism grew, and in 1919 Greater Hungary disintegrated.

The pattern which I have described, of national consciousness based on a combination of language and historical mythology, with the first of these predominant, can be found also in many of the non-Russian peoples of the European portion of the Russian/Soviet empire, of whom Ukrainians, Estonians, Latvians, and Georgians may be mentioned as examples. Another similarity between Russian and Central European experience is the attempt of rulers to impose their language on other peoples. The policy known as Russification closely resembled the Hungarian policy of Magyarization.

With this pattern in mind, we may look at some other regions and in some cases other epochs, in which language played a less dominant, though in most cases a significant role in the formation of national consciousness. In Germany and Italy we see the same combination of language and historical mythology, but with the second probably more important than the first. In Western Europe language played its part, but the main factor was the development of the centralized monarchical state, which process of course had very important economic aspects. In the new overseas nations of America economics was still more important, and language features as an instrument for nation-building after independent statehood has been won. In the central and western Muslim lands, language and historical mythology are equalled, or more probably surpassed, in importance by the pervasive influence of Islam, in which the sacred and the secular are not, as in Christendom, sharply separated. In the new states of Africa it is perhaps arguable that the phenomenon of national consciousness has hardly appeared at all.

The examples which I shall now give are but a random selection, and are intended only to provide contrasts and to stimulate thought.

The formation of national consciousness in France seems to me to be connected above all with the rise of an effective central monarchical power, a process rather slower than the old clichés would have it, since not even Louis XIV or Napoleon succeeded in centralizing power to the extent that earlier historical clichés assumed. In the process of centralization language undoubtedly played its part. One thinks of the concern of the Académie Française, founded by Richelieu, for the creation of a uniform language, and the encouragement given by both monarchical and republican rulers to French culture, right up to our own day. Even so, Weber shows that the effective triumph of French over other languages south of the Loire, through military service and universal education, is little over a hundred years old.[1] I would risk the assertion that in France language was an important instrument for spreading national consciousness rather than its cause.

The distinctive culture of the Low Countries in the late Middle Ages was very largely based on the emergence of the Dutch language with a literature of its own. This should be set alongside the other obvious factors of economic development and the rise of urban classes. However, in the three centuries which followed the partition of the Netherlands, though the language at least in its written form has remained the same on both sides of the frontier, the national consciousness of the Dutch has not extended to the southern portion of the language group. The quarrels within Belgium between Flemings and Walloons, based on language, have not led to the assertion that there exists a single Dutch nation of 20 millions, or to any significant demand for a single state.

The formation of English national consciousness is, like the French, mainly associated with the rise of the monarchy and with the inter-connected economic and social processes. However, language seems to me to have played a much greater part than in the case of either France or the Low Countries. The experts in the history of the English language speak of Old English and Middle English, the one derived from the other; but to a historian layman it seems that there was a somewhat different phenomenon—not so much that Anglo-Saxon acquired a massive influx of loan-words from French, as that two streams, the Anglo-Saxon and the Norman French, flowed together into a new language, English; and that the fourteenth century, in which this new language began to be adopted for official business, as well as being the vehicle of Chaucer, was the time when English national consciousness was formed, and the English nation born. This was not of course the end of the process. Surely pride in the English language, as used in the first translations of the Bible, as well as in the flowering secular literature of the sixteenth century, had a good deal to do with the Reformation, and with the militant assertion of English nationalism in the Elizabethan age? One may add that literature was also developing in northern English, spoken between the Humber and the Forth, and utter in passing the thought that if the court of Scotland, the source of patronage for

[1] Weber, op. cit.

literature as well as of government business, had remained in
Scotland, and if, after the union of the crowns, the King of Scotland had not preferred the obviously greater attractions of
England, the English and Scots might today have two different
languages, as do the Danes, Norwegians, and Swedes.

Language had nothing to do with the American wars of
independence against England or Spain. It had much to do with
the moulding of new nations from massive immigration, in the
United States, Argentine, Chile, Uruguay, and southern Brazil.
As for the indigenous peoples, in the north they were largely
exterminated, and their remnant swamped by the advancing tide
of immigrants; whereas in Central America and the northern
Andean regions the conquered mixed with the conquerors, but
Spanish became the language of nearly all, and remained a single
language, despite differences of pronunciation and vocabulary,
throughout the continent and islands. Indigenous languages
remained, as also in north America, but did not form the basis of
any national consciousness. Even the Quechua, of whom perhaps
six millions live in a fairly compact territory divided between
Peru, Bolivia and Ecuador, have not followed the example of
Romanians, Greeks or Serbs in demanding a single state for those
who speak their tongue.

In the central and western lands of Islam movements developed
in the twentieth century which could reasonably be called
'nationalist'. At first their motivation was simply hostility to
western rule or interference, and they were based essentially on
religion. They had both traditionalist and modernizing elements,
often in conflict with each other. It was the modernizers who took
from the west an ideology of nationalism, and began to see their
struggle as not only *against* the foreigners, but *for* the nation. The
nation came to be defined by them in terms both of historical
mythology and of language.

Of the three national consciousnesses which emerged, it was the
Turkish which laid greatest emphasis on language. Influenced
both by Balkan Christian nationalism and by the modernizing
Muslim Tatar nationalists of the Volga valley, the Turkish
nationalists insisted that the identifying mark of the Turks,
separating them not only from Greeks, South Slavs and Russians
but also from Arabs and Persians, was their language. The early
nationalists developed a Pan-Turkic idea, analogous to Panslavism, to link all those who spoke a Turkic language, from
Anatolia to Sinkiang, as a single Turkish family of nations, or even
a single nation. This dimension was however specifically rejected

by Kemal Atatürk, who after his victory over the Greeks insisted that the Turkish fatherland was only the limited territory of the Turkish Republic. In the new nationalist ideology, language was the principal component, supported by historical mythology—including fantasies about a pre-Muslim Turkish culture deriving from Central Asia, and attempts to represent the Hittites as proto-Turks. Turkish nationalism was secular, and in practice if not in theory hostile to Islam. However, after sixty years the Muslim element remains strong, and the latent conflict between language and religion in Turkish national culture is an underlying factor in the troubles of contemporary Turkey.

The second national consciousness of this region, the Arab, has been based on a fluctuating combination of historical mythology, language, and religion. If the Arabic language could be made the essential common factor, then Arabic-speakers who were not Muslims could be included within the nation. Christian Arabs, more accessible to western ideas, including the western concept of the nation, at an earlier stage than their Muslim compatriots, played an important part in the formation of Arab nationalist doctrine, and in the shift of emphasis from Islam to Arab nation. Yet the historical mythology on which the modern Arab cultural identity had to be based, with its understandable emphasis on the glories of early medieval Arabic culture, was inextricably intertwined with Islam. Co-existence of Islam and nationalism was much closer in the Arab case than in the Turkish, and it seems hardly possible for an infidel, and perhaps even for an Arab, to say which is the dominant factor.

The third national consciousness, the Iranian, arose from the movement against western interference, in which two distinct trends, one constitutionalist and enamoured of western concepts of political liberty, the other militantly Muslim, at first fought together against the Qadjar monarchy and then came to blows with each other. At that historical stage it is perhaps premature to speak of an Iranian national consciousness. The elaboration of a Persian historical mythology, which was certainly an outstanding feature of the later attempt to create a national consciousness from above, was the work of the new dynasty founded by the Cossack serjeant Reza, who imitated Atatürk in stressing the pre-Islamic past, while at the same time trying forcibly to westernize and modernize Iranian society. These policies antagonised Muslim opinion, and fifty years later a massive Muslim revolt overthrew Reza's successor. In so far as Islam in Iran is Shi'i, and Iran the only substantial state in the world in which Shi'i form an overwhelming majority, it can be argued either that the religious movement was essentially nationalist or that Iranian nationalism is essentially religious. This is an argument which no one can win. The truth is that, almost as much as in the Arab case, national consciousness and Islam are inseparable.

The problem of the relative importance of secular national consciousness and of Islam also arises, in very different circumstances, in the Soviet empire. In Central Asia the Bolshevik leaders deliberately attempted to accelerate the transformation of several Turkic dialects into distinct literary languages, and encouraged the formation of distinct national consciousnesses based on them. Fifty years of industrialization, urbanization, and education have created new social élites who express these national consciousnesses. During the same period, though the influence of the Muslim scriptures and the observance in daily life of Muslim rituals have diminished, the all-encompassing Muslim culture, embracing sacred and secular things alike, and divided by a great gulf from Russian Orthodox or post-Orthodox culture, remains untouched. Do these Central Asians view themselves first as Uzbek or Turkmen or Kirgiz, and secondarily only as Muslims, or is the priority of loyalty reversed? No certain answer is available.

If in the Muslim lands the extent of national consciousness and the rôle of language in its formation are difficult to estimate, though both are undoubtedly present, in the new states of Africa things are still more obscure. The anti-colonial movements which appeared in the African colonies of Britain, France, Belgium, and Portugal, led by intelligentzias influenced by western political ideas or at least by western catch-words, and mobilizing varying types of mass support of economic or social origin, are normally described as nationalist; but I am not sure that this is the right word. Essentially, what these anti-colonial leaders sought, and in most cases attained, with or without violence, was independence, that is to say, control over the sovereign state created, in most cases less than a hundred years previously, by European governments which had drawn arbitrary boundaries on maps in Berlin or other European capitals. Their struggles were *against* the foreign rulers, *for* possession of the *sovereign state*, but *not* on behalf of the *nation*. The sovereign states have existed under African rulers for some decades, but where are the nations?

There are two obvious examples of nations—the Amhara whose Ethiopian empire is almost two thousand years old, and who have been busily trying to Amharize their subject peoples much as the

Magyars and Russians busily tried to Magyarize or Russify theirs: and the Somalis who seek to unite all their compatriots in one state in opposition to the Amharizers, much as Romanians sought to unite their compatriots, in opposition to the Magyarizers. But elsewhere we see combinations of peoples with different languages and cultures, ruled by modernizing élites through a non-indigenous imperial language (Arabic in Southern Sudan), or an artificial *lingua franca* (Swahili in East Africa), or—in most sub-Saharan lands—through the language of the former colonial power. Nation-building is the term used for the efforts of these governments to mould their peoples into one community with a sense of national unity overriding their cultural differences. This, in the post-colonial conventional wisdom, is a good and desirable aim. Tribalism is the term used for those who put first the aspirations of their specific culture including its language. The conventional wisdom sees it as bad and undesirable. The tribe is a unit on a lower moral and political level than the nation, and fated to be absorbed in it. This of course is how the Magyarizers in Hungary saw it. In their terminology there was only one *nation* in Hungary, the Magyar; the other sub-cultures, or communities of lesser culture, were not nations but *nationalities*. This word was the Danubian equivalent of the tribe in colonial and post-colonial terminology. But the unanswerable question remains: who is qualified to say whether a community consciousness is 'lower' and 'tribal', or 'higher' and 'national'?

However, the Magyar language, culture and nation un-doubtedly did exist. The allegedly higher culture into which the Romanians, Slovaks, Serbs and Ruthenes were to be absorbed was a reality. The same is true of the Amharic culture which is intended to swallow up the Somalis, Galla and the rest. But else-where things are less clear. None of the post-colonial states has a clearly recognized single national culture. It is striking that claims for language-based national identities within multi-cultural states are not a prominent feature of African states at present, though possibly that had something to do with the Nigerian civil war, with its more than a million casualties. It is striking that African peoples have produced no Dobrovskýs, no Štúrs, no Vuk Karadžićes. Is this because Africans are immune to some European intellectual maladies, that they have escaped for good the process to which eminent African politicians some-times refer with a shudder—Balkanization? Or is it that the school systems have not yet created sufficiently numerous educated élites in the different language-groups for national consciousness to appear, and claims to be made, and resisted, on behalf of the component languages and cultures, leading to mutual frustration and conflicting nationalisms?

Perhaps in the age of television it is possible to effect cultural mobilization from above so quickly that the processes which occurred in Central Europe can be avoided altogether. Perhaps this can be done through an ex-colonial European language. There is a historical example of this, in Hispanic America, where a single Spanish language, imported by the *conquistadores* four hundred years ago, has remained both dominant and uniform, even if there are regional differences in pronunciation and vocabulary. Alternatively, perhaps there will develop within the African states or groups of states several distinct English-derived, French-derived, and Portuguese-derived languages, which will become national languages of states. Perhaps modern technology can accelerate many times this process, which in the case of the Latin-derived Romance languages of the successor states of the Roman Empire required a thousand years or more to become established. Even so, one whose experience has been Danubian and not African may perhaps be permitted a certain benevolent scepticism. That ethnic diversity has not so far created much conflicting nationalism in Africa is cause for satisfaction. Perhaps African statesmen will be able to find new ways of institution-alizing the demands of ethnic diversity without endangering the fabric of the state or provoking disruptive nationalism. If they do, they will have done better than the Austrian socialists Renner and Bauer, who produced original and constructive plans for cultural autonomy at a time when it was too late, when mutually incom-patible nationalisms were already deeply rooted, when even if in the place of Franz Josef I the House of Habsburg had produced a ruler with the reforming zeal of Joseph II he would still have found it too late. Perhaps the societies over which today's African enlightened despots rule can still be moulded into pre-nationalist, multi-cultural communities, undisturbed by conflicts between nations. Or perhaps these are not the problems which occupy the minds of African despots, whether enlightened or not.

The processes with which I have been concerned this evening cannot be quantified, and defy precise definition, yet they are realities of history and realities of the world in which we live. If my observations stimulate any of you to think about them, and in particular to encourage specialists in language and in social history to consult each other more frequently, then they will have served their purpose as a tribute to the memory of Robert Auty.

SHAKESPEARE'S MINGLED YARN AND 'MEASURE FOR MEASURE'

By E. A. J. HONIGMANN

Read 23 April 1981

THIS will not be a lecture for purists. I propose to examine a trend that troubled Sir Philip Sidney when he lamented the fashion for 'mongrel tragi-comedy'—a shift in literary taste that owed much to the genius of William Shakespeare. It started, perhaps, with the mixing of comic and more serious matter in medieval drama; Kyd and Marlowe gave it a new impetus; and it had certainly arrived by the time of *Measure for Measure*, Shakespeare's darkest comedy. But I have in mind something more far-reaching than the hybridization of kinds, or the doctrine of purity of genre. As Elizabethan drama moved towards realism, and simultaneously lurched in several other directions as well, many kinds of 'mixing' were developed—prose and verse; natural and stylized language, and stage behaviour, and acting; Elizabethan and 'historical' costume, as in the Peacham sketch of *Titus Andronicus*; plot and sub-plot—to name just a few 'mixings' that must have been in general use by the 1580s. Then Shakespeare appeared on the scene, pressed a button, and the mixer-speed accelerated remarkably, much to the disgust of purists (like Ben Jonson). Shakespeare delighted in mixed metaphor; Jonson reputedly said of some of the grandest speeches in *Macbeth*, which 'are not to be understood', that 'it was horror'. Shakespeare specialized in crazily complicated plots, cross-wooing comedies, plays with time-jumps, plays that zigzag between different countries—disgraceful 'mixings' that Jonson castigated publicly. More modern critics discover the same tendency wherever they look: Shakespeare's expert interweaving of different views of the same person, of past, present, and future, of slow time and fast time, of conflicting motives, or the interplay of many emotions in a single phrase—'Pray you, undo this button'; 'Kill Claudio'. If, as I shall argue, Shakespeare's mixing skills were of the essence, as indispensable to his success as his inventiveness in metaphor, it may be no accident that he so often peaks as a poet in scenes of intense emotion or madness

(Hamlet's, King Lear's), where a 'mixer' mechanism in the play triggers off his own special talent. I believe that these mixing skills are conscious artistry, not inspired fumbling, if only because the dramatist so often draws attention to them:

> You have seen
> Sunshine and rain at once: her smiles and tears
> Were like, a better way.   (*King Lear*, IV. iii. 16 ff.).

We need not doubt that a writer who said that 'the web of our life is of a mingled yarn' would know, even without Ben Jonson's unnecessary help, that he himself was a purveyor of intricately mingled yarns.

The 'mixing' principle in Shakespeare is my subject today. Ben Jonson was merely the first of many good critics who could not come to terms with it, and one or two other examples will illustrate the range of problems. Dr Johnson, though he defended tragi-comedy, thought that 'the poet's matter failed him' in the fifth act of *Henry V*, 'and he was glad to fill it up with whatever he could get'; in Johnson's view, Act V did not mix with the rest. Coleridge repudiated the 'low' porter-speech in *Macbeth*, which reminds us that bawdy, once removed by editors as intrusive dirt, is now praised as an integral part of the Shakespearian 'mix' in both comedy and tragedy. T. S. Eliot faulted Shakespeare's 'mixing' even more ingeniously, arguing that it is

strictly an error, although an error which is condoned by the success of each passage in itself, that Shakespeare should have introduced into the same play ghosts belonging to such different categories as the three sisters and the ghost of Banquo.[1]

These are all 'mixing' problems, and they warn us that Shakespeare's imagination scrambled the ingredients of a play in so many new ways that even the very best critics 'hoppe alwey bihinde'.

Examples of supposedly bad 'mixing' are alleged, and have to be endured, in almost every book on Shakespeare. Yet the mixing principle itself has not had the attention it deserves. This may be because criticism finds it convenient to deal with detachable units—imagery, character, genre, scene-by-scene analysis—rather than with the intermeshing of such units, which I consider the heart of the mystery. After four centuries criticism is still largely defeated by a procedural problem, how to grapple with the play as a whole: I suggest that we may solve this problem by focusing on

---

[1] T. S. Eliot, *Selected Essays* (ed. 1953), p. 116.

the mixing principle, searching for its unique functioning in each text. Not only Shakespeare criticism could benefit: we do not have to look far to discover similar needs elsewhere. Let me illustrate, tactfully, from *Juno and the Paycock*, where, it has been said, the tragic element 'occupies at the most some twenty minutes . . . for the remaining two hours and a half this piece is given up to gorgeous and incredible fooling'.[1] Who has not heard that *The Winter's Tale* consists of three acts of tragedy followed by two of comedy? Or that some scenes in *Measure for Measure* are 'tragic', others 'comic'? It is the interpenetration of comedy and tragedy that now needs our attention—or, more exactly, the interaction of everything with everything else, in these unfathomably rich plays.

O'Casey once remarked: 'I never make a scenario, depending on the natural growth of a play rather than on any method of joinery.'[2] Shakespeare criticism, when it attempts to explain the mixing principle, still tends to think too much in terms of joinery—as in a brilliant paper on *The Winter's Tale* in which Nevill Coghill showed that the bear, the famous bear, 'was calculated to create a unique and particular effect, at that point demanded by the narrative mood and line of the play. It is at the moment when the tale, hitherto wholly and deeply tragic, turns suddenly and triumphantly to comedy.'[3] Much that Coghill said about the bear seems to me perceptive, yet his is largely an explanation of joinery. Looking at the play as an organic growth, I am struck by the fact that each of its two movements ends with an addition to the story by Shakespeare—the bear, and the statue. In each case the bystanders, astounded, react aesthetically, as if the bear and statue are merely a thrilling spectacle, then struggle comically to adjust their bewildered feelings—and thus lift the scene, emotionally, in a very similar way. If the bear and statue are connected, as I think, then the mixing principle works not only in local joinery but also, more elusively, in shaping dramatic units that are far apart.

I am going to assume, in what follows, that in 'organic' drama everything joins on to everything else; that bears and statues can shake hands, as over a vast, and embrace as it were from the ends of opposed winds. The logic of our bread-and-butter world need not apply; the linear structure of events, and of cause and effect, is

---

[1] James Agate, quoted from *Sean O'Casey Modern Judgements*, ed. Ronald Ayling (1969), p. 76.

[2] Sean O'Casey, *Blasts and Benedictions* (1967), p. 97.

[3] Nevill Coghill, 'Six Points of Stage-Craft in *The Winter's Tale*', *Shakespeare Survey XI* (1958), pp. 31–41.

not the only structure that concerns us. Although we are sometimes told that a literary work grows in the reader's mind as does a musical composition, being a process experienced in time, and should not be compared to a painting, which is frozen in time, a play that lasts two to three hours differs from longer literary works, such as an epic or a novel, in so far as its process can be held in the mind as a single experience, somewhat like a painting. Aided by memorable dialogue and good acting a poetic drama will not pass away from us while we surrender to its magic, as do the trivia of day-to-day existence: such a play grows in the beholder's mind in a present continuous, partly insulated from time, a single shared experience framed by the stage, one that remains present, like a painting, even as it unfolds, challenging us to connect the ends of opposed winds, a bear and a statue, Claudio's guilt and Angelo's, Angelo's ignorance of the world and Isabella's and the Duke's. 'Only connect' is the dramatist's command, and the more unexpectedly he mixes the play's ingredients the bigger the challenge.

I would like to illustrate the 'present continuous' of drama from a soliloquy that some of you may remember—'To be or not to be, that is the question'. I find it surprising that, according to some competent editors, Hamlet here talks not of his own suicide but only of the general problem of life after death. Dr Johnson paraphrased the opening line succinctly, as follows: 'Before I can form any rational scheme of action under this pressure of distress, it is necessary to decide whether, after our present state, we are to be or not to be. That is the question . . .' Another editor soon offered a different interpretation, 'To live or to put an end to my life', which, he thought, was confirmed by the following words. Johnson had his supporters, and I find this surprising not because of the following words but because of preceding speeches that prepare us for 'To be or not to be'. Hadn't Hamlet wished that 'this too too solid flesh would melt'? (Knowing what we know about the frauds and stealths of injurious imposters, I had better say firmly that 'solid flesh' is the reading of the only authorized text . . . of this lecture.) 'You cannot, sir, take from me anything that I will more willingly part withal—except my life, except my life, except my life.' These and other passages determine our immediate impression that in 'To be or not to be' Hamlet meditates upon his own suicide; the soliloquy is not a detachable unit, it throbs with implications planted in our minds in earlier scenes.

If my example seems fanciful, let us take two that are more

straightforward. Let us take the one sentence that occurs in both *Othello* and *Macbeth*. Lady Macbeth waits for Macbeth; he appears, the daggers in his hands, blood on the daggers; the deed is done, and wrings from her a terrible, gloating cry—'My husband!' Othello explains to Emilia that the murder of Desdemona proceeded upon just grounds ('Thy husband knew it all'), and she reacts in shocked surprise—'My husband!' The same words, but the effect is totally different, because the words mingle with previous impressions, there is an inflow of power from very different sources. Lady Macbeth had taunted her husband that he was not man enough to commit the murder; when he has proved himself she cries, in effect, 'My true husband, at last!' Emilia had suspected that Desdemona had been slandered by 'some cogging, cozening slave, to get some office'; as soon as Othello names Iago it dawns on her what has happened, and she feels that she has come to a crossroad in her life. Her exclamation marks the end of a marriage, Lady Macbeth's a new beginning (as she thinks) of hers. The words that are spoken out loud are only a small part of the complex communication that goes on at the same time; whether we are conscious of it or not, these words mix with other impressions—are, indeed, completely dwarfed by momentous implications that immediately rush in upon us.

So far I have concentrated on the play's organic growth, indicating how important lines or episodes grow out of others, mixing with what we may have heard or seen much earlier in the play's 'present continuous'. The mixing principle can also be illustrated from 'joinery', as O'Casey called it—an unkind word that refers, presumably, to the way one episode is cobbled on to the next. Such local joinery, in the hands of a Shakespeare, can serve to illustrate the highest skills, where the craftsman's conscious mixing and the play's organic growth are indistinguishable. We can observe how felicitously each episode joins on to its neighbour and fits the needs of its individual play by comparing three with very similar functions—the grave-digger episode in *Hamlet*, the porter-scene in *Macbeth*, and Cleopatra's interview with the clown who brings the asp. In each case a clown's 'low' humour precedes and follows scenes of high tension, or of tragic seriousness, yet each of the three has unique features determined by its play. In *Hamlet*, where there had been much talk of suicide and the hereafter, the two clowns pick up these themes and fool around with them as naturally as grave-diggers pick up bones. Hamlet's interest in the question, 'How long will a man lie i'th'earth ere he rot?' is related to an earlier topic, how long will a man's memory outlive his life (two hours? twice two months?) — two kinds of survival after death. The play being filled with mock-interviews, in which the prince pretends to misunderstand a questioner (Rosencrantz and Guildenstern; Claudius; Osric), first grave-digger turns the tables on him, answering knavishly—so the shape of their exchanges is another thread that hooks into a larger design. 'Alas, poor Yorick' mysteriously echoes 'Alas, poor ghost'; and so on. The grave-digger episode, in short, mixes with the rest of the play in its larger themes, in specific questions, in verbal echoes, and in using a special dialogue-device, the mock-interview; and no doubt in other ways too.

A word will suffice for *Macbeth*. The dramatic irony in the porter's soliloquy is familiar: it is Macbeth who is an equivocator, who has 'hang'd himself on th'expectation of plenty'. True. I am equally struck by the porter's exchanges with Macduff—for the porter, in the delightful afterglow of his carousing, also resembles Macbeth in the previous scene in being present and not present; his tipsiness has the same effect as Macbeth's imagination—he only gives half his mind to the matter in hand. And in each case there is a cool observer and questioner, Lady Macbeth and Macduff, whose presence measures the distance of Macbeth and the porter from normality. Just as the knocking in the porter-scene spills over from the previous scene, the porter's tipsiness grew out of Macbeth's intoxicated imagination and his slowness in answering the call of the here and now and his psychic distance from Macduff were also influenced by the previous scene. It should be noted in passing that alcohol plays a part in the grave-digger *and* porter scenes, yet its effect is adapted to the needs of the play no less than is each clown's distinctive way of speaking and relating to others.

Next, Cleopatra's clown. Plutarch mentions a 'countryman', who brings the asp in a basket of figs, but not a word about his interview with Cleopatra, which is pure Shakespeare—perhaps his most daring 'mingle' in the tragedies, because here comedy modulates immediately into the tragic climax. Appropriately, it is comedy shot through with sexual innuendo, and even the chastest ears cannot miss it.

You must not think I am so simple but I know the devil himself will not eat a woman. I know that a woman is a dish for the gods, if the devil dress her not.

The richest insinuation and 'mingle' in the clown-scene, however, grows out of one keyword, repeated eight times—'Hast thou the pretty worm of Nilus there?', 'I wish you all joy of the worm'. It's a word not used by Plutarch at this point, and conjures up a very different image from Plutarch's one specific description of the asp: Cleopatra pricked the creature with a spindle, so that, 'being angered withal,' said Plutarch, 'it leapt out with great fury, and bit her in the arm'—not really what one expects from a bona fide worm. In Elizabethan English, of course, *worm* could mean reptile, or serpent, or other things—and, since no one in the play's first audience is likely ever to have seen an Egyptian asp, the uncertain meaning of *worm* was particularly useful. We are made to wonder exactly what this hidden worm may be. 'The worm will do his kind', the clown explains, helpfully. 'The worm's an odd worm.'

I have dwelt on the spectator's inability to imagine exactly what to expect because there must have been a reason for the dramatist's teasing vagueness. I am reminded of another teasing device in the play—its concealed penis imagery, a joke repeated several times, in different ways, by different characters. Since learned editors don't feel obliged to explain what can't be seen, I had better give some examples. (1) The soothsayer tells Cleopatra's ladies that their future fortunes are alike. 'Well,' says Charmian to Iras, 'if you were but an inch of fortune better than I, where would you choose it?' Reply?—'Not in my husband's nose'. (2) Cleopatra, bored, asks Charmian to play billiards; Charmian suggests Mardian the eunuch instead, and Cleopatra quips 'As well a woman with an eunuch play'd / As with a woman'. (3) A third concealed image is given to Agrippa:

> Royal wench!
> She made great Caesar lay his sword to bed.
> He plough'd her, and she cropp'd.

The wicked word is not mentioned—indeed, was not known yet, though the English language was rich in alternatives. Here, then, are three examples of concealed penis imagery—a distinctive series in the play that puts us in a state of readiness for the clown's *worm*. We have to remember at this point the infinite variety of Shakespeare's sexual imagery, and that he had used the same image before, when Lucrece exclaims against rape—'Why should the worm intrude the maiden bud?' (a traditional image long before Blake's *The Sick Rose*). Recalling also how tirelessly the Elizabethans punned on the sexual sense of *lie* and *die*, we observe that the general context also nudges us towards concealed imagery. 'I would not desire you to touch him', the clown tells Cleopatra,

for his biting is immortal; those that do *die* of it do seldom or never recover.

Cleopatra. Remember'st thou any that have *died* on't?

Clown. Very many, men and women too. I heard of one of them no longer than yesterday: a very honest woman, but something given to *lie*, as a woman should not do but in the way of honesty; how she *died* of the biting of it, what pain she felt—truly, she makes a very good report o'th'worm.

The extraordinary power and flavour of this clown-scene partly depends on concealed imagery, imagery reactivated by the puns on *lie* and *die*, by 'a woman is a dish for the gods, if the devil dress her not', but the clown's winking knowingness and by Shakespeare's teasing vagueness as to what the worm might be. At one and the same time the worm refers to the asp (a word carefully excluded until the clown has gone), to the worm in the grave, and to the sex-worm whose 'biting' is also immortal—hence the pungent rightness of the clown's parting shot to sex-obsessed Cleopatra, 'I wish you joy o'th'worm!' Here, marvelling at a treble pun that has its tentacular roots in other local puns, and in concealed imagery that acts upon us subliminally, one is tempted to cry, with Cleopatra, 'O heavenly mingle!'—for what more is possible? Yet the mingling continues:

> Give me my robe, put on my crown; I have
> Immortal longings in me.

'Longings for immortality', thought the New Arden editor. Perhaps; but, after 'I wish you joy o'th'worm' she also means 'immortal longings' as opposed to 'mortal longings'—a higher form of sexuality, a kiss from the curled Antony 'which is my heaven to have'. The sublime 'Give me my robe', a speech structured round the idea of 'immortal longings', grew out of the largely latent sexuality and low comedy of the clown-scene.

The three clown-scenes, possibly written for the same actor, have been thought to have a similar function in three of the greatest tragedies. Yet they are not merely 'comic relief', since each one builds upon ideas, images, mental states, or relationships from previous scenes—that is, flashes back to more serious concerns, mingling seriousness with laughter. (Meredith's phrase, 'thoughtful laughter', is peculiarly apt: an awareness that the clown-scene somehow mingles with what has gone before pulls us back from surrendering wholly to laughter, even though we cannot stop the play to trace all the connections.) More important for my purposes: not only are the clown-scenes sewn into the fabric of the play in so many ways—each one is sewn in in its own distinctive way. There may be superficial resemblances, but we fail to appreciate the dramatist's skill unless we see that seemingly similar devices always 'mingle' quite uniquely with their dramatic surroundings.

That brings me to the notorious 'bed-trick' in *Measure for Measure*. It was Shakespeare's error, we have been told often enough, that he chose to solve the problems of a realistic plot by resorting to pure folk-tale. After the 'realism' of the early scenes, of Angelo's passion for Isabella and of his demand that she buy her brother's life by yielding her virginity, comes the bed-trick—Angelo's betrothed, Mariana, takes Isabella's place in his bed—a hangover from folk-tale or romance, it is said, quite out of keeping with what has gone before. This account of the play assumes that Shakespeare had got into trouble with his plotting, and that the bed-trick was an attempt to slither round a difficulty. Shakespeare had departed from his sources in making Isabella a novice in an order of nuns, and in giving her a passionately virginal nature; unlike her prototype in the sources, therefore, she could not comply with Angelo's demand—so we have the bed-trick instead, a desperate expedient.

Before I argue that, on the contrary, the bed-trick is beautifully right where it is placed, no less than the bear in *The Winter's Tale*, a multiple 'mingle' in a self-consciously mingled yarn, let us examine our terminology—realism and folk-tale. So-called realistic scenes in the play do employ non-realistic devices: the low-life characters meticulously finish their sentences; Angelo soliloquises —in verse. Realism is adjustable; so, too, folk-tale episodes can be presented more or less plausibly. Much can be done to bring realism and folk-tale together, to make them tone in with one another; before we denounce the bed-trick as a desperate ex-pedient it is our duty to ask how it mingles with its surroundings.

First, though, I must correct a common misrepresentation of the bed-trick in literature. Bed-tricks, though familiar in folk-tale and romance, were not restricted to one or two *kinds* of literature: we have all read Genesis 19: 33, and *The Escapes of Jupiter*, and *The Magus*. Next: a bed-trick story can be told in the spirit of the *Reeve's Tale* or of the *Knight's Tale* or—somewhere in between. The use of significant detail will sharply differentiate one bed-trick story from another.

We can learn what Shakespeare might have done, had he thought a bed-trick too 'unrealistic' after his play's earlier scenes, by glancing at some other literary versions. Even Malory, not the most realistic of writers, felt that a drugged drink was needed to trick Lancelot into sleeping with the fair Elaine—'as soon as he

had drunk that wine he was so assotted that he wened that maiden
Elaine had been queen Guinever' (xi, 2); later Elaine's lady-in-
waiting 'took him by the finger' (there's realistic detail!) 'and led
him unto her lady'. Deloney's *Jack of Newberry*, a rip-roaring
narrative, provides a more representative example of bed-trick
realism. An English girl, Joan, had an importunate Italian lover,
who became a nuisance until Joan's kinsman taught him a lesson.
The kinsman gave a 'sleepy drench' to a young sow, put the
sleeping sow in Joan's bed, 'drawing the curtains round about',
and told the lover that his opportunity had arrived. But, he
warned, 'you must not . . . have a candle when you go into the
chamber, for . . . dark places fits best lovers' desires'. The Italian
knelt down by the bedside, saluted the invisible sow with a love-
speech, slipped into bed, ardently embraced her, and only
discovered his mistake from her non-human grunting.[1] I hesitate
to call this realism, but we may say that Deloney made room for
more 'realistic' touches than Malory. In Marston's *The Insatiate
Countess*, which is close to *Measure for Measure* in genre and date,
two ladies plot to sleep with their own husbands (the husbands
each having importuned the other's wife), 'and the better to avoid
suspicion', one wife explains, 'thus we must insist: they must come
up darkling'. 'But,' says the second wife, 'is my husband content
to come darkling?' This problem solved, she thinks of another
difficulty. 'I am afraid my voice will discover me.' 'Why, then
you're best say nothing . . .' 'Ay, but you know a woman cannot
choose but speak in these cases.'[2] The dramatist positively delights
in applying a 'realistic' imagination to the bed-trick, without
damaging his play.

It appears, then, that you can choose between comedy and
seriousness, between more and less realism. In bed-trick scenes
you can adopt almost any position, as it were. This is hard for us to
grasp today, because we have been taught to think of the bed-trick
as a purely literary device, one that belongs to literature at its
furthest possible remove from life. Before the invention of
electricity, however, the night-life of Europe must have been
much more tricky than now, and there is plenty of evidence that
strange things happened in the dark.

> Now 'tis full sea a-bed over the world,
> There's juggling of all sides . . .
> This woman, in immodest thin apparel

[1] *The Works of Thomas Deloney*, ed. F. O. Mann (Oxford, 1912), pp. 51–2.
[2] *The Plays of John Marston*, ed. H. Harvey Wood (3 vols., 1939), iii. 29.

PLATE I

The Life and Death of Sir Henry Unton. Anonymous (*c.* 1596)
National Portrait Gallery, London.

PLATE II

El Greco: *View and Plan of Toledo* (*c.* 1608)
Museos de las Fundaciones Vega-Inclán

Lets in her friend by water. Here a dame
Cunning, nails leather hinges to a door
To avoid proclamation.
Now cuckolds are a-coining, apace, apace, apace, apace!

I have laboured the point that Shakespeare did not have to fall back on a 'ready-made' bed-trick, the figmentary bed-trick of folk-tale and romance, simply to suggest that he was free to devise his own. The stark contrast that so many critics have disliked in *Measure for Measure* as 'realism' is succeeded by the bed-trick, I conclude, was entirely of his own choosing. The play was written when he was at the height of his powers, when he had fully mastered the art of mingling one episode with another, yet this bed-trick jars all expectation. Why did Shakespeare choose it, in this form, when there were other options open to him?

As I mentioned at the outset, drama in the later sixteenth century introduced many new kinds of 'mingling'. Some of the dramatists no doubt did so unconsciously. By the turn of the century, however, the mingled yarn of literature was a matter of public debate. Italian critics defended tragicomedy; Sidney moved with the times in defending pastoral, where some 'have mingled prose and verse . . . Some have mingled matters heroical and pastoral', though he was not happy about 'mingling kings and clowns'.[1] In *The Faerie Queene* Spenser aimed at variety, copying the artful confusion of Italian epic so that, as he put it, many things are 'intermedled' with one another—again, the mingling principle, artful combination. Metaphysical poetry, said Dr Johnson, experimented with the 'combination of dissimilar images . . . the most heterogeneous ideas are yoked by violence together'.[2]

Similar experiments took place at the same time in the visual arts, and they also have a bearing on *Measure for Measure*. Mannerist painters of the later sixteenth century sought out new combinations, mingling realistic detail in a recognizably non-realistic ensemble, as in Arcimboldo's *Librarian*, a deplorably bookish gentleman, or his *Autumn*, a jolly old Bacchus made out of fruit and veg whose features are recognizably those of the Emperor Rudolph II. Sometimes the Mannerists even mingled different levels of realism: Pontormo's *Joseph in Egypt* in the National Gallery playfully distorts scale and perspective, and includes clothed figures standing on pedestals like statues, wholly fanciful architecture with stairways leading nowhere—an imagined world,

[1] Sir Philip Sidney, *An Apology for Poetry*, ed. Geoffrey Shepherd (1965), p. 116.
[2] Johnson's *Life of Abraham Cowley*.

consciously deviating from nature, in no sense intended as a copy of nature.

Whether such Mannerist experiments of the late sixteenth century were influential in England is difficult to determine. We do know, however, that illustrations in sixteenth-century English books often depicted mingled scenes: a single crude woodcut may combine the creation of Eve, the Temptation, and the Expulsion from Paradise. This is a tradition that goes back to medieval art; inevitably, it appealed to later book illustrators, and English readers would know it from Harington's *Orlando Furioso* of 1591, where the engravings are copied from an Italian edition. One unusual painting of the late Elizabethan age also belongs to this tradition— *The Life and Death of Sir Henry Unton* (it hangs in the National Portrait Gallery), an attempt to bring together many scenes from the life of one of Queen Elizabeth's ambassadors: his arrival at Oriel College, Oxford; his wedding-masque; his diplomatic missions; his funeral procession and burial. Although not strictly a Mannerist painting, it mingles different scales and different degrees of realism, and each scene mingles differently with its neighbours. The artist or artists may not have been of the highest quality (some of the detail is most delicately finished), but there can be no doubt that the 'mingling principle' is consciously employed. Remember, please, how the half-length figure of Sir Henry Unton holds the whole composition together. For there is a similar centre-piece in one of the greatest Mannerist compositions, El Greco's *View and Plan of Toledo*, which belongs to the same decade as *Measure for Measure* and deserves our closer attention. According to one admirer, El Greco here did his utmost

to prevent the actual view of Toledo from dominating the picture. He put the figure of the river god of the Tagus in the left foreground. He also removed the monastery, which lay outside the town and for which he presumably painted the view of the town, from reality by transferring it from *terra firma* to a bright airy cloud. Above it he painted the vision of Mary borne high over the town by angels. . . . The painter further distorted the view of Toledo . . . by the addition of the half-length figure of a boy holding out the plan of Toledo to the spectator.[1]

Unlike the allegories of the High Renaissance, such as Botticelli's *Primavera*, El Greco's composition reassembles matter in jarringly new ways; his centre-piece, the monastery in the clouds, asserts the artist's right to make the most unexpected combinations, where heterogeneous ideas and images are yoked by violence together.

[1] F. Würtenberger, *Mannerism* (1963), p. 239.

I have digressed in order to suggest that discussions of 'mingling' problems in tragicomedy and pastoral, of 'intermeddling' in Italian epic and its derivatives, the self-conscious mingling of heterogeneous ideas and images in metaphysical poetry, and the radical rethinking of compositional norms by the Mannerists, all reflect the spirit of the age, no less than Guarini's *Compendio* of 1602, which Shakespeare could scarcely have seen, and all point forward to *Measure for Measure*. While we cannot demonstrate Shakespeare's knowledge of Italian and Spanish Mannerists, there are signs of similar experiments in England, and we can claim that he was aware of the new trends in literature. Polonius announces the actors in Elsinore—the best actors in the world for 'tragedy, comedy, history, pastoral, pastoral-comical, historical-pastoral, tragical-historical, tragical-comical-historical-pastoral, scene individable, or poem unlimited'. If even Polonius grasps that the dramatic poem no longer conforms to the traditional limits of genre, we may take it that Shakespeare and his public must have been interested in such technical developments as well.

In *Measure for Measure* Shakespeare went one step beyond any he had previously taken, not merely mingling the play's ingredients surprisingly, as often before, but making an issue of it, challenging the audience to put the pieces together and to think critically about a 'poem unlimited'. The notorious bed-trick comes at the point of no return, when a spectator *must* ask himself, even if he has previously failed to do so, 'What kind of play is this?' Terms such as 'problem play' and 'dark comedy' had not yet been invented; 'tragi-comedy' was sometimes discussed, but there was no agreed definition—in England there had been no serious attempt at definition. Up to Act III it would be reasonable to see *Measure for Measure* as a tragedy that includes a good deal of low comedy (like *Romeo and Juliet*), or as a new-formula play such as the 'tragical-comical-historical-pastoral' of Polonius, or as tragicomedy. Whichever one favours, the important thing is that one can't be certain—and, consequently, that one keeps returning to the question, 'What kind of play is it?' Even the modern spectator can't avoid this question, since he still has to fit all the bits and pieces together. 'Is Angelo's self-accusing honesty, or Isabella's torment, too life-like, placed beside a disguised duke and a comic constable, in *this kind of play*?' The question has already nagged us for a while when suddenly Shakespeare introduces the bed-trick, a twist so unexpected that now we can no longer escape our dilemma—'What kind of play?' Observe that the bed-trick, Shakespeare's addition to the story, whatever it may achieve in simplifying Isabella's problems, notably complicates the play's genre problems and the spectator's genre expectations.

The bed-trick resembles the bear in *The Winter's Tale*, and the 'Cinna the poet' scene in *Julius Caesar*, and the porter-scene in *Macbeth*, in coming at the point where the play modulates from one mood into another. It is done differently in each one, of course, but nowhere more self-advertisingly than in *Measure for Measure*. For, just at this point, the play's style joltingly changes gear several times. The Duke soliloquises in rhyming tetrameters, a new voice for him—

> He who the sword of heaven will bear
> Should be as holy as severe,
> Pattern in himself to know
> Grace to stand, and virtue go;
> More nor less to others paying
> Than by self-offences weighing. . . .

Then follows the play's only song, and shortly thereafter the Duke switches in mid-speech from verse to prose—all warning signals that the play is about to change direction. Then follows the play's most arresting modulation, Isabella's speech about the proposed midnight meeting with Angelo, a speech that the dramatist could easily have left to the audience's imagination. Shakespeare chose to give Isabella this speech, I think, because it allows him to suggest, in passing, a unique mingling of realism and romance, and the unique nature of his play: the speech combines a romantic sense of mystery, as in Mariana's song, with an insistent factualness.

> He hath a garden circummur'd with brick,
> Whose western side is with a vineyard back'd;
> And to that vineyard is a planched gate
> That makes his opening with this bigger key;
> This other doth command a little door
> Which from the vineyard to the garden leads.
> There have I made my promise
> Upon the heavy middle of the night
> To call upon him.

Despite its factualness (the garden, brick wall, vineyard on the western side, the gate, the smaller door, the two keys), this speech cannot be called 'realism'; a garden *circummured* with brick and a vineyard with a *planched* gate also carry overtones from another world, the world of Mariana of the *moated grange*, the world of *The Romance of the Rose*. The mingle, and the sense of a special creative pressure, is supported by out-of-the-way words (*circummured* and *planched*, like *moated*, occur nowhere else in Shakespeare; *circum-mured* was his coinage); and it is all bonded together by a concealed image—the Freudian slip when Isabella's imagination dimly anticipates sexual contact ('Upon the heavy middle of the night', an unusual turn of phrase that stamps her personal feeling upon this special bed-trick).

In this speech, neither realism nor romance, we are asked to give a willing suspension of disbelief to an experience as strange as the coming to life of the statue at the end of *The Winter's Tale*—a bed-trick as peculiar to this play as Hermione's statue is different from all the other statues that return to life in romances before Shakespeare. It is a far cry from Deloney's passionate Italian and his drugged sow, and from all other bed-tricks in literature, because Shakespeare (like El Greco in *The View and Plan of Toledo*) has reassembled and mingled his material in new ways. Instead of the 'clever wench' or 'clever wife' who wishes to reclaim her husband (as represented by Helena in *All's Well*) he gives us Mariana, a mere pawn in someone else's clever game; and he changed the man, a mere sex-object for the traditional 'clever wife', into the brooding, vulnerable Angelo. The bed of the 'bed-trick' disappears from view, and Shakespeare eliminates the snigger found in other plays (including *All's Well* and *The Changeling*) when one of the principals goes to or returns from copulation: instead we are asked to apply our imagination to a garden, a vineyard, a planched gate. The actors, the moral implications of the action, the feelings involved, our sense of place, our awareness of a containing society—all are changed for the specific needs of *Measure for Measure*.

Shakespeare's immense care in fitting the bed-trick into his story is also evident in his handling of Mariana. It may seem, to those who believe that the dramatist snatched the bed-trick out of the air to solve an unforeseen plot problem, that Mariana accepts it too readily. That is to presuppose that her character is reflected in the hauntingly romantic song sung for her when she first appears at the moated grange—'Take, O, take those lips away'. Producers usually cast her thus, as a dreamy romantic, for which we must partly blame Tennyson's poem *Mariana*.

> She only said, 'My life is dreary,
>   He cometh not,' she said;
> She said 'I am aweary, aweary,
>   I would that I were dead!'

Yet Shakespeare's pure and romantic maiden jumps without

hesitation at the offer of a place in Angelo's bed; the whole complicated story is explained to her by Isabella while the Duke speaks a short soliloquy, and Mariana is ready. Out of character? No: Tennyson misrepresented her. Shakespeare had previously stressed that, when Angelo rejected Mariana's love, this, 'like an impediment in the current, made it more violent and unruly' (III. i. 237 ff.). She suffers from an overmastering passion—easily conveyed to us if she has a picture or keepsake of her lover, kissing it passionately as the boy sings, 'But my kisses bring again, bring again'. Mariana's willingness to undertake the bed-trick is prepared for by what we are told about her 'violent and unruly' affection, and probably by her 'body-language' as she listens to the song; instead of being just a romantic dummy in the plot, she has character—sufficient character—to tone in with the near-realism of adjacent scenes. And she also tones in with all the other characters in the play who suffer from irresistible sexual impulses —Claudio and Juliet, Lucio, Mrs Overdone, Angelo.

To argue that Shakespeare by no means lost sight of the demands of realism, or near-realism, when he decided to intro-duce the bed-trick, may seem unwise. I would like to pursue this possibility for a moment, since the entire second half of the play appears to pull away from realism, and indeed to pull away from the first half, and this requires some explanation. The sense that the play modulates into a new mood, or changes direction, comes in Act III Scene 1, where the bed-trick is announced. Just before we hear of the bed-trick, it is important to notice, Shakespeare jolts our trust in the Duke, who proposes the bed-trick. How can the Duke say so confidently to Claudio, 'Son, I have overheard what hath pass'd between you and your sister. Angelo had never the purpose to corrupt her; only he hath made an assay of her virtue . . .'? We *know* this to be false, since we overheard Angelo's soliloquies, whereas the Duke didn't. He continues 'I am confessor to Angelo, and I know this to be true . . .'. Some critics have wondered whether the disguised Duke could be, or could ever have been, confessor to Angelo, and one has even expressed indignation that the secrets of the confessional should be revealed, contrary to the rules of the Church. The ordinary theatre-goer, however, is unlikely to encumber himself with such idle fancies: aware that the Duke's assertion, 'I know this to be true', is a fabrication, he is cued to regard 'I am confessor to Angelo' as another fabrication. Whatever his motives, the Duke appears to snatch arguments out of the air, and Shakespeare invites us to note his dexterity, and inventiveness. Then, within a few lines, the conjurer-duke produces from his hat the bed-trick—snatches it out of nothing, another brilliant improvisation, again one that he has scarcely had time to think through, any more than his right to say 'I am confessor to Angelo'.

Just as Angelo tangles himself in one deception after another, and Lucio, the comic foil, in one lie after another, the disguised Duke finds himself obliged to improvise more and more desperately—inventing the future, as it were, and becoming more and more unable to control it. We already feel uneasy about his reading of the future, I think, when he explains to Friar Thomas that he needs a disguise because he wants Angelo to clean up Vienna, and immediately adds that he half-mistrusts Angelo—

> Hence shall we see,
> If power change purpose, what our seemers be.

At this stage the Duke sees his own future role as that of an observer:

> And to behold his sway
> I will, as 'twere a brother of your order,
> Visit both prince and people.

When he reappears, however, the observer feels impelled to throw himself fully into his new role as a friar, interrogates Juliet ('Repent you, fair one, of the sin you carry?'), and then improvises impressively as he lectures Claudio on death. Has an observer the right to impose thus on another human being, merely by virtue of his disguise? The moral authority of his speech, 'Be absolute for death', is undercut by our awareness that he is playing a part—a growing uncertainty about him, corresponding to our uncertainty about the nature of the play. More unmistakably disturbing is the Duke's sudden expedient that Barnardine's head should be substituted for Claudio's; the Provost's amazement, and reluctance to comply, inform the audience, if ordinary human instincts fail to do so, that to play with life in this way is presumptuous. What, we ask ourselves, is he up to?

Everything said and done by the Duke, from his initial decision to appoint Angelo as his deputy and to look on as a 'friar', can be read as improvisation, usually as hurried improvisation. We are therefore prompted to think of the bed-trick not as an 'archaic device' placed in uncomfortable proximity to psychological realism by a fatigued dramatist, but as the Duke's device, just as much an expression of his character as his disguise-trick, and his other surprising and whimsical expedients. As the second half of the play pulls away from realism, and the question 'what *kind* of

play?' grows more urgent, we look to the Duke to solve our problems, while at the same time we half suspect that the dithering
Duke merely improvises irresponsibly. His awareness of Angelo's
intentions, and of all that happens, serves as a hint to the audience
that a tragic outcome may be prevented; yet the Duke's sheer
inefficiency, highlighted by his failure to control Lucio, by no
means guarantees a happy ending. Our uncertainty about the
nature of this mingled yarn therefore continues—augmented,
I think, by our uncertainty about the Duke's double image (as
duke and friar), and about his motives and his control.

In the second half of *Measure for Measure*, as we wonder whether
the Duke and the dramatist know where they are going, we are
teased with several possibilities. The shape of the play begins to
resemble a familiar Elizabethan stereotype—the story of the
clever man who overreaches himself, who initiates a dangerous
action, and has to improvise more and more frantically to hold off
disaster (Marlowe's Barabas, Shakespeare's Richard III and
Iago). But, if we sense this kinship, Shakespeare refuses to conform
to his model, for in this version of 'the sorcerer's apprentice' the
fumbling friar reassumes control at the end, as the Duke, and the
stereotype is shattered.

Another possibility is that the ending will be like that of *The
Malcontent*, where a disguised duke resumes his ducal authority,
forgives his enemies, and only one, the wicked Mendoza, is
punished by being ceremonially kicked out of court. Yet Shakespeare also includes intimations of a tragic outcome—a possibility that remains open, even though neither of Angelo's intended
crimes (the rape of Isabella, and the judicial murder of her
brother) has been committed. The deputy's abuse of power
deserves to be punished with death, as he himself recognizes:

> When I, that censure him, do so offend
> Let mine own judgment pattern out my death . . .

And later:

> let my trial be mine own confession;
> Immediate sentence then, and sequent death,
> Is all the grace I beg.

Angelo's death, or tragic humiliation, must be what Isabella
intends when she denounces the 'pernicious caitiff deputy' and
clamours to the Duke for 'justice, justice, justice, justice!' This
echo of *The Spanish Tragedy*, of Hieronimo's cry to his king—

> Justice, O justice, justice, gentle king! . . .
> Justice, O justice!   (III. xii. 63, 65)

—brings to *Measure for Measure* a similar tragic intensity. There are even moments when we are reminded of a play performed by the King's Men shortly before *Measure for Measure*, another play in which a ruler withdraws from his responsibilities, leaving, in effect, a deputy, whom he has raised but distrusts, a man whose abuses are closely watched by the ruler's spies, who is at last trapped and exposed as theatrically as Angelo. And in the case of *Sejanus* the outcome is tragedy.

It appears to have been Shakespeare's strategy to leave open his play's outcome and genre to the very end. We recognize several possible models, including *The Malcontent* and *Sejanus*, but not one that really answers our question, 'What kind of play is it?' Until the very last minutes the execution of Angelo remains a possibility —all the more so since some spectators would know that in some versions of this widely dispersed story Angelo did lose his head. Then, just as we think we know where we are, Shakespeare springs two more surprises. The play seems to turn into a comedy of forgiveness—until the Duke remembers Lucio, and hacks at him with unforgiving vindictiveness. In addition, we have the Duke's proposal to Isabella, which invariably comes as a surprise, despite all the efforts of producers to prepare us for it—and surely was meant to be one, the 'happy ending' of another kind of comedy grafted on here with the same careful tissue matching as we found in the bed-trick. Is a disturbing proposal not appropriate at the end of a deeply disturbing play?

It is particularly in the second half of the play that its genre is brought into question—and here Shakespeare protects himself, and teases the audience, by making it more emphatically the Duke's play. The Duke, of course, was given the role of inventor of the plot, and stage-manager, from the beginning. In the second half of the play he has to interfere more and more decisively, to resume the active responsibility that he had found so irksome, and becomes more completely the play's dramatist. After the bed-trick—*his* bed-trick, as I have said—there follows a little scene of comic misunderstanding, modelled on *The Spanish Tragedy*, that demonstrates exactly how far he may be trusted as a dramatist. Angelo's messenger arrives with a strict order that Claudio is to be executed punctually, and the Duke, all at sea, declares, preposterously, 'here comes Claudio's pardon', and again

> This is his pardon, purchas'd by such sin
> For which the pardoner himself is in.

He's wrong, and Shakespeare wants us to notice it. The dramatist-duke has lost control of his play—and as he hurriedly attempts to reorganize his plot, he, almost as much as Shakespeare, becomes responsible for its genre, and for our genre expectations. Knowing him as we do, we cannot expect artistic tidiness. He, the Duke of dark corners, is the inventor of almost all the improbable, 'non-realistic' twists of the story that make *Measure for Measure* Shakespeare's most challengingly mingled yarn before *The Winter's Tale*—his disguise as a friar; the bed-trick; the substitution of another head for Claudio's; the concealment of Claudio's escape from Isabella; the unexpected proposal of marriage. All these improbabilities, dreamed up by one man, are therefore rooted in psychological realism, being all expressions of the Duke's imagination, which is as individual as Hamlet's or Prospero's. Duke Vincentio's imagination, like that of a Mannerist painter, delighting in unexpected combinations, makes his bed-trick as necessary a centre-piece to the play's design as El Greco's monastery, which sits so solidly and improbably in a cloud of cotton wool. The Duke, in short, with his love of mystification and ingenious twists and turns, forever revising his options, was the ideal dramatist to put into this mingled yarn—the distinctive feature of which is that it mystifies and keeps changing direction, both at the level of story and of seriousness, insisting on our revising our expectations to the very last.

And what have the Duke and the bed-trick to do with all my other examples—the bear and the statue in *The Winter's Tale*; 'To be or not to be'; the cry 'my husband!' in *Othello* and *Macbeth*; the grave-diggers in *Hamlet*, the porter in *Macbeth*, and Cleopatra's clown? Only this: they demonstrate, together, how variously the 'mingling principle' works. Each example connects with its immediate context and with the present continuous of its play, but no two are the same. Isolated examples illustrate Shakespeare's habitual 'mingling' under the microscope, as it were, but of course each play consists of an infinite number of examples—reaching out in all directions, interpenetrating one another, enriching one another. *Measure for Measure* affords a different kind of example, in so far as Shakespeare also asks us to observe a violently 'mingling' dramatist, in the person of the Duke, and also a more efficient dramatist who tidies up, so to say, behind the Duke and ensures that all of the play's bits and pieces combine plausibly together.

My argument draws to its conclusion, and a scandalous conclusion it is. I have argued that in *Measure for Measure*, one of his most puzzling plays, Shakespeare wants the audience to take an

interest not merely in the story but also in the nature of the play—
an idea that we have all encountered before, in studies of other
plays and of the novel. Having bowed politely to Mannerism and
Structuralism and all things fashionable, the besotted lecturer
drags in Metadrama as well. Is it really necessary? If I am told that
a packed Bankside audience of prentices and prostitutes would be
less alert to such questions than their distinguished descendants,
whose haunt is Piccadilly, I need only remind you that *The Old
Wive's Tale* and *A Midsummer Night's Dream* also required the
audience to ponder the nature of the play, and that the same
challenge is built into the early plays of Marston and Jonson. In
Measure for Measure Shakespeare addressed an audience already
trained to query genre boundaries, and to expect the forms of
things unknown.

> And as imagination bodies forth
> The forms of things unknown, the poet's pen
> Turns them to shapes, and gives to airy nothing
> A local habitation and a name.
> Such tricks hath strong imagination.

The time has come for me to sum up, and I can do it in a single
line from Shakespeare, slightly improved:

> Such *bed-tricks* hath strong imagination.

Quotations from Shakespeare are taken from *The Complete Works* (1951),
ed. Peter Alexander. I have changed some other quotations from Elizabethan
to modern spelling.

THE RELATIONSHIP BETWEEN MONETARY AND FISCAL POLICY

By ALEC CAIRNCROSS

Fellow of the Academy

Read 6 May 1981

THE relationship between fiscal and monetary policy is one of great theoretical complexity, acute controversy, and major practical importance. Within the limits of a short lecture it is not possible to do more than indicate some of the issues involved and offer tentative judgements on them without penetrating the world of theory very deeply and avoiding altogether the lush undergrowth of econometrics that now surrounds it. It may be more helpful, on an occasion of this kind, to start with an account of the way thinking has developed on the matter before turning to some of the more obvious theoretical considerations governing the mix of fiscal and monetary policy and the limitations to which each of them is subject.

The idea of using fiscal and monetary policy to procure greater stability in output and employment—indeed the very idea of having a fiscal *policy* or a monetary *policy*—is a comparatively recent one. Before the First World War it was taken for granted that a prudent government would try to maintain a balanced budget in good times and bad, although some departure from the rules of financial orthodoxy might be inevitable in time of war. Similarly, in the days of the gold standard, monetary arrangements were designed to maintain convertibility of the currency into gold at a fixed price, an aim that paid no regard to the possibility that either inflation or unemployment might result.

This possibility, when economic fluctuations first began to be studied, was associated with the behaviour of investment which was seen as highly unstable and liable, therefore, to change abruptly in relation to the thriftiness of the public and their willingness to make the necessary finance available. The instability of investment might communicate itself to the rest of the economy: there could be no guarantee that the capital market would function in such a way as to preserve an unchanged pressure of demand on available resources. The rate of interest, seen hitherto as fulfilling this function, might not be propelled, quickly and automatically, to the level at which balance was restored between the flow of savings and the flow of capital expenditure and in the process inflationary pressure on the one hand, or a deficiency of demand on the other, might develop and continue. Capital markets, to use the modern jargon, might not 'clear' at an unchanged level of activity.

This failure of interest rates to adjust was explained initially in terms of credit creation. Bank credit might add to the flow of loanable funds when capital expenditure was expanding strongly and this would hold down the market rate of interest below its equilibrium or 'natural' rate. Conversely, a drop in the expected return from new capital investment might not be accompanied by a fall in market rates of interest on the scale necessary to offset the change in expectations.

At that stage in the development of thinking, two practical conclusions were drawn. One was that monetary policy was central to the problem of economic stability: there could be either inflation, if the banks created more credit than was needed to keep investment and savings in balance, or industrial depression, if there was an insufficiency of bank credit, the excess or shortage of bank credit corresponding to a gap between the market rate of interest and the more volatile 'natural' rate at which investment would be held within the limits of savings. The second practical conclusion was that if the source of instability lay primarily in the behaviour of investment, the state might secure greater stability by supplementing private investment in bad times through public works of various kinds. In due course this second remedy was elaborated as a scheme for advancing or retarding public investment so as to counterbalance fluctuations in private investment in the opposite direction.

These two lines of thought—one essentially monetary, the other essentially fiscal—were not necessarily consistent with one another. The rates of interest directly affected by banking policy were short-term rates which might have little or no immediate effect on long-term rates. They might, as Hawtrey argued, be of crucial importance for investment in stocks, and stock-building might be the most volatile element in investment. But if the more enduring difficulty lay in preserving stability in fixed investment, how much reliance could be put on banking policy? On the other hand, could the role of the banks be left entirely aside, as it appeared to be by those who put their faith in public works? Was it right to assume that if public investment took the place of private investment, the rate of interest would be left unaffected?

When Keynes came to consider the matter, he took a more radical line. The fundamental question to be answered was: what determined the level of output? It was not enough to consider fluctuations if these were assumed to be around a trend that represented a sustainable optimum identified with full employment or economic potential. It was necessary also to consider the possibility of persistent underutilization of available resources because of a deficiency of demand. That deficiency would only persist if there was some defect in the system preventing the kind of response in price that would extinguish the deficiency. In Keynes's view there were two such defects, one relating to the rate of interest and one relating to the behaviour of wages. Neither the capital market nor the labour market 'cleared' through price adjustments; and this failure to 'clear' was not just periodic, so that essentially intermittent departures from full employment resulted, but might be persistent and give rise to a chronic under-utilization of resources. If savers became more thrifty there was no guarantee that their access of thrift would be translated via the capital market into additional investment: on the contrary, it was entirely possible that investment might not respond, or respond perversely, and that greater thrift would serve only to impoverish the community by depressing the level of income as the only available means of keeping savings in check. Equally, if unemployed wage-earners were willing to accept lower pay, and money wages were reduced in times of depression, there was no guarantee that this would add appreciably to the number of jobs on offer since the reduction in wages could be expected to lead to a corresponding reduction in prices and this might do little or nothing to generate additional demand. Neither the real rate of interest nor the real rate of wages was determined in the way assumed in classical economic theory; and the money rate of interest and the money rate of wages did not adjust so as to allow an excess of thrift or of labour to be absorbed in the same way as a reduction in price allows an excess of some staple commodity to be absorbed in an auction market.

Keynes's ideas formed the basis of demand management in the post-war years. If a deficiency of demand may be the outcome of leaving things to market forces, policies are necessary in order to regulate demand. It also came to be accepted that there need be no presumption that these policies should bear exclusively on the level of investment rather than on other elements in aggregate demand such as consumer spending. Given the much greater weight that consumer spending has in GNP, it was obviously easier, in trying to effect a given change in total demand, to operate on consumer spending than to make an adjustment of equal magnitude in investment. The speed with which tax changes affect spending compared with the long lead times characteristic of fixed investment pointed in the same direction.

It was also a corollary of Keynesian theory that the horizon of demand management should be short-term. The preservation and prolongation of short-term stability was a natural approach to long-term stability unless there was some fundamental incompatibility between the two. Any conflict between them implied some form of instability at intervals, i.e. recurrent *departures* from a steady rate of growth. To have no concern with the size of these departures was to regard short-term stability as a matter of little importance and to express an unwarranted faith in the self-regulating character of the economic system. Not that short-term demand management and economic stability became the be-all and end-all of economic policy. The long-run balance between the different components of aggregate demand had also to be considered. There was in addition, and always has been, something that we can call supply management which looks to the longer term, may conflict with demand management, and is usually a good deal more important.

The Keynesian approach to demand management adopted in the United Kingdom after the war was couched almost exclusively in terms of budgetary action. This emphasis derived largely from pre-war experience when it appeared that, once interest rates had been brought down to a low level and the banks had ample funds, not much more could be hoped for from monetary policy and any fresh stimulus would have to come via the budget. In such circumstances, with Bank Rate held constant at 2 per cent for nearly twenty years, monetary policy was largely passive. In wartime it had been a precept of policy to refrain from raising interest rates and so adding to the tax burden. Then, and in earlier years, Keynes lent his support to efforts to keep down the long-term rate on the grounds that once investors were encouraged to think higher rates appropriate it would not be easy to induce them to return to a regime of cheap money and yet just such a regime might be required by a glut of capital.

When the war was over, fears of a higher debt burden and a possible slump again combined to induce the government to avoid the use of monetary weapons as a means of restricting demand. For this purpose it turned instead to large budget surpluses supported by rationing and other administrative controls. This preference for fiscal measures may have rested also on antipathy for the rentier and doubts as to the efficacy of high interest rates. There was an appearance of greater certainty about tax changes; Ministers could be offered a rough assessment of the magnitude of the impact of these changes on demand and output which no one would have dared to offer in respect of changes in monetary policy. When the Treasury first engaged in economic forecasting in war-time it did so in terms of an inflationary gap to be closed by budgetary, not monetary, measures. Money was left out of the picture, just as it had been in pre-war analyses of government-engineered expansions in demand and output like Lord Kahn's celebrated article in 1931 on the multiplier. In the increasingly sophisticated forecasting of post-war years this neglect of the monetary aspects of the forecast continued.

None the less, in the successive packages of measures introduced to deal with the long series of crises in the 1950s and 1960s it was usual to include a rise in Bank Rate and/or fresh guidance to the banks intended to curb the creation of credit in particular directions. The imposition of hire-purchase restrictions, which was an equally regular component of the packages and often the most important, could also be regarded as a monetary measure designed to limit consumer credit. It would be going much too far to imply, therefore, that no regard was paid to monetary conditions; on the contrary, some care was taken to make monetary and fiscal policy pull in the same direction. At no time, however, was there any government action aimed specifically at limiting the money supply; indeed, as Harry Johnson pointed out in 1959, there were no adequate figures of the money supply. The government was content to vary short-term interest rates in sympathy with its fiscal stance. At the longer end of the market it took a fairly passive line, seeking to preserve stability in the market for government debt and make what sales of gilt-edged it could at prevailing interest rates.[1]

In those days it was possible to concentrate more or less exclusively on the 'real' economy, i.e. on income flows, without bothering too much about the financial aftermath of a budget surplus or deficit. The main aim of policy was to get the level of

[1] See M. J. Artis, 'Monetary Policy', in *British Economic Policy 1960–74* (CUP for National Institute of Economic and Social Research, Cambridge, 1978), esp., pp. 229–33.

demand right, avoiding too much pressure or too little, and this aim could be fulfilled in different ways, depending on the use that was made of alternative instruments of policy. If there was pressure on the balance of payments, monetary weapons would be more likely to be brought into use. If importance was attached to a higher level of investment, monetary policy might be eased and fiscal policy tightened so as to maintain a constant pressure of demand. The choice of weapons was also affected by the urgency of the situation and the need for quick results. The monetary authorities were in a position to influence the situation more or less continuously while fiscal action was inevitably intermittent. But in a crisis both monetary and fiscal weapons were almost certain to be brought into use and to operate in the same direction in mutual support.[1]

The subordination of monetary to fiscal policy came under challenge in the 1960s from a school of thought which inverted the relationship between the two, giving clear precedence to monetary policy. The need to control inflation was put in the forefront and demand management dismissed as superfluous if not actually damaging. Control of inflation could be secured by limiting the money supply and in no other way. Monetary policy, if aimed at the level of output rather than the level of prices, would be misapplied and in the long run ineffective. Fiscal policy should be such as to comply with the need to keep the money supply under firm control.

These are propositions that have much in common with pre-Keynesian thinking. The Treasury in the 1920s would have had no difficulty in accepting all of them. In those days unemployment was explained in terms that left out any reference to the level of effective demand and in any event effective demand was thought to be beyond the power of government to influence. Government borrowing to finance public investment was officially regarded as displacing or 'crowding out' an equal amount of private investment. The quantity theory of money went without question, usually in a form that linked prices and the money supply with only a passing reference to output. It was precisely these ideas that Keynes sought to overturn: not only sought to overturn but *did* overturn.

The resurrection of these propositions does not mean that they are generally accepted. On the contrary, most economists would

---

[1] These matters are discussed in detail in 'Demand Management: Monetary and Fiscal Policy' which forms chapter 6 of my *Essays in Economic Management* (Allen & Unwin, 1971).

dismiss them on much the same grounds as Keynes did: that the capital market and the labour market do not clear in the manner of an auction market. They would suspect that, whatever may be true in academic circles, the influence on governments of such ideas rests less on their intellectual merits than on the way they chime with the temper of the times: the disenchantment with government intervention, the recognition that intervention may not achieve its professed purpose, and the greater disposition to rely on market forces.

We have heard successive Prime Ministers denounce the idea that increased public expenditure can soften the impact on employment of a trade depression. We are told almost every day that an increase in the money supply would serve only to revive inflation and would damage the long-term prospects for increased employment. We have seen an abandonment of direct intervention in the foreign exchange market in order to hold or vary the exchange rate and, what is more surprising, an abandonment of the idea that changes in real exchange rates can be accomplished by intervention. This is a retreat from demand management on the grand scale.

Of course, it is a retreat in principle only and what governments do in practice is very different. It has not resulted in balanced budgets or a steady growth in the money supply or a stable and predictable rate of exchange. The attempt to supercede discretionary government action on the level of effective demand by stated rules and targets governing the operations of the public authorities may have been intended to provide the private sector with a firm basis on which to plan ahead; but if so it has not succeeded.

The very fact that governments have adopted monetary targets and pursued fiscal policies that pay no regard to the current state of employment makes it evident that something has gone wrong with demand management. What is it that has gone wrong and how does it affect the choice of policy, if there is one, between fiscal and monetary instruments?

What has gone wrong is inflation and expectations of inflation, short-circuiting expansionary measures aimed at increasing employment and output on the one hand and out-lasting contractionary measures aimed at reducing inflation on the other. The system of ideas underlying demand management originated in a world of underemployed economies in which the danger of inflation could be almost entirely ignored and higher prices would have been positively welcomed. It was a world in which a rapid increase in the money supply excited no alarm: as, for example, in the four months preceding the conversion of 5 per cent War Loan in 1932 when clearing bank deposits expanded by over 6 per cent (i.e. at over 18 per cent per annum) while money GNP remained steady or actually fell. With over two million workers unemployed an expansion in demand was unlikely to raise wages very much and such rise as did occur was quite consistent with a downward trend in wage costs. Import prices, too, were remarkably stable in spite of the depreciation of the pound; and the terms of trade, which have so often played a central part in the inflationary process, had swung in Britain's favour to an unparalleled extent—over 25 per cent—between 1929 and 1933.

Yet even in pre-war years it was possible to foresee some of the limitations of demand management. First, there was the difficulty that neither fiscal nor monetary policy was very effective in its impact on the level of costs. Money wages—the largest element in costs—were not sensitive to small changes in demand pressure, as later experience showed, except upwards and in the vicinity of full employment. Other elements in cost were at the mercy of changes in world markets and in the rate of exchange. It followed that demand management could not by itself protect the economy from the danger of inflation.

A second limitation that became apparent in the years before the war was that the available instruments of policy are insufficiently selective. It is not enough to aim at a general and widespread increase in the pressure of demand when the increased pressure is felt unevenly and resources are not fluid. There may be bottlenecks within the economy (for example, in the building industry) or at the level of the world economy (for example, in the markets in primary commodities). Such bottlenecks can generate price increases at strategic points in the economy and if the increases spread to adjoining markets they can rapidly breed a general inflation. Where the bottleneck is of such importance as energy supplies it is capable of thwarting the response in output to an expansion in demand and such an expansion may then produce nothing but inflation.

A rather similar result may follow an over-rapid expansion of demand which gives insufficient time for supply to respond. Pre-war literature dwelt on the case of a boom in private fixed investment that enlarged the flow of expenditure and forced up the price of consumer goods until the new equipment came into use or the financial strain broke the boom. But the danger of inflation from setting out on too steep a path of expansion is not confined to cases of this kind nor is it necessarily confined to situations in which there is little slack in the economy.

These limitations all have to do with maladjustments in the 'real' economy. They all relate to the danger of inflation or to the difficulty of combating inflation without a serious loss of output and employment. When a government is pursuing an expansionary policy the crux of the matter is how much of the expansion in nominal demand will be translated into additional output and how much will spend itself in raising the price level. The bottlenecks envisaged in the second and third limitations increase the upward slope of the supply curve and dissipate more of the increase in demand in higher prices. But the first limitation—the insensitivity of costs to changes in demand—brings into question the apparatus of thought enshrined in an aggregate supply curve. If wage-earners react to a rise in the price level by claiming and obtaining a compensatory increase in money wages, costs and prices can rise progressively without any perceptible change in the level of output. If in course of time *expectations* of a rise in the price level begin to govern wage claims and wage settlements, again independently of the level of output, the notion of inflation as a movement along a rising supply curve of output becomes even more inappropriate.

In the first two decades or so after the war the interrelationship between prices, costs, and expectations did not greatly limit the effectiveness of demand management, although the pressure of demand was a good deal higher than it afterwards became. The period was one of uninterrupted and, by previous standards, very rapid inflation. But there never seemed much likelihood, except perhaps in 1950-1, that inflation would get out of hand and gather speed unpredictably at a rate that no one could afford to ignore. Once expectations became adjusted to a fairly steady rate of inflation, fiscal policy appeared to work in much the same way as it might be expected to in an underemployed, non-inflationary economy of the pre-war type. What changed matters in the 1970s was a series of jolts to the international economy that shook customary expectations and sent them into a new orbit. The first such jolt was the change in the atmosphere of the labour market after the 'events' of May 1968 in Paris. A second jolt, in 1972-3, was partly financial, involving a flight from money into commodities, and partly real, marking the abrupt end of a long period in which the terms of trade moved against staple commodities on world markets. The quadrupling of oil prices at the end of 1973 carried the movement in the terms of trade further and at the same time threw the international economic and financial system out of balance. A further jolt was given to the system by the renewed rise in oil prices in 1979–80. All of these operated to produce rates of inflation in the United Kingdom and other industrial countries unheard of in peacetime. They also introduced major uncertainties as to the adjustments that would be made both in the immediate future and eventually. These uncertainties, and the expectations to which they gave birth, transformed the task of economic management.

On the one hand, wage-earners, already reacting against the greater weight of taxation they were being asked to bear, found themselves faced with a much more rapid increase in prices, reflecting in large measure the higher cost of imports. Their expectations of real income were not adjusted to the fall by 25 per cent in the terms of trade; and their expectations of money income were adjusted sharply upwards by the observed rise in consumer prices and the uncertainty as to how they would move in future. At the same time, lenders and investors, alarmed by the way inflation was accelerating, were increasingly sensitive to any acts of government savouring of more rapid inflation. They were liable therefore to react strongly to government measures involving an increase in the supply of money or the PSBR and to the extent these reactions raised interest rates or pushed down the exchange rate they frustrated the expansionary intentions of the measures.

Opinion and expectations tended to be based on a perceived threat running from the PSBR to the money supply and from there to prices and the rate of inflation; and these expectations, like the expectations of wage-earners, tended to be self-fulfilling. The fear of inflation discourages the holding of money and titles to money (i.e. debt) and encourages a switch into real assets, titles to real assets (equities) and foreign currencies. Such switches raise the price of assets and make imports dearer, laying the basis for a broader inflationary movement. At the same time, wage negotiators stick out for bigger increases in money wages that produce the very acceleration in prices against which they are seeking to guard.

The shocks to the system over the past decade, therefore, not only precipitated much higher rates of inflation but left it with a hangover that made treatment more difficult. The central issue no longer related to the pressure of demand but to how expectations could be changed. It was not at all clear that either fiscal or monetary policy was well adapted for such purposes. There was an obvious danger that if used to expand output they would be ineffective and if used to damp down inflation would involve a disproportionate loss in output.

Once the main object of policy is to change expectations—or, to use more old-fashioned language, to restore confidence—the issue ceases to be a technical one for economists to decide. It necessarily turns on what will sufficiently impress those whose expectations must be changed before the system can function again in a normal way. It may be necessary to pander to unfounded beliefs about the causes of inflation, to play for time so as to allow current expectations to die away, or to indulge in a show of strength that arouses expectations of a different kind.

Against this historical background it would be surprising if the same mix of monetary and fiscal policy was appropriate in all situations. Which instruments are preferred must depend on what objectives of policy have priority, whether circumstances favour the use of one set of instruments rather than the other, and how it is thought the economy works. If, for example, control of inflation takes priority over getting rid of unemployment, monetary weapons have the advantage that they have an immediate and direct effect on prices just as fiscal weapons have an immediate and direct effect on employment. But it is possible to imagine circumstances in which, with unchanged priorities, monetary policy might be more effective in coping with unemployment and fiscal policy—though this is less likely—in coping with inflation. If, for example, private investment is highly sensitive to small changes in interest rates, and interest rates in turn are highly sensitive to small changes in the money supply, it may be possible, as in 1932, to exert more leverage on employment by a policy of cheap money than would be exerted by higher deficit spending. Indeed, if financial markets interpret a move to balance the budget as pointing to lower interest rates and if lower rates would not provoke a large outflow of capital, a combination of cheap money and *lower* deficit spending might in some circumstances offer the best hope of expanding employment. *Per contra* it is arguable that in the early post-war years, with large excess liquidity that would have survived much higher interest rates, it was preferable to rely on large budget surpluses to keep inflation at bay.

Leaving aside differences in policy objectives and economic circumstances, there remains a sharp difference of view over the way in which fiscal and monetary policies should be combined. On the one view, control of the money supply is the necessary and sufficient instrument for tackling inflation and without such control not much can be done to get rid of unemployment. Without quite arguing that 'money is all that matters for changes in *nominal* income and for *short-run* changes in real income', the monetarist school of thought holds that fiscal policy does not matter, or if it does, is monetary policy in disguise.[1] Neo-Keynesians, on the other hand, have been inclined to attribute prime importance to fiscal policy as a means of regulating employment and to look to some other instrument such as incomes policy for dealing with inflation. Even a neo-Keynesian would be obliged to concede, however, that if financial markets are strongly monetarist in their assessment of economic policy and if wage-earners will brook no reduction in real wages in any circumstances, while at the same time inflationary expectations are firmly shared by both groups, there may be no way in which a government can expand the economy by fiscal (or perhaps any other) policy. A mixture of wrongheaded beliefs and confident expectations, dictating the conduct of capital and labour, would be quite sufficient to put an end to the present economic system.

For our purposes it is sufficient to recognize that policy has to deal both with unemployment *and* inflation and that neither fiscal nor monetary policy can be relied upon by itself to get rid of both of them. Monetarists argue that monetary policy could always get rid of inflation but this would be true only if no limit were set to the loss in output or the length of time required. They do not propose any new instrument of policy and see a curtailment of the supply of money both as more feasible and more effective than their critics.

The monetarists are right to emphasize that an expansion in the money supply affects prices in a way that fiscal policy does not. In their view of the inflationary process the line of causation runs from money to prices to costs. An increase in the money supply causes a shift in portfolios towards other assets and hence a rise in their price (including the price of houses, foreign exchange, and— in consequence—imported goods of all kinds). It is unlikely that in those circumstances wages will for long show no response and this will reinforce the rise in import costs. But the line of causation may equally well run in the opposite direction. An increase in wages may push up costs and this in turn will push up prices and raise the demand for money. We have to reckon with both possibilities and which is the more typical and the more important is largely an empirical matter.

[1] A. S. Blinder and R. M. Solow, 'Analytical Foundations of Fiscal Policy', in *The Economics of Public Finance* (Brookings Institution, 1974), pp. 9, 59.

Where the monetarists are on weaker ground is in assuming that the money supply can be regarded as exogenous and within the control of the authorities. Given that the authorities have to operate through interest rates and not directly on the money supply, they can only control the supply in so far as they correctly gauge the demand, which responds to every wind that blows throughout the economy and from other economies as well. The more they concentrate their efforts on some target for the money supply in face of the waywardness of demand, the more volatile become the terms and conditions of credit, although the stability of these terms and conditions has an importance of its own. If, as they are bound to do, they allow some weight to the need for an element of stability in interest rates, the money supply will to that extent reflect changes in demand and not simply the intentions of the authorities. Instead of being an instrument of control, it will be a symptom of the state of the economy, a bell-wether of inflationary pressures.

By making the growth in the money supply the touchstone of policy, and fiscal policy entirely subordinate to monetary policy and little more than an aspect of it, monetarism comes near to collapsing all aspects of macro-economic policy into one and disregarding the many facets of any single line of policy—monetary, fiscal, or other. To attach overriding importance to the money supply, when the objectives of economic policy are complex and often conflicting, is to make the same mistake as to stick through thick and thin to a fixed rate of exchange and for much the same reason: that the movement of costs, especially wage costs, may not accommodate itself to some pre-arranged target. Inflexible commitments to such targets may prove very expensive: the same forces that make it difficult to go back to the gold standard or to balance the budget make it unwise in an uncertain world to put on the strait-jacket of unconditional monetary targets.

It is necessary to insist that monetary policy cannot be reduced to the single dimension of the money supply any more than the thrust of fiscal policy can be narrowed to the purely financial consequences of a budget surplus or deficit. It is possible to read an extensive history of monetary policy such as Richard Sayers's three volumes on the Bank of England[1] without being troubled by the thought that nobody knew what was happening to the money supply. But it is impossible to do so without being impressed by the wide range of central banking operations that have little or

[1] R. S. Sayers, *The Bank of England 1891–1944* (CUP 1976).

nothing to do with the money supply. Both monetary and fiscal policy cover a wide spectrum of measures with very different impacts on the economy; and it would be a travesty to boil them down to a single measure of that impact, even when only the macro-economic aspect is under discussion. If one *were* obliged to think in terms of a single dimension, it would be no more reasonable to treat changes in the money supply as a measure of the stance of monetary policy than it is to treat changes in the budget surplus or deficit as a measure of the stance of fiscal policy. The changes occurring in the money supply are the end-product of a highly complex process in which the developments set on foot by the monetary authorities spread throughout the economy. These developments include the repercussions on the rate of exchange and the balance of payments; on budgetary expenditure (e.g. higher interest payments) and tax revenue; on the lending policies of financial institutions; and on the demand for money throughout the economy. The intentions of the authorities, as expressed in the measures adopted, may differ widely from the final outcome and not necessarily in the same direction. There are good grounds for interpreting monetary policy in terms of what the authorities actually do rather than in terms of some target at which they profess to be aiming.

Just as it is not possible to regard fiscal policy as a mere adjunct of monetary policy or vice versa, so it is not possible to treat monetary and fiscal policy as if they were completely independent of one another. The different instruments of policy have to be used in combination with one another and the thrust of the various elements in the policy-mix cannot be measured separately. All economic policy instruments interact. What happens when any one instrument is used depends on the setting of the other instruments of policy and the conditions prevailing at the time. The stimulus to output that follows an increase in government spending will depend on the kind of incomes policy adopted and the success attending it. The response to a change in the exchange rate will be affected by the fiscal measures with which it is accompanied. And so on.

The 'symbiosis', as it has been called, of monetary and fiscal policy is particularly close.[1] An increase in the budget deficit requires additional borrowing and this in turn affects interest rates, the money supply, and the exchange rate. A change in monetary policy taking the form, say, of higher interest rates

[1] Ralph C. Bryant, *Money and Monetary Policy in Interdependent Nations* (Brookings Institution, 1981), p. 231.

involves a heavier burden on the Exchequer and has other effects on the fiscal balance through changes in public investment and, so far as the level of activity is reduced, through a fall in tax revenue.

These interactions are heightened in a world in which financial markets interpret a larger borrowing requirement or an increase in the money supply as inflationary and regard the second as an almost automatic outcome of the first. Under those conditions the announcement of an expansionary fiscal policy, even before any additional borrowing took place, would be sufficient to produce a rise in interest rates in anticipation, whether the government had it in mind to expand the money supply or not. Such a rise might also accompany an expansion in the money supply even if the government hoped by doing so to *lower* interest rates. Where markets are highly sensitive to the danger of inflation *any* move on the part of the government to expand demand could encounter strong, perverse market reactions. These would be the more important the more powerfully demand is influenced by changes in interest rates and credit conditions as compared with direct changes in income flows.

Although it can be difficult to disentangle monetary and fiscal policy there are clearly some objects of policy to which one set of instruments is more appropriate than the other. It has been usual, for example, to regard fiscal policy as governed mainly by domestic, and monetary policy by international, factors. This does not mean that foreign holders of sterling are oblivious to the state of the British budget or that governments feel debarred from announcing monetary targets related to purely domestic objectives. It is possible also for the budget to be used to procure balance-of-payments effects through taxes on foreign-held balances or, in opposite circumstances, on the return on British investments abroad: and for monetary restrictions to do duty for higher taxes when electoral considerations tell against additional burdens on the taxpayer. But the limits within which monetary policy can reconcile diverging national and international pressures are narrow. Just as it is difficult to control simultaneously the price *and* the quantity of money—interest rates *and* the money supply—so it is difficult to control simultaneously the quantity of money in Britain and the terms on which it can be exchanged into foreign money, i.e. the rate of exchange. If the money supply is over-expanded, some of the excess will overflow on to the foreign exchanges, pushing down the value of sterling and in this and other ways levering up domestic prices. A fall in interest rates, given high international capital mobility, will have similar—

perhaps even more powerful—effects. Conversely, if the government fixes a monetary target involving high interest rates it is in no position to resist a rise in the exchange rate and an inflow of funds that helps to relieve the contrived shortage of money. In the absence of capital controls—and usually also in spite of them—there are limits to the power of any one country to loosen or tighten credit conditions in comparison with other countries. There is, however, enough friction in the system to afford some leeway and countries enjoy more independence in their monetary policies than much current theory allows.

International factors also limit the power of individual countries to make effective use of fiscal policy in order to stabilize demand. Fluctuations in the level of activity in the international economy are almost inevitably reflected in the domestic markets of the leading participants. If they seek to mitigate or offset the fluctuations within their own economy they cannot do so by fiscal action alone without taking liberties with their balance of payments. They can only escape their 'share' of an international depression if they are able to divert resources from international to domestic uses and, even if they have large reserves or can borrow abroad, the necessary switch may not be easy to bring about.

The limits to monetary expansion would appear to be fairly narrow in normal circumstances. The monetarists are right to draw attention to the possibility that an over-issue of money may drive up prices without first generating additional income. Whether the line of causation is through a rise in the price of domestic assets or a fall in the rate of exchange, monetary expansion carries with it a danger of inflation insufficiently recognized in the past and differentiating it from fiscal expansion. It is not possible to dismiss this danger with the argument that an over-issue cannot occur since the demand for money must at all times equal the supply and that if people find themselves with too much money they will get rid of it. No doubt they will: but it is the process of getting rid of it that makes prices rise.

On the other hand, it is equally wrong to think that any increase in the money supply faster than the increase in GNP is bound to prove inflationary. It may be true that there is quite a high degree of stability in the relationship between money balances and GNP and that it would require exceptional tightness or exceptional looseness for the ratio to vary by more than a few percentage points within the year. But that does not entitle us to assume that more money must mean higher prices rather than higher output or that the demand for money balances never changes at all. All we can say is that if the ratio does show a perceptible change this should serve as an alarm bell for those who manage the economy.

In the case of fiscal policy there are limits of a different kind. A large and persistent borrowing requirement adds to the total weight of debt. What effect this will have on the economy depends on a number of factors. First, it depends upon the extent to which it does no more than take the place of private debt creation and leaves the level of economic activity unchanged. In such circumstances there is no obvious reason why rates of interest should be much affected. Second, it depends on the income yielded by the assets created out of government borrowing and whether this is sufficient to cover the debt service or leaves a residue that will swell progressively and absorb an increasing proportion of government revenue. Third, it depends on the rate of inflation. This will undoubtedly cause interest rates to rise and so add to the budgetary interest charge but at the same time it will eat away some of the real burden of debt. A fourth factor to be considered is the addition made to the net wealth of the private sector and the repercussions of this addition on the rate of saving.

It will be apparent that the last two factors interact. There will be no addition to the net wealth of the private sector if the value of the outstanding debt in private hands is being diminished by inflation faster than new debt is being created and marketed to the public. Such a situation is by no means hypothetical. In spite of the large nominal additions to the national debt occasioned by the recurrent government deficits and heavy borrowing of recent years the real value of market holdings of government debt in the United Kingdom has been falling year after year. To a large extent the deficits themselves are spurious since they are inflated by the higher interest rates that have to be offered on new issues of debt because of the very inflation that depreciates outstanding debt.

Why then should governments hesitate to borrow more in a major recession? Not, presumably, because they hold monetarist views. There is nothing inconsistent with orthodox monetarist ideas in increasing the PSBR if, as has been true in this country for the past decade, such borrowing adds little or nothing to the money supply. The hesitations of government derive in part from fear of aggravating inflation and in part from anxiety not to raise interest rates. There are circumstances in which such scruples are well grounded. If, for example, the government misjudges the amount of slack in the economy—as it would appear to have done in 1972-3—the higher borrowing requirement will be superimposed on capital requirements that already tax the available finance and will inflate demand when capacity limits have already been reached. But where there is ample slack, the effects on inflation should be rather different. As the economy expands from a low level of activity to a somewhat higher one, whatever the cause, there may well be additional pressure on prices and interest rates. But if wages rise no faster than they would otherwise, the extra pressure is likely to be small and quite different from the kind of rise occasioned by *continuing* pressure on the price level when demand becomes excessive in relation to capacity.

The effect on interest rates might be more perceptible. In the absence of an expansion in the money supply there would be a greater strain on available funds and some rise in rates might also be necessary sooner or later because of additional pressure on the exchange rate. In addition, if government spending acts as a substitute for private spending, the same level of activity may be regained only at a somewhat higher level of interest rates because the method of finance of the two kinds of spending is not the same. Private investment, especially in manufacturing, is largely financed out of profits and rarely involves extensive long-term borrowing. In a depression the profits disappear while the government's deficit spending comes from money raised in the gilt-edged market or, to a limited extent, on short term. Unless the authorities are willing to expand the money supply, therefore, interest rates are likely to be pushed up and some further 'crowding out' of private investment will then result. Normally, however, this will be no more than a partial offset to the initial government stimulus.

Thus the emphasis over the past fifty years has swung from monetary policy to fiscal policy and back again to monetary policy. The swing has gone with changes in the parameters of the economy, in the ideas of economists about how it works, in the aims of policy-makers and in the attitudes and expectations to which the system responds. The old consensus has disappeared and no new consensus has yet been achieved. In this state of uncertainty it would be a mistake for the authorities to proceed with complete confidence in any one economic model or to give priority to any one instrument of policy. Different policies interact and their separate outcomes are almost impossible to measure. What is always required is a set of policies to suit the circumstances.

From this point of view we have to recognize that we lack an instrument for reducing inflation without loss of output and that if inflation is not reduced full employment is compromised. Both monetary and fiscal policy have severe limitations in an inflationary world but they come into their own again in a world of underemployment as it becomes purged of inflation. In such a world the prime requirement is stability in money wages; only if that condition is fulfilled is it possible to exert the necessary leverage on employment through monetary and fiscal policy.

There has to be somewhere in the system an element of constancy to set limits to its instability. That constancy was once sought in the gold standard, then a fixed exchange rate and now monetary targets. The first two have been abandoned and the third is not what is really required. What is needed in order to impart the necessary inertia is a settled arrangement designed to stabilize money wages. Without such stability the system itself will be unstable and the promise of full employment illusory. But if money wages are kept reasonably stable, fiscal and monetary policy can again combine to restore high levels of output and employment without the risk of insupportable inflation.

ITALY, MOUNT ATHOS, AND MUSCOVY: THE THREE WORLDS OF MAXIMOS THE GREEK (c.1470–1556)

By DIMITRI OBOLENSKY

Fellow of the Academy

Read 1 June 1981

IN the spring of 1553 the Tsar Ivan IV (later known as The Terrible) left his capital, Moscow, on a pilgrimage. The journey, to a monastery in the far north, was intended as an act of thanksgiving for his recovery from a recent, and nearly fatal, illness. The royal party, including the Tsaritsa and Ivan's newly born child, stopped on the way in St. Sergius's Monastery of the Holy Trinity, Russia's most hallowed monastic house. Within its walls lived a man of almost legendary fame. A Greek monk from Mount Athos, over eighty years of age, he had spent the past thirty-five years in Russia, more than half of them in monastic gaols. To educated Russians he was known as a scholar of great learning, a prolific writer in their language, and a man of great constancy and courage. His name was Maximos—Maxim to the Russians. The aged monk and the young sovereign met and talked. Maxim urged the Tsar to abandon his pilgrimage and return to Moscow. Far better, he argued, to comfort the families of the Russian soldiers killed in the recent war against the Tatars than to persist on what was clearly a long and dangerous journey; and he warned Ivan that, if he did so persist, his infant son would die. The Tsar declined to alter his plans; and the child died on the way.

The story of this brief encounter between arguably the two most remarkable men in sixteenth-century Russia was told, some twenty years later, by a fervent admirer of Maxim, Prince Andrey Kurbsky.[1] This distinguished general, a former favourite of Ivan, disgusted at the Tsar's growing absolutism, had deserted to Lithuania in 1564. He surely knew much about his teacher's life: including the fact that as a young man Maxim had lived in Italy. Exactly how much of his biography Maxim revealed to Kurbsky

---

[1] *Prince A. M. Kurbsky's History of Ivan IV*, ed. with translation and notes by J. L. I. Fennell (Cambridge, 1965), pp. 76–81, 90–1.

we do not know: there were several episodes in it which, as we shall
see, he would have been wise to conceal.

Some of these episodes have come to light only recently. In 1942
the Russian scholar Élie Denissoff published in Louvain a book
entitled *Maxime le Grec et l'Occident*.[1] In it he proved conclusively
that Maxim was none other than Michael Trivolis, a Greek
expatriate who frequented the humanist schools of Italy in the late
fifteenth century. It is not often that the biography of a major
historical figure is so unexpectedly enlarged by a scholarly discovery; and Denissoff could justifiably claim that, thanks to his
book, the life of Maximos the Greek assumed the shape of a
diptych, of which Mount Athos is the hinge, and Italy and
Muscovite Russia are the two leaves.

There is no need to rehearse here Denissoff's arguments. They
are based on compelling historical, literary, and graphological
evidence, and are generally accepted today. Thus, in any account
of the life and work of Maximos the Greek, we must start with
Michael Trivolis.

The Trivolai were a Byzantine family of moderate distinction. They spawned a Patriarch of Constantinople in the mid-
fourteenth century[2] and, a little later, a correspondent of the
Emperor Manuel II.[3] One branch settled in Mistra in the Pelo-
ponnese. Michael was born in Arta, the capital of the Greek
province of Epirus, about 1470. Some twenty years earlier the city
had fallen to the Turks, and before long the family decided to
emigrate. The nearest refuge was the island of Corfu, then under
Venetian sovereignty. Greek families from the mainland had been
gathering there for some time, drawn not only by the prospect of
security, but also by the presence on the island of a group of
distinguished Greek scholars.

Michael was probably about ten years old when his family
moved from Arta to Corfu. When he was about twenty he stood
for election to the island's Governing Council. The results were
not calculated to guide him towards a public career: 20 votes were
cast for him, 73 against.[4] It was probably in 1492 that he moved to
Florence, then the leading centre of Greek studies in Europe. In

[1] E. Denissoff, *Maxime le Grec et l'Occident. Contribution à l'histoire de la pensée
religieuse et philosophique de Michel Trivolis* (Paris–Louvain, 1942).

[2] Kallistos I. See Denissoff, op. cit., p. 119, n. 5.

[3] Denissoff, op. cit., p. 119; *The Letters of Manuel II Palaeologus*, ed. G. T.
Dennis (Washington DC, 1977), pp. 24–7; J. W. Barker, *Manuel II Palaeologus
(1391–1425): A Study in Late Byzantine Statesmanship* (New Brunswick, 1969),
p. 36, n. 93.

[4] Denissoff, op. cit., pp. 84–6, 143–5, and pls. I and II.

Florence, where he remained for three years, his vocation as a scholar was shaped by the teaching of the Greek philologist John Lascaris and by the influence of the great Platonist Marsilio Ficino. Many years later, writing in Moscow, Maximos remembered Florence as the fairest of all the Italian cities he had known.[1] The influence of Plato and of the Florentine 'Platonic Academy' were to remain with him, for better or for worse, all his life.

Another, very different influence was felt by Michael during his years in Florence: that of the Dominican friar Savonarola. He probably never met him personally; but he certainly heard him preach. The full impact of this influence was to come later, after Savonarola's execution in 1498. Later still, in Moscow, he wrote for the Russians a detailed account of Savonarola's life, describing his famous Lenten sermons, his conflict with the Pope, and his grisly execution in Florence. He extolled him as a man 'filled with every kind of wisdom', and added, perhaps with a touch of tactful self-censorship, that, had Savonarola not belonged to the Latin faith, he would surely have been numbered among the Church's holy confessors.[2] Attempts have been made—not wholly convincing, in my view—to trace in Maxim's Russian writings the influence of several works of Savonarola, in particular of his *canzone De ruina ecclesiae*, and his meditation on the Psalm *Miserere mei Deus*, written in a Florentine prison, while he was awaiting his last trial and execution.[3] More easily identifiable, and more important, is the influence of the Italian friar on Maxim's later concern with moral problems, on his love of poverty, and perhaps too on his outspokenness and courage in adversity.

In one of his later writings Maxim described in some detail the University of Paris. He dwelt on its curriculum of studies, the high quality of the teaching, given free of charge thanks to a royal endowment, and its role as an international institution: its students, he wrote, who come from all over western and northern Europe, return home, to become ornaments and useful members of their societies.[4] It has sometimes been assumed that Michael

---

[1] *Sochineniya prepodobnogo Maksima Greka*, iii (Kazan, 1862), 194; Denissoff, op. cit., pp. 156–7, 423.

[2] *Sochineniya*, iii. 194–202; Denissoff, op. cit., pp. 423–8; V. S. Ikonnikov, *Maksim Grek i ego vremya*, 2nd edn. (Kiev, 1915), pp. 118–23; A. I. Ivanov, *Literaturnoe nasledie Maksima Greka* (Leningrad, 1969), pp. 156–7.

[3] K. Viskovatyy, 'K voprosu o literaturnom vliyanii Savonaroly na Maksima Greka', *Slavia*, xvii (1939–40), 128–33; A. I. Ivanov, 'Maksim Grek i Savonarola', *Trudy Otdela Drevnerusskoy Literatury*, xxiii (1968), 217–26.

[4] *Sochineniya*, iii. 179–80; Denissoff, op. cit., pp. 430–1.

visited Paris. This is unlikely; though he did announce to the Russians—quite possibly for the first time—the discovery of America, more precisely of a large land called Cuba.[1]

The next stage in Michael's life in Italy, after brief visits to Bologna, Padua, and Milan, took him in 1496 to Venice where he remained for the next two years. There he became associated with Aldus Manutius, who was then producing his celebrated editions of the Greek classics. He later told a Russian correspondent that he often visited Aldus for reasons which had to do with books.[2] It may be that Michael was actually employed in the Aldine press, and that he worked on the edition of Aristotle which Aldus was then preparing in Venice; but we cannot be certain of this. His later work as a translator from Greek into Slavonic suggests that he had been trained to edit texts; an expertise which, we shall see, was not without its dangers in Muscovite Russia.

By this time Michael must have acquired some reputation as a scholar. In a letter dated 1498 he mentions several offers of gainful employment he has recently received.[3] In the same year we find him in the service of another Italian, the distinguished Hellenist Gianfrancesco Pico della Mirandola, nephew of the celebrated Platonist Giovanni Pico. The four years which he spent at Mirandola were an important landmark in his life. Gianfrancesco Pico was not only a classical scholar, a true ἑλληνομανής, as Michael wrote to a friend in March 1500.[4] He was also a convinced Christian, a student of patristic writings, and a great admirer of Savonarola. The news of Savonarola's execution was received at Mirandola while Michael was there.

It is hardly possible to gain a clear impression of the state of Michael's mind around the year 1500. Three distinct influences undoubtedly worked on him at the time, and they must have been hard to reconcile: Platonic philosophy and classical scholarship; the Christian patristic tradition, no doubt familiar from his early youth, but now apprehended more deeply after his stay at Mirandola; and the impact of the life and teaching of Savonarola. Of the three the last, for the moment, proved the strongest. A note in an unpublished chronicle of the monastery of San Marco in Florence states that in 1502 Michael ('Frater Michael Emmanuelis de civitate Arta') was professed as a monk of that

---

[1] *Sochineniya*, iii. 44; Denissoff, op. cit., p. 423. Cf. I. Ševčenko, 'Byzantium and the Eastern Slavs after 1453', *Harvard Ukrainian Studies*, ii (1978), 13.

[2] Denissoff, op. cit., pp. 190–7, 429–30; Ikonnikov, op. cit., pp. 134–5; Ivanov, op. cit., pp. 207–9.

[3] Denissoff, op. cit., pp. 398–401.   [4] Ibid., p. 402.

monastery.[1] It is worth noting that this was the very house of which Savonarola had been the prior. Many years later Michael described to the Russians in considerable detail the life and organization of the Dominican order, while carefully concealing the fact that he had belonged to it himself.[2] His secret was to remain undiscovered for more than four centuries.

Michael Trivolis's career as a Dominican was brief. On 21 April 1504 he wrote from Florence to an Italian friend, to announce that he had abandoned the monastic life. In evident distress, he compared himself to a ship tossed by the waves in the midst of the sea, and begged for help in his present affliction (τῆς παρούσης θλίψεως).[3] Denissoff, who published this letter, concluded, no doubt rightly, that Michael was deliberately vague as to the reasons for the apparent collapse of his religious vocation.[4]

In 1505 or 1506, after yet another change whose causes remain mysterious, we find Michael, now as the monk Maximos, in the Monastery of Vatopedi on Mount Athos, back in the Church of his fathers. It is perhaps unwise to imagine a formal conversion. The hostility between Greeks and Latins had certainly hardened during the past centuries, and the ill-starred Council of Florence in 1439 had, on the whole, not helped matters. Yet in a number of Greek communities, not least in Venice and Corfu, a more tolerant attitude towards the Latin Church prevailed, and a surprising degree of liturgical concelebration and inter-communion was permitted; the rift in the body of Christendom was not yet complete. The same, in the first half of the sixteenth century, seems to have been true of one of the leading Athonite houses, the Great Lavra; though not of Maximos's own monastery of Vatopedi, where a harsher attitude towards the Latins prevailed.[5] In his Russian writings Maximos severely criticized several Latin beliefs and practices, which he roundly denounced as heretical. Foremost among them was the doctrine of the *Filioque*, the major bone of theological contention between the Greek and the Roman Churches since the ninth century. The other major issue, the claims of the Papacy to exercise direct and universal jurisdiction throughout the Christian Church, is touched upon more lightly by Maximos. Most of his strictures are directed at what he considered to be the Popes' arrogant desire to extend their own power.

---

[1] Ibid., pp. 95, 458; Ivanov, op. cit., p. 163.
[2] *Sochineniya*, iii. 182–94; Denissoff, op. cit., pp. 249–52.
[3] Denissoff, op. cit., pp. 404–6.
[4] Ibid., pp. 95–6, 261–2.
[5] Ibid., pp. 436–45.

On the whole, Maximos's criticism of the Latin Church was measured and courteous, and lacked the emotional overtones of the anti-Latin pronouncements of many of his contemporaries, Greek and Russian.[1]

The ten years or so which Maximos spent on Mount Athos were a crucial period in his life. Unfortunately, it is also the least well documented. A few writings by him have survived from this period, mostly Greek epitaphs in verse.[2] They are distinguished by elegance of form and a liking for classical imagery. On a deeper level, there is no doubt that on Mount Athos Maximos immersed himself in Byzantine literature, both religious and secular. The libraries of Mount Athos, well-stocked in the Middle Ages, had become richer still after the fall of Constantinople. Thus Maximos's former teacher John Lascaris had purchased from the Athonite monks a large number of manuscripts for the Library of Lorenzo de' Medici. It was almost certainly in Vatopedi that Maximos studied in depth the works of John of Damascus, the Byzantine theologian who seems to have been the most congenial to him, and whom he later described as having reached 'the summit of philosophy and theology'.[3] Among the early Fathers Gregory of Nazianzus appears to have been his favourite.[4] Of the secular Byzantine works, the one he used, and translated most frequently in Russia, was the encyclopaedia known today as *Suda* and formerly believed to have been written by a certain Suidas.[5]

Another feature of Mount Athos which bears directly upon Maximos's subsequent life and outlook was its cosmopolitanism. Since the early Middle Ages the Holy Mountain had been a place of meeting and co-operation between men from different countries of eastern Europe. In the late Middle Ages, partly owing to a considerable increase in the number of Slav monks, it played a particularly important role as a pan-Orthodox monastic centre. The revival of the contemplative tradition of Byzantine Hesychasm attracted men from Serbia, Bulgaria, Rumania, and Russia, as

[1] On Maximos's views of the *Filioque*, see B. Schultze, 'Maksim Grek als Theologe', *Orientalia Christiana Analecta*, clxvii (1963), 245–55; on his attitude to the Papal claims, see ibid, pp. 283–90.

[2] See Denissoff, op. cit., pp. 97–9, 412–20.

[3] *Sochineniya*, iii. 66. Cf. ibid., pp. 210, 227, 232–3. Cf. Ikonnikov, op. cit., pp. 144–5.

[4] See D. M. Bulanin, *Maksim Grek i vizantiyskaya literaturnaya traditsiya* (Avtoreferat na soiskanie uchenoy stepeni kandidata filologicheskikh nauk) (Leningrad, 1978), pp. 11–13.

[5] Ivanov, op. cit., pp. 68–79; N. V. Sinitsyna, *Maksim Grek v Rossii* (Moscow, 1977), pp. 58–60, 67–9; Bulanin, op. cit., pp. 14–18.

well as Greeks from Byzantium, to this famed nursery of the spiritual life. In the Greek and Slav monasteries of Athos, manuscripts were copied and collated, literary works were exchanged, and Byzantine texts translated into Slavonic.[1] In the early sixteenth century, despite the Ottoman conquests, this spiritual and cultural co-operation continued, and it is hard to believe that Maximos remained unaffected by this cosmopolitan Graeco-Slav environment. It must have prepared him in some degree for his future work in Muscovy.

It has been suggested that Maximos, as a product of the humanist schools of Renaissance Italy, and with the burden of his recent Dominican past, may have felt isolated, if not ostracized, in the contemporary climate of Mount Athos.[2] His superiors at Vatopedi were certainly not ignorant of his life in Italy. And it is true that his attachment to Plato, which went back to his early days in Florence, was a potential hazard in an Orthodox monastic society whose thinking, recently moulded by the teachings of the Hesychast theologian Gregory Palamas, was profoundly hostile to all forms of Platonism. Yet there is no evidence that Maximos encountered on Mount Athos any difficulties on this score. To judge from his later Russian writings, he was fully aware, from a strictly orthodox standpoint, of the pitfalls of Platonism; and he explicitly rejected some of Plato's teachings, such as the belief he ascribed to him in the co-eternity of God and the world.[3] Maximos's views on the relationship of faith to knowledge were unimpeachably orthodox. 'Do not think', he wrote in Russia, 'that I condemn all external [i.e. secular] learning that is useful. . . . I am not so ungrateful a student of this learning. Although I did not long remain on its threshold, yet I condemn those who pursue it through excessive rational inquiry.'[4] It seems that Maximos adapted quickly to his Athonite environment: certainly for the rest of his life he regarded the Holy Mountain as his true spiritual home.

It was in 1516 that the last period of Maximos's life began. In that year an embassy from the Muscovite ruler, Basil III, arrived on Mount Athos. Its purpose was to invite to Moscow a competent Greek translator. The Russian Church, from its birth in the tenth

[1] See I. Dujčev, 'Tsentry vizantiisko-slavyanskogo obshcheniya i sotrudni-chestva', *Trudy Otdela Drevnerusskoy Literatury*, xix (1963), 107–29.

[2] Denissoff, op. cit., pp. 293–301.

[3] J. V. Haney, *From Italy to Muscovy. The Life and Works of Maxim the Greek* (Munich, 1973), pp. 138–52.

[4] *Sochineniya*, i (Kazan, 1859–60), 462.

century and until the mid-fifteenth, has been subordinated to the
Patriarch of Constantinople. During this period, and especially
between 1350 and 1450, the royal library had been enriched by a
large number of Greek manuscripts brought from Byzantium.[1] By
the early sixteenth century few Russians were capable of reading
them. There was need of an expert to decipher them and translate
them into Slavonic.

The choice of the Muscovites had fallen on the Greek monk
Savvas of the Vatopedi monastery, who seems to have been a
translator of repute. Savvas, however, was too old and infirm to
travel and, as the next best, the Athonite authorities chose
Maximos. In his letter to the metropolitan of Moscow, the abbot
recommended Maximos in terms which show that the latter was
respected on Mount Athos not only for his spiritual qualities: he
described him as 'our most honourable brother Maximos . . .,
proficient in divine Scripture and adept in interpreting all kinds of
books, both ecclesiastical and those called Hellenic [i.e. secular],
because from his early youth he has grown up in them and learned
[to understand] them through the practice of virtue, and not
simply by reading them often, as others do'.[2]

On his journey north Maximos and his companions stopped for
a while in Constantinople. There can be little doubt that the
Patriarchate took this opportunity to brief him on the two vital
issues which then dominated its relations with Russia: the wish to
restore its authority over the Russian Church, which had lapsed in
the mid-fifteenth century; and the hope of obtaining from
Muscovy aid, material or political, for the Greek Orthodox
subjects of the Sultan.

Maxim (as we may now call him, using the Russian form of his
name) arrived in Moscow in March 1518. His first task was to
prepare a translation of patristic commentaries on the Psalter. On
purely linguistic grounds, his qualifications were meagre. His
abbot, in a letter to the Muscovite sovereign, stated that Maximos
knew no Russian. He may well, however, have had at least a
smattering of one of the other Slavonic languages spoken on
Mount Athos. He seems, in any case, to have acquired some knowledge of Russian fairly soon after his arrival in Moscow. And in his
old age, one of his disciples tells us, he knew Russian, Serbian,

    [1] Doubts have been cast on the existence of this library: S. Belokurov, *O
biblioteke moskovskikh gosudarey v XVI stoletii* (Moscow, 1898). See, however,
Ikonnikov, op. cit., pp. 157–66.
    [2] *Akty istoricheskie, sobrannye i izdannye Arkheograficheskoyu Kommissieyu*, i (St.
Petersburg, 1841), no. 122, p. 176.

Bulgarian, and Church Slavonic, in addition to Greek and Latin.[1] For the present, however, faced with translating the commentaries on the Psalter, it must be admitted that his equipment was poor. According to a reliable contemporary source, Maxim translated from Greek into Latin, which his Russian collaborators then rendered into Slavonic.[2] This astonishingly cumbersome procedure could hardly fail to result in errors of translation: for these Maxim was later to pay dearly.

The request to translate a collection of patristic commentaries on the Psalter was not due to a passing interest of Russian churchmen in biblical exegesis. It was prompted by hard and urgent necessities. In his introduction to the completed translation, Maxim assured the Grand Prince that the work will be useful in fighting heretics.[3] At that time, the Muscovite state and the Russian Church were struggling to eradicate the remains of the heresy of the 'Judaisers', which at the turn of the fifteenth century had posed a serious threat to the Orthodox Church in their domains. The tenets of the Russian 'Judaisers' are imperfectly known: they appear to have included a disbelief in the Trinity, the rejection of the cult of icons, and a strong attack on the hierarchy of the Church. It is possible, though not certain, that the 'Judaisers' had links with early Protestant movements in Central Europe. The heresy was first attested in Novgorod in 1470, and ten years later spread to Moscow, where it is said to have gained powerful support in government and church circles.[4] Russian society divided sharply over the right manner of treating the heretics, one party demanding their physical extermination, the other urging milder measures, particularly when they repented of their errors. The militants were led by two formidable churchmen, Gennady, Archbishop of Novgorod, and Joseph, abbot of the monastery of Volokolamsk. Gennady was a great admirer of the Spanish Inquisition. He and Joseph finally won over the Grand Prince to their view, and in 1504 the leaders of

[1] Ivanov, op. cit., p. 43.

[2] This was stated, at the time the work was carried out, by Dimitri Gerasimov, a leading diplomat who was Maxim's principal Russian assistant: *Pribavleniya k izdaniyu tvoreniy svyatykh ottsov*, xviii (Moscow, 1859), 190. Cf. Ivanov, op. cit., p. 41; Haney, op. cit., p. 46.

[3] *Sochineniya*, ii (Kazan, 1860), 303; Ikonnikov, op. cit., pp. 168-9.

[4] On the 'Judaisers', see N. A. Kazakova and Ya. S. Lur'e, *Antifeodal'nye ereticheskie dvizheniya na Rusi XIV—nachala XVI veka* (Moscow-Leningrad, 1955); A. I. Klibanov, *Reformatsionnye dvizheniya v Rossii v XIV—pervoy polovine XVI v.v.* (Moscow, 1960); Ya. S. Lur'e, *Ideologicheskaya bor'ba v russkoy publitsistike kontsa XV—nachala XVI veka* (Moscow-Leningrad, 1960).

the 'Judaisers' were publicly burned. The 'Josephians', as the militants were now called after their leader, were opposed by a group of laymen and ecclesiastics whose leaders came from remote hermitages in the north of the country, and were known as 'Elders from beyond the Volga'. They had no truck with heresy, but did not believe that the heretics should be executed. By the early sixteenth century their influence was on the wane. The militants were on the war-path, pointing to the fact that the heresy had not been eliminated by the blood-bath of 1504.

One of the texts which the 'Judaisers' used to support their teaching was the Book of Psalms. According to Archbishop Gennady, they doctored some of its passages for their own exegetical purposes.[1] It is hence not surprising that Maxim was put to work so soon on a translation of authoritative commentaries on the Psalms. It may indeed have been the main purpose of his invitation to Moscow.

Maxim took seventeen months to complete his task. This was the first of the many literary works he produced in Russia. The Soviet scholar Aleksey Ivanov, in a valuable study published in 1969, listed and briefly described 365 works attributable to Maxim, nearly half of them still unpublished at the time of writing.[2] The great majority are undated. They range over a wide variety of topics. Jack Haney, the author of the only book in English on Maxim, has divided them into four general categories: theology, secular philosophy, statecraft, and social problems.[3] The classification is useful, though it leaves out two important kinds of work: translations from the Greek (over 100 of them, mostly unpublished, are listed by Ivanov), and works on grammar and lexicography, fields in which Maxim was a pioneer in Russia. We badly need a critical edition of Maxim's writings. The only existing edition, published in Kazan in 1859–62, falls far short of this requirement.

Maxim seems to have had every reason to believe that, on completing his translation of the commentaries on the Psalter, he would be allowed to return to Mount Athos. Whether or not he was given a formal assurance to this effect,[4] the Muscovite

[1] Kazakova and Lur'e, op. cit., pp. 310, 316, 319.

[2] Ivanov, op. cit. Cf. Sinitsyna, op. cit., pp. 221–79.

[3] Haney, op. cit., p. 114.

[4] The monk Savvas of Vatopedi, the Muscovites' original choice (see above, p. 150), was given just such an assurance: Basil III of Moscow, in a letter to the *Protos* of Athos (the head of the Athonite community) dated 15 March 1515, stated that Savvas's services as a translator would be required only for a time, and that he would be sent back to Mount Athos on completion of his

authorities were clearly in no hurry to let him go home. They had other plans for Maxim. He was quickly put to work on further translations, and on the revision of the existing Slavonic texts of the Scriptures and liturgical books. These he found to be less than satisfactory: the earlier Russian translators had shown themselves deficient in their knowledge of Greek. This, Maxim observed with a touch of condescension, was hardly surprising. For the Greek language, he stressed, is difficult and complex, and requires many years of study to be mastered, especially if the student is not a Greek by birth, sharp-witted, and highly motivated.[1] It became obvious to him that the howlers committed by early translators, compounded by scribal errors, had led to mistranslations which at best were absurd, and at worst heretical. Some of the most glaring he corrected himself, unaware of the trouble he was storing up for the future.

It was not only by his correction of textual errors that Maxim sailed rather close to the wind. Through his contacts with local personalities he was becoming dangerously involved in public controversy. The first half of the sixteenth century was a period of great ferment in Muscovy: educated Russians seemed to be locked in endless and passionate debate. The momentous changes that were taking place in their society meant that they had indeed much to argue about: whether the sovereign was omnipotent, or should share his power with the aristocracy; whether heretics should be burned at the stake; what was the role of monasteries in the contemporary world; and what was the right relationship between church and state. The treatment of heretics, we have seen, was an issue over which the 'Josephians' and the 'Elders from beyond the Volga' clashed violently. We must now briefly examine another, closely related, issue, for it was to have a lasting effect on Maxim's fate.

During the late Middle Ages two different types of monasticism were prevalent in Russia. On the one hand, we find, mainly in the central areas, the large coenobitic house, owning land, often on

task: 'Akty, kasayushchiesya do priezda Maksima Greka v Rossiyu', ed. M. A. Obolensky, *Vremennik Imperatorskogo Moskovskogo Obshchestva Istorii i Drevnostey Rossiyskikh*, v, 3 (Moscow, 1850), pp. 31–2. While there is no direct evidence that Maxim was given a similar promise, he doubtless regarded the Russians as morally bound by the undertaking they had given to Savvas. It is worth noting, furthermore, that the abbot of Vatopedi, in his letter recommending Maxim to the metropolitan of Moscow (see above, p. 150), requested that he and two other monks of his monastery, who were to travel to Moscow together, be eventually sent back to Athos 'in good health': *Akty istoricheskie*, i. 176.

[1] *Sochineniya*, iii. 80; cf. ibid., p. 62; ii. p. 312; cf. Ikonnikov, op. cit., p. 178.

a large scale, exploiting peasant labour, practising works of charity and immersed in administrative and economic activity. This type of monastery came to be known as 'Josephian', after the name of Joseph, abbot of Volokolamsk, the leader of the hard-liners who wished to see the heretics physically destroyed. On the other hand, in the far north of the country, groups of small hermitages, known as *lavrai* in Greek and *skity* in Russian, clustered round clearings in the forest. Their monks came increasingly to believe that land-owning was incompatible with the monastic estate. It was in these remote *skity* that the contemplative tradi-tion burned with a brighter flame; and the leaders of this move-ment, the very same 'Elders from beyond the Volga' who urged that heretics be treated leniently, became the spokesmen in late medieval Russia of the mystical teachings of Byzantine Hesychasm.[1]

The 'Josephian' party gained a notable victory in 1503, when Ivan III was compelled to abandon his plan for the secularization of church lands. Yet the 'Non-Possessors', as the opponents of monastic estates were also called, retained some influence in government circles, and when Maxim came to Moscow in 1518, they were still far from beaten. Their leader, Vassian Patrikeev, was a resourceful and vigorous campaigner. This former general and diplomat, who belonged to a princely family, was disgraced in 1499 and compelled to become a monk. A few years later he was back in Moscow, with a powerful influence over the new Grand Prince, Basil III.[2] Vassian and Maxim were to become close friends and associates.

When Maxim arrived in Moscow Vassian had just completed, with the approval of the Church, his main life-work, a new edition of the *Nomocanon*, The Orthodox manual of canon law. Arranged by subjects and no longer, as in previous editions, chronologically, Vassian's *Nomocanon* was intended to demonstrate that monas-teries which owned landed estates were violating canon law. Maxim not surprisingly sided with the 'Non-Possessors', and placed his knowledge of Greek and experience of Mount Athos at the disposal of his new Russian friend. He was asked to arbitrate on a contentious problem of philology. The Greek *Nomocanon* permitted monasteries to own προάστεια, a word which in classical Greek means either 'suburbs' or 'houses or estates in suburbs'.

---

[1] See J. Meyendorff, *Une controverse sur le rôle social de l'Église. La querelle des biens ecclésiastiques au XVIe siècle en Russie* (Chevetogne, 1956).

[2] See N. A. Kazakova, *Vassian Patrikeev i ego sochineniya* (Moscow–Leningrad, 1960).

Previous Russian translators had taken the word to mean 'villages with resident peasants', a translation which was vigorously endorsed by the 'Possessors'. Maxim, on the other hand, assured Vassian that the true meaning of προάστεια was 'ploughed fields and vineyards', which, by restricting the scope of the word, seemed to provide ammunition to the 'Non-Possessors'. This explanation was incorporated by Vassian into his edition of the *Nomocanon*.[1]

At the same time, during his first years in Moscow, Maxim, at the request of Vassian, wrote several descriptions of the monasteries of Mount Athos.[2] He was careful to write in a non-polemical tone, and avoided any explicit reference to monastic landowning. Yet he made it clear that of the different types of Athonite monasteries he much preferred the coenobitic house, where all property was held in common and the monks supported themselves by their own labour. His accounts of Mount Athos were hardly calculated to please the 'Josephians'. As for his friendship with Vassian, it was soon to become a serious liability.

Their enemies doubtless carefully noted these words of Vassian who, unlike Maxim, was prone to overstatement: 'All our books are false ones, and were written by the devil and not by the Holy Spirit. Until Maxim we used these books to blaspheme God, and not to glorify or pray Him. Now, through Maxim, we have come to know God.'[3]

However cautious Maxim may have been in his public utterances, he seems to have behaved at times with a certain lack of elementary prudence. He allowed his cell in the Simonov Monastery to become a kind of dissident *salon*, where critics of Muscovite society, mostly members of the nobility, gathered to air their grievances.[4] This, in sixteenth-century Russia, was asking for trouble. Meanwhile, in the higher councils of church and state, his luck was running out. In 1522 the leader of the 'Possessors', Daniel, abbot of Volokolamsk and a disciple of Joseph, was appointed primate of the Russian Church; almost at once Vassian's influence at court began to wane.

Some time during the winter of 1524/5 Maxim was arrested. His arrest was followed in February 1525 by the trial of two of his

[1] See Ivanov, op. cit., p. 51; Kazakova, *Vassian Patrikeev*, pp. 62, 236; Haney, op. cit., pp. 47–8.

[2] *Sochineniya*, iii. 243–5; Ivanov, op. cit., pp. 192–8; Sinitsyna, op. cit., p. 110.

[3] Ikonnikov, op. cit., p. 409.

[4] See V. O. Klyuchevsky, *Kurs russkoy istorii*, ii: *Sochineniya*, ii (Moscow, 1957), 161–4.

regular visitors. Both these Russian associates of Maxim were charged with high treason, and found guilty. One was beheaded, the other sentenced to have his tongue cut out. In May 1525 Maxim himself was tried by a court presided over by the Grand Prince Basil III and by Metropolitan Daniel of Moscow, who also acted as chief prosecutor.

After a manifestly biased trial Maxim was sentenced to solitary confinement in the Volokolamsk Monastery (the stronghold of the 'Possessors'), put in chains, excommunicated, and allowed neither to read nor to write. His imprisonment was to last for twenty-three years. In 1531 he was tried again, at least partly because of his refusal to confess to the earlier charges, and was sentenced to imprisonment in a monastery in Tver'.[1]

The charges brought against him are known primarily from a near-contemporary document which Russian scholars have called the Trial Record (*Sudnyi Spisok*) of Maxim the Greek.[2] In fact it is not a copy of the proceedings but a literary pamphlet based on an official transcript of his trials. Until recently this document was known only in late and incomplete manuscripts. In 1968 a fuller version came to light, in a late sixteenth-century manuscript discovered in Siberia.[3] It has added much to our knowledge of Maxim's two trials. In one respect, however, this version is as deficient as the later ones. It combines materials relating to the two trials, and thus fails to distinguish between the charges brought against Maxim in 1525 and 1531. So for the present we too must be content with this unfortunate conflation.

The list of the charges is long and impressive. It included holding heretical views, practising sorcery, criticizing the Grand Prince, having treasonable relations with the Turkish government, claiming that the Russian Church's independence from the Patriarchate of Constantinople was illegal, and denouncing the monasteries and the church for owning land and peasants.

The allegation of sorcery was patently absurd, and merely shows the lack of scruples displayed by the prosecution, and particularly by the Metropolitan Daniel.[4] The accusation of heresy, equally unjust, was based on evidence no more substantial

[1] Ikonnikov, op. cit., pp. 455–97; Sinitsyna, op. cit., pp. 130–49; Haney, op. cit., pp. 64–85.

[2] See the discussion of this document, and other relevant sources, by N. A. Kazakova, *Ocherki po istorii russkoy obshchestvennoy mysli. Pervaya tret' XVI veka* (Leningrad, 1970), pp. 177–87.

[3] *Sudnye spiski Maksima Greka i Isaka Sobaki*, eds. N. N. Pokrovsky and S. O. Shmidt (Moscow, 1971); cf. Kazakova, op. cit., pp. 187–93.

[4] Kazakova, op. cit., pp. 230–1.

than some grammatical errors in Maxim's translations and occasional infelicities in his emendation of liturgical texts. These mistakes were due to his inadequate knowledge of the Russian language, a fault he readily acknowledged himself.[1] Criticism of the Grand Prince was a charge that Maxim denied: and it seems at the very least to have been unproven.[2]

The charge that Maxim entertained relations with the Ottoman government prejudicial to the Muscovite state raises more complex issues. At one or both of his trials he was accused of writing to the Turkish pasha of Athens, urging him to persuade the Sultan to declare war on Russia; and it was further alleged that he held secret meetings for the same purpose with the Turkish envoy in Moscow. Maxim vigorously denied these charges; and the recently discovered Siberian manuscript of the Trial Record makes it clear that no letters from him to the Ottoman authorities were available to the prosecution. The charges of treason and espionage could not be made to stick.[3] Yet a lingering suspicion remains that Maxim may have been less than discreet in his political table-talk. He admitted saying that one day the Sultan was bound to invade Russia, since he detested all members of the imperial house of Byzantium, from which Basil III of Moscow, through his mother, was descended.[4] As a Greek, Maxim hoped that one day the Muscovite sovereign, the most powerful Orthodox ruler on earth, would come to the help of his enslaved people and liberate them from the infidel yoke. A war between Russia and the Ottoman Empire was a necessary prelude to the liberation of the Christians of the Balkans. Maxim could hardly have concealed his irritation at the foreign policy of the Muscovite government which, faced with the hostility of the Polish–Lithuanian state and the constant military threat from the Tatar Khanates of the Crimea and Kazan', pinned its hopes on an alliance with the Ottoman Turks.

The last two charges against Maxim were straightforward, and mostly true. He never concealed his belief that the situation of the Russian Church, which had been electing its primates without reference to the Patriarch of Constantinople for almost a century, was uncanonical, and that it should return to the obedience of

[1] Kazakova, op. cit., pp. 231–3; Haney, op. cit., pp. 70–1.
[2] Kazakova, op. cit., pp. 221–6.
[3] *Sudnye spiski Maksima Greka i Isaka Sobaki*, p. 44; Kazakova, op. cit., pp. 203–21.
[4] *Sudnye spiski*, p. 70; Kazakova, op. cit. pp. 219–20.

its mother church.[1] Equally outspoken was his opposition to ownership of land by monasteries. He wrote repeatedly on this topic, denouncing Russian monks for accumulating lands and riches, exploiting their peasants, and practising usury.[2] He compared them unfavourably with the Carthusians, Franciscans, and Dominicans he had known in Italy, who led a life of dedicated poverty.[3] It was in this sensitive area of monastic ethics and economy that the Metropolitan Daniel and his minions must have felt the most threatened. In 1525, the year of Maxim's first trial, the 'Non-Possessors' were still a force to be reckoned with. It seems quite possible that Maxim's condemnation of monastic land-ownership was the main reason for the harshness of his sentence. And it is highly probable that one of the aims of his prosecutors in 1531 was to break Vassian Patrikeev. Almost at once Vassian was tried and sentenced to imprisonment in the Volokolamsk Monastery.[4] The condemnation in the same year of Maxim and his once powerful friend marked in a real sense the defeat of the 'Non-Possessors' party in Russia.

The harshness of Maxim's treatment slowly diminished in the 1530s, thanks to the humanity of the local bishop Akakiy, and especially after his chief tormentor, the Metropolitan Daniel, was removed from office in 1539. Though still at first deprived of communion, he was given his books back and allowed to write. In the mid-1540s the Patriarchs of Constantinople and Alexandria wrote to Ivan IV, requesting his release.[5] Maxim repeatedly begged his jailors to let him return to Mount Athos. The stony-hearted Russian authorities refused all his requests to be allowed to go home, at least once on the grounds that he knew too much about their country.[6]

In the last few years of Maxim's life his torments at last came to an end. He was released from imprisonment, probably about 1548, when the excommunication was lifted, and he was allowed to reside in St. Sergius's Monastery of the Holy Trinity near Moscow (in what today is Zagorsk). He spent his time reading, writing, and teaching. Despite his fading eyesight, he taught

[1] Kazakova, op. cit., pp. 196–203; Haney, op. cit., pp. 75–7, 82.

[2] *Sochineniya*, ii. 5–52, 89–118, 119–47, 260–76, iii. 178–205; Ivanov, op. cit., pp. 156–60.

[3] 'Neizdannye sochineniya Maksima Greka', *Byzantinoslavica*, vi (1935–6), 85–109.

[4] N. A. Kazakova, *Vassian Patrikeev*, pp. 75–7.

[5] Ikonnikov, op. cit., pp. 507–8.

[6] *Akty, sobrannye Arkheograficheskoyu Ekspeditsieyu*, i (St. Petersburg, 1836), 143; cf. E. Golubinsky, *Istoriya russkoy tserkvi*, ii (Moscow, 1900), 816.

Greek to a fellow monk, and wrote (a little earlier) to his chief persecutor, the Metropolitan Daniel, comforting him on his fall from power and offering him the hand of reconciliation.[1] He died in the Trinity Monastery, at the age of almost ninety.

The posthumous fate of Maxim the Greek in Russia was a curious one. His opinions on many matters of great concern to Russian society were too much at variance with official policy to make him fully acceptable, at least in the next few generations. It is true that the wonderful patience with which he endured twenty-three years of cruel torments caused him to be revered as a martyr, especially by those Russians who were at variance with the official church. He had, moreover, in his lifetime a small circle of Russian admirers, some of whom were outstanding men. It is perhaps surprising to find among them the Tsar Ivan the Terrible. It was on Ivan's orders that he was released from prison.[2] But it remains true that Maxim's influence in Russia was always very limited. It is remarkable that this Byzantine scholar was long revered in Russia for his statements on the correct way of making the sign of the cross, while his references to Greek classical literature were largely ignored.[3]

There may indeed be something symbolic in Maxim's Russian destiny. The rejection of a man who, in the depth of his spirituality and scholarship, typified what was best in the culture of post-Byzantine Greece, marked in one sense Russia's turning away from her ancient heritage of Byzantium.[4] It is true that, at the very time he was in Muscovy, the Russian churchmen were developing their egregious theory of Moscow the Third Rome, which ascribed to their capital city the role of focus of universal power and central repository for the true Orthodox faith. But Maxim's attitude to this theory seems to have been ambiguous. As a patriotic Greek, he welcomed the sixteenth-century version of the 'Great Idea'—the prospect of a victorious Russian entry into Constantinople, leading to the liberation of his people and their resurgence under the sceptre of an Orthodox tsar. In the introduction to his translation of commentaries on the Psalter, the very first work he carried out in Russia, Maxim addressed the Grand Prince of Moscow, Basil III, in these terms:

Let the poor Christians living there [in Greece] learn from us that

---

[1] *Sochineniya*, ii. 367–76; cf. Ikonnikov, op. cit., p. 535; Haney, op. cit., pp. 85–6.

[2] Sinitsyna, op. cit., p. 151.

[3] I. Ševčenko, 'Byzantium and the Eastern Slavs after 1453', *Harvard Ukrainian Studies*, ii (1978), 14.

[4] See G. Florovsky, *Puti russkogo bogosloviya* (Paris, 1937), pp. 22–4.

they still have a tsar, who not only rules over innumerable peoples and abounds in all else that is royal and is worthy of amazement, but who has been glorified above all others by reason of his justice and his orthodoxy, so that he may be likened unto Constantine and Theodosius the Great, whom your majesty succeeds. Oh, if only we could one day be liberated through you from subjection to the infidels and receive our own tsardom . . . So even now, may [God] be pleased to free the New Rome [Constantinople], cruelly tormented by the Godless Muslims, through the pious majesty of your tsardom, and to bring forth from your paternal throne an heir, and may we, the unfortunate ones, receive through you the light of freedom . . .[1]

Perhaps Maxim genuinely hoped that this rhetoric would advance the cause of his people's liberation. He wrote these words during his early days in Russia. His belief that Moscow, as the successor of Constantinople, was the third and last Rome, if it ever was sincere, soon foundered on the reality he saw around him. He was too much of a Byzantine at heart to be taken in for long by this meretricious substitute of the East Roman ecumenical idea, propounded in Russia by his sworn adversaries, the 'Josephian' monks. And he was probably too much of a realist not to observe how, in sixteenth-century Russia, through the narrowing of cultural horizons and in the wake of the *realpolitik* of its rulers, the Christian universalism of Byzantium was being transformed and distorted within the more narrow framework of Muscovite nationalism. Perhaps this is why Maxim's vision of the Christian commonwealth was, in the last resort, pessimistic. In a passage of pointed allegory, written in the early 1540s, he tells us that, toiling one day down a hard and wearisome road, he encountered a woman dressed in black, sitting by the roadside and weeping disconsolately. Around her were wild animals, lions and bears, wolves, and foxes. 'The road', she said to Maxim, 'is desolate and prefigures this last and accursed age'. Her name, she told him, was Vasileia (which in Greek means 'empire' or 'kingdom').[2]

It is not easy to assess precisely the place which should be allotted to Michael–Maximos–Maxim in the cultural history of each of the three worlds to which he belonged. Before this can be done satisfactorily we need, I think, a fuller answer to three questions: what was the nature of his Platonism, and how did he square it with his Christian beliefs? What led him to leave the

---

[1] *Sochineniya*, ii. 318–19. I have, in the main, followed the translation of this passage by Haney, op. cit., p. 163.

[2] *Sochineniya*, ii. pp. 319–37; cf. Haney, op. cit., pp. 164–7.

Dominican order and retire to Mount Athos? And what impact did his writings have upon later Russian literature? In the meantime we can perhaps agree to accept the following conclusions: Maximos, though not a creative thinker, was at least a sound and wide-ranging scholar, with an excellent training in ancient philosophy and textual criticism; though he played an important role in the controversies that shook sixteenth-century Muscovite society, his learning was, with a few notable exceptions, above its head; and he lived in a cosmopolitan world where the Byzantine heritage, the late medieval Italo-Greek connections, and the traditional links between Russia, Mount Athos, and Constantinople were still to some extent living realities. He was one of the last of his kind.

'NEW MEN, STRANGE FACES, OTHER MINDS': AN ARCHAEOLOGIST'S PERSPECTIVE ON RECENT DISCOVERIES RELATING TO THE ORIGINS AND SPREAD OF MODERN MAN

By J. DESMOND CLARK

Fellow of the Academy

Read 24 September 1981

Introduction

SIR MORTIMER WHEELER always emphasized that archaeologists are digging up, not things, but *people* (Wheeler, 1954, 13). He then went on to show that it is field-work—systematic survey and excavation—that is the only acceptable basis for the hypotheses on which the archaeologists make their interpretations or, in modern parlance, construct their models. But *things* reflect the ways in which people make and use them—the technological proficiency of the makers, their mode of livelihood, even their thought processes and ethical beliefs. For the more remote periods of prehistory, however, when the earliest manifestations of tool-making occurred of which evidence is sometimes found associated with the hominid fossils, as much reliance is placed on the anatomical characteristics of the fossils themselves as on the tools for showing how these earliest ancestors may have behaved. But, with the advent of Modern Man, early in the later Pleistocene, the variability by that time manifest in the archaeological assemblages in all inhabited regions of the Old World and the adaptive patterning this implies are the clues to understanding something of the behavioural diversity that is the special characteristic of our own species.

In what I now have to say we will pass in review the facts concerning the fossil remains of man and his tools over that crucial period of time when Modern Man, *Homo sapiens sapiens*, made his entrance upon the world stage. Some of these bones and stones represent substantial evidence. Others are less satisfactory and some are probably downright misleading did we but know it! The palaeoanthropologist today is only too conscious of the variable nature of the data but, through the interdisciplinary team approach that is nowadays the norm, we are better equipped than ever before to analyse them and to make more consistent use of the synthesizing process. Even so, we are still a very long way from producing answers to some of the questions and problems of which this review will treat. However, even though the conclusion must be, so to speak, inconclusive, I hope the review will show the vitality and enthusiasm with which the planned search is conducted and the understanding it is providing of where we have come from and wherein our chances of survival may lie as well as the sheer excitement of the future potential of palaeoanthropology.

The appearance of Modern Man is the most significant event in the whole long record of mankind's biological and cultural evolution. He successfully replaced the Neanderthalers and all other contemporary hominid forms within a few thousand years and, by the end of the Pleistocene, 10,000 years ago, he had pushed into almost every corner of the Old and New Worlds. The speed with which these developments took place was phenomenal when compared with the change from *Homo erectus*, via the earliest forms of *Homo sapiens*, to Neanderthal. The accompanying change from the Lower through to the end of the Middle Palaeolithic took nearly twice as long. And the evolutionary process that brought about the transition from the earliest tool-making hominids with their basic and generalized stone tool equipment to the early *Homo sapiens* stock represented by the Neanderthalers with their much more varied tool-kits, lasted nearly fifty times longer (Clark, 1975, 179-84).

Theories of Man's Descent

It seems evident that such rapid and accelerating biological evolution was made possible in great part by the increasing efficiency of man's technical skill and the success with which hominids were able to adapt their behaviour to ecological change and to the occupation of new environmental niches. That Modern Man—*Homo sapiens sapiens*—was possessed of intellectual and technical abilities in advance of all other forms of men, effectively eliminated any possible competition and, down the ages, these qualities have manifested such potential that they have given him mastery of the world with prospects of also extending this to outer space before too long. Recent discoveries show that modern forms

of man were everywhere dominant from 35,000 to 30,000 years
ago and it is unlikely that any archaic *sapiens* or Neanderthal
remains will be found that are younger than 30,000 BP (Trinkaus
and Howells, 1979).

'Modern Man' is characterized by a lighter skeleton showing
reduced muscularity as compared to the Neanderthalers. His
brain was the size of ours. He had a high brow with a shorter face
and a jaw with a chin and small, regular teeth. Rearrangement of
the organs of the throat, especially the pharynx, enabled him to
develop the complex speech systems we use today, while the
artistic and aesthetic achievements of his culture show intellectual
capacities and a reasoning ability akin to our own. By contrast,
Neanderthalers were more muscular and robust, with a flatter
forehead, a protruding face, and a chinless jaw. Otherwise they
were not all that different from ourselves though intellectually
less flexible. This change in muscularity and robustness is perhaps
one of the most significant since it implies a major modification
in the way they performed the assorted tasks of daily life (Campbell, 1976).

The earliest populations with fossils that are anatomically
modern belong in contexts which are interpreted in either of two
ways. They can be regarded as showing *hybridization* of early
modern stock with Neanderthalers, or as being representative of
the genetic modification inherent in the emergence of a *new* stock.
Resolution as to which hypothesis is the more likely must rest with
the anatomists and anthropologists and does not lie within the
competence of the present writer. Since also it is the cultural
evidence that will mostly be discussed here, the fossils themselves
will be reviewed only for the implications and inferences that can
be drawn from them about the nature of the technological component with which they are associated and thereby the abilities of
these early modern populations.

Crucial to the problem of man's origins and evolution is the
reliability of the dating evidence. Although, since the advent of
radiocarbon, this is very much more acceptable, it is still far from
adequate since the lower limit of the method extends back only
to the end of the Middle Palaeolithic and of Neanderthal man.
However, there are now prospects of being able to extend reliability back to 100,000 years ago by various carbon isotope
enrichment processes (Muller, 1977; Hedges and Moore, 1978).
By correlating results from these with others obtained using the
uranium decay series dating, fission track, thermoluminescence
and archaeomagnetism methods, a great deal of the present

uncertainty in archaeological correlation of Middle Palaeolithic assemblages and Neanderthal fossils is likely soon to be eliminated or considerably reduced. In particular, where *suites* of dates are available, we can have confidence that cultural assemblages and fossils can be correctly chronologically ordered.

For the present, therefore, the general consensus among archaeologists and anthropologists is to recognize a 'Neanderthal grade' of hominid evolution showing a wide range of variation and lasting from about 100,000 to about 35,000 years ago. This includes not only the better known classic and early Neanderthal populations of Europe, concerning which a large bibliography exists, but also the related and contemporary populations and individual fossils of 'progressive Neanderthalers' from the Middle East and central Asia. Less closely related anatomically but sharing similar general characteristics are fossil remains from Africa, north and south of the Sahara. From the original *Homo erectus* stock in Africa (e.g. Koobi Fora ER3733 and ER3883; Olduvai OH9; Ternifine) there appears to have emerged, early on during the late Middle Pleistocene, perhaps 300,000 years ago, an early *Homo sapiens* grade of man possessing heavy brow ridges and a large, robust face but a relatively less robust post-cranial skeleton (e.g. Kabwe, Saldanha, Ndutu, Bodo). Sometimes known as 'rhodesioid' after the *Homo rhodesiensis* fossil from Broken Hill (now Kabwe), these are not classic Neanderthalers though they have shared attributes. They are examples of a very variable African *sapiens* grade in which the early emergence of modern characteristics is clearly demonstrated. Associated faunal and cultural remains and other evidence suggest that these fossils fall within the chronological range of other early sapient fossils such as Swanscombe, Steinheim, Arago, Petralona, and early Neanderthal man in Europe (Howells, 1973, 83–128; Campbell, 1976, 293–313; Trinkaus and Howells, 1979).

The fossils from Ngandong on the Solo River in Java were first described as having characteristics that related them to Neanderthalers and as being of comparable age (von Koenigswald, 1958). More recent assessments, however, suggest that they are appreciably older than the early Upper Pleistocene and more closely related, morphologically and chronologically, to the earlier hominid *Homo erectus* (Jacob, 1976). From China also come fossils which are contemporary and share anatomical traits with both the classic Neanderthalers of Europe and with Modern Man (Howells, 1977; Lanpo, 1980, 37–60; Wu Xinzhi, 1981). Taken as a whole, therefore, this evidence clearly shows, in each of the cases, an *in situ* evolutionary development, so to speak, of the early Upper Pleistocene hominids from the older, archaic *Homo erectus* stock via an early *Homo sapiens* grade, so that there is probably general agreement among anthropologists that the various regional populations of the early Upper Pleistocene derived a large part of their genetic composition from the ancestral indigenous populations (Howells, 1980). In Europe, however, while the Neanderthal populations appear to have evolved relatively gradually from the pre-existing regional stock, their final disappearance was sufficiently sudden to suggest that an autochthonous transition from Neanderthal to Modern Man need not necessarily have taken place there.

With the possible exception of Europe, therefore, it would seem that a transition from the Neanderthal grade to Modern Man undoubtedly did take place, though there are still those who adhere to the hypothesis that an as yet undetected stock, derived from the original tool-maker *Homo habilis*, was the progenitor.

The Neanderthal Hypothesis (Fig. 1)

Part of the disinclination to accept Neanderthalers as immediate ancestors of Modern Man derives from the old misconception that they were subhuman, brutish, and bad: a repelling, crude, and shambling ape-man that could never have given rise to ourselves (Boule, 1911–13). Such a view—based on a series of preconceptions, false hypotheses, incorrect reconstructions, and inaccurate measurements—has now disappeared though there is still a

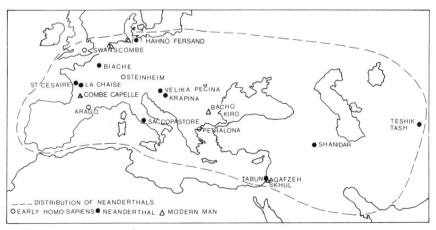

FIG. 1. Map of Europe, west and central Asia to show the distribution of Neanderthalers and location of sites with hominid fossils referred to in the text. (After Trinkaus and Howells, 1979.)

reluctance on the part of some anthropologists and prehistorians to accept the evidence that—the classic European Neanderthals apart—these fossils (of which more than one hundred now exist) represent a gene pool that, by 50,000 years ago, was capable of producing a range of individuals, some classically Neanderthal and others showing characteristics that link them with Modern Man. Indeed the ranges of variation of Neanderthal and Modern Man overlap (Campbell, 1976, 307).

As we have said, another way of interpreting these 'progressive' fossils is that they are hybrids between Neanderthalers and a contemporary and, as yet, unidentified modern population. That such a population *may* have existed cannot be totally excluded because of the vast areas of the Old World that still remain to be investigated. The Pleistocene populations of the Indian peninsula, for example, are quite unknown and large parts of south-east Asia and the Far East remain to be explored. But, with the increase in investigations in the Middle East, Russia, eastern Europe, and northern and southern Africa, the existence there of such a population now appears less likely and the 'prae-*sapiens*' hypothesis, once favoured on the basis of the cranial evidence from European Middle Pleistocene fossils, must fall away since the new fossils from Petralona and Arago show that they belong, morphologically and chronologically, midway between *Homo erectus* and the Neander-thalers (Stringer, 1981). If, therefore, there is now less likelihood of finding an isolated modern stock that, suddenly some 35,000 to 40,000 years ago, manifested itself by a rapid expansion that successfully eliminated all Neanderthalers, then the Skhul and Qafzeh fossils from Israel must be seen as representing a popula-tion in which the genetic changes leading to Modern Man were already well under way (McCown and Keith, 1939; Campbell, 1976, 302–3, 311).

This seems to me the more acceptable explanation though the circumstances leading to this transformation still remain to be identified, as well as the ways in which it was effected. Which, for example, of the two models that have been postulated is the more probable?—that these genetic mutations were sufficiently com-plex to have taken place only once in some, as yet, unidentified region from where Modern Man spread throughout the world? or, alternatively, that he evolved in each of several regions of Eurasia and Africa from the autochthonous hominid populations derived ultimately from *Homo erectus*? Some say the first of these models seems the more likely for genetic reasons. However, a third model might also be possible, namely that, although the changes were effected in only one region among a relatively isolated population, they were of sufficient significance for mankind that the population explosion they initiated resulted in very wide dispersal of the new stock which, through hybridization with some of the older indigenous populations with which they came into contact, ensured some genetic continuity with what went before and provided a gene pool that contributed to later behavioural specialization and so gave us the racial differences in the present-day world populations.

Each of these models will be viewed in the light of the cultural evidence described below but, before doing so, it is necessary to look at the main reasons for advocating a Neanderthal ancestry for Modern Man. First, they have many anatomical character-istics in common though, clearly, there are important differences, especially in the head and face and in the general robustness and muscularity of the Neanderthalers. However, for the present thesis, the shared characteristics outweigh the dissimilarities. Secondly, populations with the Neanderthal grade of character-istics are very widespread, stretching from China to southern Spain, from northern Europe and central Asia to South Africa and south-east Asia. Thirdly, there is considerable variability both among these populations as a whole and between individuals of a single population. The Middle Eastern Neanderthalers and some of the African fossils are closer to early modern repre-sentatives than is the classic European Neanderthal population with which, until recently, they have always been compared (Trinkaus and Howells, 1979). Fourthly, they appear to have been sufficiently well adapted, socially and economically, to be able successfully to occupy a broad range of ecological niches. They were competent foragers and efficient hunters of large game, organized to a transhumant pattern of occupation of base camps, sometimes in caves, and more temporary dwellings in the open. Their technical understanding and varied tool-kits permitted them to perform efficiently a number of different tasks and to exploit a very diverse range of resources from the tundra to the tropics. They were clearly capable of some abstract reasoning (Bergounioux, 1958) which can only have been possible by means of a relatively efficient communication system (Lieberman and Crelin, 1971; Campbell, 1976, 345–6). This is manifest in the number of deliberate burials of both adults and children. Food for the dead was included (cf. the pig bones at Skhul (McCown and Keith, 1939) or the goat at Teshik Tash (Movius, 1953)) and there were other grave goods, notably the 'flowers' with the burial

at Shanidar (Solecki, 1971, 246-50). The more esoteric ritual
represented by the Monte Circeo skull in its circle of stones (Blanc,
1958) and the use of pigment seen at a number of sites (Campbell,
1976, 347-8; Clark, 1982, 337-8) suggest some basic ceremonial
practices and magical beliefs while the care extended to living
handicapped members of the group, as seen in the arthritic old
man of La Chapelle-aux-Saintes (Campbell, 1976, 306) and the
man with the withered arm at Shanidar (Solecki, 1971, 212,
195-6; Trinkaus and Zimmerman, 1982) bespeaks a social
responsibility little different from our own.

Notwithstanding the above similarities with ourselves, it is clear
that Neanderthal and Neanderthal-related populations were less
efficient, biologically and culturally, and were more limited as to
what they *could* do—and wanted to do—with their technical
equipment. It is claimed that one important advantage possessed
by the early representatives of Modern Man in many regions was
the standardization of the primary form from which the stone
tools were made. That is, they were able to produce blades which
greatly facilitated the manufacture of a wide range of retouched
pieces that could be mounted in traditional ways as the working
parts of tools and weapons. At the same time, other materials
began to be much more widely used.

Although bone, antler, and ivory had been worked into simple
tools in earlier times, there is nothing older that compares with the
efficient Upper Palaeolithic bone and antler equipment. This is
also true for the unique Upper Palaeolithic cave and home art,
though the first crude attempts at engraving do occur somewhat
earlier (de Sonneville-Bordes, 1974).

Upper Palaeolithic in Europe

The first fossil evidence of Modern Man from sites in Europe
occurs in association with the early Upper Palaeolithic blade
traditions of which there are two major divisions. One is the
Chatelperronian which Bordes has shown (1972*b*) is probably
derived from the Mousterian of Acheulian tradition but which
others see as intrusive with a possible origin in south-west Asia.
The other is the Aurignacian which *could* have evolved somewhere
in eastern Europe. Because of this association it has come to be
assumed that Modern Man and the Upper Palaeolithic are indivisible. In addition, because the break between the older
industries and the early Upper Palaeolithic was considered an
abrupt one, it was assumed that the makers of the Upper Palaeo-

lithic blade tools were all moderns whereas the makers of the earlier industries—generally known as Mousterian—were all Neanderthalers. However, artefacts (cultural evidence) associated with early hominids cannot, of themselves, be used as an indicator of what kind of men made them and the morphology of artefacts is always an extremely poor indicator of the complexity of the behaviour of their makers. Moreover, ethnographic evidence shows that it is the nature of the working edges of tools alone that is significant (e.g. Hayden, 1977). It is not the actual tools that are important, therefore, but what their makers *did* with them.

Stringer's multi-variate metrical analysis (1974) of later Pleistocene crania also strongly suggests that, in Europe, the late classic Neanderthalers were not ancestral to the early Upper Palaeolithic modern population since they resemble them even less than do the earlier Neanderthalers. Possible support for this view is provided by the recent discovery in a cave at Saint-Césaire in western France, of a classic Neanderthal skeleton that is as young as or younger than 34,000 BP. However, the associated industry is not Mousterian but early Upper Palaeolithic (Chatelperronian) (Lévêque and Vandermeersch, 1980; ApSimon, 1980) confirming Bordes's (1972b) hypothesis that the Chatelperronian is evolved from the Mousterian of Acheulian tradition. However, if the modern Combe Capelle fossil also belongs with the Chatelperronian as is claimed (though there is some doubt), this does present a problem. At the same time Aurignacian assemblages and modern human remains are as old as 30,000 years and Aurignacian and Chatelperronian are sometimes found interstratified, so that it is possible that Neanderthal and *Homo sapiens sapiens* may have existed contemporaneously for a time in south-west France. Additional support, though needing confirmation, comes from another Neanderthal fossil from West Germany (Hohnöfersand) dated to about 36,000 BP which also shows some modern features (Bräuer, 1981) and from the earlier existence of the Aurignacian in eastern Europe—namely, from the Bacho Kiro cave in Bulgaria where it appears to date to as early as 43,000 BP and is claimed to be associated with fossil remains of anatomically modern appearance (ApSimon, 1980; Wolpoff, 1981, and reply by ApSimon). It is unlikely that this question of overlap between Neanderthaler and Modern Man, of transition from Mousterian to the Chatelperronian and contemporaneity of Mousterian, Chatelperronian, and Aurignacian, will be resolved until considerably closer and more refined dating evidence becomes available. Only then also will the question of origins—whether *in situ* or from external migration—

become clearer. If established opinion favours an external origin for the European Upper Palaeolithic and its makers, Modern Man, the new evidence that is becoming available could require some substantial revision or redefinition of this view.

The Middle East

In the Middle East the situation is just as complex but rather different. Here we have fossil evidence of a fully modern population associated with a Mousterian industry at Qafzeh cave in Israel (Vandermeersch, 1977). There is a very similar situation at Skhul (Mount Carmel) where the modern form is associated with Neanderthalers and, again, with a Mousterian (McCown and Keith, 1939). On the other hand, at Wadi Amud, a Neanderthal is associated with an industry considered transitional between the Middle and Upper Palaeolithic (Watanabe, 1970). These anatomically modern forms are believed to be older (40,000–50,000 BP) than the classic Neanderthalers of Europe and recent uranium series dates for Skhul cave suggest ages between 80,000 and 350,000 BP (Bar-Yosef and Goren, 1981). There is also evidence from this region of an early Upper Pleistocene blade tradition older by some 12,000–15,000 years than the Levantine Aurignacian. This evidence comes from the Negev where Marks's investigations have shown the Mousterian industries there to contain blade elements that resemble and anticipate the Upper Palaeolithic (Marks, 1977) and this is the same also in Lebanon (Copeland, 1975, 337–9). The first true blade industry immediately post-dating the Mousterian is more than 45,000 years old in the Negev (Boker Tachtit) and comprises 55 per cent of blades (Fig. 2). The tradition can be seen to continue here (Boker A) down to 27,000 years ago and its earlier stages have been correlated by McBurney (1977, 26–30) with the earliest Upper Palaeolithic at Ksar Akil (Layer 25) in Lebanon of which the estimated age is 43,000 BP. The same industry occurs at Abu Halka, also in northern Lebanon, and McBurney has gone on to demonstrate the close relationship also with the Dabban industry from Cyrenaica which, he convincingly argued, was intrusive from the Levant as well as being some 3,000 years more recent, making its first appearance around 40,000 years ago.

This early Upper Palaeolithic tradition appears appreciably earlier in the Levant than does the Aurignacian which, though inadequately dated there to around 32,000 BP, is unquestionably stratigraphically younger at Ksar Akil. In the Upper Palaeolithic

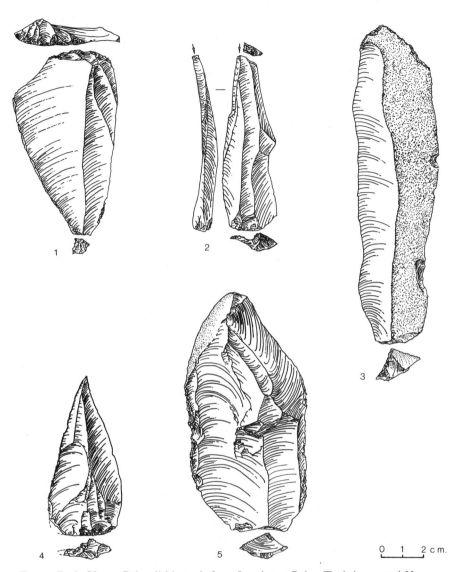

FIG. 2. Early Upper Palaeolithic tools from Level 4 at Boker Tachtit, central Negev: (1) end scraper; (2) burin on truncation; (3) distally retouched blade; (4) point; (5) modified flake. (After Marks, 1977, vol. i, pp. 69–71.)

of Iran (the Baradostian) appearing at about the same time (42,000–40,000 years ago) McBurney saw the same tradition which spread not much later to Afghanistan and thence to north central Asia and Japan (McBurney, 1975, 201–19; 1977, 30). On the other hand, the claimed antiquity of the Aurignacian in Bulgaria may be an indication of an independent development

of a second, unrelated but equally early, Upper Palaeolithic
tradition originating somewhere in eastern Europe which only
later spread to the Levant.

Outside Europe, the Middle East, and northern and central
Asia, the fossils that are ascribed to fully Modern Man, *Homo
sapiens sapiens*, are nowhere found associated with industries of
Upper Palaeolithic type, though general contemporaneity is
established. The Upper Palaeolithic blade, burin, and elaborate
bone work industries were clearly efficient and helped to support a
thriving, expanding population that was far more numerous than
that of the Neanderthalers and which occupied habitats that they
did not, or could not, use. However, in other regions where quite
different and often simpler-looking stone tool-kits were made,
anatomically modern populations also flourished, expanded, and
became ecologically diversified. Thus, it would appear that the
success of Late Pleistocene Modern Man was *not* specifically tied to
Upper Palaeolithic technology. Perhaps it was related to more
general and fundamental innovations such as improved language
capabilities and strengthened social organization.

Africa (Fig. 3)

In north-west Africa, two cave sites in coastal Morocco have now
yielded human remains in association with Aterian industries
(Débenath, 1975; Roche and Texier, 1976) (Fig. 4). The Aterian
complex is the north-west African and Saharan equivalent of the
later European, north-east African, and Levantine Mousterian
and carbon dates suggest that it is all older than 40,000 BP (Clark,
1982). The fossil remains (Ferembach, 1976a) from the Dar-es-
Soltan and Temara (ibid. 1976b) caves have fully modern
characteristics and are clearly different from and younger than
the Neanderthalers from Jebel Irhoud, with a Mousterian industry (Howell, 1982, 137–40). However, the Aterian, whose
makers were credited with the invention of the tang as an adjunct
to efficient hafting of stone working-parts, shows quite clearly its
close affiliation with the Mousterian.

Moving to the Sudan in north-east Africa, the Singa cranium is
that of another early modern hominid considered to belong in the
early Upper Pleistocene where it is contemporary with a Middle
Stone Age flake and chopper industry (Wells, 1951; Lacaille,
1951).

In eastern Ethiopia from the Porc-Epic cave, the Dire Dawa
mandible fragment for which both Neanderthaloid and Modern

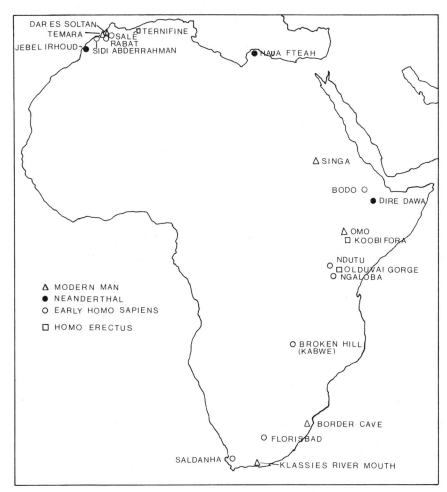

FIG. 3. Map of Africa to show location of sites with hominid fossils referred to in the text.

characteristics have been claimed (Vallois, 1951) has now been shown to be associated with a Middle Stone Age (Levallois and disc core) technology with points and side scrapers and is more than 32,000 years old (Clark and Williams, 1978). From the lower Omo valley in south-west Ethiopia come fossils with a date of around 120,000 years BP that exhibit an association of more archaic features (Omo II) with those of fully Modern Man (Omo I) (Day, 1972) and other fossils (Guombe in east Turkana and Kanjera (Oakley *et al*. 1977, 60)) contribute to the broad degree of variability which is comparable to that seen in the Middle East and early Upper Pleistocene hominids.

The nearly complete Ngaloba skull recently reported from

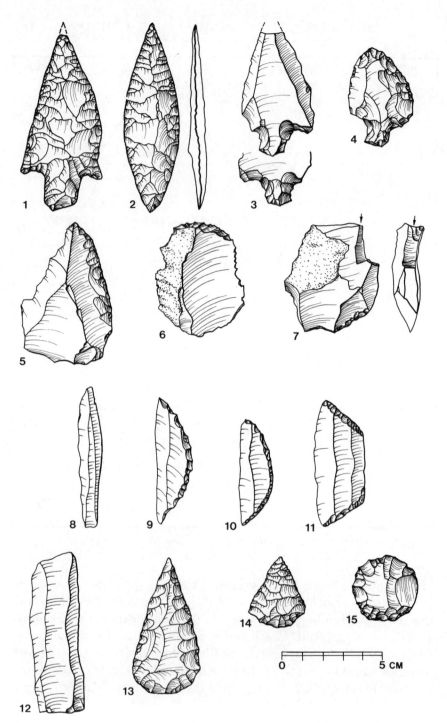

FIG. 4. *Nos. 1–7*. Aterian artefacts from sites in north-west Africa and the Sahara:
(1) pointe marocaine; (2) point; (3) tanged flake; (4) tanged scraper; (5) side scraper;
(6) end scraper; (7) burin. *Nos. 8–11*. Howieson's Poort (Epi-Pietersburg) and *nos. 12–15*.
Pietersburg artefacts from Border Cave, South Africa: (8, 12) blades; (9, 10) large
lunates; (11) trapeze; (13, 14) points; (15) scraper. (Nos. 1–7 after Clark, 1982, p. 263;
nos. 8–15 after Beaumont *et al.* 1978, p. 411.)

Laetoli, northern Tanzania (Day *et al.* 1980) is also, though robust, fully sapient. With it is a Middle Stone Age industry and Middle to early Upper Pleistocene fauna. It is associated with a volcanic tuff that also occurs at Olduvai Gorge where it is dated to 120,000 BP and where Middle Stone Age tools are again present.

The Middle Stone Age in East Africa and Ethiopia most probably begins *c.*200,000 years ago (Wendorf *et al.* 1975; Clark, 1982, 274–85) and it had most likely disappeared by 35,000 years ago while the earliest blade industries—the equivalent of the Upper Palaeolithic—are dated in the Galla Lakes region of Ethiopia to more than 27,000 years ago (Street, 1980).

In South Africa, three fossil assemblages are significant in the present context and are relatively firmly dated to the end of the Middle or the beginning of the Upper Pleistocene. The partial cranium from Florisbad in the Orange Free State probably belongs with an early Middle Stone Age industry and is now thought—on multivariate analysis—to be intermediate between the older archaic *Homo sapiens* stock (represented by Broken Hill, Saldanha, and other fossils) and modern humans (Howells, 1980, 9–11). In age it is more comparable to the early Neanderthalers of Europe (Saccopastore, Biache, and La Chaise) but may well be even older (Rightmire, 1978).

In the Klasies River Mouth complex of caves on the south coast of South Africa, human remains have been recovered from occupation layers containing the earliest Middle Stone Age assemblages resting immediately on the Last Interglacial raised beach (about 120,000 years old) from which the sea had just begun to retreat. These are fragmentary fossils but are reported as almost all anatomically modern (Rightmire, 1976). The stone industry with which they are associated is typologically early Middle Stone Age (Middle Palaeolithic), a tradition which continues, except for one abrupt break in artefact technology, for some 50,000 years. The break in question is dated between about 80,000 and 90,000 years ago and consists of an industry (Howieson's Poort Complex) made on blades with retouched tools that include backed blades, large lunates and trapezes, and various scraper forms. While blade technology dominates, artefacts in the Middle Stone Age flake-blade tradition are also present (Deacon, 1979, 87–102). There are a number of other sites in South Africa, in Lesotho (Carter and Vogel, 1974), and in Zimbabwe also (Cooke, 1971) where blade technology appears at this early time only to disappear and not reappear again until some 35,000 years later at around 25,000–20,000 years ago with the first Later Stone Age industries.

Even more significant than the Klasies River Mouth fossils are the discoveries in the Border Cave (Ingwavuma) on the edge of the escarpment in south-east Africa near the border between Natal and Swaziland (Beaumont *et al.* 1978). Here the artefacts from the lower levels are all older than 35,000 BP and belong in the Middle Stone Age tradition with again a layer containing the Howieson's Poort blade complex that divides the Middle Stone Age proper into earlier and later stages (Fig. 4). The main occupation levels span four lengthy periods of frost-weathering and, on extrapolation and correlation with the stratigraphy at Klasies River Mouth and other South African cave sequences, and oxygen isotope stages, there is reason to believe that the cave was first occupied by Middle Stone Age man at a time before the Last Interglacial (Butzer *et al.* 1978) about 195,000 years ago.

The human remains comprise a partial adult cranium, mandible, and post-cranial fragments found by a farmer digging for guano. An infant burial was excavated from a shallow grave in the top of the earlier Middle Stone Age (Pietersburg) layers just below the Howieson's Poort blade complex level and a second adult mandible comes from that level itself. The inferred age of this blade tradition level is about 90,000–95,000 BP (Butzer, 1979, comment on Rightmire) so that, if this estimate is correct, some of the fossils may be even older.

While some doubt may exist as to the level from which the specimens found by the farmer came—though it is claimed that sediment in the interior of the cranium is the same as that from the layer in which the infant burial was found—the latter and the second adult mandible appear to be dated securely in the Middle Stone Age. All these hominid fossils are anatomically modern without a trace of 'archaic' features and can be regarded as 'an already partially differentiated basal stock from which the Khoisan peoples, amongst others, ultimately arose' (Beaumont *et al.* 1978; Rightmire, 1979).

Summarizing, the fossil evidence from Africa indicates the early differentiation south of the Sahara of an 'archaic' early *sapiens* stock (represented by Broken Hill and other fossils) which appears first with the assemblages of Acheulian bifaces during the later Middle Pleistocene. By the beginning of the Upper Pleistocene an early modern population had evolved from them, represented by Singa, Omo, Klasies River Mouth, Border Cave, and other eastern and southern African fossils (Rightmire, 1981; Bräuer, 1978); they were making tools in the Middle Stone Age flake and blade tradition. In north-west Africa, individuals of fully modern appearance were also present well before 35,000 years ago. Possibly evolved from the Jebel Irhoud Neanderthal stock, they are the ancestors of the late Pleistocene populations there and were the makers of the Aterian Industrial Complex. If the dating is correct, these fossils are both older than and contemporary with the classic Neanderthalers of Europe and the modified populations of the Middle East.

The early blade industries—the Howieson's Poort in southern Africa (Deacon, 1979) and the pre-Aurignacian in Cyrenaica (McBurney, 1967, 75-104) and the Amudian in the Levant (Garrod and Kirkbride, 1961), both of the latter being stratigraphically older than the Mousterian—remain difficult to explain. However, they show clearly that some very widely dispersed populations were, by the beginning of the Upper Pleistocene, capable of devising and manufacturing blade-dominated industries with their potential for standardized preforms for a multiplicity of tool types. Whatever the technique used to make them —whether punch or direct percussion—if blades were so much superior, as has been claimed for the Upper Palaeolithic, why did not this tradition continue instead of giving way to the Mousterian flake tradition? There is, as yet, no convincing explanation supported by factual data. The reason does not appear to be ecological but one possibility that needs investigating is that, at this time, stone tools were still hand held and it was only later, during the Middle Palaeolithic, that efficient hafting techniques were developed. In such circumstances, much of the superiority of a standard blade preform might not have been so apparent and its abandonment would be more readily understandable when conditions dictated the advantage of the Mousterian flake tradition. No hominid fossils have been found with the pre-Aurignacian and Amudian in the eastern Mediterranean but the southern and eastern African fossils, as also those from the Moroccan coastal caves, show that populations within one end of the range of variability resembling modern humans were broadly dispersed in the continent well before 40,000 years ago and that they were the makers of tool-kits in both the prepared flake and blade manufacturing traditions.

Southern Asia (Fig. 5)

It is a matter for considerable regret that no hominid fossils have been recovered from the Indian peninsula that are more than 10,000 years old. They must, however, be present there when one takes into account the *Homo erectus* fossils from Java (Sangiran, Trinil, Sambungmachan) and China (Choukoutien, Lantien) and their discovery is certainly overdue. At present still, as Sir Mortimer Wheeler said twenty-two years ago, Pleistocene man's 'solitary memorial (there) is an infinitude of stones' (Wheeler, 1959, 34). The Middle Palaeolithic of India is probably no younger than 35,000 years and, in its later stages, shows a tendency to produce long blades with faceted platforms, as in the Levant.

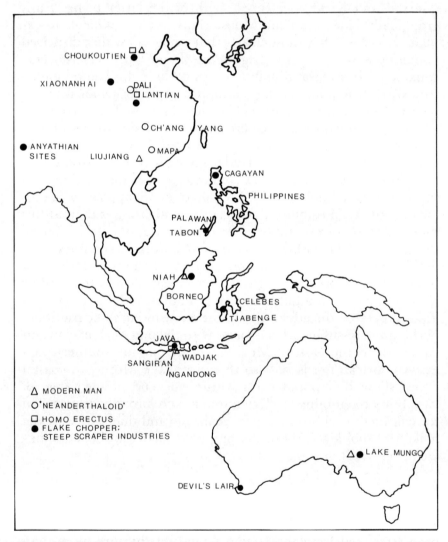

Fig. 5. Map of the Far East and Australia to show the location of sites with hominid fossils and early Upper Pleistocene artefact assemblages referred to in the text.

The earliest true blade industries there have dates showing them to be between 30,000 and 20,000 years old (Sali, 1974; Sharma *et al.* 1980; Murty, 1979), though a probably older industry from Renigunta (Murty, 1968) in south-east India, may be the equivalent of the South African Howieson's Poort Complex. In their final form, at the close of the Pleistocene, the small blade assemblages have resemblances to the Zarzian of Iraq and Iran (Sharma and Clark, 1982, 268–9). Their ancestry, therefore, may be linked with the early Upper Pleistocene blade tradition (antedating the Aurignacian) in the Levant. In the light of the Wadjak fossils from Java (Day, 1977, 310–12), that from Niah in Borneo, and the Australian fossils, we can expect to find anatomically Modern Man in India at least in a 40,000-year-old context.

The Wadjak fossils are fully modern and, though undated, they are likely to be earlier rather than later in the Upper Pleistocene. The juvenile from the great cave at Niah in Sarawak is also modern with no trace of more archaic traits (Brothwell, 1960). It is associated with artefacts and an early radiocarbon date of 40,000 BP. In view of the inferred correlation of Modern Man and Upper Palaeolithic blade industries, it is further significant that the artefacts associated with the Niah fossil, with those from the Tabon Cave on Palawan in the Phillipines (Fox, 1978) and those from Lake Mungo in Australia, bear no relationship at all to what we know as the Upper Palaeolithic (Fig. 6). The Niah artefacts are choppers and large flake tools with some worked bone (Harrisson, 1978; Shutler and Shutler, 1975, 20–2). They are comparable to other early upper Pleistocene chopper and flake assemblages from Tabon Cave and Cagayan in the Phillipines; Tjabenge in Celebes and Ngandong and Sangiran in Java as well as the Anyathian sites in Burma so that this tradition is clearly long established and very widespread in Indonesia.

Australia

Especially significant is the evidence now available for the first peopling of Australia. The three fossils now recovered from Lake Mungo belong to a horizon dated to more than 32,000 BP. They are associated with hearths and stone artefacts showing that they were burials, incidentally the oldest-known cremations, relating to temporary camp sites close to one of the many freshwater lakes existing in the interior of the continent at that time (Bowler *et al.* 1970). The most recent excavations have shown that artefacts are

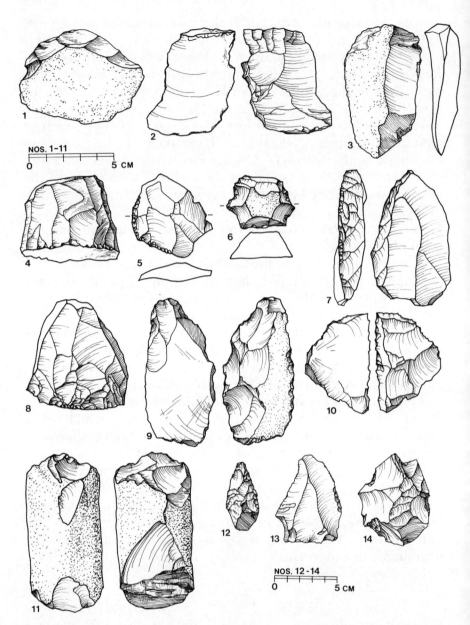

NOS. 1–11
0   5 CM

NOS. 12–14
0   5 CM

FIG. 6. *Nos. 1–4.* Flakes (1–3) and core scraper (4) of the south-east Asian Tabonian tradition. (Nos. 1–3 from Niah Cave, Sarawak and no. 4 from Tabon Cave, Palawan.) *Nos. 5–8.* Scrapers (5–7) and horsehoof core (8) of the core tool and scraper tradition from the Lake Mungo cremation site, Australia. *Nos. 9–14.* Flake tools and chopper from Locality 15, Choukoutien, northern China: (9–11) flake scrapers; (12) small core chopper; (13) point; (14) flake. (Nos. 1–3 after Shutler and Shutler, 1975; no. 4 after Fox, 1978; nos. 5–8 after Mulvaney, 1975; nos. 9–14 after Movius, 1949.)

present in the deposits up to 1.5 m below the horizon with the burials (Shawcross, 1957). Devil's Lair, Western Australia, is another such later Pleistocene occupation site (Dortch and Merrilees, 1973). There can, therefore, now be no doubt that the interior desert parts of Australia had been populated by man at least 40,000 years ago, probably considerably earlier. Moreover, these fossils show no trace of archaic *Homo erectus* characteristics but are ancestral to the present-day Australian aborigines (Shaw-cross and Kaye, 1980). The Australian artefacts comprise—to use the Australian terminology—horsehoof cores, steep edged scrapers, and flat scrapers belonging to what is termed the 'Australian core tool and scraper tradition' (Bowler *et al.* 1970, 50; Mulvaney, 1975, 172–80).

China

The evidence for the first appearance of Modern Man in mainland China is much less well dated. The recently discovered cranium from Dali (Wu Xinzhi, 1981; Howells, 1980, 7–8), associated with a late Middle Pleistocene fauna, is an example of an early *Homo sapiens* grade with characteristics intermediate between *Homo erectus* and Modern Man; so that, here again as in Europe and Africa in this time range, the 'phyletic gradualism' model is applicable. Dali man is associated with a scraper industry in flint and quartzite. The Neanderthal-like Mapa (Maba) skull and the maxillary fragment from Ch'ang-yang are not associated with artefacts but the fauna belongs in the late Middle or early late Pleistocene (Lanpo, 1980; *Atlas of Primitive Man in China*, 1980, 86–90; Aigner, 1978a, 142–3). However, other sites with the same fauna (Localities 15 and 22 at Choukoutien (*Atlas*, 1980, 61–5, 69), Xindong Cave (*Atlas*, 1980, 66–8), Gezidong Cave (*Atlas*, 1980, 82–5, for example) have all produced numerous artefacts in the flake and chopper tradition (Fig. 6, 9–14; Fig. 7). Some of the flake tools are not unlike those found with some of the African Middle Stone Age industries. Later are the Liujiang (*Atlas*, 1980, 139–42), Ziyang (*Atlas*, 1980, 147–8), and Upper Cave, Choukoutien (*Atlas*, 1980, 110–19) fossils, all are representative of early Mongoloids. Although the associated artefacts tend to be smaller, these still unquestionably belong in the flake and chopper tradition (e.g. Xiaonanhai—Hsiao-han-hai), though well-shaped bone tools also now occur (Aigner, 1978a and b; Freeman, 1977).

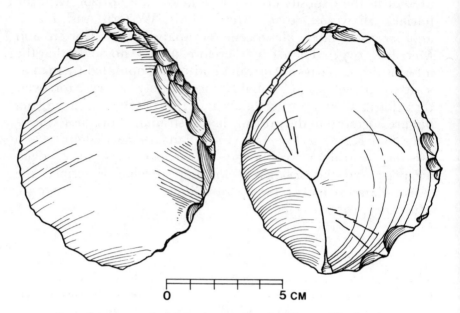

FIG. 7. Large retouched flake chopper from Locality 15, Choukoutien.
(After Movius, 1949.)

Conclusions

One undeniable conclusion to be drawn from this review is that
the available chronology (Fig. 8) suggests that fossils which are
anatomically modern appear earlier in south-east Asia where they
are associated with a flake and core culture, and in Africa where
the association is with the Middle Stone Age, than they do in
Europe or northern Asia where the cultural tradition is that of
the Upper Palaeolithic. Obviously, therefore, it is particularly
dangerous to assume that Modern Man is synonymous with
Upper Palaeolithic tools since, in large parts of the Old World,
the Upper Palaeolithic does not occur though Modern Man was
there by the early Upper Pleistocene. This is not to say that in the
regions where the Upper Palaeolithic is found such a connection is
not valid: of course it is. Though even here considerable caution
should be exercised in equating genotype and culture over the
time of transition.

In every instance in the respective continents, the hominid
fossils that date to the time of the late Middle Pleistocene (some
300,000 to 100,000 years ago) and the early Upper Pleistocene
(about 100,000 to 40,000 years ago) show features intermediate
between the older *Homo erectus* stock and the Neanderthal and

modern grades of evolution, thus demonstrating that a gradual-istic model for hominid evolution in more than one region is not inconsistent. The cultural evidence is, moreover, in accord with this in that the early *Homo sapiens sapiens* fossils are associated with markedly different technological traditions in Europe, Asia, and Africa.

The evidence presented in this review, however, might be interpreted in other ways and the one which is closest to the truth will only be determined after very much more precise dating evidence becomes available. We need to be able to place a fossil or an artefact assemblage accurately within a thousand, rather than ten thousand, years, so rapidly does it appear that both biological and cultural transformation came about. Besides refinement in conventional radiocarbon dating and the need to be able to

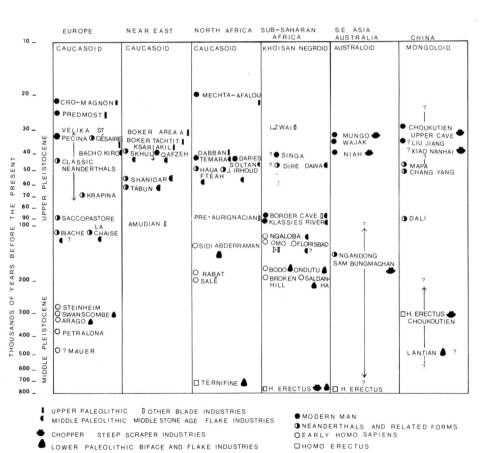

FIG. 8. Chart to show the temporal relationships of hominid fossils and artefact traditions referred to in the text.

extend the possibility of obtaining finite results back at least 100,000 years, it is necessary to date the fossils themselves *directly*. This is now possible since only a minute amount of material is needed to obtain a date. Until these improvements are realized there is little chance of obtaining the conclusive chronological evidence that will help in deciding between the 'phyletic' or the 'replacement' models (Cronin *et al.* 1981; Trinkaus and Howells, 1979; Sarich, 1971).

If—and I believe the evidence for this cannot be disputed—Modern Man evolved within the 'Neanderthal evolutionary grade' by a 'phyletic gradualism' then it was not so much the actual artefacts of his technology as the conception and manner of their use deriving from intellectual superiority made manifest through a full communication system that was responsible for the population explosion that took place some 40,000 years ago. Improved nutritional standards resulting from the new hunting and gathering strategies, increased protein intake, and a more sustained diet, favoured the spread of the genotype by shorter spacings between births and larger band size, so necessitating expanded and more intensive use of the land and its resources. Was it therefore, culture—*language* and technology—that was the catalyst behind Modern Man's dispersal? I suspect it was. At the Palaeolithic level populations must still have been sufficiently sparse, however, to have cushioned competition as there was generally somewhere to move to. Where 'empty areas' were available population spread was particularly rapid thereby lending support to the 'punctuated equilibrium' or replacement model. Such was the case in the Congo basin after the recession of the forests with the onset of the Last Glacial (Clark, 1980, 45). Or again, in the populating of the Americas where groups of hunters crossed the Bering Strait at least 14,000 years ago and, by 9,500 years ago, had reached the tip of South America some 14,000 km away (Haynes, 1969). The open nature of the continually changing group composition in hunting and gathering societies can be expected to have set up a chain reaction very advantageous to dispersal of genes and technological skill. This is likely to have led, if the 'replacement' model has validity, to hybridization with pre-existing populations so that, by social selection, the more archaic genotypes were eliminated. A similar diffusion of genes and cultural technology is to be seen in the much later spread of food production into Europe from the Near East (Ammerman and Cavalli-Sforza, 1971), by way of the 'bow wave' which left also in its wake pockets of older peoples and technology that changed more slowly in less favourable habitats. Another comparable example is the equally rapid spread of Iron Age/Bantu-speaking populations in sub-Saharan Africa in the first few centuries of the present era (Phillipson, 1975; Van Noten, 1982). The mechanism whereby Modern Man spread throughout the world is, therefore, not so much in question as the sequence of events whereby this came about.

In these earliest Upper Pleistocene human fossils exhibiting a blending of archaic and modern characteristics, are we witnessing a trend towards the modern form to which the full transformation took place by evolutionary gradualism in several areas of Africa, Asia, and, perhaps, Europe? or was this transition effected only once? in which case, many of these intermediate populations must have become extinct. Only better dated, more complete and culturally associated fossils can provide the answer. The replacement model might favour eastern Africa and the Middle East as a single or two separate regions of differentiation and dispersal. Here fully modern representatives make an earlier appearance and the demonstrated variability would indicate that these were areas close to the centre of speciation (Thorne, 1980). The incompleteness of the evidence does not, however, rule out southern Asia or the Far East though, taken as a whole, intermediate fossil forms and the associated industrial diversity in each region suggest that both the biological and cultural data better support a model of 'evolutionary gradualism' that might have been hastened or sometimes overlain by migration or replacement. One thing at least is clear—that one must not confuse acculturation, on the one hand, with biological change, on the other. These are separate issues and are not *necessarily* related.

If this discussion must close on a note of uncertainty as regards the fossils themselves, I hope I have shown that the search for the source of the Upper Palaeolithic may be in the nature of a red herring where it comes to looking for the *origins*, as opposed to the *later spread*, in certain parts of the world, of the modern genotype. This is one of the most intriguing problems in palaeoanthropology today and a systematic programme of interdisciplinary and international investigation of the Asian tropics is long overdue. This is probably the most pressing need in this field and is certain to bring exciting and decisive new discoveries and rewards that will enable us to re-evaluate the existing data. When such a programme has got under way, when investigation in Africa is intensified and the chronologies have been improved, then we can expect that the uncertainties prevailing today will be considerably reduced. Our interpretative models will be narrowed down and the 'new men, strange faces, other minds' that the record reveals and that Sir Bedivere was so worried about, will assume their true significance and relationship and the sequence of events whereby 'the old order changeth yielding place to new' (Tennyson: 'Morte d'Arthur') will in time be much better understood.

Note. Grateful thanks are recorded here to my colleagues Glynn Ll. Isaac and Timothy D. White who kindly read the manuscript at different stages and made very helpful comments; to Jane Dill and Judith Ogden for the illustrations; and to my wife for the final typing of the lecture.

REFERENCES

AIGNER, J. S. (1978a). 'Pleistocene faunal and cultural stations in south China.' *In* F. Ikawa-Smith (ed.), *Early Palaeolithic in South and East Asia* (Mouton, The Hague), pp. 129–62.
—— (1978b). 'Important archaeological remains from north China.' Ibid., pp. 163–232.
AMMERMAN, A. and CAVALLI-SFORZA, L. L. (1971). 'Measuring the rate of spread of early farming in Europe', *Man*, vol. 6, pp. 674–88.
APSIMON, A. M. (1980). 'The last Neanderthals in France?' *Nature*, vol. 287, pp. 271–2.
Atlas of Primitive Man in China (1980). Science Press, Beijing, China.
BAR-YOSEF, O. and GOREN, N. (1981). 'Notes on the chronology of the Lower Palaeolithic in the southern Levant.' *In* J. D. Clark and G. Ll. Isaac (comp.). Las industrias más antiguas pre-acheulense y Acheulense, Preprint, Comisión VI, *X Congreso UISPP* (Mexico, Oct. 1981), pp. 28–42.
BEAUMONT, P. B., DE VILLIERS, H., and VOGEL, J. C. (1978). 'Modern Man in sub-Saharan Africa prior to 49,000 years BP: A review and evaluation with particular reference to Border Cave', *S. Afr. J. Sci.*, vol. 74, pp. 409–19.
BERGOUNIOUX, F. M. (1958). '"Spiritualité" de l'homme de Néanderthal.' *In* G. H. R. von Koenigswald (ed.), *Hundert Jahre Neanderthaler—Neanderthal Centenary 1856–1956* (Utrecht), pp. 151–66.
BLANC, A. C. (1958). 'Torre in Pietra, Saccopastore, Monte Circeo. On the position of the Mousterian culture in the Pleistocene sequence of the Rome area'. Ibid., pp. 167–74.
BORDES, F. (ed.) (1972a). *The Origin of* Homo Sapiens. UNESCO, Paris.
—— (1972b). 'Du Paléolithique moyen au Paléolithique supérieur: Continuité ou discontinuité?' Ibid., pp. 211–18.
BOULE, M. (1911–13). 'L'Homme fossile de La Chapelle-aux-Saintes', *Annales de Paléontologie*, nos. 6, 7, and 8.
BOWLER, J. M., JONES, RHYS, ALLEN, H., and THORNE, A. G. (1970). 'Pleistocene human remains from Australia: A living site and human cremations from Lake Mungo, Western New South Wales', *World Archaeology*, vol. 2, pp. 39–59.
BRÄUER, G. (1978). 'The morphological differentiation of anatomically

modern man in Africa with special regard to recent finds in East Africa', *Z. Morph. Anthrop.*, vol. 69 (3), pp. 266–92.

—— (1981). 'New evidence on the transitional period between Neanderthal and modern man', *J. of Human Evolution*, vol. 10, pp. 467–74.

BROTHWELL, D. R. (1960). 'Upper Pleistocene human skull from Niah Caves', *The Sarawak Journal*, vol. 9 (15–16 NS), pp. 323–49.

BUTZER, K. (1979). 'Comment on Rightmire, 1979', *Current Anthropology*, vol. 20 (1), p. 28.

—— BEAUMONT, P. B., and VOGEL, J. C. (1978). 'Lithostratigraphy of Border Cave, Kwazulu, South Africa: A Middle Stone Age sequence beginning *c*.195,000 BP', *J. Archaeol. Sci.*, vol. 5, pp. 317–41.

CAMPBELL, B. G. (ed.) (1976). *Humankind Emerging*. Little Brown, Boston.

CARTER, P. L. and VOGEL, J. C. (1974). 'The dating of industrial assemblages from stratified sites in eastern Lesotho', *Man* (NS), vol. 9, pp. 557–70.

CLARK, J. D. (1975). 'Africa in prehistory: Peripheral or paramount?', *Man*, vol. 10 (2), pp. 175–98.

—— (1980). 'Early human occupation of African savanna environments.' *In* D. R. Harris (ed.), *Human Ecology in Savanna Environments* (London), pp. 41–72.

—— (1982). 'The cultures of the Middle Palaeolithic/Middle Stone Age.' *In* J. D. Clark (ed.), *The Cambridge History of Africa, Volume I: From the earliest times to c.500 BC* (Cambridge), pp. 148–341.

—— and WILLIAMS, M. A. J. (1978). 'Recent archaeological research in south-eastern Ethiopia (1974–1975): Some preliminary results', *Annales d'Éthiopie*, vol. 9 (Addis Ababa), pp. 19–44.

COOKE, C. K. (1971). 'Excavation at Zombepata Cave, Sipolilo District, Mashonaland, Rhodesia', *S. Afr. Archaeol. Bull.*, vol. 26, pp. 104–27.

COPELAND, L. (1975). 'The Middle and Upper Palaeolithic of Lebanon and Syria in the light of recent work.' *In* F. Wendorf and A. E. Marks (ed.), *Problems in Prehistory: North Africa and the Levant* (Dallas), pp. 317–50.

CRONIN, J. E., BOAZ, N. T., STRINGER, C. B., and RAK, Y. (1981). 'Tempo and mode in hominid evolution', *Nature*, vol. 292, pp. 113–22.

DAY, M. H. (1972). 'The Omo human skeletal remains.' *In* F. Bordes (ed.), *The Origin of Homo Sapiens* (Paris), pp. 31–5.

—— (1977). *Guide to Fossil Man*, (3rd edn.), Chicago.

—— LEAKEY, M. D., and MAGORI, C. (1980). 'A new hominid fossil skull (LH 18) from the Ngaloba Beds, Laetoli, northern Tanzania', *Nature*, vol. 284, pp. 55–6.

DEACON, J. (1979). *Guide to Archaeological Sites in the Southern Cape*. Mimeograph, Southern African Association of Archaeologists Excursion, 30 June–4 July, 1979.

DÉBENATH, A. (1975). 'Découverte de restes humains probablement atériens à Dar-es-Soltane (Maroc)', *C.r. hebd. Séanc. Acad. Sci.* (Paris, 281-D), pp. 875–6.

DORTCH, C. E. and MERRILEES, D. (1973). 'Human occupation of Devil's Lair, Western Australia, during the Pleistocene', *Arch. and Phys. Anth. in Oceania*, vol. 8 (2), pp. 90–115.

FEREMBACH, D. (1976a). 'Les restes humains atériens de Témara (campagne 1975)', *Bull. Mém. Soc. Anthrop. Paris*, ser. 13, vol. 3, pp. 175–80.

—— (1976b). 'Les restes humains de la Grotte de Dar-es-Soltane 2 (Maroc) campagne 1975', ibid., pp. 183–93.

Fox, R. B. (1978). 'The Philippine Palaeolithic.' *In* F. Ikawa-Smith (ed.), *Early Palaeolithic in South and East Asia* (Mouton, The Hague), pp. 59–86.

Freeman, L. G. (1977). 'Palaeolithic archaeology and Palaeoanthropology in China.' *In* W. W. Howells and P. J. Tsuchitani (eds.), *Palaeoanthropology in the People's Republic of China* (Nat. Acad. Sci., Washington), pp. 79–113.

Garrod, D. A. E. and Kirkbride, D. (1961). 'Excavation of Abri Zumoffen, A Palaeolithic rockshelter near Adlun in south Lebanon, 1958', *Bull. Musée de Beyrouth*, vol. 16, pp. 7–45.

Harrisson, T. (1978). 'Present status and problems for Palaeolithic studies in Borneo and adjacent islands.' *In* F. Ikawa-Smith (ed.), *Early Palaeolithic in South and East Asia* (Mouton, The Hague), pp. 37–57.

Hayden, B. (1977). 'Stone tool functions in the Western Desert.' *In* R. V. S. Wright (ed.), *Stone Tools as Cultural Markers* (Canberra), pp. 178–88.

Haynes, C. V. (1969). 'The earliest Americans', *Science*, vol. 166, pp. 709–15.

Hedges, R. E. M. and Moore, C. B. (1978). 'Enrichment of 14C and radio-carbon dating', *Nature*, vol. 276, pp. 255–7.

Howell, F. C. (1982). 'Origins and evolution of the African Hominidae'. *In* J. D. Clark (ed.), *The Cambridge History of Africa, Volume I: From the Earliest Times to c.500 BC* (Cambridge), pp. 70–156.

Howells, W. W. (1973). *Evolution of the Genus Homo.* Menlo Park, California.

—— (1977). 'Hominid fossils.' *In* W. W. Howells and P. J. Tsuchitani (eds.), *Palaeoanthropology in the People's Republic of China* (Nat. Acad. Sci., Washington), pp. 66–78.

—— (1980). '*Homo erectus*—who, when and where: A survey', *Yearbook of Phys. Anthrop.*, vol. 23, pp. 1–23.

Jacob, T. (1976). 'The puzzle of Solo man.' *In* G. J. Bartstra and W. A. Casparie (eds.), *Modern Quaternary Research in southern Asia* (Rotterdam), vol. 4, pp. 31–40.

Koenigswald, G. H. R. von (1958). 'Der Solo-Mensch von Java: ein tropischer Neanderthaler.' *In* G. H. R. von Koenigswald (ed.), *Hundert Jahre Neanderthaler—Neanderthal Centenary 1856–1956* (Utrecht), pp. 21–6.

Lacaille, A. D. (1951). 'The Stone Age industry of Singa.' *In* A. J. Arkell, D. M. A. Bate, L. H. Wells, and A. D. Lacaille (eds.), *The Pleistocene Fauna of Two Blue Nile Sites* (British Museum (Nat. Hist.), London, Fossil Mammals of Africa, No. 2), pp. 43–50.

Lanpo. J. (1980). *Early Man in China.* Foreign Languages Press, Beijing, China.

Lévêque, F. and Vandermeersch, B. (1980). 'Les découvertes de restes humains dans un horizon castelperronien de Sainte-Césaire (Charente-Maritime)', *Bull Soc. Préhist. Franç.*, vol. 79, p. 35.

Lieberman, P. and Crelin, E. S. (1971). 'On the speech of Neanderthal man', *Linguistic Enquiry*, vol. 2, pp. 203–22.

McBurney, C. B. M. (1967). *The Haua Fteah (Cyrenaica) and the Stone Age of the south-east Mediterranean.* Cambridge.

—— (1975). 'Early man in the Soviet Union: The Implications of some recent discoveries', Albert Reckitt Archaeological Lecture, *Proc. British Acad.*, pp. 172–221.

—— (1977). *Archaeology and the Homo sapiens sapiens Problem in Northern Africa.* Kroon Memorial Lecture, 1977, Netherlands Museum for Anthropology and Prehistory, Amsterdam, Haarlem.

McCown, T. D. and Keith, A. (1939). *The Stone Age of Mount Carmel, Vol. II The Fossil Human Remains from the Levalloi–Mousterian.* Oxford.

MARKS, A. E. (1977). 'The Upper Palaeolithic sites of Boker Tachtit and Boker: A preliminary report.' *In* A. E. Marks (ed.), *Prehistory and Palaeoenvironments in the Central Negev*, vol. i (Israel, Dallas), pp. 61–80.

MOVIUS, H. L. (1949). 'The Lower Palaeolithic cultures of southern and eastern Asia', *Trans. Amer. Philosophical Soc.*, ns, vol. 38 (4), pp. 329–420.

—— (1953). 'The Mousterian cave of Teshik-Tash, south-eastern Uzbekistan, Central Asia', *Amer. School of Prehist. Res. Bull.* vol. 17, pp. 11–71.

MULLER, R. A. (1977). 'Radioisotope dating with a cyclotron', *Science*, vol. 196, pp. 489–94.

MULVANEY, D. J. (1975). *The Prehistory of Australia* (rev. edn.). Penguin Books, Harmondsworth.

MURTY, M. L. K. (1968). 'Blade and burin industries near Renigunta on the southeast coast of India', *Proc. Prehist. Soc.*, vol. 34, pp. 83–101.

—— (1979). 'Recent research on the Upper Palaeolithic in India', *Jour. Field Archaeol.*, vol. 6 (3), pp. 301–20.

OAKLEY, K. P., CAMPBELL, B. G., and MOLLESON, T. I. (1977). *Catalogue of Fossil Hominids, Part I, East Africa* (2nd edn.), London.

PHILLIPSON, D. W. (1975). 'The chronology of the Iron Age in Bantu Africa', *Jour. Afr. Hist.*, vol. 16, pp. 321–42.

RIGHTMIRE, G. P. (1976). 'Relationships of Middle and Upper Pleistocene hominids from sub-Saharan Africa', *Nature*, vol. 260, pp. 238–40.

—— (1978). 'Florisbad and human population succession in southern Africa', *Amer. Jour. Phys. Anthrop.*, vol. 48 (4), pp. 475–86.

—— (1979). 'The implications of Border Cave skeletal remains for later Pleistocene human evolution', *Current Anthropology*, vol. 20 (1), pp. 23–35.

—— (1981). 'Later Pleistocene hominids of eastern and southern Africa.' *In* J. Jelinek (ed.), *Homo Erectus and his time, II, Anthropologie*, vol. 19 (1), pp. 15–26.

ROCHE, J. and TEXIER, J.-P. (1976). 'Découverte de restes humains dans un niveau atérien supérieur de la grotte des Contrebandiers à Témara (Maroc)', *C.r. hebd. Séanc. Acad. Sci.* (Paris, 282-D), pp. 45–7.

SALI, S. A. (1974). 'Upper Palaeolithic research since Independence', *Bull. Deccan Coll. Research Inst.*, vol. 34 (1–4), pp. 154–8.

SARICH, V. (1971). 'Human variation in an evolutionary perspective.' *In* P. Dolhinow and V. Sarich (eds.), *Background for Man* (Boston), pp. 182–91.

SHARMA, G. R. and CLARK, J. D. (eds.) (1982). *Palaeoenvironments and Prehistory in the Middle Son Valley, Madhya Pradesh, North Central India*. Allahabad, India.

—— MISRA, V. D., MANDAL, D., MISRA, B. B., and PAL, J. N. (1980). *Beginnings of Agriculture*. Allahabad, India.

SHAWCROSS, W. (1975). 'Thirty thousand years and more', *Hemisphere: Asian Australian Monthly*, vol. 19 (6), pp. 26–31.

—— and KAYE, M. (1980). 'Australian archaeology: Implications of current interdisciplinary research', *Interdisciplinary Science Reviews*, vol. 5 (2), pp. 112–28.

SHUTLER, R. and SHUTLER, M. E. (1975). *Oceanic Prehistory*. Menlo Park, California.

SOLECKI, R. S. (1971). *Shanidar: The First Flower People*. New York.

SONNEVILLE-BORDES, D. DE (1974). 'The Upper Palaeolithic c.33,000–10,000 BC.' *In* S. Piggott, G. Daniel, and C. B. M. McBurney (eds.), *France Before the Romans* (London), pp. 30–60.

STREET, F. A. (1980). 'Chronology of late Pleistocene and Holocene lake-level fluctuations, Ziway-Shala basin, Ethiopia.' *In* R. E. F. Leakey and B. A. Ogot (eds.), *Proc. 8th Pan-African Congress on Prehistory and Quaternary Studies, Nairobi, Sept. 1977* (Nairobi), pp. 143–6.

STRINGER, C. B. (1974). 'Population relationships of later Pleistocene hominids: A multivariate study of available crania', *Journ. Archaeol. Sci.*, vol. 1, pp. 317–42.

—— (1981). 'The dating of European Middle Pleistocene hominids and the existence of *Homo erectus* in Europe'. *In* J. Jelinek (ed.), *Homo erectus and His Time, II, Anthropologie*, vol. 19 (1), pp. 3–14.

THORNE, A. G. (1980). 'The centre and the edge: The significance of Australasian hominids to African palaeoanthropology.' *In* R. E. F. Leaky and B. A. Ogot (eds.), *Proc. 8th Pan-African Congress on Prehistory and Quaternary Studies, Nairobi, Sept. 1977* (Nairobi), pp. 180–1.

TRINKAUS, E. and HOWELLS, W. W. (1979). 'The Neanderthalers', *Scientific American*, vol. 241 (6), pp. 118–33.

—— and ZIMMERMAN, M. R. (1982). 'Trauma among the Shanidar Neanderthals', *Amer. J. Phys. Anthrop.*, vol. 57, pp. 61–76.

VALLOIS, H. V. (1951). 'La mandibule humaine fossile de la grotte du Porc-Epic près Dire Daoua (Abyssinie)', *L'Anthropologie* (Paris), vol. 55, pp. 231–8.

VANDERMEERSCH, B. (1977). *Les hommes fossiles de Qafzeh (Israël)*. Vols. I and II, D.Sc. thesis, Université Pierre et Marie Curie, Paris, 6, CNRS.

VAN NOTEN, F. (1982). *The Archaeology of Central Africa*. Graz, Austria.

WATANABE, H. (1970). 'A palaeolithic industry from the Amud cave.' *In* H. Suzuki and F. Takai (eds.), *The Amud Man and His Cave Site* (Tokyo), pp. 77–114.

WELLS, L. H. (1951). 'The fossil human skull from Singa.' *In* A. J. Arkell, D. M. A. Bate, L. H. Wells, and A. D. Lacaille (eds.), *The Pleistocene Fauna of Two Blue Nile Sites* (British Museum (Nat. Hist.), London, Fossil Mammals of Africa, No. 2), pp. 29–42.

WENDORF, F., LAURY, R. L., ALBRITTEN, C. C., SCHILD, R., HAYNES, C. V., DAMON, P., SHAFFIQUILLAH, M., and SCARBOROUGH, R. (1975). 'Dates for the Middle Stone Age of East Africa', *Science*, vol. 187, pp. 740–2.

WHEELER, SIR M. (1954). *Archaeology from the Earth*. Harmondsworth.

—— (1959). *Early India and Pakistan to Ashoka*. London.

WOLPOFF, M. H. (1981). 'Allez Néanderthal' and Reply by A. M. ApSimon, *Nature*, vol. 289, pp. 823–4.

WU XINZHI (1981). 'A well-preserved cranium of an archaic type of early *Homo sapiens* from Dali, China', *Scientia Sinica*, vol. 24 (4), pp. 530–9.

REALISTIC ART IN ALEXANDRIA

By PROFESSOR NIKOLAUS HIMMELMANN

Read 15 October 1981

IT is now almost a century since Theodor Schreiber started his crusade for the discovery of Alexandrian art. In his first article in *Athenische Mitteilungen* in 1885 he maintained, among other things, that the metropolis on the Nile had been the true birth-place of Hellenistic genre in painting and sculpture.[1] The evidence he produced was not very impressive, consisting of a few original bronzes from Alexandria in the Dimitriou Collection in Athens, which he had not even seen himself. He suggested, however, that famous genre sculptures in Rome like the so-called shepherdess in the Palazzo degli Conservatori were also Alexandrian works.

As is well known Schreiber's provocative thesis met with a very strong reaction. His opponents immediately and rightly objected that the interest in realistic topics was a common trait of Hellenistic culture and art and not at all confined to just one part of the Hellenistic world.[2] There followed lengthy polemics on the question, whether such masterpieces of Hellenistic realism as the Fisherman in the Vatican or the Drunken Woman in Munich had their origin in Alexandria or in Asia Minor. Not one of these problems was solved and still in 1950 in his handbook on Greek sculpture Lippold philosophically remarked: 'Of the types representing everyday people some go back to Alexandria, others certainly belong to Asia Minor.'[3]

Returning to these questions I would like to begin with some observations about those sculptures which have been passed down through ancient copies. I must say, however, beforehand that regarding this group I have no decisive arguments either and cannot solve the problem for any given case. Nevertheless it may be useful to rehearse some of the existing evidence. The origin of the Drunken Woman is mostly sought in Asia Minor, since Pliny

[1] *Athenische Mitteilungen*, 10 (1885), pp. 380 ff., 391.
[2] e.g. G. Cultrera, *Saggi sull'arte ellenistica* (1907).
[3] G. Lippold, *Griechische Plastik* (1950), p. 331.

mentions a statue of that type in Smyrna.[1] This hint is seemingly corroborated by the fact that the influence of the Drunken Woman can already be detected in the art of Asia Minor at the turn of the third and second century BC.[2] But whether these observations can decide the question seems doubtful. The ivy-crowned lagynos, which the old drunkard is hugging in her lap, had a special meaning for Alexandria where the popular feast of the Lagynophoria was named from it.[3] The vase reappears with a type of small bronze showing a hunchback on the way to the picnic connected with the feast. Pl. VII*d* is an early example of the series recently acquired by our Akademisches Kunstmuseum in Bonn.[4] In his left hand the bald-headed cripple holds a basket with victuals and a cock for sacrifice; in his right he is carrying the lagynos. Bronzes of this type were very popular in the Hellenistic world and were reproduced still in the first century BC. One example was even excavated in Strasburg, considered to be an Alexandrian import rather than a Gaulish imitation (another such specimen was found in Augst near Basle). That a creation like the Drunken Woman is possible in Alexandria typologically as well as stylistically may be proved by a plastercast from Memphis in Hildesheim, which still belongs to the third century and represents the same figure squatting on the ground and with the same heavy and ornament-like folds in her garment.[5] The extremely fine ivy pattern in the background makes it clear that this picture also is to be seen in a Dionysiac setting. Controversial as the arguments are, I dare not decide whether Alexandria or Asia Minor has a better claim to the statue.

The situation is almost the same as with the spinario of the Castellani type, the influence of which on the art of Asia Minor is proved beyond all doubt by the well-known caricature in terracotta from Priene in Berlin which dates from the late second century.[6] Despite this evidence, however, it should not be forgotten that there are strong arguments for Alexandria as well. I am thinking not only of the structural relationship between the spinario and Alexandrian statuettes, like the bronze beggar in Berlin, whom we shall discuss later, but of even closer similarities.

---

[1] *NH* xxxvi. 33. Cf. Cultrera, loc. cit., pp. 72 f.

[2] Himmelmann, *Drei hellenistische Bronzen in Bonn* (1975), pp. 17 f.

[3] O. Rubensohn, *Archäol. Anzeiger*, 44 (1929), 204 ff.

[4] Bonn, inv. no. C 656. Cf. Ch. Picard, *Gallia*, 16 (1958), 183 ff.

[5] C. Reinsberg, 'Studien zur hellenistischen Toreutik' = *Hildesheimer ägyptologische Beiträge*, 9 (1980), 321, no. 57, Abb. 82.

[6] Himmelmann, loc. cit., pp. 26 ff.

The head may be compared to the terracotta fragment in the Benaki Museum, which has tentatively been identified with Philopator, in whose reign I am sure the prototype of the spinario is to be dated.[1] As to imitations, there are several of them from Egypt—for example, a statuette in Hartford, whose Egyptian origin is likely because of the material used.[2]

A third magnificent masterpiece of Hellenistic realism, the Fisherman in the Vatican, was well known in Asia Minor as is shown by numerous copies from imperial times.[3] The excellent head in the Konya Museum is perhaps the best replica in the whole tradition. On the other hand, the earliest hint of the statue is found on a sherd from Alexandria, allegedly in Dresden.[4] It belongs to a very rare species of relief vases, which to my knowledge has not as yet been described and classified, but whose origin in the third century cannot be doubted. Obviously the fragment reproduces a kindred type of figure with loincloth, stooping frontally and standing with parallel legs. The Fisherman, whose origin in my opinion must be sought in the late rather than in the early third century, is one of the most influential creations of Hellenistic art. The impression this statue made on contemporaries is even testified to by an Athenian witness, i.e. the magnificent terracotta from the Kerameikos, which cannot be much later than the prototype.[5] Unfortunately it is a stray find without context and still unpublished (Pl. XI*d*).

Among the less well-known works of Hellenistic realism I would like to mention the obvious similarity which exists between the head of a peasant or fisherman in Dresden and a terracotta fragment from Alexandria in Budapest.[6]

These sculptures, of big or moderate size and known to us through copies, do show connections with Alexandria, but the evidence is ambiguous and other centres may raise their claims as well. A clearer answer may be expected from the original statuettes in bronze, faience and terracotta, which exist in great numbers. As for the bronzes, their provenance is mostly unknown

[1] H. Kyrieleis, *Bildnisse der Ptolemäer* (1975), pl. 39. 3, 4.

[2] Himmelmann, *Drei hellenistische Bronzen in Bonn*, pls. 18, 19*a*.

[3] Th. Wiegand, 'Torso eines Fischers aus Aphrodisias' = *Jahrbuch der Preußischen Kunstsammlungen* (1916), 1. The head in Konya, *The Art Bulletin*, 9. 69, figs. 126–7.

[4] *Expedition v. Sieglin*, ii. 3, pl. xxvi. 1.

[5] Photograph no. KER 10073–4 of the German Archaeological Institute in Athens.

[6] Terracotta Budapest inv. no. T. 376. Dresden Hermann 178 = Brunn-Bruckmann, pl. 395. 1.

but in many cases their Alexandrian origin can be demonstrated by technical criteria. Alexandrian bronzes are rarely touched up or polished after the casting process, but usually show the dull wax-like surface of the original model.[1] Closely related to the bronzes are the figurines of faience and terracotta, which may be assigned to Alexandria on material, technical, and iconographical grounds. Since on this occasion the terracottas are my main interest, I will make only a few remarks about the bronzes.

Specialities of the Alexandrian workshops are the exquisite, small bronzes of crippled beggars and hunchbacks, which obviously served as apotropaic table decoration. A related type of dwarf figurine is once mentioned as a $\pi \acute{a} \tau a \iota \kappa o s$ $\dot{\epsilon} \pi \iota \tau \rho a \pi \acute{\epsilon} \zeta \iota o s$.[2] The attribution is controversial in the case of the famous statuette in Berlin, its origin having been sought in Asia Minor as well as in Alexandria.[3] The problem is easily decided by a fragment of faience in Geneva showing a head very similar to that of the bronze in Berlin.[4] The motif of the whole figurine was probably also the same, since a small remnant gives evidence that the cripple touched his chin with one of his fingers. The bronze in Berlin has its nearest relative in a statuette of the Hamburg museum, which has not yet been attributed to any known school.[5] The picture of the crippled idiot here reaches the utmost macabre pathos, very reminiscent of similar tendencies in the Hellenistic epigram. That it too comes from Alexandria is proved by similar heads from Memphis in the Petrie Museum of London University College.[6] The elongated skull is clearly an Egyptian element as is the small pigtail at the back of the head. Dorothy Thompson has made a very good case for the Alexandrian origin of the dancer in the Baker collection, which, because of modern cleaning but also because of its exceptionally high artistic quality, defies the usual technical criteria.[7] Among other arguments used, Dorothy Thompson has shown that the thin veil covering the face is a detail often found in Alexandrian terracotta figurines. Her impression is corroborated by a wonderful faience fragment in London Uni-

[1] Kyrieleis, *Antike Plastik*, xii (1973), 138.

[2] Pauly–Wissowa, *Real-Encycl.* xviii. 2, 2551.

[3] K. A. Neugebauer, *Die griechischen Bronzen der klassischen Zeit und des Hellenismus* (1951), no. 62, pl. 30.

[4] Geneva, inv. no. 13225.

[5] D. G. Mitten–S. F. Doeringer, *Master Bronzes from the Classical World* (1967–8), no. 116.

[6] G. M. A. Richter, *Coll. Latomus*, 48 (1960), pl. 26, figs. 129–30.

[7] *AJA* 54 (1950), 371 ff.

versity College (Pls. X*a*, *b*).[1] It belongs to the still unpublished finds from Petrie's excavations in Memphis and makes especially refined use of the motif, showing beneath the veil the features of an attractive negroid woman. The fragment seems to represent *in nuce* the refinement of Alexandrian life, the enchantment of which is so often attested by ancient authors. I take the opportunity to attribute to Alexandria a small bronze in Baltimore showing a figure of uncertain sex in a garment with long sleeves.[2] I think the type is identical with that of a big marble statuette in Florence.[3] The Alexandrian provenance of this piece was long ago demonstrated by Amelung. The meaning is controversial and I cannot offer a new interpretation. The very rough surface is typical of Alexandrian bronzes. Compared to the Florence marble with its flat, one-dimensional view, the statuette in Baltimore shows a more complicated composition and a more plastic treatment of the garments; it is obviously the older one.

I must leave the bronzes since today I am mostly concerned with the Alexandrian terracottas of which there are considerable numbers but which offer great difficulties for classification. At a first glance there are two large groups.[4] The terracottas from the early cemeteries like Sciatbi and Hadra are usually of tolerable artistic quality but they only show types which are also known from the repertoire of the Greek homelands. Realistic and Egyptianizing statuettes seem to be lacking. On the other hand, we have huge numbers of that coarse material called 'Fayumi', which are perhaps the most ugly products of ancient art. In this group realistic and Egyptian features are very prominent indeed. The term 'Fayumi' originally meant terracotta figurines coming from the oasis of that name. Many authors still use it as a geographical term to mark the presumed difference between the coarse products of the province, the χώρα, and the more refined manufacture of the metropolis. I am not going to deny that there is such a difference, but on the whole this concept is misleading. Fayumi-like terracottas have also been found in Alexandria itself and in the fashionable resort of Kanopos, so that it is much more likely that the phenomenon marks a chronological rather than a geographical difference. The transition from the earlier group to the later

---

[1] Inv. no. UC 2321.

[2] D. Kent Hill, *Cat. of Classical Bronze Sculpture in the Walters Art Gallery* (1949), pl. 33, no. 139.

[3] M. Bieber, *Sculpture of the Hellenistic Age*[2], fig. 333. From this statuette it is obvious that a male figure is meant.

[4] R. A. Higgins, *Greek Terracottas* (1967), pp. 129 ff.

one is difficult to detect and has even been denied by such a
connoisseur as Gerhard Kleiner. He hypothetically maintained
that there was a gap in the tradition and that the manufacture in
Alexandria was reopened only in the middle of the first century BC
under the influence of Myrina in Asia Minor. On an historical
basis this is anything but convincing. So our main task will be to
inquire whether there are not still realistic or Egyptianizing
terracottas which can be dated to the period, let us say between
250 and 175 BC. For that purpose we shall mostly use stylistic
arguments, but we have some criteria based on materials too.
Very often early Alexandrian terracottas are made from imported
clay. Small statuettes are usually made of it alone; for bigger ones
it is mixed with cheap local material.

For reasons of both style and material an old servant in Berlin
may be accepted as an Alexandrian work of the third century,
as has been proposed by Hanna Philipp.[2] The block-like composition and the heavy treatment of the garments are very near to
that of the well-known marble statuette of a servant in the Therme
Museum in Rome.[3] This type has already been vindicated for
Alexandria by earlier authors on the basis, however, of erroneous
assumptions. It is nevertheless interesting that a fragment of a
variant in the Vatican shows the old woman with a statuette of
Harpocrates in her arm.[4] This, of course, is not sufficient to attribute the original type to the Alexandrian school.

Before considering the next type, I would like to look at two
terracotta heads, the meaning of which is not yet clear. The
fragment in Budapest (Pl. III*c, d*) seemingly wears a ribbon and is
distinguished by its very individual features.[5] For these reasons
it has been identified with a late-Hellenistic ruler. Next to it we
have a head excavated in Alexandria and of the typical local
material, according to Perdrizet who published the piece in the
catalogue of the Fouquet collection.[6] The man wears a close-
fitting cap and therefore has been baptized as a Dioscuros (this,
however, with a question mark, since here the individual features
are conspicuous too). I must add that the Budapest head also

---

[1] G. Kleiner, 'Tanagrafiguren' = *15. Ergänzungsheft des Jahrb. Deutsch. Arch.
Inst.* (1942), pp. 255 ff., 257.

[2] H. Philipp, *Terrakotten aus Ägypten* (1972), no. 4, fig. 3.

[3] Helbig[4], iii, no. 2424.

[4] G. v. Kaschnitz-Weinberg, *Sculture del Magazzino del Museo Vaticano*, pls. 35,
196.

[5] *Bulletin du Musée National Hongrois des Beaux-Arts*, 22 (1963), 18 ff.

[6] P. Perdrizet, *Terres cuites Fouquet*, pl. 52, no. 253.

wears a cap, because no hair is shown above what is presumed to be the ribbon, and neither a knot nor ends are visible at the nape of the neck. The riddle of the two heads can be solved by a more completely preserved statuette in Hildesheim (Pls. IV, V), where only the arms and part of the legs are lacking.[1] The head of the man is very similar to the Alexandrian fragment, not only in the features but also in the cap, which is very distinct here because of the white colour and the brown hair which projects from beneath. The short mantle, which is draped over the prominent belly and leaves the greater part of the legs uncovered, and in addition the close-fitting tricot make for easy identification. The man is a comedy actor who needs the cap as a pad for the heavy mask worn on the stage. The meaning is already clear from an oinochoe of the late fifth century in Leningrad, where comedy actors prepare themselves for a performance.[2] Hellenistic terracottas of men with this sort of cap, then, belong to a much older iconographical tradition. It is the representation of the actor without mask, the point of which lies in the contrast between the rigid mask and the individuality of the living face behind it. On the well-known vase-sherds from southern Italy in Würzburg, for example, the noble features of the tragic mask are contrasted with the vulgar head of the actor and his bristly beard.[3] One may doubt, however, if the statuette in Hildesheim and related Hellenistic types always carried masks in their hands. The contrast here may have been more subtle and of a merely physiognomical kind: between the pretentious attitude of the actor and the prominent belly of the comic role on the one hand and that sceptical, knowing expression of the almost suffering face on the other. This melancholy of the professional entertainer reminds one very much of the expression on the face of the comic poet as represented most distinctively by the portrait of Menander.[4] Later tradition regarded Menander as a hypochondriac and this was probably suggested by his portrait as well as by some of the characters in his plays. For further comment, see Aristotle on melancholy in the 30th book of the *Problemata*. The role the actor of the Hildesheim terracotta performed was probably that of the parasite.

The provenance of the statuette in Hildesheim is not known,

[1] *Die Denkmäler des Pelizaeus-Museums zu Hildesheim* (1921), p. 172, fig. 72 (2235).
[2] M. Bieber, *The History of the Greek and Roman Theatre* (1961), fig. 184.
[3] *Festschrift für James Loeb* (1930), pp. 5 ff., fig. 1, pl. 2.
[4] G. M. A. Richter, *The Portraits of the Greeks*, ii (1965), 224 ff.

but it obviously comes from Alexandria and must belong to the third century BC. The well-preserved colours speak for an Egyptian find; the clay is rather coarse and typical of Alexandrian products. There are very close stylistic parallels among terracottas in the museum of Alexandria, as, for example, a thick man with himation, which may have been of a kindred type.[1] The similarity of the face to the head from Alexandria has already been noted.

The type of actor with close-fitting cap is probably an Alexandrian creation, which, however, was imitated in other places. The only alternative would be an Athenian origin, the Athenian manufacture of this time being much richer and much more original than is obvious from the publications. Dorothy Thompson told me, however, that there is as yet no trace of this type in the very comprehensive material from the Agora. Besides the head in Budapest already mentioned there are heads from Pergamon and Smyrna and even nearly complete figures from Myrina.[2] All of them are considerably later than the statuette in Hildesheim, which must belong to the middle of the third century. As a contrast, I cite the head from Smyrna in the Louvre. As if made of rubber, the elongated form, the bloated face, and the pathetic expression betray an origin in late Hellenistic times. A counter-check can be made with a fragment from Egypt in Amsterdam, which, with its terse and dry forms, leads back into the third century.[3]

There is another echo of the type preserved in a miniature terracotta from Egypt in Hildesheim (Pl. IIIa, b) showing the same man with prominent belly and a short mantle covering it.[4] He too looks upward with a suffering expression which here, however, is rather exaggerated. This is most probably a caricature of the actor, still belonging to the third century, as is shown by the strongly divergent axes. The same complicated and dissonant rhythm is met in a statuette of another motif, a crippled spastic beggar in Hamburg.[5] He is clad in a mantle, which covers his head and his haunch, but leaves his bottom bare (Pl. VIIc). Very similar to this figurine is a naked beggar of fine clay in Hildesheim which shows

[1] E. Breccia, *Terrecotte figurate greche e greco-egizie del museo di Alessandria* (1930), i, pl. 20. 1, no. 466.

[2] E. Töpperwein, *Terrakotten von Pergamon* (1976), pl. 73, no. 493. S. Besques, *Catal. figurines . . . en terre cuite Louvre*, iii. 2, pl. 287 h = D1532. F. Winter, *Die Typen der figürlichen Terrakotten*, ii. 428, 8. 10.

[3] Inv. no. 7439.

[4] Ibid. 2375.

[5] *Arch. Anzeiger*, 75 (1960), 96 ff., figs. 36, 37.

PLATE III

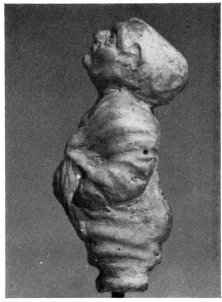

a.   *b.*

Caricature of an actor, terracotta figurine, Hildesheim, Roemer- und Pelizaeus-Museum

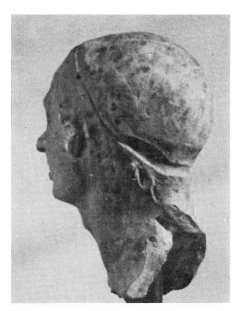

c.   *d.*

Terracotta head, Budapest, Museum of Fine Arts

PLATE IV

Terracotta figurine of an actor, Hildesheim, Roemer- und Pelizaeus-Museum

PLATE V

Terracotta figurine of an actor, Hildesheim, Roemer- und Pelizaeus-Museum

PLATE VI

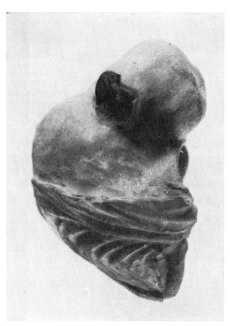

a.

b.

c.

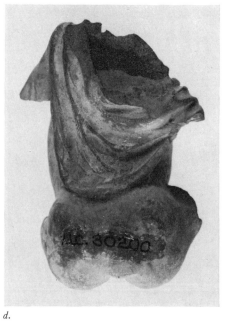

d.

Torso of grotesque cripple from Memphis, University College London, Petrie Museum

PLATE VII

a.   *b.*

Terracotta of grotesque cripple, Hildesheim, Roemer- und Pelizaeus-Museum

c.   *d.*

Terracotta of grotesque cripple, Hamburg,   Bronze figurine of hunchback with lagynos,
Museum für Kunst und Gewerbe   Bonn, Akademisches Kunstmuseum d.
                                              Universität

PLATE VIII

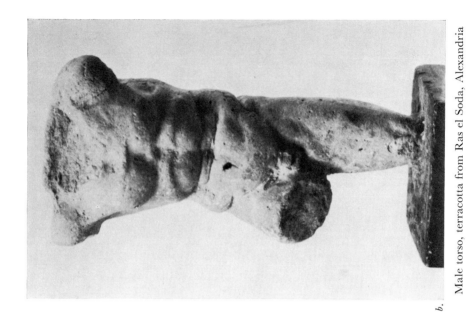

b.   Male torso, terracotta from Ras el Soda, Alexandria

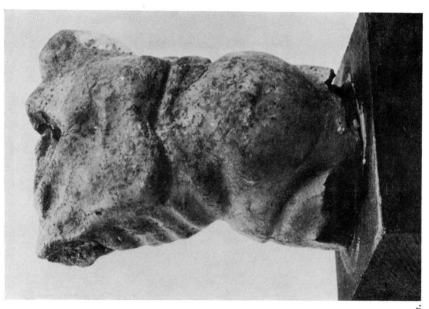

a.   Grotesque torso, terracotta from Ras el Soda, Alexandria

PLATE IX

b. Egyptianizing figurine, terracotta from Ras el Soda, Alexandria

a. Torso of Priest, terracotta from Ras el Soda, Alexandria

PLATE X

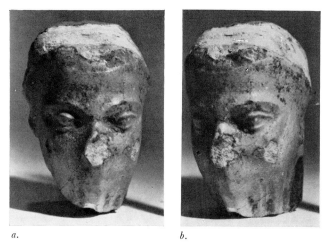

a.   *b.*

Fayence head of veiled woman, University College London, Petrie Museum

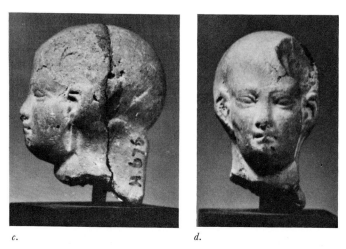

c.   *d.*

Terracotta head, Karlsruhe, Badisches Landesmuseum

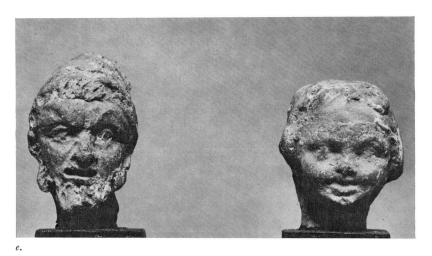

e.

Terracotta heads from Ras el Soda, Alexandria

PLATE XI

a.   *b.*

Terracotta head of an old woman from Ras el Soda, Alexandria

c.   *d.*

Fayence fragment of Ptolemaic queen from
Ras el Soda, Alexandria

Terracotta head from the Kerameikos,
Athens

PLATE XII

b. Terracotta figurine, Berlin-Charlottenburg,
Ägyptisches Museum

a. Terracotta figurine, Olympia

the same spastic attitude (Pl. VIIa, b).[1] Notwithstanding the small size and the disgusting motif, these statuettes are of a high artistic quality. There is, for example, a remarkably different treatment of the fleshy and flabby face, the thin skin over the swollen belly, and the backside, where the bony structure of the body is rendered underneath the covering flesh. This differentiation is still lacking in a torso (Pl. VI) of a very bold composition in University College London.[2] It comes from Memphis and is made from imported clay. The attitude is not as complicated as that of the other ones, showing more parallels instead of distortion. It probably dates from before the middle of the third century and represents the earliest example of the crippled beggar type I have been able to find as yet.

Seeking for a lower limit for this group of statuettes, I would like to compare the head of the Hildesheim cripple with a grimace-making head in Hamburg, which clearly shows a different kind of treatment.[3] No longer is there a rendering of the material values of the surface but strongly accentuated and tense globular forms. The same principle of bulging, protruding forms, flatter and with less tension, however, is found in an Alexandrian terracotta from Olympia (Pl. XIIa), which is probably meant as the caricature of a comic poet sitting on a theatrical throne.[4] This statuette comes from a pit, the contents of which were not later than the middle of the second century BC, according to Heinrich Bartels. One may already compare it to a so-called Pataikos in Berlin (Pl. XIIb), a bald-headed freak with the lock of Harpocrates and a huge phallos.[5] Please note the round vase on his left-hand side, which will be of use to us later. The head is very similar indeed, showing the same flat swellings of the face. This, however, is already a typical product of the Fayumi group. The gap noted by Kleiner, then, does not exist: there is continuity of develoment from the late third to the middle of the second century. Concluding this chapter, I would like to illustrate the difference between the two stages once more by comparing two terracottas of exactly the same motif, a pygmy dancer in a tightly draped mantle.[6] Both are on the same plate in an article by Adriani. On the left-hand side there is a fine difference of treatment between loose and stretched parts of the

---

[1] Inv. no. 992.
[2] UC 30200.
[3] *Arch. Anzeiger*, 75 (1960), 113, fig. 40.
[4] *VIII. Olympia-Bericht*, pp. 251 ff. (H. Bartels), pls. 120, 121.
[5] Philipp, loc. cit., pl. 9, no. 11.
[6] *Röm. Mitt.* 70 (1963), pl. 41. 1, 2.

garment; this must belong to the late third century. On the right-hand side, on the contrary, we have these tense swellings of face and body, over which the mantle is stretched tightly and uniformly.

After this preparation we may endeavour to classify a large find of terracottas, which came to light in 1940 near Alexandria in a place called Ras el Soda.[1] Since this group comprises a considerable number of realistic and Egyptianizing types, the chronology is of great interest for us. The find had no stratigraphical context, being probably the contents of a favissa, which was emptied in later times. Among the datable objects there were three coins of imperial times and two Megarian bowls of the second century BC. Adriani, who published the material, saw that it was mainly pre-Roman and dated it to 'the second half of the Hellenistic epoch', whatever that may mean. Reynold Higgins proposed the first century BC, but this is not likely as I will try to show.[2] Apart from these two authors, the find is mentioned only as far as I can see by Peter Fraser, who shares Adriani's opinion.[3]

I would like to begin with a selection of grotesque heads showing globular forms and heavy ornament-like features.[4] They are still very different from the grotesque head in Hamburg mentioned before, being smaller and less tense. One might think of a late Hellenistic origin, but this is precluded by a head of this time in the Vatican.[5] Compared to its rugged, open form, the heads in Alexandria are quite compact. Nor is a date possible in imperial times, represented in the Vatican collection by the flat-faced head of a Fisherman.[6] The shrill expressionism of his head produced by the linear treatment of the features is completely lacking in the fragments from Ras el Soda. Symptomatic of their style is the head of an old woman (Pl. XIa, b) from the same find showing heavy bulging forms, still lacking, however, the tension characteristic of terracottas of the early second century.[7] Symptomatic also of the style of the group are some grotesque torsi (Pl. VIIIa) which may be inspired by models of the early fifth century, like the well-known statues

    [1] A. Adriani, 'Trouvaille à Ras el Soda' = *Annuaire du Musée Gréco-Romain*, iii (1940–50), 28–46, pls. 13–29.

    [2] Higgins, loc. cit., p. 132.

    [3] P. M. Fraser, *Opusc. Athen.* iii. 12 f.

    [4] Adriani, loc. cit., pl. 20. Cf. pl. 17 ff. Average height 2.5–3.0 cm.

    [5] D. Facenna, *Rend. Pontif. Accad. Rom. di Archeologia*, 29 (1956–7), pl. 10, no. 67.

    [6] Ibid. no. 65.

    [7] Adriani, loc. cit., pl. 19. 4 (centre), 5 (centre).

from Paros.[1] The terracottas, however, betray their Hellenistic origin by the different treatment of the surface rendering the physical qualities of the body: the bony ribs, the flabby flesh of the breast, and the tense swollen belly. It is useful to compare this with a late Hellenistic torso of the Sieglin collection, which reproduces the Fisherman of the Vatican.[2] This statuette is lacking the clear structure of the older ones; it is just a bloated surface. The same may be said of a jumper from Smyrna in Budapest, the bones of which are treated like rubber.[3] Having checked the catalogues of the big collections, if only superficially, my impression was that none of the grotesque statuettes from Smyrna was much earlier. The much disputed question as to whether Alexandria or Smyrna has the priority in this field may be decided with good conscience in favour of Alexandria.

I would like to offer for Ras el Soda not only a relative but also an absolute chronology. Among the terracottas there is the fine torso of a man (Pl. VIII*b*) with raised right leg and stooping body.[4] Here again we have the bony structure and dry treatment of flesh characteristic of all the naked figures in the find. This very much resembles the famous statue of the dying Gaul in the Capitoline museum, for which the same differentiation in treatment is symptomatic. Since the dying Gaul belongs to a group erected shortly after 225 BC, it is very likely that the related terracottas from Ras el Soda were made in the last quarter of the third century. It is an open question, of course, whether the find also comprises later material. At a first glance, for example, the contorted dancer with thick belly and thin limbs may give the impression of a much later date.[5] But I do not think that this is necessary, comparing it with the cripple of University College London mentioned above (Pl. VI). This figure shows a comparable boldness of composition and the same contrast between belly and limbs. There may be only a short period of development between the two terracottas, the younger one from Ras el Soda showing a greater contortion with divergent axes and a softer treatment of flesh.

If this opinion is sound, we may be able to classify the earliest Egyptianizing figures among Alexandrian terracottas. The find from Ras el Soda comprises several statuettes of crouching or

[1] Ibid., pl. 15. 1, 4. Height 5.5 cm. Torsi from Paros A. Kostoglu-Despini, *Problemata tes parianes plastikes tou 5tou aiona* (1979), pl. 39 ff.
[2] *Expedition v. Sieglin*, ii. 2, pl. 57. 6.
[3] Inv. no. T. 345.
[4] Adriani, loc. cit., pl. 16. 1 (left), 2 (left). Height 7 cm.
[5] Ibid., pls. 13. 1, 2, 16. 1 (right), 2 (right). Height 11 cm.

sitting young men with large phalloi, naked or wearing a fringed himation.[1] These are forerunners of the corresponding types which play a prominent part in the repertoire of the Fayumi. As an example, I show only one naked figure (Pl. IX*b*) in the familiar Egyptian sitting position and with the two folds under the breast typical also of the Egyptian tradition.[2] The head, however, resembles Egyptian prototypes less than Ionian faces of the late archaic period. We find the same mixture of Egyptian and archaic Greek elements in a small terracotta head in Karlsruhe (Pl. X*c, d*), which is made from fine imported clay.[3] Here the Ionian face goes together with the elongated skull and the support in the nape of the neck, also common in Egyptian art. For technical and stylistic reasons, the fragment must belong to the last quarter of the third century when native Egyptian influence made itself felt elsewhere.

If the whole find belongs more or less to this epoch, as I assume, we can classify some more realistic types represented in this context. There is a priest of Isis (Pl. IX*a*) clad in a fringed mantle, an elegant terracotta which may be compared to figures on late Ptolemaic oinochoai.[4] The head may have been similar to that of a more complete statuette in Berlin, which is of a somewhat earlier date but has already the same realistic rendering of the shrivelled breast.[5] A very lively head (Pl. X*e*) with shaggy beard, open mouth, and raised brows may represent a fisherman.[6] Finally, I would like to mention two objects of faience, both being of interest for the chronology. One of them shows a well-known type of farmer with basket and has already been dated to the late third century by Dorothy Thompson.[7] I will consider another copy of this type at the end of my paper. The other fragment (Pl. XI*c*) comes from the miniature portrait of a Ptolemaic queen in the guise of Isis.[8] It is a pity that just the face is destroyed but anyway the type of hairdo is identical with that of a big statuette in New York which, according to the inscription, represents Arsinoë II.[9] The fragment then shows Arsinoë II, whose cult, however, lasted for

[1] Adriani, loc. cit., pls. 14. 5, 16. 4, 25. 4, 6.

[2] Ibid., pl. 25. 6.

[3] Inv. no. H 676.

[4] Adriani, loc. cit., pl. 22. 1.

[5] Philipp, loc. cit., pl. 4, no. 6.

[6] Adriani, loc. cit., pl. 18. 6.

[7] Ibid., pl. 23. 1, 2. D. Burr Thompson in *Studies in Classical Art and Archaeology*, for P. H. von Blanckenhagen (1979), pp. 175 ff., pl. 50, 3–4.

[8] Adriani, loc. cit., pl. 23. 7.

[9] Kyrieleis, *Bildnisse der Ptolemäer*, pl. 71.

centuries, or one of her immediate successors. This seems likely because of the parallel locks of hair, which on the latest Ptolemaic oinochoai are replaced by a more complicated pattern. This speaks for a date before the end of the third century.

I would like to conclude with a big bronze statuette in the Metropolitan Museum of New York, acquired in 1972.[1] With a height of 40.5 cm and finely worked, it is a masterpiece of realistic art from antiquity. The bronze shows an old man with short unathletic legs, flat feet, and sagging belly. He wears the exomis, having put a closed diptychon behind the fringed girdle. His left shoulder and arm are naked, the withered flesh of the old man being rendered in a very naturalistic way. The left arm is across the body; the lost right arm must have been raised against the head, which is looking downward with an expression of deep thoughtfulness. The head corroborates the impression that the man is a banausos. His forehead is bald and he wears a short beard. The wrinkled front and the eyes, which are set close together, add to the picture of a narrow-minded character. All these features make it impossible to recognize here a philosopher merged into 'les profondeurs de la pensée'. A philosopher of course would wear a himation, not the exomis as we have it here. This is rather the mark of a banausos and, more specifically, a craftsman. The statuette resembles very much indeed the type of Daidalos as we meet him on Roman sarcophagi or on gems. I give only one example, where the short legs and flat feet and the prominent sagging belly are the same.[2] On a sarcophagus with Pasiphaë in the Louvre Daidalos is clad in an exomis and is in attitude just like the New York bronze.[3] Thus it would be legitimate to name the man Daidalos, were it not for the brooding expression which needs a special explanation.

This interpretation is complicated by the fact that the type of the New York banausos can be found also among Alexandrian terracottas. A statuette from the Sieglin collection, formerly in Leipzig and lost during the last war, shows the same man with short legs and his left arm across his body.[4] The figurine proves that we were right to think the right arm was raised and probably supported the head, though there is no trace of this on the bronze. The identity of type is clear also from the diptychon sticking in front of the belly. Other details, however, are different. The man

[1] Inv. no. 1972, 11, 1. *Mon. Piot*, 54 (1965), 25 ff.
[2] G. Lippold, *Gemmen und Kameen des Altertums und der Neuzeit*, pl. 48. 1.
[3] C. Robert, *Die antiken Sarkophagreliefs*, iii. 1, pl. x, no. 35.
[4] J. Vogt, *Expedition E.v. Sieglin*, ii. 2 (1924), pl. 71. 1.

wears a shawl with fringes at the end. His head is without beard and he does not concentrate on thinking but looks rather bored and impudent. This makes it very probable that a waiting slave is meant, the typical attitude of whom we already find on so many red-figured vases. The fringed shawl perhaps gives him a special Alexandrian note, the exact meaning of which eludes us.

The type of terracotta described must have been very popular in Alexandria and was reproduced there for centuries. I cite another example in Berlin, which dates from the late third century AD.[1] There are other copies from the same mould in Hildesheim and elsewhere. At a first glance the identity of type with the terracotta in Leipzig is not obvious but this is due to the difference of style over such a long time (the figurine in Leipzig being probably of the first century BC). The terracotta in Berlin not only shows the same attitude but also details, such as the short legs and the fringed shawl. That we were right to connect the type of terra-cottas with the New York banausos is proved by the head, which does not follow the statuette in Leipzig but returns to the type of the bronze, repeating the bald forehead, the short beard, and the brooding expression. On his right-hand side the man is flanked by a pillar with a globular vase on it. This may hint at the context of the figure, but it does not help us very far. You may remember the identically shaped vase represented with the Pataikos in Berlin, where this was obviously meant as a symbol of the cult of Harpo-crates, who often holds this sort of vase himself. Here (together with the fringed shawl) it may mean that the man is a slave in a precinct of Harpocrates, but the point of the character and especially of his brooding expression remain an enigma to us.

As to the date of the New York bronze, it is much easier to reach plausible results. I compare it to a faience in the Benaki Museum showing a farmer with basket of a type already mentioned.[2] The attitude of the figurine with parallel legs and one arm across the body is very similar and adds to the impression that the New York banausos comes from this typological tradition. The style of the faience, however, is quite different. In spite of its much smaller size it shows stronger accents and the rendering of naturalistic details is more powerful. The belly bulges over the girdle, the arm is not flat but seen in profile. The contour is disturbed by the basket and by the diagonal roll of the himation. The faience type has been dated to the late third century by Dorothy Thompson and this is quite convincing. If you compare the New York bronze it is much flatter

---

[1] Philipp, loc. cit., pl. 46, no. 48. Perdrizet, loc. cit., pl. 91, no. 441.
[2] Burr Thompson, loc. cit., pls. 49 f.

and its contours speak very clearly. The next parallel to this kind of composition is the statuette of a waiting slave in Lyon, which also may be of Alexandrian manufacture or at least an imitation of an Alexandrian prototype of the second half of the first century BC.[1] I think that this is the date of the New York banausos too. This tradition is still continued by figures like the late bronze of a fisherman from Volubilis, who follows a very similar scheme of composition.[2]

Last but not least there is the provenance of the New York statuette which speaks for an Alexandrian origin. It was found in the sea off North Africa, probably not far from Cherchel, ancient Iol-Caesarea. There was always a very close cultural contact between Alexandria and the Numidian capital. It had its climax when in 20 BC Juba II, the famous connoisseur on the throne, married Cleopatra Selene, daughter of the last reigning Ptolemaic queen. It is obvious that the family saw themselves in the tradition of the Ptolemies, as is shown by the name of the crown prince. There was also a gallery of ancestral portraits, among which the heads of probably the first Ptolemy and Cleopatra VII were found.[3] Against this background it becomes very likely that the New York bronze is an original work from Alexandria bought for Iol-Caesarea in the time of Juba II. As one of the few masterpieces of ancient art preserved, it is a late but outstanding witness to the high artistic level of realism in Alexandrian art, to which my brief remarks were dedicated.

My thanks are due to Homer Thompson for reading and correcting my English version. My studies profited much from a stay at the Institute for Advanced Study in Princeton during the first months of 1981. For the provision of photographs and the permission to publish them I should like to express my gratitude to A. Adriani, W. Brashear, A. Eggebrecht, G. Grimm, R. Hall, G. Hübner, W. Hornbostel, D. Johannes, U. Knigge, B. Schmitz, J. G. Szilagyi, J. Thimme.

[1] St. Boucher, *Bronzes grecs, hellénistiques et étrusques des musées de Lyon* (1970), 50, no. 29.

[2] C. Boube-Piccot, *Les Bronzes antiques du Maroc*, i (1969), 169 ff., no. 180, pls. 103–7.

[3] *Die Numider* (Exhibition in the Rheinisches Landesmuseum, Bonn, 1979–80), pp. 516–19.

LOCKE'S LOGICAL ATOMISM

By MICHAEL AYERS

Read 4 November 1981

ALL our ideas are either simple ideas or else complex ideas constructed out of those simple ideas. What made Locke adopt this compositional model for thought? The answer seems to go without saying. Compositionalism seems no more than the natural model for anyone who wants to claim that all our ideas come from experience. It seems only natural to explain the idea of a centaur, which cannot have been acquired in experience, as a fiction constructed out of elements which have been so acquired. It seems only natural that Locke should have tried to extend that explanation to the ideas of God and infinity, to mathematical ideas, to the ideas of material and spiritual substance, to the ideas of right and wrong, and to other ideas commonly held to be innate in his time because they seemed to transcend experience or to be independent of it. Yet to stop there is to fail to discern the full meaning of compositionalism for Locke, the special significance of 'simple' and 'complex' in his philosophy.

One proposal as to such a deeper meaning may appeal to some just because it finds the source of Locke's model outside the abstractions of pure philosophy. That is the view, given graphic expression by Sir Isaiah Berlin, that Locke was captivated by the methods of contemporary physics. Just for that reason, Berlin suggests,

> The mind was treated as if it were a box containing mental equivalents of the Newtonian particles . . . These 'ideas' are distinct and separate entities . . ., literally atomic, having their origin somewhere in the external world, dropping into the mind like so many grains of sand inside an hour glass; there they continue in isolation, or are compounded into complexes, in the way in which material objects in the outer world are compounded out of complexes of molecules and atoms.[1]

A similar suggestion has recently been made by Dr M. A. Stewart, of Lancaster University. Stewart argues, I am sure rightly, against

[1] I. Berlin (ed.), *The Age of Enlightenment* (1956), p. 31.

those eminent commentators[1] who have claimed that compositionalism became, in later editions of the *Essay*, a somewhat half-
hearted component of Locke's concept-empiricism. He offers
evidence that even in his latest thoughts Locke enjoyed finding
rather detailed analogies between his theory of ideas and Robert
Boyle's theory of particles or corpuscles. For Stewart, so it seems,
the question whether Locke remained faithful to compositionalism just is the question whether he continued to take the analogy
with physics seriously.[2]

There is one big problem with this story. No doubt every
thinker, however revolutionary, has to work within a tradition
using, for whatever fresh purposes, the conceptual tools supplied
by his context. But conceptual tools are not just words and
phrases. For a philosopher, to construct a theory by means of such
tools and to define his relationship to the tradition is one and the
same act. Even to refuse to employ certain available concepts is a
positive contribution to the latter task. If it is true that Locke took
over the notion of combination from physical theory, then one
must expect some intelligible relation between that theory and
what he saw himself as doing. One might, for example, expect—to
be rather obvious—that he took himself to be offering a theory of
the mind with the same status as Boyle's theory of matter. The
trouble is that we know just how he saw himself in relation to
Boyle, because he tells us, and it has nothing to do with any
analogy between simple and complex in 'the material and intellectual worlds'.[3]

Boyle's method included two distinct components, experi-
mental and theoretical. The first, generally known as 'natural
history', was a process of observation and experiment leading to
empirical or merely descriptive generalization such as, indeed,
Boyle's Law. The second consisted in speculative and usually
rather general explanation in accordance with the hypothesis of
corpuscles and the void. This speculation was valuable in
explaining how material variety and change might arise from a
few simple principles. Yet it is to 'natural history' that Boyle's
specific discoveries were credited. Now consciousness for Locke is
an attribute of the mind or thinking thing at the level of observa-

---

[1] Cf. J. Gibson, *Locke's Theory of Knowledge* (1917), ch. iii; R. I. Aaron, *John Locke* (2nd edn., 1955), ch. iii.

[2] M. A. Stewart, 'Locke's Mental Atomism and the Classification of Ideas', I and II, *Locke Newsletter*, 1979 and 1980. See especially II, pp. 46–60.

[3] The phrase is adapted from *Essay Concerning Human Understanding*, ed. P. Nidditch (1975), II. xii. 1.

tion: the real and underlying nature or essence of 'that which thinks' is unknown, a matter for speculation.[1] He sees his theory of ideas and knowledge as the application of what he calls the 'historical, plain method' to the experienced operations of the mind.[2] Consequently, whereas absolutely simple material particles would be ontologically or, to use Berlin's word, 'literally' atomic, simple ideas are only 'simple' at the superficial level of appearance and mere description. That is why Locke disclaims any Cartesian intention to 'meddle with the Physical Consideration of the Mind' ('physical' here meaning 'natural' rather than 'material'.)[3] He even refuses to arbitrate between materialism and immaterialism as explanations of the natural basis of consciousness.[4] The theory of material atomism itself was for Locke far from perfect, although a hypothesis for which he fears 'the Weakness of humane Understanding is scarce able to substitute another'.[5] All this is part and parcel of the strong anti-dogmatism which constitutes a major theme of the *Essay*. It is therefore incredible that he was predisposed by any respect for Boyle's method to find the structure of Boyle's speculation replicated at the level at which we observe or experience the mind.

In other words, the analogy between the composition of ideas and the composition of physical particles does no theoretical work for Locke, but arises as little more than a decorative conceit. Its elaboration may be significant if we are interested in the literary style or tone of the *Essay*, a not unimportant topic, but we should look elsewhere for the answer to the question with which we began. I would suggest that we should look, not towards physics, but less adventurously at the context of existing logic and epistemology. For the truth is that these branches of philosophy had been heavily compositionalist since Plato.[6] It is that background which gives the compositionalism of the *Essay* its philosophical depth and significance, making it the vehicle by means of which Locke could express systematic opposition, above all, to the followers of Aristotle and Descartes. He does so, very crudely

[1] Cf. *Essay*, II. i. 9; IV. iii. 17; IV. iii. 29; IV. vi. 14; IV. xii. 12; etc.
[2] *Essay*, I. i. 2.
[3] Ibid.
[4] Cf. *Essay*, IV. iii. 6.
[5] *Essay*, IV. iii. 16.
[6] Cf. *Theaetetus* 203, where Plato uses the alphabet analogy employed by Locke at *Essay*, II. vii. 10. Although Stewart may well be right that Locke got the idea from Boyle (who follows Lucretius in using it to expound physical atomism) it seems possible that seventeenth-century compositionalism is directly indebted to the argument of *Theaetetus*.

speaking, by arguing that what is a paradigm of simplicity for the rival theory is in fact complex; or that what is held by others to be self-evidently complex, is better regarded as simple.

It seems that the doctrine which was uppermost in Locke's mind when he first began to set out the theory of the *Essay* (in what is now known as 'Draft A')[1] was the Aristotelians' notion of a simple term or 'simple apprehension'. That notion arises in the context of Aristotelian theories of the proposition, in which predication was regarded in three associated ways as it pertains to words, to things, and to thoughts. First, in predication words or terms are combined in sentences. Such combination, Aristotle tells us, must at least implicitly include a verb, paradigmatically the verb *to be*, before something capable of truth or falsity is achieved.[2] Second, we are also invited to regard the proposition as the association of things or beings or entities. For example, the species *man* may be said or predicated or affirmed of the individual man; and one thing, its quality *white*, exists 'in' another thing, the white object.[3] Third, Aristotle takes it that something corresponds in the mind to both these levels, a thought which does not differ from nation to nation as language differs.[4] For later Aristotelian theory the act of mind which corresponds to a term is the 'simple apprehension' of its meaning, or a 'concept'. 'Judgement' or mental 'affirmation' corresponds in the mind to the ordering or combination of terms in the sentence or statement. Sentences or propositions can in turn be combined in syllogism, and judgements or affirmations, correspondingly, in reasoning, 'ratiocination', or 'mental discourse'. Hence logic was traditionally divided into three parts, concerned with terms, with propositions, and with syllogism.

This straightforward model of increasing complexity seems to have had, right from its origin in Aristotle himself, an interesting qualification relating to the first stage. The chief part of Aristotle's theory of terms is his doctrine of 'categories' or 'predicaments' which distinguishes various sorts of predicate or, if you like, of being or attribute. 'Man', 'horse', 'gold' fall under the category of substance; 'four-foot' falls under quantity; 'white', 'musical' under quality; 'larger' under relation; 'in the Lyceum' under place; and so forth. Each of these predicates was held to be simple,

---

[1] *Locke's Essay: An Early Draft* (1936), eds. R. I. Aaron and J. Gibb (written 1671).

[2] Cf. *De Interpretatione*, 17a11–15.

[3] Cf. *Categoriae*, ii.

[4] Cf. *De Int.* 16a3–9.

however many words it may contain. It is incapable of truth or falsity by itself, without combination.[1] Yet this conception of simplicity, tying it to the categories, leaves open the possibility of compounds which combine items from different categories but which are not straightforwardly or fully propositional. For example, 'musician' combines *man* and *musical*. Like any term, such expressions assert nothing by themselves, yet their compound nature shows itself in predication. 'John is a musician' means the same as 'John is a man and John is musical'.[2]

Here we may ask why the term 'man' is the paradigm of simplicity if, as Aristotelians believed, it can be defined, for example as *rational animal*. Their answer is that 'man' denotes a *thing* which is simple and unitary, while 'musician' does not. 'A man', 'a horse', 'gold', 'lead' answers the question 'What is it?' asked of a natural individual or naturally homogeneous quantity of stuff. That is to say, it classifies the individual or stuff according to its whole unitary nature or essence, rather than just by its size or quantity, or by its qualities or relations and so forth. It places the individual in a natural kind or species. (This narrow but natural understanding of 'What is it?' is perhaps more natural in Greek.) The unitary nature or essence of the species is expressed in a 'real', that is to say, scientific definition: *man* was commonly defined as *rational animal*. But that nature is supposed not to have parts corresponding to the linguistic parts of the definition. Musicians, by contrast, do not as such belong to a species with an essence, but rather to a class arrived at by arbitrary combination. Correspondingly musicians are not natural individuals *qua* musicians but *qua* human beings. To come or cease to be a musician is not to come or cease to exist.

This distinction is elaborated in the theory of predicables, the explanation-schema of Aristotelian science and another way of dividing up and relating predicates. The predicables are (after Porphyry) genus, species, difference, property, and accident. The 'real' or 'simple' definition of the essence of the *species* is by *genus* and *difference*. *Properties* are attributes common to all members of the species: they flow from, or are explained by, the essence, as our having hands or language or the capacity for laughter was supposed to flow from our being rational animals. *Accidents* are attributes which are not so connected with the essence, and which any member of the species may have or lack, as it chances. Thus there could be no single word which meant *man who is rational* or

---

[1] *Cat.* iv.
[2] Cf. *Metaphysica*, *Z* iv; *De Int.* v, viii, and xi.

man who has hands, since these conceptions or expressions add nothing to *man*. To try to introduce such a word would simply introduce a synonym for 'man', another name for the species. 'Musician', by contrast, does add to *man*, just because musicality is an accident.[1] The paradigmatic Aristotelian compounds thus compound substance with accident.

In the Port Royal *Logic*, a work in which Antoine Arnauld attempts to graft the Aristotelian logical tradition on to Cartesian metaphysics and epistemology, the Aristotelian distinction between simples and compounds seems to be given recognition in a discussion of complex expressions, in which 'two or more words are joined together to express one idea'. All such expressions are treated as quasi-propositional: the notion of a 'transparent body' is the notion of a 'body which is transparent'. But a distinction is drawn between explicative complex expressions, like 'man who is an animal endowed with reason', and determinative complex expressions, like 'transparent bodies'. In the former, the relative clause adds nothing and leaves the extension of the term unaffected. In the latter, the adjective or clause is an addition which further restricts the extension—there are fewer transparent bodies than bodies. But the whole explanation notably avoids recourse to Aristotelian ontology or epistemology. There is no appeal to a conception of man as a simple being, or of 'rational animal' as a simple definition. 'Man who is rational' is an explicative complex expression just because 'man' means the same as 'animal which is rational', which is a determinative complex expression.[2]

Locke's attitude to the Aristotelian theory is similarly reductive, but more elaborate and more explicit. His theory of ideas is essentially a theory of terms. Ideas are, in effect, Aristotelian 'simple apprehensions': that is to say, they constitute that which corresponds in the mind to terms or 'names', to expressions capable of standing in subject or predicate place. Ideas, he tells us in Draft A, are joined or separated 'by way of affirmation or negation, which when it comes to be expressed in words is called proposition, and in this lies all truth and falsehood'.[3] In the *Essay* he asserts that '*Is*, and *Is not*, are the general marks of the Mind, affirming or denying', and he draws attention to those other 'Words, whereby [the Mind] signifies what connection it gives to the several Affirmations and Negations, that it unites in one

---

[1] Cf. *De Int.* 20b31–21a8.

[2] *Logic, or the Art of Thinking* (1662), I. vii. (*Later note*: This paragraph now seems misleading. A more direct response to Aristotelian compounds is the category of *choses modifiées* of *Logic* I. ii.)   [3] 'Draft A', pp. 19–20.

continued Reasoning or Narration', for example 'but', 'therefore', and so on.[1] Here he is following closely in the tradition, treating the language of the second and third parts of logic in due place. He is famous for his supposed principle that all words stand for ideas,[2] but it is in fact essential to his theory that he is in agreement with earlier logicians that some words, 'which are not truly, by themselves, the names of any Ideas, are of . . . constant and indispensible use in Language'.[3]

Locke's classification of ideas as 'ideas of substances', 'simple ideas', 'ideas of simple modes', 'ideas of mixed modes', and 'ideas of relations' should therefore be read as, above all, a rival to the Aristotelian categories. Since there were ten or eleven of the latter he has at least achieved a striking economy. But it is equally striking that only one of his categories is allowed to be truly simple, namely simple ideas, ideas of simple modes being simple only by courtesy and in a limited sense. The relationship to Aristotelian theory, however, is quite explicit. For example, bearing in mind the logic-books' definition of a 'simple apprehension' as the understanding of a term, he tells us in Draft A that those simple ideas 'are properly simple apprehensions to which we apply the names that others doe'[4]—a point considerably less crude than a straightforward identification would have been. The first active composition of simple ideas, we are told, is the formation of specific ideas of substances. It is entirely unsurprising that Locke sees this composition as propositional: as he puts it, 'the first affirmation or negation of our minds are about those material objects in the frameing of our Ideas of them'.[5] He thought that in forming the complex idea of a species of thing out of simple ideas of sensible qualities we 'in effect'[6] affirm that the qualities do in general exist together in the same substance: 'yet the whole compounded idea being knowne under one name and taken altogeather considerd as one thing as man horse water lead etc they may be treated of as simple apprehensions'—that is, as single concepts corresponding to terms.[7] He is thus attacking the Aristotelian view of the names of the species of substances as paradigmatically simple terms from within an Aristotelian conception of complexity. To unpack

---

[1] *Essay*, III. vi. 1–2.

[2] Cf. *Essay* III. ii. 2: '*Words in their primary or immediate Signification, stand for nothing, but the Ideas in the Mind of him that uses them.*' At the end of the previous chapter he more accurately promises to consider, 'To what it is that Names . . . are immediately applied'.

[3] *Essay*, III. vii. 2.

[4] 'Draft A', p. 14.

[5] Ibid., p. 5.

[6] Ibid., p. 7

[7] Ibid., p. 17.

what is understood by the name is to unpack a quasi-propositional compound.

In the *Essay* Locke drops the suggestion that the complexity of complex ideas is propositional, for reasons which we need not go into. What does quite emphatically remain is the contrast with Aristotelian theory. Simply to entitle his chapter 'Of our Complex *Ideas* of Substances' was to throw down the gauntlet to the Aristotelians, but the contrast is immediately spelt out. The famous, much misunderstood, passage which opens the chapter constitutes an insulting diagnosis of their error:

> The Mind . . . takes notice . . . that a certain number of . . . simple *Ideas* go constantly together; which being presumed to belong to one thing, and Words being suited to common apprehensions, and made use of for quick dispatch, are called so united in one subject, by one name; which by inadvertency we are apt to talk of and consider as one simple *Idea*, which indeed is a complication of many *Ideas* together.[1]

He later returns to the same topic, even more explicitly: 'These *Ideas* of Substances, though they are commonly called simple Apprehensions, and the names of them simple Terms; yet in effect are complex and compounded.'[2]

Why is it important for Locke that our ideas of substances are complex? The answer is one small part of a story too long to tell here. Briefly, however, Locke believes that we are doomed to conceive of natural species and genera in terms of lists of observable qualities and powers, commonly experienced in conjunction but, as far as we are concerned, otherwise unconnected. This experienced variety lies not in the object, but in the circumstances and our modes of sensibility. For we must suppose that it can in principle be explained by an underlying material structure affecting observers and surrounding objects in a variety of ways. That is why, included in the complex idea of the species, is the idea of an unknown substratum or subject of the observable qualities and powers, 'which Qualities', as Locke says, 'are commonly called Accidents'.[3] To know the thing itself would be to know its essence, but all we know are accidents.

This last claim is expressed in another well-known, but also much misunderstood, passage, one which contains a clear allusion to traditional logical theory:

> when we speak of any sort of Substance, we say it is a *thing* having such or such Qualities, as Body is a *thing* that is extended, figured, and capable

[1] *Essay*, II. xxiii. I. [2] *Essay*, II. xxiii. 14.
[3] *Essay*, II. xxiii. 2.

of Motion; a Spirit a *thing* capable of thinking; and so Hardness, Friability, and Power to draw Iron, we say, are Qualities to be found in a Loadstone. These, and the like fashions of speaking intimate, that the Substance is supposed always *something* besides the Extension, Figure, Solidity, Motion, Thinking, or other observable *Ideas*, though we know not what it is.[1]

It is paradigmatically accidents which, on Aristotelian theory, exist 'in' a subject. Locke is saying that our concept of the species is nothing but that of certain accidents in an otherwise unidentified substance: that is to say, the concept is compound.

Another part of Locke's argument denies the existence of objective specific essences at all. Although he has doubts about Boyle's version of mechanism, he is convinced that some mechanist theory is true. That means that the only essence or nature in the material world is the essence of matter itself, the nature from which flow the necessary laws of mechanics, whatever they may be. The particular species and genera, *horse*, *bird*, *gold*, *metal*, and so forth, are each, Locke thinks, arbitrarily distinguished by us through a defining set of observable attributes which he calls the 'nominal essence'. The only serious candidate for the 'real essence' of a species is that complex aspect of its unknown material structure which is responsible for the concurrence of those observable attributes by which the species is defined. There is nothing truly substantial or distinct or permanent about a 'real essence' so conceived. It exists as something distinct only relatively to the arbitrary nominal essence through which it is indirectly picked out.[2] All these doctrines are advanced in a complex but brilliantly effective and influential attack on the doctrine of predicables—'this whole mystery of Genera and Species'[3]—which I have attempted to unravel elsewhere.[4] One small element in this attack is a point which is the obverse of the claim that our ideas of substances are complex: namely, that there is no ground for distinguishing an Aristotelian simple term, such as 'horse', from an Aristotelian compound term, such as 'palfrey', defined as a *horse which ambles*. It would therefore follow that the latter is logically as good a name of a species as the former, even if not so useful for the practising biologist.[5] The question how many species there are is for Locke the question how many names there are. Ice is a distinct species, he claims paradoxically, while molten gold

---

[1] *Essay*, II. xxiii. 3.   [2] Cf. *Essay*, III. vi. 6.
[3] *Essay*, III. iii. 9.
[4] 'Locke *versus* Aristotle on Natural Kinds', *Journal of Philosophy* (1981).
[5] Cf. *Essay*, IV. viii. 6.

is not, just because there is a distinct name for the former but not for the latter.[1] As he says in another allusion to Aristotelian theory, if we see something which falls outside our classification, we ask 'what it is, meaning by that Enquiry nothing but the Name'.[2]

For all that may be wrong with Aristotelian essences, these provocative contentions are today beyond belief, which may suggest that the truth lies somewhere between the two philosophies. For many reasons natural taxonomy, especially above the level of species, is a much more arbitrary business than the Aristotelian model allows. Yet Locke's solution, that it is a matter of entirely arbitrary, if informed, definition in terms of observable criteria fails to catch the semantic significance of the underlying affinity, whether evolutionary or structural, which is presumed to exist when items are placed in the same class. The issue is still an area of hot dispute in both biology and philosophical logic. As far as the latter is concerned, we still lack an agreed and convincing account of the significance of the Aristotelian distinction between what is simple and what is composite, and will no doubt continue to do so until we have a better theory of the relation between individual and species. What is certain is that the distinction cannot be safely ignored.

Locke's inclusion of the ideas of body and spirit among his examples of complex ideas of substances indicates that he was fighting on two fronts, bearing Descartes in mind even in the act of challenging Aristotelian substantial forms. Descartes, however, stands clear of traditional logic in a number of ways. In particular, the distinction between terms and propositions is irrelevant to his conception of simple and complex. His notion of a simple idea itself embraces what is propositional. One reason for this somewhat unorthodox approach to thought must lie in his famous theory of judgement. On the current Aristotelian doctrine, as we have seen, 'judgement' or mental 'affirmation' was the act of combining 'simple apprehensions'. Such terminology conflates propositional thought with acceptance or belief, a definite propositional attitude. Yet Descartes holds that assent to a proposition is voluntary, an act of will which comes after the work of the understanding. For him, whatever can be believed can be held in mind or 'perceived' prior to acceptance, rejection, or suspense of judgement. By this two-stage model he explains error, which is supposed to occur only when we judge rashly in the absence of

---

[1] *Essay*, IV. vi. 13.   [2] *Essay*, II. xxxii. 7.

clear and distinct perceptions or ideas. The term 'idea' therefore covers whatever is an object of the understanding antecedently to assent or dissent. An 'idea' is typically what Descartes calls 'material' for a belief. He does say that an idea is not capable of truth or falsity in the strict sense, but that is only because he regards beliefs as the primary bearers of truth and falsity, while ideas occur within the context of other mental states, such as desire. It is not because ideas are never propositional in form. Accordingly ideas can be said to be 'materially' true or false, in whatever context they occur.[1]

There are other considerations which may help to explain Descartes's approach. He holds that every conscious state or act involves an idea, and that every idea is an idea *of* something. That is to say, an idea is essentially referred or related to an object, and such reference seems to be interpreted as itself a kind of propositional thought.[2] Another motive may be supplied by the point that to have a Cartesian clear and distinct idea of something is to understand it. It is difficult to separate our understanding—for example, what identity is, from our grasping such principles as that, if A is identical with B and B with C, then A is identical with C. That particular principle is, as it happens, included explicitly in Descartes's sample list of 'simple notions'.[3]

All this seems to have set a problem for Descartes's followers, for Aristotelian logic was too impressive and too prestigious simply to be jettisoned. Besides, empiricists like Hobbes and Gassendi were already incorporating it into their systems with some popular success. Arnauld's solution, in what was to become the standard Cartesian logic, takes the bull by the horns. The Cartesian distinction between perception and assent, the understanding and the will, is simply identified with the distinction between the simple apprehension of the meaning of terms and the mental affirmation of propositions. As on the traditional account, a propositional content comes into existence only with a propositional attitude. Arnauld seems prepared to deal with the content of wishes and other non-cognitive states of mind simply by postulating other sorts of combinatory act than judgements.[4] The traditional conception of combination was, then, securely re-established by the time Locke began to write, despite what may seem the obvious objection that, as Thomas Reid was to put it,

---

[1] Cf. *Meditations*, III (with Descartes's reply to Arnauld's objections) and IV.
[2] Cf. *Passions of the Soul*, I. 22–5.
[3] *Rules for the Direction of the Mind*, xii.
[4] A. Arnauld and C. Lancelot, *A General and Rational Grammar* (1662), I. ii. 4.

'it is one thing to conceive the meaning of a proposition; it is another thing to judge it to be true or false'.[1] For Locke 'perception' and 'judgement' are acts of propositional composition and it is for that reason that he calls ideas the 'materials' of knowledge and belief. It is not because they constitute, as Descartes holds, propositional material for assent.

One line of approach to Descartes's employment of the notion of simplicity is to see him less as the questing philosopher of popular imagination, endeavouring as best he can to escape from scepticism to certainty by some rigorous linear argument, than as a philosopher struck by the need to explain what he takes to be our—especially his own—remarkable capacity for knowledge. For Descartes was convinced that all material change is in accordance with simple and necessary mechanical laws; and that, with the aid of some theological bolstering, these laws can be derived *a priori* from a suitably refined understanding of what it is to be material, that is, from the intelligible essence of matter.[2] He supposed that the intellect can penetrate—that his own intellect had penetrated—to the hidden principles of things. But how could such a thing be done? The problem is like Kant's problem—How is synthetic *a priori* knowledge possible?—but Descartes saw nothing wrong with a metaphysical answer. The intellect can spin knowledge from its own entrails because God created it with the means to do so. We have innate ideas, capacities for knowledge of fundamental principles which can be made explicit if we adopt the proper method.

A first principle of Descartes's method is that what is complex and not understood should be broken down into what is simple and intelligible and evidently true.[3] These simple ideas, as Spinoza tells us in his exposition of Descartes, must be examined individually: 'For if he could perceive simple ideas clearly and distinctly, he would doubtless understand all the other ideas composed of those simple ones, with the same clarity and perspicuity.'[4] Analysis is to be followed by synthesis.[5] The theory is full of Aristotelian overtones. The Aristotelian principle that what is uncombined is incapable of either truth or falsity is replaced by the principle that only what is complex can be false. 'Simple natures', we are told, 'are known *per se* and are wholly free from

---

[1] *Essays on the Intellectual Powers of Man* (1785), i. i. 8.
[2] Cf. *Principles of Philosophy*, ii. 36–44.
[3] Cf. *Rules*, v–vi.
[4] Spinoza, *Principles of Cartesian Philosophy* (1663), introduction.
[5] Cf. *Rules*, xiii.

falsity.' There is nothing in a simple nature not completely known because 'otherwise it could not be called simple, but must be complex—a compound of the element we perceive and the supposed unknown element'.[1] As the Aristotelian stripped away accidents to leave bare the essence and properties of the species, Descartes strips inessentials from our everyday conception of a body to reveal the simple idea of extension and other simple ideas, such as mobility and duration, which are necessarily connected to extension. The simplicity and intelligibility of these ideas is for him a kind of guarantee, through the goodness of God, that they are 'true' and pertain to reality. They constitute a dependable link between the subjective realm of ideas and what is objective and external.

Locke's epistemology is the antithesis of all this, but is expressed in remarkably similar terms. The link with reality is not innate and intellectual but adventitious and sensory. He states the problem very explicitly, like Descartes, in the form of a hypothetical scepticism:

'Tis evident, the Mind knows not Things immediately, but only by the intervention of the *Ideas* it has of them. *Our knowledge* therefore is *real*, only so far as there is a conformity between our *Ideas* and the reality of Things. But what shall be here the Criterion? How shall the Mind, when it perceives nothing but its own *Ideas*, know that they agree with Things themselves?[2]

But the question is not put in any spirit of perplexity, as many critics have assumed. It is simply the prelude to a summary statement of Locke's clear, confident, highly theoretical and deliberately anti-Cartesian answer to it. That answer, like Descartes's, hinges on the distinction between simple and complex ideas. It also hinges on a neat causal theory of representation.

Simple ideas, as we know, are necessarily received through the senses or reflection. That is to say (to ignore the special case of 'reflection'), they are caused in us by external things acting on the senses. For that very reason simple ideas must be taken to correspond to their objects in regular and orderly ways, even if we do not know the nature of those objects or how they act on us. A simple idea is therefore a natural sign of its cause. It is naturally fitted to represent in thought that attribute of reality, whatever it may be, which is in general responsible for our receiving ideas or sensations of that type.[3] Thus the simple idea or appearance of

[1] *Rules*, xii.   [2] *Essay*, IV. iv. 3.
[3] Cf. *Essay*, IV. xi. 2.

white received in sensation and capable of being recalled in the imagination represents in thought whatever in the object underlies its general disposition or power regularly to cause just that sensation in us. This power Locke calls the 'quality' of the object.

It follows that simple ideas are all necessarily 'real' and 'conform' to things. They cannot be 'fantastical':

> simple Ideas *are not fictions* of our Fancies, but the natural and regular productions of Things without us, really operating upon us; and so carry with them all the conformity which is intended . . . Thus the *Idea* of Whiteness, or Bitterness, as it is in the Mind, exactly answering that Power which is in any Body to produce it there, has all the real conformity it can, or ought to have, with Things without us.[1]

Similar arguments go to prove that simple ideas are necessarily adequate and also 'true', in the loose sense in which ideas can be said to be true if something exists conforming to them.[2] For Locke as for Descartes, falsity and inadequacy only arises when there is complexity.

It is significant that the very ideas which for Locke epitomize simplicity, ideas of colours, were taken by Cartesians to exemplify composition. Descartes took the ordinary idea of a colour to include both the bare image or sensation and an 'obscure judgement' as to its unknown cause. Two other sorts of ideas of a colour are possible: first, the rash and false idea which incorporates the judgement that the cause of the sensation is qualitatively like the sensation, that the sensation of colour represents its cause as it is in the object; and, secondly, the clear and distinct, materially true idea which refers the sensation to mechanical causes in the object.[3] All, however, are complex. For Locke, on the other hand, the sensation or image *is* the idea, and his criterion for its simplicity is phenomenal, the limits of phenomenal discrimination. Each simple idea, being 'in it self uncompounded, contains in it nothing but *one uniform Appearance*'.[4] This simple appearance *represents* something, but the causal relation which constitutes the representative relation does not enter into the content of the idea, as it does for Descartes. Still less do speculations as to the intrinsic nature of the unknown cause: simple ideas do not, Locke tells us, 'become liable to any Imputation of *Falshood*, if the Mind (as in most Men I believe it

---

[1] *Essay*, IV. iv. 4. Cf. II. xxx. 2.
[2] Cf. *Essay*, II. xxxi. 2; II. xxxii. 14.
[3] Cf. *Principles*, I. 66–73; *Meditations*, III and VI. Cf., too, Arnauld, *Logic*, I. ix.
[4] *Essay*, II. ii. 1.

does) judges these Ideas to be in the Things themselves'.[1] For they are 'as real distinguishing Characters, whether they be only constant Effects, or else exact Resemblances of something in the things themselves'.[2] With phenomenal simplicity goes indefinability, for the idea of a colour, like any simple idea, cannot be conveyed in words. This familiar point was taken by Leibniz, but he remains obdurately Cartesian. Five years before the publication of the *Essay*, he had written,

we are not able to explain to the blind what red is; nor can we make manifest to others any object of this kind except by bringing the thing before them, so that they may be made to see, smell or taste the same; . . . It is nevertheless certain that these notions are composite, and may be resolved, since they have their several causes.[3]

Despite this disagreement over paradigms, there are some ideas which are simple for both Locke and Descartes: for example, very general ideas like *existence* and *unity* which figure in Cartesian 'eternal truths'. For Locke, however, such ideas are mere abstractions from experience, and there are no eternal truths outside our own minds. A different problem is raised by the question, 'What are the simple ideas of extension?' Here Locke is pulled in two directions. He sees the claims to be simple of the general or determinable concept, which any Cartesian would have chosen, but he unsurprisingly prefers what he calls 'a sensible Point', 'the least portion of Space or Extension, whereof we have a clear and distinct *Idea*'. As he recognizes, his paradigms do not fit extension very neatly, but he is no more in real retreat than Leibniz was over colours. As a footnote to the Fifth Edition of the *Essay* reports him, '. . . if the *Idea* of Extension is so peculiar, that it cannot exactly agree with the Definition that he has given of those *Simple Ideas*, so that it differs in some manner from all others of that kind, he thinks 'tis better to leave it there expos'd to this Difficulty, than to make a new Division in his Favour. 'Tis enough for Mr. *Locke* that his Meaning can be understood.' The objection is dismissed as a pedantic nicety which does not touch the real issues.[4]

We can say, then, that a fundamental difference of view over the nature of what ties thought to reality—innate structural interpretive principles versus reliable experiential building-blocks—found expression within the general framework of a

[1] *Essay*, ii. xxxii. 14.
[2] *Essay*, ii. xxx. 2.
[3] Leibniz, 'Reflections on Knowledge, Truth and Ideas' (written 1684).
[4] *Essay*, ii. xv. 9, with footnote in 5th edn.

compositionalist theory of ideas.[1] Unless we recognize that relationship and the methodological and epistemological point of Locke's variety of compositionalism, it is easy to exaggerate both the limitations which it placed on his thought and apparent inconsistencies in his argument. In a notorious passage he seems ready to allow that, after all, no idea whatsoever enjoys absolute simplicity, since all ideas, 'when attentively considered', include 'some kind of relation' in them. 'And sensible Qualities,' he asks, 'what are they but the Powers of different Bodies, in relation to our Perception . . . And if considered in the things themselves, do they not depend on the Bulk, Figure, Texture, and Motion of the Parts?'[2] Yet the point is not an abject capitulation to the Cartesian conception of the complex idea of a sensible quality, nor is it an even more abject flight from compositionalism altogether. It is part of an argument for including ideas of powers in the class of simple ideas, by contrast with ideas of substances. Locke has in mind that ideas of substances may be formed more or less well and appropriately and carefully, whereas our idea of the power of a thing, say the power of wax to be melted by gentle heat, an idea which we acquire when we take note of its regular observable behaviour, leaves, so Locke thought, no comparable room for error. The appearance of the regular effect adequately 'represents' a power both in the agent, the source of heat, and in the patient, the wax. In other words, it represents whatever in each object underlies or causes the observed tendency, just as the idea of white adequately represents whatever in the object regularly causes that idea in us. No mere analytical method applied to our ideas will take us further in either case, for our knowledge and thought about the world stands on such 'simple' representative relationships, founded on experience. It is this epistemological simplicity which really counts as simplicity in Locke's eyes.

What, then, is the role of analysis for Locke? I can give only a rough and partial answer now. Like Descartes, he recommends that we examine our complex ideas part by part as a route to what he calls 'clear and distinct' ideas. Yet this Cartesian phrase has been radically reinterpreted in line with Locke's conviction that no method will enable us to penetrate with certainty and full understanding beyond the limits of observation. We are condemned to speculative hypothesis employing only experiential concepts. One thing method can do, however, is to keep us pressed

[1] The possibility of such a comparison is briefly mentioned, but not explored, by Gibson, p. 48.

[2] *Essay*, II. xxi. 3.

up against this barrier by eliminating mere unclarity of thought. Here the impediment is not a veil of ideas so much as a veil of words which can entangle and impose on us especially with respect to the formation of complex ideas. To overcome this impediment we need a systematic, settled, and public way of thinking about nature and human affairs, that is to say, orderly and settled systems of complex ideas and an orderly and settled vocabulary to express them. Ordinary or 'civil' language is for various reasons inadequate, and a strict or 'philosophical' language needs to be introduced. Locke is here acting as spokesman for the programme of linguistic reform, especially in chemical and biological classification, initiated by Bacon's denunciation of the 'Idols of the Market-place' and taken up by the Royal Society. This programme, in Locke's eyes, concerns complex ideas. For simple ideas, just as they are necessarily 'adequate' and 'true' in their relation to reality, so are they almost inevitably, even if not necessarily, 'clear and distinct' and all that is good in their relation to a public language.[1] That is to say, problems of meaning and communication can arise (or arose in the seventeenth century, in Locke's reasonable view) when men talk and think in chemistry of 'liquor', 'salt', or 'metal', in biology of 'fish' or 'shrubs', and in ethics of 'honour' or 'justice', but they do not in general arise in respect of such simpler predicates as 'blue' or 'square'. The chief remedy for such problems, therefore, to which Locke devotes a significant part of the *Essay*, consists in the analysis of the complex into the simple.

There are many gaps in the present argument,[2] but I have tried to give at least an impression of the depth and complexity of the context which supplied Locke both with the tool of compositionalism and with the problems on which he brought it to bear. In studying such relationships between thinker and context I believe that we are studying human rationality itself. Perhaps what is chiefly wrong with the proposal that Locke adopted compositionalism in emulation of physical theory is that it grossly underestimates that rationality in his case.

[1] Cf. *Essay*, II. xxix. 7; III. iv. 15.
[2] I have discussed only certain Lockean simple and complex ideas, and I have not considered how much Locke owes, e.g., to Hobbes or Gassendi.

THE GREAT LITTLE MADISON:
FATHER OF THE CONSTITUTION

By PROFESSOR ESMOND WRIGHT

Read 5 November 1981

JOHN F. KENNEDY in 1962 described James Madison as 'the most underrated President in American History'.

At first glance this seems a strange description of one who was by general consent the Father of the Constitution, the author of twenty-nine of the eighty-five *Federalist Papers*, the major architect of the Bill of Rights, one of two major campaigners against the Alien and Sedition Acts in 1798, Jefferson's chief lieutenant, his Secretary of State, and, in 1809, his successor as the fourth President of the United States.

But there are paradoxes and contradictions in the man's thinking that go some way to explain John Kennedy's assessment. Madison was a dedicated republican with a firm faith in popular sovereignty, and the *Federalist Papers* were a superb piece of propaganda in the struggle for the ratification of the Constitution. Yet much of his thinking is conservative: in *Federalist* 10 he emerges as tough, cautious, and ultra-realistic, both in his appreciation of the primacy of economic forces and in his awareness that, at the centre of democratic politics, there is a struggle which he saw as a clash of factions, and which we in Europe, accustomed to a Marxist dialectic, would call a war of classes. The *Federalist* emphasis is on the protection of property interests against the attacks of popular majorities, not on the protection of 'the people' from the tyranny of the executive. Popular government, yes, but awareness also that a popular majority could wield a tyranny all its own. He could have said, with Burke, that the tyranny of the multitude is a multiplied tyranny.

Again, he introduced the Bill of Rights in 1790—having argued in 1787 that it was unnecessary.

And there is another paradox: the contrast between his achievement, for as such, two hundred years later, we can see it to have been, and the man's limitations of physique and experience.

How did he acquire the reputation that he did—a man of no special family standing, born in what he called 'an obscure corner of the world', a remote part of Virginia, so shy that he did not speak in public before the age of thirty, so physically unimpressive that he was incapable of military experience when a public career required it, with a voice that was all but inaudible? Neither in fluency of speech, nor in literary style nor in natural combativeness, was this a Tom Paine; his prose could be not only tortuous but ambiguous.

If we look beyond 1789, the paradoxes can be continued. The nationalist of 1787 broke with Hamilton in 1790, and became the nullifier and near-secessionist of 1798, so his otherwise consistent federalism was tarnished. In 1812 he took his country into a war for which it was ill-prepared, which one section of it did not support, a war the main cause of which had been already abandoned by Britain, and a war which, when it ended, had not dealt with those alleged causes anyway, like impressment and freedom of the seas. Later he denied himself a role as a Southern apologist, by his doubts over slavery, by condemning nullification and secession, by refusing to permit the pro-slavery men to exploit for their own purposes his attack on the Alien and Sedition Acts, and by refusing to endorse the pro-slavery and pro-states rights' positions of John C. Calhoun or Robert Y. Hayne.

The answer—if I may give it at the outset—is that Madison was creating something new, and intellectually he was sailing in uncharted waters. His more philosophic associates did not attempt this. Jefferson in 1776 had contended:

Whether I had gathered my ideas from reading or reflection I do not know. I know only that I turned to neither book nor pamphlet while writing it. I did not consider it as any part of my charge to invent new ideas altogether, and to offer no sentiments which had ever been expressed before.

Adams more pungently put it, 'not an idea in it but what had been hackneyed in Congress for 2 years before'. The Declaration of Independence, they both agreed, said nothing that had not been said repeatedly over the previous century. But, translated into the Articles of Confederation, in which sovereignty—if it could be found—was exercised by thirteen distinct and sometimes rival republics, the ideas of 1649 had proved themselves totally inadequate as a system of government. Madison's task was to do nothing less than to devise a new theory and a new system that would reconcile empire and republic, liberty and large size, the ability to command allegiance at the centre but permit autonomy at the peripheries. His preoccupation was with 'an empire for liberty'. He had to build nothing less than an extensive, federal, representative republic when many abroad and some at home, including Hamilton and at times Jefferson, denied that it would last, and he had to develop a political theory that would be a guide to preserving it for posterity. Madison was moving into totally new ground, and mere literary grace was not enough. What mattered was knowledge, wisdom, patience, total dedication, and that political skill some would call prudence, others opportunism, and others even inconsistency. The parallels are with Burke, and —dare it be said?—with Aristotle.

My concern tonight is with the man, and the source and nature of his political ideas, not with the final document, which is all too familiar. Who was he? Where did his ideas come from? Was he a mere imitator, as he was certainly an admirer, of Thomas Jefferson?[1]

The tactics came with the personality. He was dwarfed physically and in manner by the Virginian giants, Washington and Jefferson, even pushed into the shadows later (after marriage in 1794 when he was forty-three) by the stronger personality of his wife, and by the irresponsibility of her son by her first marriage, John Payne Todd. There was little charisma in the 5 foot 6 inch figure, with his hair carefully combed to hide a low forehead, almost always dressed in black, diffident and weak-voiced—so weak that it was suitable neither for the pulpit nor the law. He refused to go abroad, and travelled reluctantly—there was a chronic fear of sickness, and a frequency of 'bilious' attacks. The Virginian political leaders were by contrast impressive physically and in resources, men of many acres, and if they were not always of long-tailed families or of hereditary wealth, they made it—or married into it—easily: witness the careers of Washington and Pendleton, George Mason and Peyton Randolph. They were squires by heredity, and, almost by heredity, justices of the peace and vestrymen, hiring and firing rectors, collecting taxes for

[1] For reasons of time, I omit from this paper reflections on Madison's views on religious toleration, slavery, and the West. On these, see my article, 'The Political Education of James Madison', in *History Today*, 31 (Dec. 1981).

The quotations from Madison's writings that follow in this paper are drawn from *The Papers of James Madison* (eds. Rutland *et al.*, Universities of Chicago and Virginia Press, 1956—12 vols. to date). The best one-volume biography is by Ralph Ketcham (1971), but Irving Brant's six-volume life (1941-61) and one-volume abridgement (1970) are indispensable.

support of the Anglican Church, serving as county militia officers. Almost all of them came from the Tidewater or the Northern Neck, trading with Britain and the West Indies, sophisticated in their fashion, leaders chosen by open and oral elections, by men who usually went merry to the Court House.

Despite his small stature, his lack of military experience, and his remote frontier home, Madison did in many respects conform to this pattern: his first public post, as a delegate to the Virginian Convention in 1776 which drew up the Virginian Constitution, was uncontested; he went aged twenty-five as his father's son representing the sparsely settled county of Orange; his father was landowner and vestryman, justice and county lieutenant, and chairman of the Orange County Committee. He was accompanied by his uncle William Moore as a fellow delegate and went as a member of a local committee, all of whom were interrelated, and not from any merits of his own. A year later, he was defeated at the polls, a defeat he later ascribed to his youthful refusal to supply free liquor to the voters.

The people not only tolerated but expected and even required to be courted and treated. No candidate who neglected those attentions could be elected. His forbearance would have been ascribed to a mean parsimony, or to a proud disrespect of the voters . . . It was found that the old habits were too deeply rooted to be suddenly reformed. Particular circumstances obtained for me success in the first election, at which I was a candidate. At the next, I was outvoted by 2 candidates, neither of them having superior pretensions, and one particularly deficient in them; but both of them availing themselves of all the means of influence familiar to the people. My reserve was imputed to want of respect for them, if to no other unpopular motive.[1]

The man who won, Charles Porter, happened to be the local tavern-keeper. The limitations went deeper. He had three years at home, part of the time suffering from melancholia, and frequently admitting that he did not expect to live long; he was rejected by the first girl he sought, a fourteen-year-old Kitty Floyd from New York; and it was not until he was thirty—four years after he began his legislative career—that he first spoke in public. None of this sounded auspicious.

Montpelier was in Orange County in the Piedmont, where the Rapidan emerged from the mountains to meet the Rappahannock, 30 miles north of Monticello, 80 miles north-west of Richmond, which became the capital in 1779. When Madison

---

[1] 'Autobiographical Notes, 1832', cited in W. C. Rives, *The Life and Times of James Madison* (3 vols. 1859–68), i. 181.

first visited Richmond in May 1784, it had only three hundred buildings. The fall line settlements and all beyond them were frontier country reached by neither postriders nor coaches so that letters waited for the passing of trustworthy travellers. In political terms this was, in Madison's phrase, 'the most spirited part of the country'; here Loyalists were few indeed. But it was remote. When he went to the Continental Congress in Philadelphia in March 1780 the journey took twelve days, owing to 'the extreme badness of the roads and the frequency of rains'.

At his birth, the estate of some 5,000 acres was still raw with stumps and slash, more forest than field, rich in oak and hickory, pine and poplar, chestnut and dogwood. There were then some forty slaves, many of them children, and the rich red clay produced tobacco, corn, and wheat. His father was his own manager, aided by the younger sons, notably Ambrose, whose death in 1794 coincided with James Madison's own marriage and with his return to Montpelier—it may even have been its cause. There was here a firm and happy agrarian base, comfortable certainly but not rich. In his years as Congressman, he was constantly short of money. The state was slow in paying his salary and, without the services of moneylender Haym Solomon, he and many others could not have continued. He was self-sufficient, however, and in 1801 on his father's death he inherited the estate. It was no Westover, and no Monticello. He could devote himself to public affairs but never without anxiety; after his death his widow survived only by the sale, first, of his notes on the Convention (for $30,000 in 1837), then his other manuscripts for $25,000 (in 1848), and finally by selling Montpelier itself.

The family could trace their origins back to John Madison, a ship's carpenter of Gloucester County who died before 1683, and who had received 600 acres of land for immigrants whose passage was paid, and increased this by adding to it another 1,300 acres on the York and Mattapony rivers. This is, however, one generation further back than Madison himself traced his roots. On neither side were they, he thought, 'among the most wealthy of the country, but in independent and comfortable circumstances'. They were, he said, respectable but not opulent. At his grandfather's death in 1732, there were twenty-nine slaves, of whom fourteen were children. In the next fifty years the number quadrupled. In 1782 there were 118 slaves. His grandfather owned twenty-eight books—on religion, practical medicine, and a 'manual for plantation living'. In his father's library, when he died in 1801, there were eighty-three titles, mainly medical and religious, among them: *The Art of Midwifery*; *Cold Bathing*; *Gospel Mystery of Sanctification*; and *Life of Man in the Soul of God*.

Madison was the eldest of twelve children, five of whom died in infancy. The Piedmont countryside was dotted with Beales and Willises, Madisons and Taylors. His grandmother, Frances Taylor, widowed when thirty-two, was a strong character; she died when he was ten. There was a swarm of Taylor relatives, since Frances Taylor's four sisters had fifteen children, and her four brothers had dozens of male heirs. His father had forty or more first cousins on the Taylor side alone. Among the connections were Edmund Pendleton and John Taylor of Caroline County. On his death, Madison left the estates to some thirty nephews and nieces. Dolley said the house was once filled with more than a hundred friends and relatives. A second cousin James, born at Staunton in the Valley and brought up at Madison Hall in Augusta (now Rockingham) County, became a professor at William and Mary College, and in 1777 its president; after the Revolution he was to be first bishop of the Protestant Episcopal Church in Virginia. In 1777 Madison lodged with this cousin, the Reverend James, in Williamsburg, a town then of 150 families, and often dined—so it seems—at table in College. One of his second cousins married the sister of Patrick Henry, another, and two daughters as well, married the children of Andrew Lewis, kinsman of Washington and a victor in 1774 of the battle of Point Pleasant with the Indians. It was a family-based system. In Virginia, kinship counted. It still does.

In his education there were three periods: aged 11 to 16 at Donald Robertson's school on the Innes plantation on the Mattapony, near Dunkirk, and near the Madison tidewater lands in King and Queen County; aged 18 to 21 at Nassau Hall (the largest building then in North America) the college of New Jersey (Princeton); and not least the three years 1772–5 of—on the whole—gloomy and melancholy but sustained reading at home at Montpelier, much of it in theology and law. Each of these was of major significance.

At school he studied the classics, French, and Spanish, and discovered later in life that his French sounded more Aberdonian than Parisian.[1] Robertson's library gave him access to

---

[1] Robertson was born in 1717, educated at Aberdeen and the University of Edinburgh, and came to Virginia in 1753. He was tutor in the family of Col. John Baylor of Caroline County, and was one of many pre-Revolutionary Scots schoolmasters who dispensed 'learning with a burr'.

Montesquieu, Montaigne, Fontenelle, Locke's *Essay Concerning Human Understanding*, and to the *Spectator*, as much an influence on him as on Franklin. An eight-volume set of the *Spectator* was ordered by his father two years before James Madison was born.

From 1767 to 1769 Madison was educated at home, since the newly appointed minister of the Brick Church the family attended, Thomas Martin, lived with the family at Montpelier (and died a year later). Martin was a graduate of the College of New Jersey, then under the guidance of the zealous New Light Presbyterians Samuel Davies and Samuel Finley. It was Martin's persuasions that led Madison (stage 2) to Princeton, rather than to William and Mary. Williamsburg was from July to October, 'the sickly season', a malarial area; and even worse was the fear that the president of William and Mary, James Horrocks, might become the first American bishop, as part of that Episcopal design which was, rightly or wrongly, attributed to British policy. Moreover, as Governor Fauquier reported, former President Thomas Dawson had too often applied 'for consolation to spirituous liquors'; an unnamed group of professors in 1773 were known to have 'played all Night at Cards in publick Houses in the City, and . . . often [were] seen drunken in the Street'.[1] By contrast, John Witherspoon, who had become president of Princeton the year before, came from Paisley and was an active Presbyterian, happily free from any taint of being a Pisky. He owed his popularity, and the call to Nassau Hall, to his satirical pamphlet *Ecclesiastical Characteristics, or The Arcana of Church Policy*, a savage attack on churchmen who put social duties before Christianity, and to whom Socrates mattered more than St. Paul. It would not stop the same Dr Witherspoon mixing his own religion with politics. His staff consisted of only two tutors but with him he brought 500 books. The Princeton library, largely the gift of Governor Belcher, had 2,000 books, but it was Witherspoon who introduced the ideas of the Scottish Enlightenment.

Madison's Princeton years are, I believe, the most important in his life, since they shaped his basic attitudes and gave him his intellectual equipment. He worked intensely hard, packing a four-year course on Scottish lines into two (August 1769–September 1771), followed by a few months with Witherspoon studying Hebrew, law, and ethics. Clearly he was attracted to the idea of

[1] W. S. Perry (ed.), *Historical Collections Relating to the American Colonial Church*, i. 517; cf. Burk, *History of Virginia*, iii (1805), 333, and Dumas Malone, *Jefferson the Virginian* (1948), p. 52.

a career both in divinity and in law, but in the end chose neither, presumably because of his weak voice and personal timidity. He worked so hard that he thought he would not survive the strain. He was too ill to attend his own graduation exercises. He remained shy and introspective. His health, he said in his *Autobiography*, written at the age of eighty, was 'too infirm for a journey home'. He was, however, dauntingly well prepared: Latin and Greek, mathematics and natural philosophy, and, notably, public law, the Law of Nature and of Nations which Witherspoon taught himself. His texts were Locke, Harrington, and Montesquieu in government, Grotius, Pufendorf, Barbeyrac, Cumberland, Selden, Burlamaqui, Hobbes, Machiavelli, Harrington, Locke, and Sidney. Montesquieu, Adam Ferguson, Lord Kames, and Hume appear elsewhere on his reading lists. Rousseau was ignored, and to Witherspoon Voltaire and Hume were anathema —as were Plato, More, and Utopians generally. The emphasis was on clarity in thinking and clarity in speech, with public disputations in English and Latin, which Witherspoon had introduced. The goal, of course, was knowledge, but, more than that, philosophic enquiry into the causes of things. The method was by reason not revelation.

This course of study can be described as 'philosophic' in the eighteenth century (and still in the Scottish) sense, a study *de rerum natura*. It was Scottish in the most direct sense, and it was in Scotland, and especially in Edinburgh, that what we would now call not philosophy but political sociology, and what Scots still call 'political economy', had been developed: in the work of Francis Hutcheson and David Hume, Adam Smith, Thomas Reid, Lord Kames, and Adam Ferguson, not to mention Principal Robertson as historian. Their writings in history, ethics, politics, economics, psychology, and jurisprudence, in terms of 'a system upon which natural effects are explained', had become standard texts. These Scottish writers made one common assumption. The assumption was

that there is a great uniformity among the actions of men, in all nations and ages, and that human nature remains still the same, in its principles and operations. The same motives always produce the same actions; the same events follow from the same causes . . . Would you know the sentiments, inclinations, and course of life of the Greeks and Romans? Study well the temper and actions of the French and English.

Thus wrote David Hume, presenting the basis of a science of human behaviour. The method of eighteenth-century social science followed from this primary assumption, the constancy of the human reaction. Again Hume:

Mankind are so much the same, in all times and places, that history informs us of nothing new or strange in this particular. Its chief use is only to discover the constant and universal principles of human nature, by showing men in all varieties and situations, and furnishing us with materials from which we may form our observations and become acquainted with the regular springs of human action and behaviour.[1]

Moreover, the aim of studying man's behaviour in the past was for the purpose of prediction—philosophy would aid the legislator in making correct policy decisions. Comparative historical studies of man in society would allow the discovery of the constant and universal principles of human nature, which, in turn, would allow at least some safe predictions about the effects of legislation 'almost as general and certain as any which the mathematical sciences will afford us'. 'Politics' (and again the words are Hume's) to some degree 'may be reduced to a science'. This was the orthodox enlightenment view. It raided history for evidence, but it was in itself profoundly unhistorical.

In his 'Of Ancient and Modern Confederacies', Madison accepted this Age-of-Reason concept: 'the past should enlighten us on the future: knowledge of history is no more than anticipated experience. Where we see the same faults followed regularly by the same misfortunes, we may reasonably think that if we could have known the first we might have avoided the others.'[2] In his recent studies of the impact of Scottish thinkers on the American revolutionaries, *Inventing America* and *Explaining America*, Garry Wills has argued that the predominant influence on Thomas Jefferson and his writing of the Declaration of Independence was not John Locke and possessive individualism but rather the moral-sense philosophers of the Scottish Enlightenment, particularly Francis Hutcheson and William Small. Wills contended that Jefferson, like the eighteenth-century Scots, was a moral sentimentalist, not a contractarian; and that he believed that society was held together not by legal or contractual ties but by ties of affection, benevolence, and moral feeling. With the Scots having captured Jefferson's mind so completely, 'the question arises', Wills writes in the preface to *Explaining America*, 'whether any other political thinkers of our early national period were

---

[1] Hume, 'Of Liberty and Necessity', in *An Enquiry Concerning Human Understanding* (1748).

[2] *The Papers of James Madison*, ix (1975), 4–22.

influenced by the Scottish Enlightenment'. The answer, he says, is emphatically yes, that Madison was Hume's man.[1]

To the Age of Reason there was another basic, and to Americans, more disturbing, premise. To both Adams and Hamilton history proved (so they believed) that sooner or later the American people would have to return to a system of mixed or limited monarchy—so great was the size of the country, so diverse were the interests to be reconciled, that no other system could secure both liberty and justice. Similarly, Patrick Henry's prediction on 9 June 1788, in the Virginia Ratifying Convention, 'that one government [i.e. the proposed constitution] cannot reign over so extensive a country as this is, without absolute despotism', was grounded upon a 'political axiom' scientifically confirmed, so he believed, by history.[2] They all followed Montesquieu in this. It is indeed hardly surprising, since the men of the Enlightenment in Europe had no alternative but to seek their reforms through despots. And the seventeenth-century thinkers they read—Hobbes, Grotius, and Pufendorf—were advocates of the absolutist state. It was natural for Americans in moments of pessimism to talk of Cincinnatus, or even, as Hamilton did, of Caesar.

Again, Enlightenment thinking rested on a solid groundwork of historical knowledge, in spite of the essentially unhistorical nature of its theoretical foundations. History is invoked more often than philosophy. Montesquieu, Mably, and Delolme were called on less for their philosophical views than for their factual material. The history of Greece and of Republican Rome form for the Founding Fathers a first frame of reference. Besides this, the authors of the *Federalist* show acquaintance with the later history of the Holy Roman Empire—thanks, no doubt, to the invaluable Robertson—and with the separate histories of Great Britain, France, the Low Countries, and Switzerland. Although the *Federalist* was published in the same year as the last volumes of Gibbon, its authors are true to their century in their neglect of the Middle Ages. History ends with the establishment of the Roman Empire, and begins again in the second half of the fifteenth century—all between is decadence or feudal anarchy. And even in those stretches of familiar history, there were peculiar emphases: Trenchard and Gordon and *Cato's Letters* of the 1720s made Harrington as well as Locke fashionable; and consideration of the Interregnum years, 1649 to 1660, gives Cromwell hardly a

[1] Wills, *Inventing America: Jefferson's Declaration of Independence* (1978) and *Explaining America: the Federalist* (1980).
[2] Cf. Elliot's *Debates*, iii (1838), and Henry's contributions, *passim*.

mention. In all the discussion of constitutions as binding charters, why the neglect of Cromwell and the 'Instrument of Government', of Cromwellism and of republican tyranny and for that matter of British seventeenth-century Federalism?[1]

Into this historical–philosophic context it was easy to fit Locke but it is Locke the psychologist, rather than Locke the politician, the Locke of *Human Understanding* with his preoccupation with the universal laws governing Human Nature. In one way Locke reinforced Harrington. The origin and purpose of the state Locke found in property.

> The reason why men enter into society is the preservation of their property, and the end why they choose and authorize a legislature is that there may be laws made and rules set as guards and fences to the properties of all the members of the society. It is the cause of the origin and it is the end of the state. The supreme power cannot take from any man part of his property without his consent.[2]

But it was the Scots, Witherspoon the Whig and Hume the Tory, who were the decisive influence on James Madison.

The impact of Princeton was important not just in this dedication to the study of political ideas, but in emphasizing the study of public law and government. Witherspoon pushed the college into the public arena. 'The spirit of liberty', he said, 'breathed high and strong'. He declared himself to be 'an opposer of lordly domination and sacerdotal tyranny',[3] and this role Madison was glad to inherit. At Madison's first commencement, honorary degrees—the first ever awarded—were given to John Hancock, John Dickinson, and Joseph Galloway, three revolutionary heroes; as early as 1770 the seniors wore American-spun coats—as Madison would himself at his own Inaugural as President in 1809; and, in the commencement that followed the Boston Massacre, the president's son James—who was in 1777 to be killed at the battle of Brandywine—upheld the affirmative case in the debate in Latin on the thesis 'Subjects are bound and obliged by the law of nature, to resist their king, if he treats them cruelly or ignores the law of the state, and to defend their liberty'. They also proved conclusively—and that in the presence of royal governor

---

[1] This is an area on which it is proper to salute three path-finding articles: Caroline Robbins, 'When it is that Colonies may turn Independent', *William and Mary Quarterly*, xi (April 1954) and Douglass Adair, 'That Politics may be Reduced to a Science', *Huntington Library Quarterly*, xx (1957), and his 'The Tenth Federalist Revisited', *William and Mary Quarterly*, viii (1951).

[2] Locke, *Second Treatise*, chap. 9 sec. 124 and chap. 11 secs. 134, 138.

[3] *New Jersey Archives*, xxviii. 227, 345. Cf. Ketcham, op. cit., p. 38.

William Franklin—that 'Omnes Homines, Jure Naturae, liberi sunt'. His closest friend, William Bradford, in his valedictory address in 1772 spoke on 'The disadvantages of an Unequal Distribution of Property in a State'. At Nassau Hall the young man from Orange County was drinking heady wine.

The studying did not stop at Princeton but continued (stage 3) through the next three years. Basic to it was the buying of books through Jefferson and William Bradford; the list of books he recommended for the use of Congress in 1783 included, along with many standard religious works, books by Bayle, Leibniz, and even Diderot, still little read in America. In his correspondence with Bradford and with Philip Freneau, his Princeton friends, he refers to Hume and Fielding, Pope and Kames, Swift and Samuel Butler. These years were marked by an ill health which he believed to be due to epilepsy, but much of which seems to have been in his own mind, and much talk of imminent death. But his friend William Bradford told him that 'persons of the weakest constitutions, by taking a proper care of themselves, often outlive those of the strongest'. Despite the hypochondria, the physical handicaps which kept him out of military service and the threats of visitations of malaria, smallpox, and yellow fever, he was saved by long walks, by riding, and by regular visits to Berkeley Springs in the Catoctin Mountains, still a popular spa with Virginians. He lived of course, like many hypochondriacs, to a ripe old age: he died aged eighty-six.

There was a further stage in his education: on-the-job training as a politician. His knowledge of government was distilled not merely from books, or from reports of 'turbulent scenes in Massachusetts and infamous ones in Rhode Island', as he called them. By 1782, at thirty-six, he was a seasoned legislator. He had served three years in the Virginia Assembly, eleven months in Richmond in the 1784 to 1786 years, and four in Congress. He possessed clear insight into the ways of politicians. He had that necessary ingredient for political success: experience of defeat— having failed to be re-elected because he refused to hand out free whiskey. He knew the nature of pressure groups; he had worked for Virginia's commercial interests against New York's; he had fought religious factions in politics; he had helped push his political foe, Patrick Henry, out of the legislature upstairs into the weakest governorship in America. He was suspicious of oratory— Henry he called 'a forensic member'; he saw him as a trimmer keen on applause, lazy, and careless. He knew the Byzantine manœuvres of local politicians. But throughout all his activity he read voraciously. In 1785 and 1786 he studied the federacies of Ancient Greece, of the Holy Roman Empire, the Swiss Confederation, and the United Provinces. He catalogued the various devices used for financial support, for diplomatic representation, for cooperation in time of war, for the regulation of commerce, for the coercion of members who disobeyed confederacy orders, with the troubles in mind that had bedevilled the states under the Articles of Confederation. He sought especially to identify the constitutional bonds of union, the way these bonds worked or failed to work in practice, and the particular causes of the demise or enfeeblement of confederations. He concluded his account of the several leagues with a section entitled 'Vices of the Constitution'. The 'regular fault' of the ancient and modern confederation was that 'the Deputies of the strongest cities awed and corrupted those of the weaker', and Greece thus 'was the victim of Philip . . . [and later] proved [no] Barrier to the vast projects of Rome'. In the United Provinces of the Netherlands Madison noted that though the confederacy seemed on paper to be strong enough, 'the jealousy in each province of its sovereignty renders the practice very different from the theory'. Furthermore, there were 'numerous and notorious' examples of foreign ministers who intrigued with deputies and otherwise interfered in the internal affairs of the Netherlands. Everywhere, Madison found that weak unions courted disaster.

He recorded the facts and lessons about the ancient and modern confederacies in a booklet of forty-one pocket-sized pages, easy to use in debate or writing. It became his vade mecum for the debates in the Federal Convention in 1787 and the Virginia ratifying convention in 1788. He also inserted large parts of his notes almost verbatim in the eighteenth, nineteenth, and twentieth *Federalist Papers*.[1] He became steadily but all but inevitably not a theologian nor a lawyer but a politician. His years at Princeton and then in the continental Congress, along with his interest in the west, emphasized his continentalism, though he was originally a States Rights man. The years of reading and studying—making an advantage out of the disadvantages of physical frailty—made him dedicated, conscientious, well-informed and, at a desk, untiring. Georgia Congressman William Pierce left this description:

Mr Madison . . . blends together the profound politician with the scholar. In the management of every great question he evidently took

[1] Cf. *Papers*, x (1977), notes to p. 324. Cf. also Carl Becker, *The Heavenly City of the Eighteenth-Century Philosophers* (1932), p. 95.

the lead in the convention, and though he cannot be called an orator, he is a most agreable, eloquent and convincing speaker. From a spirit of industry and application which he possesses in a most eminent degree, he always comes forward the best informed man of any point in debate. The affairs of the United States, he perhaps has the most correct knowledge of, of any man in the Union. . . . Mr. Madison is about thirty-seven years of age, a gentleman of great modesty—with a remarkable sweet temper. He is easy and unreserved among his acquaintance, and has a most agreable style of conversation.[1]

He was assiduous in recording the debates, hour after hour, day after day through the long muggy four months of Philadelphia heat. But he was no mere recorder. The Federal Convention saw him now give many major speeches. And he wrote twenty-nine articles in the *Federalist*. In 1787 he has to be judged not by his philosophy but by his statecraft, for he was not a political philosopher but a practical politician drawing solutions from past experience, not theory, and always putting his knowledge to the search for solutions. If in a sense he was doing in 1787 what Locke had done for South Carolina in drawing up a constitution, he nowhere left major philosophic testaments as did Locke and Burke, in England, as did Hamilton in his Convention Speech of 18 June 1787, and John Adams in his *Defence of the Constitutions of the United States* (1787) or his *Discourse on Davila*. The *Federalist* essays apart, and the essays for Freneau's *National Gazette*, written in the winter of 1791-2, there is no state paper that serves as his testament or as a model. His views have to be gleaned from innumerable contributions to debates, or from attitudes on particular experience as a Virginia Congressman under the first Constitution of Virginia which he helped to draft, as a councillor of state in Virginia, as a Federal Congressman from 1780 to 1783 and again in 1787, and as a Virginia Assemblyman from 1784 to 1786. This is the penman of the revolution, staying at his desk and close to home. Adrienne Koch described him as 'the most cosmopolitan statesman never to have quit American shores.'[2] Clinton Rossiter's phrase for him was 'a single-minded political monk'.[3]

What had this education given him? What ideas recur in his

---

[1] Pierce, 'Characters of the Convention', in A. T. Prescott, *Drafting the Federal Constitution, a Re-arrangement of Madison's Notes* (1941), pp. 32-3.

[2] Koch, *Jefferson and Madison, the Great Collaboration* (1950). His longest journey was in 1784, in Lafayette's extrovert and attention-hungry company, to the Mohawk Valley.

[3] Rossiter, *1787: the Grand Convention* (1966), p. 126.

writing? Intellectual activity in any culture is not of course a one-way flow between great minds and passive recipients; it is a discourse, as Gordon Wood has said in reviewing Garry Wills's recent book, 'a complex marketplace-like conglomeration of intellectual exchanges involving many participants all trying to manipulate the ideas available to them in order to explain, justify, lay blame for, or otherwise make sense of what is happening around them'.[1] It followed from this long indoctrination that, first, it was all but instinctive for Madison to speak the language of the social contract. The idea of a contract, he wrote to Nicholas Trist (15 February 1830), is 'a fundamental principle of free government'. The confederation was the result of 'a compact among the States'. He never captured Paine's fire, however, nor Jefferson's skill as phrase-maker. There is nothing here of the simple grandeur of those sixteenth-century citizens of Aragon who when asked to swear allegiance to their sovereign replied: 'We who are as good as you swear to you who are no better than us allegiance as Prince and Heir to our Kingdom, on the condition that you preserve our laws and liberties; and if not, not.'[2] In number 43 of the *Federalist* he justified the revolutionary action of the Philadelphia Convention in discarding the Articles of Confederation by referring to 'the transcendent law of nature and of nature's God, which declares that the safety and happiness of society are the objects at which all political institutions aim and to which all institutions must be sacrificed'. Natural law, and natural rights, the notion that there was a higher law binding on all governments, these were the basic doctrines of 1787, as of 1776. There was no organic view of the state, no rolling Burkeian phrases, nothing on the colonial origins and British roots and not a great deal on what might be called the argument from continuity. Everything turned on choice, either by individuals or by states, and on choice being exercised now. Madison appealed to the 'transcendent and precious right of the people to alter or abolish their governments as to them shall seem most likely to effect their safety and happiness'. All government is formed by agreement, not by tradition or inheritance, by agreement made here and now, and sovereignty can be alienated or divided. Madison had no use for the Blackstonian idea that sovereignty is absolute, indivisible, and inalienable—*un roi, une foi, une loi* was a monarchic notion and redolent

---

[1] Gordon Wood, 'Heroics', in *NY Review of Books* (2 Apr. 1981), p. 16.

[2] John Dunn, *Political Obligation in its Historical Context* (OUP 1980), p. 204; Ralph E. Giesey, *If Not, Not. The Oath of the Aragonese and the Legendary Laws of Sobrarbe* (Princeton, 1968), Appendix I, p. 247.

of Divine Right. Ultimate sovereignty lay with the people, the ultimate sovereign authority, 'the only legitimate fountain of power'. They, and not the individual states, must ratify the Constitution in specially summoned conventions. On them as individuals it operated. Its basis of support lay in 'the enlightened opinion and affection of the people'. In this sense he was a thorough Whig.

But it followed, secondly, that he was implicitly conservative. Property was important, and to be secured. It is property that ensures wisdom and responsibility in the citizen and stability in the state. The prime function of government, he says, is the protection of the different and unequal faculties of man for acquiring property.

From the protection of different and unequal faculties of acquiring property, the possession of different degrees and kinds of property immediately results . . . The most common and durable source of factions has been the various and unequal distribution of property. Those who hold, and those who are without, property have ever formed distinct interests in society. Those who are creditors and those who are debtors fall under a like discrimination. A landed interest, a manufacturing interest, a mercantile interest, a monied interest, with many lesser interests, grow up of necessity in civilized nations, and divide them into different classes, actuated by different sentiments and views. The regulation of these various and interfering interests forms the principal task of modern legislation, and involves the spirit of party and faction in the necessary and ordinary operations of government.

He defined a faction as 'a number of citizens, whether amounting to a majority or a minority of the whole, who are united and actuated by some common impulse of passion, or of interest, adverse to the rights of other citizens or to the permanent and aggregate interests of the community'. Government by faction is to be condemned since it permits the same men to be parties and judges in their own cause. In a controversy between creditors and debtors, both are parties, and neither should have the right to impose its will upon the other. 'Justice ought to hold the balance between them.' In like manner any question involving the mercantile or manufacturing or landed interest, or the apportionment of taxes, should not be decided at the behest of a powerful faction concerned with its own aggrandizement, but by legislators acting with an exact impartiality, and with a sole regard for justice and the public welfare. Thus Madison recognized class conflict as the basis of politics, but he refused to regard a class dictatorship as either necessary or desirable.

The latent causes of faction were sown in the nature of man.

All civilized societies [he had written in New York in the spring of 1787] are divided into different interests and factions, as they happen to be creditors or debtors—rich or poor—husbandmen, merchants, or manufacturers—members of different religious sects—followers of different political leaders—inhabitants of different districts—owners of different kinds of property, etc., etc.

Even where there was no real basis for conflict, the most frivolous and fanciful differences could excite passionate hatreds.

How control these factions? In particular under a republican government, where the majority rules, how prevent that majority from trampling on the minority or on individuals? By enlightened self-interest? But statesmen with vision would not always be at the helm. By public opinion? But the average man—even the average legislator—was likely to think in terms of local interests. Did a Rhode Island Assemblyman, Madison demanded, care what France or even Massachusetts thought of his paper money? By religion? But this did not restrain men as individuals, and it had even less effect on the masses. Indeed, religion could lead to persecution as often as it did to righteousness.

Madison inherited the idea of the individual motivated by self-interest voluntarily leaving a state of nature to live in a free government because it will protect his life, liberty, and property. What was new in his thinking was that he saw the main threat to free government arising from its own creation, from its ambitions, and from its factional spirit. How, then, to curb 'the notorious factions and oppressions' of corporate towns and little republics? Madison's answer brought him back to the grand strategy of the Philadelphia convention. The solution was not to try to remove the causes of faction, for a free society would always produce differences among men. The solution was to use man's vice as a political virtue, and allow the growth of factions to be itself a guarantee of liberty. There would be a healthy and positive 'conflict of ambition countering ambition'. This was ultra-realistic, complex, and sophisticated. And it was devoid of illusion.

Mass unrest was often perceived in the spirit of young Gouverneur Morris: 'The mob begin to think and reason. Poor reptiles! . . . They bask in the sun, and ere noon they will bite, depend upon it. The gentry begin to fear this.' Madison spoke of the Shays Rebellion in scathing terms. Nowhere in America or Europe—not even among the great liberated thinkers of the Enlightenment—did democratic ideas appear respectable to the

cultivated classes. Whether the Fathers looked to the intellectuals
of contemporary Europe or to their own Christian heritage of the
idea of original sin, they found ample confirmation of the notion
that man is an unregenerate rebel who has to be controlled.

Human beings are generally governed by base and selfish
motives, by suspicion, jealousy, desire for aggrandisement, and
ambition. In *Federalist* 55, he said, 'As there is a degree of
depravity in mankind which requires a certain degree of circum-
spection and distrust, so there are other qualities in human nature
which justify a certain portion of esteem and confidence.' He was
more realistic and cynical than Jefferson. There is no talk in him of
the infinite perfectibility of man. 'The purest of human blessings
must have a portion of alloy in them; the choice must always be
made, if not of the lesser evil, at least of the greater, not the perfect
good' (*Federalist* 41). 'What is government itself but the greatest of
all reflections on human nature? If men were angels, no government would be necessary. If angels were to govern men, neither
external nor internal controls on government would be necessary.'
(*Federalist* 51).

This was thus Whig theory but of a traditional and conservative
kind. He would not assume, as did Hobbes, that the absolutism of
Leviathan was the price to pay for self-preservation. But he would
not move towards the aristocratic, plutocratic, and centralizing
policies of Hamiltonian federalism either, when they ran counter
to what he considered to be the interest of the people and their
republican rights. Madison rejected the views of older republicans
like Machiavelli and certainly of 'democratic' theorists like
Rousseau. Just as he refused to look to the notion of a disinterested
monarch or of an aristocracy, since neither could in practice be
above the battle, just as his realism led him to reject the idea of the
'General Will', so he poured an equal scorn on concepts of a
'Legislator' or a 'Dictator' who would magically resolve the
people's problems and then, equally magically, ride away into the
sunset. Even a Cromwell, he might have said (but did not),
acquired ambitions of his own, if not for himself, then for his
posterity.

The foundation of the 'American science of politics', then, was a
hard-headed and, we would now say, 'realistic' view of human
nature. Rejecting the belief of a few of the more radical thinkers of
the European Enlightenment in the perfectibility of man, the
Founding Fathers were virtually unanimous in their distrust of
the human animal. Man was an imperfect creature whose actions
and beliefs were often shaped by passion, prejudice, vanity, and

self-interest, and whose boundless ambition, though sometimes diverted into socially desirable channels by his craving for public approval and fame, made it difficult for him to resist the temptations of power and vice. Man's feeble capacities for resistance thus turned power and vice into corrupting and aggressive forces, the natural victims of which (in the public arena) were liberty and virtue, those central pillars of a well-ordered state. Long ago Horace White observed that the Constitution of the United States is based upon the philosophy of Hobbes and the religion of Calvin. It assumes that the natural state of mankind is a state of war, and that the carnal mind is at enmity with God. The men who drew up the Constitution in Philadelphia during the summer of 1787 had a vivid Calvinistic sense of human evil and damnation; they believed with Hobbes that men are selfish and contentious. They were men of affairs, merchants, lawyers, planter-businessmen, speculators, investors. Having seen human nature on display in the market-place, the courtroom, the legislative chamber, and in every path and alleyway where wealth and power are courted, they felt they knew it in all its frailty. To them a human being was an atom of self-interest. They did not believe in man, but they did believe in the power of a good political constitution to control him. Virtue was an important word. Everyone of Madison's teachers was either a clergyman or a devout Christian layman. The concept of the worth of the individual soul, like the faith in the republic itself, came out of a Christian and a classical tradition.

The government to be set up, however, was republican. In *Federalist* 43 he defended the provision of the Constitution which authorizes Congress 'to guarantee to every State in the Union a republican form of government'. Nor should it casually be overthrown, or changed with frequency. Stability was as important as liberty itself. As a realistic interpreter of human behaviour, as the practical builder of a constitution, he had to dissent from Jefferson's conceit of a political change every generation, whether that meant nineteen years or thirty-four. 'Stability in governments is essential to national character . . . as well as to that repose and confidence in the minds of the people, which are among the chief blessings of civil society' (*Federalist* 37) and, as events would show, he would oppose rights of nullification or secession. The centralist, the nationalist, and the conservative in him was dominant.

If he was both contractarian and conservative, he was also, thirdly and most important, the pragmatist, the problem-solver. Government is set up to curb faction and to curb man's capacity for error and for sin, and this means that it must (1) be balanced,

(2) have its powers separate, though overlapping, (3) be extensive, (4) be representative, and (5) be strong. In his letters of 1786 and 1787 to Jefferson, Washington, and Randolph he developed his practical ideas on constitutional reform: he wanted a stronger national government—and he called it 'national'—with the right to regulate trade, and with a negative on the legislative acts of the states, 'in all cases whatsoever'. He wanted it to have the right to raise money, by an impost on trade. He wanted a national judiciary with supremacy over state courts; he wanted a bicameral legislature, with a seven-year term for senators, a council of revision, and an executive, about which, in 1787, he admitted that he had 'scarcely ventured' to think in detail. He sought 'tranquility' within each state, the right of coercion against delinquent or fractious states, and, 'to give a new system its proper validity and energy', he wanted the new charter ratified by the people and not merely by the legislatures of the states. Moreover, when the Founding Fathers met, they would meet in secret. Open government openly arrived at was a twentieth-century not an eighteenth-century illusion; it was an invitation, Madison knew, to disaster. The Constitution, of which he was the main shaper, was the work of a few—all men, and not one a journalist.

The verdict? A modest man, with no presence and little money who by studying and by reason constructed—in all its omissions—the most intricate and longest-surviving Constitution in human history. Its very restraint and its brevity may have helped to allow it to be the acceptable form of government for three million farmers on the Atlantic coast in 1787 and today for 230 million people of every race and colour from coast to coast. He knew what was important: balance, separation of powers, property rights—and federalism. He came to his conclusions from his own reflection and experience. His reading could do little for him here. Past revolutionary and republican theory had guided the Founding Fathers when it came to the defence of the revolution, the establishment of independence, and the temporary ordering of their own state and national affairs. But now, farsighted republicans were disturbed by the unhappy thought that the Articles of Confederation were not adequate to the task of establishing a more enduring republican union. On the problem of establishing republican government in a large state, previous republican thinkers were either silent or pessimistic.

Even the great classical models were silent. Aristotle had little or nothing to say about a republican federal state, and Madison mentions him only once. He could derive from his reading of the classics a healthy respect for the farming class as the backbone of a polity, but he could have found little or nothing about a federal polity comparable to the actual political situation he faced in America. He may have found in Cicero a conception of natural law which had become so deeply embedded in western thought that it had become a basic premise of constitutional theorists in the sixteenth, seventeenth, and eighteenth centuries. Cicero spoke eloquently of a true law which men might know by reason, an eternal law which 'summons men to the performance of their duties', an unchangeable law which 'restrains them from doing wrong', a law which cannot morally be invalidated by human legislation, a higher law to which the state and its rulers are subject.[1] But, again, there was in Cicero and in most other advocates of natural law, nothing on the problems of a large federal commonwealth. And Cicero, like Plato, Machiavelli, and Rousseau, in any case gets no mention at all. Moreover, he was empiricist not dogmatist. If he was sometimes zealously committed to key ideas, he never insisted that a theory for democratic Greece or republican Rome or constitutional England could be transferred automatically to popular government in America. Aristotle, Machiavelli, Calvin, Harrington, Locke, Montesquieu might suggest 'lessons', but they did not have solutions. He had to devise a theory that would take into account a large expanse of land, the spirit of liberty and equality, the prevalence of local self-government, the widespread distribution of property, an enterprising economic spirit, a deeply rooted constitutional ethos, and some kind of federal division of powers. He made it work not because of *Federalist* 10, or new states having parity with the original thirteen, but because he rested a strong central government on acceptance by the people in the states; by making it national and Federal. And the way of life it secured was prosperous enough to give the people—in all their greed and ambition, and their proneness to faction, which he fully recognized—the will to make it work. This is more than can be said for any *philosophe*. He was the rarest of beings, a very successful and creative politician, or, more accurately, a political mechanic in what he himself called 'a workshop of liberty'.

[1] Cicero, *On The Commonwealth* (Columbus, Ohio, 1929 ed.), pp. 129, 215-16.

THREE POETICAL PRAYER-MAKERS
OF THE ISLAND OF BRITAIN

By GWYN JONES

Read 11 November 1981

IT is a humbling admission for a Welshman to make—and humbly I make it—that in the course of a life which while not yet grown long grows longer by the hour, and a career much given over to trafficking in history and legend, fiction and myth, I have never once invented a triad. Let me, under your protective shield and benevolent helm, here and now redress this injustice to the Threeness of Three, and begin by hanging three small flower baskets of verbal amplification on the bare trellis-work of my would-be triadic title. Thus:

Three Poetical Prayer-Makers of the Island of Britain: Cynddelw the Great Poet, who praised the Princes of Earth and the King of Heaven, and requested his dues of both; James Kitchener Davies the Deathbed Poet, who in extremis prayed to God to deny him all those things he had most worked and prayed for; and Saunders Lewis the Poet of Arduous Causes, who prayed that the Good Thief who died with Jesus on the Cross should pray for us, that we too may know Him in the hour of our extremity.

Which brings me to the second paragraph of my preamble. Having read my terms of reference I am aware, acutely aware, that the Warton Lectures of the British Academy are unambiguously entitled the Warton Lectures on English Poetry. I am even more acutely aware that my Warton Lecture is strictly speaking *not* precisely, entirely, exclusively, or even predominantly on English poetry, and lifetime apostle of the blurred edge though I am, I would expect no one to believe me if I said it was. So I need indulgence—and as I hope, with good reason. For Cynddelw Brydydd Mawr most decidedly was not an English poet. His praise-poems to his patrons the Welsh princes made all they could of the mischief, murder, and mayhem those same princes tirelessly inflicted on the English foe, who it must be admitted as tirelessly inflicted an equal uncharity on them.

In arms against Angles, in Tegeingl's lands,
Blood spilling in streams, blood pouring forth . . .
In strife with the Dragon of the East,
Fair Western Dragon, the best was his.
Ardent the lord, sword bright above sheath,
Spear in strife and outpouring from sword,
Sword-blade in hand and hand hewing heads,
Hand on sword and sword on Norman troops,
And constant anguish from the sight of death . . .
I saw war-stags and stiff red corpses,
It was left to the wolves, their burial;
I saw them routed, without their hands,
Beneath birds' claws, men mighty in war;
I saw their ruin, three hundred dead,
I saw, battle done, bowels on thorns;
I saw strife cause a dreadful uproar,
Troops contending, a rout collapsing . . .
I saw lances red with Owain's rush,
I saw for Saxons sorry corpses . . .

Not an English poet, did I say? He wasn't even pro-English. Nor was James Kitchener Davies pro-English, though somewhere along the line (he was christened James) he must have been pro-Kitchener. Nor is Saunders Lewis pro-English either. He is pro-Welsh. The dearest wish of his political life has been to preserve the Welsh language, achieve Welsh self-government and national independence, and arrest and reverse the twentieth-century process of anglicization and alienation which seeps and creeps through much, indeed most, of Wales today. But to drive my own horses and fly my own hawk—it has been my conviction throughout most of my adult life that it is not only our Welsh business to know what we can of English poetry, but the Englishman's business to know what he can of Welsh poetry. These separate businesses being part and parcel of our common business of being and belonging with and to each other and to the ever-expanding sphere of family, locality, region, country, and as far thereafter as our modest fund of humanity may carry us. This isn't as pious—and certainly not as pi—as it may sound, for I am also a convinced believer in what, within the law and the bounds of regard, is separate and different and individual in us all. Welsh poetry has various characteristics, qualities, ambitions of manner and matter, and above all of metrical and verbal patterns and congruences of sound, not much met with in English poetry. Few among you have more love for English poetry than I—or a warmer admiration—but it is without any constricting modesty, as it is entirely without arrogance, that I am seizing my opportunity to touch lightly, and with the help of two inspired translators,[1] on a subject that the mildly aberrant and erratically inquiring Thomas Warton would, I am sure, approve of.

Which brings me urbanely to the three less than urbane poetical prayer-makers of my lecture this evening. They belong, be it noted, to widely separated centuries. Cynndelw's *floruit* was the second half of the twelfth century, one of the outstanding ages of Welsh poetry. He acquired the cognomen *Brydydd Mawr* during his lifetime, and though at first it may have remarked the width of his shoulders, it served soon to acknowledge the magnitude of his mind. He was thus not only the Large Poet but also the Great Poet, and either way accepted the appellation without demur.

He was a poet of the Gogynfeirdd. The first great age of Welsh poetry was that of the Cynfeirdd, literally the First or First-Come Poets. The Gogynfeirdd were the Next-to-the-First or Next-Come Poets. They are also known as the Court Poets and the Poets of the Princes. The Cynfeirdd or First Poets produced and in part preserved a substantial body of heroic and tragic verse, exemplified by the poems associated with the names of Taliesin and Aneirin on the one hand, and the saga-names of Llywarch the Old, Heledd, and Cynddylan on the other. The emphasis was on the heroic kinds: eulogy, elegy, and commemoration. Gnomic and nature poetry survive too, vaticination and religion; but the age was a Heroic Age, and its verse mirrored and portrayed it.

The circumstance is relevant to Cynddelw and his peers. The Gogynfeirdd were in every good sense of the word professionals, who inherited, practised, and transmitted not so much an art as a highly organized and strictly regulated craft of verse-making. What you did and how you did it—in what words, in what form, and with what techniques—these things were prescribed. One has heard the phrase, 'a painters' painter'. Cynddelw was of all things a poets' poet. He knew all modes, all means, all measures, and knew that he knew them. His patrons knew it, his fellow-poets knew it, his disciples knew it, and after eight hundred years we know it. He was the greatest of the Gogynfeirdd for two chief reasons. The first is that just mentioned: he was so accomplished a performer (and I stress that word) that whatever task he took in hand he performed superlatively. Like his fellows he had taken over from

---

[1] The translations of Cynddelw (in *The Earliest Welsh Poetry*, Macmillan, 1970) and of J. Kitchener Davies are by Professor Joseph Clancy of New York. Those of Mr Saunders Lewis are by Dr Gwyn Thomas of Bangor. I owe them warm thanks, as I do Mrs Mair K. Davies and Mr Saunders Lewis.

Taliesin and Aneirin the poetic kinds proper to a professional poet. He seems to have begun his career as court poet to Madawg ap Maredudd, lord of Powys, for whom he composed a classical eulogy while he lived, and a classical elegy when he was dead. Ah, that we might all have our Cynddelw!

Madawg dead and dirged, Cynddelw went on to ply his skills before other great ones of the Welsh world, Owain Gwynedd in the north, and the lord Rhys down south, and again and again discharged with resource and authority whatever a patron might properly require and a craft would rightly permit. Which brings us to the second reason why he was the greatest of the Gogyn-feirdd. Word-master, song-master, rule-master though he was, the very personification of the bardic ideal, he brought something more to verse-making: he brought himself. He made a little more room within the tradition, a little more elbow-room for the poet to work in. And so we find Cynddelw addressing Madawg's young daughter Efa in an innovatory poem which combines ardent respect with respectful ardour, private devotion with public regard, the innocent friendship due to a child (and your lord's child at that) with the awakening compliment welcome to a young woman. Cynddelw was gallant in his ode to Efa as Dryden in his day would be gallant in his address to the Duchess of Ormond, all things wondrously subdued by a master of his craft and made concordant with the purpose, the pleasure, and the duty of a court poet who is also a Great Poet, Brydydd Mawr. He made use of the *llatai* or love's messenger in a fashion prophetic of Dafydd ap Gwilym; somewhat surprisingly wrote a poem after the death in battle of his own son; and in the grammarians' discussion of the modes of versification there is reference to the 'manner of Cynddelw', with its suggestion that he experimented there too. And on everything he composed he set his own unmistakable stamp and impress.

I came to Cynddelw late—and that not to my regret. There is much to be said for postponing some major delights and en-lightenments till one is old enough to appreciate just what it is one has been missing. He instantly looked a poet for me. His con-fidence appealed to my feeling for authority, his courtly arrogance to my courtly humility. Here was a man who at all times was con-scious of what God had given him. 'Be silent, bards—a bard is speaking!' I judged him true brother of my old friend, the tenth-century poet Egill Skallagrímsson of Borg á Mýrum out in Iceland, who stepped before kings, opened his mighty jaws (which were also melodious), and instantly had silence; and to my still older friend the unknown author of *Culhwch and Olwen* in the *Mabinogion*, that exultant master of early Welsh narrative prose. Like Cynddelw, because they were supreme craftsmen they could meet the severest demands of their art; and like him, because they were supreme artists, they left a savour of their unique selves with the products of their craft.

But I resist the temptation I find almost irresistible, and approach, as Cynddelw had to in the end, that prayer to God which makes him part of my talk this evening. Like Egill a skald, bard, court poet, and friend of princes, and a warrior whose sword knew the colour of red, Cynddelw would have acquitted himself well at Ragnarok, had Christianity boasted such a luxury. Since it didn't, he would write a set piece in classical form, with every rule of language and structure obeyed, stamp it with his bardic authority, and concurrently make it eloquent of his distinctively eloquent personality. This set piece was the verse-composition known as *marwysgafn* (that is, Deathbed Poem), addressed by a bard not to his lord on earth but to his Lord in Heaven. Let me at this point again remind you of the secular inheritance of the court poets of the twelfth and thirteenth centuries, who had taken over the traditional rights and duties of their British or Celtic heroic age predecessors. Theirs was an essential and indispensable function of the society they lived in. For behind the bloody catalogues and brutal exultations of heroic poetry (and believe me, they *are* bloody and brutal, and none more exultantly so than the Welsh), behind these lies a deep, enduring, and imperative grasp on reality. In a heroic society, if the hero-king had need of his people, his people had equal need of him; and it was the bard as celebrant and memorialist who could do most to enhance him in life, sustain him and his house before posterity, and (perhaps most important of all) define and hold up for approval and emulation those standards of personal and public worth and conduct which were a man's best, most precious, and least alienable possessions in life and death. It was these standards and their expression in terms of war, valour, service, reward, loyalty, contempt of death, and love of fame everlasting, which were the bond and buttress, shield and stay, of tribe, confederacy, people, and nation, in a warlike and hierarchical age.

Of all these matters Cynddelw was fully seized and cognizant. Had he not said so, many times, to many princes?

> Britain's regal hawks, I chant your high song,
> Your honour I bear,
> Your bard, your judge I shall be,
> Your assistance is due me.

What more natural, and what more inevitable, than to enunciate these patent truths yet again, this time to the Prince of Princes and King of Kings, with whom in justice and mercy they would count most? Which he did, in a formal composition of an established kind, the *marwysgafn* or Deathbed Poem, a mode of address at once personal and public to Almighty God, and one which he brought more into line with secular eulogy than his contemporaries did.

The Deathbed Poem opens with our author's customary ease, authority, and assurance:

> I salute God, asylum's gift,
> To praise my lord, bounteous, benign,
> Sole son of Mary, source of morn and eve
> And teeming river-mouths,
> Who made wood, and mead, and true measure,
> And harvests, and God's overflowing gifts,
> Who made grass and grove and mountain heather . . .

The entire introduction is excellent in manner and exemplary in sentiment. So is his second section, which begins with Cynddelw nudging God's elbow—or was it the lesser though still exalted humerus of the Archangel Michael?

> I salute God, I solicit acclaim
> For the piece I perform . . .

And less ambiguously than is usual he speaks of a gift to be given, a reward to be received. In the third section his eloquence heightens, and he lets sound his grand diapason of words, phrases, and poetic counters. This is the very stuff of twelfth-century poetic rhetoric, and from first line to last Cynddelw is in control of it.

> Almighty Ruler, when you were born,
> Came mercy for us, came redemption,
> Came Adam's sons from faithless faction . . .
> Came Christ incarnate, mainstay, master,
> Came in Mary's womb the wished-for Son,
> Came the world's five ages from torment . . .
> And He is our helm and our haven
> Who judges our deeds by our doing,
> And He, heaven's Lord, portion of peace,
> Brought us forth from perdition when pierced,
> And He rose for us, and won His reward,
> And the Lord will not deny us His help.
> And as a reward He was seated
> In full might, the sun's road His domain.

> The man whose hand will give his tithe to God,
> He is not thwarted of his reward.
> I am a bard, flawlessly fashioned:
> In my Creator's hold, legion's Lord,
> I, Cynddelw the singer, grace I ask;
> Michael, who knows me, welcome be mine!

The masculine strength of the diction, the compulsive appeal of the imagery, the pressure and timing of the emotional sequence would conceal, if concealment were possible, or even desirable, the gradual merger of redemption and reward which grows explicit in the second half of Cynddelw's exposition of God's justice and mercy. Christ won his reward, the man who pays his tithe wins his reward: shall not God's bard, flawlessly fashioned, win his too? Something well past reason if short of commonsense tells me, Why not? If we can approve of the juggler of Notre Dame who brought the tribute of his one skill to a private performance before Our Lady, why not a performance, public or private, to the glory of God by that conjuror with words and magician with metre, Cynddelw Brydydd Mawr? 'Be silent, bards; a bard is speaking!'

> Almighty Ruler, when of you I sang,
> Not worthless the piece I performed,
> No lack of fine style in the lyric . . .

And so to the poem's ending. Cynddelw's skills, his largeness of utterance, his power and conviction, do not for one moment desert him as he moves from claim to appeal, and from appeal to his plea for salvation. I will read it, then leave it to speak for itself, for its poet, and for the poetical resources, intellectual, emotional, linguistic, and metrical, of Welsh twelfth-century poetic prosody:

> Almighty Ruler, deign to receive,
> Reverent request, harmonious,
> Flawless in formation of language,
> My song in your praise, fair land's candle.
> Since you are master, since you are monarch,
> Since you are prophet, since you are judge,
> Since you are kind, since you are benign,
> Since you are my teacher, banish me not,
> In your wrath, from your fair land.
> Refuse me not your grace, exile's Lord,
> Scorn me not amidst the wretched crew,
> Spill me not from your hand, vile dwelling,
> Throw me not to the black loveless throng.

And so, leaving Cynddelw the Great Poet behind us, to confront God with his greatness, we approach over the gulf of

eight centuries the second and third close-set spider-legs of my
wide-spanned poetical tripod. By way of a bridge it was my
intention, as it is still my hope, to proffer a few sentences about
religious poets and their poetry in Wales today, in both our
languages; a remark or two about the erosion of Christian belief
which we share with the rest of Great Britain; and the sparest of
spare words about the decline of Nonconformity and Methodism,
which to me, as to so many of my South Wales born and bred
generation *were* Christianity in those kingfisher days when life's
pasture is green and youth's cup runneth over.

I would not, of course, be misunderstood as saying that Welsh
poets are more notoriously or even more numerically backsliders
from the Lord than their readers or the generality of their English,
Scottish, and Irish peers. On the contrary, mighty exceptions at
once spring to mind. In the English-language literature of Wales,
for example, that so-called Anglo-Welsh writing whose flowering
over the last half-century or so has been so variously rich, R. S.
Thomas and David Jones are not just religious poets: they are
specifically and eminently Christian poets, the one a priest of the
Church in Wales, the other a convert to Roman Catholicism.
A Christian upbringing and a Christian witness are not in themselves, need I say? enough to make even a religious man a religious
poet. Nor can a religious fiction greatly avail. Dylan Thomas, who
despite Swansea and 'Where Tawe Flows', belonged at heart with
uberous Dyfed and tidal Towy, fostered a poetical attachment to a
deity who was old before Zeus and Yahweh were young—a deity
human–animal–divine, part Polar Bear, part Father Christmas,
with a spoonful of Merlin to taste.

> Animals thick as thieves
> On God's great tumbling grounds
> Hail to his Beasthood!

And why not? But it is a long way off from the Whitsun Walk of
childhood and the Easter Sacraments of age. Any religion
deserving of the name, though the dictionaries are beginning to
give ground, requires a God, and demands that he be worshipped.
Pleasure before a sunset, awe on a mountain's height, wonder at
the struts and hinges of a seagull's wing, are not enough. The
'Author's Prologue' to the *Collected Poems* of 1952, whose hundred
lines, we are told, it took Dylan a whole year to compose, may well
be the most discreetly evasive poetic evasion of the Christian God
in twentieth-century literature.

Then there was John Cowper Powys, a giant—nay, Titan—of

our age, whose life was a baffling search for Truth between the sulphurous chasms of the First Cause and the sleety highlands of the Fourth Dimension. And what was the Truth he came up, or down, with? 'To be at the death of God is my single quest.' Few of us had thought to go as far as that. We were modest, tolerant men with no taste for Deicide, but rather a disposition to find old beliefs grown empty of meaning, so that we let them go. For better, and partly for worse, men like Gwyn Thomas, Idris Davies, Raymond Williams, Rhys Davies, and myself, took shape in the evening of our teens as religious men without a religion, men of faith without a faith, who had still to learn the saddening lesson that Pelagius was a born loser, and his genial Celtic heresy concerning the goodness of man a non-starter from the start.

Hedge and dyke a little and who will be surprised to hear that the situation in Welsh-language poetry is not too dissimilar? The last eighty years or so, the years encompassing T. Gwynn Jones, R. Williams Parry, T. H. Parry-Williams, Saunders Lewis, Gwenallt, Waldo Williams, and Alun Llywelyn-Williams (I have drawn a birthday line under the outbreak of the First World War), have been the most splendid age of Welsh poetry since the Age of the Cywydd. Of religious poets three are outstanding: Saunders Lewis, Gwenallt, and Waldo Williams. Of the three the best for my purpose is Saunders Lewis, which implies no criticism of the others; for there is no doubt in my mind that a handful of his religious poems, and especially 'Mary Magdalene' (*Mair Fadlen*), 'To the Good Thief' (*I'r Lleidr Da*), and 'Ascension Thursday' (*Difiau Dyrchafael*), are our supreme modern Welsh artefacts of their self-declared unequivocally Christian kind. Here is a man who in Thomas Merton's phrase is 'writing for God', and bringing to that exalted task every literary skill, every exercise of care, and every quality of unremitting exactitude of which he is capable. You don't have to share Mr Lewis's religious convictions to feel this. Each one of these poems, as a made and finished thing, has a completeness, a 'truth' which is its own, even more than it is the poet's—a statement which may well seem to you in need of explication. But a poem, we should from time to time remind ourselves, is not a poet, though it sometimes coincides with, and is quite often confused with, its maker or his supposed outlines. Rather, it is a poet's artefact, a poet being a man with the will and means to make and perfect a statement in verse entirely adequate in its manner and matter to fulfil the intention of its maker and the expectancy of its hearer, or reader.

That expectancy need not precede acquaintance. A poem can

arouse and gratify expectancy simultaneously, at a first hearing or a fiftieth. As we hear it, possess it, and are possessed by it, we acknowledge the highest and most effective mode of communication of which human speech, our highest human communicant, is capable. Something significant and necessary has been stated, made manifest, in the best words and in the best structured form. This is the empyrean function of a craft employed in the service of what we nowadays call an art. This is what Cynddelw believed, though he would certainly have expressed himself differently. There can be found (indeed, there *has* been found) a right way of expressing a theme of general rather than private import (to be merely private, personal, self-exploratory, and self-indulgent—such is the theory—is to diminish, to slough significance), and to achieve that rightness is the first and full business of a poet.

One speculation always leads to another. Were Saunders Lewis to write a Deathbed Poem, after the fashion of the Masters, it would certainly be found one of the most striking and effective of its affecting and formalized kind. Most of our mortal vicissitudes have befallen him, often as though by personal invitation, his longings higher and his disappointments correspondingly deeper than those of his fellows. Like his friend David Jones a convert to Roman Catholicism, unlike his friend an authoritarian by temperament and conviction, he is in all things a man of burning and self-sacrificing beliefs, in religion, national and nationalist politics, and unaccommodatingly devoted to the preservation and enhancement of the Welsh language and his concept of our Welsh destiny. He has been a lifelong fighter, braced by the knowledge that you must not take on only those battles you expect to win. That would be the easy satisfaction of fighting for glory. You must fight for your cause because it *is* your cause, even though it may carry with it the bitter lesson that the majority of your fellow-countrymen neither approve your struggle nor want your sacrifice. For much of his life he has been among the most notable public figures in Wales, and is certainly one of the most distinguished Welsh poets, dramatists, and polemicists of the century.

By his own definition he is a craftsman who has learnt to trust technique, and knows that a good poem is an impersonal thing. It can be so, no question of it; but for me there is equally no question that a good poem may also be found a personal thing. But there is no particular dilemma: the inexactitude of language and the imprecision of thought, personal weightings, and private refinements (of which I recognize a great many in myself), make many literary disagreements more apparent and soluble than real and permanent. But before I go on to look at an 'impersonal' poem of his which impresses me as a poignantly 'personal' one, let us consider a poem, not his, where the critical proposition that a poem has its own truth, which is not necessarily or wholly the truth of its poet, brings comfort and admiration, whereas a belief in its literal, professed personal truth would bring desolation and grief to the reader. This is James Kitchener Davies's *Sŵn y Gwynt Sy'n Chwithu*, 'The Sound of the Wind that is Blowing'. I have no wish to deal in absolutes and bests, but this poem, because of its autobiographical content and social commentary, its cry of pain for the self and despair for the nation, the Old Testament nature of its appeal to God in hope's destruction; and because it shows the selection, shaping, and reshaping of material proper to a work of art; and because of its effect upon every kind of reader, whatever his politics, religious faith, social background, and life's history; for these reasons, along with its command of words and metre, it is among the most remarkable statements made about industrial South Wales and its people during the harsh decades of poverty and strain between the two world wars.

It coheres with my general purpose in that like Cynddelw's Deathbed Poem (and not unlike the effigy of some early seventeenth-century divine portrayed while still alive in his chosen shroud and coffin), it is an address to God postmarked for Earth as well as Heaven. *Sŵn y Gwynt*, as it fell out, was literally a deathbed poem, commissioned by Radio Wales, and composed in hospital between two surgical operations a short time before its author's death in 1952. Most of it he was himself too weak to write down. 'It was from a few notes of his on paper,' wrote his wife, 'and from listening to my husband's spoken words line by line, that I set it down on paper, there by his bedside.' It is a work simple in structure but complex in intention. The poet's life was neither commonplace nor, in South Wales terms, all that remarkable. At the age of twenty-four he had left the farm and fields of Tregaron in Mid-Wales for the fields and pits of the Rhondda Valley in South Wales, where he became a teacher, married, wrote some interesting plays for a playless land, espoused the Welsh national-ist cause with fervour, 'ventured in elections', and played an active though not dominant part as orator and preacher in what Gwyn Thomas has called the 'fermenting disquiet' of the busy, harassed, can't-be-kept-down life of the strung-out Valley townships.

He was, let us say, dedicated to good causes. Certainly to good intentions. A life so dedicated, so occupied (and preoccupied), so demanding, so prone to set-backs, and so slow to harvest—who among us, trapped in the murk of disappointment and the opacity of doubt, but might ask himself, 'Why do I do it? Why should I? And, God help me, to what end?'

> Remember,
> There was no need for you, more than the rest of your fellows
> To scream your guts out on a soap-box
> on the street-corners and the town squares;
> no call for you to march in the ranks of the jobless,
> your dragon-rampant hobnobbing with the hammer-and-sickle;
> there was no need for you
> to dare the packed Empire and the Hippodrome on Sunday
>   evening,
> —you a dandy bantam on the dung-heap of the spurred cocks
> of the Federation and the Exchange—
> but you ventured,
> and ventured in elections for the town Council and the County
> and Parliament all in good time
> against Goliath in a day that knows no miracle.

When I say I don't know how much of this is hard fact, and how much is metaphor, that is not indifference. If I add that their precise boundaries require no drawing, that is not heartlessness. Truth in a court of law is one thing: the truth of distilled or rearranged experience is another, especially in a poet's auto-biography, and perhaps above all in his *marwysgafn* or Deathbed Poem.

> For it not only blows where it will, the tempest,
> But blows what it will before it where it will.

And one thing it can blow before it, shedding a little here and heaping a little there, is literal truth, which is a commodity that Ancient Mariners and Cider-drinkers with Rosie have always managed to do very nicely without. May we not assume that Kitchener Davies at a fraught period of his life entered as many men must within the dark night of the soul, and from that unset-tling experience of insight and self-deception, anxiety and regret, together with such incidentals as every writer's longing for a subject to write about, our human need to explain our uniqueness, to tell how it was and is with us (reinforced by the Welsh tradition of the poetic set piece and work of public significance), Kitchener's being in hospital and undergoing surgery for abdominal cancer, his wife's sustaining presence—from these things, and others guessable, came incomparably the best poem he ever wrote, and the one by which he will be remembered.

To recall past happiness (he was to say that the tumbledown walls of the farmhouse of Y Llain set a brand as of Cain on him in the Rhondda); to have literary, professional, and political ambitions, and know oneself grown older with no great matter accomplished; to brood on pain and survival—these are the black crows of middle age. To suspect oneself a failure, and fall prey to self-doubt, self-pity, self-accusation—these make the crows look bigger and blacker. 'What shall I cry?' saith the Preacher. 'Birds build' was Gerard Manley Hopkins's cry in Crowland:

> Birds build—but not I build, no, but strain,
> Time's eunuch, and not breed one work that wakes.
> Mine, O thou lord of life, send my roots rain.

The wind that in childhood ruffled the sheltering hedges of Y Llain and spared the shelterers in its protective ditch; that made squirrels of boys in the tossing branches; the wind that blew broken hopes and soiled ambitions with yesterday's tins and newspapers along the gutters of the Rhondda; the wind he had courted and challenged to brace and cleanse his soul—

> May God who is slow to anger forgive my presumption,
> pulpiteering, singing hymns and praying to Him . . .
> I asked for the wind that was probing the skeletons
> to breathe into my dry bones the breath of life.
> I pleaded with the tempest to winnow with the whirlwind
> my desert's draff, and drench with its rains
> my wasteland's parched ground till it bloomed as a garden.
> I appealed with fervour without considering—
> without considering (O terror) He could take me at my word,
> He could take me at my word and answer my prayer,
> And answer my prayer.

Self-accusations, however unjust and unnecessary, are a destructive burden for a man wasted by a cruel illness, a weight of foreboding, and a longing for the lost normality of home, family, peace and quiet. But God is merciful: Can one yet unpray one's prayers, unhope one's hopes, undream one's dreams? Can one by God's grace renege? It was of the Father of Mercies that Kitchener asked this impossible boon.

> O Father of Mercies, be merciful,
> Leave me my comrades' company, and my acquaintances' trust,
> And the strength that is mine in my wife and children . . .
> Atonement who purchased freedom,
> Do not tangle me in my prayers like Amlyn in his vow,
> do not kill me at the altar by whose horns I have blasphemed,—

but let me, I pray, despite each wound, however hideous,
fail to be a saint.
 O Saviour of the lost,
save me, save me, save me,
from your baptism that washes the Old Man so clean:
keep me, keep me, keep me,
from the inevitable martyrdom of Your elect.
Save and keep me
from the wind that is blowing where it will.
So be it, Amen,
 and Amen.

When I first read this astonishing exercise in self-revelation, as
one born in the crumpled blanket of the coal valleys, bred to the
innocence of book-learning, and raised on the breast of religion, it
seemed to me the almost unbearable expression of a poet's truth.
Nowadays, for all the seas and cities in between, still Antaeus
to my native plot; my judgement sharpened but my ideals un-
impaired; my theology under snow but my sympathies vernal in
leaf and flower; I see it rather as the *poem's* truth, to which the
poet's narrower truth has been legitimately accommodated. It is
no compliment to a work of the creative imagination to catalogue
it as a factual record. Our poem is not fact unadulterate and unadorned, but fact transmuted, selective, coloured, re-emphasized,
re-ordered. *Sŵn y Gwynt*, 'The Sound of the Wind that is Blowing',
is a deeply moving poem because it is a beautifully contrived
poetic artefact, whose truth is to human nature and experience.

There can be no doubt that for all its public aspects *Sŵn y Gwynt*
is an intensely personal poem, a poem of Me and Mine and Here
and Now. We left Saunders Lewis after remarking his opinion that
a good poem is an impersonal thing, and after my promising to
read an 'impersonal' poem of his which impresses me as being not
only personal but poignantly so. It is a poem called *Caer Arianrhod*,
which means 'The Fortress of Arianrhod', *arian* meaning 'silver'
and the whole phrase the apt Welsh name for the Milky Way. It is
a poem of just eight lines, and purports to be the soliloquy of
Owain Glyndŵr (Owen Glendower) before he was encountered
on the Berwyn mountain in North Wales early one morning by the
early rising Abbot of Valle Crucis. 'You have risen early,' said
Owain. 'No,' answered the Abbot; 'It is you who have risen early
—a hundred years before your time.' Whereupon Owain disappeared. It was Owain Glyndŵr, you remember, who last led a
revolt in arms to restore an independent kingdom of Wales, was
defeated by the English monarchy, disappeared, and died in

1410–17. Whatever the rights and wrongs of it, Glyndŵr's rising and its failure remains a somewhat throat-constricting episode in Welsh history. Here are the thoughts, the words, one national leader found for a predecessor of 500 years before:

> I saw the night closing its wing over the moor,
> Over a few frail homesteads, fallow land, infrequent furrows,
> And the stars came and the Milky Way, a dense miracle,
> To spatter the feathers of the firmament with their myriad peacock-eyes.
>
> I spread the wing of my dream over you, my country,
> I would have raised for you—had you willed it—a joyful stronghold;
> But my lot is like a shooting star that's cast out from among the stars
> To stain the darkness with its hue and to burn out.

Earlier I congratulated Dylan Thomas on a masterpiece of evasive evasion. Now I congratulate Saunders Lewis on a triumph of personal impersonalism. The impersonalism is there, all right, in the distancing of the subject, the appeal to history and legend, the vast unrolling of landscape and stars, the loftiness of the diction and control of the emotion, the balanced structure. Paradoxically, these same things make it a deeply personal poem. The protective wing of the night, the wing of my dream; the raising of Caer Arianrhod, and the joyous stronghold I would have raised for you, my people; the dense miracle of a myriad stars, and the star which was not chosen, but was rejected to fall alone; the more public and impersonal, the more private and personal, with the truth of the poem and the truth of the poet in classical equipoise. And a poem of painful ironies, for poet and reader alike.

But our real business with Saunders Lewis is not in respect of this beautifully designed allegory, parable, metaphor—what shall we call it?—of a poem. It is rather with him as one of our Three Poetical Prayer-Makers of the Island of Britain. In prayer, as in eulogy and elegy, in patriotic diatribe and vaticination, he belongs with the bards, the men of professional skill and technical exactitude, above all the men of high and noble utterance. Like Cynddelw's, his voice is the voice of a living tradition. And like Cynddelw he made a little more room within the tradition. During my meditations and procrastinations and changes of direction for this evening's talk, I at one time thought to choose a poem each from Medieval Welsh, Old Norse, and Old English, to illustrate—no, just to proclaim—the fascination they have for me: Cynddelw's *Deathbed Poem*, the *Sonatorrek* of Egill Skalla-grímsson, in which the poet, shattered by the loss of his sons but canny even in his grief, railed at Othin, threatened him with his sword—and then took him back into favour for his poetry's sake—and that most beautiful, tender, and moving of all Old English religious poems, *The Dream of the Rood*. It was not to be, but it would be a present enrichment if the last of these, *The Dream of the Rood*, were in your minds now, as I begin to read, without comment, without explication, without praise—for the poem needs none of these things from me—Saunders Lewis's poem *I'r Lleidr Da*, 'To the Good Thief'.

> You did not see him on the mountain of Transfiguration
>   Nor walking the sea at night;
> You never saw corpses blushing when a bier or sepulchre
>   Was struck by his cry.
>
> It was in the rawness of his flesh and his dirt that you saw Him,
>   Whipped and under thorns,
> And in his nailing like a sack of bones outside the town
>   On a pole, like a scarecrow.
>
> You never heard the making of the parables like a Parthenon of
>   words,
>   Nor his tone when he talked of his Father,
> Neither did you hear the secrets of the room above,
>   Nor the prayer before Cedron and the treachery.
>
> It was in the racket of a crowd of sadists revelling in pain
>   And their screeches, howls, curses and shouts
> That you heard the profound cry of the breaking heart of their
>   prey:
>   'Why hast thou forsaken me?'
>
> You, hanging on his right; on his left, your brother;
>   Writhing like skinned frogs,
> Flea-bitten petty thieves thrown in as a retinue to his shame,
>   Courtiers to a mock king in his pain.
>
> O master of courtesy and manners, who enlightened you
>   About your part in this harsh parody?
> 'Lord, when you come into your kingdom, remember me,'—
>   The kingdom that was conquered through death.

Rex Judaeorum; it was you who saw first the vain
    Blasphemy as a living oracle,
You who first believed in the Latin, Hebrew and Greek,
    That the gallows was the throne of God.

O thief who took Paradise from the nails of a gibbet,
    Foremost of the nobilitas of heaven,
Before the hour of death pray that it may be given to us
    To perceive Him and to taste Him.

DIPLOMACY AND WAR IN LATER FIFTEENTH-CENTURY ITALY

By MICHAEL MALLETT

Read 19 November 1981

'IT is obvious that ever since the Roman Empire . . . Italy had never enjoyed such prosperity, or known so favourable a situation as that in which it found itself so securely at rest in the year of our Christian salvation, 1490, and the years immediately before and after.'[1] The famous words of Francesco Guicciardini at the beginning of the *Storia d'Italia* have been in the minds of all historians who have involved themselves in the debate about the state of Italy in the second half of the fifteenth century. Guicciardini's golden age of peace and stability has been echoed by those who have wished to stress the constructive balance of power, free of outside interference, achieved by the Italian League of 1455, by the growth of permanent diplomacy, and by the activities of far-sighted politicians.[2] It has been denounced by those others who have attached more importance to the tensions and fears of the period, to declining military effectiveness, to intrigue, deception, and growing social unrest.[3] But on both sides there has been a

The following abbreviations will be used in the footnotes: ASF—Florence, Archivio di Stato; ASMa—Mantua, Archivio di Stato; ASMi—Milan, Archivio di Stato; ASMo—Modena, Archivio di Stato; ASV—Venice, Archivio di Stato.

[1] Francesco Guicciardini, *La storia d'Italia*, ed. C. Panigada (Bari, 1929), i. 2; English translation by Sydney Alexander, *The History of Italy* (London, 1969), pp. 3-4.

[2] For differing approaches to this view of the period, see particularly G. Soranzo, *La lega italica* (1454-5) (Milan, 1924); E. W. Nelson, 'The Origins of Modern Balance of Power Politics', *Medievalia et Humanistica*, i (1943); R. Cessi, 'La lega italica e la sua funzione storica nella seconda metà del secolo XV', *Atti del R. Istituto Veneto di Scienze, Lettere ed Arti*, cii (1942-3); Garrett Mattingly, *Renaissance Diplomacy* (London, 1955), pp. 91-100; V. Ilardi, 'The Italian League, Francesco Sforza and Charles VII (1454-61)', *Studies in the Renaissance*, vi (1959).

[3] Among critics of the 'optimistic' approach, see particularly E. Pontieri, *L'equilibrio e la crisi politica italiana nella seconda metà del secolo XV* (Naples,

tendency to emphasize Italian military unpreparedness in 1494, either as a result of intense disunity or of peaceful coexistence. The wars of the period have tended to be described as brush-fire wars, temporary aberrations and breaks in the normal pattern of diplomatic relations, or as the result of the ambitions of over-powerful *condottieri*. Both interpretations, therefore, place emphasis on a certain separation between war and the normal course of politics.

It is the aim of this lecture to question some of these interpretations, particularly in the light of the unfolding publication of the letters of Lorenzo the Magnificent which has provided the opportunity for sustained and detailed research into the Italian politics of the period.[1] This work, in which I have had the good fortune to become involved, is confirming some of the older ideas and hypotheses; it gives substance to Garrett Mattingly's vision of the importance of systematic diplomacy, and to some extent supports the views of the powerful influence of the leading military captains. But above all it is setting before our eyes the intimate connections between this diplomatic scene and the ever present threat of war and preoccupation with war.

A balance of power has been defined as a way of conducting international relations to avoid major wars by constantly adjusting alliance systems in accordance with changing military and economic strength. It involves a shift from a preoccupation with the purely local and immediate to a concern for areas not necessarily contiguous to the frontiers of the main powers involved. All this is to some extent true of Italy between 1454 and 1494, but it is particularly important in the Italian context not to see balance of power as a sort of panacea for all political ills, a universal acceptance of the need for peace and harmony, a kind of political enlightenment. It was rather a stalemate produced by economic exhaustion and a realization that the days of easy conquest had passed, even though the hegemonic aspirations remained. It was a situation which called for incessant alertness, a need to be constantly informed about the military strengths and

1946); B. Barbadoro, 'Il problema dell'equilibrio e la crisi della libertà d'Italia', *Questioni di storia medioevale*, ed. E. Rota (Milan, n.d.), pp. 455-73; F. Catalano, 'Il problema dell'equilibrio politico e la crisi della libertà italiana', *Nuove questioni di storia medioevale* (Milan, 1964), pp. 357-94; G. Pillinini, *Il sistema degli stati italiani* (1454-94) (Venice, 1970).

[1] Lorenzo de' Medici, *Lettere*, eds. R. Fubini and N. Rubinstein, i-iv (Florence, 1977-81). The volumes so far published cover the period 1460-80; vols. v and vi will be devoted to 1480-4.

intentions of rival powers, a determination to be prepared both to seize opportunities for minor gains and to counter such opportunistic moves by others. It was also a situation which was both fostered by, and itself encouraged, the growth of permanence in regimes, bureaucracies, diplomatic activity, and military establishments.

There is, of course, a danger in seeing the period too much as a whole. It is possible to suggest that the first ten years after the peace of Lodi saw a more positive balance achieved in which some Italian leaders, notably Francesco Sforza, Cosimo de' Medici, and Pius II, worked for peace, and that thereafter, despite the amount of information available to regimes through their diplomatic networks, despite the continual state of military preparedness, the tensions mounted. The shifting alliances of the post-1466 period on the whole failed to take account of changing military and economic strengths. The regimes themselves become more insecure internally and more inclined to thoughtless bellicoseness in the search for quick advantage. But behind such interpretations of gradual breakdown there tends to lie the dangerous assumption of historians that the main interest of the period lies in understanding the events of 1494. The roar of Charles VIII's guns has filled the ears of those who have studied the preceding years and conditioned their historical perspectives. One of the great advantages of the work on the Lorenzo letters is that it has concentrated the mind of the researchers involved on specific moments in the period and isolated them to some extent from the Guicciardinian 'crisis of Italy'. Such an approach suggests that while there were undoubtedly shifts in emphasis, and climactic moments, like Otranto, which profoundly affected the political scene, the underlying tensions between the Italian states remained surprisingly constant between 1454 and 1494. Milan, usually linked to France, was always suspect to Naples, fearful of Angevin, and later French, claims to its throne. Venice's fears of the Turks and of Milanese reprisal for the Lombard lands lost before 1454 were constant factors. The rising economic and naval power of Naples frightened all the other Italian states, while the hegemonic aspirations of King Ferrante in Genoa and southern Tuscany, as he sought to turn the western Mediterranean into an Aragonese lake, affected Florence and Milan in particular. The Papacy, inevitably mutable in its policies, yet had a consistent fear of Naples on its southern frontiers and of a possible Medici *signoria* on those to the north. Florence, beset by financial problems and open to interference and infiltration from all sides, conducted an economic rivalry with Venice and an increasingly apparent territorial and jurisdictional rivalry with the Papacy. In the midst of it all was the Romagna, the one significant political vacuum left after 1454 in which all the powers sought advantage and spheres of influence. Nor can the pressure on the system from outside Italy be said to have varied in any consistent manner. The dangers of French intervention and interference, and of Turkish incursion, were ever present.

It would be wrong to overturn traditional thinking to the extent of suggesting that these tensions, which created a sort of cold-war situation in Italy, generated a positive arms race. The maintenance and improvement of artillery trains was certainly a part of the military planning of most of the Italian states, and there was a growing awareness of the formidable potential of the new weapons. The Milanese artillery train in 1472 consisted of 16 large cannon which required 227 carts and 522 pairs of oxen to transport them and all the miscellaneous accessories for their use.[1] By 1471 Bartolomeo da Cremona was training 20 gunners at a time in the Venetian arsenal,[2] and in 1498 the Senate declared that 'the wars of the present time are influenced more by the force of bombards and artillery than by men at arms'.[3] But it was more the maintenance of permanent establishments of traditional forces which preoccupied governments. The Italian League of 1455, and all subsequent alliances of the period, sanctioned, encouraged, and yet sought to limit, such standing armies. The terms of the League set the size of the armies at 6,000 cavalry and 2,000 infantry for Milan, Venice, and Naples, and 2,000 cavalry and 1,000 infantry for Florence and the Papacy.[4] But undoubtedly all the states, with the exception of Florence, exceeded these levels of permanent troops in the years which followed. Galeazzo Maria Sforza in the early 1470s had detailed plans drawn up for the speedy mobilization of an army of nearly 43,000 men and the permanent effectives at his disposal numbered over 20,000.[5] Venice could count on a standing cavalry force of about 8,000 men during the 1460s and 1470s, supplemented by 2,000 professional infantry and an increasingly effective and trained select

---

[1] M. E. Mallett, *Mercenaries and their Masters; Warfare in Renaissance Italy* (London, 1974), p. 161.

[2] ASV, Senatus Terra, reg. 6, 49ᵛ (7 Oct. 1471).

[3] ASV, Senatus Terra, reg. 13, 64ᵛ (27 Dec. 1498).

[4] Soranzo, op. cit., pp. 192–3.

[5] E. C. Visconti, 'Ordine dell'esercito ducale sforzesco, 1472–4', *Archivio storico lombardo*, iii (1876).

militia.[1] Paul II, throughout his pontificate, deployed an army of 8,000 to 10,000 men for a series of minor campaigns designed to strengthen his control over the papal state.[2] The Aragonese kings of Naples were more interested in building up naval than military strength, but by the 1470s the military ambitions of Alfonso, Duke of Calabria, ensured that a large standing force was available, and the influential *Memoriale* of one of his principal lieutenants, Diomede Carafa, indicated the degree of permanence and pro-fessionalism expected of this army.[3] The maintenance of these forces consumed, in peace-time, about half the annual income of the Italian states. Florence, for reasons which I have explored elsewhere, was reluctant to undertake such expenditure and normally maintained its standing forces at or below a minimum level to conform with its alliance obligations.[4]

With this build up of permanent forces there was inevitably a decline in the mercenary nature of the leadership. Captains were encouraged to take out long-term contracts and to settle per-manently within the frontiers of the state which they served. Most of the Italian states resorted increasingly to relying on their own subjects to provide military leadership; this was particularly true of Naples, Milan, and the Papacy, less so of Venice; Florence remained once again exceptional in this respect. At the same time the increasing dependence of military forces on the state led to the states themselves adopting that traditional feature of *condottiere* warfare—the tendency to conduct wars of manœuvre and attri-tion, with the avoidance of battle and heavy loss one of the key features. As the main responsibility for maintaining expensive and precious troops passed from captain to state, so the anxiety not to take unnecessary risks was also transferred. This reinforced the whole framework of fifteenth-century war policy which was oriented towards wars of attrition which damaged the rival state's

[1] M. E. Mallett, 'Preparations for War in Florence and Venice in the Second Half of the Fifteenth Century', *Florence and Venice: Comparisons and Relations*, i (Florence, 1979), 150.

[2] Mallett, *Mercenaries and their Masters*, p. 117; G. Zorzi, 'Un vicentino alla corte di Paolo II; Chierighino Chiericati e il suo trattatello della milizia', *Nuovo archivio veneto*, NS xxx (1915); A. Da Mosto, 'Ordinamenti militari delle soldatesche dello stato Romano del 1430 al 1470', *Quellen und Forschungen aus italienischen Archiven und Bibliotheken*, v (1902), 31-3.

[3] I. Schiappoli, *Napoli aragonese: traffici e attività marinara* (Naples, 1972), pp. 25-32; P. Pieri, 'Il "Governo et exercitio de la militia" di Orso degli Orsini e i "Memoriali" di Diomede Carafa', *Archivio storico per le provincie napoletane*, xix (1933).

[4] Mallett, 'Preparations for war', *passim*.

economy and aimed at minor territorial gains—rather than at the annihilation of the enemy. Thus the whole tendency in the late fifteenth century for the tempo of Italian warfare to slow down and to rely heavily on tactics of manœuvre was more the result of the policy of governments than of the preferences of the captains. However, the War of Ferrara, which will be the focus of the later part of this paper and which is sometimes described, quite erroneously, as 'the last medieval war in Italy', was to prove somewhat exceptional in this respect.[1]

The fact that most of the Italian states in the second half of the fifteenth century had large permanent armies in a greater or lesser state of constant preparedness undoubtedly affected the conduct of relations between those states. But it would be wrong to overestimate the extent to which those permanent forces were normally ready for war or themselves fostered a willingness to go to war. While it was certainly true that contingents of heavy cavalry could be alerted at very short notice, and dispatched to counter or support aggressive political moves, full-scale mobilization was a very different matter. Milan was able to move relatively large bodies of cavalry to the Bolognese within days in response to tensions in the Romagna, as in June 1470 when 1,500 cavalry were sent,[2] and in May 1480 when Roberto da Sanseverino went with 3,000 cavalry to counter a papal threat to Pesaro.[3] But the mobilization of the permanent forces meant moving them over to wartime rates of pay and in some cases filling out the ranks with new recruits. It meant the paying of large advances or *prestanze* before the troops could be moved out of quarters. It meant the rounding up of additional horses and oxen for the baggage trains and the levying of the militia and pioneers to accompany the army. All this took time, and above all ready cash—a commodity of which fifteenth-century states were always short. A state like Venice, which had access to the assets in the vaults of its banks in emergency, was thus able to mobilize much more quickly and effectively than the other Italian states. This was clear in April 1480 when 400,000 ducats was needed, and quickly available, to get the army and a huge river fleet ready for the war of Ferrara. This advantage, as much as

---

[1] F. Secco d'Aragona, 'Un giornale della guerra di Ferrara (1482–4), *Archivio storico lombardo*, 8th ser. vii (1957), 344. For the best account of the War of Ferrara, see E. Piva, *La guerra di Ferrara del 1482* (Padua, 1893).

[2] Lorenzo de' Medici, op. cit. i. 158.

[3] ASMi, Archivio sforzesco, Potenze Estere, Firenze 299 (18 May and 2 June 1480); Dukes of Milan to Filippo Sacramoro in Florence.

any other factor, accounts for the general fear of Venetian imperialism in this period.[1]

If the presence of permanent forces contributed significantly to the conditions of *equilibrio* in which the Italian states found themselves in the second half of the fifteenth century, it was diplomacy which provided the mechanism of the system. Diplomacy to avoid war, diplomacy to prepare for war, diplomacy to end war; the two were crucially linked. Garrett Mattingley in his seminal book on *Renaissance Diplomacy* rightly countered the claims of the diplomatic theorists themselves that their main object was to preserve peace, but he underestimated the intimate connections between diplomacy and war in fifteenth-century Italy. He introduced, in fact, an unnatural separation between the two by ascribing the growth of permanent diplomacy in Italy to the unreliability of the mercenary system, and by suggesting that 'diplomacy was for rulers, war for hired men'.[2] This second suggestion is the result of a peculiarly Florentine view of Renaissance development, a view which, particularly in the field of international relations, leads to severe distortions. While it is on the whole true that the Florentine political élite had little direct experience of war and regarded diplomacy as a laudable, and indeed necessary, occupation for the good citizen, the same generalization is less applicable to the other Italian élites. In Venice the very experienced military *provveditori* and the ambassadors came from the same small social group, and were often the same men.[3] Many Milanese and Neapolitan diplomatic envoys had military experience, and not a few of them were 'hired men' in the sense of not being native-born subjects of the states which they served. Among the leading Milanese diplomats of the period were Prospero Camogli, Nicodemo Tranchedini, Sacramoro and Filippo Sacramori, Antonio Bracelli, and Sforza Bettini, all of whom were not Milanese by origin and some of whom served other states during their careers.[4] Giovanbattista

---

[1] D. Malipiero, *Annali veneti*, in *Archivio storico italiano*, vii (1843), 253. For a discussion of the fear of Venetian imperialism in this period, see N. Rubinstein, 'Italian Reactions to Terraferma Expansion in the Fifteenth Century', in *Renaissance Venice*, ed. J. R. Hale (London, 1973).

[2] Mattingly, op. cit., pp. 61–2.

[3] M. E. Mallett, 'Venice and its *Condottieri*, 1404–54', in *Renaissance Venice*, pp. 135–7.

[4] For short biographies of some of these men, see L. Cerioni, *La diplomazia sforzesca nella seconda metà del Quattrocento e i suoi cifrari segreti* (Rome, 1970), i; on Prospero Camogli, see P. M. Kendall and V. Ilardi, *Dispatches with Related Documents of Milanese Ambassadors in France and Burgundy, 1450–83*, ii (Ohio, 1971), xvi–xxi.

Bentivoglio in the service of Naples, Zaccaria Saggio da Pisa, the Mantuan envoy in Milan in the late 1470s and early 1480s, Antonio da Montecatini, Ercole d'Este's man in Florence for a number of years, are other examples of this phenomenon.[1]

That the military context within which these diplomats operated was no longer one of errant, and potentially faithless, mercenary captains is a point which has already been made. This is not to deny that a small group of prestigious captains did maintain a degree of independence and mobility in their allegiances and this enabled them to influence, but not I suggest control, the relations between the Italian states. The political roles of men like Federico da Montefeltro and Roberto da Sanseverino were of great significance in the years round the War of Ferrara and these can be well studied through the diplomatic correspondence of the period. One of the main functions of the resident ambassadors was the negotiation of the *condotte* of such men who provided the high command of the permanent armies. This was one of the points at which military organization and diplomacy were inextricably intermeshed. Similarly the negotiation of the alliances and leagues which dominated the period required detailed consideration both of those high-level contracts and of the general level of the maintenance of permanent forces.

But it was in their role as information gatherers that the diplomatic agents of the period had their closest contacts with the military world. Ambassadorial dispatches were filled with information on troop movements and dispositions, on the state of preparedness of companies, on the activities of paymasters and commissaries as indicators of impending mobilization. A dramatic improvement in the quality and flow of information was one of the principal characteristics of Italian statecraft in the second half of the fifteenth century. The resident ambassadors, more informal spies and informers, and the development of patron–client relationships in which one of the main obligations on the client was to keep his patron informed, all contributed to this. The information provided was not, of course, just military information. Reports on revenue, proposed taxes, and on the popular reactions to taxes were always welcome, although interestingly enough ambassadors rarely reported on economic conditions of a more general nature. The other main area of interest to ambassadors was the

[1] For Giovanbattista Bentivoglio, see *Dizionario biografico degli italiani*, viii. 633–4. Zaccaria Saggio was the Mantuan representative in Milan throughout the 1470s and the early 1480s. Antonio da Montecatini arrived in Florence in October 1478 and remained well into the 1480s.

unity of the regime to which they were accredited. The role of ambassadors in noting, seeking out, and even fostering factions within the Italian states is a fascinating area of research. The envoys of the other powers in Florence clearly encouraged the existence of pro-Milanese, pro-Aragonese, and pro-Venetian factions within the Florentine political class. This was not just a way of gaining additional inside information, but a form of calculated subversion and interference which could affect policy decisions and if necessary be directed towards undermining the political will of the Republic. Ambassadors seem to have been a good deal less scrupulous in these matters than Mattingly suggested and the question clearly has important implications for both external and internal affairs. However, it is too big a topic to open up in this paper and I want to move on from this rather general discussion to consider some detailed examples which illustrate the points I have been making, chosen from the period of the War of Ferrara.

The signing of the peace which ended the Pazzi War on 13 March 1480, and of the league between Naples, Florence, and Milan on the same day, initiated a period of two years uneasy tension which can be described as the preliminary to the War of Ferrara which broke out on 2 May 1482.[1] The alliance systems which confronted each other in the opening stages of that war were forged two years earlier in March and April 1480. The League of Naples was the recreation of an *entente* of the late 1460s and the league between Sixtus IV and Venice, signed on 16 April, was a natural counterbalance to it. The papal–Venetian league grew out of the dissatisfaction of both parties with the peace of 13 March and the desire of Girolamo Riario to find support for his Romagna ambitions. It was negotiated by Cardinal Foscari with Riario and the Pope, with active encouragement from Federico da Montefeltro who was angry at the preference being given to other *condottieri* in the Neapolitan League.[2]

In fact the Neapolitan League itself was in a good deal of difficulty in the summer of 1480. The idea, which was floated in early May, that the League should be reformulated in the light of the emergence of the rival papal league, took three months to materialize. The main reason for this delay was the difficulty which the three allies had in agreeing on a military command structure. This stemmed partly from the rivalries among the *condottieri* concerned, Ercole d'Este and Roberto da Sanseverino

[1] Lorenzo de' Medici, op. cit. iv, particularly, 367–402.
[2] E. Piva, 'Origine e conclusione della pace e alleanza fra i Veneziani e Sisto IV', *Nuovo archivio veneto*, NS ii (1901).

supported by Milan and the Duke of Calabria supported by
Naples. But more importantly the difficulty arose because of the
deep-rooted suspicion in Milan and Florence of Neapolitan
hegemonic intentions, because of the temporary internal crisis in
Milan caused by the erratic behaviour of the Duchess Bona and
the ambitions of Ludovico Sforza, and because of Florence's
apparently adamant refusal to make the financial contributions
expected of it towards the cost of the *condottieri*. The first of these
issues was exacerbated by the fact that the Duke of Calabria and
his troops were still occupying the Senese and appeared to be
bringing to fruition the long-term Neapolitan ambition to
establish a foothold in southern Tuscany. As Pierfilippo Pandolfini
remarked in a letter of 9 July to Lorenzo de' Medici, it was necessary 'to have the King as kinsman and companion, and even as
father, but not as Signore', and the Milanese appeared to concur
with this view.[1] But at the same time it was the Florentine
ambassador in Milan, Pierfilippo Pandolfini, who was most outspoken in his comments on the critical internal situation in Milan
itself, and his male chauvinist remarks about the instability of
female rulers were scarcely calculated to promote collaboration
between the two states.[2] However, it was the Florentine obstinacy
over money which was the most recalcitrant of the problems. This
was only in part a reflection of genuine financial difficulties
following the heavy costs of the Pazzi War. Feeling was growing in
Florence that it was being milked by its allies and that it was time
to make a stand and demonstrate that the Florentine treasury was
not bottomless.[3] Lorenzo was particularly sensitive to public
unrest over taxes, and was anxious to use the *condotta* issue to put
pressure on King Ferrante to give back the Florentine towns in
southern Tuscany which had been occupied by the Neapolitans
and Sienese during the Pazzi War.[4] These were to be persistent
themes in Florentine diplomacy in the next two years and they
illustrate well the interrelationship between military organization,
finance and broader political considerations, both external and
internal, which preoccupied the diplomats of the period.

[1] ASF, Signoria, Otto e Dieci; legazioni e commissarie, missive e responsive,
10, 263-4ᵛ (9 July 1480): '. . . se fe havere il Re per parente et compagnio, et per
padre, ma non per Signore!'

[2] Ibid. 169ᵛ-171 (2 Apr. 1480) and 177-79ᵛ (8 Apr. 1480); Pierfilippo
Pandolfini in Milan to Lorenzo.

[3] L. Landucci, *Diario fiorentino del 1450 al 1516*, a cura di I. del Badia
(Florence, 1883), p. 35.

[4] ASMi, Archivio Sforzesco. Potenze estere, Firenze 299 (25 June 1480):
Filippo Sacramoro from Florence to Dukes of Milan.

The Neapolitan League was finally renewed on 25 July 1480 and the *condotta* of Ercole d'Este as lieutenant-general of the League, which was a part of the agreement, included secret clauses specifically guaranteeing Ferrara against Venetian aggression.[1] Throughout the negotiations the threat of war in the Romagna to frustrate the ambitions of Girolamo Riario had been another constant theme which helped, in fact, to bring the League to fruition.[2]

But war in a different form was about to erupt in Italy. On 27 July, two days after the signing of the League, a Turkish fleet of 150 sail appeared off the coast of Puglia. Within days Otranto had fallen and for over a year events in Italy were to be crucially conditioned by the threatening presence of the Turk on Italian soil.[3] The Duke of Calabria and the bulk of his troops were withdrawn from Tuscany to face the new threat, and Florence saw the possibility of taking advantage of the withdrawal, and of Ferrante's new difficulties, to reclaim the lost towns. The 'insperato accidente' of Otranto, as Machiavelli described it, seemed to give diplomatic advantage not only to Florence.[4] Sixtus IV seized the opportunity to strengthen his prestige through vociferous championing of a crusade and to humiliate Ferrante by forcing him to beg for crusading funds.[5] Ludovico Sforza was able to resolve the internal crisis in Milan by taking control from the Duchess Bona without fear of Neapolitan interference. While in Venice the Senate pondered what advantage could be drawn from the embarrassment and preoccupation of Naples.

There was, of course, a widespread belief that Venice had

[1] F. Fossati, *Per l'alleanza del 25 luglio, 1480* (Mortara–Vigevano, 1901). For the *condotta* of Ercole d'Este, see ASF, Riformagioni, atti pubblici, cxxxviii (25 July 1480).

[2] E. Piva, 'L'opposizione diplomatica di Venezia alle mire di Sisto IV su Pesaro e ai tentativi di una crociata contro i Turchi, 1480–81', *Nuovo archivio veneto*, ns v, vi (1903); F. Fossati, 'Nuovi documenti sull'opera di Ludovico il Moro in difesa di Costanzo Sforza, *Atti e memorie della Dep. di storia patria per le Marche*, ns i–ii (1904–5); F. Fossati, *A proposito di una usurpazione di Sisto IV nel 1480: documenti milanesi* (Vigevano, 1901).

[3] C. Foucard, 'Fonti di storia napoletana dell'Archivio di Stato di Modena: Otranto nel 1480 e nel 1481', *Archivio storico per le provincie napoletane*, vi (1881), 82–3; P. Egidi, 'La politica del regno di Napoli negli ultimi mesi dell'anno 1480', ibid. (1910), 699–705.

[4] N. Machiavelli, *Istorie fiorentine*, a cura di F. Gaeta (Milan–Feltrinelli, 1962), p. 546.

[5] Foucard, op. cit., pp. 609–28; E. Carusi, 'Osservazioni sulla guerra per il ricupero di Otranto e tre lettere inedite di Re Ferrante a Sisto IV', *Archivio della società romana di storia patria*, xxxii (1909).

actually engineered the Turkish assault, and a general fear that
the Venetians would use the situation to their positive advantage
by initiating some aggressive move in northern Italy.[1] However,
their apparent reluctance to take advantage of the situation is
perhaps an indication of their passive involvement in the whole
affair. It is tempting to suggest that growing tension over Ferrara
and the eventual outbreak of the war was somehow linked to the
Turkish invasion, but the chronology of the events does not really
bear out such a hypothesis. The build up of that tension was a slow
and erratic process and there is little evidence of Venice seizing
with both hands the opportunity offered by the distraction of
Naples.

The position of Ferrara as a Venetian satellite had been a cause
of tension between the two cities for centuries. The famous *capitoli*
which gave Venetians extensive commercial concessions in
Ferrara, free access to the Po, and the right to maintain a
Visdomino in the city who presided over the Venetian community, went back to the twelfth century.[2] In 1405 Venice had
established control over the salt pans at Comacchio and forced
Ferrara to buy from the Venetian monopoly, but this in turn
created constant irritations over Ferrarese salt smuggling. During
the Lombardy wars the Polesine had been ceded by Venice to
Ferrara in return for military support and this served to create a
strident faction of Venetian landowners in the area which took
every opportunity to press for aggressive action against Ferrara.
The marriage of Ercole d'Este to Eleanora d'Aragona, the
daughter of King Ferrante, in 1472 further aroused Venetian
suspicions, and it was soon clear that Ercole intended to use his
new relationship with Naples and his position in the Neapolitan
League of July 1480 to strengthen his position *vis-à-vis* Venice.
During the negotiations over the League in the summer of 1480
Lorenzo de'Medici had expressed his concern that Ercole d'Este
was likely to draw the League into a war with Venice.[3]

All this suggests that Venetian aggressiveness was not the only
explanation of the war of Ferrara, and that such aggressiveness
was at least in part the result of pressure from a private interest

[1] Piva, 'L'opposizione diplomatica', i. 75–89; F. Fossati, 'Alcuni dubbi sul
contegno di Venezia durante la ricuperazione d'Otranto', *Nuovo archivio veneto*,
NS xii (1906); A. Bombaci, 'Venezia e l'impresa turca di Otranto, *Rivista storica
italiana*, lxvi (1954).

[2] ASV, Miscellanea atti diversi, 6A, *Rei Ferrariensis liber*; Piva, *La guerra di
Ferrara*, i. 9–12.

[3] ASMo, Carteggio degli ambasciatori, Firenze 2 (15 July 1480): Antonio da
Montecatini to Niccolo Sadoleto in Naples.

group within Venice.[1] These indications are borne out by the events of 1481 and early 1482. The first significant flickers of alarm came in January 1481 when the Venetians, after protesting about the building of houses on the Polesine frontier which were being used by salt smugglers, sent in troops to burn them down. The tremors caused by this episode ran through the diplomatic correspondence of all the Italian courts.[2] But it was like one stone dropping into a pool; the ripples had largely dispersed when in May Vettor Contarini, a fanatical anti-Ferrarese noble, arrived in Ferrara as Visdomino, and was within weeks engaged in a row with the ecclesiastical authorities which led to his excommunication.[3] Protests from Venice and harassment of Venetians in Ferrara followed. By late August Venetian protests were changing to positive counteraction and once again the diplomats of Italy were beginning to register reactions to the increasingly threatening situation. However, throughout this period there was no evidence of a Venetian military alert.

Then on 16 September Girolamo Riario arrived in Venice. He came ostensibly to cement the papal–Venetian alliance, to negotiate a *condotta* for himself, and to receive the rank of honorary noble of the city. But his ambitions in the Romagna were well known and there were even indications that he aspired to the throne of Naples itself.[4] Venetian help was crucial to these aspirations and Venetian help could perhaps be bought by a papal offer of Ferrara. It is not known how complete the agreement was between Riario and Venice at this stage, but clearly papal favour was an essential preliminary and a decisive encouragement to any move against Ferrara. Equally clearly, however, Riario was not much liked in Venice. He earned for himself a reputation for meanness by refusing to tip the oarsmen of the *Bucentaur* and the servants in the palace that were placed at his disposal, and seemed to attach little importance to the privileges conferred upon him.[5]

By this time Otranto had finally been recaptured and in a sense Venice's opportunity had passed without the Republic having made any real effort to grasp it. But by late September decisive

[1] Piva, *La guerra di Ferrara*, i. 16 and 55.

[2] ASMo, Carteggio degli ambasciatori, Firenze 2 (3 Jan. 1481): Antonio da Montecatini to Ercole d'Este.

[3] Piva, *La guerra di Ferrara*, i. 19.

[4] ASV, Dieci, misti, 20, 32 (9 Nov. 1480); Sigismondo de' Conti, *Istorie dei suoi tempi* (Rome, 1883), i. 114–15.

[5] Piva, *La guerra di Ferrara*, i. 50–3.

moves were being made. Venice began to construct three great bastions within the Ferrarese frontiers and the tide of protest now flowed the other way.[1] For two months the League debated an appropriate response; dispatches and instructions shuttled backwards and forwards between Milan, Florence, Rome, and Naples. By December Milan and Naples began to mobilize and ambassadors of the League were sent to Ferrara to offer support to Ercole d'Este and consider putting diplomatic pressure on Venice. By January Venice seemed to be set on a course for war; troops were being called out all over Lombardy, and moved from the eastern frontier to billets in the Padovano.[2] In late January Alberto Cortese, the Ferrarese ambassador in Venice, took fright at the rising tide of feeling against him and fled from the city.[3]

It was at this stage, however, that both inevitable delays in military mobilization and the intricacies of diplomatic manœuvre intervened. None of the members of the League were anxious for war; Naples was bankrupt and not very concerned about the defence of Ferrara; Florence declared categorically in February that it could spare no men or money for Ferrara until the question of the Sienese towns was resolved;[4] Milan was preoccupied with the growing rift between Ludovico Sforza and Roberto da Sanseverino and with the rebellion of the Rossi family; all felt it essential that agreement should be reached with Federico da Montefeltro about a *condotta* with the League before there could be any question of war with Venice. But Federico refused to negotiate actively until March when his current *condotta* with Naples and the Pope was approaching its expiry date.[5] There was a widespread belief that Venice was merely trying to force Ercole d'Este out of the League and would stop short of war. This may

[1] ASV, Senatus Secreta, 30, 33 (24 Sept. 1481). On 4 Jan. 1482 1,500 Venetian infantry were ordered to garrison the new bastions (ASV, Senatus Secreta, 30, 46).

[2] ASF, Otto, responsive, 2, 161 (report of Bongianno Gianfigliazzi from Ferrara of 7 Jan. 1482); ibid. 200 (report of Pierfilippo Pandolfini from Naples on 26 Jan. 1482).

[3] Piva, *La guerra di Ferrara*, i. 67.

[4] ASF, Signoria, missive, minutari, 12, 138ʳ–138ᵛ (instructions of Otto to Gianfigliazzi in Ferrara of 11 Feb. 1482); ASMa, Archivio Gonzaga, 1627 (Zaccaria da Pisa in Milan to Federigo Gonzaga, 16 Feb. 1482).

[5] ASF, Archivio Mediceo avanti il Principato (henceforth MAP), xlv. 198 (Giangaleazzo Sforza to Lorenzo de' Medici, 5 Dec. 1481). Federico finally agreed to open negotiations with the League on 7 Mar. 1482 which was three months before the expiry of his *condotta* with Naples and the Papacy (ASF, Otto, responsive, 2, 224; Pierfilippo Pandolfini from Naples to Otto, 4 Feb. 1482).

have been true initially but Venice was increasingly encouraged by the hope of gaining the services of Roberto da Sanseverino if he defected from Milan, and by the assurances of Riario that he would bring the Pope on to its side. In late March ambassadors of the League were in Urbino waiting impatiently while Federico consulted with his astrologers about a suitable date for signing his new *condotta*,[1] and Sanseverino was on his way to Venice to conclude terms with the Republic. On 3 April this contract was signed and Venice had a significant accretion of strength to its already powerful and by now largely mobilized standing army.[2] Venice now began to prepare a large river fleet for use on the Po and some money and infantry began at last to arrive in Ferrara from its allies.[3] On 15 April Federico da Montefeltro finally signed with the League as captain-general having persuaded the allies to accept an elaborate military plan for concerted attacks on Rome and across the Adda.[4] On 30 April Sixtus IV finally offered Ferrara to Venice.[5] Two days later Roberto da Sanseverino crossed the Tartaro on a five-mile causeway prepared by Veronese pioneers and threw his army into the heart of the still largely defenceless Ferrarese state.[6]

This complex and rather abbreviated story brings out clearly some of the interconnections between diplomacy and war which I have been seeking to stress. Ambassadors were active at every point; in Ferrara they were seeking to advise and encourage Ercole d'Este in his dilemma of whether to give in or resist; in Milan they were trying to help Ludovico Sforza resolve his internal problems and get his army ready; in Florence their role was to find a solution to the problem of the Sienese towns without driving Siena into the arms of the Venetians. Meanwhile in Rome the ambassadors of the League and of Venice were alternately

[1] ASF, MAP, LI. 103 (Luigi Guicciardini and Pierfilippo Pandolfini from Urbino to Lorenzo de' Medici, 31 Mar. 1482).

[2] R. Predelli, *I libri commemoriali della Repubblica di Venezia, Regesti* (Monumenti storici pubblicati dalla R. Dep. veneta di storia patria, 1st ser. *documenti*, vols. 3, 7, 8, 10, 11. Venice, 1879–1901) v. 268–9.

[3] The Bishop of Parma, the Milanese envoy in Ferrara, reported in early April both on the Venetian preparations and that 'in quella terra non si parla altro che di guerra benchè i vecchi et più savi non la volessino' (ASF, MAP, LI. 106; Bernardo Rucellai from Milan to Lorenzo, 4 Apr. 1482).

[4] ASF, MAP, LI. 122 (Luigi Guicciardini to Lorenzo de' Medici, 15 Apr. 1482).

[5] E. Piva, 'La cessione di Ferrara fatta da Sisto IV alla repubblica di Venezia (1482)', *Nuovo archivio veneto*, NS xiv (1907), 415.

[6] Piva, *La guerra di Ferrara*, i. 76–7.

cajoling and threatening Sixtus IV; in Naples the Milanese and Florentines had to convince Ferrante of the necessity for war; and in Urbino they had to cope with the vagaries and ambitions of that great prima donna, Federico da Montefeltro. Alongside all this activity the stage was at least partly taken up by the commanding figures of Federico and Roberto da Sanseverino without whose participation the war was unlikely to start, and by the 50,000 men who were gradually preparing themselves in their billets.[1]

The war itself revealed a combination of both surprisingly new and predictably traditional elements. Bloody battles like Campomorto and Argenta were interspersed with periods of manœuvre and stalemate; Albanian stradiots and Turkish janis-saries, retained in his service by the Duke of Calabria after the fall of Otranto, fought alongside heavily armed veterans of the wars of the 1450s; Venetian gunners experimented with gas shells and shrapnel while their traditional river fleets were blown out of the water by Ferrarese guns massed on the banks of the Po; tortuous and treacherous peace negotiations alternated with the extra-ordinary summit strategy conferences of princes at Cremona in February 1483 and Milan in January 1484. Through it all the suspicions and rivalries amongst the allies remained and Venice emerged beleaguered, outnumbered, but with the main gains at the peace of Bagnolo in August 1484.[2]

I have deliberately avoided placing too much emphasis on the role of Lorenzo de' Medici in the events I have been describing, partly because he was the subject of the brilliant Italian Lecture given four years ago to the Academy by Nicolai Rubinstein,[3] partly because I think that, at least for this period, his political pre-eminence in Italy has been somewhat exaggerated. Guicciar-dini's identification of him as the 'ago del bilancio' has been enormously influential in later writing, and one's view of the judgement must be conditioned not only by one's perceptions of his actual political contribution but also by one's understanding of the whole nature of the balance of power and the possibility of it being influenced or controlled by individual statesmen. However, as a well-documented example of the relationships between one

[1] For lists of the troops prepared by the various states for the early stages of the war, see Biblioteca Nazionale di Firenze, Magl. xxv. 161.

[2] C. Bonetti, 'La Dieta di Cremona', *Archivio storico lombardo*, 4th ser. x (1908); R. Cessi, 'La pace di Bagnolo dell' agosto 1484', *Annali triestini di diritto, economia e politica*, xii (1941).

[3] N. Rubinstein, 'Lorenzo de' Medici: the formation of his statecraft', *Proceedings of the British Academy*, lxiii (1977).

Italian political leader and the ambassadors of his state, his case obviously has a great relevance to any discussion of the role of diplomacy.

What exactly was Lorenzo's role in the formation of Florentine foreign policy? How did he relate both to the formally appointed ambassadors and to the official foreign-policy committees of the Republic? Through what other mechanisms did he or might he have operated to influence that policy and the political affairs of Italy? The answers to these questions cannot be the same throughout his career, nor, I suggest, can they be along the lines of steadily tightening control. In my view, a growing authority in the 1470s was to some extent interrupted and reduced in 1480, and was only gradually recovered in the later years of the decade with Lorenzo's important links with Rome and Naples.

Lorenzo's role in Florentine foreign policy depended on a number of factors. It depended, of course, on his natural position as one of the leaders of the oligarchy, a man whose opinions were influential in the *pratiche* and whose personal influence affected the way others thought and voted. This influence was increased by his carefully cultivated and well-known contacts outside Florence and by his position at the head of Florence's leading bank, with all that that meant in terms of economic standing and access to commercial and political information passed back by Medici banks agents. Equally carefully cultivated were his contacts with the foreign ambassadors in Florence all of whom tended to regard him as their main contact within the city and some of whom would bring the letters and instructions which they received from their governments to him to see before taking them to the official foreign-policy committees of the Republic. But, there is a danger in attaching too much importance to this essentially 'external' view of Lorenzo's pre-eminence in Florence. Princes, and the ambassadors of princes, disliked dealing with republican committees and were always anxious to find a leader in Florence, a stable point with which to negotiate, and through which to influence and control the city. The Milanese ambassador, Sacramoro Sacramori, reported in 1471: 'The affairs of this city have reached the point where everything depends on a nod from Lorenzo, and nobody else counts for anything.'[1] This was patently untrue but it was the way Milan wished to see it, and the way that Sacromoro, who had Lorenzo's ear, wished to see it. But in

[1] A. Brown, *Bartolomeo Scala (1430–97); Chancellor of Florence* (Princeton, 1979), p. 68: 'sono reducte le cose di questa città in locho che tutto consiste in uno cenno di Lorenzo, ne crediate che altri ce siano se non per uno zero . . .'.

practical terms such contacts were clearly important for Lorenzo's reputation as knowledgeable about foreign affairs.

Lorenzo also relied to some extent on personal envoys for particular missions and negotiations. But, up to 1484 at least, he does not seem to have made much use of any system of permanent personal agents and secretaries within the embassies abroad, as Guicciardini suggested.[1] Ambassadors selected their own secretaries in this period and there is very little evidence of Lorenzo corresponding with individuals in the embassies other than the ambassadors themselves.

But, finally, Lorenzo's role did depend heavily on his personal contacts with Florence's ambassadors and the extent to which they corresponded with him while on their missions. The ambassadors during the years 1480 to 1484 can be divided into three broad categories in terms of their relationship with Lorenzo. There were those who can be best described as 'Lorenzo men', whose careers depended very largely on their links to Lorenzo and whose appointment as ambassador was presumably owed to his influence. Men such as Francesco Gaddi and Baccio Ugolini come into this category and clearly regarded themselves as primarily his agents and only formally accredited by the Republic.[2] Their correspondence with Lorenzo tended to be detailed and comprehensive; all important information was passed to him. Then there was a middle group of men who were clearly closely linked to Lorenzo and on terms of intimacy with him—either through family ties, shared interests, or neighbourhood relationships within the city—and yet who had a role and an influence in the

---

[1] Francesco Guicciardini, *Storie fiorentine*, ed. R. Palmarocchi (Bari, 1931), p. 79.

[2] Francesco d'Agnolo Gaddi, a noted humanist and literary figure, was one of Lorenzo's most trusted envoys. He was sent to the French court in 1479, and again in May 1480 when he remained for nearly two years, first as Lorenzo's personal envoy and from Dec. 1480 as accredited ambassador of the Republic. He had the same dual role on a mission to Naples and the Duke of Calabria in the autumn of 1482. For fuller details of his diplomatic career, see L. Sozzi, 'Lettere inedite di Philippe de Commynes a Francesco Gaddi', in *Studi di bibliografia e di storia in onore di Tommaso de Marinis* (Verona, 1964). For his letters to Lorenzo during his second mission to France which indicate his very divided allegiances, see ASF, Signoria, Otto, Dieci; legazioni e commissarie, missive e responsive, 75 *passim*.

Baccio di Luca Ugolini was another of the literary figures of the Platonic Academy and the Lorenzan circle. He was sent to France and Germany in Aug. 1478, and to the abortive Council of Basle in Sept. 1482. He was also a confidant of the Gonzaga and was frequently in Mantua (A. Della Torre, *Storia dell'Academia Platonica di Firenze* (Florence, 1902), pp. 796–800).

oligarchy of their own right. Pierfilippo Pandolfini, Bernardo Rucellai, and Bernardo Bongirolami fit naturally into this category.[1] Such ambassadors tended to be more selective in the material which they sent to Lorenzo; letters to him would contain the more confidential information and news which the writer thought would be of particular interest to him personally—but referring him to their reports to the official organs of the Republic for more standard information. Finally, there were the envoys who owed nothing to Lorenzo, who stood entirely on their own feet in the oligarchy and whose attitude to him was one of differing degrees of personal friendship. Such men tended to come from an older generation—like Antonio Ridolfi, Guidantonio Vespucci, and Luigi Guicciardini.[2] The correspondence of this group of ambassadors with Lorenzo tended to be intermittent, in so far as we can tell, and rather arbitrary in the issues which were discussed.

For all these men, however, prior to 1480, there was a tendency

[1] Pierfilippo di Gianozzo Pandolfini was described by Antonio da Monte-catini as 'la mano drita cum la quale se segna Lorenzo, et praecipue ne le cose de fora' (ASMo, Carteggio degli ambascratori, Firenze 2; 6 Feb. 1481). But he was also a leading member of the Florentine oligarchy and the Republic's ambassador in Milan (Oct. 1479-July 1480), Naples (Nov. 1481-Mar. 1482), Rome (Feb.-May 1483), and at the peace negotiations at Bagnolo in Aug. 1484. His surviving correspondence both to Lorenzo and to the Otto is very extensive. Bernardo di Giovanni Rucellai was Lorenzo's brother-in-law and another noted humanist (G. Pellegrini, *L'umanista Bernardo Rucellai e le sue opere storiche*, Livorno, 1920). He was ambassador in Milan from Feb. 1482 to Oct. 1483.

Bernardo di Giovanni Bongirolami was a lawyer and a relative newcomer to the Florentine political élite, and hence perhaps more dependent than some on Lorenzo's support. He also was ambassador in Milan from Nov. 1483 to June 1484, following on important embassies to Naples and Rome in the early 1470s.

[2] Antonio di Lorenzo Ridolfi came of the older generation of Florentine politicians and had a distinguished record of public service in the 1460s and 1470s. He was chosen as ambassador to Rome in Apr. 1480 because he was known to be on good terms with Sixtus IV (ASF, Signoria, missive originali, 4, 67-8; 16 May 1480). He remained in Rome until Dec. 1480.

Guidantonio di Giovanni Vespucci was a lawyer and very experienced diplomat. He was ambassador in France in 1479 and 1480, and in Rome for much of the period between 1481 and 1484. His letters to Lorenzo, many of which survive in ASF, MAP, are notable for their selectivity in the matters discussed, and a tendency to draw a clear distinction between his official duties as ambassador and the private business of the Medici which he handled.

Luigi di Piero Guicciardini was, like his brother Jacopo, one of the most experienced politicians in Florence and a man whose prestige and seniority made him something of a rival to Lorenzo. He was ambassador in Venice in the first half of 1480, and together with Pandolfini negotiated the *condotta* with Federico da Montefeltro in Mar./Apr. 1482.

to use Lorenzo as a sort of filter for secret and confidential information, for unverified rumour and gossip, and for expressions of opinion by the ambassador himself. At this time dispatches were addressed to the Signoria in peace-time and were frequently discussed in the Pratica and read out to ambassadors of the foreign powers.[1] These were not the best forums for the discussion of confidential issues and the revelation of the secrets which the Florentine ambassadors had learnt. So, such information was sent to Lorenzo in the knowledge that he would know how to insert it into the policy-making process. Up to 1480 Florence lacked a small semi-permanent foreign-policy committee which could appropriately handle confidential business and long-range policy like the Consiglio Segreto in Milan, and so 'the secret affairs of this government will now pass through the hands of Lorenzo, as they passed through those of his father' as the Ferrarese ambassador put it in 1469.[2]

However, part of the constitutional reforms of April 1480 was the setting up of such a foreign-policy committee—the Otto di Pratica.[3] Eight leading members of the new Council of Seventy held the responsibility for six months and ambassadors were specifically encouraged to report fully on confidential and secret affairs to the new committee.[4] The development was seen as an extension of the special authority and continuity which the Dieci di Balia had in war-time to a period of peace.[5] The Otto, indeed, had responsibility for all military affairs as well as foreign policy but could always refer particularly controversial issues to a full debate in the Council of Seventy. The impact of the setting up of the new committee on ambassadorial reporting was immediate. The ambassadors clearly felt freer to report confidential matters direct to the Otto and this accounts in part for the more intermittent

---

[1] For discussion of the conduct of Florentine foreign policy and the role of ambassadors, see E. Santini, *Firenze e i suoi oratori nel Quattrocento* (Florence, 1922) and G. Pampaloni, 'Gli organi della Repubblica fiorentina per le relazioni coll'estero', *Rivista di studi politici internazionali*, xx (1953).

[2] Rubinstein, 'Lorenzo de' Medici', p. 87.

[3] N. Rubinstein, *The Government of Florence under the Medici, 1434 to 1494* (Oxford, 1966), pp. 199–201.

[4] ASF, Signoria, Legazioni e commissarie, 21, 7–8ᵛ (to Antonio Ridolfi and Piero Nasi, 2 May 1480), and ASF, Otto di Pratica, Legazioni e commissarie, 1, 7 (to Luigi Guicciardini, 2 May 1480).

[5] *Memorie e ricordi di Ser Giusto di Giovanni Giusti d'Anghiari*, in Biblioteca Nazionale di Firenze, ii. ii. 127, 135ᵛ: 'Quelli trenta della Balia di Firenze elessono otto cittadini di Firenze che havessino la cura del governo loro per di fuori della terra che si può dire sieno in luogo de' Dieci di Balia' (19 Apr. 1480).

quality of the letters of some of the senior ambassadors to Lorenzo in this period.[1] Lorenzo was not a member of the first two groups of the Otto di Pratica, and although he continued to be consulted on all major issues and he clearly had access to the official ambassadorial reports, one gets the impression of him dropping a little into the background in this key area of Florentine policy-making. Undoubtedly there were many occasions within the following two years when there were fierce debates over foreign policy and military affairs; Lorenzo frequently found himself defending a minority position, both inside the Otto and outside, against hardliners who disliked the way in which Florence was seeming to be manipulated and exploited by its allies.

These insights into Lorenzo's role in foreign policy-making within Florence in these years obviously have some bearing on one's view of his influence in Italy as a whole. Foreign observers, in this period, frequently remarked that Lorenzo's reputation and authority within Florence depended to a large extent on his links with other Italian and foreign powers, and that without these his position in the city would be considerably weakened. But it is equally true that the reputation and influence of Lorenzo outside Florence depended on the extent to which he was seen by the powers to have control of the Republic's foreign policy. However, the influence of Lorenzo in the wider 'concert' of Italy was also dependent on the economic and military strengths of Florence itself. But militarily it was clearly the weakest of the five major powers and its growing reluctance actually to contribute money to the leagues in which it was involved tended to nullify its economic strength. The lack of regard for Florentine opinions and interests which was clearly apparent in the intrigues and negotiations of this period tended to negate the value of Lorenzo himself as a sort of arbiter in Italian politics, although this was a role for which both Milan and Naples occasionally cast him.

The fusion of diplomatic and military affairs in peace-time and the need for small long-serving committees that could discuss such

[1] The impact of the change in foreign policy direction is most apparent in the letters of Pierfilippo Pandolfini in May 1480 (ASF, Signoria, Otto, Dieci; legazioni e commissarie, missive e responsive, 10, 196–224). When Antonio da Montecatini approached Lorenzo to seek his help in persuading both the Florentine *signoria* and, more importantly, King Ferrante that Ercole d'Este's *condotta* should be agreed before the League was redrafted, Lorenzo referred him to the Otto di Pratica which had been specifically set up 'per fare le cose loro più segrete'. He refused to write direct to Naples because this would 'rompere lo ordine di questo governo apena cominciado' (ASMo, Carteggio degli ambascratori, Firenze 2, 24 May 1480).

matters in confidence and with the benefit of continuity of experience was summed up in the establishment of the Otto di Pratica in Florence. Exactly the same process was taking place in Venice with the gradual involvement of the Council of Ten in such matters. Here the development was more gradual and informal, but it was in 1480 that the Council first began to get involved in secret diplomacy while at the same time it was extending its authority over many aspects of military organization.[1] Foreign policy, diplomacy, and war, were thus playing their parts in that crucial consolidation of power which was so much a feature of the Italian political scene in the later fifteenth century.

[1] Zaccaria Barbaro, sent to Rome at the end of May 1480, was the first Venetian ambassador to write extensively to the Consiglio de' Dieci (ASV, Dieci, misti, 20, 4^v–5 f.). For an extended discussion of the growth of the power of the Dieci in military affairs, see J. R. Hale and M. E. Mallett, *Venice: the Military Organisation of a Renaissance State, 1400–1617* (Cambridge, forthcoming). Other recent discussions of the role of the Dieci are G. Cozzi, 'Authority and the Law in Renaissance Venice', *Renaissance Venice*, pp. 303–8; M. Knapton, 'Il Consiglio dei Dieci nel governo della Terraferma: un' ipotesi interpretativa per il secondo '400', *Atti del convegno 'Venezia e la Terraferma attraverso le relazioni dei rettori'* (Milan, 1981).

THE FABRIC OF DRYDEN'S VERSE

By RICHARD LUCKETT

Read 26 November 1981

THE modern and the seventeenth-century meanings of 'fabric' have common elements, disparate emphases. When Dr Johnson wrote of Pope that 'he used almost always the same fabrick of verse' he meant that he wrote almost exclusively in the heroic couplet.[1] Johnson's sense is the modern sense, the manufactured material of which an object, most usually a building or a dress, is made. I shall have something to say about that aspect of Dryden's verse, but my aim is to try to go beyond it, to suggest its relation to what I believe to be the principal seventeenth-century sense of fabric: that is, the building itself, the sum of the parts. The seventeenth-century sense and the modern sense are not obviously exclusive; it is precisely their interrelation that is useful for my argument.

I shall begin with prophecy, a device about which Dryden was certainly as dubious as you may be, but which, once he had hedged his bets, he never hesitated to use. As he wrote in his *To Sir Robert Howard*, of 1660:

> Yet let me take your Mantle up, and I
> Will venture in your right to prophesy.
>
> 'This Work, by merit first of Fame secure,
> 'Is likewise happy in its Geniture:
> 'For since 'tis born when *Charls* ascends the Throne,
> 'It shares at once his Fortune and its own.'

I shall hedge my own bets by modifying the word to 'prediction'. I anticipate, if only because of the inadequacies of the available editions, that in the field of Dryden scholarship more and more evidence will come to light of his borrowings of words, of phrases, images, and procedures, but particularly the first two, from his immediate predecessors, and from his contemporaries amongst the English poets. I think, that is to say, that the convenient and

---

[1] Samuel Johnson *Lives of the English Poets*, int. Arthur Waugh, 2 vols., London, 1906 (1952), ii. 305. Johnson's *Life* also provides another relevant usage; of the *Essay on Man* he observes that it 'plainly appears the fabrick of a poet' (ibid., p. 274).

prevalent notion of 'common stock', which is in itself testimony to the situation that I am about to outline, will disappear, and that scholars will find increasing numbers of sources for Dryden in which it seems probable that he has drawn directly on particular poems because they had a relation to his immediate concern in composition—in other words, an exploration of what Eliot was describing when he said, with a sufficiency which is in itself a critical challenge: 'The capacity of assimilation, and the consequent extent of range, are conspicuous qualities of Dryden.'[1] In fact, this process is already under way, and it is its bearing on criticism that to an extent I want to anticipate.

The kind of thing I have in mind can best be illustrated by attempting a reconstruction of the way Dryden may have worked in writing one of his most famous odes. I cannot demonstrate that he did work in quite the sequence I propose; I think also that one obvious question—was he consciously or unconsciously proceeding in such a manner?—does not answer to the circumstances of the kind of process of creation that I hope will emerge from this account. But that is something I must endeavour to substantiate in the description.

When Dryden accepted the commission to write an ode for the 1687 feast of the Gentlemen Lovers of Musick he was dealing with a genre established as recently as 1683, and having for its exemplars a contemptible piece by Christopher Fishbourn, an even more contemptible piece by Nahum Tate (which has the distinction, remarkable in criticism, of being described as 'sugary, simpering, and mincing with almost incredibly bad taste' by so latitudinarian a commentator as Montague Summers), and a workmanlike poem, which Dryden would certainly have known, by John Oldham.[2] What is at once evident in these poems, even in the Oldham, is a lack of structure. That the need for an appropriate structure for a Cecilian Ode concerned Dryden we know from his copy (now in the library of Trinity College, Cambridge) of Spenser. Stanza 12 of the second of the Mutabilitie Cantos contains a reference to how, at the marriage of Peleus and Thetis:

> . . . *Phoebus* self, that god of Poets hight,
>   They say did sing the spousall hymne full cleere,
>   That all the Gods were ravisht with delight
> Of his celestiall song, and Musicks wondrous might.

---

[1] T. S. Eliot, *Selected Essays* (London, 1951), p. 312.

[2] Thomas Shadwell, *Complete Works*, ed. Montague Summers, 5 vols. (London, 1927), i, p. ccxi.

Against this, Dryden wrote: 'groundwork for a song on St. Cecilia's Day.' He never used it, though the 'Power of Musick' is of course the theme of *Alexander's Feast*. But what is suggestive is the subject of the Canto as a whole: Dame Mutabilitie's plea to

> This great Grandmother of all creatures bred
> Great *Nature*, ever young yet full of eld,
> Still mooving, yet unmoved from her sted

and Spenser's extraordinary extended exploration of, and meditation upon, change, time, immortality, eternity, and the universe, which raises so many of the questions that were to preoccupy philosophers and theologians (and, of course, poets) for the next century. It is no great jump from the Mutabilitie Cantos to Sir John Davies's discussion in *Nosce Teipsum* of the proposal 'That the Soule cannot be destroyed':

> *Perhaps* her *cause* may cease and she may die;
> God is her *cause*, his *word* her maker was,
> Which shall stand fixt for all eternitie,
> When heaven and earth shall like a shadow passe.

> *Perhaps* some thing repugnant to her kind
> By strong *Antipathy* the *Soule* may kill;
> But what can be *contrarie* to the mind,
> Which holds all *contraries* in concord still?

> She lodgeth heate, and cold, and moist and drye,
> And life, and death, and peace, and warre, together.

Which brings us to the actual language of the *Song*:

> Then cold, and hot, and moist, and dry,
> In order to their stations leap,
> And MUSICK'S pow'r obey . . .

as well as back to that paradox of uncreation to which Spenser had alluded with: 'And *Natur*'s selfe did vanish, whither no man wist.' We are in contact with both the actual language of the *Song* and with its form when we turn to Cowley's Pindarick on 'The Resurrection', which would unavoidably have come to Dryden's mind since its second stanza was drawn on quite directly by John Oldham in his *Ode* for 1684, 'Begin the Song'. Oldham, however, used only the opening of the stanza, which tells how the years

> All hand in hand do decently advance,
> And to my *Song* with smooth and equal measures *dance*.

It was the continuation of Cowley's stanza which stirred Dryden's imagination:

> Whilst the *dance lasts*, how long so e're it be,
> My *Musick*s voice shall bear it companie,
>   Till all *gentle Notes* be drown'd
>   In the *last Trumpet*s dreadful sound;
> That to the *Spheres* themselves shall *silence* bring,
>   Untune the *Universal String*.
>   Then all the wide extended *Skie*
>   And all th'*harmonious Worlds* on high
>   And *Virgil*'s sacred *work* shall dy . . .

We are also in contact with the essential dramatic device of the *Song*, a point that can be made more explicit by turning to another Pindarick on 'Nature's great solemn Funeral', John Norris's *The Consummation*. Norris was a friend of Dryden's, and his ode was published shortly before the composition of *A Song*. It is an ambitious, not very successful, piece. It draws, as it could scarcely avoid doing, on the Cowley. And so there are good ideas in it. Norris gets Cowley's 'untun'd' into his last line, the position that it occupies in Dryden's poem, thus terminating his creation with uncreation:

> And now the World's *untun'd*, let down thy *high-set* string.

It also introduces one important new device: Time, by means of a somewhat drastic pun, becomes an actor, 'The Antient Stager of the Day', and the image of the theatre stays in Norris's mind:

>   See how the Elements resign
> Their numerous charge, the scatter'd Atoms home repair . . .
>   They know the great Alarm,
>   And in confus'd mixt numbers swarm,
> Till rang'd, and sever'd by the *Chymistry* divine,
> The Father of Mankind's amaz'd to see
> The Globe too narrow for his Progeny.
>   But 'tis the *closing* of the Age
> And *all* the *Actors* now at once must grace the *Stage*.

The theatre evidently stayed in Dryden's mind also, and I do not think it fanciful to suggest that Norris's 'globe' may have triggered a recollection of a passage which he had once had occasion to excise from *The Tempest*—the pageant becoming not 'insubstantial' but 'crumbling', the transformations ultimate, the ending of the revels final, the Globe, the theatre, itself the operative image. For the essential dramatic device of *A Song* is functional, turning, just as Shakespeare does, the occasion, the gathering in Stationers' Hall, into a part of the poem's imagery. The last trumpet becomes a real trumpet, the assembly of the Gentlemen Lovers of Music becomes 'This crumbling pageant', and a synecdoche of the Last Judgement. The literalism is stark; the equation, 'trumpet' 'last trumpet', almost naïvely obvious, if not brazen; the effect is totally shocking. Dr Johnson thought the use of the image of the Day of Judgement 'so awful in itself, that it can owe little to poetry'; but the Cowley and Norris Odes by their comparative insignificance (though Johnson admired part of the Cowley) show that it owes everything to poetry.[1] Dryden even manages to extend what we might normally presume to be the scope of the art itself; and yet: 'owes everything to poetry'? Norris, Oldham, Cowley, Davies, are all drawn upon directly; from a distance, Spenser and Shakespeare make their contributions. But what is so striking is the unlikeness of Dryden's material, animated in his poem, as compared to what we might think of as its inert form in his sources—the radical reformation that it has undergone. Dryden has contrived simultaneously to find in the occasion itself his principal image, to use this image of the creation and uncreation of the world as his plot, to introduce as the logical subplot the history of music—Jubal, Orpheus, and Cecilia are each progressively more gifted exponents of the art—and then within this double frame to create a series of character parts which comes, again with an irresistible logic, directly out of an account of the invention of the first musical instrument, and ends its passage from the profane to the sacred with a further movement, where no further movement had seemed possible, into the most awful dimension of the sublime. The affects of the viol (Jubal's chorded shell, the *testudo*), the trumpet and drum, flute, lute, violin, and organ, provide a conspectus of the primary human emotions. In perceiving this Dryden not only found but fixed the form of the Cecilian Ode in perpetuity, and it is as much a musical as a literary innovation, a feat of design which, if it does not impress as such, only fails to do so because it appears so obvious; a kind of 'Try sparrowhawks, Ma'am', which makes a perfect order in a field where disorder doubly prevailed, should we allow Pushkin's opinion that 'Ecstasy does not require any intellectual power capable of relating the parts to the whole. . . . Homer is immeasurably greater than Pindar, the ode . . . stands on the lowest rungs of poetry . . .'[2] and take in addition Dryden's own view of English

---

[1] Johnson, op. cit. i. 311.
Tatiana Wolff (ed.), *Pushkin on Literature* (London, 1971), p. 170.

Pindaricks. These he appears to have recognized for what they were: an invention of the 'happy genius of Mr. Cowley', which gave an apparent classical license for something wholly unclassical, a poem 'like a vast tract of land newly discovered. The soil wonderfully fruitful . . . overstocked with inhabitants, but almost all salvages, without laws or policy.'[1]

I believe that similar accounts could be given of the creation of many of Dryden's poems: of *To the Pious Memory of Mistress Anne Killigrew*, for example, of which Jonson's *To the Immortall Memory . . . of Sir Lucius Cary and Sir H. Morison* is an obvious source, contributing a strategy (in that both poems are not about the historical characters of their subjects, but about the virtues that those characters could be taken to illustrate), a fundamental structural device (the introduction of the poet's person into the poem), and verbal echoes. Less anticipatable as a source is Anne Killigrew's own verse, which Dryden had evidently read with attention and which gave him the basis for:

> Mean time her Warlike Brother on the Seas
> His waving Streamers to the Winds displays,
> And vows for his Return, with vain Devotion, pays.
> Ah, Generous Youth, that Wish forbear,
> The Winds too soon will waft thee here!
> Slack all thy Sailes, and fear to come,
> Alas, thou know'st not, Thou art wreck'd at home!

The *Dies Irae* in Roscommon's translation, Nathaniel Lee's *Theodosius* (where the Dioscuri also appear), which provided the image of

> 'Twas *Cupid* bathing in *Diana*'s Stream,

besides two poems by Cowley on the matchless Orinda, together with some others of the poems prefaced to Katherine Philips's works—a connection obvious enough, but topically strengthened because both Katherine Philips and Anne Killigrew died of smallpox—also play their part. Nor does Dryden hesitate to borrow from himself, making extensive use of motifs (the comparison of poetry and painting, the Last Judgement), and details from his earlier work—indeed, even from his earliest work, his *Upon the Death of the Lord Hastings* of 1649. These things all come together in what Johnson called, with reason, 'undoubtedly the noblest ode that our language has ever produced', and are united and transformed by Dryden's development of

---

[1] *Letters upon Several Occasions* (London, 1696), pp. 55-6.

a dominant theme: an attempt to answer the question 'How shall the poet be saved?' which Anne Killigrew's life, death, and innocence are all made insistently to demand.[1] Jonson's strategy is carried a stage further, and the problem of writing an acceptably panegyrical elegy on a young lady who practised, with at best a modest talent, the 'two Sister-Arts of Poësie, and Painting' is resolved by writing a poem overtly introducing Dryden himself, as practitioner of the arts of poetry and playwriting, and the reflections prompted by the idealization of Anne Killigrew that her death has made incumbent upon him. But this very issue is explicit in the first stanza of James Tyrell's *To the Memory of the excellent Orinda* which, like Dryden's canonization of Anne Killigrew, sees Katherine Phillips as a saint, yet in the order of the poets, and which suggests the problem of the pure tribute from the impure vessel. Moreover, in a manner almost alarming in the context of my argument, the second stanza of Tyrell's poem raises abruptly the whole question of design, of scheme, in the Pindarick. What Dryden has done is to implement the notion structurally, and this is the aspect of his poetic gift that I am now concerned to urge.

This is not just a way of looking at Dryden: it is an identification of a method of composition to which he himself admits, and which attracted comment (albeit in an oblique and sometimes disparaging form) from his contemporaries, the most notable, since it cannot disguise a qualified admiration despite its disapproval, being Gerard Langbaine's description of Dryden as the 'skilful Lapidary'. Dryden was fascinated by the process of creation, to the extent that the *Epistle Dedicatory of the Rival Ladies* is sometimes cited, a little implausibly (since it neglects Hobbes, and, of course, Shakespeare) as the first account in English of the psychology of composition:

This worthless present was designed you, long before it was a play; when it was only a confused mass of thoughts, tumbling over one another in the dark; when the fancy was yet in its first work, moving the sleeping images of things towards the light, there to be distinguished, and then either chosen or rejected by the judgment.... And, I confess, in that first tumult of my thoughts, there appeared a disorderly kind of beauty in some of them, which gave me hope, something worthy my Lord of Orrery might be drawn from them.

'Judgment' is the operative faculty, 'distinguishing' the instrumental process, 'order' (and here I think we should recollect the

[1] Johnson, op. cit. i. 310.

French *ordonnance*) the principle of Beauty. Or we can turn to the
first prologue to *Secret Love*:

> He who writ this, not without pains and thought
> From *French* and *English* Theaters has brought
> Th' exactest Rules by which a play is wrought.
>
> The Unities of Action, Place, and Time;
> The Scenes unbroken; and a mingled chime
> Of *Johnson*s humour, with *Corneille*s rhyme.
>
> But while dead colours he with care did lay,
> He fears his Wit, or Plot he did not weigh,
> Which are the living Beauties of a Play . . .

to *To my Dear Friend Mr. Congreve, On His Comedy, call'd The Double-
Dealer*, where a sustained architectural analogy with a precise
allusion to what was contemporaneously happening at the top of
Ludgate Hill introduces a listing of the excellencies of Congreve's
predecessors which concludes with his subsumation of their
virtues, to the *Essay on Dramatic Poesy*, and Crites on Ben Jonson,
the 'greatest man of the last age', who was willing 'to give way' to
the Ancients 'in all things':

he was not only a professt Imitator of *Horace*, but a learned Plagiary of all
the others; you track him every where in their Snow: if *Horace, Lucan,
Petronius Arbiter, Seneca*, and *Juvenal* had their own from him, there are
few serious Thoughts which are new in him; you will pardon me, therefore, if I presume he lov'd their fashion, when he wore their Cloaths.

Tracking Dryden, but in the snow of his contemporaries, is
precisely the tendency in Dryden scholarship that I am predicting
and that I have endeavoured, in a particular instance, to demonstrate; and it is an activity for which I now wish to suggest a
perspective, a perspective in perhaps a distressingly literal sense,
since it has to do with the architectural proclivity of the Restoration, with which I am anxious to associate the underlying processes that seem to me the common factors in the fabrication of
Dryden's verse. These processes have it in common that they are
structural; and this I take to be an element in English poetry that is
both uncommon and, to a certain extent, unpopular. It is certainly
untypical.

The architectural proclivity of the Restoration is neatly
summed up by Evelyn, who in his diary entry for 4 February 1685,
which is, in effect, an obituary for the King, wrote that Charles II
loved 'Planting, building, & brought in a politer way of living,
which passed to Luxurie & intollerable expense'. Did Evelyn
then reflect that on 28 October 1664 he had recorded a con-

versation with Charles, occasioned by his presentation to the King of his *Sylvae* and his translation of Roland de Fréart's *Parallèle de l'Architecture*? My point is not that Evelyn might have done more than a little to whet that appetite the effects of which he subsequently deplored, but that the irony reveals the way in which the two concerns, which have as their common factor the necessity of design, imbued the culture of the Restoration, a culture with which Dryden quite consciously identified himself, of which he was, to an extraordinary degree, the deliberate emissary, a culture which had to it a quiddity, a sense of its own particularity, perhaps unique in English history. 'All, all, of a piece throughout': Dryden's summary in *The Secular Masque* from *The Pilgrim* reveals his absolute awareness of the way he had come to adumbrate a period; and in a sense this is what his poems do too.[1] My account of *A Song for St. Cecilia's Day* may have suggested the manner in which that poem made a number of other poems redundant. 'Who now reads Cowley?' Few people, since what Cowley did was better done by Dryden. Why should Pope have tried to suppress his *Ode on St. Cecilia's Day*? One reason must be that he had come to see that there was nothing in it that had not been better done by Dryden. But *The Secular Masque* is not, as it happens, merely inspired hindsight. It was the Restoration itself that enabled Dryden to speak as a poet. At that time, by which he was twenty-eight, he had, so far as we know, written only four poems. From 1660 onwards until his death in 1701 there is not a year in which he fails to publish. And here I must return to my beginning and bring the poem *To Sir Robert Howard* back into play: his prophecy is in fact far apter for his own career than for Howard's, and the poem tells us why:

> this is a piece too fair
> To be the child of Chance, and not of Care.
> No Atoms casually together hurl'd
> Could e're produce so beautifull a world.
> Nor dare I such a doctrine here admit,
> As would destroy the providence of wit.

No event in English history was ever more witty than the providential Restoration, and when that Restoration was jeopardized Dryden used the model of wit-writing established by Davenant in *Gondibert* to indicate why. *Annus Mirabilis*, which follows *Gondibert* not only in its stanzas and manner, but also in its latent five-act organization (I cannot at all assent to Ker's description of it as

---

[1] Thomas Rymer makes the necessary point quite explicitly when he writes, in his *Tragedies of the Last Age* (1678): 'I have thought our Poetry of te last Age as rude as our Architecture . . .'.

a 'series of fragments, with no more than an accidental unity'),
confounds prophecy with wit.[1] The Republicans had claimed that
God was with them, and saw in the course of history their justification of that claim. The year 1660 had turned their proposition to
dead sea fruit, and was, consummately, a witty providence. But
1666, when England suffered the aftermath of plague, the Dutch
in the Medway, and the Great Fire, threatened to be, and was
represented by adherents of the Old Cause as being, its reversal. In
Annus Mirabilis Dryden propounded a possible way of seeing the
events of that year, a year of darkness, or, if you consented to his
vision, of wonders, interpreting it on the same principle, in a poem
which was a triumph of design.

The poet as architect is sufficiently familiar as both a topos
of debate with which Plato and Quintillian made play, and as a
subject of debate which no reader of Ben Jonson could ignore.
I am not now concerned with the metaphor, but the particular
status of architecture in the Restoration, a status demonstrated, in
its poetic context, by John Webb's complaint when John Denham
was appointed Surveyor General of the King's Works in 1660:
'Though Mr Denham may, as most gentry, have some knowledge
of the theory of architecture, he can have none of the practice, but
must employ another.'[2] It is as gentleman, not as poet, that
Denham has some knowledge of the theory of architecture, and it
is to this aspect of Webb's assumption, the assumption equally
attested to by Sir Roger Pratt's observation: 'if you be not able to
handsomely contrive it yourself, get some ingenious gentleman
who has seen much of that kind abroad . . . to do it for you', that I
want to draw attention.[3] The tardiness of Sir Christopher Wren's
discovery of his avocation as architect is as striking as the tardiness
of Dryden's discovery of his avocation as poet. What is more,
Wren had himself, in his translation of Horace's *Epistle to Lollius*,
essayed poetry, and in 1663 in conversation expressed views on wit
sufficiently striking for his friend Thomas Sprat to write them
down, develop them, and then report them back to their originator: the Wit of Discourse

uses the best and easiest Words, is not the first that takes up new ones,
nor the last that lays down old ones. But above all, its chiefest Dominion
is in forming new Significations, and Images of Things and Persons.
And this may be so suddenly practised, that I have known in one

[1] John Dryden, *Essays*, ed. W. P. Ker, 2 vols. (Oxford, 1900), i, p. xxxiii.
[2] Howard Colvin, *A Biographical Dictionary of British Architects and Craftsmen*
(London, 1978), p. 258.
[3] Sir Roger Pratt, *The Architecture*, ed. R. T. Gunther (Oxford, 1928), p. 60.

Afternoon, new Stamps, and Proverbs, and Fashions of Speech raised, which were never thought of before, and yet gave Occasion to most delightful Imaginations . . . Wit consists in a right ordering of Things and Words for Delight.

Sprat ends by lamenting, in verse wittily symptomatic of the disease he describes, the fact that 'All the World are at present Poets', and by asking 'What is to be done with this furious Generation of Wits and Writers?'[1]

I think this offers a clue as to Dryden's discovery of himself as a poet, and his practice as a writer. It is debatable whether Sir John Denham was ever the architect of a building, but there has never been any question that he was the architect of a poem in which the two senses of fabric coinhere. The achievement of *Cooper's Hill*, which opens with an allusion, by means of Waller's poem on the occasion, to Inigo Jones's beautifying and regularizing of Old St. Paul's, is the stance of the poet, independent of Royal Windsor and rebellious Runnymeade, who equates himself with the river upon which both places stand:

> O could I flow like thee, and make thy stream
> My great example, as it is my theme!
> Though deep, yet clear, though gentle, yet not dull,
> Strong without rage, without o'erflowing full;

lines which Dryden both commended in his criticism, and, in his poem to *Sir Robert Howard*, imitated:

> Yet as when mighty Rivers gently creep,
> Their even calmnesse does suppose them deep,
> Such is your Muse: no Metaphor swell'd high
> With dangerous boldnesse lifts her to the sky . . .
> So firm a strength, and yet withall so sweet,
> Did never but in *Sampson*'s Riddle meet.

It is Dryden's prompt perception of the importance of this, rather than his imitation, that signifies. This is not to deny that he responded to the fabric of the heroic couplet as it was employed by Denham: he manifestly did so, to the extent of writing blank verse which is really disguised couplets, and using broken couplets, as the normative and restraining form, in his Pindarick Odes. But what I think him to have found far more compelling was Denham's equation of viewpoint and Archimedean point; the balance of the couplet inherent in the balance of the composition.

In his *Declaration of the Aeneis* to the Marquess of Normanby Dryden recounts that he

---

[1] Stephen Wren, *Parentalia* (London, 1750), pp. 258-9.

had also studied *Virgil*'s Design, his disposition of it, his Manners, his judicious management of the Figures, the sober retrenchments of his Sense, which always leaves somewhat to gratifie our imagination, on which it may enlarge at pleasure; but above all, the Elegance of his Expressions, and the harmony of his Numbers. For . . . the words are in Poetry, what the Colours are in Painting. If the Design be good, and the Draught be true, the Colouring is the first Beauty that strikes the Eye.[1]

'If the Design be good, and the Draught be true'; it is the essential precondition, and the metaphor runs throughout Dryden's criticism: 'But in a room contrived for state, the height of the roof should bear a proportion to the area: so in the heightenings of poetry, the strength and vehemence of figures should be suited to the occasion, the subject, and the persons.' Dryden's admission in his dedication to *Troilus and Cressida* (1679) that he was 'often put to a stand, in considering whether what I write be the Idiom of the Tongue . . . And have no other way to clear my Doubts, but by translating my English into Latine, and thereby trying what sense the words will beare in a more stable Language', is interesting not so much for what it may or may not have to tell us about the state of English, or Dryden's Latinity, as for what it reveals about Dryden's reflex of thought, his capacity for an immediate shift into another mode of conceptualizing the matter. Dryden's translations also signify here, first in their quantity, the extent to which they are his preferred mode (over half his published verse, it has been estimated, is translation), secondly in their customary procedures—the use of a multiplicity of texts, commentaries, and existing English versions. There is, in this process, an assumption of an underlying recoverable form, which is equally the assumption that could cause him, in the *Fables*, to make a passage of Chaucer comprehend a passage of Lucretius—and the effect is not of anything applied, not of superimposition, but of something derived from the essence of the concerns which Aristotle, Lucretius, Chaucer, Robert Burton, and Dryden had in common. And I must emphasize that I consider this as much a matter of the ectomorph as of the endomorph, of the perception of the space created by a structure as of the scaffolding itself, the space implied by Dryden when he said of 'piety' in its Virgilian application to Aeneas, that 'the word in Latin is more full than it can possibly be expressed in any modern language' and which he himself consistently exploited, as when, in *To the Pious Memory* he described Anne Killigrew as '. . . yet a young Probationer, / And Candidate of Heav'n'.

This radical cast of mind in Dryden emerges in many different ways: in the way he takes over existing mythologies or devices and inverts them: the prophecies of doom (and the title of the poem itself) in *Annus Mirabilis*, Shadwell's claim to the Jonsonian inheritance in *Mac Flecknoe*, Marvell's sardonic glimpse of Charles as Saul in *Absalom and Achitophel*, the Whigs' emblematic token in *The Medall*, the title of Lord Herbert's deistical tract in *Religio Laici*, the fable out of a low church pamphlet in *The Hind and the Panther*, in the mordant critique of empire ('Here let my sorrow give my satyr place') in the same poem.[1] It finds expression in his recurrent concern with origins—of painting in *To Sir Godfrey Kneller*, of poetry in *To the Earl of Roscommon*, of music (as we have seen) in *A Song for St. Cecilia's Day*—a concern that is as naturally extended to scriptural text as to Stonehenge. This same radicalism has a clear relation to the aspect of Dryden which must have some bearing on the psychology of his conceptual brilliance: that is, his taking of risks.

Such a taking of risks can assume many forms. A fascination with the subject is in any case implicit in the recurrent images of gambling and trade as in the superficially unlikely contest of *Threnodia Augustalis*, where we find both the assertion that

> Never was losing game with better conduct plaid . . .

and the equivocal

> The vain *Insurancers* of Life,
> And He who most perform'd and promis'd less,
> Even *Short* himself forsook th'unequal strife.

Money is a constant topic in Dryden, but it is never far removed from the question of chance. In *Annus Mirabilis* we have the possibility that 1667 will reverse 1666, the King's prayers be denied, the Dutch enter the Thames, the plague break out anew. In *Absalom and Achitophel* the risk is that the mockery of Charles would not, by its subject, be regarded as worth the end that it achieves (after all, what would James have said had Dryden chosen to treat him in such terms?). In *Religio Laici* the risk is that the acceptance of the critique of scriptural texts will lead to an entire dependence on embodied tradition, and here, of course, for Dryden, it ultimately did. Dryden's Catholicism, in *The Hind and the Panther*, and the position of political absolutism (however humane and qualified) set out in the postscript to the translation of *The History of the League*, are both in a sense compensatory, symptomatic of a desire for certainty impelled by

[1] For *The Hind and the Panther*, cf. Paul Hammond, *Notes and Queries*, 29, no. 1 (February 1982), pp. 55–7.

that almost involuntary clarity of vision that could make Dryden
in his first play, *The Wild Gallant*, anticipate virtually every argument for the rights of women that would be advanced in the next
three centuries, and in his penultimate, *Amphitryon*, present as
bleak a view of the human condition and the nature of human
happiness as the context of comedy has ever allowed. It is this
vision, too, that informs Dryden's conditionality, his tendency to
say, in criticism, 'on the one hand there is this, on the other that',
and to plump for neither, just as the opening stanzas of the *Anne
Killigrew* Ode begin by postulating two opposing notions of the
history of the soul after death, and two opposing notions of the
origins of poetic inspiration, resolve neither of these conundrums
and, for all that, proceed unembarrassed, Dryden having from
these contradictory hypotheses, to which he in no way commits
himself, derived a wealth of rich and effective imagery. Hence
also, I suspect, the appeal for Dryden of *The Knightes Tale*, that
fable in which, so notably, events occur, but in which the moral
questions seem deliberately unresolved, are indeed challenged as
the kind of questions that we might assume them to be, and which
has, as Dryden handles it, that acutely uncomfortable emphasis,
so disconsolatory, on the fact of tragedy as, in fact, tragedy. And
who, in the seventeenth century, but Dryden would think to
compare Virgil to a tightrope walker, even though the image has
its precedent in Horace?

Some kind of insight into this state of mind is to be obtained
from a reading of Joseph Glanvill, whose sermons, particularly
that on 'Catholic Charity', so aided and influenced Dryden in the
composition of *Religio Laici*:

> He that is extreme in his Principles, must needs be narrow in his
> Affections: whereas he that stands on the middle path, may extend the
> arms of his Charity to those both sides: It is indeed very natural to most,
> to run into extremes: and when men are faln Out with a Practice, or
> Opinion, they think they can never remove to too great a distance from
> it, being frighted by the steep before them, they run so far back, till they
> fall into a precipice behind them. *Every Truth is near an Errour*: for it lies
> between two Falshoods.[1]

This awareness of not at all an easy or comfortable middle way
(the emphasis is Glanvill's) seems to touch a particular chord in
Dryden, and Glanvill continues:

> The Apostle tells us, that we *know but in part*, and makes Confidence

[1] Joseph Glanvill, *Some Discourses, Sermons and Remains*, ed. Anthony Horneck
(London, 1681), p. 119.

an Argument of Ignorance. If any man think that he knoweth any thing, he knoweth nothing yet, as he ought to know. And *Solomon* reckons it as an argument of Folly; *The Fool rageth and is confident*: and there is nothing that discovers it more.

So we have in Dryden this architectonic tendency, his faculty for strong design, and at the same time a characteristic which might seem to point in quite another direction, though it is repeatedly an essential part of the plotting of his poems: the instant of absolute seriousness that is most frequently achieved by introducing the poet in his proper person, but is also often an apartness, an abstraction, as in the recurrent songs for aerial spirits, or the pellucidity of

> Hark, hark, the Waters fall, fall, fall;
> And with a Murmuring sound
> Dash, dash upon the ground,
>   To gentle slumbers call.

The moment itself can be illustrated by the King's prayer in *Annus Mirabilis*, when any notion of wit-writing is abruptly damped down, or by the elegy for the Earl of Ossery in *Absalom and Achitophel*; or by the introduction of the poet through the way in which *Annus Mirabilis* is submitted as the offering of a non-combatant who nevertheless, as a gentleman, should have been in the war—'a due expiation for my not serving my King and Country in it. All gentlemen are almost oblig'd to it . . .'. In *Mac Flecknoe* he uses his own creation of Maximin (from *Tyrannick Love*) against himself, just as in the same poem he sardonically inverts his own triumphant naming of London as Augusta, which has been the apogee of *Annus Mirabilis*. In *Religio Laici* the repudiation of Dryden's own poetic gift which is the climax—or rather the climactic humility—of the poem, is clinched in terms of the invocation of '*Tom Shadwell*'s *Rhimes*', the shabbiness of which it has been one of the major achievements of the exercise of that gift to establish. In the Oldham elegy he attaches to his criticism of his subject's poems a criticism of his own, the two in conjunction substantiating each other in a manner that confirms the seriousness of feeling, precision of sentiment and absence of hyperbole in the poem. In *To the Pious Memory of . . . Anne Killigrew* he assesses the moral worth of his dramatic writings in terms that go beyond anything that Jeremy Collier was to suggest. In the Prologue and Epilogue to *All for Love* he makes as devastating a self-criticism in terms of craftsmanship. In *The Cock and the Fox* he introduces a disrespectful reference to *Alexander's Feast*. His radical eye was always turned upon himself (some of the self-criticisms in the prose are quite as remarkable); that it could be so was in large measure a consequence of his adoption of, proclivity for, underlying designs independent of the patterns of human volition and of emotional fulfilment in the sense of the gratification of appetite. When he perceives the 'groundwork' of a *Song for St. Cecilia's Day* it is significant that he sees it as that, as a foundation, as the artist's draught: such a scheme is the necessary armature of his imagination. Indeed, in the *Dedication of the Aeneis* we can discover Dryden discerning his own manner of composition in another poet:

I have already told your Lordship my Opinion of *Virgil*; that he was no Arbitrary Man. Oblig'd he was to his Master for his Bounty, and he repays him with good Counsel. . . . From this Consideration it is, that he chose, for the ground-work of his Poem, one Empire destroy'd, and another rais'd from the Ruins of it. This was just the Parallel.

Saintsbury attributed 'the frantic rage which Dryden's satire provoked in his opponents' to 'a coolness always to be discovered at the centre of his scorn'—an opinion which is quoted where one might least expect to find Saintsbury approved, in the first of Wyndham Lewis's Enemy Pamphlets, *Satire and Fiction*. Yet it is a context that I find revealing. Lewis, in his practice of two arts, aimed for a similar coolness (and it is worth pointing out that the word is Dryden's own: he refers, in the Preface to *The Fall of Man*, to 'the Coolness and Discretion which is necessary to a Poet'). In literature, at least, Lewis seldom achieved this. But when he did it was because of a perception of a form, a structure, the allegedly 'abstract' form upon the necessity of which post-Impressionist theory (not at all, ultimately, a theory of abstraction) so forcefully insisted.

I want to end by postulating two further parallels. Picasso's saddle and handlebars of a racing bicycle that have become a bull seems to me to have been inadequately discussed in the available criticism. There is a way in which the object speaks rather than looks. It is a statement about Picasso's mixed allegiances, to Paris and the north (the land where the bicycle race is a predominant passion) and to the South and Tauromachy. It is also a political statement, since it was made in 1943 in a France divided politically along just such a line as the device, in its construction, premises, and denies. My second parallel is quite simply Handel's setting of *A Song for St. Cecilia's Day 1687* where Handel drew on a recently published volume of keyboard music by Gottlieb Muffat, the *Componimenti . . . per il cembalo*, to an extent breathtaking even for the hardened student of Handel as a borrower. Yet the work is magnificent, no part more so than the elaborate fugato of the final chorus, which Handel has constructed simply by orchestrating a conjunction of Muffat's (unaltered) music, and Dryden's words. As with the poems, the act of composition is the perception of this conjunction, the fabrication a transformation. Matthew Arnold, who of course claimed Dryden for prose, nevertheless said something, if unwittingly, for the other side, when he reminded readers of the Preface to the 1853 edition of his *Poems* that:

What distinguishes the artist from the mere amateur, says Goethe, is *Architectonicè* in the highest sense; that power of execution, which creates, forms, and constitutes: not the profoundness of single thoughts, not the richness of imagery, not the abundance of illustration.

In just such a way Dryden created—and often with an economy comparable to that of Picasso and Handel—from fabric, a fabric.

THE CULT CENTRE OF MYCENAE

By G. E. MYLONAS

Read 1 December 1981

I T is a great honour to be with you today in this special gathering, to bring to you the fraternal greetings of the Academy of Athens and to lay before you the results of the final clearing of an important section of the west slope of the acropolis of Mycenae.

The title of my presentation contains two provocative elements. The first deals with the locality involved: Mycenae, as is well known, has kept the interest of scholars and laymen alike ever since Heinrich Schliemann, in 1876, and Christos Tsountas, in 1886, brought to light the royal tombs of Grave Circle A and the reputed Palace of Atreus respectively. Since then the extensive excavations and publications of British scholars, especially of Alan B. Wace, and of Greek and American scholars in Mycenae and Pylos, especially of C. W. Blegen, have kept interest alive. The second element deals with the religion of the Mycenaean world in contrast to the Minoan. We know less about the second subject than we do about the life story of the Cyclopean city, in spite of the pioneer work of Sir Arthur Evans and Martin P. Nilsson, the monumental achievement of Ventris and Chadwick, the important studies of Professor Palmer, and the efforts of a pleiad of international scholars. Consequently every piece of evidence, however small, that can add to our knowledge is, I believe, of great interest and of the utmost importance. Such evidence was obtained in the last thirty years by British and Greek scholars on the west slope of the acropolis of Mycenae; part of this evidence will form the substance of my discussion today, which is also offered as a tribute to the memory of Alan B. Wace.

The section of the west slope that is of interest to us at present lies to the east of the so-called Hellenistic Tower of the West Cyclopean Fortification wall. In 1886 the area was tested by Tsountas. Within the space of 30 × 28 m, he uncovered foundations of structures partially published in the *Praktika* of 1886 with an architectural drawing by Wilhelm Doerpfeld. Since that early time, Wace, his collaborators, and Greek scholars have further explored the slope. The foundations revealed by Tsountas seem to have belonged to two different structures, occupying three rising terraces. Those on the higher level are indicated by the letter Γ on Doerpfeld's plan. The foundations on the middle and lower terrace level are known now as Tsountas's House.[1]

Among the maze of foundations that were in evidence at the beginning of my investigation, the dark end of a conglomerate block which covered the calvert of the drain was visible high up the slope. The westward flow of the drain was uncovered by Tsountas along the stepped street that lines the south-west wall of the house named after him. A massive wall built across the conglomerate block, covering its upper face, proved to be of Hellenistic date and served to retain the slope of the hillside. The removal of a small part of this massive wall revealed the complete block and proved that it was a threshold measuring 2.5 m in length and 0.9 m in width. Cut ledges and two pivot holes, some 0.12 m in diameter, indicate that a two-leaf wooden door swung inward. Burnt remnants of the door were found on the threshold. The area behind the doorway, as proved by the threshold, was filled with a mass of calcined debris that had rolled from higher levels. Evidently the burning mass caused the destruction of the doorway and its prothyron, 1.15 m in depth. The east-flanking wall of this prothyron is preserved to a good height, while the west-flanking wall was destroyed at the time of the building of the Hellenistic retaining wall. On the lower part of the surviving east-flanking wall of the prothyron were found the remains of a painted dado. A chariot procession is painted on one fragment and on another multi-coloured wavy bands.[2]

A lane some 1.9 m in width and 9.0 m in length leads to the prothyron and doorway. At its southern end it turns at right angles to the east and forms a raised platform 1.75 m in length, 3.2 m in width, and 0.1 m in height. That lower landing did terminate in a stairway, running approximately from north to south, which is partially preserved. Originally it seems to have had fourteen steps, eight of which are partially preserved. The remnants are sufficient, however, to prove that the stairway had a width of 1.7 m, that its steps were 0.36 m broad, and had a rise of only

[1] The remains of the structure on the higher level were investigated again by Wace in 1950. His brief report in the *JHS* (1951) was only known to me in 1968 when I began to clear the area again. That work continued till 1975.

[2] Conglomerate thresholds in private houses have not as yet been found at Mycenae. Our example also precedes that found by Lord William Taylour in the so-called 'anteroom' of his 'two cult areas'.

o.1 m. The dimensions give the stairway a monumental aspect. Above the steps were found traces of a larger landing, at which a path from the Palace apparently ended. Unfortunately the excavation could not proceed beyond the higher landing.

Fragments of pottery found indicate that the stairway as well as the doorway were constructed in the second half of the LH III B period, that the doorway was abandoned, after its destruction by fire at the very end of that period, and that the stairway continued to be in use, perhaps serving a different purpose, until the end of the LH III C period. Under the slab of step No. 2 (counting from the top) the grave of a small child was found belonging to the end of that period, and at the north-east edge of the lower platform a column base typical of LH III C times. A deep crater, pieced together from many fragments, painted in the dense style, is the most important vase found of those times.

From the doorway an interior corridor or passageway leading northward begins. It was noted by Tsountas, who, however, uncovered but a small section of its length. In the area around the doorway and even at a length of 10 m, its width is destroyed but along its eastern edge survive traces of the lime-plaster pavement which enable us to follow its course.[1] The clear-cut edge of the fragment of pavement by the doorway made possible the examination of the fill below it and proved the existence of an earlier coated pavement, some 0.23 m below the uppermost, proving two periods of use of the corridor. From the doorway the corridor proceeds northward in a gradual and easy incline. At a distance of 12 m from its beginning, the west-flanking wall is preserved to the level of its upper pavement, thus establishing the width of the corridor at 1.90 m. At its 18th metre of length, the course of the corridor is interrupted by a cross-wall built at a higher level, at whose base, still above the level of the corridor, was revealed a stretch of cobble-stone pavement strewn with sherds of the LH III C2 period establishing the date of the cross wall. Below the cobble-stone pavement, only 0.09 m above the uppermost pavement of the corridor, set in a thick layer of plesia the greater part of a circular hearth, made of clay enclosed by a solid ring of lime, was found. Its greatest diameter is 0.81 m. On either side of the hearth stone bases of wooden columns, some 0.18 m in diameter were still

---

[1] The corridor was found covered with calcined debris, similar in character to that noted around the doorway, for a length of 1.5 m from the doorway. The Hellenistic retaining wall noted before was built on this calcined debris. Clearance of the debris brought to light the Mycenaean east-flanking wall of the corridor plastered with a thick coat of clay and chopped straw.

in situ. The stratigraphy of the area proves that the corridor was abandoned at the end of the LH III B period and that shortly afterwards a building was constructed over its area to which the hearth belonged; in still later times in the LH III C2 period, a building was constructed over the area of the hearth to which the cross-wall and cobble-stone pavement belong. The last building was destroyed at the end of the LH III C period.

Evidence of modern disturbance of the lime-plaster pavement of the corridor was revealed at a short distance from the area of the hearth and at that point along the east edge of the pavement a drain was found leading northward and continuing its course into the gallery of Wace's building (the Citadel House). The corridor in its northward course and at its 28th metre reaches a broad platform. The gallery of Wace's building seems to have terminated at that same platform. The relation of that gallery to the platform and the corridor, indicated also by the drain, will be determined when Wace's observations and final reports are published.

On reaching the platform and at its 28th metre from the conglomerate threshold, the corridor turns at an acute angle to the south proceeding southward in an opposite direction to that originally followed. Near its turn, at a distance of 1.5 m from the platform and against its west-retaining wall, a bench survives to a length of 2.3 m, 0.4–0.45 m wide and with an average height of 0.4 m. It is made of clay interspersed with tiny stones and is coated with white earth mixed with a small quantity of lime.[1]

At the 8th metre of its southern course the corridor is flanked by a stairway, five steps of which survive; to this we shall return later. From that point the corridor continues southward to terminate at the façade of Tsountas's building *Γ*. That building has a complex history and is of great importance. Most of it was excavated by Tsountas in 1886; in 1950 Wace continued its exploration which was completed by us between the years 1966 and 1975. The building is composed of two parts, the smaller of which to the south was called by Tsountas Building *Γ*. It measures 4.9 × 3.2 m and its area to the rock level was dug by Tsountas. From it he

---

[1] Almost across the corridor from the bench and along the west side of the corridor the floor of a room is exposed opening to the south-west. It stands on an artificial terrace and at its centre, standing 0.1 m above the floor, there is a small frame of clay recalling a hearth or altar. No information is available about that building, which we may call Building X. It stands almost above and to the side of the 'Room of the Idols'.

Six metres beyond the sharp turn the corridor narrows to 1.4 m.

reported a number of small objects most important of which is the well-known plaster tablet with the painted representation of a scene of worship. The painted fragment of a goddess(?) with a griffin, found by us in the fill dumped by Tsountas beyond the south wall of the room, may also have belonged to this room. In the general area of Γ, not specified exactly, Tsountas found the plaster female head usually called the head of a sphinx. In his diary Tsountas states that it was found in the fill of the stepped way. The date of Γ was not determined by its excavator,[1] but its location and its relation to the megaron of the House of Tsountas, indicate that it is the oldest structure in the area.

Another room, Γ_1, was added at a later stage to Room Γ as an extension to the north-west, in such a way that Room Γ was enclosed by the walls of that extension; apparently a special meaning was attributed to Γ.

Tsountas revealed the length and what was surviving of the east, west, and south walls of Γ_1 so that a tentative ground plan of the composite structure could be drawn, but he did not clear its area to rock level, as he had done in the case of Room Γ. Apparently he found a floor some 0.57 m above rock level and there stopped his work. It is unfortunate that he did not give details regarding the nature of that floor, but the surviving fragment of pavement around the circular object drawn by Doerpfeld, at the north-east corner of Γ_1, some 2 m in length and with a maximum width of 1 m, indicates that this may have been Tsountas's floor.

In 1950 Wace, realizing that Γ_1 was not fully excavated, again cleared the part revealed by Tsountas and dug below the level reached by the early explorer. Some 0.37 m below that level Wace found the pavement of lime-plaster considered to be the floor of the extension of Room Γ_1. On that floor he found important remains which he described briefly in his note published in the *JHS* for 1951, concluding that the building was a 'shrine, the first of its kind to be discovered at Mycenae'. The complete second clearing of Room Γ_1 in 1971–2 proved his conclusion to be correct. Room Γ_1 stretches from north-east to south-west with its entrance at the north-east. (For easier and clearer description hereafter we shall use the cardinal points of the compass, north, south, etc., instead of north-east and south-west.) The west side of Room Γ_1 is not entirely preserved, but the bottom course of its foundation

---

[1] He did mention the discovery of sherds in its fill though these apparently were not studied.

still exists making certain the dimensions of the extension; its length is 6.45 m and its average width 4.5 m. The north side is entirely open, and with it the interior corridor comes to an end. The damaged end of the corridor again gave us the chance to examine its fill and to find the existence of two pavements with a distance of 0.21 m between them. The lowest pavement belonged to Γ_1 and stood 0.36 m above its floor. Traces of two steps of smoothed flat stones, running along the entire front of the building, bridged the difference between the end of the corridor and the pavement of Γ_1. Thus a stepped open entrance occupied the north side of Γ_1.

At a distance of 0.8 m from the south rear wall of Room Γ_1 is preserved a horseshoe-shaped low altar, cleared first by Wace in 1950 and again by us in 1972. Built of clay mixed with plesia it has walls covered with seven different coats of lime plaster; none of these was painted. It rises, at an average, 0.2 m from the pavement and possesses a slightly concave surface exhibiting three thin coats of lime plaster. From north to south it measures 1.33 m and from east to west 1.29 m. At its south-west end was added a circular projection (0.57×0.4 m) in the middle of which is preserved a circular hole 0.16 m in diameter and 0.12 m in depth. The walls of the cavity are not vertical, but lean slightly and are coated with lime. At its bottom there was a very soft fill, ashy in colour, 0.07 m in depth; between it and the rock below a compact fill of earth contained a few sherds of MH times. To the side of the altar is also attached a bulk of clay leaving a groove of 0.08 m in width between it and the circular projection. The groove was also plastered, and proceeded away from the altar. It is now preserved to a length of 0.6 m. Wace reported that the neck of an amphora, set in the floor, terminated the groove.[1] On the concave surface of the altar can now be detected slight traces of smoke proving that the structure could not have been used for household needs, such as cooking or heating, but was used for religious rites. Wace assumed that the round hole of the circular projection at the south-west edge was used to secure a rhyton, reporting that in the area he found a fragment of such a vessel. The large diameter of the hole, its small depth, and its slanting walls rule out such a use. Apparently the hole was used for libations and this use agrees well with its function as an altar. Besides, near the altar Wace found a 'shallow dish probably

---

[1] We found neither trace of that fragment nor indications of its previous existence.

intended for offerings, and in or near this room were two small vases not much larger than thimbles and probably votives'. He also reported a thick layer of plesia in the space between the south side of the altar and the south wall of the room. (This should be borne in mind for later reference.)

To the north of the altar and slightly west of the axis of Rooms Γ and Γ_1 a large boulder is still *in situ* (1.15 × 0.7 × 0.65 m) wedged securely in place against the rock that rises below it. Its top is not worked, but presents a rough, anomalous surface. On average, that surface is 0.24 m above the floor. Its size and its surface prove that the boulder could neither have been used as the base of a column or similar support, nor was it lowered subsequently into position to serve a later structure, as has been assumed. Its surface is some 0.12 m below the floor of the later structure, and furthermore on its vertical sides can be seen even to this day traces of the lime plaster of the floor of Γ_1. These definitely prove that boulder and altar, surrounded by the same pavement, are contemporary. The inescapable conclusion is that both were used for religious rites, and I suggest that the boulder is a 'slaughtering stone' on which sacrificial animals were laid to be killed and their blood carefully collected to be used for libations.

Along the east side of the shrine its builders left the rock of the slope to project within the area of the room; in fact the foundations of its east wall were built on the projecting rock. The top of that rock was hammered level to take a pavement, a method used by the Mycenaeans in other similar situations, as is proved in particular by the working of the rocks in the area between the south and north corridors of the Palace on the summit of the citadel. It is now important to note that the levelled top of the rock is in line with the fragment of pavement, the existence of which is marked in our plan of the north-east corner of the room. It is on the same level as the uppermost pavement at the end of the corridor before the east front of the shrine and it is at this level that Tsountas stopped his excavation. All indications point to the conclusion that some time in the life of the structure and for some reason that cannot be definitely proved Room Γ_1, i.e. the area of the shrine, was filled in and another floor was laid 0.37 m above its pavement to serve a room of a later period. That room we may call Γ_2, since it was enclosed by the same walls and had the same dimensions as Γ_1. The entrances of the south wall of Γ_1 and north wall of Γ were raised to the new level and new wooden thresholds were placed. That the new Room Γ_2 served the same rites as those celebrated in Room Γ_1 is indicated by another structure revealed in front of the north-east corner of Γ_2, and at the east side of the end of the corridor ending at the shrine.

The structure is only partially preserved, but its two parts are evident. Facing the corridor we find a rectangular platform made of clay and earth mixed with a few sherds which rises 0.3 m above the pavement of the corridor. Its surface and the vertical walls of its sides are covered with three layers of fine lime plaster of excellent quality, the nearest approach to stucco. At present the platform measures 1.15 m from east to west and 1.55 m from north to south. Apparently its south side is not preserved to its original extent and in consequence we cannot be certain about the right dimension of its width. At the broken edge of the south side, and what could be near its south-west corner, is preserved the greater part of a round hole, originally 0.24 m in diameter, at the bottom of which were found ashes, fragments of burnt bones of small animals, and a few plain unidentifiable sherds.

Along the east side of the platform, forming its second part, two worked porous blocks are *in situ* measuring together 1.75 m in length from north to south and from 0.58 to 0.44 m in width. A third block, now missing, is indicated by the cuttings on the porous blocks. These consist of shallow rectangular dowel holes and a wide band worked along the edge. These further prove that the blocks served as a base on which a light structure was secured, possibly of wood. The rear ends of the blocks toward the slope were secured by rough stones wedged against each other, against the rocks and the porous blocks. Finally we should note that beyond the south side of the porous blocks and in the north-east corner of Room Γ_2, an almost elliptical ring was again cleared. With a diameter of some 0.75 m at its widest, it was made of thick clay strengthened with sherds, and was noted first by Tsountas and then by Wace. In 1971 it still contained ashes and burned matter. There can be no doubt that the surviving remains of the structure belong to a rectangular altar, perhaps similar in form to that depicted on the gem from Myrsinochorion–Routsi found by Marinatos. In that composition, a woman worshipper places flowers, her offering, on a small rectangular altar. Our rectangular altar with a wooden table could have been used for similar offerings of flowers and fruit. Its first section, the platform of earth, was the prothesis of the altar. We should perhaps note that a ditch was dug in modern times along the north side of the platform damaging the area.

The rectangular altar is certainly connected with Room Γ_2, built over the shrine, which suggests that Room Γ_2 also served as

PLATE XIII

a. General air view of the central section of the west slope of the acropolis of Mycenae.

A Area below the lane to the conglomerate threshold. K Conglomerate threshold. E△ Processional Way. △ Lane to doorway. 0 Stepped lane. I Shrine. Y Room of the Idols. VIII Area of Round altar.

b. Blocked doorway of Room T₇.

PLATE XIV

a. General view of Shrine Γ₁ from the North. B. Rectangular altar.

b. Remains of the rectangular altar in front of the north-east corner of
Shrine Γ₁.

PLATE XV

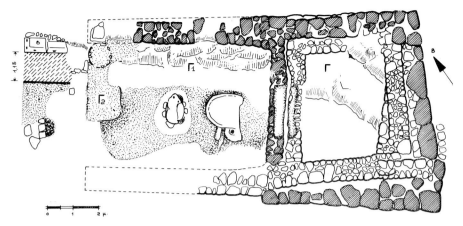

a. Ground plan of Shrines Γ, Γ₁ and Γ₂ of Mycenae.

b. Round altar of Mycenae T₁. Area of the Room of the Idols.

PLATE XVI

North-west end of the Processional Way. *a*. LH III C Wall. δ. Platform and turn to south of Processional Way.

a shrine succeeding Γ_1, when it was filled in.[1] There can be no doubt that the corridor, connecting successive shrines and altars, was the only passage in Mycenae whose entrance was closed with a door. It could be reached from higher points on the slope and from the Palace itself. Its length and graduated incline was designed with much labour and ingenuity to enable priests and priestesses to process in state to the shrines and altars at its southern end: it was a veritable 'Processional Way'; a πομπικὴ ὁδός. We may now note that a *terminus ante quem* for the construction of the ensemble of corridor and shrines is provided by the calcined debris that was found filling its doorway, debris that should be placed to the end of the LH III B period. As a tentative general conclusion regarding this ensemble we can now state: (1) The corridor was a 'Processional Way' leading to shrines and altars on the west slope of the acropolis of Mycenae. (2) That 'Processional Way' was abandoned at the end of the LH III B period, when Tsountas's and Wace's buildings were destroyed and abandoned. (3) In LH III C1 times, a structure was built over the area of the abandoned corridor. To this structure belong the hearth with two columns, which was used for secular purposes, and the pavement of plesia overlying the pavement of the corridor. (4) In still later times, in the LH III C2 period, the cross-wall over the corridor with its pavement of cobble-stones was built. The child's grave under the main stairway also belongs to the end of the LH III C2 period. Sherds found everywhere in the area as well as structural details confirm this historical outline.

We have already noted the existence of a small stairway at the west edge of the 'Processional Way' and at a small distance from the rectangular altar. Five steps of that stairway are still *in situ*. Tsountas, who uncovered the stairway, speaks of six stairs and there must originally have been at least as many. The topmost step is still covered by the lime plaster of the pavement of the corridor, thus indicating that the two were in existence at the same time. From the foot of the stairway begins a narrow paved passage leading to the outer court of 'Tsountas's House' which occupies the second and third and lowest platforms of the slope.[2] The

---

[1] The raised door openings on the south wall of Γ_1 and that on the north wall of Γ, corresponding in height to the depth of the fill, would indicate that Γ was in use continuously until the end of the LH III B period when the shrines were destroyed and the corridor was abandoned.

[2] In that outer court Tsountas found two porous stones so worked as to form a shallow basin some 0.4 m in diameter with a hole in its centre (0.16 m in diameter) in the shape of an ivy leaf. Below the opening, to a depth of 0.35 m, a

character of the building with its Megaron, side chambers, and basement rooms, cannot be definitely established; the use of the building remains uncertain, although Wace suggested that it might have served as the house of a priest. A test in the court of the Megaron proved that an older paved floor underlies the one in view today. Two periods of use are also indicated by the stairs leading to the basement rooms of the building; of these the uppermost three are an addition of later times. Thus we have a correspondence with the two periods represented by the pavement of the 'Processional Way' and of the shrines on the higher platform of the area.[1]

In the lowest terrace of the slope within the fortification walls a narrow area of fill was left unexcavated between the excavations of Tsountas and of Lord William Taylour and his collaborators. That strip we cleared in 1972–3. Within the area and some 0.25 m from the edge of Lord William Taylour's excavation, there came to light a round altar rising above the floor 0.68 m. Made of clay mixed with small stones, it has a diameter of 1.4 m and its sides were covered with a thick coat of plesia. Its surface, covered irregularly by larger stones, does not exhibit strong signs of burning. A thick layer of plesia, averaging 0.25 m, covered the altar and its immediate area, sealing and preserving them.

At a distance of 1.2 m west of the altar, below the level of plesia, a shallow pit was found, 0.3 m in depth, 1.0 m in width and 1.15 m in length. It was filled with ashes, bones of small animals, and sherds. It is evident that the contents were the remnants of offerings used in the rites performed at the altar. Superficial examination of these bones did not disclose signs of thorough burning or evidence of breaks or cuttings. Fragments of a three-legged pyxis, beautifully decorated in brilliant black with details in dull white, belong to the vases found below the sealing of plesia. In the upper layer of the fill of the pit, corresponding to the bottom of the plesia fill, there was found a spouted phiale which could have been used for pouring libations, while two deep skyphoi, with their interiors painted black, come from the second uppermost layer above the plesia sealing. Immediately above

hollow space was found filled with ashy earth mixed with burned pieces of charcoal and fragments of bones. He accepted this as a bothros in which libations were poured. This element is the only one found which might indicate a religious purpose for the building. However, it is not sufficient to establish that function.

[1] The building we have named Building X opened on to the outer court of Tsountas's House with which it communicated by a paved passage.

that sealing was found the fragment of a stirrup vase bearing an inscription in Linear B script, a two-letter word reading κα-λα or even γα-λα. The fragmentary figurines, found also in the fill below the plesia sealing, are of special interest. One, only 0.065 m tall, represents a man with hands extended forward and upwards in an attitude of worship. His long garment may indicate that he was a priest. The other, 0.07 m in height, is female with hands crossed on the chest covered by a shawl-like wrap that is carried around the back.[1]

It is interesting to note that on the floor of the room of Taylour's area, in Room T9 as we called it, we found the neck of an amphora embedded in the floor, used perhaps for libations, and near it a headless ivory female figurine, preserved to a height of 0.05 m and elaborately and delicately carved.

The characteristic sherds found in the area of the altar prove that it was used well into the LH III B2 period, and in those later years the altar was sealed by plesia. The fill above the plesia layer has not yielded evidence to prove that the area was again used for religious rites. No foundations or relics were found in the lowermost section of the upper fill, or in its topmost layers. Both contained only sherds and those in small numbers. Thus it seems that after the sealing of the altar its area was no longer used for religious rites. This was also indicated by the architectural evidence obtained in 1973 during the second clearing of rooms belonging to the complex first revealed by Lord William Taylour and his collaborators. It was found that originally these rooms opened on to the platform or area of the altar; later their original door openings were blocked by walls and, after raising the level of the floor, their users turned them away from the altar to the direction of what Taylour called the 'ante-room' and the later shrines of his complex. Changes in construction are evident in the walls of a number of rooms of the complex, including the west wall and the front south wall of the 'Room of the Idols'. All these and other characteristics and conclusions have to await the publication of Taylour and his collaborators' work, to which will then be added our own evidence. Meanwhile we may recall the layer of plesia, found by Wace in the shrine Γ_1. Could that have been part of an enveloping coat corresponding to that placed over the round altar, an enveloping coat with which shrine Γ_1 was sealed and his area filled in to be replaced by shrine Γ_2? We may now wonder what forced the Mycenaeans to fill in shrines and altars and

[1] It recalls the wrap of the famous ivory group of two seated women and a boy found by Wace high on the north slope of the acropolis of Mycenae.

maybe to abandon others. Certainly only an event of great destructive power which suddenly befell them can account for their action. They may have decided that the event caused the desecration of their shrines and forced them to fill in their areas or even abandon them. The destructive event could not have been caused by conflagration, since the evidence of fire is not indicated by the ruins. It seems to me that an earthquake is the most likely agent of destruction. Evidence of an earthquake is to be found in various parts of the Mycenaean territory. In the area of the round altar we have definite evidence. The south-west side of the court of the altar was lined by a shallow stoa roofed by thin slabs of schist. A number of these were found against the west side of the altar in different slanting and semi-erect positions indicating clearly that they slid from their position when a tremor caused the collapse of the slightly built south-west wall of the stoa. Let us also recall the dislocated corner of the shrine Γ_1 which could have been caused by an earthquake. The skeleton of a man, crushed by the fallen north wall, was found in Room 2, of the Southwest House or the House of the High Priest. The house 'I', discovered and cleared by Mrs Ione Shear in the area of the Treasury of Atreus in 1962, provided further evidence. There, even the skeleton of a woman was found in the doorway with the skull broken by fallen stones. Even more striking evidence was revealed in 1975 in a house at a short distance north of the citadel at a place known today as 'Plakes'. In the basements of that house three victims of an earth-quake were found below the fallen stones of its walls; furthermore, walls were displaced and their lining and corners were put out. The pottery found with the victims indicates that the earthquake must have occurred shortly before the end of the LH III B period.

Whatever the explanation of the abandonment of earlier altars and shrines may be, the fact remains that two levels exist in the course of the 'Processional Way', that a new altar was constructed and the round altar was sealed just before the end of the LH III B period. The surviving 'Processional Way', with its doorway which only allowed entry to the area at certain times, and the accumula-tion of shrines and altars around it, leads one to the conclusions that the shrines were filled in and reorientated in the area exca-vated by Lord William Taylour and his collaborators before the end of the LH III B period, and that the area described was used for religious rites and that it was the Cult Centre of Mycenae.[1] The boundaries of that area are defined by the walls of Wace's building (or Citadel House), by the stepped street of Tsountas, to the north

[1] Cf. the 'Room of the Idols'.

and south, and by the higher reaches of the west slope of the hill and the West Cyclopean wall, to the east and west.

Further to the west and south of the cult area, Tsountas in 1886 brought to light a maze of foundations for which unfortunately no definite information exists. To obtain such information we cleared the area again revealing here and there some unexcavated parts. One of these was found against the Cyclopean West Fortification Wall, immediately to the south of Tsountas's stepped street. It comprised the well-preserved remains of three basements and rooms, with others stretching along the West Cyclopean Wall. I do not intend to discuss the work done there, but I must mention the discovery in the fill of these rooms of fragments of wall paintings of great beauty and significance. Among them is the large fragment of the well-known 'Mycenaean Lady' or 'Goddess with the necklace' and others belonging to figure-eight shields. Apparently these formed part of a frieze in a room above the basement No. 2, in the fill of which they were found. On another fragment we have a seated figure, almost three-quarters size, holding in her hand a figurine, evidently an offering. The striking painted decoration as well as the wealth of objects found, among which were fragments of elaborately carved ivory, indicate that the inhabitant of the building must have been an important personality. He lived in a remote corner, far from the Palace, located next to the cult centre. It is perhaps permissible to suggest that the personality was the High Priest of Mycenae in charge of its Cult Centre. The foundations stretching along the slope to the south separated from this house by a wide corridor remind one of cells in a medieval monastery and perhaps these cells were occupied by the personnel of the Cult Centre. Interestingly enough, in the centre of Room B_1 of that area a low rectangular frame, another altar-hearth revealed by Tsountas, is well preserved even today, while around the walls of the room survive remnants of a continuous low bench. Was the room used for rites or for religious instruction to younger members of the priesthood?

For our closing remarks I may use a photograph taken from the air by balloon at the completion of our work there. The striking accumulation of altars and shrines to which access was obtained through a Processional Way becomes clear; we can almost see processions of priests and priestesses coming slowly down the Processional Way to reach the altars and shrines for the performance of imposing rites.[1] The uncovering of the Cult Centre on

[1] As well as the evidence illustrated in the photograph, the important work

the west slope of the acropolis of Mycenae, with its shrines and altars and its monumental Processional Way, along with the information obtainable from the inscribed tablets of Linear B script which can now be read, thanks to the monumental work of Ventris and Chadwick, will establish a firm foundation for our knowledge and research of the Mycenaean religion. It will widen the religious horizon of the period and will help clear a number of notions developed into axioms that seemed not to require proof. The notion, for example, that the main Shrine of State was located in the Palace is now proved untenable; no shrine was uncovered in the Palace although its area to the rock below has been totally cleared and, in contrast, a cult centre was found away from the area of the Palace with what their characteristics would indicate are actual shrines. Consequently, the opinion that the Palace was considered sacred because the Shrine of State was incorporated in it now becomes unfounded. The possibility that the king should be considered sacred because he lived in an assumed sacred palace, and that he was the high priest as well as a king because he officiated in a non-existent shrine of state in the Palace, can no longer be maintained without further proof; this is not easily found. Such a high priest would have been stationed near the Cult Centre, near the shrines and altars he served: in the building covered with paintings may we not have his house? Let us hope that present knowledge will be enhanced, both in depth and in extent, by the work of younger scholars who will continue the search, and that they will find in the work of their predecessors a good and lasting foundation on which they and others will continue to build. To them I wish '*Τύχην ἀγαθήν*'.

May I now be allowed to end my presentation by expressing my appreciation for the chance of placing before such a special audience the results of the work of Greek and British scholars of the last thirty years in only one corner of Mycenae, the capital city of Agamemnon.

of Lord William Taylour and his collaborators has contributed greatly to our knowledge of the area.

THE THEORY OF DESCRIPTIONS

By T. J. SMILEY

Read 2 December 1981

To set the scene, here are three contemporaneous quotations from Meinong, Russell, and Moore:

Things may be said to be more or less real, according to the proportion of truth in the assertions that they do or do not exist . . . Being is an absolutely universal term; i.e. not only 'realities' and 'actualities', but propositions, whether true or false, and any terms that can be used in a proposition, have being or are entities.

Existence is not a predicate.

It is plain that *ı* is a fundamental logical notion, and that it would be merely shirking to invent a dodge for getting on without it.

From Meinong, Russell, Moore; but not in that order. Half-real beings, which exist as much as they don't, were Moore's idea. It was Meinong who had to remind Russell that existence is not a predicate. And it was Russell himself who, only a year or so before writing *On Denoting*, condemned as shirking the very thing that he there declares to be imperative; for his Theory of Descriptions is the claim that it is necessary as well as possible to get on without descriptions and kindred expressions. I shall argue that it is impossible as well as unnecessary, and defend a theory in which they are treated as genuine singular terms.

I

The interesting thing about descriptions is that so many of them are functions in disguise. *Principia Mathematica* explains that its notation for descriptions is chiefly needed to lead up to what it calls descriptive functions—terms with free variables like 'the king of x' or 'the revolution of x round y'—and the examples of descriptions in *On Denoting* are all substitution instances of descriptive functions. Other descriptions may actually have to be reconstrued as descriptive functions, as when 'the woman every tribesman loves' (i.e. his wife) becomes 'the woman x loves' governed by a quantifier 'every tribesman x' elsewhere in the sentence. The same goes for descriptions in temporal or modal contexts, where 'the so-and-so' may need to be read as elliptical for 'the so-and-so at time t' or 'in state of affairs w'.

As well as descriptive functions there are terms involving explicit function-symbols like . and $+$. Function terms of both kinds are central to logical theory because they are central to mathematical practice, and the real test of a theory of descriptions comes with its handling of functions. Neglecting them encourages the false belief that empty terms (terms that fail to stand for anything) represent mere waste cases which can be disposed of more or less arbitrarily. It also encourages a confusion between a logic of descriptions and an account of the uses of 'the', to the point where a proponent of a 'natural logic' of descriptions can put forward 'the same N' (as in 'John and Bill live in the same house') as being a definite description.

Function terms are special partly because they can be nested, producing $fx, f(gx), f(g(hx))$, etc. This makes it possible to express concisely and manipulate easily, i.e. with little or no use of quantifier logic, information of great complexity. In Russell's theory, however, terms containing function-symbols have first of all to be replaced by descriptive functions, for example by postulating a relation $+(x,y,z)$ with the same meaning as (whisper it!) $x+y=z$, and reintroducing $x+y$ as short for 'the z such that $+(x,y,z)$'. Then these and any other descriptive functions have to be eliminated in the well-known way. Thus the move from $2+3=5$ to $2=5-3$, instead of being a simple instance of the simple move from $a+b=c$ to $a=c-b$, becomes the move from $(\exists x)((y)(+(2,3,y)\equiv y=x)$ & $x=5)$ to $(\exists x)((y)(-(5,3,y)\equiv y=x)$ & $2=x)$. This is only the beginning: an equation like $2x^4+3x^2=5$ requires fourteen more quantifiers to deal with the extra function-symbols. The numerals too must be eliminated, and even assuming the simplest zero-cum-successor notation this adds another twenty-six quantifiers to each of our examples. Russell's theory fails the function test by making the expression and manipulation of mathematical information humanly impossible.

Russell was aware that his theory would have 'horribly awkward' consequences; none the less he thought it could be proved to be correct. Let a *singular term* be whatever can be the logical subject of a sentence; then his semantical theory supplies these premises: singular terms stand for things and other expressions stand for concepts; sentences express propositions, which are non-linguistic wholes composed of things and concepts, and a sentence is true if the constituents of the proposition are related in the way indicated by the sentence. There are then two proofs that descriptions cannot be singular terms, and that sentences containing them cannot have the simple logical form that their grammar might suggest. First, any true equation must be obviously true, for if $a = b$ is true a and b must stand for the same thing and so $a = b$ expresses the same proposition as $a = a$. But 'Scott is the author of *Waverley*' is true without being obvious. Second, any sentence containing an empty singular term will express something with a gap where there ought to be a constituent: not a whole proposition but a 'nonsense' like a jigsaw puzzle with a missing piece. But what is expressed by 'the king of France is bald' is not nonsense since it is plainly false. Parallel arguments apply to function terms.

The first proof is the more far-reaching of the two, for it implies that only logically simple expressions can be singular terms. As originally formulated, however, Russell's semantics contained a complication calculated to frustrate the proof. This was the idea that certain 'denoting phrases' stand for more than one propositional constituent; in particular, descriptions will express a concept and denote a thing. If a and b denote the same thing but express different concepts $a = b$ can after all be true without expressing the same proposition as $a = a$. It was therefore to be one of the chief tasks of *On Denoting* to refute and undo the complication and produce the simplified version of the semantics for which the proof is valid. The refutation takes the form of a dilemma over how to specify the concept expressed by a description. *Using* the description is no good, because that only serves to specify the thing the description denotes. But if the concept can only be specified by *mentioning* the description, on the lines of 'the concept expressed by "a"', then the relation between concept and denotation, which ought to be a logical one, is made out to be 'merely linguistic through the phrase'.

To me this argument is noteworthy for the way it brings out an extraordinary feature which Russell's semantics inherited from his mentor Moore. This is the idea that the study of propositions and their constituents, which here is called logic, can be divorced from any study of language. The latter may perhaps provide a 'useful check on the correctness' of the former, but 'meaning, in the sense in which words have meaning, is irrelevant to logic'. Only someone imbued with this idea could so briskly dismiss linguistic relations as 'mere' or be so confident that a relation mediated through a phrase cannot be 'logical'. Russell himself presented the dilemma as if it were a criticism of Frege's theory of sense and denotation, which, though different from Russell's in almost every other respect, has the same effect of frustrating his first proof. But until it is shown that Frege's theory shares the feature we have been discussing, the 'mention' horn of the dilemma presents no threat to it. As for the 'use' horn, the second most prominent contention of *Ueber Sinn und Bedeutung* is a flat denial of it, through the doctrine of indirect denotation. There may or may not be serious criticisms of this doctrine as an answer to the problems of indirect speech, but an argument that overlooks its very existence can hardly be one of them.

Turning now to the second proof and its minor premiss that it is false that the king of France is bald: this has been challenged, notably by Strawson's championing the 'nonsense' alternative (more on this later). Even if it had not been challenged the premiss would in any case be inconclusive until it has been shown why the label 'plainly false' shouldn't be covering Russellian nonsenses, much as 'nonsense' is a common label for very plain falsehoods. What we need are examples of empty terms occurring in sentences that are plainly *true*. Clearly they won't be found occurring as subjects, but for any other sort of occurrence the theory of partial recursive functions is an unimpeachable source of examples. Outside mathematics there are plenty of examples of the form 'there is no such thing as *a*', but for other forms we need to look at cases where there is dispute rather than agreement over the existence or non-existence of something. Thus if one consults the literature of astronomy for the 1860s or geology for the 1920s one does indeed find scientists, agnostic or sceptical about the existence of the now-debunked planet Vulcan or the debunked and then rebunked continent Pangaea, using these names to propound true conditionals—and to ask questions, which is another difficulty for the 'nonsense' alternative.

Another assumption of the second proof is that if 'the king of France' is a singular term it does not stand for anything. This needed to be defended against Frege, who proposed to secure by fiat that all descriptions stand for something or other, and against Meinong, who held that there is a king of France in some sense weaker than 'exists'. Russell understandably found Frege's proposal artificial and Meinong's contention incredible, but thought that Meinong could also be convicted of actual logical error:

the chief objection is that such objects, admittedly, are apt to infringe the law of contradiction. It is contended, for example, that the existent present King of France exists, and does not exist; that the round square is round, and also not round, etc. But this is intolerable; and if any theory can be found to avoid this result, it is surely to be preferred.

We have seen Russell misrepresenting Frege in the course of his other argument; here it is Meinong's turn. As a German speaker he naturally used the definite article where English usually has the indefinite article or a plural noun, namely to express generic propositions. So where he says 'Das runde Viereck ist rund' we should translate 'a round square is round' or 'round squares are round'. No wonder he maintained that (as we would put it) 'round squares are round and square', far from being contra-dictory, is analytic. No wonder that (anticipating Moore's celebrated contrast between 'tame tigers growl' and 'tame tigers exist') he distinguished the true 'existent golden mountains are existents' from the false 'existent golden mountains exist', pointing out that 'exists' is not a predicate and that predication here has no existential import: 'so gewiß das Dasein kein Sosein und auch das Sosein kein "So"'. In short, what Russell calls the 'result' of Meinong's theory of objects is actually a travesty of the data which that theory attempted to explain.

To vindicate Meinong's data is not, of course, to vindicate his theory, either applied to those data or as it might be applied to descriptions. For a genuine refutation both of Meinongian and Fregean theories of descriptions we may apply the function test, looking at their handling of the theory of partial recursive functions. The simplest Fregean method is to convert each partial function f into a total function f^* by setting $f^*(n) = 0$ whenever fn is undefined. The trouble is that the class of functions obtained in this way from the partial recursive functions is not recursively invariant; that is to say, it is not stable with respect to recursive numerical transformations (the proof is sketched below, among the references). But recursive invariance is the condition which, in the words of Rogers's *Theory of Recursive Functions and Effective Computability*, 'characterizes our theory and serves as a touchstone for determining possible usefulness of new concepts'. The objec-tion in short is that what is offered as a surrogate for a branch of the theory of computability fails to constitute an intelligible theory of anything. The argument can easily be adapted to apply to Meinongian or sophisticated Fregean versions which go outside the domain of numbers for their total functions. For lying behind it is the fact that there are three possibilities for any computation, whether numerical or not: it may produce an appropriate output or halt without doing so or soldier on for ever; but a theory restricted to total functions can only represent the first two cases.

I began this section by using the function test to argue that Russell's theory of descriptions is untenable, but there is an *ad hominem* argument to the same effect. This concerns the notion of the variable, which Russell took as fundamental, thinking not of a symbol like *x* but of the 'essentially and wholly undetermined' propositional constituent that such a symbol would have to stand for. Moore seized on this as soon as *On Denoting* appeared. Referring to Russell's claim that the constituents of any proposition we understand must be entities with which we are immediately acquainted, he asked 'Have we, then, immediate acquaintance with the variable? and what sort of an entity is it?' Russell replied

I admit that the question you raise about the variable is puzzling, as are all questions about it. The view I usually incline to is that we have immediate acquaintance with the variable, but it is not an entity. Then at other times I think it is an entity, but an indeterminate one. In the former view there is still a problem of meaning and denotation as regards the variable itself. I only profess to reduce the problem of denoting to the problem of the variable. The latter is horribly difficult, and there seem equally strong objections to all the views I have been able to think of.

Could there be a more candid admission that he had as much reason to reject the Theory of Descriptions as for rejecting the alternatives to it?

Either way, whether his theory is rejected on external or internal grounds, the direction of Russell's proofs becomes reversed, and they turn into a *reductio ad absurdum* of his semantic premisses. The first proof incidentally becomes an argument in favour of Frege's theory of sense and denotation (naturally, since it was to explain the existence of unobviously true equations that the theory was propounded). The second proof becomes a warning that there must be some way other than Frege's of accommodating empty terms within his theory.

II

Why then did Frege reject empty terms? He says they breed fallacy and error, and it has to be admitted that even professionals are not immune: *Principia*'s treatment of descriptive functions is muddled by the idea that 'the wife of *x*' is ambiguous, rather than empty, when *x* has more than one wife. But fallacy and error could never be a reason for rejecting empty terms out of hand. They are no more than an invitation to the logician to earn his living by devising a systematic remedy, and it remains to be seen how drastic the remedy has got to be.

His polemic about partial definition needs to be mentioned next. The definition of division may be called partial, since 'sun/moon' is senseless. Frege heavily criticizes those who treat such definitions as unfinished and so extendible, because they do not see that a definition fixes the senseless as much as the sensible side of its boundary of application. He goes on to condemn partial definition itself and to argue that a sense must be given to celestial arithmetic and to expressions like $(2 = 2) = (2 + 3 = 5)$. This paradoxical conclusion is not, however, supported by his arguments. The proper conclusion is not that domains of definition must be universal but that they must be decidable. This would explain why they are appropriately mirrored by grammatical rules of well-formedness, and it would incidentally dispose of Hilbert and Bernays's theory of descriptions. It also has the corollary that at a certain level it must be decidable what sort of thing a singular term stands for. This will be achieved for descriptions through the relevant common noun or through one used in defining it, and for function terms through the definition of the relevant function-symbol; while for proper names it invites the systematic use of symbols to do the job done in, for example, 'Fujiyama' or 'Mount Fuji' (status symbols?) But even if Frege were right about partial definition, this wouldn't tell against empty terms. It only appears to do so because of an ambiguity in ideas like 'domain of definition' or 'undefined'. We say that division by the moon is undefined, meaning that '1/moon' has no sense; but we say too that division by zero is undefined, meaning merely that '1/0' has no denotation. (It is because it has a perfectly good sense, namely 'the number which gives 1 when multiplied by 0', that we can tell it has no denotation.) We ought to distinguish between partial definitions, which make fa sometimes meaningless, from definitions of partial functions, which make fa meaningful but empty for some non-empty a; and only the latter are relevant here.

We come, finally, to Frege's argument that the presence of an empty singular term prevents a sentence from having a truth-value. The outcome of this is similar to the outcome of Russell's argument that an empty term prevents a sentence from expressing a proposition: similar enough to present the same difficulties. The difference lies in the mechanism. In Russell's semantics the things terms stand for are literally parts of what sentences express, but in Frege's semantics things are only mapped on to truth-values in the notional way that a function maps things of one sort (its arguments) on to things of another sort (its values). He must therefore be assuming that a function can't map nothing on to something, i.e. that if a is empty fa must be empty too. But this is false. An obvious counter-example is the set-forming function $\{\ldots\}$, for the term $\{$the king of France$\}$ is not empty but stands for a set—the empty set. Other counter-examples are the constant functions; these have been noted by Scott, who calls them 'non-strict' functions. Anyone who is used to partial functions, which map some things on to nothing, will find nothing disconcerting about non-strict ones, for the two are merely opposite sides of the same coin. And if the functions mapping things on to truth-values need not be strict, this reason for supposing that empty terms create truth-value gaps collapses.

III

The proposal, then, is to enrich the classical predicate calculus by adding a description operator and provision for function-symbols, using them in the obvious way to create a class of logically complex singular terms. Some of these may be empty, and we stipulate that every atomic sentence containing an empty term is false. Sketchy as this is, it suffices: the logician only has to push his canoe so far into the stream for the semantics of the connectives and quantifiers to bear him on inexorably.

Our stipulation about the truth-value of atomic sentences agrees with Russell's verdict on 'the king of France is bald', but it turns out that at most one person in three shares his feeling that this is 'plainly' false; indeed a comparable minority feel that it is plainly neither true nor false. If we reject a truth-value-gap semantics we need an alternative explanation for these truth-value-gap responses. And one plausible explanation is that those who respond in this way do so because, for them, calling 'the king of France is bald' false involves more than simply denying its truth; it also involves being willing to subscribe to the truth of its contrary, 'the king of France is not bald'. The interest of this for the logician lies in the challenge to enrich the formal system so as to allow for the expression of such contrary pairs of predications, to see if the idea can be extended to cover sentences in general, and to explore its consequences. But this calls for a lecture to itself, and I pass right over it to deal with two other grounds of objection to our stipulation.

Identity. Most of the literature treats $a = a$ as true even for empty a, and some of it appeals to the evidence of intuition. On putting a simple numerical example to a group of innocents I found that three-quarters did indeed feel that $a = a$ was plainly true for empty a—but the proportion halved as soon as the wording was changed to 'a is the very same number as a', while as many people's intuitions told them that $a = a$ was true but $a \leqslant a$ false as that both were true! One couldn't hang a dog, let alone a point of logic, on such evidence.

If $a = a$ is an atomic sentence the Russellian line makes it false for empty a, but controversy over this is liable to be spurious. For anyone who takes partial functions seriously soon finds that he needs two readings of identity, call them $=$ and $\equiv$. They are interdefinable and agree in every case except that $a = b$ is false and $a \equiv b$ true when a and b are both empty. Algebra needs $=$ which, unlike $\equiv$, excludes empty roots of equations and allows terms to be freely moved across equations; but $\equiv$ is right for expressing, for example, the basic law of functions $a \equiv b \supset fa \equiv fb$, or identity conditions like $(x)(fx \equiv gx)$.

The coexistence of $=$ and $\equiv$ is an instance of a phenomenon that is not peculiar either to identity or to the logic of singular terms. A look at English sentences of the form $F(\text{an } \mathcal{N})$ seems to show up two large classes of predicates. One class calls for an existential reading of the sentence, i.e. equating 'an $\mathcal{N}$' with 'some $\mathcal{N}$'. The other leaves room for a generic reading in which 'an $\mathcal{N}$' is roughly equated with 'any $\mathcal{N}$' or 'whatever is an $\mathcal{N}$'. The continuous present tense, for example, seems to belong to the first class while the simple present may or may not belong to the second: compare 'a tame tiger is growling', 'a tame tiger growls', and 'a tame tiger exists'. Sentences containing descriptions seem to exhibit a similar division, as befits the equivalence between 'the $\mathcal{N}$' and 'an $\mathcal{N}$ but for which there are no $\mathcal{N}$s'. It therefore in no way impugns the Russellian line over truth-conditions to concede that many simple sentences with empty subjects can be read as true. For this will be because they can be read as $F(\text{whatever is } a)$ and so are to be formalized by $(x)(x = a \supset Fx)$ rather than by the atomic Fa. This seems to be the route that leads to $\equiv$, with its intuitively gratifying corollary that $a \equiv a$ is always true. There is also the counter-intuitive corollary that $a \equiv b$ is true whenever both terms are empty, but this is like the counter-intuitive truth of $(x)(Fx \equiv Gx)$ whenever both predicates apply to nothing. It is part of the price of using truth-functional connectives to help formalize 'whatever ...', and it would be inconsistent to put up with it in the predicate calculus and balk at it over singular terms.

Free logic. Free logic is conceived as a version of the predicate calculus that accommodates empty singular terms without taking any stand over the truth-value of atomic sentences containing them. Qualified by an adjective, the name has also been applied to logics that do take a uniform stand, and my own proposal would thus be called negative free logic. If I reject this description it is because it implies an acceptance of the methodology of free logic which I do not share. Consider, for example, 'John prevented the accident at the corner of such-and-such streets', 'Ponce de Léon sought the fountain of youth', or 'Heimdal broods' (Heimdal coming from Norse myth). These are typical of test sentences routinely cited by the leading free logicians, and it can hardly be a coincidence that they appear to vindicate the refusal to take a uniform line over the truth-values of atomic sentences with empty terms. A negative free logician is supposed to say that the non-existence of the accident or fountain or Heimdal makes them false. I should certainly not want to say this, but in trying to account for their truth or potential truth I should start by denying that any version of the predicate calculus was an appropriate vehicle, or that they were of the aRb or Fa form. Surely the first involves a counterfactual (there was no accident but there would have been if he had not acted); the second requires expansion in a non-extensional logic; and the third calls for a distinction between language used with tacit reference to a story (legend has it that . . .) and its use within a story or as a record of everyday fact. As I see it, the business of a theory of descriptions is to do for singular terms what the predicate calculus does for 'and' and 'every' and so on; and this does not include a logic of prevention or seeking or myth. These are separate—and quixotic—undertakings which are given no unity by accidents of grammatical form, nor by the fact that they all involve singular terms: descriptions occur everywhere, but a logic of descriptions is not a logic of everything.

IV

Given our stipulation about atomic sentences, $F(\imath x Gx)$ is equivalent to $(\exists x)((y)(Gy \equiv y = x)\ \&\ Fx)$, and this provides the start for a proof that any sentence is equivalent to a descriptionless one. This in turn makes up half of a demonstration that descriptions are eliminable, in the sense that the 'outer' system containing them is equivalent to the 'inner' system which would have obtained if they had not been introduced. The other and more difficult half lies in showing that the introduction of descriptions is conservative, i.e. that it does not affect logical relationships within the inner system. I mention eliminability to caution against exaggerating its importance. For the equivalence between sentences with and without descriptions, on which the equivalence between the outer and inner systems depends, only means that they have the same truth-conditions, not the same sense or the same behaviour under logically significant operations. Talk of 'equivalent' systems and 'eliminability' is therefore liable to beg the question. In particular, going back to my original argument against Russell's theory and considering functions along with descriptions, the equivalence between the outer and inner systems does not alter the fact that the outer one is a possible vehicle for mathematics as practised by human beings while the inner one is not.

Whatever one thinks of the eliminability of descriptions, one needs to stress the difference between it and Russell's 'elimination' of them, for the whole point of Russell's theory is the denial that there can be an 'outer' system. The contextual definitions offered by *Principia Mathematica* are a substitute for a logic of descriptions, not a corollary of one. Could one then meet Russell halfway by developing a logic of descriptions in which they do not figure as singular terms? Yes, by treating them as quantifier expressions. The idea goes back to a remark of Geach's thirty years ago, and several logicians have propounded systems in which description is represented by a binary quantifier, producing sentences on the lines of $(\imath x)(Fx, Gx)$. I should only like to stress something that the binary quantifier approach implicitly or explicitly rejects, namely a place in logic for general terms, i.e. nouns and noun phrases like 'number', 'prime number', 'prime number that divides ten'.

Logic has never been at ease with such terms. Sometimes they are replaced by singular terms under the guise of class-names; other times they are replaced by predicates (Russell was an influential advocate of this); and other times again they are simply ignored, leaving the choice of a domain of individuals for the predicate calculus as the sole evidence of a systematically suppressed general term calling for interpretation. Actually, general terms differ from singular terms and predicates as much as either differs from the other. In particular, predication presupposes that (in Dummett's crisp phrase) the world has already been sliced up into objects, whereas general terms determine the principles by which the slicing is effected. Hence predicates but not general terms can be negated, and there are universal predicates but no universal general term, for 'same non-number' or 'same thing' fail to supply the requisite principles. The exclusion of general terms is also a waste of good workaday logic. It leaves no place to explore the nesting of restrictions in complex terms, or the interplay between more and less complex terms exemplified on the one side by 'some N that Fs, Gs' and 'there are no Ns that F' and on the other by 'some N Fs and Gs' and 'no Ns F'. Nor does it do justice to the syntactic variety of quantifiers, which besides the familiar ones that go with a single term and a single predicate, and the 'binary' ones that go with a single term and a pair of predicates (more Ns F than G), include, for example, those that require more than one term (more Ms than Ns F) and the especially interesting class that require terms but no predicates (there are Ns, there are more Ms than Ns). The addition of a descriptive quantifier to a logic of general terms leads at once to an equivalence between the quantifier expressions 'the M' and 'some $(M$ but for which there are no Ms$)$'; and if we take the special case where M is of the form 'N that Fs', and use the interplay cited above to eliminate the complexity of the bracketed general term, we obtain a 'Russellian' equivalence between 'the N that Fs, Gs' and a sentence with quantifier expressions involving only the bare N, namely $(\exists Nx)(Fx \ \& \ (Ny)(Fy \supset y = x) \ \& \ Gx)$.

It is all very well to say that description can be treated as quantification, but why should it be? One answer is interesting but irrelevant. This is that every singular term is paralleled by what, following Faris, we should call a singular quantifier. For as well as seeing Fa as predicating F of a we can see it as predicating something of F, namely that it applies to a. In other words, for each singular term a it is possible to introduce a quantifier $(a \ \ )$, which might be read 'a is such that it . . .' and which goes to make up sentences on the lines of $(ax)Fx$. Given descriptions as singular terms, the possibility—one might say the inevitability—of singular quantification is interesting as explaining their apparent ability to double as quantifier expressions. But the pressing question is whether it was right to admit them as singular terms in the first place or whether they must be treated as quantifier expressions exclusively.

If one asks why the standard quantifier expressions are not singular terms, a decisive answer is the presence of ambiguity in sentences like 'everyone R someone', which would be inexplicable if they were logically of the aRb form. Frege's proposal to reconstrue quantifier expressions as second-level predicates allows these ambiguities to be explained as straightforward cases of ambiguity of scope, just as $\log x^2$ involves an ambiguity of scope between a pair of first-level functions. It has been argued, notably by Prior, that sentences like 'it is not true that the king of France is bald' create the same difficulty and call for the same solution. The argument rests, however, on overstretching the analogy between the formation of composite predicates and the standard formation of composite functions. The latter takes a pair of functions f and g and produces a new function (fg), defined so that $(fg)a \equiv f(ga)$ for every choice of a. The two sides here have a quite different structure—f and g occur on the right in their normal role as functions while on the left they occur rather as arguments, namely of a second-level composition function—but the equivalence allows us to write fga indifferently without coming to harm. In an analogous way a connective like $\sim$ and a predicate F can be used to form a new predicate $(\sim F)$. This is naturally defined so that wherever possible $(\sim F)a \equiv \sim(Fa)$, but equally naturally the two sides diverge for empty a. In that case $(\sim F)a$ is false, following the general rule for a subject-predicate sentence with empty subject; while $\sim(Fa)$, which is the negation of such a sentence, is true. Here, therefore, it is not safe to omit the brackets, any more than in $a^{(2^3)}$ and $(a^2)^3$, and that is all there is to it. To suppose that $(\sim F)a$ cannot possibly differ from $\sim(Fa)$ is to suppose that there cannot be more than one useful notion of composition. As with non-strict functions, the moral is that the approach to logic in terms of function and argument, profound and liberating though it may be, is a potent source of error if handled uncritically.

Descriptions are also alleged to create scope ambiguities in temporal and modal contexts. Description is only incidental to this phenomenon, which pervades the logic of general terms: the ambiguity of 'the king was bald' or 'the king could be bald' is all of a piece with that of 'several kings were bald' or 'every king could be bald'. And to talk of scope here is to prejudge the issue. Perhaps these ambiguities can be explained as ambiguities of scope as between a quantifier and a tense or modal operator. But it seems to me that they can be explained as well or better in terms of ellipsis, i.e. 'king' being read as elliptical for 'king at t' or 'king in w'. In the temporal case this merely follows up the natural distinction between 'the present king' and 'the then king'. In the modal case it might be objected that it depends on a possible-worlds semantics. This is true, but the scope solution calls for quantification through modal operators, and how is this to be explained if not through a possible-worlds semantics? Anyone who wants to use modal ambiguities to show that descriptions are not genuine singular terms has both to produce some other and better way of explaining quantification into modal contexts and show that it rules out the invocation of ellipsis.

V

It may have sounded odd to cite Strawson as championing Russell's 'nonsense' alternative, for surely one of his principal criticisms was that the disjunction between nonsense and falsity is a bogus one, reflecting Russell's failure to distinguish between sentences and the statements they may be used to make in different contexts of utterance. As to Russell, I think there is abundant evidence, e.g. his use of 'about' as a technical term belonging to his theory of propositions and his regular use of quotation marks to refer to propositions, to suggest that the disjunction between nonsense and falsity in *On Denoting* is a perfectly coherent one, concerned not with sentences but with what they express. And Strawson's own language is so strikingly consistent with this way of construing Russell—Russell's idea of a proposition reduced to nonsense by the absence of a constituent reappears as the idea of a statement 'suffering from a deficiency so radical as to deprive it of the chance of being true or false'—as to suggest a disagreement within the Russellian semantics rather than about it.

Tempting though it is to depict Strawson as a rival player in the same game as Russell, he is really trying to take over the pitch for a different game altogether. I'm not thinking here of his discussion of Russell but of his claim that the significant truths about descriptions, including whatever can be salvaged from the Russellian equivalences, are 'necessarily omitted from consideration' by *any* formal logic. For, he argues, formal logic by its very nature ignores questions of context, and hence the formal logician's ideal is the sentence whose truth is unaffected by context. But the vast majority of contingent sentences are highly sensitive to context, and perhaps the only ones that meet the ideal are the quantified sentences of the predicate calculus. And this, he says, explains the 'acharnement' (a French word meaning 'desperate eagerness') with which logicians try to reduce subject-predicate sentences to quantified ones in the way typified by Russell's theory. For naturally 'the formal logician is reluctant to admit, or even envisage the possibility, that his analytic equipment is inadequate for the dissection of most ordinary types of empirical statement'.

If this is true I have been wasting my time, but is it true? Granted that formal logic takes no account of context, does it follow that it cannot handle context-sensitive sentences? Some logicians have said so, including at times Russell—the same Russell whose short list of singular terms comprised 'I' and 'this'.

But they are wrong. All we need do is assume the same context of utterance for the sentences on each side of an implication, say. Provided they are affected by context in matching ways they can then be handled for all the world as if they were context-independent. This assumption can be made explicit by mentioning the sentences, on the lines of

the statement made by uttering 'I am taller than you' in any context implies the statement made by uttering 'you are shorter than me' in the same context

a formula which naturally gets shortened in practice to

'I am taller than you' implies 'you are shorter than me'.

Alternatively the assumption can be left tacit by using both sentences, as components of one on the lines of

the statement that I am taller than you implies the statement that you are shorter than me.

The only essential is to treat both sides the same way. Mention on one side and use on the other leads either to

the statement made by uttering 'I am taller than you' in any context implies that you are shorter than me.

or else to

the statement made by uttering 'I am taller than you' in any context implies that the person or persons addressed are shorter than the speaker.

The first is absurd and the second introduces Strawson's 'very special and odd sense of "implies"', but neither exposes any inadequacy on the part of formal logic. They are simply the products of a gratuitously lopsided form of expression.

The Russellian truth-conditions for descriptions are a prime example of all this. Imagine the assertion 'the table is covered with books' eliciting the query 'which table?', and this getting the answer 'there is only one table'; and you see how the two assertions have that matching sensitivity to context which makes possible a strictly formal treatment of the implication between them. How could Strawson of all people have overlooked this? How explain the *acharnement* with which he adopts the lopsided form of expression I have just been discussing? Can it be that the informal logician is 'reluctant to admit or even envisage the possibility' that his contribution is limited to such theorems as

the word 'I' is correctly used by a speaker to refer to himself; the word 'you' is correctly used to refer to the person or persons whom the speaker is addressing . . .?

Fortunately there is a more interesting explanation. If we spell out the truth-conditions of 'the table is covered with books' not as $(\exists \text{ table } x) \ldots$ but as $(\exists x)(x \text{ is tabular } \& \ldots)$, with the general term replaced by a predicate and a variable ranging over everything whatever, then we are asking for Strawson's criticisms. For, as he has observed, general terms are typically highly sensitive to context while predicates are not. And though I do not believe that the desire to get away from context-dependence played the slightest part in Russell's policy of replacing general terms by predicates, Strawson's observation provides further evidence that the policy is profoundly mistaken. It is a mistake that can easily be avoided in a theory of descriptions, so the threat of a contextual takeover evaporates; but Russell shares the blame for the misunderstanding that gave rise to it.

VI

I have been advocating a theory of descriptions that admits them as genuine singular terms, allows for empty terms, and accepts the Russellian truth-conditions for the relevant sentences. The resulting logic adds little of direct philosophical interest to the classical predicate calculus on which it builds, for it calls neither for any radical change in the expression of our thoughts nor for any departure from bivalence. It throws up no discoveries to compare with Church's theorem or the Löwenheim–Skolem theorem, and for better or worse it is unlikely to emulate the work of Gentzen or Tarski by inspiring a philosophical programme that would have been inconceivable without it. What makes it remarkable is that the one thing on which the philosophers who have written most influentially upon the subject are agreed is that it is wrong in principle: recall Frege's rejection of empty terms, Strawson's takeover bid on behalf of informal logic, and above all Russell's claim that a description is really a wff in sheep's clothing. If I am right, then, the philosophical significance of the logic of descriptions is like the curious incident of the dog in the night-time:

'Is there any point to which you would wish to draw my attention?'
'To the curious incident of the dog in the night-time.'
'The dog did nothing in the night-time.'
'That was the curious incident', remarked Sherlock Holmes.

REFERENCES

Moore: (on degrees of reality) *Baldwin's Dictionary of Philosophy and Psychology*, 2 (1902), 420f.; (on the variable) letter of 23 October 1905 in the Russell archives at McMaster University.

Russell: (on shirking and on its awkward consequences) 'On Meaning and Denoting', unpublished manuscript in the McMaster archives; (on the logical versus the linguistic) *The Principles of Mathematics*, pp. 42 and 47; (on the variable) 'On Denoting' in, e.g., *Logic and Knowledge*, p. 42, and letter of 25 October 1905 in the McMaster archives.

Meinong versus Russell: Meinong, *Über die Stellung der Gegenstandstheorie im System der Wissenschaften* (1907), p. 17; Russell, 'On Denoting', p. 45, in *Logic and Knowledge*, and reviews in *Mind*, 14 (1905), 531-3 and in *Mind*, 16 (1907), 439. It should be added that a decade later Meinong was to dig for himself something akin to Russell's trap, in his *Über Möglichkeit und Wahrscheinlichkeit* (1915), but that is a chapter in another story.

'The same N' as a description: Lakoff, 'Linguistics and Natural Logic', in *Semantics of Natural Language*, eds. D. Davidson and G. Harman.

Recursive invariance: the arguments for which a partial recursive function takes a given value have to form a recursively enumerable set, but those for which it is undefined need not do so. It thus turns out that for some f^* in our class the set of n for which $f^*(n) = 0$ is not recursively enumerable. Consequently the recursive transformation that consists of swapping 0 and 1, say, transforms f^* into a function that cannot belong to the class, since for every partial recursive function g the set of n for which $g^*(n) = 1$ has to be recursively enumerable.

Frege and empty terms: (his arguments for condemning partial definition) *The Philosophical Writings of Gottlob Frege*, pp. 165 and 169f.; (non-strict functions) Scott, 'Identity and Existence in Intuitionistic Logic', in *Applications of Sheaves*, eds. M. P. Fourman, C. J. Mulvey, and D. S. Scott (1979). Scott also uses the same terminology as I do for the two readings of identity.

Free logic: Lambert, 'On the Philosophical Significance of Free Logic', *Inquiry*, 24 (1981); van Fraassen, 'The Completeness of Free Logic', *Zeitschrift für Mathematische Logik*, 12 (1966), 219f. and 233; van Fraassen and Lambert, 'On Free Description Theory', ibid. 13 (1967), 240.

Description as quantification: Geach, *The Philosophical Writings of Gottlob Frege*, p. 51; J. A. Faris, *Quantification Theory* (1964); Prior, 'Is the Concept of Referential Opacity Really Necessary?', *Acta Philosophica Fennica*, 16, 196-9, and 'Nonentities', in *Analytical Philosophy*: 2nd ser., ed. R. J. Butler.

The logic of descriptions advocated here: Hailperin, section 2 of 'Remarks on Identity and Description in First-order Axiom Systems', *Journal of Symbolic Logic*, 19 (1954); Smiley, section 1 of 'Propositional Functions', *Aristotelian Society Supplementary Volume*, 34 (1960); Burge, 'Truth and Singular Terms', *Nous*, 8 (1974).

Strawson: (on 'a deficiency so radical') *Logico-linguistic Papers*, p. 82; (on formal logic and context) *Introduction to Logical Theory*, pp. 176 and 211-17; (use of lopsided formulations), section III of 'On Referring', e.g. in *Logico-linguistic Papers*.

PLATE XVII

S. S. Prawer

ROBERT AUTY

ROBERT AUTY

1914–1978

ROBERT AUTY, who was elected Fellow of the Academy in 1976, was born on 10 October 1916 in Rotherham as the son of a schoolmaster and educated at Rotherham Grammar School and Gonville and Caius College, Cambridge. He took Firsts in both parts of the Modern and Medieval Languages Tripos and was awarded the coveted Tiarks German Scholarship which enabled him to study at the University of Münster. He made very good use of this opportunity and in the short space of two years he completed the work for a doctoral dissertation on the later Minnesang under Günther Müller.[1] He returned to Cambridge in 1937 as Faculty Assistant Lecturer in German with special responsibility for medieval and philological studies. On the outbreak of war in 1939 he joined the Czechoslovak government in exile as an interpreter and transferred to HM Foreign Office in 1943. In 1945 he went back to Cambridge and soon became University Lecturer in German. His interest in Slavonic studies began to outweigh that in German and in 1948 his lectureship was redefined as one in German and Czech; in 1957 he became a full-time Slavist.

His own college had no opening for a fellow in German, for the subject was in the care of E. K. Bennett, whose pupil Auty was. He spent some years in the wilderness as a University Teaching Officer without a college home, and when Selwyn College made him a fellow and lecturer in 1950 it was a happy day for him and for the college. He stayed there until 1962, when he left for the chair of Comparative Philology of the Slavonic Languages in the University of London in succession to Grigore Nandriş, which, however, he did not occupy long. In 1965 he went to Oxford as successor to Boris Unbegaun in the chair of Comparative Slavonic Philology, held with a fellowship at Brasenose College.

---

[1] *Studien zum späten Minnesang mit besonderer Berücksichtigung Steinmars und Hadlaubs.* The *rigorosum* was on 30 June 1937. The dissertation was never printed; the times were not propitious, and in the meantime Auty's interests had shifted. Auty's own typescript copy is now in the Slavonic section of the library of the Taylorian at Oxford. He expressed his thanks to Günther Müller at the end of the curriculum vitae in much warmer terms than are usual on this highly formal occasion ('Zu ganz besonderem Dank bin ich Herrn Professor Günther Müller verpflichtet, ohne dessen anregende und bereitwillige Hilfe mir diese Arbeit nie gelungen wäre') and he retained a lifelong respect and affection for him.

Here he remained until his death on 17 August 1978. He maintained his contact with the School of Slavonic and East European Studies in London and served it faithfully for years on its Council, latterly as chairman. After his death the Academy established a named lecture in his memory; the lecture was given in March 1981 by Hugh Seton-Watson, an old friend, on 'Language and National Consciousness' (a subject very dear to Auty's heart) with a generous tribute to him. (This lecture appears in the present volume of the *Proceedings* (1981).)

Many aspects of his career have been dealt with in previous notices; a select list will be found on pages 354–5 below. The intention of the present memoir is to complement them, not to replace them. There are many testimonies to his personal qualities, his genius for friendship, his loyalty, his courage and his generosity, his humane good sense, his sense of humour, and his quiet authority; there is no need to dwell on them here, though illustrations of some of them will be found in the pages which follow. In particular, as a non-Slavist I cannot carry out the duty of 'historical research and evaluation' to which Sir Kenneth Dover referred in his Presidential Address in 1979. Fortunately this task has been ably discharged by Gerald Stone in his assessment of Auty's contribution to Slavonic studies as a whole in *Oxford Slavonic Papers*, NS xii (1979). Only one point need be made here. West European Slavists tend to be Russian-based and Russian-centred. The fact that Auty's approach was different was part of his strength as a Slavist and it enabled him to make a quite individual contribution to Slavonic studies.

One of his outstanding characteristics was his remarkable facility in the acquisition and use of languages, the feeling for structure and idiom which enabled him to speak them correctly, and the phonetic and rhythmic sense which enabled him to speak them without accent. The atmosphere in his undergraduate days was favourable to this accomplishment. Among students of German at Cambridge in his generation there were half a dozen (all of them his friends) who already had a command of spoken German such that they could keep Germans guessing about their nationality for an appreciable time. This was partly due to the inspiration of a young don, Trevor Jones (then of Trinity Hall), who had just returned to Cambridge after a period of research as Tiarks Scholar in Germany and who believed that gifted students could and should aspire to the near-native mastery of foreign languages which he had himself achieved.[1] Later there came the

[1] Trevor Jones: see *German Life and Letters, Special Number for Trevor Jones* (October 1975), introductory notice by Leonard Forster and Siegbert Prawer.

excitement of the example of N. B. Jopson, a dazzling practitioner
in many languages, especially Slavonic. Years later Auty wrote his
obituary; it is remarkable how much of what he said about Jopson
is applicable to himself, e.g.

> As a practical linguist, with a brilliant command of the main Western
> European and Slavonic languages and of several others besides, he was
> unrivalled. [. . .] Regarding languages, of whatever period, as living
> organisms whose spoken form was as important as the written, he
> succeeded in showing his pupils that philology need not be a dryasdust
> study but something related to the real life and activity of human beings,
> with a profound fascination for those prepared to find it.[1]

Auty's ability was no mere parrot-like flair but was backed
by formidable philological knowledge, as was Jopson's. I remember in the week before sitting examinations in 1934 comparing
notes with Auty about the revision work we were each doing, I
for Part II of the Modern Languages Tripos, he for the Preliminary to Part II. He told me that he had spent the previous night
dreaming vividly that he was following the etymology of various
German and English words through all the intermediate stages
back to Primitive Indo-European. Here, I realized, was someone
in quite a different street from the rest of us run-of-the-mill
philologists.

Jopson's great gift was inspiring to his pupils, but it was
academically unproductive. He rejoiced in his remarkable powers
and enjoyed exercising them, but his output of research was
minimal. Auty went beyond this, and the list of his publications
shows that the example of Jopson's limitations was not lost on him;
he was not only a superb practitioner but a productive scholar.
Though language for him always came first, an important factor
in this development was his concern with literature. His dissertation had been on a literary subject and he retained his interest in
literature and literary scholarship throughout his life, reading
widely and discriminatingly in several languages. In this way he
covered a quite extraordinarily broad spectrum, so broad indeed
that he could step easily from one specialized field into another
and bring some significant contribution to it.

A decisive event was his shift from Germanic studies to
Slavonic. Here too Jopson was important in helping him, as he
said in his London inaugural lecture, 'to transform a marginal

---

[1] *Slavonic and East European Review*, xlvii (1969), 304. Auty's obituary of
Unbegaun in *Oxford Slavonic Papers*, NS vii (1974) also contains observations
equally applicable to himself.

interest in Slavonic languages into the main preoccupation of my
academic life'.[1] In the increasingly specialized world of academe
such shifts are unusual; it is worth sketching the background to
this one and attempting to determine how this 'marginal interest'
arose.

The study of German in the 1930s in Britain was still largely
determined by the first holders of chairs and headships of department who, with few (but important) exceptions, were all Germans
or Austrians. They had spent the difficult years of World War I in
this country and were Anglophile to a man, but their education
had been in the German nationalist tradition of the early years
of this century, which had concentrated on certain aspects of
German literature and culture to the exclusion of certain others.
The moving force in German history was seen to be Prussia; we
learned German history at school from J. A. R. Marriott and C. G.
Robertson's *Evolution of Prussia*; there was no German history
but Prussian history. The Teutonic component in medieval
civilization was firmly stressed, in accordance with contemporary
research in Germany itself. The literature of Austria and Switzerland was neglected as such, though of course Grillparzer and
Stifter, Keller and Meyer took their place as figures in *German*
literature. This state of affairs led several young Germanists to try
to fill this gap for themselves by visiting Austria and even
Hungary. The Austro-Hungarian cultural complex attracted
interest. Auty was affected by this atmosphere, and so it is not
perhaps surprising that he should have devoted much of his life to
the study of the languages of the Habsburg Empire, and fitting
that the Austrian Academy of Sciences should have made him a
corresponding member in 1975. Another important feature of
German studies at that time was the lack of any reference to one
of the formative events in German cultural history, the great
movement of colonization of Eastern Europe in the Middle Ages
(largely because it was not directly reflected in German vernacular literature of high quality). So we were ill-equipped to understand what we read in the press about German irredentism in
Eastern Europe and, for instance, the Polish Corridor; we had
been brought up to believe that all that sort of thing had been
settled by President Wilson, and official Germanistics avoided the
subject. We were thus mostly unaware of the large Slavonic component in the German population and the role of the Slavs in
German history, both of which were carefully played down,
despite their decisive importance in the history of Prussia. (The

---

[1] *Slavonic and East European Review*, xlii (1964), 257.

World War I propaganda about Huns was quite rightly discounted.) When, for instance, I went to Leipzig in 1934 all this burst upon me as a new and exciting experience. On my way there I had bought in Bonn a volume of polemical essays *Der ostdeutsche Volksboden* (Breslau, 1926) edited by Wilhelm Volz. Their object was to emphasize the German element in the development and culture of the regions east of the Elbe and to play down the Slavonic. To the unprejudiced—because ignorant and unprepared—young English reader this had the opposite effect and inspired him to find out as much as he could about the Slavs and their relations with Germans. I seized the first opportunity and visited Prague from Leipzig at Christmas 1934. When I became English Lektor at Königsberg in 1935 I began to study Polish in the expectation of being able to explore the Slavonic world from there, but things turned out differently. Until then I had been moving in the same general direction as Auty was to move, and for much the same reasons, though I never had his commitment and strength of purpose; my interest in Slavonic things remained marginal and dilettante.

If I have spoken of myself here it is in order to illustrate the situation in which members of our generation of young Germanists found themselves and what the factors were which turned the interest of some of us towards the Slavonic world. Auty's studies on the later Middle Ages in Münster would have made him aware of the German colonization of the regions east of the Elbe (in which Westphalians played a major part) and the importance of the Slavs; this may well have been one of the reasons why he decided to visit Prague in 1937. His sister Phyllis[1] was already interested in Slavonic history (a subject to which she has devoted her life). Emlyn Garner Evans, a friend of both Autys, had been approached (when President of the Cambridge Union) by the Slovak politician Alexander Kunoši to participate in what became a series of International Youth Conferences on Czechoslovak and Eastern European problems in general held at Tatranská Lomnica in Slovakia. It was in this connection that Garner Evans led an all-party British youth delegation which visited Czechoslovakia on a fact-finding mission in April of that year.[2] Robert Auty joined this group; it was a turning-point in his life.

[1] Phyllis Auty: Lecturer and from 1970 Reader in Southeast European History at the School of Slavonic and East European Studies; Professor of Modern History at Simon Fraser University, British Columbia, 1974–8.

[2] Emlyn Garner Evans was at Caius with Auty. He had just founded the World Youth Congress Movement in 1936. See *Who was Who*, vi. On its

His love for the country was instantaneous. James Mark,[1] a Cambridge friend also studying in Münster, wrote: 'He came back to Münster like Moses having seen the promised land.' He had gone on the delegation as an interpreter, using German as a vehicular language, and so his first contacts with that polyglot Republic were necessarily through the German cultural component. He was met at the station in Prague by a young student of German at the Charles University, Vilém Fried,[2] who was to act as his guide. Their first common ground was the poetry of Rilke (a sort of *genius loci*), but of course they soon discussed other things as well. To foreigners studying in the constricting atmosphere of Nazi Germany German politics looked different seen from Prague; the atmosphere of free political discussion was stimulating and exciting; the threat posed by Konrad Henlein and his party was clear to anyone coming from Germany, and to such a person the ideology of Masaryk was naturally more attractive than that of Hitler. Auty's time in Münster had shown him where Nazism was leading. Prague impressed him therefore as a centre of free and enlightened German culture in an era, as Hugh Seton-Watson has written, 'of political freedom and of immensely fertile intellectual and cultural activity, which could not fail to impress any sensitive visitor in those years'. Others felt like him, especially after the German annexation of Austria in 1938. One of the representative figures there was Hubert Ripka, with whom Auty became friendly.[3] A further factor was the phenomenon of the symbiosis of Germans and Czechs; but more important still was the impact of a new world, a Slavonic world, its sheer strangeness an attraction and a challenge; all these were subsumed in the professional challenge presented to a keen young philologist by the Czech language itself. He completed his doctorate at Münster in June of that year and took up his duties as Faculty Assistant Lecturer in

return the delegation published a brochure, *We saw Czechoslovakia*, with a preface by Wickham Steed. There seems to be no copy in this country, though the New York Public Library has one; I am grateful to Leo Miller of New York for getting me a photstat of it. Auty appears in the list of delegates as of 'Caius College, Cambridge and Union of University Liberal Societies'.

[1] James Mark: see *Who's Who*.

[2] Vilém Fried, now Professor of English at the Gesamthochschule Duisburg: see *Kürschners deutscher Gelehrtenkalender* and the notice by Helmut Schrey in the *Festschrift* for him, *Forms and Functions*, eds. Jürgen Esser and Axel Hübler (Tübingen 1981), pp. 5 f.

[3] See Hubert Ripka, *Eastern Europe in the Post-War World* (London 1961), with a memoir of the author by Hugh Seton-Watson, from which the above quotation is taken.

German at Cambridge in October. Alongside his teaching in German he devoted himself intensively to the Slavonic languages, Czech in the first instance but also Russian and for a trained philologist and medievalist, of course, Church Slavonic. He and I attended the classes in Church Slavonic given by N. B. Jopson, which Auty recalled with pleasure in his obituary of Jopson as 'a rewarding and unforgettable experience'. He learned enough Russian to take part in two Russian plays and later in life had a good command of the language.[1] Nearly every vacation was spent in Czechoslovakia, usually in the flat belonging to Fried's parents in Prague but occasionally in summer schools elsewhere. In this way he acquired a good knowledge of the country not only through its language and literature but also, as his Czech and Slovak friends recall with pleasure, through its folk-song and its gipsy music, its food and its drink. At a summer school of Central European studies at Tatranská Lomnica he had a traumatic experience which he recounted afterwards with amusement. The participants had gone on a mountain excursion in warm summer weather and gathered at a restaurant where lunch had been arranged for the whole party. Dispersed at intervals down the long tables were carafes of a clear colourless liquid which Auty assumed to be water. Thirsty after his exertions he poured himself out a tumblerful and drank it off, only to discover that it was slivovitz. . . .

Thanks to these frequent contacts his progress in the Czech language was rapid and he made a large number of friends in the country, many of them young people active in political life, but some, like Hubert Ripka, more senior. An important friendship, which left its mark upon his life, was that with Hana Škobisová, a twenty-year-old student of English. He met her through Fried, who remembers her as 'a real beauty'. Auty was very attached to her, and his friends assumed that his sudden precipitate visits to the Continent in 1938 and 1939, of which more below, were connected with her. She was half-Jewish, so that in the event of a German take-over, which was generally considered imminent, she would undoubtedly be in danger. When in March 1939 the Germans occupied the rump of Czechoslovakia Auty telephoned her from Cambridge and asked her to marry him; quite apart from his feelings for her this seemed the simplest and quickest way of ensuring her safety and her freedom; it was offered by a number of idealistic young Englishmen to Jewish girls in those days, and Auty's case is not an isolated one. It was an unforgettable night of

[1] Information from Professor Alexander Myl'nikov of Leningrad.

15 March 1939, when some of Auty's friends called on him in his lodgings at 17 Portugal Place to express sympathy and concern and stayed with him until the small hours, drinking horse's neck to keep their spirits up, while he repeatedly tried to telephone Hana. Communications with Prague were understandably disrupted, but he succeeded eventually and made his proposal, which was refused. The following day he went to Prague to see her and got there on the last international train before the frontier was closed. It seems that Hana despite everything could not contemplate marrying an Englishman. He made a final attempt in July 1939, after his political activities on behalf of Jews and anti-Nazis had made it impossible for him to enter what was by then called the Protectorate of Bohemia and Moravia (he had been expelled by the Gestapo on 8 April). He went to Leitmeritz/Litoměřice, by that time in the Reich, which was as near as possible to where she then lived, and, at a point where the Elbe formed the new frontier between the Reich and the Protectorate, Auty on one side of the river saw Hana and Fried on the other side waving to him. He could not swim, so they swam across, under the noses of the frontier guards on both sides. This was the last he saw of Hana; she and Fried swam back and she, with her mother and one of her brothers, later died in Theresienstadt. Fried managed to escape to Britain and joined Auty in London in 1940. I have a postcard from Auty dated Leitmeritz 20 July 1939: 'It being impossible for me to enter Bohemia I have come to the nearest possible point—the frontier in fact. It is very unlikely that I shall be a married man next year.' The final sentence suggests something of his despair: 'Fortunately they still have slivovice here.' It was not until I had collected the material for this memoir that I realized the full significance of this card, for Auty never mentioned the episode to me.

He had at an early stage made acquaintance with the Slovak component in the Republic. He was particularly attached to his Slovak friends; they seemed to him more relaxed and less complex than the Czechs, and their easy companionship appealed to him. Characteristically he devoted himself seriously to the study of the Slovak language as distinct from Czech (Slovaks noted that he was the first West European philologist to do so) and rapidly acquired a mastery of it which became legendary. His first contacts with the Republic had been made through the Slovak, Alexander Kunoši, who also escaped to England and joined Auty in London. (He later became Czechoslovak ambassador in South America, returned to political life in Slovakia, and died after a period in prison). Many of Auty's scholarly publications were devoted to the Slovak language; during the war he broadcast from London both in Czech and Slovak, and his listeners, both Czech and Slovak, would not believe that he was not a native speaker.

His Slavonic interests, intense though they were, did not impair his concern with Germans and German things, especially Jews and other endangered persons. After the *Anschluss* it became particularly acute and together with Richard Samuel he helped a number of refugees to leave Austria. Samuel was an older man with a good record in World War I and already a scholar of distinction, who had escaped from Hitler to become German Lektor in Cambridge, a man whose mild and gentle exterior concealed great courage and determination.[1] He visited Prague with Auty in March 1938 and was concerned with him in helping Czech Social Democrats to leave the country before the German take-over. One of those whom they got out was Wenzel Jaksch, the leader of the German Social Democratic Party (*Deutsche Sozialdemokratische Arbeiterpartei*) in the Czechoslovak parliament, a fierce opponent of Konrad Henlein. Jaksch came to England and addressed an undergraduate society in Cambridge in the autumn of that year; he spent the war years in London and went to West Germany after the war, having vainly tried to prevent the expulsion of Sudeten Germans from Czechoslovakia when the war was over.[2]

This activity seems to have been the start of Auty's courageous and determined rescue work for Jews in Nazi-controlled lands. An anonymous but well-informed obituary in *The Jewish Chronicle* (15 September 1978) describes how, at the time of the *Kristallnacht* pogrom he was woken in the early morning of 10 November 1938 and asked to go to Munich to find persons on a list given him and to arrange for their release.

By the time Auty reached Munich [the account continues] some of the people he was seeking had already been taken to Dachau. He set about finding them and negotiating for their release. But it did not stop there. With a list of names provided by the Cambridge Refugee Committee, but also in answer to the many personal appeals on the spot, he set about tracing innumerable Jews right across Germany, and negotiating with the German authorities for their release and their departure from the country. He was deeply moved by the suffering he saw in those first few weeks. Eventually a system was evolved whereby people in England could guarantee individual Jews to secure their release. One such person

[1] Richard Samuel, later Professor of German in the University of Melbourne: see *Kürschners deutscher Gelehrtenkalender* and *Who's Who in Australia*.

[2] Wenzel Jaksch: see *Neue deutsche Biographie*, x.

has described how she guaranteed a whole family: Robert Auty had secured the release from concentration camp of the father, who was joined in England by his wife, his two daughters and his mother-in-law. There were many such cases. I have heard that the number of people whom he helped in this way must have run to hundreds. He was known to such people as 'the modern Pimpernel'.

Among those whom he helped to escape was the philosopher Werner Brock,[1] who became a familiar figure to Cambridge modern linguists until he returned to Freiburg after the war.

He never spoke of this activity to those not immediately concerned with it, and many of his close friends were quite unaware of it until after his death, as the author of his obituary in *The Times* evidently was. As one of his friends wrote: 'I did not know he was the modern Pimpernel and always thought he visited Czechoslovakia to see a young woman.' His friends among themselves used to make fun of the way he would turn up suddenly on the doorstep, with a taxi waiting, borrow £50 (a lot of money then), and disappear; they thought he was just chronically improvident, for they knew nothing of the Samaritan background. It was characteristic of the man to keep his own counsel on such a matter for over forty years. Many young Englishmen of his generation (the present writer included) were in possession of the same or similar information and exposed to the same stimuli but had not the compassion and the resolution to take the practical measures he took.

At the outbreak of war it was natural that he should make contact with the Czech government in exile. He worked as a translator for the Czech Ministry for Foreign Affairs in London until he transferred to HM Foreign Office in 1943. He and his sister Phyllis, who worked for the Foreign Service of the BBC, shared a flat with Emlyn Garner Evans in Notting Hill Gate; their hospitality during the blitz was memorable. The German Air Force compelled us all to adopt Jorrocks' recipe: 'Where the M.F.H. dines he sleeps, and where the M.F.H. sleeps he breakfasts'; there were mattresses on the floor, some of us slept in armchairs; the comradeship was heartening, especially to the exiles from Eastern Europe like Kunoši and Fried, who soon found their way there. Fried remembers being kept awake by an air raid and trying to while away the time by reading the newspaper; Auty was calmly reading a Turkish grammar (he read grammars like novels). My own memories are similar. He frequently acted as interpreter for

---

[1] Werner Brock: see *Kürschners deutscher Gelehrtenkalender*.

President Beneš and other members of the Czech government in exile on official occasions. He remembered with a smile the occasion when he accompanied Beneš on an official visit to Cambridge. The party was conducted round King's College by the Provost, J. T. Sheppard. Auty gave a running translation of his remarks, but he was puzzled by continual references to 'our young king', which he obediently put into Czech, somewhat to the bewilderment of his audience, for in 1941-2 George VI was no longer young. It was not for some time that he realized that Sheppard was talking about Henry VI. . . . In the course of these duties he became personally acquainted with the leading Czech political figures, especially Beneš and Jan Masaryk; Ripka he already knew from Prague. Some of his Czech friends thought that he got rather tired of the personal and political intrigues which flourish in closed groups of highly strung people working under constant strain; though he never said anything to this effect he was evidently relieved when he was asked to join the Foreign Office.

It was there that he met Kay Milnes-Smith whom he married shortly before the end of the war. They had one son and adopted a daughter. The union was later dissolved, and it may be that Auty was one of those sociable people who did not find fulfilment in marriage. No doubt this circumstance played some part in his decision to leave London for Oxford in 1965; shortly after this the marriage was finally terminated.

On his return to Cambridge he resumed his German teaching and in August 1947 he took part in an international summer school at his old university of Münster. He gave a lecture on 'Das Studium des europäischen Mittelalters und sein Wert für die heutige Zeit'.[1] The city of Münster was largely in ruins, modern and strictly local problems were pressing, and it seemed paradoxical to point to the study of the Middle Ages in Europe at large. But Auty was able to show convincingly that the past was still relevant. His peroration summed up his plea for a new, European, non-nationalistic, study of the Middle Ages of the sort that at that very time was being advocated by Ernst Robert Curtius:[2] 'das, was uns verbindet, kann man sehr oft bis in das Mittelalter zurückverfolgen; das, was uns trennt, ist oft neuerer Herkunft'. From this point the way could lead to Germanistics or Slavistics,

[1] The papers delivered at this course were published in *Das Auditorium* (1947) nos. 11-12 under the title *Weltprobleme vom Ausland her gesehen*.

[2] Auty was already aware of Curtius's work at this early stage and quoted from one of his recent articles; his great work, *Europäische Literatur und lateinisches Mittelalter*, had not yet appeared.

and in the event the pull of Slavistics was stronger. Apart from this lecture (his dissertation was never printed) his only publications in German studies were two book reviews in 1948 and 1950; even while he was officially a lecturer in German he had begun to publish in the Slavonic field. It was a natural and a welcome development when he went to a chair of Slavonic philology, first in London and then in Oxford. His contribution to Germanistics had, however, been far from negligible. It did not take the form of print but of inspiration to younger scholars; among them were D. H. Green, Marianne Wynn, H. D. Sacker, D. M. Blamires, and R. A. Wisbey, all of whom have achieved prominence in medieval German studies. He himself never lost touch with German things.

His Oxford years were surely the happiest of his life. The easy though not undemanding social life in Brasenose as a 'bachelor' fellow was the right environment for him, and the generous provisions of the Oxford chair left him free to pursue his own bent to an extent which would have been barely possible elsewhere. One immediate result was frequent travel in Slavonic lands and a stream of publication, mainly short pregnant articles and authoritative reviews over a wide field, written in eight languages besides English. His interest was now increasingly focused on the languages of the Austro-Hungarian Empire as vehicles of culture, on their development under the impact of the ideas of Herder and the nationalisms of the nineteenth century and, not least, of the demands of government and administration in the succession states. This work led him to study questions of linguistic resources —what languages can do, what writers can make them do. This interest led him outside the Indo-European field, first to Hungarian, of central concern for any study of the languages of the Habsburg Empire. He developed a great affection for the Hungarian language, for Hungarian literature, and Hungarian music. He was concerned with a translation by Ninon Leader of the works of the Hungarian poet Endre Ady, whom he greatly admired, and he translated a number of the poems himself. He took up Estonian in his later years and made several prolonged visits to Tallinn. His interest in Estonian language and culture was increasing and had he lived he would certainly have done some work in the Finno-Ugrian field. This interest did not go unappreciated both in Estonia itself and among Estonian communities in exile. When he was the de Carle Lecturer at the University of Otago he learned Maori. It was in these lectures in New Zealand that he summed up a lifetime of research on

'Language and Nationality in East Central Europe 1750-1950' (published in *Oxford Slavonic Papers*, NS xii).

Among the Slavonic languages to which he devoted particular attention were those of Yugoslavia. His relations with that country were greatly facilitated by his sister Phyllis, an authority on Yugoslav history and a biographer of Tito, but they went back to contacts made initially at the conferences at Tatranská Lomnica (at which Southern Slavs were well represented) and later through friends of N. B. Jopson's. He visited Yugoslavia in the late summer of 1939 with English friends; as the political situation worsened they made a dramatic dash for home by car from Belgrade with the frontiers closing behind them as they drove from country to country. He went back again repeatedly after the war. Year by year, from 1953 to 1961, he contributed the section on Serbo-Croat language and literature to *The Year's Work in Modern Language Studies* in collaboration with Rudolf Filipović, professor of English at Zagreb, who became a close friend (he wrote an obituary of him for the Yugoslav Academy of Sciences). At the time of his death a proposal was going forward for his election to the Yugoslav Academy as a corresponding member. He worked on Slovene and Macedonian as well as on Serbian and Croatian, again in the context of the emergence of literary languages, but he also devoted attention to medieval Serbian and glagolitic texts. His interests were diachronic as well as synchronic.

It was, however, Czech and Slovak which absorbed him from start to finish, and the list of his publications in this field is a long one. In 1968 the Czechoslovak Academy awarded him the Josef Dobrovský gold medal for distinguished work in Slavonic studies. He was friendly with members of the Cercle Linguistique de Prague and derived great stimulus from their ideas, though he was not a structuralist and maintained his independent position. It was a great satisfaction to him that our Academy on his initial recommendation elected Bohuslav Havránek a Corresponding Fellow in 1977. He kept up his contacts with the country and maintained good relations with the official bodies, despite divergent political views. This was not a case of sitting on the fence, for his views were known. It was another instance of his ability to command respect while maintaining his own position. He was almost unique in the world of international Slavistics, riven in all directions by political allegiances, personal enmities, and warring ideologies, in that he was trusted by East and West alike. For this reason he played an important part in international Slavistic conferences as one of the few who could talk to everybody and who retained the respect of everybody. 'The dignified white-headed figure on the podium seemed to be an essential part of international Slavists' meetings' wrote Dimitri Obolensky and Anne Pennington, and they went on to tell how 'at the eighth International Slavists' Conference at Zagreb, just a fortnight after his death, there was an unprecedented number of public tributes; he was commemorated at every session in which he should have participated and there were innumerable private tributes also'.[1] The list of the functions he discharged on international academic bodies (it may be found in his entry in *Who's Who*) is a long one; here too his linguistic facility was a great asset. So was the skill he had developed over the years in university administration. It seemed at one time as though he would have no time left for scholarship but would develop into a mere member of the academic establishment. The list of his publications shows that what some of his friends feared did not in fact come about.

It was characteristic of his involvement with Czechoslovakia that he should have chanced to be in that country at the two climacteric moments, September 1938 and August 1968. In September 1938 he was in Prague with his sister and a small group of English friends; they followed with mounting embarrassment and shame the policies of the Chamberlain government, some-what heartened by the stand made by Kingsley Martin in the *New Statesman*; when even he began to waver they wrote a letter to the journal from Prague in protest, which, however, was not printed (the editor was flooded with letters on this subject). In August 1968 Auty observed the Soviet invasion from close to and was escorted to the frontier by the Austrian consul, who was also responsible for seeing that some other visitors emerged safely. On arrival in Vienna Auty telephoned a letter to *The Times* which appeared on 24 August. Besides description of what he had seen and a call to HM government to 'initiate and persist in the strongest action' it contained a statement which represented his own deep conviction: 'Since September 1938 this country has owed a heavy debt to Czechoslovakia.' Much of his life was devoted to making that debt good.

---

[1] *Slavonic and East European Review*, lvii (1979), p. 93. It is probably significant that no mention is made of these remarkable tributes in the very full account of this conference in the Czech journal *Slovo a slovestnost*, xl (1979), pp. 333–44, which had, however, published a—short—notice of Auty's death earlier that year (p. 75).

It was with some diffidence that I agreed to write this memoir. Though we had been close friends for more than forty years, when it came to the point I realized how little I really knew him, and I found this feeling shared by many to whom I applied for impressions of him or information about him, even by some of those who felt his death as a personal loss. And yet all are agreed on the warmth of his presence and his gift for friendship across all barriers. When you met him after a long absence, it was as though your last meeting had been yesterday; contact and rapport were immediate. A Selwyn colleague wrote:

He was 'companionable and communicative' and generous with his time in dealing with his friends. I once heard him say aloud while he walked around the S.C.R. after a feast: 'I like people, I like people'.[1] For all that, I didn't find Auty easy really to get to know deeply; no doubt my own fault.

There was a private central sphere, a *for intérieur*, to which only very few were admitted. His sister Phyllis came near to defining it when she said: 'He was a great romantic'. A basic idealism and an emotional engagement combined with strong determination lay behind his 'Pimpernel' activities as well as the more humdrum devotion which he gave to his college and his university, to all the multifarious bodies on which he served, to his students, to his research, and to his friends.

There was little trace of romanticism in his exterior. He dressed very soberly. His face was long and narrow, with a long chin and upper lip, and—except when he laughed—quite remarkably unexpressive; it was difficult to guess what he was thinking. In his student days in Germany he, like me, found, somewhat to his surprise, that he was what Germans then called a 'blonder nordischer Langschädel'; blonde was a good thing to be in those days and could be extended to cover lightish brown, as in his and my case; he was certainly 'nordic' and dolichocephalic. His hair bleached very early; he was grey before he was thirty and white before he was forty. This was a great asset to him in his Civil Service career and later; in hierarchical contexts he appeared to have more seniority than he actually possessed and he was quick to realize this. His walk was characteristic—his stride was a shade longer than normal for his (medium) height. His laughter was infectious. He died in the midst of life the way most scholars would wish: his scout found him in the morning of 18 August 1978 lying

[1] On a similar occasion he took the same theme a stage further and said: 'I like people, but the people one is with do not always like people.'

dead in bed with the light on and a book open in front of him; the radio was still tuned in to Central Europe. A memorial service was held for him in the University Church on 28 November; his college had rightly assumed that its chapel would prove too small. In fact the great church was packed with visitors from far and near to hear Dimitri Obolensky's moving address. His successor in the chair, Anne Pennington, planned a conference on 'The Formation of the Slavonic Literary Languages' in his memory. It was held in Oxford in July 1981, but she did not live to take part. She died in May of that year, not yet fifty years old, and so the conference was in her memory as well. The Serbian poet Vasko Popa wrote lines for her which are also appropriate to her predecessor:[1] he too until his last breath enlarged his Oxford home built in Slavonic vowels and consonants.

LEONARD FORSTER

I have been greatly helped in the composition of this memoir by personal communications, written and oral, from many quarters, for which I am extremely grateful, especially from Professor Phyllis Auty, who provided me with a great deal of material over and above her own memories, and Professor Vilém Fried, upon whose personal reminiscences I have drawn heavily. Others whose help I am glad to acknowledge are Professor Richard Griffiths, Professor Richard Samuel, Professor Rudolf Filipović, Professor Eric Herd, Professor R. A. Wisbey, Dr P. J. Durrant, Mr Trevor Jones, Dr Mary Beare, and Dr James Mark. I have also profited by various previous obituary notices, of which the following are the most important:

The Times, 24 August 1978, with a follow-up notice by R. M. Griffiths on 4 September.
Selwyn College Calendar, 1978–9, by Peter Hutchinson.
Jewish Chronicle, 15 September 1978, by Herta Simon.
Almanach der Österreichischen Akademie der Wissenschaften, cxxviii (1978), pp. 377 ff., by Josef Hamm (in German).
Slavonic and East European Review, lvii (1979), pp. 89 ff., by Dimitri Obolensky and Anne Pennington, with a list of Auty's publications.
The Brazen Nose (1978), pp. 29 ff., by R. M. Griffiths, repeated with minor alterations in *The Caian* (November 1979), pp. 58 ff.
Slovo a slovestnost, xl (1979), pp. 75 f., by Ivan Lutterer (in Czech).
Slavica slovaca, xiv (1979), p. 79, by Eugen Pauliny (in Slovak).

[1] Vasko Popa, 'Anne Pennington', translated by Peter Jay, Anthony Rudolf, and Daniel Weissbort, *Times Literary Supplement* (26 June 1981).

Filologija, ix (1979), pp. 245 ff., by Rudolf Filipović (in Croatian).

Earlier, Vilém Fried had written an appreciation of Auty's work for his fiftieth birthday in *Naše řeč* (1964), pp. 244 ff. under the title 'Bohemistika a slovakistika ve Velké Británii'.

I have not traced any notice in Soviet journals.

PLATE XVIII

Walter Stoneman

E. R. DODDS

ERIC ROBERTSON DODDS

1893-1979

I

ERIC ROBERTSON DODDS, who died at his home at Old
Marston, just outside Oxford, on 4 April 1979, had been Regius
Professor of Greek at Oxford from 1936 to 1960, and a Fellow of
the Academy since 1942; in 1971 he received the Kenyon Medal.

Many memoirs could be written of this many-sided man; but
whatever aspect of his life and scholarship one tries to describe,
there is first the business of coming to terms with his autobiography, the carefully documented study which he put together
in the years following his wife's death, partly as a consolation to
himself. *Missing Persons*, which was published in 1977, is a book of
much elegance and appeal, presenting a personality to which
many readers have been strongly attracted. It received deserved
acclaim, and was awarded the Duff Cooper Prize for Literature.
But it certainly sets the memoirist a problem. Here surely is the
votive tablet where the old man's life lies exposed. It is a mine of
personal information, otherwise beyond reach. But, like everything this instinctive stylist wrote, it is a studied composition.
Though he called it *Missing Persons*, recalling the potential Eric
Doddses who one by one failed to develop, and though he clearly
thought of the total picture as fragmented and incomplete, it
strikes most people—as it struck Philip Toynbee in a review at the
time—as presenting an unusually consistent and coherent character. Dodds's instinct, as he looked back on his life, seems to have
been to focus on two things: on his independence and individuality, especially when manifested in opposition to authority; and on
the way in which his growth and his experiences exemplify our
common condition, as the psychologists of our age have seen it. Of
his academic achievement and the particular cast of his scholarship he says comparatively little. This is partly because it is not the
primary stuff of autobiography as he conceived it, but partly also
because he habitually professed a certain shyness about it. He was
writing for a public whom he believed inclined to view professors
of Greek as extinct monsters (the phrase is his own)[1] and their
occupations a barely tolerable eccentricity. But he was, of course,

---

[1] *Presidential Address to the Classical Association* (1964).

a scholar of outstanding success, whose achievements both as an editor of important texts and as an innovative interpreter of Greek civilization have had immense influence, probably more than those of any British Hellenist of our time.

In attempting here to outline this achievement and the course of his professional life, I have of course made much use of *Missing Persons*, but I have tried not to repeat too much of what is better said there, assuming that the reader will have read it himself. There is, however, an obvious initial difficulty arising from the fact that there were a number of large concerns in Dodds's intellectual life, not directly connected with his profession as a scholar, but none the less affecting it and affected by it. These concerns are more fully, but still not quite fully, set out in *Missing Persons*. First in importance among them is his role as a man of letters, a respected observer and participant in a significant chapter of English literary history. Was he not himself a poet? Did he not know Eliot and Yeats, Auden and MacNeice? True, his relations with the first two were comparatively slight, for Eliot's general views were poles apart from his, while Yeats was a much older man, and Dodds never found it easy to learn from the old. But his links with Auden and MacNeice, both dating from his Birmingham period (1924–36), were important to all concerned. MacNeice, whom he appointed to a lectureship in his department, he seems to have regarded as in some sense his creation; Auden was a more accidental acquisition. It is perhaps worth recalling here Auden's last tribute to one whom he regarded as a very wise man, the *Nocturne for E. R. Dodds*.[1] It is an apt tribute, for it abounds in allusions to Greek poetry, from Hesiod to Ptolemy, and combines this with a measure of disturbing contemporary reference; but it is also very penetrating, for the sense of wonder at a universe 'where weak wills find comfort to dare the Dangerous Quest' is a fundamentally optimistic one and Dodds was, for all his austerity and his air of expecting the worst, nevertheless an optimist. Not everyone could see this in him, but Auden evidently understood. What is difficult to assess, however, is how far Dodds's concern with contemporary poetry affected his scholarly attitudes. I suspect it was not very much. One common factor, indeed, was a love and mastery of words, instinctive and obvious in him from childhood. Like his poets, he readily abandoned conventional stylistic decorum for

[1] Published in the volume of the *Journal of Hellenic Studies* 'in honour of E. R. Dodds' (1973), p. 2. Humphrey Carpenter's recent *Life of W. H. Auden* contains many extracts from Dodds's correspondence, and is illuminating on all this aspect of his life.

the vivid word, even it if stuck out a mile in the context, and he did so with a sure touch. He could clearly have been a notable translator: witness the *Antigone* chorus at the end of Chapter II of *The Greeks and the Irrational*. Indeed, he sometimes regretted not having done more of this; Gilbert Murray's example might have urged him that way—or did it deter, by demonstrating that translation dates so soon?—and so might his awareness that the preservation of Greek studies rested more and more on the translators. But he did not respond, and we can only guess why. Another thing he shared with some at least of the poets was a passion (also to be discerned in him as a boy) for psychological analysis and exploration. But the main thrust of his mature scholarship was towards ideas, not words, and towards psychological generalization rather than the purely individual.

It seems to me, therefore, that it is the second of his extra-professional lives that probably impinged more strongly on his scholarship, and this indeed is how he saw it himself. This second life was his enduring activity in the realms of psychical research. He often took part in seances and experiments; the *Proceedings of the Society for Psychical Research* contain some of his most characteristic writing;[1] and he served as President of that Society in 1961–3. In all this, Gilbert Murray and a whole group of late Victorian classicists were his exemplars; but his interest seems to go deeper than theirs. It is not that he was more credulous—far from it; but the effort to state the probabilities and demolish the pretences and fallacies was something that he took very seriously indeed, and in which he felt his intellectual integrity at stake. This interest certainly squared with what became his central scholarly topic: the Greek reaction to what he called the 'surd' element in the world. The psychical researcher and the author of *The Greeks and the Irrational* were labourers in the same vineyard.

The third of these sets of extra-professional concerns was his public life. Dodds never ducked public issues. From his Fenian and non-combatant days onwards, he was a serious and austere judge of attitudes to public affairs. Where he could, he joined in—as in the affairs of the local school at Marston in his latter years. In this again, he was in the tradition of Murray, though his work was inevitably much more limited; and the links between his social conscience and his scholarship were always strong. It never

---

[1] Especially his personal statement, 'Why I do not believe in survival' (1934), his account of Murray's telepathic experiments (1957), and 'Supernormal phenomena in Classical Antiquity' (1971, reprinted in *The Ancient Concept of Progress*).

slipped Dodds's mind that the study of the ancient world had its lessons for the political world in which he and his pupils lived. The most notable example of this is to be seen in his *Gorgias*. The book arose, he tells us in the Preface, from 'lecturing to undergraduates who were soon to be soldiers' in circumstances which 'brought sharply home . . . the relevance of this dialogue to the central issues, moral and political, of our own day'.

'Our own day' covered two world wars, many persecutions, and two periods of distress and disturbance in his native. country: ample evidence of 'failure of nerve' and 'flight from reason'.

II

He was born at Banbridge, Co. Down, on 26 July 1893. His father, Robert Dodds, was a graduate in classics of Queen's College, Galway, and headmaster of the grammar school at Banbridge. He died, an alcoholic, when Eric, who was the only child, was seven. The boy's upbringing thereafter fell on his mother, Anne Fleming Allen. Two or three years after Robert Dodds's death, they moved to Dublin, and Eric went to school there for a time; but in 1908 he was sent as a boarder to Campbell College, Belfast. Here the foundations of his classical learning and of his literary understanding and sensitivity were laid; he acknowledged his debt in an obituary of R. F. Davis, his principal teacher, published in *The Campbellian* in 1937. Here also he had the first of his tussles with authority, later recalled and recorded with pride, to the point of being expelled in the end for 'gross, studied and sustained insolence to the headmaster'. But there survives a diary for 1910–11 —the sole survivor of his early diaries, presumably the 'minor exception' alluded to in *Missing Persons*, 11—and it is no farouche rebel that is revealed, but a lively boy with a great many very ordinary tastes and ambitions, healthy, tough, and handsome. He is pleased with a faultless Greek prose, which even Davis could not scrawl over, but even more pleased at a successful game of rugby. He shows a good deal of anxiety about getting his prefect's duties over quietly. But the most striking thing is what seems today a quite extraordinary felicity of language (though perhaps it was not so unusual in 1910) and an uncannily mature taste for dissecting people's motives and reactions.

England, and especially Oxford, provided a great cultural shock. But Dodds's undergraduate career at University College was a distinguished one. He duly won his First in Honour Moderations (1914) and his Craven (1913) and Ireland (1914).

He attracted Gilbert Murray's attention, it seems, mainly by his efforts at the 'Art of Translation' class—an enterprise Dodds was to repeat for himself twenty-five years later—but it was in his third year, which was also the first year of the war, that he had the academic experience which seems to have had the most effect on him. He attended J. A. Stewart's class on Plotinus, at which T. S. Eliot was the only other persistent attender. The interest aroused —or was it already there?—lasted a lifetime. Plotinus' psychological insight, his imagery of illumination,[1] especially the grappling of his ratiocination with the unknown, remained in the centre of Dodds's scholarly concerns till the end. Indeed, if he identified himself with any ancient thinker—and he was interested in the way scholars do so identify themselves—it was with Plotinus, whom he saw, no doubt too simply, as a lone bearer of the light of reason in a darkening world of fear and superstition.

The war, however, made a rude break. Unable to comprehend or share English patriotic feelings, Dodds nevertheless volunteered in 1915 for service as a medical orderly in Belgrade; but the episode was a brief one, and he was back in Oxford in January 1916. The Easter rebellion of that year redoubled the difficulties of an outspoken Fenian in a shocked and bereaved England; on Dodds's own account, he expressed himself fairly forcefully, and was therefore 'advised' to leave Oxford in the summer, prepare for Greats at home, and come back to sit the examination in June 1917. All went according to plan; but when it was all done, he had to find a job, and proceeded to look for teaching posts and examinerships in Ireland. In the event, he spent about two years teaching classics in various schools—St. Columba's College, Rathfarnham; Kilkenny College; Dublin High School. He used later to urge that every university lecturer should have a spell in the school classroom; and it may well be that his always admirable power of putting things clearly, interestingly, and unpatronizingly was fostered in these years. The first break from the uncertainties and insecurities came with his appointment to University College, Reading, in 1919. Here he was encouraged and influenced by the Spinoza scholar W. G. de Burgh, with his broad smile and genial heart, and by his own departmental head,

---

[1] Professor A. H. Armstrong draws my attention to the importance of this. He adds: 'My last memory of him is of going round the great Turner exhibition at the R.A. with him, and of his pleasure in the way everything turned into light in the latest pictures: this was, he thought, a good way to see the world when one was old. Perhaps here we return to a deep reason for his affection for Plotinus, the philosopher of light.'

P. N. Ure. Here too he made friendships that lasted till his old age (as with J. D. Mabbott); and here he found his wife, Annie Edwards Powell—'Bet'—who was then a lecturer in the English department at the College. His knowledge of the Neoplatonists was now steadily deepening; and about the time of his Reading appointment we find him recommended by Stephen McKenna[1] to the SPCK as the possible compiler of an anthology of Neoplatonic texts, part of a series devoted to the origins and background of Christianity. He agreed, and the work, when submitted, was read for the publisher by W. R. Inge, who was enthusiastic about it. The two little volumes of these *Selections*—the translation volume (1923) preceded the texts (1924)—represent a very great deal of original work in a field still relatively uncultivated. Interest in these things had indeed been growing, thanks partly to Inge's own work and T. Whittaker's *Neoplatonists*, and it is certainly not true to say that Dodds initiated it in English scholarship. Still, it was an unusual speciality, and not one calculated to appeal to the classical orthodoxies of the time. He tells himself (*Missing Persons*, 75) the amusing story of how he tried to interest T. E. Page in a Loeb Plotinus—an enterprise effected many years later by his friend and disciple A. H. Armstrong.

He remained at Reading till 1924, but in 1922 (in the year before his marriage) he applied for a Fellowship by examination at Magdalen College, Oxford. He was not successful; it was H. H. Price who was elected—a man with whom he had, as it happened, a good deal in common. J. A. Smith wrote to de Burgh to explain why they had not chosen Dodds, and commented on Dodds's 'self-consciousness' and the excessive number of 'I holds' that marked his written style: a revealing comment, and one that rings true.

Dodds's appointment to a chair of Greek at Birmingham in 1924 (a year or so after his marriage) marks off the rest of his career from the formative and often stormy period that had preceded it. He was only thirty-one, and had published very little—and all of it on Plotinus and the Neoplatonists. So it was a bold move, and it was a brilliant success. For the next twelve years he and Bet lived happily among congenial colleagues and pupils and enjoyed a literary and cultural life, avant-garde and left-wing, which seemed to them, as *Missing Persons* makes plain, something of a paradise. There was a lot to do: teaching, building

---

[1] MacKenna, whose Journal and Letters Dodds edited, with a memoir, in 1936, had been working on Plotinus since about 1905; he often acknowledges Dodds's help, and Dodds for his part regarded this remarkable Irish patriot and scholar as something of a hero.

up a department, undertaking major tasks of scholarship—and making a garden, for Dodds now became a very knowledgeable and expert gardener.[1] Most important was the circle of friends, and especially perhaps Louis MacNeice, now a junior colleague, and W. H. Auden, the son of a Birmingham doctor. This was one of the last periods in which an English provincial city, prosperous and secure, could have a cultural life, even a rather radical one, of its own; and there can be no doubt that Dodds loved this and contributed to it greatly. He was also training young scholars who were to contribute notably to Neoplatonic and other studies; B. S. Page and R. E. Witt were research pupils of his at this time. At the same time, his own work went forward. In 1928 he published a very influential and original article on Plato's *Parmenides* and its importance to the Neoplatonists[2]—a milestone in the understanding of the relation between these later 'Platonists' and their master's works. In 1929, an article on 'Euripides the Irrationalist' appeared in the *Classical Review*; and here, for the first time, the future course of Dodds's researches could be seen. But as yet, this was a side line; he was busy on his exemplary edition (1933) of Proclus' *Elements of Theology*, the most concise and comprehensive handbook of later Neoplatonism, the interpretation of which demanded a thorough understanding of the whole system. The edition remains what it was soon seen to be, a model of editorial technique and the most lucid introduction available to Neoplatonic ways of thinking. It established Dodds as a scholar with a mastery of all the approved skills; but so far as his own intellectual development was concerned, it was something of a dead-end. In later life, he was not particularly interested in Proclus, or in Iamblichus or Syrianus; and the large amount of work done in recent years to deepen understanding of this school received from him only rather distant encouragement. Much of Proclus was tedious, and there was a nasty air of superstition about it; perhaps only the taut, schematic *Elements* was worth a serious man's time.

It must largely have been the Proclus that made Dodds a possible candidate for Gilbert Murray to suggest as his successor at Oxford in 1936. It appears that A. D. Nock, whose *Sallustius* had made him an expert in the same sort of field, also lent his voice. The offer was made, and reluctantly—really reluctantly—accepted. It was an appointment that surprised many and

---

[1] He used to say at a later date that there were two jobs in Oxford for which he thought he might qualify: the Regius Professorship, and the post of Head Gardener at St. John's, also vacant.

[2] *Classical Quarterly*, 22 (1928), 129-42.

disappointed some. Not only were there likely local candidates—
J. D. Denniston, C. M. Bowra—but there was the whole business
of Dodds's repute as a non-combatant, if not an actual pacifist, in
the Great War, not to speak of his Irish nationalism and his left-
wing point of view. Neither he nor Bet was happy in the early years
at Oxford; indeed, she hardly ever took any part in the life of a
university which she plainly found distasteful. There were un-
happily no children; and her life in the centre of Oxford, with few
sympathetic friends, cannot have been easy. It is pointless now to
apportion blame; Dodds was not a man to smooth his own way,
and those who were antagonized by him were not easily reconciled.
Coming two years after the appointment of Eduard Fraenkel, also
controversial and also marvellously beneficial, this new and hardly
less alien intrusion will have been hard for some to bear. In a long
view, the antagonisms were childish. Undergraduates at least soon
saw in Dodds a worthy successor of Gilbert Murray. His splendid
delivery (no one ever forgets the cadence of his voice), his sharp
mind and lucid exposition of knotty problems, the modernity of
his culture, his obvious social concern, and the absence of any sort
of talking down to the audience—all this made him a natural
charmer of serious youth. It is this side of him that appears in his
rather pretentious inaugural lecture, in which he emphasizes the
need to make technique in scholarship the servant and what he
called 'humanism' the mistress. *Mutatis mutandis*, this was the old
Stoic image of Penelope and her maidservants; and it was not a
very apt lesson for the time and place.[1] Dodds did indeed fight
against the worse excesses of the D.Phil. industry most of his life,
but Oxford in 1936 was not the battlefield on which to encounter
that particular adversary. None the less, the lecture is worth re-
reading, both for its faith in scholarship as a road to an honourable
intellectual life, and for its prescience; for, as with other things that
Dodds wrote, the problems he adumbrated were in the future.

   The years before the war enabled Dodds to do most of the work
for his commentary on the *Bacchae*, though it was not published till
1943. This is the most exciting volume in the series of which it
forms part, for it shows Dodds's editorial mastery displayed in
many thorny passages and also the understanding of Dionysiac
religion hinted at in the Euripides article of 1929. Many people
have testified to the protreptic power of the *Bacchae* commentary,

---

[1] So Dodds himself came to feel (*Missing Persons*, 127); compare also the
slightly different account of these events in the excellent obituary by Dodds's
successor, Hugh Lloyd-Jones, in *Gnomon* 52 (1980), 78 ff., reprinted in *Blood for
the Ghosts* (1982), 287 ff.

as an exemplification both of the exactness of scholarly argument and of its subordination to important historical and literary issues.

The war of 1939 roused very different sentiments in Dodds's mind from that of 1914; moreover, the Irish complication was temporarily somewhat out of mind. The cause was righteous, and he was prepared to spend both mind and body in its service. His mind was called on first; he did a lot of work, under Arnold Toynbee's general direction, on German education, and in 1941 he published a pamphlet in which he set out his discoveries. Both Eduard Fraenkel and Rudolf Pfeiffer approved of *Minds in the Making*; Fraenkel 'read it as carefully as if it were Plato' and called it 'one of the occasions where one feels proud to be a British subject'. It also has its prescient moments, and it is tempting to quote a passage from near the end (p. 30):

> Occasionally . . . I have met innocent young people who assured me quite gravely that they were unable to make any distinction of kind between 'fascists' like Hitler and 'crypto-fascists' like Mr. Churchill or 'social-fascists' like Mr. Bevin. If any such are among my readers . . . I would ask them very seriously to apply for help to the nearest refugee. Even the young should not permit themselves to use important words—especially abusive words—without attempting to find out what they really mean in terms of living.

More strenuous times were to follow. He has himself recorded his experiences in Kuomintang China in 1942–3, when he went out with Joseph Needham to lecture in universities and report on ways in which academic co-operation between Britain and China could be fostered when better times came. Around the end of the war, too, he had spells abroad: a visit to America to investigate their ways of providing for the teaching of Oriental languages; and another to the universities of the British zone in Germany in the winter of 1946.

By this time he was already back lecturing and teaching. Few traces of the pre-war coldness remained. Those of us who first knew Dodds well in the late forties can recall only a few: some common-room embarrassments, and a sense (actually quite unjust) that it was not very generous of Christ Church to provide the Regius with nothing more than a time-share of a small and rather dark room, however friendly and accommodating his fellow-sharer. But in fact, the war had changed almost everything, and his *auctoritas* grew with startling rapidity. This was in part due to his work on Homer, his lectures on whom set a new standard of presentation, and were accompanied by some splendid 'hand-outs' which circulated very widely; the fruit of this appeared in his chapter on Homer in *Fifty Years of Classical Scholarship* (1950), a balanced account of 'unitarians' and 'analysts' which held the field a long time, and is still worth reading. He was now on the point of producing his most characteristic and influential work, *The Greeks and the Irrational* (1951), the published version of his Sather lectures given at Berkeley in 1949. The book has eight chapters: the first is about Homer, and takes its start from Agamemnon's apology in the nineteenth book of the *Iliad*; the last—just like the last chapter of Gilbert Murray's *Five Stages of Greek Religion*—gives a view of a post-classical failure of nerve, or, in Dodds's metaphor, 'the refusal of the rider to jump'. For breadth of reference and apt choice of instances, it has few equals among modern works on Greek thought; and its notes and appendices are a very rich quarry. It made new links between psychology and anthropology on the one hand, and classical studies on the other, and this was widely recognized by experts in all these disciplines, as the fame of the book slowly grew. But it took—as Dodds recognized—an oblique look at Greek religion and philosophy, viewing the development less from the front, and so less completely, than either Rohde's *Psyche* or Murray's *Five Stages*, the two books which most influenced its structure and selection of material. It is in fact quite easy to criticize, and accordingly gave rise to a good deal of stimulating debate. What does he mean by the 'irrational'? No clear definition of Greek rationalism emerges in the book; and the beliefs which it does discuss are heterogeneous, for what is the necessary connection between orgiastic cults, consciousness of guilt, and belief in magic and dreams? Again, is it really possible to discuss these things, given our fragmentary knowledge, with such a tight historical framework? For this is very much a historian's book, in the sense that it is the chronological sequence, the movement of opinion from decade to decade and generation to generation, that poses the questions it attempts to answer. The *Iliad* is seen to reveal different attitudes from the *Odyssey*, the Archaic Age brings its innovations, and gets to know the shamans from somewhere in northern Asia, Euripides is 'a dramatist in an age of doubt'. It is this way of posing questions, this eagerness to label generations, that makes the book vulnerable to critics who question the fact of such changes or take more account than Dodds did of the literary sophistication and conventions of the poetry that inevitably forms the main body of evidence.

Meanwhile, the *Gorgias* edition, planned in the war, was moving forward. It was published in 1959, arguably the best all-round edition of any dialogue of Plato that we possess. Dodds did a good deal for the still imperfectly known tradition of the text, and his exegesis of the argument is hard to fault. All this time, too, his local *auctoritas* was still increasing; this is by no means the place to touch on the parochial affairs of the Oxford faculty, but it was important during these years that there should be a professor who was generally respected, not only among his immediate colleagues but outside, and especially by historians and philosophers. Greek studies, as personified in Dodds, were by no means wholly linguistic and literary; the point was that his mastery of these realms could be seen to serve wider and more obviously serious issues.

The success of *The Greeks and the Irrational* made Dodds well known in the world of anthropology and psychology and he made many new contacts and friendships. One of these is worth singling out. About 1960, the psychiatrist and sociologist George Devereux sent Dodds a paper he had written about Oedipus. They met— I am not sure whether before or after this—at a conference at Royaumont, and evidently took to each other. At any rate, Dodds persuaded Devereux to add a knowledge of Greek to his remarkable polymathy, and a flood of correspondence and discussion followed. It may well be that Devereux's influence, and the contacts it opened up, gave Dodds's next book—*Pagan and Christian in an Age of Anxiety*—a more sophisticated psychological basis than *Greeks and the Irrational* had had. *Pagan and Christian* was based on the Wiles lectures given at Belfast in 1963, after Dodds's retirement from Oxford. *Age of Anxiety* in the title is a phrase of Auden; it thus acknowledges both Dodds's desire for links with the literary world and his passion for labelling and defining generations—a passion which went on to the end, witness Devereux's account of his last visit to Dodds, who answered the question 'What are you working on now?' with the remark 'I am trying to understand our own age better'.[1] *Pagan and Christian* is a sequel to the earlier book but uses a smaller stage, a rather artificially defined period between Marcus Aurelius and Constantine, and deals mainly in individual cases. It has four chapters, dealing with attitudes to the material world, the daemonic world, and the gods, and then with the dialogue between pagan and Christian. It is a brave and important book, and contains some classic passages—for example, the survey of late pagan views of the universe and much of what is said about Aelius Aristides—but it does, I think, suffer like its predecessor from some lack of subtlety in handling literary texts: for example, Dodds apparently took Lucian's *Peregrinus* as pretty straight historical

[1] Preface to *Païens et Chrétiens dans un âge d'angoisse* (Paris, 1979); a very valuable piece.

material, and confessed to Devereux that if he had been a novelist, he would have made that extraordinary person his hero. None the less, it is all vintage Dodds; and it is fascinating to see how he sets his individual cases in the general framework without—as Devereux again pointed out—either succumbing to the heresy that we are all puppets of society or attributing to society a *psychē* of its own.

The early years of retirement were both happy and active. Dodds was himself not much troubled by ill health, except for a seasonal asthma that sometimes kept him home in the summer months; he was, as he would say, 'an old toughie', and the impression he made was one of an exceptionally hale, spare, and serene old age. Louis MacNeice's death in 1963 was the first blow: it was not only a great personal loss, but led to Dodds's involvement in a great deal of work as literary executor, an obligation he had accepted many years before, and which proved a much more demanding commitment than he had expected. Far worse was Bet's long and distressing illness; with her death in 1973, as he said, his 'occupation' was gone. There was little time for continuous academic work; but at eighty it is proper to *colligere sarcinulas* and this is exactly what Dodds did in 1973, by collecting some old essays and some new ones in a volume which took its title from an essay on the 'Ancient Concept of Progress' written in 1969 and arising largely out of his being asked to review L. Edelstein's posthumous *Idea of Progress* (1967).

The few years left to him after Bet died revealed him once again in a new light. His resilience asserted itself, and his ever energetic *daemon* made him embark on another and more complex gathering up of luggage, the composition of *Missing Persons*. This gave not only comfort but recognition; old acquaintances renewed contact, Ireland at last claimed him—or at least the Ulster radio and television services did. All this time he was encouraged and comforted by many friends at home. Some were old neighbours and colleagues; others were younger people (he often let rooms in his house to carefully chosen graduates or other lodgers) who knew a wise man when they saw one, and surrounded him with the kind of independent affection and respect that he liked. He died at home, in the seventeenth-century 'Cromwell's House' to which he and Bet had moved in 1946. When his obituary appeared in *The Times*, after the long interruption of publication, it chanced to be on the same page as that of Sir George Clark, who had lived in the same house before him. Dodds liked the touch in Clark's history of Marston, in which he contrasts the 'mediocrity of its human population' with the distinction of the terrier bitch bought by the sporting parson Jack Russell in 1815.[1]

III

There can be little doubt about what Dodds did for Greek studies in this country. For one thing, he extended their range, and made the later phases of antiquity respectable, at least in their philosophical and religious aspects. But, more important, he made them, as Peter Levi succinctly put it,[2] completely modern and serious. The modernization was effected by constant reference to anthropology and even more to psychology; this was his way of bringing his life's work into what he guessed to be the mainstream of contemporary thinking. Perhaps he was too optimistic, perhaps he attached himself to ways of thinking that have not stood the test of time, perhaps he was too determinedly historical. In so far as that is so, his work is bound to have an ephemeral element; but how small this is, and how easily discounted, is evident when one thinks of the solidity of the Proclus, the controlled scholarship of the *Bacchae* and the *Gorgias*, and the range and precision of the material adduced to support, for example, his interpretations of maenadism and theurgy. Of course, his pattern of work and interests was of his time and place, and reflection on Gilbert Murray and Jane Harrison,[3] and on the disappointment of rationalist hopes in the twentieth century will go a certain way to explain it; but what endures, both of scholarship and of humane temper, is infinitely more important.

This enduring humanity is bound up with what Peter Levi called his seriousness. And this in turn raises certain questions. Was it of choice or because he had a blind spot that Dodds avoided talking or writing much about comedy or Hellenistic poetry or Latin poetry, or indeed anything (except Plato) where the qualities of urbanity and irony prevail over the meaningful and serious? He was certainly no stranger to fun; but he does seem to have had a horror of the frivolous and a suspicion of verbal point and sophistication which may have developed into a failure to understand and take account of what is, after all, a central feature of most ancient literature. For example, he was a magnificent

[1] *VCH Oxfordshire*, vol. 5, p. 215.

[2] *Classical Review*, 29 (1979), 134.

[3] This connection is well seen, from an outside point of view, by G. Mangani, 'Sul metodo di Eric Dodds . . .', *Quaderni di storia*, 11 (1980), 173-205.

interpreter of the *Gorgias*, where the message is impassioned and the humour destructive, but less at home with the *Phaedrus*, to judge by the solemnity with which he handles its 'blessings of madness' in a much-read chapter of *Greeks and the Irrational*.

Anyone who knew him will ask such questions, for the fascination of his personality and his learning was great; and I mean 'fascination' in a pretty strict magical sense. Many people found him austere and astringent. Disciples speak of his 'constructive discouragement', the rigorous criticism that urged putting the book away for nine years before publishing; others know that he could be warm and encouraging and that the born teacher understood who needed the spur and who the curb. Any pupil of his is bound to acknowledge, with much gratitude, the value, both in itself and as an example, of his perceptiveness and sympathy. If one tries to sum him up, it is in a series of paradoxes. He was at once rebellious and magisterial; diffident and serene; wise and immature. He was a master of words, but suspicious of rhetoric; a rationalist, but with an eye always open to the numinous; a passionate and rigorous scholar, and at the same time a man whose moral vision gave him a deadly hatred—or was it fear?—of the trivial and the *Nichtwissenswertes*.

Missing Persons does not wholly unravel the mystery. It rather intensifies our curiosity about a great scholar in whom many have properly seen something of a hero and something of a prophet.

Donald Russell

Note: I have naturally incurred many debts to people who have helped me and talked to me about Dodds; I should like particularly to thank Dr Norman Heatley, Professor A. H. Armstrong, and the late Mr C. W. Macleod.

PLATE XIX

R. W. HUNT

RICHARD WILLIAM HUNT

1908-1979

I

ANY account of Richard Hunt and his place in contemporary British scholarship has a peculiar shape imposed upon it by the surviving materials as well as by the nature of the man and of the positions which he occupied for most of his life. He shunned publicity and the posts he held for over forty years—a lectureship at Liverpool University followed by the Keepership of Western Manuscripts in the Bodleian Library—gave full scope to his instincts for withdrawal from the limelight. Moreover, his publications were relatively brief, by-blows (one might say) in a life of scholarship, the results of chance encounters with Festschriften and meetings of societies. His main influence was exercised in personal contacts with scholars from all parts of the world. He was not an expansive writer, whether in public or private. He looked on the written word as a vehicle for conveying information as briefly as possible and he almost never allowed his private feelings of grief or disappointment or frustration or, for that matter, of joy, to rise to the surface of speech, much less of writing. To one who expressed sympathy with him in the bitterest of his personal griefs—the loss of his first wife and expected baby after only one year of marriage—he made a brief acknowledgement and passed without a pause to the description of manuscripts. It was not that he was heartless, far from it; but, when there was nothing to say, he said nothing.

In these circumstances it might seem an impossible task to write a memoir of these years without event. It must largely be a record of an unremitting pursuit of learning, and even here there are obstacles to be overcome. If we may crudely divide scholars into those who seek to know in order to solve problems, and those for whom problems are just incidental occurrences in exploring as wide an area of learning as possible, Richard Hunt is almost as pure a specimen of the second category as it is possible to find. He solved many problems in scholarship, but only in the way in which he wrote articles or gave talks: they were by-products of scholarship. It is not easy to arrange his work around any central issues. His learning can only be understood in the broader picture of scholarly developments in his lifetime, especially, but not exclusively, in medieval studies. In this context, nearly everything he wrote is significant, whether he published it or not, and whether or not it was intended for any eyes but his own.

It is at this point that his biographer has an incomparable asset at his disposal. Although Richard Hunt published only a small proportion of what he wrote, and wrote only a small proportion of what he knew, he threw away very little. He was a most tenacious preserver of the written word. He may sometimes have destroyed papers, but not many. When he died he left a large mass of manuscripts, notes, descriptions of manuscripts, scholarly correspondence, lectures, and papers in chaotic abundance. These papers constitute a remarkable archive of scholarship. They contain the materials for several learned works, of which two or three are already in course of preparation. Hidden within the mass of paper there are hints and insights which may provide the starting points for many future enquiries. The devoted labour of Dr Bruce Barker-Benfield has brought order into this chaos and in due course it is to be hoped that these papers will be available in the Bodleian Library for the use of other scholars. The essential task for a biographer, however, is not to catalogue the contents of these papers nor to forestall later enquirers, but to give some idea of the ways in which they illuminate Richard Hunt's scholarly interests and provide a guide to the development of medieval studies in this country in the last fifty years.

The events which I shall have to record are few and unremarkable; but the learned lines to be traced in these papers are of the highest interest, and they will sometimes require a lengthy explanation for their elucidation. By way of introduction it should be said that the half century after 1930 was a period of remarkable change in British medieval scholarship, and Richard Hunt was a central figure in this change. At the beginning of the period, medieval studies in Britain, apart from the study of vernacular literature, were still firmly contained within the secular and institutional limits broadly delineated by Stubbs and his successors since about 1850. Of course, there were and had always been some exceptional scholars who looked beyond these limits— such men as Edmund Bishop, Henry Bradshaw, M. R. James, to name only the most remarkable. But these men had had little influence on the main body of work in British universities. They had no patronage at their disposal and consequently they had little power to encourage young scholars in what were widely looked on as eccentric lines of enquiry. The result of this powerful canalization of effort was that British scholars had taken almost no part in some of the most important new areas of medieval study. The most striking example of this British isolation was in the study of medieval scholastic thought, which had undergone a huge expansion, largely as a result of the patronage of Pope Leo XIII, following his encyclical of 1878. The policy of this pope had been one of many influences which extended the area of intensive enquiry into every corner of medieval philosophy, theology, and canon law, and to every other aspect of the disciplines of the medieval schools. The influence of this work had scarcely penetrated into British scholarship before 1930. The fate of the young C. R. S. Harris, who as a young Fellow of All Souls in the early 1920s had undertaken a study of Duns Scotus, may be mentioned as an indication of the total isolation of Oxford from medieval scholastic studies: in Oxford he could find neither supervisor nor guide in even the simplest matters of medieval disputations and their transmission. Despite his great ability, his two-volumed work on Scotus, which appeared in 1927, was fatally flawed by his ignorance of the basic disciplines of medieval scholastic thought.

The importance of the 1930s for British medievalists was that these rigid lines of demarcation which separated 'serious' history from eccentricity began to dissolve. A very important influence in bringing this about was the Regius Professor of Modern History in Oxford, F. M. Powicke; but there were also more general influences working in the same direction which need not, at present, be elaborated. Suffice it to say that Powicke was concerned about Richard Hunt's future, partly because it was not easy for anyone with Hunt's interests to get a job at that time, and partly because he saw that in Hunt there was a young scholar capable of taking his place in an area of scholarship from which Britain had hitherto been isolated.

II

With these preliminaries I turn to the details of his career. He was born on 11 April 1908, in the Derbyshire village of Spondon, where his father was a general medical practitioner. His mother, Mabel Mary Whitely, came from a family of Nottinghamshire lace manufacturers. Their family consisted of three sons and a daughter, of whom Richard was the second son. As a family, they never left Spondon except for holidays in Suffolk and family visits to a grandmother in Felixstowe. They were not great travellers. In this steadfast immobility we may detect something which came naturally to Richard in later life. The family had the usual rather spartan comforts and interests of the professional class to which they belonged. They were brought up to have a love of Dickens and Scott and to engage, at a fairly low level of competence, in family games of golf and tennis, activities to which Richard long remained unexpectedly addicted. Financially they were only moderately well off, and scholarships were needed to send the sons to public schools. It seems to have been this need which determined the choice of Haileybury for Richard. In later years he never mentioned his school days, and he seems to have been mildly oppressed by the barbarities of boarding school life. Nevertheless, he made some lasting friendships, among them (Aelred) Sillem, later abbot of Quarr Abbey, and J. R. Liddell, who shared, and perhaps stimulated, his early interest in the Middle Ages.

If Haileybury was lacking in general intellectual stimulus, it provided him with a sound classical education. The Classics master was a former Balliol undergraduate and later Fellow of Merton College, R. G. C. Levens, and it may have been as a result of his encouragement that Richard tried for a Balliol scholarship. He failed to get a scholarship, but with some help from a family trust he was able to go to Balliol as a commoner in 1927. Here he came at once under the influence of his Balliol tutor, R. A. B. (later Sir Roger) Mynors, who will appear frequently in the following pages. In the arts of composition, which then dominated the Oxford study of Latin and Greek, Hunt was only moderately successful, but in his notes and essays which have survived from his undergraduate years we find some remarkable foreshadowings of his later interests and habits of thought. At that time, all undergraduates at Balliol during their first two terms were required to write a general essay each week on subjects chosen by the Master. All these early essays of Hunt's have survived, with careful notes of the tutors to whom they were read, and the remarks which they made about them. With hindsight, it is possible to see that these essays gave evidence of some unusual intellectual powers, and it is perhaps not very creditable to the search for brilliance which the tutorial system encouraged that they seem to have evoked no more than mild commendation. His essay on Lewis Carroll, written in his second term, already shows his extraordinary faculty for picking out bibliographical details which could be used to illustrate important themes. Moreover, at a time when the importance of logic in Lewis Carroll's writing was not as widely appreciated as it now is, Hunt saw that it was one of the mainsprings of Carroll's life and a permanent influence in his books.

It also made him [he continued] very precise and meticulous. We are told that from January 1861 to the time of his death he kept a précis of every letter he wrote. There are 98,721, and all indexed with an ingenious system of cross-referencing devised by himself. . . . His poetry was not the merely imaginative nonsense poetry of Edward Lear. It is mostly either parody or composed on scientific principles. Take the quatrain which appears in *Through the Looking Glass*, ''Twas brillig and the slithy toves . . .': this was made up in 1855 long before the rest of the book was thought of, and was originally meant as a parody of Anglo-Saxon poetry and fitted with a glossary. . . . These books are thoroughly a part of our nursery tradition, itself perhaps the greatest in any language.

I do not know how competent he was at that time to pronounce on the nursery tradition in any language other than English, but the remark has the stamp of his mature years, and no one who knew him in later life can read these sentences without seeing the man who later wrote about the indexing symbols of Robert Grosseteste and the logical grammarians of the twelfth century.

More immediately important for the future, these years also saw the beginning of his lifelong habit of transcribing with meticulous accuracy the unpublished contents of medieval manuscripts. Among the earliest of these is a transcript of verses in a Trinity College manuscript (no. 34). Hunt noted its date (quite in his later style): 's.xii ex.' and the record of his transcription: 'copied in J. R. H. Weaver Esq.'s room in Coll. Trin. Nov. 1930'.

Several notebooks survive which testify to the range of his undergraduate reading—not only Helen Waddell's *Wandering Scholars* and Haskins's *Twelfth Century Renaissance*, which many an undergraduate of that time read with a thrill of discovery, but also (which very few undergraduates can ever have looked at) the recently published edition (1930) of *Carmina Burana* by Alfons Hilka and Otto Schumann. His notes on this last publication show that Hunt had already thoroughly grasped the principles of the exhaustive German method of editing.

These are trifles, but they may be mentioned as the earliest symptoms of what was later to become his life's work. Practically, however, the main need for him in these years was to make sure of a First-Class degree if he was to have much hope of an academic career. This gave him a good deal of anxiety; but, after getting only a Second Class in classical Honour Moderations, he got a First in Greats, and this was followed by his election to a Senior Scholarship at Christ Church for two years from October 1931. In the circumstances of the time, and in view of Hunt's repugnance to presenting himself in a favourable light, it was an imaginative choice.

Without delay he set off for Munich, the fountain-head of the modern study of palaeography, with the declared intention of working under the direction of Paul Lehmann. Lehmann in Munich and E. A. Lowe in Oxford were the most distinguished pupils of Ludwig Traube, who at the beginning of the century had shown how the scientific study of manuscripts could be used as an instrument of literary and intellectual history. Lehmann's contributions to medieval studies, like those of Traube himself, were far more than merely palaeographical. He was an innovator in the study of medieval literary forms and in the study of medieval German libraries. It may be conjectured that it was this last interest which was the most powerful influence in taking Hunt to study under him. As long ago as 1907, Lehmann had started under Traube's inspiration to work on the library catalogues of Switzerland and Germany. In 1918 he had produced the first, and in 1928 the second, of the massive series of volumes containing the texts of these catalogues, and there were (and still are) more to come, in 1932, 1933, 1939, 1962, 1977, 1979.

The main inspiration in turning Hunt's attention in this direction came from Mynors, who was at this time urging Hunt to take on, or collaborate in, some kind of similar publication of English library catalogues. Hunt's first reactions were distinctly cool. The sight of Lehmann's icy persistence in a publication which, with all its scholarship, had many of the qualities of a telephone directory, was enough to chill the most enthusiastic admirer. Hunt spoke to Lehmann about it, and Lehmann was not encouraging: it was work, he rightly observed, which could not be undertaken as a spare-time occupation. Lehmann's scholarship made a deep impression on him. Looking back many years later, when he could see his development in perspective, he recorded: 'I always feel grateful to Lehmann for putting me on to an analysis of a big fifteenth century *florilegium* which made me look around for sources.' This work, dry though it was, taught him as nothing else could have done to understand the texture of medieval thought. He worked assiduously in Lehmann's seminar, visited the manuscript collections of Prague in his company, and generally learnt the trade of being a medievalist at its roots.

At the same time, stimulus of a different kind was coming to him from Powicke, who wanted him to write a D.Phil. thesis on Alexander Nequam. Here too Hunt's reactions were cool. If medieval library catalogues seemed too horrendous a task, Alexander Nequam somehow failed to satisfy the breadth of his interests. Yet Powicke was undoubtedly right. Alexander Nequam was a perfect subject for a D.Phil. thesis: he was an important scholar whose works covered a wide range of grammatical, scientific, and theological learning. His works are preserved in a large, but not overwhelmingly large, number of good manuscripts. They were (and still are) largely unprinted and unstudied; and they are a mirror of a large area of thought at a central moment in the Middle Ages. The arguments for 'adopting' him as a subject were strong, but the impulse was weak.

This nagging choice overshadowed Hunt's last months in Munich in the summer of 1932, while around him a more horrific choice was reaching its fatal issue. Before long Lehmann would be starting his lectures with a Nazi salute. Meanwhile, Hunt certainly benefited from his technical expertise, and by the time he returned to England, he was probably better equipped than anyone in the country at that time with the skills necessary for using manuscripts for studying the literary and intellectual history of the Middle Ages.

His year in Munich had completed his technical education, but the problem of his future was becoming urgent. He had only one certain year of his Senior Scholarship left and he needed something to show for it. Wisely (but perhaps with a slight sense of desperation) he chose Alexander Nequam, and registered as a D.Phil. student at Oxford under Powicke's supervision. In 1933, his Senior Scholarship was extended for a third year so that he could finish his thesis, and in 1934 he successfully applied for a Lectureship in Palaeography at Liverpool in succession to J. A. Twemlow. In 1935 he reported that Alexander Nequam was still hanging heavy on his hands, and though he completed his thesis in 1936, it was by then clear that his heart was not in it.

As soon as the thesis was finished, for all practical purposes Hunt forgot about it. Then and later, his friends begged him to publish it, and common prudence urged the need for publication. As late as 1961, he was persuaded to bring it up to date for publication, and he took some half-hearted steps in this direction. Now, after nearly fifty years, it still remains and still deserves to be published, and it is being prepared for publication by Dr Margaret Gibson. It is a treasury of accurate information about many manuscripts and many points of learned detail over the wide range of subjects covered by Alexander's works. Even in its unpublished state, it has been used more extensively than most theses in the Oxford History Faculty. Why Hunt was indifferent to its publication remains something of a mystery. Of course, everyone is apt to lose interest in a subject after writing about it, and there are always more important things to do than refurbishing exhausted thoughts for publication. But Hunt's indifference to his longest piece of learned writing has deeper roots than this. Even while he was working on it, his mind was on other subjects, and among these subjects the history of medieval British libraries, which he had not been able to see his way through in 1932, was the most important. This was to be the biggest single interest of his scholarly life, combining, as it did, his early work as an under-graduate in Oxford, when he first discovered the fascination of medieval manuscripts, with his experiences in Munich, when he saw the subject in its full European setting. To understand the way in which the work developed a certain amount of background explanation is needed.

III

An interest in the contents of medieval libraries was not new in England. It had a long and continuous history going back at least to the thirteenth century. But in modern scholarship, a new age of careful and scientific investigation began in France with the great Leopold Delisle's *Cabinet des Manuscrits de la Bibliothèque Impériale* (3 vols. 1868–81) followed in Germany by Becker's *Catalogi Biblio-thecarum Antiqui* (1885), and then by Gottlieb's and Lehmann's long series of German and Austrian catalogues from 1895 on-wards. In England the only scholarly work of comparable impor-tance was that of M. R. James, notably in his publication of the catalogues of Canterbury and Dover (1903) and—most impor-tant for our present subject—his short analysis, published in 1922, of the catalogues associated with a fifteenth-century bibliographer, whom James identified with John Boston of Bury St. Edmunds.[1] It was from James at Eton that Mynors had learnt to study medieval manuscripts, and it was from Mynors that Hunt's interest in medieval manuscripts was given its first distinct impulse. Mynors saw Hunt as the scholar who could carry on James's work with the learning and method which had character-ized the work of the continental scholars. As we have seen, Hunt was at first reluctant; but no sooner was he fully committed to Alexander Nequam than the libraries of medieval England be-

---

[1] Dr R. H. Rouse has shown ('Bostonus Buriensis and the author of the *Catalogus Scriptorum Ecclesiae*', *Speculum*, 41 (1966), 471–99) that the compiler of the catalogue was not 'John Boston' but a Henry of Kirkstede (probably Kirstead in Norfolk), a monk and librarian of Bury who died in about 1380. But since Hunt and his colleagues referred to the author as 'Boston of Bury' in all their discussions, I have retained this label.

came a major feature of his thoughts and efforts. The evidence for this growing interest can be found in countless notes from the years from 1933 onwards. His earliest sketch of the subject goes back to an unpublished paper on *English Monastic Libraries* which he read to the undergraduate History Society of Keble College in the spring of 1934. Like his thesis, from which it was then an imprudent diversion, it deserves to be printed even after this long lapse of time, for it contains a sketch of the physical and mental conditions under which scribes and authors pursued their tasks in the face of wind and weather, neglect, imperfect information, and the disapprobation of their superiors, which can be found nowhere else so well portrayed. There is one passage which deserves to be quoted, for it contains the key to a great deal of Hunt's later career:

In conclusion I should like to touch on the subject of how far books in one monastery were available to others. Little has been done on it so far. I think we may safely say that books were lent from one house to another for the purposes of transcription, though I cannot remember an instance of it later than the ninth century. . . . Some scholars, as William of Malmesbury, journeyed round in search of materials. But if a book was not in the library of one's house, was there any means of discovering it without writing round until you struck a copy? It may be surprising to some people to discover that there was. The earliest example comes from France. There existed in the seventeenth century (two Benedictine scholars saw it) a catalogue of the library at Savigny, and bound up with it the catalogues of Mont St. Michel, Caen, Bec, Jumièges. The date is variously given as 1210 or 1240. Of it, Delisle says (*Cabinet des Manuscrits*, i, 527), 'I do not know any document that shows so clearly how abbeys in the Middle Ages gave a real publicity to their catalogues, and how monk-scholars knew where to find books which were not in the library of their own house'. A fragment (*ib.* ii, 42, 196, 513) has also been found of a general catalogue of the Paris monasteries for the use of students at the Sorbonne.

In England we have a much more ambitious scheme. There exists more than one copy of a work which contains the names and works of all the commoner writers (mainly theological) used in the Middle Ages. The number varies [in different versions] from seventy to ninety-two. Against each work, there is a number or a series of numbers. Each number represents a monastery. Thus if we turn up Alexander Nequam, the first work given is his commentary on the Song of Songs; and against it are the numbers 142, 108, 15, XII, 46. These numbers stand for the following monasteries: Rievaulx, St. Peter's Gloucester, St. Albans, Buildwas and St. Neots. The catalogue was almost certainly compiled by the Franciscans, for it arranges England into seven Custodies, and among the Custodies appears Salisbury, which ceased to exist before 1331. Further, there are very few libraries of friars mentioned, and those that do occur are almost certainly a later addition. Therefore, it looks as if it were drawn up before the friars had collected large libraries. It is closely connected with another composite work, a collection of references to the incidental comments of the fathers on the Scriptures, and both together are known as the *Tabula Septem Custodiarum*. Thus, on Prov. XXXI.10 it gives references to Ambrose on Luke, Augustine Sermon 35, Bede on Luke, and St. Bernard's second homily on '*Missus est Angelus*'. It indicates whether these references are anagogical, allegorical or tropological and gives exact references to book and chapter, in each case using subdivisions 'a' to 'g' and the opening words of the passages. Together they were meant to be a help to the theologian and preacher.

In the fifteenth century it was much enlarged by, it seems, a monk of Bury called John Boston. His list includes 672 authors and gives some slight account of their lives, where there is an easily available source. For many works it does not note the existence (of any manuscripts). Of course it contains many mistakes. But so far as is known, there is no parallel in the rest of Europe.

The importance of this passage is that it was a first attempt to put in the larger setting of their purpose as aids to theological study the remarkable series of documents to which M. R. James had called attention in 1922. The passage also shows that, already in the spring of 1934, Hunt had done a great deal of detailed work on these lists. By the middle of 1935, with his thesis still unfinished, Hunt had prepared a transcript of the earliest of this series of texts, preserved in the Bodleian MS Tanner 165. Hunt reported this achievement to Mynors on 28 March, adding that he had also got some distance in understanding the method of compilation and the causes of confusions which were later to give much trouble to its editors. He had worked out that the composite catalogue was based on reports of manuscripts actually seen in the libraries enumerated. To this extent, therefore, it contained first-hand evidence of existing volumes; but reassuring though this was, there was the warning that 'the compiler must have been absolutely at the mercy of the contributions sent in', Mynors's reaction to this news was immediate. On 5 April he wrote: 'It is heroic of you to have transcribed already the vast mass of Tanner. . . . It clearly ought to be the first volume of a Corpus Catalogorum under the auspices of the British Academy.' On 30 May, after studying the transcript, Mynors wrote again: 'it marks an epoch in medieval studies.' Almost certainly by this time Hunt had already completed some of the remarkable studies identifying the works and manuscripts mentioned in these lists, which are to be found among his notes. Two years later Mynors himself contributed to this venture by completing an elaborate annotated transcript of the later, larger, and even more baffling catalogue associated with John of Boston. By 1937, therefore, the study of this collection of catalogues and the identification of the works and manuscripts mentioned in them was well advanced. Why then, did it not appear? Why is it still, even now, a project adopted by the British Academy for *future* publication?[1]

The main part of the answer to this question is that the project grew in complexity as it developed. The number of detailed enquiries necessary for turning bare lists of books and libraries into reliable accounts of real men, real libraries, and actual manuscripts became larger and larger. So far as Hunt was concerned, the range of these enquiries was soon extended to embrace a complete survey of all the existing British manuscripts of which the medieval provenance could be established. This soon became a distinct project on its own, and like the 'Boston of Bury' project, it also had a tendency to grow as it progressed. The earliest evidence for the existence of such a project in the Hunt papers is a letter from Mynors of 9 April 1932, mentioning that he had started a 'slip catalogue of manuscripts of known provenance, which has quickly reached over 800 slips'. More collaborators, notably Hunt and Liddell, were quickly drawn in, and the accumulation continued from several different sources. Among Hunt's papers there is a list of manuscripts of monastic provenance in Cambridge University Library, with a note in his hand: 'copied by Pink and given me by J. R. L(iddell), 1936'. In this list the evidence for continuing activity is clearly apparent. The original list contained about 100 manuscripts, but there are many additions in Hunt's hand. So the process of collection was going ahead vigorously in the years from 1932 onwards, and it was given still further momentum under the impulse of C. R. Cheney. In November 1937 he suggested that a collaborative effort should be made to produce a list of all extant British manuscripts of known monastic provenance. From this time, work on this project (very soon extended to include secular as well as monastic libraries) went ahead with increasing vigour with a uniform system of descriptive cards, a single collecting centre, and with N. R. Ker emerging as its editor and chief collector and executive, while Hunt was increasingly the member of the group to whom everyone turned for criticism, information, and an authoritative judgement on doubtful points. The team was remarkable in bringing together

[1] The work is now well advanced, and the long-awaited edition of these catalogues, edited by Richard and Mary Rouse, will appear before long.

in total harmony and mutual confidence four or five men of different talents but with a single object. Their work in the years before 1940 did more than anything else to lay the material foundations for the later study of intellectual life in England in the Middle Ages: in a unique way, it linked learning to the harsh realities of physical objects and available resources. It is hard to believe that this could have been accomplished in so short a time by any other combination of scholars. But there was a price to pay: quite abruptly the 'Boston of Bury' project began to take second place to *British Libraries*. Hunt recognized that the later project was a necessary preliminary to the completion of 'Boston'. It will, he wrote, 'save an endless labour' in locating manuscripts, and 'be a means of making available the things we find by the way'.[1] The consequence was that *British Libraries* took an increasing proportion of his time. His correspondence with Ker (it has survived on both sides in remarkable completeness) gives a picture of scholarly co-operation worthy of a better age. It will not be out of place to quote a small part of one long letter from Hunt to Ker as an example of the kind of co-operation which was quietly bringing about, at this most unfavourable moment, the publication of a remarkable piece of historical scholarship. The letter is dated from Liverpool 25 September 1940:

I have been going through M(edieval) B(ritish) L(ibraries) with great enjoyment, slightly tempered by fears for the safety of the MS. The notes I have made speak for themselves, though some of them may give you some trouble, I am afraid, because I have not always been able to verify my queries: and some of them may turn out to be mare's nests.

I have only checked thoroughly those houses, whose MSS. or catalogues I have gone into at one time or another. I would have done more, but have not had time. The library A.R.P. regulation is that everyone 'without exception or excuse' either leaves the building or descends to the lowest stack floor, which isn't furnished with books.

Will you look up Berlin Phill. 1805 and 1904? We haven't the Berlin catalogues here and my notes are insufficient to show whether their

[1] The question of priority between the two projects was probably never explicitly faced, partly because M. R. James's judgement that the publication of the 'Boston' catalogue was an essential preliminary to 'any really thorough investigation of ancient English libraries' was accepted without dispute. Hunt's contrary judgement was the result of several years' work, which had shown that 'Boston' presented a mass of problems, which could only be resolved by a detailed study of the surviving books from the constituent libraries. For M. R. James's initial judgement, see his study of the library at Bury St. Edmunds in *Cambridge Antiquarian Society Octavo Publications*, xxviii (1895), 34; and R. W. Pfaff, *M. R. James* (1980), p. 201, for a general account of these developments.

provenance can be determined. According to my notes, C(orpus) C(hristi) C(ollege, Cambridge, MSS) 28 and 182 both have erased inscriptions, but the MSS. were in CCC when Jock (Liddell) and I went through them, and we didn't try the ultraviolet.

If there are things in my notes which are not intelligible, just send them back with fierce comments and I'll try to elucidate them.

This letter was almost the last which passed between Hunt and Ker on this subject before the volume, *Medieval Libraries of Great Britain*, was printed. On 1 August 1940, Cheney ('at three in the morning' after 'pretty long hours in a government office') had written to Hunt: 'Here is a sample page of our Med. Brit. Libraries for your comments and criticisms. If we can finish it off soon, we can get it printed and published by the R. Hist. Soc. at once—the printer has *just* enough paper and the Society is willing.' The volume was in fact 'finished off soon', and it was published by June 1941.

With this part of the 'medieval libraries' enterprise successfully completed, the way was clear for a final push to finish the earlier 'Boston of Bury' project. But the war was now pressing more closely than before. So far as Hunt personally was concerned, his second marriage in 1942, his growing family, and above all his increasing obligations towards Liverpool University (the Professor of Medieval History, Coopland, had retired in 1940; no successor was appointed till 1945, and in the interval a large part of his work was done by Hunt) all combined to make immediate progress on 'Boston' impossible.

It was the fate of 'Boston' to be continually thrust aside by other projects which appeared to be necessary to it either as a foundation or overflow. It was in this guise that, in the last months of 1937, yet another project began to present itself. This was a plan for a new periodical which would gather up the flow of new discoveries. On 29 November 1937, Hunt wrote: 'I have been discussing lately with a friend (Dr. Raymond Klibansky) the possibility of starting a periodical to deal with medieval thought and learning. Such a periodical is badly wanted. There is no English periodical which will print material on medieval thought: it has to be sent abroad.' The discussions thus started continued and broadened in scope during 1938. By the middle of the year the outline of the first number of the new periodical had been determined. It only remained to find a publisher, printer, subscribers, and to put out a prospectus. The indomitable energy of Dr Klibansky was largely engaged in canvassing and solving these problems, and in the last days of 1938 a prospectus was issued for a periodical, familiarly and (in the circumstances of the time) sardonically known as MARS: it announced that *Mediaeval and Renaissance Studies* would appear twice a year, starting in October 1939 with an appetizing list of thirty contributions promised for the first numbers. The first number was ready in the summer and was sent to Belgium to be printed. It was lost in the turmoil of the following year, printed again in England, and finally appeared in 1941, with a further instalment in 1943. Planned under the imminent threat of war, and brought into existence in the presence of war, it represented a concentration of the new spirit of medieval research which was stirring at that time. The periodical struggled on after the war with four further numbers from 1950 to 1968. The high standard of editing persisted and the need did not diminish, but the periodical languished amid manifold distractions. It deserves to be mentioned here as an expression of the hopes and efforts of the pre-war years.

IV

When the war ended, the 'Boston of Bury' project was immediately revived. But two new obstacles now appeared. The first of these was a minor international incident which, however slight its practical importance, elicited contrasting statements of rare interest from the groups of continental and British scholars interested in the project. To understand the continental point of view we have to go back to M. R. James's article of 1922 which first brought to light the importance of the 'Boston of Bury' group of library catalogues. One of the earliest scholars to grasp the significance of the discovery was the Belgian scholar, Fr. Joseph de Ghellinck, SJ. He wrote briefly about the discovery in a paper for a Congress of Librarians in 1923, and at greater length in a paper of extraordinary brilliance, 'En marge des catalogues des bibliothèques médiévales', in 1924.[1] A brief quotation from this paper will give a clear idea of the point of view and personality of this highly gifted scholar. The dry lists of books in medieval library catalogues, he writes,

sont tout autre chose qu'une pétrifaction de la bibliographie rudimentaire antique . . . Elles recèlent la matière de tout un chapitre dans l'histoire de l'esprit humain; . . . ces notices anonymes jouent le rôle de témoins dans l'histoire de la diffusion des écrits et de la transmission des idées; . . . elles nous donnent un tableau, souvent très net, de la transmission de la culture, de ses moyens de propagation et de leur

[1] *Miscellanea Francesco Ehrle*, vol. 5, *Studi e Testi*, 41 (1924), 331–63.

rapidité, de la proportion des divers éléments qui y entrent; elles nous apprennent la mesure du succès des ouvrages, le rôle des pays et des époques, des écrivains et des groupements d'écrivains, dans la formation de la pensée médiévale.

It would be difficult to make greater claims than these for any single body of evidence. In Fr. Ghellinck's paper, they were supported by a scintillating array of examples, including the 'Boston of Bury' group of catalogues, of which it is not unfair to say that, dazzling though they are in their variety, they scarcely provide the illumination of *la transmission des idées* promised in the first paragraph. Fr. Ghellinck, however, was certainly the first to appreciate the wider importance of the 'Boston' catalogue which M. R. James had brought to his attention, and the English scholars always, though somewhat quixotically, accepted that he had a prior claim to any future publication. They were, therefore, reluctant to take any step towards publication without his agreement.

After the war, when contact with foreign scholars was re-established, it soon became apparent that the kind of work which Hunt and Mynors had been doing before the war was not what Fr. Ghellinck wanted. He was not at all interested in the identification of the precise manuscripts referred to in these catalogues, nor in the detailed history of the libraries to which they belonged. He was interested only in the evidence which they provided for the use or disuse of the various works mentioned in the catalogues. That is to say, he was interested only in the light they could throw on the general history of Christian thought along the lines which he had laid down in 1924. A bare publication of the lists as they stood would (as he thought) satisfy his needs. With the raw material in front of them in print, it could be left to him and other widely ranging scholars to draw their own conclusions.

This view was entirely consistent with Fr. Ghellinck's earlier writings on the subject. But it struck at the foundations of the detailed work of Hunt and Mynors. With a view to getting a favourable hearing for their point of view they sought the help of W. A. Pantin, who wrote to Fr. Ghellinck giving the views of the English scholars. Ghellinck replied in a letter which is a masterpiece of wit and learned polemic. He first analysed the contrasting points of view of the English and continental scholars: he and his colleagues (he wrote) were interested only in this material as evidence for the diffusion and transmission of literary works, as a contribution to the history of thought and doctrine. Whatever went beyond this was superfluous: 'non pas inutile, mais tout à fait secondaire'. The English scholars, by contrast, were interested in the history of libraries, or what he called 'la documentation d'histoire bibliothéconomique'. This latter constituted 'la belle tradition anglaise dans l'histoire des bibliothèques, des Botfields, des Edwards, des Bradshaws, des James, etc.' The English scholars were conducting an investigation into points of detail in which he and his friends had no interest. Nevertheless, despite his prior claim to these documents, he did not wish to deprive the English scholars of their chance of realizing their aim 'essentiellement anglais par son object et ses matières'; but he pointed out that the researches of his English colleagues would take many years, and during this long time the learned world would be deprived of the use of documents which in their simple unadorned state would render 'd'énormes services' to those who could use them for literary and intellectual history. What he and his committee therefore suggested was that the English scholars should prepare the documents for immediate publication with a minimum of introduction, and without any attempt to identify individual manuscripts or to describe the state of individual libraries. Once published, they could get on with their own researches at leisure without depriving the learned world of the documents which it needed. This manner of proceeding was, he claimed, a well-established practice. It would release the documents in a form that would provide 'un remarquable ensemble de renseignements pour la tradition littéraire du moyen âge et pour les inspirateurs de sa pensée' and it would give the English scholars ample time for their secondary investigations.

The contents of this letter must have given its recipients a *mauvais quart d'heure*. If Fr. Ghellinck was right they were relegated to the position of humble toilers at the coal-face, extracting ore to fuel the intellectual powerhouses of Europe, free in their long leisure to potter about among the old books, harmlessly engaged in finding out who had owned them, leaving the more serious work of tracing the intellectual history of Christian Europe to others. The strength of this view of the matter depended upon the correctness of Ghellinck's assumption that the material could be used for his grand purposes without further refinement. It was, therefore, essential, if the contrary view were to be maintained, to demonstrate that nothing could be made of these documents without the most careful assessment of the individual manuscripts, and the clarification of the many confusions embodied in the material available to medieval librarians. To neglect these facts could lead only to a superficial view of the European intellectual tradition.

It was left to Hunt to draft the reply to Fr. Ghellinck. His draft is a monument to his judgement. It also expresses an important principle in intellectual history—the principle that intellectual history cannot seriously be undertaken without the most exact attention to the material circumstances of intellectual work. The draft was later improved by his colleague, but this is the main part of what Hunt wrote:

Dear Fr. Ghellinck,

We thank you very sincerely for your letter in which you state so clearly the grounds for producing a 'provisional' edition of the *Catalogus librorum Angliae* and of Boston of Bury.[1] We very much welcome the frank and open exchange of views on the means of achieving the aim we all have in view, namely of making accessible to scholars the long awaited texts, so valuable, as you say, for the literary history of the Middle Ages.

From the point of view of the wider plan for a *corpus* of English mediaeval Library catalogues it would be a very great advantage to have printed texts of CLA and of Boston to work on; but we are not wholly convinced that a text with the minimum of introduction and a summary critical apparatus, but without any attempt to identify the works of the various authors, would be of great value to scholars. In view of the way the texts were compiled, some attempt at identification of the works mentioned seems necessary, and would surely be appropriate in a series like yours which is notable for the excellence of its apparatus. The examples of 'provisional' texts to which you refer, the edition of the *Martyrologium Hieronomianum* by De Rossi and Duchesne and that of the *Corpus Juris Canonici* by Friedberg are on rather a different footing. There were many editions of both texts in existence already, and Friedberg does give the references to sources.

Here we should like to correct a false impression which our earlier letter created. You say that 'l'œuvre que vous projetez se manifeste tout de suite comme une œuvre de documentation d'histoire biblio-théconomique', while the interest of the *Spicilegium* is in 'la documentation . . . dont peut tirer parti l'histoire littéraire'. We are no less anxious than you to make CLA and Boston really usable for scholars working on the literary history of the Middle Ages. The point we wished to emphasize was that they are texts *very dangerous to use for such enquiries* without a knowledge of the way their compilers worked and of the sources upon which they drew; and it would be impossible to bring this out by a few brief general observations in the introduction.

We think that the best way to make the point clear is to send you one

[1] The first of these texts (generally abbreviated to 'CLA') was the thirteenth-century catalogue made by the Franciscans preserved in the Bodleian manuscript which Hunt had transcribed in 1935; 'Boston of Bury' was the catalogue derived from this and preserved in the Cambridge University Library manuscript which Mynors had transcribed in 1937.

or two specimens of the method of identification we should propose to adopt, (a) for patristic and (b) for mediaeval authors. For patristic authors we should give only a reference to a printed edition (normally Migne, *Pat. lat.*) without any discussion of the true authorship of individual works. For mediaeval authors we should go a little further and indicate summarily, as far as we can, the true author of any particular work. For there is a difference in the weight to be attached to the evidence of CLA and Boston for patristic and mediaeval authors. For patristic authors they merely reflect the manuscript tradition; for mediaeval authors, they may do something more. In both cases we refer to manuscripts only where a special point has to be made, e.g. where the attribution of particular works (or groups of works) to a particular author would be otherwise unintelligible, as in the enclosed specimen of Athanasius, or when the evidence derived from extant manuscripts makes certain the identification of works otherwise only to be guessed at, as in the enclosed specimen of Augustine.

To sum up, we should be prepared to attempt to construct a 'provision' edition of CLA and of Boston, but we should be very reluctant to see such an edition appear without the identification of the works included in them. . . .

. . . We should be glad if you would consider these observations, and send us the comments of the board of Directors of the *Spicilegium*.

So far as I know Fr. Ghellinck's answer has not survived, but in practice the views of the English editors prevailed.

I have described this controversy at some length for two reasons. The first is that, in the light of such criticisms as those of Fr. Ghellinck and, indeed, of thoughts which may arise in the minds of even sympathetic observers, Hunt's lifelong dedication to the task of describing the minutiae of a huge number of individual manuscripts requires justification, and here is its justification in his own words. I have said that Hunt did not easily or frequently think it necessary to explain himself. On this occasion he did so, and it is a striking tribute to the confidence which his colleagues had in his judgement that they left it to him to draft the reply to so formidable a critic as Fr. Ghellinck. His draft shows that their confidence was well justified. No one else could have demolished the thinly veiled dismissal of his and his colleagues' learned activity with more devastating brevity and force.

A second reason for dwelling at some length on this point is that a memoir of Hunt can only be of interest if it makes clear—what he himself never found it necessary to clarify in print—the general purpose served by the many detailed enquiries on which he was engaged throughout his learned life. This debate brings his work and that of his collaborators into the context of the general development of medieval scholarship during the period from 1930 to 1980. This half-century saw the culmination and decline of two great efforts in medieval scholarship: the English *constitutional*, and the continental *scholastic*, interpretation of the Middle Ages. The first was defective in its parochialism; the second in its lack of parochialism. The first was strong in its grasp of times and places, but limited in its ideas; the second was strong in its grasp of doctrines, but weak in relating these doctrines to practical situations. The first was inspired by the belief that the institutions of government preserved all that was most important in the doctrines of the Middle Ages. The second was inspired by a conviction that the medieval tradition of scholastic thought was the continuing central theme of European civilization. Under the influence of this conviction, a mass of work was produced of great historical and intellectual importance. Its weakness was that it touched only lightly on the conditions which promoted scholastic thought and the pressures to which it responded. The conflict between Ghellinck and the group of scholars with whom Hunt associated was a confrontation between those, like Ghellinck, who wished to describe the stream of thought as an object in its own right, and those who insisted that material circumstances and limitations were an essential part of any realistic intellectual history. It is this contrast which gives the controversy a place of general interest and lasting importance in the history of medieval studies.

Whether or not Fr. Ghellinck was right in thinking that the bare lists of books and libraries would have rendered *d'énormes services* to medieval intellectual history, he was certainly right in predicting that the world would have to wait a long time to have the texts in the form which, as the English scholars insisted, alone made them capable of being used. One reason for this was that the end of the war brought new duties and distractions to all participants. Consequently, the project scarcely moved forward during the next fifteen years, until Richard and Mary Rouse took it up and brought new minds to the task. This is not the place to attempt to assess how much still remained to be done in editing the texts, identifying their contents, and investigating the circumstances in which they were planned and carried out. That is a story which will be told elsewhere.

V

In October 1945 Hunt left Liverpool and returned to Oxford as Keeper of Western Manuscripts at the Bodleian Library. Earlier,

he had refused to be considered for important librarianships—
notably at Liverpool—on the ground of his lack of administrative
experience and skill. But he viewed the Bodleian offer with
enthusiasm: 'there is so much to be done in Bodley', he wrote on
15 November 1944, 'and there surely ought to be possibilities for
trying to be of some use to people who are working on manuscripts, though I am very vague about the actual duties of the
Keeper'. His enthusiasm grew as he learnt more: 'It is a marvel-
lous prospect', he wrote on 14 January 1945. 'When telling me the
duties of the Keeper, Craster (then Bodley's Librarian) put first
helping and advising readers, for which I was very glad.'

His immediate impressions on arrival confirmed these high expectations: 'The work of the library is very exhilarating', he wrote
in describing a sale of Harmsworth Trust manuscripts. 'I fixed my
attention on several manuscripts very inadequately described.'
This was his first venture to the sale-room to pick up manuscripts,
which were not expensive, but which made significant additions to
the Bodleian collections. The decade after the war was a golden
age for acquiring unspectacular but interesting manuscripts. A
number of important collections came on the market—not least
the large residue of the Phillipps library—and the group of friends
who before the war had collaborated in *British Medieval Libraries*
and 'Boston of Bury' were now largely instrumental in selecting
manuscripts to add to the Bodleian collections. Until the mid-
1950s prices were still low; yet the Bodleian expenditure on new
acquisitions rose from an average of about £400 a year before the
war to £3,450 in 1952–3 and to £13,362 in 1962–3. In 1975–6 (the
year of Hunt's retirement) it reached the quite exceptional total of
£58,472. This was not a symptom of lavish or indiscriminate buying, but of constant watchfulness. Hunt's eye for significant detail
was equally active in finding sources of finance for new acquisitions and manuscripts which were worth buying.

In addition to purchases, his authority and persuasive power
encouraged gifts and deposits. In 1958 Hunt wrote of the arrival of
185 boxes of personal papers of Sir Thomas Phillipps ('they will
take some digesting'), followed by the remaining hoard of English
topographical manuscripts: 'They only arrived [Hunt wrote on
Sunday, 15 June], on Thursday afternoon, 15 tea chests. We still
have these chests to unpack and haven't counted them, but there
are over 500 vols., so we have our hands full'—this (he added) at a
time when 'the university has just decided that we shall keep the
whole library open till 10 p.m. in term time and have given us no
money for extra staff'.

Another aspect of his new job, which he was quick to appreciate and act upon, was his responsibility for modern as well as medieval manuscripts, and for administrative as well as literary documents. Nothing was more conspicuous in his thirty-year tenure of the office than his concern for papers of every date and every type. Court rolls and modern diocesan records were among the earliest objects of his energy. On 28 April 1946, he wrote: 'I am having a list of Court Rolls completed for the Register of Manorial Documents, and I am at work with a helper on the conspectus of shelf marks. . . . It is exasperatingly fiddly work.' Almost exactly a year later a new source of trouble made its appearance. On 28 April 1947, he wrote: 'I've been a good deal concerned with Diocesan Records of late. We have taken in a large fresh batch of the Oxford ones. . . . An old mill-stream rose up during the floods and entered the cellar of Church House where the records were kept. . . . I got a team of volunteers and we removed all the wet papers and parchments, and tied each parish into a parcel and carted them all off to our New Building.' These diocesan records kept on arriving for several years as they were released from ecclesiastical custody. Troublesome though they were, they proved to be an endless source of interest to him. He never looked at any documents, however mundane his immediate purpose, without going deeply into the reason for their existence and the forms of life of which they were the record. When the papers of Bishop Wilberforce were being sorted out, he wrote: 'We have been able to learn from them how insufficient is our knowledge of the precise nature of ecclesiastical records.' Characteristically, the chance which brought a growing bulk of diocesan records under his care caused him to revise several long established judgements on the condition of the clergy in the eighteenth and nineteenth centuries, and also helped him to deal with practical problems when he was churchwarden of St. Barnabas in Oxford.

Everywhere in his work we see this same interplay between cataloguing, describing, understanding, and forming new judgements on men and their affairs. His judicious buying of manuscripts for the Bodleian was informed by a deep sense of the nature of the collections under his care and of their gaps. He had a special tenderness for the memory of those who were connected with the collections, as we can see in his researches into Archbishop Laud's books, and in his sympathy for Shelley whose letters form one of the main modern acquisitions among the Bodleian manuscripts. Some of Shelley's letters had been the subject of a forgery scare which he thought ill-judged, and he dealt with it firmly in the course of other business. On 18 March 1945, he wrote:

I went up to London last Monday, partly to look at a MS. that was being sold at Sotheby's (a collection of fifteenth century theological treatises of some interest, which we got for the modest sum of £34), partly to see some of the B.M. people about the authenticity of a much disputed letter of Shelley to Mary. It belonged to the notorious T. J. Wise, but I am convinced it is genuine. To my joy it had an erased number on it which connects it with a series of letters Shelley wrote to Mary while he was eluding the sheriff's officers, and which were stolen from a desk they left at Marlow when they went to Italy (at least I think so). They were bought back by Mary from a disreputable man who pretended he was a natural son of Byron. He made forged copies of some of them which have caused the trouble. But most of it would have been avoided if only people would take the trouble to look at the originals.

This is a good example of the combination of sympathy and acumen which went with his daily work. This combination was nowhere more needed or more freely exercised than in his dealings with the growing number of researchers from all parts of the world who wanted advice, information, and help. It was the appearance of this growing army of workers which transformed the Bodleian from a quiet and scholarly institution with a small income and staff and an ingrained distrust of readers, into a big business with an annual budget of £1.6 million, a growing staff, and all the complications of a rapidly expanding number of readers. This was something which those who persuaded Hunt to return to Oxford in 1945 had not reckoned with. Another thing which they had not fully appreciated was his extraordinary devotion to readers and students of all kinds and ages. In 1945 he had welcomed the Librarian's assurance that the Keeper's first duty was to help and advise readers; but he carried out this duty with a zeal that was almost ferocious—he was a formidable and outspoken critic of shoddy work, and he had a genius for knowing what a reader needed. To all who came to him, whether casual readers, or members of his staff, or colleagues, he was a lavish source of help on a very wide range of subjects. Often he did not need to be asked: he simply noticed the need and met it. On one occasion it is recorded that he happened to notice that a reader had ordered two manuscripts, from which he deduced that a third, in a college library, would also contain relevant material. He promptly informed the reader, and added yet another to the long list of scholars who were indebted to him for timely information which they could have obtained from no other source. It was this part of his work which inspired the awe and devotion of scholars from all parts of the world: perhaps no one in this country except Henry Bradshaw at the Cambridge University Library a hundred years ago has made anything like the same impression on the workers in a library.

Some might think that his energies were dissipated by his availability to every caller and to every call on his time. This was the nature of the man. It was one aspect of his total absorption in the task of the moment. In his earlier years he had been a central point of reference on all points of scholarship for a few friends whenever they needed a steady judgement and a sharp eye backed by a retentive memory. In the second and longer phase of his career after 1945 he performed this function for all who came to study western manuscripts in the Bodleian. His scholarly work during the last thirty-five years of his life must largely be looked for in the books and articles published by others, and in his contributions—generally anonymous—to the cataloguing of manuscripts under his care. The acknowledgements of his help in prefaces and footnotes are beyond counting, and even if they could be counted they would give no idea of the extent to which his suggestions and knowledge of the sources, and above all his instinctive understanding of what other scholars were getting at, had transformed many of the works which he helped to bring into existence. He was content with this role. He felt no proprietorship in his learning. He knew that he was not a fluent writer, and he may have sensed that he lacked something—whether selfishness or ambition or a creative instinct—which makes for great productivity. He had none of the unease which lies at the root of a desire to create something new. His own imaginative life was in the writings of the past. He was in daily contact with one of the world's greatest collections of scholarly work, and he enjoyed this contact. He knew and had handled a large part of it. He gave his close personal attention to the work of cataloguing new accessions and revising the old catalogues of the main collections. His historical account of these collections, in the first volume of the *Summary Catalogue*, besides being lucid and accurate, is filled with little touches, which show that he understood the problems of his predecessors. In everything relating to books his judgement was both firm and clairvoyant. He had none of the instability of enthusiasm, but he was capable of explosive outbursts of joy in the presence of a sudden discovery, whether his own or another's. One colleague recalls 'the day when he walked into my study just as I was about to return an Exeter College manuscript which had been deposited for photography. He opened it, and almost shouted, "That's Petrarch's hand!"' It was this kind of incident which makes his memory live in the Bodleian. From 1945 onwards, his life was dedicated to an ideal. After he had been some years in the Bodleian, he wrote: 'The more I reflect on librarianship in big "research" libraries, the more I am sure that the librarian ought to be a scholar—not that he will have much time for scholarship, unless he has the energy of a Delisle. But without it, the place becomes devitalized, and the staff sink to be library clerks.'

Although the pursuit of this ideal took up most of his time and left him 'not much time for scholarship', it would be wrong to think of him only as a reference system for others. Although he got little pleasure from original writing, he got intense satisfaction from bringing to light and making intelligible the writings of scholars of all periods. He had early begun the practice of copying texts, and he continued this practice to the end. To copy texts which are difficult in subject-matter as well as script is not a mechanical process, but a process calling for deep knowledge and powers of interpretation. It was a process which gave him pleasure in exercising many kinds of skill. In his later years, his transcripts were largely of medieval grammatical texts. He was drawn to this subject partly no doubt because nearly all the writers whom he dealt with had had to learn Latin in the painstaking way in which he himself had learnt it, and their problems had been his problems. But later, the twelfth-century grammarians drew him into the higher reaches of the subject. Long before grammar had become a fashionable branch of modern philosophy, he had discovered that it was the foundation of all medieval thought and had deeply influenced their approach to philosophy and every-thing else. His first serious work on the subject was stimulated by the need to write something for the new periodical *MARS*. In July 1938 he visited Durham to study a twelfth-century manuscript in which he had found grammatical notes by a number of masters of the late eleventh and early twelfth centuries, and he went on to Paris to see two related manuscripts. This led to the first of his grammatical studies which appeared in *MARS* in 1943, followed by a continuation in 1950. The latest of his articles on this subject appeared in 1975.[1] Among his papers there are five boxes of gram-matical texts and descriptions of grammatical manuscripts, of which some extracts will appear in the invaluable *cahiers* of the medieval Institute of the University of Copenhagen: an interest-

[1] These articles have now been collected and republished, not altogether satisfactorily, in a single volume.

ing illustration of the continuing truth of Hunt's remark in 1938 about the lack of a suitable periodical for such work in this country.

It would weary the reader, and make no essential addition to this sketch of his scholarly character and achievement, to record the many contributions which he made during the last thirty years of his life to co-operative works and learned committees. It must suffice to mention only one publication and two committees.

The publication is the revised edition of the *Oxford Dictionary of the Christian Church*, edited by Miss E. A. Livingstone and published in 1974. Hunt's contribution to this was second only to that of the editor herself. He read and revised nearly all the medieval articles, and he entirely rewrote several, notably those on Stephen Langton, Gottschalk, Florus of Lyons, Heiric of Auxerre, Gilbert de la Porrée, and Albertus Magnus. This was the kind of writing in which he excelled—correcting mistakes by stealth, adding new information anonymously, and bringing a wide range of up-to-date scholarship to bear on an article that might occupy half a page.

Of committees, the one which he enjoyed most was the Library Committee of Lambeth Palace, on which he served for many years. He liked it because it was a small and informal gathering of congenial colleagues, and it got things done—nothing less than the restoration and reorganization of a great historic library after its destruction in the war. The other committee which 'got things done' was the manuscripts Sub-committee of the Standing Conference of National and University Libraries, of which he was chairman from 1957 to 1975. It sounds like an administrative nightmare; but it was from this unglamorous height that he exercised an effective leadership in promoting scholarly publications which will form part of the permanent equipment of future medievalists. He succeeded in this, not by administrative skill or dominating personality, but simply by knowing the jobs that needed to be done and the people who could do them, and being obviously right. Two volumes of N. R. Ker's *Medieval Manuscripts in British Libraries* (with two more to come) and Andrew Watson's Catalogue of dated and datable Latin manuscripts in the British Library, already testify to the efficacy of this unobtrusive form of leadership. It was work which he could promote and encourage without strain and without formality because he saw the whole field with the eye of a master and a friend.

A final extension of his genius for collaboration was occasioned by his election as a Fellow of this Academy in 1961. This led to his becoming a member and then chairman of the Committees on the

Medieval Latin Dictionary and British Medieval Texts. The editors of all the projects connected with these committees soon learned like everyone else to draw abundantly from his overflowing well of knowledge.

VI

In the peculiar circumstances of Hunt's life and work—the brevity of his published work and the abundance of unpublished material, together with his wide and deep influence on contemporary scholars conveyed in short notes and verbal observations—it seemed proper to make this memoir a record of co-operative enterprises in which he played a major part even though his name was seldom publicly associated with them. I have tried to give a view of his work as it appeared from near at hand, and as it can still be found in his voluminous papers. To go further and attempt to portray the man, as he appeared to the many scholars who came to him in the Bodleian for work and in his home in Walton Street for refreshment, would go beyond the scope of what I have attempted. Everyone found him helpful to an astonishing degree —helpful both in the range of his original observations and in his willingness to communicate them freely. Everyone found his home life—largely shaped and coloured by the immense good nature and exuberance of his second wife, Kit Rowland—a scene of warm and abundant hospitality. Everyone who knew him will remember his characteristic attitude at home, puffing his pipe under the eaves of his remarkably expressive eyebrows, often silent while others talked, breaking out at times into a deep chuckle or a body-shaking laugh. Not so many saw his rare outburst of indignation, or his stubborn persistence in defending some scholarly truth, or his outspoken enforcement of some simple rule like not smoking in a non-smoking compartment. With all his faculty for appreciating others, he could be very formidable, and even ruthless, as a critic.

The story would be seriously incomplete if these aspects of his personality were omitted. But one example of his absolute rigour on questions of scholarship or the plain rules of life must stand for all. I owe the example to Dr Myres, formerly Bodley's Librarian, and I give it in his words:

Did I ever tell you the tale about Richard's encounter with the old King of Sweden—another learned man—when he visited Bodley? Richard had set out for his inspection some MSS. to take his fancy in Selden End, including the one which figures Noah's Ark portrayed as a Viking Long Ship. The King was delighted with this, and ventured a date for it. 'No, *No, NO!*' thundered Richard, thumping the table with indignation, and announced a different century. But the King stood his ground, pointing to details of construction and rigging, in justification of his date. Richard replied with equally decisive palaeographical considerations, and soon they were hard at it, like a couple of terriers, whom I and the royal equerries, with their eyes on the clock, had the greatest difficulty in separating. When they were eventually persuaded to let go of their respective ends of the bone of contention, both seemed equally delighted with the learned rough and tumble, and equally oblivious of the tattered and irrelevant protocol.

There, in all his simplicity, is the scholar whom we knew.

After the death of his wife in December 1977, the vivacity went out of his domestic life, but he continued to work, and he was still at work when death came suddenly in the night of 13 November 1979.

R. W. SOUTHERN

Note: The compilation of this record has been made possible by the help of many friends of Richard Hunt. I am especially indebted to Dr N. R. Ker, Sir Roger Mynors, and Mrs Joan Varley who have allowed me to use a large collection of letters in their possession, which illuminate different phases of the works described above. They, together with Dr Beryl Smalley, Professor and Mrs Richard Rouse, Mrs G. D. G. Hall, Dr J. N. L. Myres, Dr Bruce Barker-Benfield, Dr A. C. de la Mare, and other members of the Bodleian staff, have enabled me to fill many gaps and correct many errors in my memory of events and in my knowledge of the complicated business of the Bodleian.

PLATE XX

G. W. H. LAMPE

GEOFFREY WILLIAM HUGO LAMPE

1912-1980

GEOFFREY LAMPE was a giant in many senses—tall and fine in physical presence, large-hearted and generous and without a trace of pettiness, broad in his sympathies and wide in his range of learning. In our youth, some of us were brought up on a popular rendering of τὸ ἐπιεικὲς ὑμῶν in Phil. 4: 5 as 'your sweet reasonableness', and this well describes Geoffrey's temperament and outlook. Reasonableness was important to him. He detested anything superstitious or irrational and, still more, anything pretentious or 'bogus'. His instinct was to deflate the pompous and to explain and reduce to orderly comprehensibility everything he possibly could—and this, with a genial and tolerant grace. He felt that if a matter could be explained, then he had come to terms with it and, in a sense, mastered it. To within half an hour of his death, having long before come to terms with his medical condition, he was quietly and serenely ordering his affairs down to the last detail of his own memorial service.

He was born on 13 August 1912, and died on 5 August 1980, a few days before his sixty-eighth birthday and less than a year after superannuation from the Regius Chair of Divinity at Cambridge.

His father, who came from Alsace, with forbears from Utrecht, had been a successful conductor of the Bournemouth Symphony Orchestra, but left England before the outbreak of the 1914–18 war, and Geoffrey was brought up by his remarkable mother who lived to see him become Ely Professor of Divinity at Cambridge. He went to Blundell's School and then, with a scholarship, to Exeter College, Oxford, where he had a first-class record in both Greats and Theology Schools. He had chosen Theology because, by then, it was clear to him that he should seek Holy Orders, and he went for training to the Queen's College, Birmingham, whence, in 1937, he was ordained deacon. After a short curacy at Okehampton (1937–8), he became an assistant master at King's School, Canterbury, marrying Enid Elizabeth Roberts from Tiverton in 1938. In 1941, after the school had been evacuated to Cornwall, he joined up at the earliest opportunity as an army chaplain, and quickly won universal respect and affection from officers and men. This was due to his devoting his gifts and natural charm quite simply to the service of all, without the slightest discrimination. Whether it was playing bridge with officers while waiting in England before the Normandy landings—apologetic and apparently surprised when he won, as he usually did—or inviting an NCO up to sit with him and the other officers at a concert; whether it was grinding through dull routines before the invasion, or, in the trenches, repeatedly risking his life in bringing in the dead and ministering to the wounded (in the action in which his conspicuous courage won him the MC); whether he was black with mud and smoke and haggard with the appalling things he had seen, or enjoying a regimental dinner—it was all the same: always, a consistent humanity, free of self-concern, and at the disposal of others.

As soon as the issue of the war was decided, and before demobilization, his gifts were enlisted for finding and training recruits for the ordained ministry in the Church of England. He was among the leading agents of the Church's Advisory Council of Training for the Ministry, engaged in running selection courses in Germany. Here, the theological learning which as an army chaplain he had sedulously concealed became evident in lectures and courses for the ordinands.

After demobilization there followed the unbroken academic career, from the Chaplaincy and Fellowship at St. John's College, Oxford, to the Edward Cadbury Chair at Birmingham (1953-9), where he became also Dean of the Faculty of the Arts and Vice-Principal of the University, then to the Ely Chair (1959-71), and finally to the Regius Chair of Divinity at Cambridge. Honours accrued: honorary doctorates from Edinburgh (1959) and Lund (1965), election as a Fellow of the British Academy (1963) and as an Honorary Fellow of St. John's College, Oxford (1976), Honorary Canonries of Birmingham and Ely. In 1978 the King of Sweden created him a Commander of the Northern Star for his distinguished services in conferences between Anglicans and Scandinavian Lutherans.

All through, the priorities remained the same. His career unfolded itself without ambition or scheming. Each step was taken in simple response to some immediate demand. His publications are equally eloquent of his aims. An early work, *The Seal of the Spirit*, was concerned with a current matter of debate in the councils of the Church closely affecting questions of Anglican relations with other communions. The great lexicon of Patristic Greek is designed to put at the disposal of scholars not Lampe's own theories but the facts of patristic language and thought. The Bampton Lectures, at the end of his life, sum up, in terse and lucid prose, his understanding of the rationale—so far as he could reduce it to reasoned speech—of a lifetime's devotion to God revealed in Jesus Christ. Apart from the massive achievement of the lexicon, he published comparatively little. He did not write much for learned journals, since he was more interested in reaching a wider and less specialized audience. Most of his writing was directed to the elucidation of the theology behind urgent, practical decisions. His time and talents were lavished on teaching and on pulling his weight in university and college administration and in church policy-making. As a chairman of a university board or committee, if he appeared sometimes to cut through complexities in administrative debates by ignoring the niceties of a situation, it was his considered method of dealing with the legalists and nit-pickers and getting on with the important business. He was (as an observer wrote in *Theology*) 'often able with a smile or rueful comment to defuse a grumpy or irritable colleague or to dispose of some too fanciful suggestion without the maker of it feeling put down'. Very little that was of real moment escaped him. At Birmingham, he carried his responsibilities as Dean of the Arts and (for a period, simultaneously) Vice-Principal of the University, if not lightly, at any rate without neglecting scholarship or social life. At Cambridge, while discharging his academic duties fully and faithfully, he generously undertook many duties in his own college, Caius, of which he was a loyal Fellow, and in the University, and, when Ely Professor, also as a residentiary Canon of the Cathedral. In the Cathedral and city of Ely, he and his wife took their social responsibilities seriously. From their hospitable home in the great Norman 'Black Hostelry' light and enjoyment spilt over into the neighbourhood.

In the University, as well as the faculty administration that fell to him and a spell on the General Board of the Faculties, he was for many years a member, and latterly the devoted chairman, of the Board of Extramural Studies. In addition, he was an indefatigable lecturer for that Board. After a full day in the University, he would drive through foul weather to lecture to some small group of non-specialist seekers in a remote corner of the fens. He was a born communicator and he cared about those who would not normally come within range of theological study, or might not count themselves Christians until someone could untangle their confusions. His enthusiasm and excellence as a teacher would transform a handful into a large and still growing audience.

In addition to such local ministries, he was for many years the University constituency's representative in Convocation or, as it became, the General Synod of the Church of England. Much as he detested the boredom or worse of long hours in London witnessing discussions of sometimes merely administrative matters, he established a reputation as a formidable orator, bringing learning and logic to bear on matters of importance that were close to his heart, 'on guard' [as a writer in *Theology* put it] 'at the intersection of theology and practical affairs'. He eloquently championed the cause of intercommunion between churches and of the removal of sexual discrimination. What has been called the greatest single step towards reunion since the war was largely due to his advocacy—the admission of communicants from other denominations to receive Holy Communion in an Anglican church. He was chairman for many years of the Anglican Group for the Ordination of Women to the Historic Ministry of the Church. He took a strong and reasoned line against the recognition of exorcism—not because he denied the need for man's release from the grip of evil, but because he believed that this method was intellectually indefensible and theologically retrograde.

He also found time and energy to devote to the important conferences between Anglicans and Scandinavian Lutherans which met periodically in England or abroad. The Lampes's hospitality when they were hosts became legendary. Equally, they extracted a great deal of enjoyment and amusement from the occasions when they were guests. After the delegates had spent a long evening at a hospitable Scandinavian dinner, Geoffrey was once heard to say that at last he understood what the Psalmist meant when he said 'I am become like a bottle in the smoke' (Ps. 119: 83). But his serious contribution to theological understanding, both by speaking and writing and by intensive listening, was incalculable, and he won respect and friendship from the Lutheran theologians, of which the accolade already alluded to was a symbol.

Lampe had the greatest difficulty in saying 'No', and occasionally this led to the acceptance of two simultaneous commitments at opposite ends of the earth. Graceful apologies and the selection of a suitable friend as deputy would soften the blow for the loser.

As a scholar, Geoffrey Lampe was held in deep respect, not because he produced original theories but because of his massive learning, especially in the patristic field, and the soundness of his judgement. His first substantial book, constituting, in part, his claim to the Oxford BD and DD degrees, for which he was approved in 1953, was *The Seal of the Spirit* (1951). This was a thorough and well-documented investigation into the relation between baptism with water and the reception of the Holy Spirit in Christian initiation in New Testament times and in the sub-apostolic period. It was designed partly to show that it was only after that that 'the long period of confusion and obscurity has begun, in which we still find ourselves groping today' (p. 190). But, as usual with Lampe, it was more than a history of doctrine. Most of all it was designed to show, whatever the importance of the rite of confirmation, that

if we keep in mind the implications of the teaching of the New Testament and the early Church, we shall refuse to accept the doctrine that it is in this rite [confirmation] alone that a man can receive the seal of the Spirit by which he is signed for eternity; we shall not see in it the means by which alone one can be made a full Christian. (p. 322.)

This conclusion, carefully supported by New Testament and patristic learning, was important for the Church of England, because one party, whose most learned spokesman at that time was Dom Gregory Dix of Nashdom Abbey, was insisting on the acceptance of episcopally administered confirmation as an in-dispensable prerequisite to reunion with other Christian com-munions. Anybody who took sides in this debate thereafter ignored Lampe's powerful advocacy to the contrary at his peril. The book was followed by papers or summary statements on the same theme, such as '*Baptisma* in the New Testament' (*Scottish Journal of Theology*, 5, 1952), 'The Place of Confirmation in the Baptismal Mystery' (*Journal of Theological Studies*, NS 6, 1955), and *What is Baptism?* (Mowbray, 1958).

The study of the relation of water-baptism to the reception of the Spirit of God reflects one of Lampe's major doctrinal concerns — the doctrine of the Spirit. Many of his papers and contributions to collective works (such as *The Interpreter's Dictionary of the Bible*) are devoted to the subject, and it is possible to trace a growing conviction that in the conception of God as Spirit there is likely to be found the best hope of expressing today the relations between God, Christ, the world, and ourselves. The fourth-century debates had led to the formulation of this in terms of 'Father, Son, and Spirit' as defined by Greek ontological words—οὐσία, ὑπόστασις, πρόσωπον, and the rest; but Lampe was among those who question whether those terms can still serve. His convictions culminated in the Bampton Lectures for 1976, published in 1977 under the title *God as Spirit*.

The thesis had already been adumbrated in 'The Holy Spirit and the Person of Christ', contributed to a symposium, *Christ, Faith and History* (1972), and after the Bamptons a short sermon followed the same lines in 1978, entitled 'What Future for the Trinity?' posthumously reprinted in *Explorations in Theology*, 8, 1981. His answer to that question, if it was expanded to mean 'What future is there for the traditional, classical *doctrine* of the Trinity?' was 'Not much'. Lampe regarded it as impossible, as long as one used the fourth-century substance-language, to do justice today to the conviction that God, as Creator, operates from within his creation and not by invasion from without, and approaches human beings on a fully personal level. 'Incarnation', in its specialized doctrinal use, distinguishing it from inspiration, consequently fell under the same strictures. If, instead, one worked in terms of God's approach to humankind through inspiration—that is, through the fully personal approach of the divine to the human spirit—one might get somewhere. The Bamptons were concerned to show that the distinctively Christian religious experience, reflected from various angles in the New Testament and known ever since in the Christian Church, could be translated into terms of God as Spirit. The success of the attempt has been variously estimated. Nobody reading the book attentively could fail to see that, if pressed ruthlessly to its logical conclusion, its argument would lead to some kind of unitarianism, since essential to the argument are the interpretation of Jesus as an inspired man (albeit supremely and decisively inspired), and the restating of the resurrection of Jesus in terms of a new experience of the Spirit of God in the light of the life and teaching of Jesus. Correspondingly, it would mean an 'exemplarist' interpretation of how Christ brings new life (though Lampe is at pains to point out that 'mere' is a misleading epithet for exemplarism). Lampe himself knew all this better than anybody; but he had no intention of abandoning the essentials of Christian faith and practice, of which he was a shining and inspiring example. The essay in *Christ, Faith and History* shows a masterly grasp of the history of doctrine and of the issues at stake in this matter. One by one Lampe anticipates the objections to his interpretation and tries to meet them. In most cases he is able to show at least that the orthodox proposals raise formidable problems of their own. It is when he comes to the finality of Christ that he has most difficulty in logically defending his own position. In the end, he can only say that it is inconceivable that Christ should ever be superseded—which seems hardly to follow from the premisses. His statement of his stance in the sermon referred to is this:

I believe we should rethink the use of doctrinal models which led to the formulation of this doctrine [i.e. that of the Trinity]—but not the faith which they are intended to express. If we do substitute unitarianism for trinitarianism it must not be the unitarianism that denies the divinity of Christ. On the contrary, I believe we can assert that God was in Christ, without using the model of 'God the Son'. It must not be a unitarianism which postulates a deistically-conceived God remote from the world, separated from our human hearts and minds; we must acknowledge the present reality of God with us and in us; yet without, I hope, the confusions of the fourth-century theology of the Holy Spirit. We have to preserve and safeguard the reality of Christian experience and faith; but there is room to try to find fresh forms of theological expression for it. (*Explorations*, pp. 36f.)

It would be foolish to underestimate the deep and prolonged reflection behind such statements or (most impressive of all) the personal devotion which inspired Lampe's whole life and work and made him eager to find an acceptable modern statement about it. It may be that even his severest critics will not find it easy to meet his comment on conciliar language about the third 'person' of the Trinity: 'no one has ever ventured to suggest what the difference is between generation and procession' (*Explorations*, p. 36).

Whatever posterity makes of his doctrinal work, the Patristic Lexicon is an impressive monument to his learning and ability. It had been conceived a generation earlier by H. B. Swete, and a beginning had been made under the leadership of Canon H. Moore. Dr Darwell Stone, the first officially appointed editor, had been succeeded by Dr F. L. Cross. Cross, however, who became Lady Margaret Professor at Oxford, was soon engaged on another big project—his *Oxford Dictionary of the Christian Church*—and it was thus that Geoffrey Lampe came on the scene. He had recently come back from war service and had been elected into a Fellowship as Chaplain of St. John's College. It was an inspired choice when he was invited to become editor of the Patristic Lexicon in 1948. With his flair for the practical—and the practicable—he saw at once that the only hope of bringing the project to completion reasonably soon was to enlist more regular paid staff, and he set about raising money by successful appeals to various organizations (including the Academy) as well as to individuals. This enabled him to take on a small but dedicated staff. Miss Graef and Miss Grosvenor had already been recruited. Ultimately, he came to be assisted, for longer or shorter periods, by some dozen scholars. The Bodleian lent a room, Cuddesdon College and Pusey House lent texts, and the work proceeded, thanks to the genial and tactful pressure applied by their master to 'the slaves of the Lampe' as they were affectionately called. They were rewarded by an annual picnic in Bagley Wood, which became famous. Lampe himself amazed his friends by his own capacity to work at high speed and accurately, using even the spare half hour, snatched from a heavy teaching and pastoral routine, to draft some short article. He himself undertook some of the major articles. The Patristic Greek Lexicon was designed to be complementary to Liddell and Scott and Jones, whose declared policy was to omit words, other than those of the New Testament, which were found only in Christian writers. Incidentally, Lampe points out in the preface the anomaly by which L. S. J. had not included the Neoplatonist Synesius simply 'because he ended his career as a Christian bishop'. Ideally, then, the Patristic Lexicon should have taken account of all words, whether of theological importance or not, which belonged—or of which some particular use belonged—only to Christian authors and which mirrored the idiom of such writers. Inevitably, however, the emphasis had to be laid mainly on the theologically significant. The decision of the Delegates of the Oxford University Press to publish the Lexicon was a vote of confidence in Lampe's learning and judgement. It began to appear, a fascicle at a time, and was first published as a whole in 1968, after Lampe had become Ely Professor at Cambridge. The Press excelled itself in the accuracy and excellence of this extremely complicated piece of printing. New critical editions of some of the patristic texts were coming out while the cards were in preparation or even when fascicles were going to press, and nobody knew better than the editor that, had time and money been no consideration, it could have been improved; but the fact that it was completed, and so excellently, despite all the difficulties which, to a less able editor, might have seemed insuperable, is a tribute to his capacity both as a scholar and in personal relations. It is characteristic, too, that this, his largest work, should have been the work of a team, and should have been an indispensable tool for the use of other scholars.

To come from the gigantic to the miniature, one of Lampe's posthumously published essays, obscurely entitled 'The "Limuru Principle" and Church Unity', illustrates exactly the same dedication of massive learning and expert ability to practical purposes. A conference held in Limuru in Kenya had been a landmark in the formation of the South India Church from Anglican, Presbyterian, and Congregationalist components. In his article, Lampe analysed the doctrinal options confronting the uniting communions.

The choice . . . is nothing new. Basically, it is whether we understand episcopal order in terms of a 'pipeline' transmission of the grace of orders, or whether we interpret it as an expression, within the complex variety of the work of the Spirit in the church's life and ministry, of the unity of Christian people in the historic and continuing apostolic mission to the world.

In stating his own belief that non-episcopal ministers were 'ordained by Christ with his ordination' and that the important question was whether they could be brought into communion with the bishop in an episcopally ordered church, he was able to appeal to Augustine who 'could recognize that by abandoning their schism and coming into communion with the Catholic church the Donatist clergy nullified the irregularity of their ordination'. In the same posthumously published collection, there is a hard-hitting and devastatingly clear statement on women and the ministry of priesthood. It shows Lampe's awareness of present circumstances as well as his antiquarian learning. In the last paragraph he meets the objection that alleged theological arguments for the ordination of women are really a smoke-screen to cover the advance of a purely secular liberation movement. On the contrary, he says, there is a much deeper question at stake. There has indeed been a revolution on the economic and social level, but

we should be cautious about using the word 'secular' to describe these changes. They do not come about without God's providence. God speaks to the church through the world as well as to the world through the church, and it is through the interaction of the church with the world that we may, if we listen, hear God's word.

There are other hitherto unpublished papers which deal purely with exegetical questions without direct application to the concerns of the church in the world today. These show how fresh and original his academic acumen was to the end, but they are not so characteristic of his attitude as are his essays in applied theology.

He enjoyed debate, and could be a formidable opponent. At one meeting of the Cambridge Theological Society he listened to a distinguished visitor delivering a frothy and jargonistic paper, and, when it was over, fired a few simple questions across his bows which brought him virtually to a standstill and compelled the chairman to intervene with a rescue operation. At the New Testament Seminar, of which he was a regular member, he used sometimes to indulge in a little dignified slumber while some aspirant to originality unfolded an improbable or impossible thesis, but would wake in time to ask innocently about the exact meaning of a passage in the text under discussion. This usually led to the downfall of the theory and some hasty sweeping of the fragments under the carpet. For his sixty-fifth birthday his friends devised, appropriately, not a Festschrift but a Fest for him and Elizabeth, his wife—two days of festival, including a thanksgiving Eucharist in Great St. Mary's Church, with Geoffrey Lampe himself as celebrant and a close friend, Canon William Purcell, as preacher; a dinner in Clare College; and a colloquium in Westcott House, at which papers bearing on Lampe's theological positions were read and debated. He said afterwards that it seemed to him rather like a prolonged D.Phil. viva at the end of which the candidate was not sure whether he had been approved; but his enjoyment of every moment of it was evident. So was his enjoyment of all friendly contact with persons, whether inside or outside university life, whether academic or social. Here was a scholar wearing his learning and ability lightly, because his priorities were dictated by Christian humaneness.

At the end of his life the courage that had won the MC became evident again. In 1976 extensive cancer was suddenly diagnosed and he underwent drastic surgery followed by exhausting radiotherapy. He and his wife together faced the situation and came through with quiet determination. In an amazingly short time he was back in circulation again, shirking no duties and refusing no social invitations—indeed, living with more verve than ever, perhaps because he knew it was borrowed time. He talked openly about his illness, yet with a dismissive casualness that made it seem a mere incident in an enjoyable life. He celebrated his retirement from the Regius Chair by doing a 72-mile walk along the South Downs Way with his son Nicolas and his daughter Celia; and the next year, he and Elizabeth did one more of the adventurous tours they so much loved, in the Balkans and Greece and Italy. He returned a very sick man, but lived to baptize his second grandson as he had baptized the first, and to plan his daughter's wedding service: it was a close and affectionate family and they planned everything together. He died a month before the wedding took place.

C. F. D. MOULE

Note. The writer is indebted for much of this information to contributions to *G. W. H. Lampe, Christian, Scholar, Churchman—a Memoir by Friends*, ed. C. F. D. Moule (London: Mowbray, 1982), and must express thanks to the publisher for permission to quote a few sentences verbatim.

PLATE XXI

C. A. MACARTNEY

CARLILE AYLMER MACARTNEY[1]

1895–1978

CARLILE AYLMER MACARTNEY was born on 24 January 1895. His father was a barrister, and his family of Northern Irish, and more distant Scottish, origin. His mother's name before marriage was Louisa Gardiner.

Macartney won a scholarship at Winchester, and was in College from 1909 to 1914. He won the school prize for Greek verse and the Kenneth Freeman classics prize, as well as the Goddard Exhibition, the school's award for outstanding classical scholarship. In his last year he held the school office of Prefect of Library. He won an open scholarship at Trinity College, Cambridge, in 1914.

He did not go up to Cambridge in October, as war had meanwhile broken out in Europe. He joined the army as a private. Many years later he used to say that the master in charge of the Officer Training Corps at Winchester had disliked him, and refused to recommend him for an immediate commission; and that he had remained eternally grateful to this man, since he would otherwise almost certainly have been killed. Seven out of fifteen scholars of his year were in fact killed, but Macartney survived. He was commissioned in November 1914, served in the Hampshire Regiment for two years, and was then transferred to Royal Field Artillery in January 1917. He was wounded at Potisje near Ypres in July 1917. After two months in hospital in England, a training course and another period in hospital in Ireland, he returned to France in June 1918 and served in an anti-aircraft battery until the end of hostilities.

After the war he returned to take up his scholarship at Trinity, but did not stay to complete his degree.

[1] In my research for this memoir, I received valuable help from the following persons, to whom I should like to record my gratitude: Mr G. C. W. Dicker, Keeper of Old Wykehamist Records, Winchester College; Miss Alex Ward, Head of Army Historical Branch, Ministry of Defence; Miss Dorothy Hamerton, then Librarian at Chatham House and in charge of its archives; Dr László Péter, of the School of Slavonic and East European Studies in the University of London; and most of all Miss Elizabeth Barker, the historian of wartime British diplomacy in Central Europe, for her unfailingly generous advice and assistance in tracing papers in the Public Record Office, and for her personal memories of C. A. Macartney's activities. To all of these my grateful acknowledgements.

In 1919–20 he spent some time in Central Europe as a journal-ist, and it is from then that his study of the languages, politics, and cultures of that region began. In 1921 he was appointed vice-consul in Vienna, a position which he held for four years. In this period his knowledge of the intricacies of Danubian life deepened, and he became personally acquainted with many of the persons and problems thrown up by the convulsions of the perished Habsburg Monarchy. In 1923 he married Nedella, daughter of Colonel Mamarchev of the Bulgarian army.

After leaving Vienna, he worked for the *Survey of International Affairs*, produced at the new Royal Institute of International Affairs at Chatham House, under the direction of his friend and elder fellow-Wykehamist Arnold Toynbee. Macartney wrote the second volume of the 1925 *Survey*. In 1926 he joined for two years the editorial staff of the *Encyclopaedia Britannica*. In 1928 he moved to the League of Nations Union, and worked in its intelligence department for eight years, partly in Geneva and partly in London, becoming their chief specialist on the national minorities of the new multi-lingual states of Central and Eastern Europe, and indeed an expert in this field unsurpassed in any country of Europe or beyond. During these years his first books appeared: *The Social Revolution in Austria* in 1926; *The Magyars in the Ninth Century* in 1931; *Hungary* (a general history in the 'Modern World' series) in 1934; and *National States and National Minorities* in the same year.

Macartney was eager to obtain an academic appointment, and applied for the Sir Ernest Cassel Chair of International Relations at the London School of Economics. His referees were Gilbert Murray, Arnold Toynbee, and Monty Rendall, and he also had supporting testimonials from Sir James Headlam-Morley, J. L. Garvin, and R. W. Seton-Watson; but his application was unsuccessful. In November 1931 Toynbee recommended him for the Stevenson Chair at LSE, but this too was unsuccessful. The scholar appointed to this chair was C. K. (later Sir Charles) Webster. Macartney's impressive scholarly achievements, how-ever, received recognition with his appointment to a Fellowship at All Souls, in 1936. His association with the college lasted for more than forty years, and was undoubtedly a blessing for him, since it enabled him to study and write in a university setting, without being compelled to do regular teaching or academic administra-tion, for which tasks he was probably not temperamentally suited. He made his home at Boars Hill, within easy reach of All Souls, and could travel to and from London when required. In 1937 he published another major book: *Hungary and Her Successors*.

During the Second World War he was a leading member of the enlarged Research Department of the Foreign Office, directed by Toynbee, located in Oxford, and consisting largely of persons formerly closely associated with Chatham House, together with the small but extremely efficient secretarial infra-structure of that institution. Macartney's task was to supply expert advice to the Foreign Office in connection with Central Europe in general, and Hungary in particular. Possibly more important was his contribution to the Hungarian Section of the BBC Overseas Service. His regular broadcasts, in Hungarian with a strong English accent, were immensely popular in Hungary, where he became known more widely than ever before as Makartni Elemér (the latter Hungarian Christian name being pronounced approximately as his own Christian name of Aylmer). It was a tribute both to his reputation and to a certain surviving liberalism in wartime Hungary that his series of volumes of *Studies in the earliest Hungarian historical sources*, which had begun to appear in Budapest in 1938, could continue in that city despite the state of war between the two countries, parts 4 and 5 being published in 1942 (but with the false date of 1940 printed on them in order to satisfy censorship!). The series was completed by parts 6 and 7 in Oxford in 1951.

After the war Macartney returned to All Souls, and his literary output once more revived. His *Medieval Hungarian Historians* (1953) summarized his conclusions on the seven-part series of 1938–51. In 1957 he published a two-volume work curiously entitled *October Fifteenth*. The title refers to the date of Admiral Horthy's abortive attempt to break away from Hitler in 1944; but the book is a detailed history of internal and foreign policies in Hungary from 1929 to 1944. While working on this book, Macartney held the Montague Burton Chair of International Relations at Edinburgh University, a part-time post whose lecturing duties were not arduous, but permitted him to remain in Oxford and to travel northwards from time to time. A short history, entitled simply *Hungary*, appeared in 1962. In 1968 Macartney published his last major work, *The Habsburg Empire 1790–1918*, a detailed narrative of Austria and Hungary in the nineteenth century and up to the collapse of the Monarchy, with special emphasis on the history of institutions. Having hitherto specialized in the early Middle Ages and the twentieth century, Macartney applied himself in his last years to the Early Modern period. The result was two slighter but valuable works, *Maria Theresa and the House of Austria* (1969) and a collection of well-chosen documents with explanatory notes, *The Habsburg and Hohenzollern Dynasties in the Seventeenth and Eighteenth Centuries* (1970), this latter appearing in his seventy-sixth year.

Macartney was an individual scholar, in the tradition of European learning in the age, long since expired, when scholars sought both to learn and to diffuse the results of their learning, and when universities had not become extensions of state bureaucracy. He was also a participant in international politics, with opinions passionately held and with a sense of duty to exert political influence. This account of his life will therefore have two themes, which cannot be effectively unscrambled from each other: his major historical works and his involvement in the field of international affairs and foreign policy.

His first book, *The Social Revolution in Austria*, was published in 1926. Not quite 300 pages long, it was divided about half-and-half between a summary of Austria's recent history and a discussion of the main social classes, institutions, legislation, and unsolved problems. It began with a short penetrating essay on the Habsburg Monarchy, and then described in much greater detail the period of defeat and attempted revolution, and the emergence of a democratic republic. There followed two chapters on the Social Democratic Party, the conflicting groups within its leadership, the institution and operation of works councils in factories, and socialist achievements in housing in Vienna. Then came a chapter each on the peasants and the Church, on the middle classes, and on the relations between Jews and Germans, in the broader economic and cultural spheres as well as in political life. This book showed Macartney to be a shrewd observer as well as a promising historian, commanding the clear straightforward style, with no words wasted and with no needless erudite obscurities, and the ability to put scenes and incidents vividly before the reader's imagination, which were to mark most of his published works. The book was at the same time a personal statement, with irony and occasional venom. These were, however, rather impartially distributed. Financial speculators, left socialist demagogues, anti-socialist Roman Catholic priests, and Galician Jewish immigrants might each in turn resent some of his judgements.

His next book, *The Magyars in the Ninth Century*, published in 1930, was a study of a little explored corner of early medieval history. Using Byzantine and Latin sources, as well as passages translated for him from Arabic and Persian authors, besides secondary works by German and Hungarian historians, he endeavoured to distinguish from each other the Magyars and the other peoples of the steppe—Cumans, Kavars, Petchenegs, and many others—of whom very little was known, and to reach conclusions about the origins of the ninth-century invaders of Central Europe who founded the Hungarian state. In 1934 came *Hungary*, a volume in Ernest Benn's Modern World series edited by H. A. L. Fisher. It followed approximately the pattern of his Austria book, with about two-fifths devoted to history and the rest to analysis of the Constitution, the Church, the main social classes and the problems of foreign policy. The differences between aristocratic magnates and gentry, and the role played by the latter in political leadership and in administration, were clearly explained. So also were the problems of the peasantry, which comprised landless labourers on vast estates, dwarf holders with too little land, and prosperous farmers found chiefly in the west and south-west. The inadequacy of such land reform legislation as had occurred was also made abundantly clear. The position of Jews in business was another important theme: Hungarian Jews emerged in a more favourable light than had Austrian Jews in the earlier book. A fault of the book was the very small space devoted to education and to the role of the intellectual, as opposed to the business, section of the middle class, whether Jewish or Magyar.

It is convenient to mention at this point Macartney's later works in the history of Hungary, an important part of European history and one in which he attained high standards of scholarship, but a field of study of less widespread interest than his publications, from the 1930s on, in international politics.

Outstanding was his series of 'Studies in the earliest Hungarian historical sources', of which eight successive parts appeared between 1938 and 1952. The first five were published in Budapest, the last in Oxford. In this obscure and specialized field there was and is certainly no one in Britain, and few if any in Hungary capable of a critical judgement of Macartney's work, which remained an object of admiration mingled with awe. His last book on a Hungarian theme was a short comprehensive history of that country, published in 1962 and bearing the same simple title as his 1934 book, *Hungary*, with which it should not be confused.

His fourth book, *National States and National Minorities*, of 1934, was a major work of scholarship, the most original, and possibly in the long term the most valuable, of all his writings. It was a result both of very wide historical reading and of experience of the activities of the League of Nations in Geneva and of its most influential champions in England. He traced the emergence of the concept of nationality from medieval western Christendom; the intricate pattern of conquests, and coexistence of successive dominant and subject peoples, in Central and Eastern Europe; and the concepts of individual nationality within a multi-national empire, as they were embodied in the *millet* system of the Ottoman Empire, or discussed by political thinkers in Austria-Hungary. He then examined the nationalist movements that grew in the Danube basin and the Balkan peninsula in the nineteenth century and up to 1914; the adoption by the Allies of the aim of national self-determination in the Great War; and the redrawing of frontiers and creation of new states which followed the war. Almost half the book was devoted to a detailed analysis of the purposes and the operation of the Minority Treaties, placed under the supervision of the League, which nine states were obliged to sign. His conclusions were pessimistic. Where a community which shared a national consciousness was broken by a frontier (and he recognized that this was sometimes unavoidable), a nationally conscious group was torn away from its community and placed in a state where another nationally conscious community was dominant. (This situation was different from one in which a whole nationally conscious community was placed under the rule of another, though writers on nationalism often confused, and still confuse the two.) Macartney's conclusion was that 'a national state and national minorities are incompatibles'.

As Macartney saw it, there were three possible solutions to the problem. One was to change the frontiers so that they should greatly reduce the numbers left on the 'wrong sides'. This remedy, which became generally known as Revisionism, had severe limitations, and was not applicable at all to certain regions. The second was an exchange of populations. This was in fact adopted in several cases, the most important being between Greece and Turkey, where tremendous hardships were caused, but the two governments, recently at war with each other, made concerted efforts to mitigate them. Both these solutions were discussed at length in Macartney's book, but he himself preferred a third, which was to replace nationality as the basis of legitimacy of government by some higher principle. Essentially, he believed that the problems of national minorities could only be solved by the abolition of national states. He quoted with approval Lord Acton's condemnation of modern nationalism: 'A state which is incompetent to satisfy different races condemns itself; a state which labours to neutralise, to absorb or to expel them, destroys its own vitality; a state which does not include them is destitute of the chief basis of self-government.' Looking at the world of 1934, he could not see examples which offered much immediate help or hope to victims of national discrimination in Central Europe. The two cases which came nearest to this were the Soviet Union and the United Kingdom. In the first case, while lacking enthusiasm for the Bolshevik form of government, he nevertheless took seriously the claim of the Soviet authorities to have introduced genuinely equal treatment of all nationalities. In the second case, as a result of a long history, it had become true of Britain that 'the state can fairly be said to be equally the state of all nationalities inhabiting it'. But as Macartney would not have wished to see a re-enactment of the Bolshevik Revolution in the Danube valley, and it was useless to advise the Danubians to repeat six hundred years of British history, there was little comfort to be derived from either example.

In the next years Macartney concentrated on the Hungarian minorities, and in 1937 published *Hungary and Her Successors*. This book, like its predecessor exceeding 500 pages, examined in detail the status of the Hungarian minorities in lands which had been ceded by the peace treaties to Austria, Czechoslovakia, Romania, and Yugoslavia. In stating his conclusions he had in mind the situation at the time of the collapse of the old Hungary and the situation as it was in the mid-1930s. At the time of writing it was clear to him that Hungarians both in the residual Hungarian state and in the minority areas of neighbouring states bitterly resented the situation created by the peace treaties, and that this resentment was by no means confined, as opponents of Hungary especially in Czechoslovakia liked to argue, to the landowning upper class. It was equally clear to him that the non-Hungarian nations which had formerly lived under Hungary had no desire to be reunited with Hungary: in his view this had been true of Romanians and Serbs already in 1918 but only partially of Slovaks, but in 1937 was equally true of all three. He therefore rejected the 'maximum' revision advocated by nationalists in Budapest—that is, the restoration of the old frontiers. He did, however, favour a 'minimum' revision, which he specified in detail. He believed that it would be not only an act of justice to the Hungarians but a measure beneficial to the peace of Europe if Hungary were to recover from Czechoslovakia the Grosser Schütt island between the two branches of the Danube east of Bratislava, and some portion of the plain north of the Danube; and from Romania the plains lying west of the Bihar mountains. The second of these changes would restore 400,000 Hungarians to Hungary while placing only 40,000 Romanians under Hungarian rule. Apart from this he believed that Ruthenia, formerly the north-eastern corner of Hungary and now the eastern province of Czechoslovakia, should be restored to Hungary. The Ruthenes were not Czechs or Hungarians, and would be a minority in either state. Their national identity was by no means clear (Ukrainian, or Russian, or a distinct Ruthene people), but in Macartney's view their economic situation would improve if they were included in Hungary. Macartney was thus advocating adoption, within limits, of the first of the three solutions which he had set forth in his earlier book. He remained, however, convinced that the third solution was still the best. He reiterated his opinion that in Central Europe the 'national state' (Hungarian from 1867 to 1918, the three Successor States since 1918) had proved a failure. He still held out as an ideal the state which stands above nationalism, and offers equal respect to all cultural communities existing within it. He believed that ultimately the best candidate for such a state would have been a reconstituted Hungary. His reasons were that the Hungarian state before 1918 formed, within its natural frontiers, an admirable geographical and economic unit, and that there was an earlier Hungarian tradition, long antedating the age of nationalism, which fitted Lord Acton's criteria. It was summed up in the advice given to his son by St. Stephen, the pagan chief who became the first crowned Christian king of Hungary and was later canonized by Rome: *Regnum unius linguae uniusque moris imbecille et fragile est.*

A year after the appearance of the book, the Munich surrender brought about the mutilation of Czechoslovakia, in consequence of which Hungary regained from Slovakia substantially more territory than Macartney had proposed, but did not acquire Ruthenia. The latter was given far-reaching autonomy within the rump republic, and was designed by Hitler to be a centre for Ukrainian nationalist activities directed against the Soviet Union and Poland. While the new Czechoslovak–Hungarian frontier was still being negotiated, Macartney published, on 26 October 1938, in *The Times* a 2,500-word article, in which he set forth in precise and unemotional language the Hungarian case. Essentially the article was a concentrated summary of the facts and arguments of his book; but it was remarkable for almost totally ignoring the international situation which had made revision of frontiers possible. Its opening paragraph contained the following words:

This is one of the rare occasions on which it may prove possible to get a settlement founded on acknowledged principles of justice; to prove that revision need not necessarily strike a blow at peace, but may lay the foundations for a more enduring order. For in so far as a settlement affording honourable satisfaction to both parties can now be reached, a new era of cooperation in the Danube valley may open.

This extraordinary complacency infuriated those who felt that the destruction of the old democratic Czechoslovakia was in itself a tragedy, and still more that Hitler's diplomatic success had created a solid base of German domination in Central Europe from which it would be able to threaten the rest of the continent and the world. Among these was Macartney's older colleague R. W. Seton-Watson, who in previous years had greatly admired Macartney's work, and encouraged and tried to help his career. A painful exchange of letters took place between them, after which their relations, though outwardly correct, remained irreparably strained.

Five months later came the complete dismemberment of rump Czechoslovakia, and this time Hungary, without the approval of Hitler, forcibly annexed Ruthenia. This won Macartney's approval, for the reasons stated in his earlier writings, and also because it put an end to the Ukrainian schemes. As Hungary had acted against German wishes in this case, though in accordance with them after Munich, it showed, he believed, that her rulers placed Hungarian interests first, and had not become vassals of Hitler.

At the outbreak of war in September 1939 Macartney joined the Research Department of the Foreign Office located in Oxford. In November 1939 the British Minister in Hungary, Mr (later Sir) Owen O'Malley requested that Macartney should come to Hungary. The Foreign Office, and Arnold Toynbee as his immediate chief, agreed to this, and he spent February and March 1940 there. He met a great number of Hungarians, including his old friend Count Paul Teleki, a distinguished academic geographer as well as an elder statesman, who had become Prime Minister for the second time in February 1939. Macartney's findings were summarized in a long memorandum forwarded by O'Malley to the Foreign Office on 29 March 1940. Teleki and the Regent, Admiral Horthy, were essentially pro-Western. Teleki had preserved a considerable measure of political liberty, making Hungary an oasis in the Danubian fascist desert. This was recognized by Hungarian Jews and socialists, who knew that they could only lose by any further changes. However, the ability of Hitler to promise more gains of territory, at the expense of Romania and Yugoslavia, which Britain could not do, made it difficult for any Hungarian government to resist German pressures.

The Vienna Award of 30 July 1940, dictated by Ribbentrop and Ciano to the governments of Hungary and Romania, divided Transylvania between the two, leaving hundreds of thousands of each nation on the 'wrong' side of the line, but representing very large gains for Hungary. It was discussed in a memorandum by Macartney for the Foreign Office of 9 September 1940. His recommendation for policy was that Britain should remain uncommitted to either the Romanian or the Hungarian side. 'Keep the carrot dangling . . . Do nothing irrevocable.' He outlined various possible future settlements: an independent Principality of Transylvania; a restoration of the Trianon frontier; cession to Hungary only of the western plainland region; either of two earlier official Hungarian proposals which differed from the Vienna Award; a treaty compelling the Romanian government to grant the Hungarians autonomy within a united Transylvania; a transfer of populations; or the retention of the existing partition. The first, though attractive, he considered irrealizable; the second unjust; population exchange so brutal and so expensive as to be unacceptable; promises of autonomy worthless; and the various Hungarian proposals of the past open to serious objections. Paradoxically, he ended up moderately in favour of what the Axis dictators had imposed: the present line '. . . not entirely to be sneered at as an attempt to secure a not very inequitable ethnographic line . . . may well be regarded as impermanent, but so must any solution'.

In April 1941 German pressure, and the strongly pro-German command of the Hungarian army, brought Hungary into the war against Britain's ally Yugoslavia, and this was rewarded by annexation of territory from that country. Unable either to consent to this policy or to prevent it, Count Teleki shot himself. On 27 June Hungary went to war with the Soviet Union. The rulers of the now much enlarged Hungary showed little sign of following the advice of St. Stephen or of Lord Acton. They displayed a national intolerance towards their new non-Hungarian subjects not less than that of the Succession States between the wars. In January 1942 reprisals against Yugoslav partisan activities culminated in a massacre in Novi Sad (Újvidek), the main city of the annexed region of Yugoslavia, on the Danube, in which it was estimated that some 2,250 Serbs and 700 Jews lost their lives.

Nevertheless pro-British and democratic forces not only existed, but were tolerated by the government to a much greater extent than anywhere in Europe outside neutral Sweden and Switzerland. Liberal and socialist ideas could be expressed in print, and part of the press supported the concept of an Independence Front—which in the circumstances could only mean united action by opponents of the Third Reich. Miklos Kállay, who became Prime Minister in March 1942, was himself bitterly anti-German, protected the democratic elements, and sought for an opportunity to withdraw from the war against Russia. His emissaries established contact with the British authorities during the summer of 1943. The surrender of Italy aroused hopes that the Allies would be able to move into Yugoslavia from Italy, in which case he would have brought Hungary over to their side. However, the inability of the Allies to occupy more than southern Italy, and the fate meted out by a vengeful Mussolini and his German patrons to those Italians, including his own son-in-law, who had abandoned him, destroyed such hopes. In March 1944 German forces occupied Hungary, and forced Horthy to accept a puppet government, recruited from reliably Germanophile politicians of the upper and middle classes, which provided further support to the war effort against Russia and obligingly sent hundreds of thousands of Hungarian Jews to their deaths in the German extermination camps. In October 1944 Regent Horthy made a last attempt to break loose from Germany, ill planned and quickly crushed. Hungary was placed under the joint rule of German forces and of a semi-criminal rabble of Hungarian fascists, and became the main battleground between the southern forces of the German and Russian armies. At the end of the fighting Budapest was in ruins, the economy collapsed, and the people at the mercy of Russian soldiers encouraged by their commanders to wreak vengeance for the sufferings of Russia on any one who fell into their hands.

During these two years Macartney continued to produce learned comments on the Hungarian situation, with diminishing effect. He must have been generally informed at the time of Kállay's peace efforts, but took no part in the negotiations and contacts, which were handled through the channels of the Special Operations Executive under the direction of the Foreign Office, in consultation with the United States and Soviet governments. As the victory of the Allies approached, Macartney hoped that Britain would use its influence to secure a settlement in Central Europe that would be just to all peoples concerned. In particular, since both Romania and Hungary had been allies of Hitler, he hoped that the Transylvanian problem would be considered without prejudice either way. It is arguable that his influence may have contributed to the use, in the terms of armistice given by the

Allies to Romania in September 1944, of the qualified formula that Romania would be given 'Transylvania, or the greater part of it, subject to confirmation at the peace settlement'. In practice, it was the Soviet government alone which decided the frontier, and Stalin preferred simply to restore to Romania what she had had before, while keeping for himself the eastern half of Moldavia, or Bessarabia. At the peace conference with the lesser enemy states, held in Paris in the summer of 1946, neither the British nor the American government raised any objection.

Macartney's six years as a government specialist on Central European affairs may thus be said to have achieved nothing, even if he did provide much well-digested information. More important were his broadcasts, which were widely listened to, highly popular, and maintained or increased the sympathy for Britain felt by many Hungarians. They were, however, an object of fierce attack by the Czechoslovak exiles. A feature of this quarrel was the hostility between Macartney and the exiled Count Michael Károlyi, the ill-fated radical Prime Minister of 1918–19, who was excluded from the BBC broadcasts, essentially on the ground that his memory and his name were anathema to the effective political class in Hungary. Károlyi's claim to be heard was espoused by the Czechs, and this further strengthened Macartney's objection to him. The inability of these two men to do each other justice, Károlyi a somewhat quixotic aristocrat with a noble record of struggle on behalf of social reform and political liberty, Macartney a devoted friend of Hungary with deep understanding of its social and political issues, must be a source of some surprise and great regret to an observer of modern Hungary.

Macartney's broadcasts, however, also raised a serious question on which there was genuine disagreement among British officials concerned with Hungary. One view was that by maintaining indirect communication with the rulers and the wider political class of Hungary, by showing understanding for these men's difficulties while firmly insisting that the alliance with Germany would prove, and was already proving, disastrous for Hungary and should be abandoned, the broadcasts were encouraging those who were trying to minimize Hungary's military effort in Russia, and who were trying not without success to preserve liberal decencies in Hungarian political life. Thus, it could be claimed, the broadcasts were promoting Allied interests. The opposite view was that, admirably intentioned though they were, the broadcasts were encouraging Horthy, Kállay, and their friends to believe that they could go on fighting the Soviet Union without incurring any real displeasure from the Western powers. It was not denied that Macartney emphasized the solidity of the Western–Soviet alliance and urged the Hungarians to break with Hitler. But the mildness of his tone, their personal knowledge of his affection for Hungary and of the sort of Hungarians who were his friends, and the fact that the British government used him as its spokesman, caused them to ignore his warnings and to believe that they could get away with a policy of fighting against one ally and seeking the protection of the others. The broadcasts were thus, it was argued, more harmful than beneficial to Allied interests.

In August 1943 Macartney's broadcasts were stopped. It seems likely that this was due rather to the prevalence of the second over the first of these two British views than to successful intrigues by Czechs. Macartney, however, was deeply hurt by the decision, which he remembered with bitterness in later years.

After the war Macartney returned to the calm of All Souls and Boars Hill, and took up again his literary labours. The last thirty years of his life produced two major works and several others of lesser but substantial value.

The first was *October Fifteenth*, published in two volumes in 1957 by Edinburgh University Press, at a time when Macartney held his part-time chair there. The title is taken, as already noted above, from the date in 1944 when Regent Horthy made his unsuccessful attempt to break away from Germany, and was instead arrested and deported by his former allies, being rescued from comfortable incarceration in a German castle by the liberating American army. It is an extremely detailed exposé of Hungarian history between 1929 and 1945. It is based on his own experience, spread over more than thirty years, on conversations with leading persons (including visits to both Horthy and Kállay in their immediate post-war captivity), on massive study of the Hungarian press, on such official documents as had been published or were available up to the time of writing, and on more interesting documents given to him by various Hungarians who had been able to acquire them, as well as on private diaries and on published memoir literature. The rather large portion devoted to foreign policy partly duplicates what has been done by others, and may be faulted in detail as greater quantities of official documents are studied by historians. But the narrative of internal politics, and the presentation of the personalities and motives of all the prominent, and many less prominent, figures is of incomparable value. Individuals come to life in these pages as they are portrayed by an author who combines insight into character with remarkable literary skill. No other writer, Hungarian or foreign, has done this job, or is or ever will be in a position to do it. It is safe to say that this book will be a source of knowledge for all who may ever wish to study this particular place and period in history. It is also arguable that any one who gives himself time to peruse attentively these 1,000 pages (an enjoyable but protracted experience) will emerge with a better understanding of the tragic predicament of small nations and of persons charged with small bits of power and responsibility in mid-twentieth-century Europe, and indeed of the human political condition *tout court*.

The other major work was a history of Austria-Hungary from the death of Joseph II to the abdication of Charles, entitled *The Habsburg Empire 1790–1918*, published in 1968 and running to nearly 900 pages. The emphasis is on constitutional developments, and these are viewed mainly from the centre, which means Vienna rather than Budapest, let alone the lesser centres such as Prague or Lemberg. Even Hungary, of which he knew so much, recedes into the background, and his interest returns to Austria, where his concern with Central Europe had begun nearly fifty years earlier. Habsburg rulers and their bureaucrats are the leading figures, and Macartney shows in his handling of them the empathy and the clarity of expression that mark so much of his work. His grasp extends to the intricacies of the financial bureaucracy, which do not make easy reading, and he reveals thorough knowledge of peasant problems and of their interconnection with national conflicts. In the Preface he expresses mild disdain for the 'tribal histories' produced in profusion in recent years by members of the lesser 'nationalities': one sees what he means, but this is to do less than justice to a good deal of valuable scholarship that has seen the light in neighbouring states, despite difficult intellectual conditions. Macartney's distaste for nationalism as legitimacy was unabated, but he was no longer concerned to find a new legitimacy: this book was devoted only to the past.

The statement of the late Professor Pribram, quoted in this Preface, that a historian of the Monarchy needed fourteen languages, was exaggerated: half that number from within its borders, plus French and very marginally Russian, would suffice, and of these Macartney had sufficient command. The difficulty of the subject is only partly linguistic. It is rather that the essence of this empire's history is that it produced a culture, with its own unity, to which all the arts, literature, physical and human landscapes, and a way of life contributed, but which was more than any of these. Literature can more easily be treated in words than the other aspects. There was such a thing as 'Austrian' literature, if we may use that adjective to cover the whole *Kulturraum* (no English equivalent). However, this 'Austrian' literature is marvellously elusive. Most of the best of it was expressed in one language—German—yet much that was essential remained embedded in other languages from which it could not be fully extracted. At the same time the fact that German was the language of a wider great literature in no way permeated by an 'Austrian' spirit made any clear demarcation impossible. Macartney in his Preface stated that he felt compelled to leave out 'all *Kulturgeschichte* proper, as distinct from literary etc. activities which had their importance for the development of national movements'. This is a perfectly reasonable decision, but it does mean that the innermost essence of the subject is missing. But could any mortal grasp that essence? No one yet, certainly in English, and probably in any other language, has better described the anatomy of the many-limbed and many-headed creature than Macartney, and it seems unlikely that any one will do a better job for some time yet.

Macartney was elected a Fellow of the British Academy in 1965. He was also made a Corresponding Member of the Austrian, and was awarded the Grand Decoration of Honour, with gold, of Austria in 1974. He revisited Hungary several times after the war, the first being in 1945 and the last at a historical colloquium in Budapest in 1971. He was elected a Corresponding Member of the Hungarian Academy in 1947, but two years later, at the height of the Stalinist terror under Mátyás Rákosi, his membership was terminated. Though Hungarian historians working under the communist regime held him in high regard, and he had good personal relations with them, they were not able to obtain a reversal of this insulting and unjust action, doubtless imposed on the Academy by the party leadership; and this was a source of lasting bitterness to him. He also made one lecture tour in the United States, and was elected a Freeman of the City of Cleveland (Ohio), the centre of the largest population of Americans of Hungarian descent.

Mention must be made in conclusion of his activities on behalf of Hungarian exiles in Britain. He was one of a small group of British academics who visited Austria immediately after the Hungarian Revolution of October 1956 to see what could be done for students from Hungarian universities who had escaped from the Soviet invasion. He took a personal interest in those who came to Britain and were enabled to continue their studies in this country. He was also a founder, and for many years President, of the Anglo-Hungarian Fellowship, which held regular meetings in the hospitality of the Polish Hearth in South Kensington, at which lectures were given and problems discussed which interested cultured Hungarians uprooted from their homeland.

In Macartney's lifetime two world wars started in Central Europe; not only did crises in that region trigger off two human catastrophes, but among the deeper causes of both disasters were forces at work in those lands, which were little understood in the north and west of Europe at the beginning of this century, though they became more familiar as they spread to Russia, the Muslim lands, and the whole world beyond Europe and North America.

The tragedy of twentieth-century Central Europe had its social, national, constitutional, and international aspects. All four strikingly foreshadow developments in Asia and Africa in the mid-century.

The social scene was marked by the antagonism, sometimes latent and sometimes brutally evident, between pre-industrial upper classes, with privileges and mentalities that had disappeared in most of northern and western Europe, and a peasantry with too little land and primitive methods of agriculture, growing poorer as its numbers increased and its needs were neglected by rulers overwhelmingly interested in cities and industry. That part of the peasantry which became uprooted from the village and swelled the population of the new urban agglomerations, added to the confusion and the unrest.

In multi-lingual and multi-confessional Central Europe social discontents became inseparable from national. From subcultures based on minority languages emerged educated élites no longer willing to be treated as members of second-class communities, ruled by persons who considered themselves to belong to the only, official, nation in the state. Mere cultural diversity was slowly transformed into national consciousness; leaders appeared who claimed that their peoples too were nations, and as such demanded their own sovereign states; and more and more members of these peoples followed their lead.

Increasingly, the old political legitimacy was undermined, and the attempts to replace it had small success. The political challengers of the old order spoke of democracy, but whether that was a suitable word to describe what they got, is rather doubtful. Democratic constitutions were duly enacted, but old methods of government remained. Majority rule was exploited by demagogues, or obstructed by officials, or both processes occurred together. Universal suffrage, distorted in this way, could not so much liberate the peoples as offer the masses to the demagogues as a bludgeon with which to beat their rivals; and after years of confusion new tyrants emerged.

Each new state was nominally sovereign, but each was constrained not only by unsettled frontier disputes with small neighbours but also by the rivalries of neighbouring Great Powers. The relationship between small and large states was not simple. The big bullied the small when they had the chance, but the small used the big for their own ends too.

Macartney was well aware of all four sets of problems. His first book gave precedence to the social factor. The policies and leadership of the Austrian social democrats gave him grounds for cautious optimism—which the tragic events of the mid-1930s proved wrong. He also well understood the yawning social gulf in Hungary between great landowners and landless workers or dwarf holders. He was never—as his critics at times portrayed him—indifferent to the need for a land reform; but he did not see why the fact that Romania and Czechoslovakia had carried out land reforms should in itself justify their retention of lands inhabited by Hungarians.

As the years passed, he gave greater attention to the problems of nationalism, which in fact assumed first place in the politics of the 1930s. He continued to regard nationalism as a bad basis of legitimacy for a state. He would always have preferred to see forms of government based on some higher principle, under which citizens would have had freedom to develop their own national cultures. But no such state appeared in Central Europe after the collapse of the Habsburg Monarchy, and the Habsburg Monarchy had not been such a state.

He preferred democracy, at least in the sense in which that word was habitually used in the West in his lifetime, to dictatorial forms of government, but he was sceptical of its prospects in Central Europe. Hungary's government in the 1920s was a kind of Whiggish constitutionalism, with a parliament comparable to the British before 1832, and with a large measure of civil liberties, at least for city dwellers. Yugoslavia's attempts at democracy broke down by 1929. The agony of Romanian democracy was more protracted, but it was never a very healthy organism. Czechoslovakia came much nearer to a Western democratic model, and Macartney gave it credit for this, yet remained sceptical of a state in which the dominant nation formed less than half the population. As for Hungary, in the 1930s the old oligarchic landowning élite lost a great deal of its power, and some democratization certainly occurred, in the sense of drawing much wider social forces into political life, but this did not make for more of the Western type of democracy. Macartney's scepticism was increased, but it is a fair criticism of him that he modified it in the case of Hungary by giving it the benefit of more doubts than he was willing to concede elsewhere.

Preoccupied as he became with the need to repair injustices done to national minorities by the Versailles peace settlement, Macartney saw the growing rift between the Western and Central Great Powers in Europe as a struggle between Have-Nots and Haves. He saw that Hungarian revisionism inevitably received more support from Mussolini and Hitler than from French or British leaders; but the fact that Hungary drifted towards a status of satellite of the Axis did not diminish his sympathy for the Hungarian cause, either before or after a state of war existed between Britain and Germany. He would not admit that, since the Third Reich represented a threat to all civilized values, any person or government which followed its lead was thereby betraying humanity.

Many years later he made to the present writer, in the most friendly manner, the comment that R. W. Seton-Watson's mistake had been to think that if the national discontents which beset the Habsburg Monarchy could be removed by national self-determination Central Europe would have a happy future; and that Seton-Watson's son had made an essentially analogous mistake in thinking that if the social oppressions and discontents of the same region in the 1930s could be removed by socialism, there could be a happy future. He was right in both cases, but he could not himself produce a better cure. The Hungary whose wrongs he tried to right proved as fiercely nationalist in its aims and its practice as the Successor States had been to their Hungarian subjects. The peace settlement of 1918-20, inspired by Wilsonian principles of self-determination, was followed not by a community of free peoples but by a *Kleinstaaterei* of mutually hostile neighbours. The revolution of 1917-21 in Russia, made in the name of socialism, created not a brotherhood of workers' republics, but a totalitarian empire that crushed all national cultures, including the Russian, even if it used Russians to that end; and its extension to the Danubian lands artificially froze some national antagonisms and exacerbated others. Restoration of the old super-national or pre-national legitimacies of monarchy or of the universal church might be greatly preferable, but their chances seemed negligible.

The twentieth century appeared stuck with the facts of nationalism, in Europe and further afield. The disintegration of the overseas colonial empires reinforced this conclusion. Indeed their fate placed the fate of Austria-Hungary and its Succession States in a different perspective: how far Macartney was aware of this is not clear from his writings. As for the remaining land-based colonial empire, from the Elbe to Kamchatka, no doubt in time it would be one with Nineveh and Tyre, but the time-scale was not predictable.

No way was visible in Macartney's lifetime of preventing the national consciousness which arises from economic and cultural development from turning into political nationalism. Economic prosperity and social transformations could, and sometimes did, make nationalism milder, but they did not seem able to cure the illness, or to prevent recurrent outbreaks. The *Kleinstaaterei* of the Danube basin between the world wars was repeated, with strikingly similar ugly features, by the *Kleinstaaterei* in other continents which followed the Second World War. Yet if a proliferation of small sovereignties was dangerous, attempts to suppress them, and attempts within multi-national states to suppress national cultures or to deny national consciousness, proved no less dangerous. The lessons of Austria-Hungary and of the Successor States were clear, but they were not being learnt.

There was one important problem of these decades in Central Europe, of which Macartney was well aware, which deserves a few more words—the Jewish problem.

Jews and Magyars in the nineteenth and twentieth centuries were interwoven in a web of love–hate relationships which cannot easily be unravelled. When in the first decades of the nineteenth century Jews began to pour into Hungary from the formerly Polish territories which had been annexed by Russia and Austria, they encountered the same grass-roots hostility which had characterized all pre-modern Christian societies. However, the dominant land-owning classes soon found that Jews could be useful to them in the task which they set themselves of transforming Hungary into a strong modern national state. Jews revealed talents for industrial entrepreneurship, and for the modern intellectual professions, which Magyar gentry-folk lacked, and did not particularly wish to acquire. As these skills were clearly useful to a modern state, the Hungarian political élite encouraged Jews to develop them, and made their task easier for them. This was especially true after 1867, when Hungarian governments acquired, under the Habsburg Crown, almost complete internal sovereignty. For their part Jews eagerly embraced the Magyar language, became Magyar patriots—even to the extent of espousing and promoting the official policy of pressing Slovaks, Romanians, and others to turn themselves into Magyars—and increasingly inter-married with Magyars and sought assimilation. The flourishing new urban economy and literary–scientific culture of Hungary at the turn of the century was thus largely the product of an unusually fruitful synthesis, within the growing educated élite, of Magyar and Jew. Meanwhile at the lower levels of the Hungarian social pyramid latent hostility to Jews remained.

In politics Hungarian Jews tended to be liberals or socialists. This did not worry the Magyar rulers. Most of them subscribed to some sort of liberalism, and they were not much worried by socialism among industrial workers. The two forces in which they did see potential danger were nationalism among the non-Magyars and agrarian revolt among dwarf-holder peasants and agricultural labourers. Hungarian Jews had virtually no contact with, or sympathy for, either of these forces.

Things changed dramatically in 1919. Socialism, especially its left wing, communism, briefly triumphed when defeat in war overthrew the old regime in Hungary, and many of the socialist and communist leaders were Jews. Overthrow of the communist regime brought a wave of anti-semitism in Hungary. Although the re-establishment of an orderly oligarchical form of government, with elements of liberalism, under Count Stephen Bethlen in the 1920s, brought improvements, the old honeymoon period between Magyars and Jews was past. In the 1930s new motives for anti-semitism arose with the world economic depression: aspirants for jobs in business and the professions, and persons thrown out of such jobs, saw the Jews, who were numerous in those fields, as rivals or exploiters. As the hold of the old oligarchy relaxed, and middle-class or even plebeian elements were drawn into political life, pressure for restrictions on Jews grew. It reached its climax when the Sztojay government of March 1944—a government, it must be noted, not of wild fascist fanatics but of highly respectable middle-class politicians—sent hundreds of thousands of Jews to Hitler's extermination camps. The destruction of most Hungarian Jews (those of Budapest were spared deportation), was not the work of the old reactionary oligarchy, but was a result of the relative democratization of the 1930s.

These processes Macartney closely observed and understood. He knew that the social and cultural forces involved were too complex for simple denunciation. He avoided the usual pejorative adjectives of both left and right, but he sometimes spoke and wrote bitingly about Hungarian Jews, as well as about Hungarian Christians, and his expressions in matters in which he felt emotionally involved were not always judicious; but though perhaps it is true that on the whole he disliked Jews, it is not fair to call him, as he sometimes was called, an anti-Semite, and absurd to call him a fascist. This was recognized by the Israeli organizers of a conference held in Haifa in April 1972, on the tragically sensitive subject of relations between Jews and their host peoples in Eastern Europe in modern times, who invited Macartney to read a paper on Hungary. Both in his formal presentation and in informal discussions his sincerity and straightforwardness impressed conference participants.

Macartney had a rather retiring nature, was at times truculent, and could bear grudges for a long time. His career did not follow the normal academic *cursus honorum*, but intellectual excellence was something which he admired in others and which he himself attained. Neither the bland pieties of the academic world, to which the words 'liberal values' were conventionally, though often misleadingly, attached, nor the bureaucratic mechanisms of the institutions which are still called universities because no more suitable name has yet been found for them, held much attraction for him. Yet he was in a broad sense a teacher, and exercised influence not only through his books, and the many lectures which he gave both to academic and to wider audiences, but also through the help and advice which he generously provided for individuals who sought it.

His basic opinions, in so far as one can judge in so reticent a person, were far from the public ethos of the 1970s. An important part of his code was loyalty to friends, and this he unhesitatingly extended to those, in Hungary or elsewhere, who fell victim to political catastrophe, including those who might be said to have brought their fate upon themselves. One example is an old friend from Macartney's Vienna days in the 1920s, General Hindy, who in January–February 1945 was the joint commander, with the Germans, of the garrison of Budapest when besieged by the Soviet Army. By holding out to the bitter end Hindy could be said to have caused the destruction of most of the capital and the loss of many thousands not only of Russian military but of Hungarian civilian lives. Taken prisoner by the Russians, he was tried as a war criminal and executed. Macartney dedicated his book *October Fifteenth* 'to the honoured memory of Iván Hindy, General,

† August 26th 1946'. The rights and wrongs of that particular case must be left to future historians, or to a higher authority still, but Macartney's gesture shows the man. *Victrix causa deis placuit, sed victa Catoni.*

Popularity of person or opinions, intellectual fashions, and the polished image did not stand high on his scale of priorities, but he valued honest praise and resented its absence. These aspects of his character no doubt have various origins, all unknown to the present writer; but it is perhaps not fanciful to attribute them in part to that peculiar combination of humility and arrogance, of respect for the truth and for those who seek it with contempt for all kinds of self-advertisement, which formed the Wykehamical ethos of his day. He will often, as a schoolboy, have heard the words: 'grant that we, whose lot is cast in so goodly a heritage, may strive together the more abundantly to share with others what we so richly enjoy; and as we have entered into the labours of other men, so to labour that other men may enter into ours'. Whatever may have been his inward vision, his outward performance—fallible judgements and perverse actions included—does not greatly diverge from that prayer. He laboured mightily, and left behind him works which others will use, and using, remember him.

G. H. N. SETON-WATSON

PLATE XXII

T. B. MITFORD

TERENCE BRUCE MITFORD

1905-1978

TERENCE MITFORD was not a man to fit easily into the patterns of the scholarly world. During the final phase of the German occupation of Crete he led a group of Greek partisans in the White Mountains. The diary he kept then is the true epitome of the man: lists of weapons and equipment, records of enemy positions and partisan movements are interspersed with notes on villagers needing help and transcriptions of Greek inscriptions (as on 4 January 1945: 'rough stele of blue grey limestone: *ΕΥΚΡΙΝΗΣ ΜΕΓΑΛΟΚΛΗ*. Letters prob. late 2nd or early 1st B.C.'). Not a few classical scholars from Britain in both wars combined action and scholarship, sometimes in rather unexpected ways. We will never know whether Mitford saw himself a heir to such a tradition. But men like D. G. Hogarth or J. N. L. Myres may well have been an inspiration to him.

Terence Bruce Mitford was born in Yokohama on 15 May 1905, the eldest son of C. E. Bruce Mitford, journalist and writer, and of Beatrice Jean, née Allison. As he rarely, if ever, talked about his childhood, it is difficult to assess in which way family atmosphere (his mother seems to have been a remarkable person) and life abroad formed certain traits of his character in those years. Dulwich College, to which he was sent towards the end of the First World War, opened the way to Oxford when he won a scholarship in Classics to Jesus College.

Life at Oxford unfolded diverse and fascinating prospects. It also revealed already in the undergraduate a contrast that made itself felt throughout Mitford's life: the contrast between his deep love for the Classics and his ardent passion for active life. At first the Senior Classical Scholar for Jesus seemed to live up to his promise, taking a First in Mods. But gradually sports took up so much of his time and energy (he very nearly won a Rugby blue in a 'vintage year') that his final degree could not exactly be described as a good one.

Fortunately for Mitford athletic prowess counted as much as scholarly achievement with the Principal of St. Andrews University at that time. Thus he was appointed temporary assistant to the great Latin scholar W. M. Lindsay, who was Professor of Humanity at St. Andrews until 1936. The move from Oxford to

Scotland was a more momentous decision than Mitford can possibly have imagined at the time: it marked the beginning of an association with the Department of Humanity at St. Andrews which lasted for half a century. After a four years' term as Warden of St. Salvator's Hall Mitford was appointed Lecturer in Humanity in 1936. The bonds with Scotland were strengthened greatly when he married in the same year Margaret, daughter of Professor P. T. Herring of St. Andrews. Serving herself on the staff of the University as a Demonstrator in Anatomy, she proved to be through all his life a staunch partner in his many activities—kind, humorous, firm, and quietly distinguished.

There is a strange divide between the teacher and the scholar in Mitford's academic career at St. Andrews. His duties as a Lecturer and later (from 1952) as a Reader in Humanity and Classical Archaeology were confined nearly exclusively to teaching Latin prose composition and to lecturing on Latin texts—prose authors mostly, but sometimes also a poet such as Catullus. Mitford was a painstaking and conscientious teacher, assessing shrewdly the individual talents and merits of each pupil. He kindled a love of the Classics even in students who were frankly uninterested in the beginning, and he took special pains with his lame ducks. For these he founded the famous 'Gamma Club' which saved quite a number of its members from being sent down. Much of Mitford's impact as a teacher rested on his personality. His warmhearted and compassionate humanity, although sometimes hidden under a bluff manner, attracted even those who did not share his strong opinions and won him the lifelong devotion of many of his pupils. They used to come regularly to the Mitfords' large house, being made to feel at home by Margaret Mitford in the lively and delightful household where the five Mitford children grew up.

Mitford's interests as a scholar were focused on Greek epigraphy. He was attracted early by the study of inscriptions, and after his first travels in Cyprus in the mid-thirties (characteristically by bicycle) he devoted most of his energy to research in Cypriot epigraphy. At that time neither history nor classical archaeology was part of the St. Andrews curriculum, but Mitford was fortunate in that successive Professors of Latin encouraged him to pursue his particular scholarly interests. Although he sometimes felt this strongly marked separation of teaching and research rather acutely, he never applied for other posts and never seems to have contemplated seriously moving from St. Andrews. He had taken roots in Scotland where his family now lived and where he had formed a wide circle of friends. St. Andrews gave him a kind of life that suited him very well and the Preface to his last major work (*The Nymphaeum of Kafizin*), written in 1975, expressed once more his strong attachment 'to the University of St. Andrews which I have the honour and the pleasure still to serve'.

The long summers in Scottish Universities enabled Mitford to pursue one of the most constant aims of his life: to travel and to explore abroad in Classical lands. His achievements as a scholar in the field and his war experiences were closely interwoven. Although the war was for him a decisive phase of life, he retained an extraordinary reticence about it; of his experiences he would rarely speak. Yet what we know of his service has the ring of a heroic tale of old. Commissioned into the Dorset Regiment in 1939, he was soon seconded to Special Air Services and sent to serve under Pendlebury in Greece. During the German attack on Crete in 1941 he commanded a troop of raiders based on an island in the mouth of Suda Bay. He managed to escape to Egypt, one of the last to leave the island. Transferred to Special Operations Executive, he was given the task of raising and maintaining a force of Kurds in Syria—meeting there N. G. L. Hammond as an expert in demolition, Patrick Leigh Fermor as chief weapon instructor. A very tough, cheerful lot, enormously strong, with huge moustaches and lambskin kalpaks, these Kurds were trained to sabotage the Turkish railway route into Iraq in the event of Turkey joining the Axis powers, one of the reconnoitred objects being the suspension bridge over the Euphrates at Deir-es-Zor. As Turkey remained neutral, there was no chance of performing Lawrentian feats. Mitford then took his Kurds to Iraq on a mission still shrouded in mystery, thus gaining an opportunity to explore the desert route down to the eastern shore of the Persian Gulf in the steps of Alexander.

He returned to the Aegean theatre with the Special Boat Service. When the Italian armistice seemed to offer an easy chance to occupy the Dodecanese islands, Mitford led an SBS patrol in a minute caique and captured Patmos with a crew of four. His rule there—parleying with the venerable abbot of St. John's monastery, distributing food to starving islanders, reopening the local school—lasted a few days only. But SBS gave him another opportunity for secret and daring service: he was one of those preliminary invaders of Sicily who greatly facilitated the task of the first landing formations.

Late in 1944 Mitford returned to Crete, landing one night by parachute in the Omalo plain in the heart of the White Mountains.

He trained partisans with the machine gun, cleared mines in the Chania and Rhethymnon areas, and at the same time looked around for inscriptions. 'Pistol in one pocket, squeeze paper in another', as he once casually told me—and his diary bears out the tale. Quiet, thoughtful and imperturbable, he had a strong hold over his *andartes*, amongst them the famous Paterakis brothers (it was Antonis Paterakis who with Leigh Fermor captured the German GOC). In the high villages up in the White Mountains he is remembered to this day with affection as 'Mitsos'.

Mitford's war record shows the extraordinary courage, resilience, and endurance of the born soldier. And the war strengthened his innate love of hardships and simple life. His craving for the open air and his utter disregard for comfort were such that in Athens, rather than spending the night in the British School, he would take a bus out of the city in the evening to sleep under an olive-tree. What made him the model of a travelling scholar was the combination of such war-tried habits with a natural sympathy for all manner of men and an unusual talent for forming easy relationships with the most diverse people—a talent which owed a good deal to his command of Modern Greek and Turkish.

The love of the wild grew even stronger over the years, and so grew his dislike of the changing world of today with all its 'modern contraptions'. His marked distrust of mechanical contrivances reflected this attitude. When he transferred his field of activity from Cyprus to Turkey, this was due primarily to the Enosis crisis. But it was also a retreat into the wilderness—a wilderness which (as he once complained) was in the end also 'softened up by the arrival of the bus, the Landrover, and the transistor radio'.

Cyprus and Cilicia were the two areas to which he exclusively devoted his post-war field-work. Cyprus has cast her spell over many visitors to the island, captivating and firmly holding their interests. So it was with Mitford. The island's classical past, at that time rather neglected by scholars, had aroused his curiosity already in the years before the war. The title of the first article he ever published defined his future field of study: 'Contributions to the Epigraphy of Cyprus' (*Journal of Hellenic Studies*, 1937), and there he outlined his research programme: 'studying the Greek and Roman inscriptions of the island, with the intention of ultimately producing a small Corpus'. Edition and interpretation of the epigraphic texts of Cyprus indeed retained the central place in Mitford's scholarly interests throughout his life. Constant travel, often in very primitive conditions, and meticulous study of the original texts over many years made him the unrivalled master of Cypriot epigraphy. A long series of learned articles on Hellenistic, Roman, and early Christian texts contributed to a better understanding of the history, culture, and economy of the island during these periods. Mitford did not attain his original aim of producing a corpus for the whole of Cyprus (which would have formed volume xv of *Inscriptiones Graecae*). But he edited in a comprehensive way the inscriptions of two of the island's most important Greek cities: *The Inscriptions of Kourion* (1971) and *The Greek and Latin Inscriptions from Salamis* (with I. Nicolaou, 1974).

When the political situation in the island put a temporary end to his activities there in the late fifties, he began another ambitious research project: the collection and edition of the inscriptions of Rough Cilicia. This plan was not simply an *ad hoc* expedient. Mitford had set his eyes on southern Turkey a long time before; as early as 1953 he advised a young epigraphist to work in Pamphylia, promising him a rich harvest of new texts. The inscriptions of Rough Cilicia were to be published as volume vi of the *Tituli Asiae Minoris*, edited by the 'Kleinasiatische Kommission' of the Austrian Academy. Mitford thus established a connection with that learned body which meant much to him in the later years of his life. He spent long months in Vienna working through his squeezes, photographs, and field notes, profiting from the Academy's copious archives.

The epigraphic journeys into the rough mountains and valleys of western Cilicia and Pamphylia he undertook first with the late Professor G. E. Bean, an explorer of the same fibre and an indefatigable walker. Later he was accompanied by his wife and by his son Timothy, himself an ancient historian. Well over fifty, he had not lost his powers of resilience and endurance. He walked quite literally into the Taurus and existed off the land for weeks, undaunted by the roughest conditions. His courage and physical stamina, his genial habits and sense of humour won him the respect of the originally suspicious Turkish villagers. Such a mode of travel (which very few of his colleagues would care to imitate) had its rewards, presented in two volumes with the title *Journeys in Rough Cilicia*, published with G. E. Bean as *Denkschriften der Wiener Akademie* (1965, 1970). These volumes show that Mitford's method of field-work enabled him to discover many hitherto unpublished inscriptions and to locate for the first time a number of Classical sites in a region notoriously difficult for archaeological explorers—quite apart from the enjoyment he drew from the hard life and the beautiful wild country.

As an epigraphist Mitford was painstaking and infinitely

patient in his factual scholarship—revising (as his notebooks show) again and again the inscribed stones down to minute detail, and building up over the years a vast store of information about the intricate problems of Cypriot inscriptions. He belonged with that school of epigraphy which thinks it both possible and desirable to restore even severely mutilated texts to a large extent, if not completely. Consequently he did not always escape the hazards inherent in this method. Once Mitford had convinced himself of a certain solution to a textual problem, he could not easily be induced by arguments of other scholars to change his mind. In matters of scholarship as in many other respects he set great store by his independence.

It was to 'Nikokles, King of Paphos' that one of Mitford's earliest articles was devoted (*Anatolian Studies Buckler*, 1939). Again a note was struck which was to be an important and recurrent theme in his field-work. It was one of the minor side effects of the war that Mitford met in the Middle East J. H. Iliffe, director of the Palestine Archaeological Museum, but at that time seconded to the staff of Sir Alec Kirkbride in Amman as Assistant British Resident. Bicycling through Cyprus in the full heat of August 1949, Mitford and Iliffe learnt about the discovery of some Archaic limestone statues in a mound outside the village of Kouklia, the ancient Old Paphos. Once more an excavation project was sparked off by a sheer accident occurring at the appropriate moment. From 1950 to 1955 the Kouklia Expedition of the University of St. Andrews and the Liverpool Museums (of which Iliffe had become the director) excavated at Old Paphos, until work had to be suspended due to the growing unrest created in the island by the Enosis movement. At a time when Cypriot archaeology had not yet gained its present interest and importance, the Kouklia Expedition did vital pioneer work, discovering *inter alia* the first Late Bronze Age cemeteries of Old Paphos and a unique siege ramp dating from the Ionic Revolt.

The overall archaeological direction of the Expedition's work rested with Iliffe, while Mitford was responsible for the actual policy in choosing the staff, selecting the sites, and taking care of the dig's organization in general. He cheerfully bore the burden of arranging labour and procuring supplies at at time when the island was far from offering the easy commodities of today. Mitford was the driving spirit of the Expedition, both respected and beloved in the village by Greeks and Turks alike (some of his Homeric tales are still told in the *kapheneion* today). He soon became a well-known figure in the whole Paphos district, equally

well at home with the Colonial Secretary as with the local *mukhtar*
or the poorest of workmen.

Mitford, although not trained as an archaeologist, took an
active part in the excavation of the Late Bronze Age necropolis
and of a Roman house next to the Temple of Aphrodite. But at
Kouklia as elsewhere inscriptions, and now especially Syllabic
inscriptions, remained his dominating interest. Syllabic texts
occur sporadically already in his earlier articles. But it was only in
the late forties that his growing involvement with that particular
domain of scholarship began. The Classical Cypriot script had
played some part in the decipherment of the Cretan Linear B
texts. But the Syllabic inscriptions are also of intrinsic value for the
history of Cyprus, where the Greek alphabet was only adapted
(and hesitatingly at that) from the end of the fourth century BC.

Mitford not only revised or published a number of isolated
Syllabic inscriptions, many of these from the collection of the
Cyprus Museum: he had the good fortune to discover (or to re-
discover) three large and important groups of Syllabic texts. At
Kafizin, a small cone-shaped hill near the Nicosia–Larnaca road,
Mitford excavated in 1949 together with the then Curator of the
Cyprus Museum, the late P. Dikaios, the remains of a sanctuary of
Nymphs. In this project he also profited from the dedicated
support of an English hotel proprietor at Nicosia who would rush
out his slightly inebriated customers in a fleet of taxis for
emergency operations when heavy rains had washed inscribed
sherds down the steep slope of the hill. The graffiti with dedications and prayers, left by the worshippers at Kafizin, constitute
important new evidence for the religions of Hellenistic Cyprus.
They prove at the same time that the Syllabic script was used in
the island right down to the end of the third century BC, at least for
cult purposes.

At Rantidi, a few miles south-east of Kouklia, a number of
Syllabic inscriptions from a Sanctuary site were excavated by
R. Zahn in 1910 on behalf of the Prussian Academy. During his
last campaign at Kouklia, in 1955, Mitford carried out (with the
help of M. R. Popham) a survey of the area which produced
twenty-two new inscriptions from the site. At the same time he
began a thorough study of the surviving 1910 texts which he
caused to be assembled at the Kouklia Museum.

Finally, his own excavations at Kouklia yielded an unexpected
harvest when more than 250 Syllabic texts were discovered in
the siege ramp which had been erected in 498 BC by a Persian
army outside the North East Gate of Old Paphos. Many of the

inscriptions are fairly short dedications. But it is of prime importance that all these texts have a definite *terminus ante quem*— the more so, as the Archaic Paphian syllabary represents an intermediate stage between the Cypro-Minoan script of the Late Bronze Age and the Classical Syllabic script. The tenacious study of these documents made Mitford a leading authority on the Syllabic texts of Iron Age Cyprus with all their intricate problems. Thus it seems most appropriate that during his last visit to Kouklia, in April 1977, mosaic restorers in the North Hall of the Temple of Aphrodite accidentally discovered a large fragment of a Syllabic text dating from the reign of King Nikokles, of which Mitford published a first description and short commentary (*Bulletin de correspondance hellénique*, 102, 1978).

Fortune was less kind as far as the publication of these three important text groups was concerned. Battling already against ill health, he was able to see through the proofs of *The Nymphaeum of Kafizin. The Inscriptions of a Hellenistic Cult Site in Central Cyprus* (1980), although the volume was published only after his death. Of the Rantidi texts he left a nearly complete manuscript, of the Paphian siege mound inscriptions a very thorough documentation. (Both texts groups will be edited by O. Masson in the series 'Ausgrabungen in Alt-Paphos': a series destined, by agreement with Mitford, for the publication of all excavation results from Kouklia since 1950.) But although Mitford's untimely death on 8 November 1978 prevented him from finishing these tasks, the debt the history and epigraphy of Cyprus owe to his untiring work is immeasurable.

Yet recognition of his scholarly work came slow and late; this may have been because he concentrated so exclusively on a fairly circumscribed field of research. In 1961 and 1967 he was a member of the Institute of Advanced Study at Princeton. The German and the Austrian Archaeological Institutes elected him a Corresponding Member; Oxford gave him a D.Litt. in 1973. He was made an FBA in 1974, and a few months before his death the Austrian Academy elected him a Corresponding Fellow.

His own university gave him the title of Honorary Emeritus Professor and Research Fellow when he retired in 1973. It was a well-earned honour: that ancient history and classical archaeology are taught at St. Andrews is in no small way due to the efforts of Mitford. He created the little Museum of Archaeology at St. Andrews, providing a number of exhibits from his own excavations in Cyprus. He also took a great interest in the Committee of the Scottish Universities for an Archaeological Field School, of which he was chairman for a time. But his most important contribution was the time and energy he devoted over long years to the St. Andrews Archaeological Society. Under his inspiring guidance the Society, with its lectures and its annual archaeological picnic, created an ever-increasing interest in the subject, both in university and town. That the Society attracted for many years scholars of international repute as visiting lecturers to distant Scotland, was not only due to Mitford's wide network of acquaintances in the scholarly world. It was at the same time a proof of the strong incentive formed by the combination of Margaret Mitford's generous hospitality and of Terence Mitford's strong personality.

He was a man of very individual character; and yet it seems difficult, if not impossible, to evoke the impression he made on those he met or worked with. It is certainly significant that one never remembers him in a city or in a library, but out in the country: striding down the hill below the Chiftlik of Kouklia, or walking up Lucklaw Hill in Fife. On such walks he would point out rare birds, as bird-watching increasingly became his key interest besides epigraphy. Ardlogie, the solitary house far out in the country into which the Mitfords moved in later years, was an ideal place for such an occupation. But his ornithological interests were not confined to Scotland. He took part in the study of migratory movements in Scandinavia, and in 1975 he acted as 'Adviser to the Jordanian Government on Bird Conservation'.

A first impression of the man, with his marked reticence and his military bearing (which was underlined by a certain facial likeness to Vespasian), could be misleading. His true character was far from being one-sided. Mitford could of course be direct, laconic, and sometimes stern; for small talk he had no taste. But he could also be a most delightful companion, a great raconteur with an unfailing sense of humour. And he was always sensitive and kind, showing in small acts or gestures how he cared for others.

Yet, with all his humanity and understanding, he was in certain respects set and unyielding in his ideas, disdaining what he considered 'the modern vice of flexibility at all costs'. He was deeply conservative, not only in a political sense: averse to change which seemed to him nowadays almost everywhere change for the worse, *teste* his introduction to the Kafizin publication: 'As universities proliferate, so do seats of learning become the rarer and more precious'. There would, however, be exceptions when he had convinced himself of a cause being just—as when he, a firm believer in the infinite superiority of a classical education, supported Principal

Sir Malcolm Knox against conservatives in St. Andrews in his fight for scientific expansion of the University.

Terence Mitford will always be remembered for the man he was: single-minded, courageous, independent. The lament of pipes that ended the simple burial service in Kilmany church has gone: but his deep laughter is still with us.

FRANZ GEORG MAIER

I am most grateful to Mrs M. Mitford, Professor J. N. Coldstream, Sir Kenneth Dover, Mr P. M. Fraser, Professor N. G. L. Hammond, Mr Patrick Leigh Fermor, Dr T. Mitford, Dr R. L. S. Bruce-Mitford, Professor G. E. Rickman, and Professor J. K. S. St. Joseph for their help in composing this memoir.

PLATE XXIII

Luther Ramsey

ROY PASCAL

ROY PASCAL

1904–1980

Roy Pascal was born on 28 February 1904, to C. S. Pascal and Mary Edmonds, who carried on a grocery business in Birmingham. It was to this city, centre of the industrial heartland of modern Britain, that he was to return for the last four decades of his life; it was also Birmingham's ethos of hard work, hard-headedness, and diligence that coloured his own serious-minded, conscientious outlook and impelled him to produce a steady and impressive output of academic scholarship spanning half a century and embracing several disciplines. The whole corpus of his work can be claimed as evidence that Roy Pascal was perhaps the most distinguished Germanist this country has produced, with a justifiably international reputation.

As both a Foundation and a King Edward scholar Pascal's schooling took place at King Edward's School, Birmingham, which was of somewhat less repute then than now. Certainly, in the period after the First World War few schools prepared pupils for Modern Language studies and Pascal was in the first Modern Languages Sixth at King Edward's School. He acquired his German in a rough and ready way from one Miltiades Acatos, who was Greek and had studied in Germany. Literary texts were treated only as linguistic exercises; indeed, the study of literature hardly existed at the school, least of all in English.

In 1921 Pascal unsuccessfully took the Entrance Scholarship examination at Sidney Sussex College but a year later did gain a Scholarship at Pembroke College, Cambridge, which was awarded on the results of the Higher Certificate Examination. On his arrival at Cambridge in 1923 Pascal found the German teaching there overwhelmingly dull and lacking in stimulus; the Professor, Karl Breul, gave an unsystematic course on Goethe's *Faust* from notes 'brown with age' and an equally enthusiastic but uncritical course on the Ballad, and Pascal always regretted having been under a professor who gave him so little. Elsie Butler, too, though a delightful companion and an adventurous and imaginative investigator, did not inspire Pascal as a lecturer. It was left to E. K. (Francis) Bennett, who was devoted to his students and made immense efforts to cater for their needs, to guide and support Pascal's undergraduate studies. His lectures, though eschewing method and theory—that would have been nectar to the young Pascal—nevertheless communicated his own sensitive feeling for literature and awakened an appreciation for good writing in his students. Above all, he encouraged them to follow their own tastes, and Pascal learned from him to go directly to the literary texts and make his own critical way through them. Of course, Pascal later learned a great deal about scientific method, but to the end clung to the habit of direct confrontation with the text that Bennett had instilled in him. From being a supervisor Francis Bennett became a close companion; he took Pascal to theatres, concerts, and operas, and introduced him to his friends; and they shared holidays together in England, France, and Germany. Later Pascal was to acknowledge his 'immense debt to his kind, generous personality'.

Apart from Bennett, however, and sporadic courses on Schiller's aesthetic writings and on Romanticism by Edward Bullough that for the first time brought him into contact with a teacher of a subtle, penetrating mind, Pascal found little stimulus inside German studies. The best part of his education at Cambridge came from his connections with people in other disciplines— English, History, Philosophy, and the Sciences—and the college and university societies he attended like the English Club or the Heretics (of which he became President). Here he acquired that natural breadth of interest that enabled him in later work to ignore disciplinary frontiers with easy disdain. In fact, the impetus to make his career in German did not arise from narrow literary or linguistic considerations. In those days it was uncommon for a student of German to visit Germany, and Pascal's first trip was to a Summer School at Berlin in 1924 (financed by a personal loan—never repaid—from Pascal's Director of Studies at Pembroke, H. G. Comber). Here Pascal first met modern Germany (for his literary studies at Cambridge closed with Hauptmann, the early Rilke, and George). To his astonishment he listened to a course on contemporary history in which Great Britain was fiercely attacked, and to lectures on art that employed *völkisch* criteria that he later recognized to be close to those of the National Socialists. He found the staid world of his upbringing challenged in many ways, met *Wandervögel* and the youth movement, a world in which ideas and culture seized hold of people. From that time on he decided to devote himself to German as his main study. The memory of the shock that this unknown world gave him provided him later with one of his main avowed purposes as a professor of

German: to relate academic studies as far as possible to the contemporary world of Germany.

After graduating in 1927 with First Class Honours in French and German Pascal was awarded the Tiarcks scholarship and went to Germany to embark on his research on Novalis. Supervision was negligible, apart from one perfunctory talk with Breul, and Pascal wrestled alone for some time with the problem of finding the links between the philosophers Fichte and Schelling and the writers Novalis and Friedrich Schlegel. After a year or two he abandoned the theme. On the whole, Pascal made very few acquaintances and got little profit from his academic courses in Berlin (Winter Semester) and Munich (Summer Semester), perhaps, he thought later, because he was both too shy and too headstrong. The stimulation of this year came, as was to be expected, from life and culture outside the university sphere. Pascal was fascinated by the scintillating musical productions in Berlin, by the great early German silent films and the new Russian films of Eisenstein and Pudowkin, by the magnificence of Reinhardt in the theatre, and above all the dimly understood innovations of Piscator and Brecht, well worth the sacrifice of living poorly—often on meals of black bread and sausage. It was also in Berlin that he met Feiga (Fania) Polianovska, a lady of Russian origin whom he married in 1931 and who bore him two daughters. Fania was to remain with Roy as a warm, intelligent, and intellectual companion to the end.

Roy Pascal's teaching career began on his return from Germany in the autumn of 1928 when he became supervisor of Modern Language Studies at Pembroke, to be elected a Junior Research Fellow the following year. At first he was required to teach French literature as well as German, but numbers of students were now increasing so rapidly that he could soon concentrate on German. In spite of being called a 'research' Fellow, he was required to teach about sixteen hours a week supervision with about four students in each class who wrote an essay every fortnight. Despite his protestations he failed to get any notable improvement for several years; his income (Fellowship £250 plus per capita fees) was soon near £1,000 a year, but he could do his own work only in vacations and had difficulty keeping up with the reading necessary for his classes. He had many excellent pupils—some of them becoming themselves Germanists of note—and able men like C. P. Magill, Trevor Jones, F. J. Stopp could be relied on to write disconcertingly long essays. The first university lectures Pascal gave, on his own admission with very inadequate preparation, were on Reformation and Baroque literature. He had become a devotee of Baroque architecture during his stay in Munich and must have been one of the first English scholars to lecture on Baroque, a term hardly known in England then. The Reformation period attracted him even more, and his lectures on Luther matured into his first book, *The Social Basis of the German Reformation: Luther and his Times*, published in 1933. Like most of the dozen books and numerous articles he wrote, this volume, focusing as it does on the ferment of class struggle and the Peasant Wars, is symptomatic of that earlier resolution to study German literature in the broader context of history, society, and culture. In the library of Birmingham University it is to be found in the History section, as are many publications by Pascal, while yet others appear on the shelves of English, Comparative Literature and Literary Theory. Further lectures, on *Aufklärung* and *Sturm und Drang*, generated the selection of critical voices and inter-pretations, *Shakespeare in Germany 1746–1815* (1937), that 'arose out of certain practical needs of teaching' and through which Pascal sought to show 'that the attitude to Shakespeare in this period is not merely a matter of aesthetic appreciation, but is, even more, a part of a changing moral and social outlook'.

Moral and social attitudes always preoccupied Pascal, and politics was their practical manifestation. Returning frequently to Berlin during vacations, Pascal became ever more aware of the political tensions there. It was the period of the great economic crisis and party and ideological strife was becoming acute; literature became a battlefield and a literature of the left (Brecht, Toller, Döblin, Heinrich Mann, Arnold Zweig) made a great impact. Pascal had joined the Labour Party on returning to Cambridge, and meeting Hugh Dalton, then Under-Secretary of State in the Labour government, he tried to persuade him to advocate a more generous policy on Reparations towards Germany, since Snowden's intransigence at the Hague Conference (1929) was destroying the moderate parties in Germany. It was difficult for Englishmen at the time to imagine the radi-calization going on in Germany and even though Pascal saw the growing demonstrations of Nazis he did not understand the danger fully. He got into bad odour with his very conservative College for speaking in favour of Stresemann and the admittance of Germany into the League of Nations. More damaging to his career prospects was his increasing sympathy with the Communist Party and the extreme Left as the political crisis sharpened, though whether he actually became a member of the Party is a matter of dispute. For this reason Pascal's Research Fellowship was not renewed in 1934 (though he managed to obtain a University Lectureship in German), and he was elected into a full Fellowship only after death had removed certain of the senior Fellows of the College (an Honorary Fellowship of Pembroke followed four decades later, in 1976). Pascal's political views, though the outcome of many factors, were at this time much influenced by the situation in Germany, and in their turn influenced his German studies. They led him to a field of investigation much neglected by Germanists—to the early Marx, whose philosophical manuscripts were now first being published and becoming more widely known. The influence of these writings was profound in many fields at this time—among philosophers, theologians, and sociologists—and Pascal found them illuminating both for the history of German thought and the methodology of cultural studies. In 1938 he published, with the help of two former pupils, a translation of parts of *Die deutsche Ideologie*.

In these years, and particularly in the National Socialist period, the position of a Germanist was exposed, responsible, and in any case difficult. The least politically minded was affected. All the Cambridge Germanists—and nearly all in Great Britain—were appalled at the militarism and radicalism of Hitler, and horrified by what happened after his accession to power. Democratic and Jewish colleagues were dismissed and forced into exile, and many outraged Germanists like Pascal involved themselves in public protests and organizations to aid the imprisoned or exiled. Their relations with official German bodies, university authorities, the German Embassy in London, the officially sponsored Anglo-German Association, were awkward, to say the least, though opinions differed as to how far they should associate themselves openly with public and hostile criticism. At the Conference of University Teachers of German held in Cambridge in 1936, the first he attended, Pascal proposed that Conference should send a protest to the German government over the victimization of Jewish academics, but the Conference thought it unwise to take a collective step of this kind. Yet many members who spoke against his proposal assured him privately of their sympathy for it, among them Collinson and Barker Fairley. It was certainly difficult both publicly to criticize Hitlerism and to maintain contacts with Germany; Pascal's own links with Germany were severed, and were replaced by association with refugee scholars of all types. As early as 1934 Pascal made his position plain with a book *The Nazi Dictatorship*, roundly condemning the new regime in Germany as a manifestation of monopoly capitalism and expressing the not uncommon view that Hitler was preparing for war. After 1934 Pascal visited Germany hardly at all, preferring to work in Switzerland.

Pascal's fervently held political views and left-wing stance were rooted in the first instance in a genuine disgust with the class and cultural snobbery he found so frustrating and painful in England. Yet this emotional proclivity was confirmed by systematic and assiduous study of the structures and historical developments that produced the injustices of a class society in the twentieth century. Marxism appealed to both Pascal's feeling and his intellect. In the ferment of the 'Pink' thirties, when Cambridge was alive with political energy and idealism, international situations—whether the Spanish Civil War, Hitler in Germany, or the Utopian hope of the Soviet Union—provided ample opportunities for action from self-immolation to treason. In this fertile ground Pascal's political awareness, intellectual capabilities, and social concern combined in the denunciation of Nazi Germany. During the war years he deliberately abstained from 'pure' literary studies, giving priority to the need to combat the menace of National Socialism as an intellectual, lending what weight he could to this struggle with his pen. An integral and sustained part of this purpose was the explication of the modern political and historical development of Germany to an English readership. *Karl Marx: his Apprenticeship to Politics* appeared as a Labour Monthly shilling publication in 1942; its closing sentences serve as well to describe Pascal's own reluctance to retreat into the shelter of academe and cut himself off from the great events shaping the world:

As contributor and editor Marx was brought to observe the real condition of men, the actual functions of the state; his attention was directed away from abstractions to realities; he left the philosopher's coterie and entered social life. This meant a great theoretical as well as practical progress. His intellectual method was to link these practical problems to the general framework of his ideas, to measure his philosophy against them; and so, at one and the same time, to fashion a policy and refashion his philosophy.

A year later there followed another Labour Monthly pamphlet, *Karl Marx: Political Foundations*; in 1945 an article on 'The Junkers' appeared in *The Contemporary Review*, sounding a warning about the danger of this 'tough, violent, ruthless' caste, and another in 1946, 'A Prussian Officer in France, 1940', which attacked Ernst Jünger as a member of the 'conservative opposition' which was nevertheless a buttress of Hitler's power and little to be trusted. A further study of the phenomenon of aggressive German nationalism and its roots, 'The Frankfurt Parliament, 1848, and the *Drang nach Osten*', was published in the *Journal of Modern History*; it displays Pascal's accustomed authoritative mastery of historical detail, underpinned by an insatiable reading of memoirs and autobiographies. Again in this year, 1946, Pascal ventured wholly into the realm of the historian with *The Growth of Modern Germany*, another work of mediation between the German and the English mind. In it he seeks to outline, not diplomatic or political history, but the 'main mass of social movement', and convincingly elaborates objective historical reasons for the rise of Nazism. Two years later he returned to the theme of *The German Revolution of 1848* in the Birth of Socialism series by Fore Publications.

It will be seen that Pascal was much preoccupied at this time with important aspects of Germany that were of more pressing importance than literary studies for an understanding of that country in the dangerously amorphous immediate post-war period. By now, of course, Pascal was well established as Professor of German at Birmingham University and was fast building a national reputation with his forthright yet discriminating writings. But he found time for more run-of-the-mill things: he became President of the Association of University Teachers in 1944–5, and it was no doubt this office as well as his preoccupation with contemporary Germany that led him to being invited to join an AUT delegation which visited the British Zone in January 1947 at the request of the Control Office for Germany and Austria. Before the delegation was finally appointed there appears to have been some resistance at the Foreign Office against Pascal's participation, on the grounds of his left-wing views. In the event Pascal was largely responsible for the final report in which his pragmatic imprint can be detected; many practical suggestions were made for a comprehensive range of measures to be immediately implemented, with the aim of revitalizing and democratizing the German universities, by injecting younger blood to break the dominance of cliques of senior professors and by bringing them into closer touch with public opinion in the outside world.

Pascal's move to Birmingham had come partly as a result of his growing disillusionment with the academic world of Cambridge which he saw as too narrow and exclusive. In addition, the numbers of students grew considerably during the thirties and he felt that the pressures of teaching and other practical duties (including extraneous college chores) were little by little exhausting his energies and making it difficult for him to do a sustained piece of scholarly work. He began to think of leaving Cambridge and the occasion arose on the retirement of Professor F. E. Sandbach in Birmingham. Pascal applied for, and was appointed to, the vacant Chair, moving house with his family on the very day that Hitler opened the attack on Poland. His salary, which in the last years at Cambridge came to about £1,400 (from Fellowship, Lectureship, and supervision, with some addition when he acted as assistant tutor), fell abruptly to £1,000, and he maintained later that he had never since reached the heights of affluence he enjoyed in the privileged Cambridge of the 1930s.

But there was probably a deeper dissatisfaction prompting Pascal to leave Cambridge. The German School there was not a Department or School proper, in no sense a combined force. Its members, though friendly, never met to discuss a programme or syllabus, or to hear a paper. R. A. Williams, who came from Belfast in 1932 to succeed Breul as Professor, was, like his predecessor, a completely ineffective head, according to Pascal. German studies were governed directly by the Board of Modern and Medieval Languages, the members of which, apart from the professors, were elected by the vote of lecturers, and the numbers from each language-school were restricted. Pascal was somewhat galled by never becoming a member of this Board and he thought it a regrettable handicap that the possibilities of new departures in German were severely restricted by this structure of government. It was a great relief to him, on coming to Birmingham, to find that a Department could shape its own syllabus with relative autonomy and respond swiftly to new demands and new ways of thinking, though this was to have disastrous repercussions a score of years later. At this time too the decisive intellectual stimuli for Pascal's own thinking came from outside German and Modern Language circles—from philosophers, historians, English criticism, scientists. Traditional 'language and literature' studies seemed inadequate to the challenge of Hitlerism and he felt the need for a broader base to support the struggle against the Nazi cultural ideology. He saw this struggle as the first obligation of a Germanist and he entered on it on the philosophical–political basis of the early writings of Marx, which in his view provided the best formulation of the historical, ideological, and cultural principles to resist Nazism. During the war the more pragmatic, non-academic ambience of industrial Birmingham enabled him to occupy himself, as far as publications went, mainly with such matters; it was only as the pressure of these problems relaxed after 1945 that he felt free to devote himself again to more purely literary history and criticism, though in this later work too the impetus of the thirties is evident. Throughout this period Pascal was to some extent an oddity in German studies, and for many colleagues there always clung to him, quite erroneously, the aura of a scholar with a political axe to grind that made his literary criticism faintly suspect. His academic history is nevertheless of interest in reflecting (as did that of William Rose at London University) quite directly the tensions in German studies in this agitated period.

At the time that Pascal arrived in Birmingham in 1939 he found a small department of two or three colleagues and only a handful of Honours students. Sandbach, a quiet, sober, tolerant man, had established a slow tempo which persisted throughout the war years, despite Pascal's quick and impetuous nature. The universities were then all in the doldrums, with the country occupied with other matters and both staff and students disappearing into national service. Pascal suffered from a stomach ulcer and, though he volunteered, he was turned down by the Navy; thereupon he joined the ARP Wardens and carried out fire-watching duties at the Edmund Street site of the University in the centre of Birmingham. During these years, when academic life was just ticking over, Pascal played an active part in the University as well as working closely with outside bodies like the Workers Educational Association. He reflected on the different life-styles of red-brick Birmingham and venerable Cambridge and came to the conclusion that the structure of the former offered more. College intimacies were lacking, but relationships with members of other Arts departments were intellectually more productive. One missed the wide choice of personalities at Cambridge but was brought into daily proximity with a greater variety of persons; and though there was always the danger that members of one department might become isolated from others, Pascal felt that, given the will, the Faculty organization at a modern university gave a better basis for intellectual academic life than the Cambridge college system.

The end of the war saw a resurgence of German studies and before 1950, to cope with the rapid increase in students of German, Pascal had appointed three new lecturers—R. Hinton Thomas, W. B. Lockwood, and S. S. Prawer—all of whom were subsequently to occupy Chairs elsewhere. The transformation was not only numerical: with the defeat of Nazi Germany and the influx of young enthusiastic colleagues, Pascal began again to publish articles and books on literary subjects, prolifically and, characteristically, with no heed to the limitations of period or specialization. *The German Sturm und Drang* (1953) seeks to encompass the 'wide scope', the 'totality of range', and the 'multiple achievement' of this complex and chaotic stage in the formation of German literature. Pascal here set himself the task of assessing the fundamental principles and significance of the *Sturm und Drang* in the broadest sense, within a European framework and in the context of its century. This was to be a work of explanation and elucidation, and the chapter headings indicate its wide sweep: the *Sturm und Drang* and the State, and the Social Classes, Religion, The Creative Personality, Thought and Reality, The Idea of History, the Revolution in Poetics, Achievement. Sadly, he never wrote the promised complementary volume on the poetic qualities of the often startling imaginative works of the movement.

Three years later, in 1956, came his full-length study, *The German Novel*, which displayed magisterially his solidity of taste and self-assurance of judgement. Here he set out to discuss 'the novels I hold to be of the highest worth, with the object of finding out, as far as I might, what it is that makes them good novels'. What it is that makes this good criticism and an authoritatively standard work on the genre is his fearlessly capable grasp of thorny and controversial ideas and terminology, his bold consideration of none but the best in the literary canon, his skill at conducting aesthetic argument at a high level, and his avoidance of the banalities of histories of literature. Pascal's next major work, *Design and Truth in Autobiography* (1960), arose out of the urgent personal need to grapple with the enigma of this genre so neglected in literary criticism. His own constant surprise at the fixed image others had of him and the realization that his own view of himself as an unpredictable, protean being was not accurate either, led him to muse on both the subjective and objective aspects of auto-biography. This became an 'insistent moral pressure', seeking to understand the problematic concept of the tenuous continuity of the individual personality, the desire to prove to oneself that the new grows organically out of the old, as if 'freedom could mean something to me only if it was destiny, as if a choice was satis-factory only if it imposed itself as my nature'. This study reveals a great deal about Pascal himself while at the same time the ideas he voices are an ironic comment on the very task I am engaged on in this memoir—to put down on paper a certain, necessarily defined, image of a man. Pascal's book, bridging as it does the major cultures of our continent, is a thoughtful and penetrating study of the most intimate conundrum facing a man—the reason for existence—especially as the cult of the individual personality has permeated the European imagination since the Renaissance. This search is best encompassed in Pascal's own words:

> I mean a need for meaning. I do not believe that an individual life has a religious or transcendental meaning, and I cannot even comfort myself with the metaphysical despair, the Angst, of the existentialists. Nor is it enough to prove to myself that I am fulfilling a social purpose in a useful job. The meaning had to be personal, subjective. I did not pitch my hopes extravagantly high, and felt one could be content if one could feel one's self to be consistent, to have developed naturally and organically, to have remained 'true to itself', and if within this framework one could order certain intense experiences whose significance defied analysis but which were peculiarly one's own.

The deep earnestness of Pascal's reflections on the significance of life has its counterpart in his serious dedication to the improvement and reform of university German studies. In the 1950s he was already thinking of changes that would allow students to be guided towards knowledge of, and contact with, the present, living people and their culture. While preserving the study of the language and literature of the past he wanted to give it this modern cutting edge, in a modest way initially: by including living authors in the literary syllabus, and by an introduction to the structures of modern Germany, its social and political institutions and thought. These ideas adumbrated in the pre-Robbins era were developed beyond the embryonic stage and put into practice in the early sixties; a programmatic description of the changes in the Birmingham course was formulated by Pascal in a celebrated article 'New Directions in Modern Language Studies', which appeared in *Modern Languages* in June 1965. The sharp thrust of pragmatism appeared in certain general considerations that were taken as guide-lines: the intellectual bent of students applying to enter Modern Language courses, the need to provide a programme with an intellectual discipline, and the perspective of social usefulness (careers). The most novel—and contentious—aspect of the restructured undergraduate course was the socio-logical analysis of contemporary (German) society, for which Pascal enumerated four principles:

(1) Social studies are desirable for their own inherent importance and usefulness, and the students' interest in the foreign people gives a hopeful basis for them.

(2) Our courses should centre on social fields immediately accessible to the students—the family, the city, and such—and build outwards from these towards the larger political organisations.

(3) A preliminary course in sociological principles and methods is necessary so that students may understand something of the technique of social study.

(4) The fields they are to study should as far as possible link up with data and problems they meet in other courses, literary, linguistic, and philosophical.

But Pascal's laudable desire to broaden the basis and the substance of German studies backfired; and within a few years the 'liberated', free-choice undergraduate options—together with a well-structured and successful MA course initiated in 1965—had become the domain of pseudo-sociologists, students with a glib command of a few superficial, often platitudinous principles of the social sciences. The slogan words were 'relevance' and 'participation'. Many in the late 1960s returned from their year abroad at one of the German universities seething with rebellion and determined to implement the tactics and achieve the disruption they had seen in Germany. Pascal became the target: as Head of Department he stood for authoritarianism, and was subjected to a campaign of vituperation and vilification which led to his seeking early retirement in 1969. The 'alien thinking' he protested against had been imported from Germany and purported to be Marxist in inspiration—an ironic contrast to Pascal's own lifelong endeavours to fructify literary criticism in this country with Marxist elements. But Pascal was caught unawares; he realized too late in his ordeal that reasoned discussion and rational argument stood no chance against aggression and hysteria, that the tactic of loud and raucous defamation would quite simply drown his quiet voice. A handful of ruthless individuals in the Department, with all the appurtenances of the fascistoid tendencies they so reviled, browbeat and bullied students and even staff to such an extent that Pascal felt isolated and exposed. On this sour note he resigned from his Chair, a disillusioned and disappointed man.

Colleagues in many countries were saddened at this abrupt and abrasive close to Pascal's long teaching career; that his distinguished and continuing contribution to German studies was held in the highest regard is evidenced by the *Festschrift* in honour of his sixty-fifth birthday in 1969, a collection appropriately entitled *Essays in German Language, Culture and Society*. Pascal accepted an invitation to spend the year immediately after his resignation as a Visiting Professor at McMaster University, Canada, and he returned from this to settle down in Birmingham to a decade of research and publication untrammelled by the exhausting demands of administration, teaching, and grappling with student 'protest'. In his later years a number of honours, not unexpectedly, came his way. He was awarded the Goethe Medal in 1965 and the prestigious Shakespeare Prize of the FVS Foundation, Hamburg, in 1969. A year later he was elected Fellow of the British Academy. In 1974 Birmingham University conferred on him the degree of LLD *honoris causa*, and three years later an Hon. D.Litt. was bestowed on him by Warwick University (where he had been Visiting Professor).

During the 1970s, until his health began to fail, Pascal pursued his researches with undiminished enthusiasm and vigour, and he was still an assiduous visitor to both University Library and Common Room. In 1973 he completed and published a full-length study of the complex emergence of 'modernism' in German culture, *From Naturalism to Expressionism: German Literature and Society 1880–1918*, generated by his lasting conviction 'that all art . . . is rooted in the artist's life-experience, and that the type of experiences available, the insights and values discoverable, are, if not decided, then profoundly influenced by the structure of society and the character of social life'. In his maturity Pascal was well aware that 'social life' is not a firm and reassuring thing outside individuals and is 'never experienced raw, but always indirectly through the mediation of habits, ideas, purposes that interpret it and give it a prearranged shape'. Discerningly, he explored the verbalizations of social life that give it form and meaning through that delicate area of 'contemporary opinion and interpretation of aspects and problems of society' rather than the social facts themselves. The symbiosis of literature and society was always for Pascal a dialectical and mutually enhancing process; and the strong undercurrent of his thinking and his perception of literature was still as powerful as ever—the themes of different chapters recall the method and assumptions of *The German Sturm und Drang*, written twenty years earlier. That Pascal could switch effortlessly from the social to the aesthetic was shown in 1977 with his last published book, *The Dual Voice*, an investigation of free indirect speech and its functioning in the nineteenth-century European novel. Like his unique earlier work on autobiography this study adds much valuable analysis to the body of theory of *le style libre* and *erlebte Rede*. Again Pascal moves with sovereign ease from one literary culture to another, and though confining himself deliberately to one century, he shows himself in his conclusions to be fully aware both of the multiplicity of narrative forms in our century as well as of more untraditional and iconoclastic aesthetic approaches. At the time of his death, on

24 August 1980, Pascal was engaged in a series of studies of the enigmatic work of Franz Kafka, one of which had already appeared in print. It is to be hoped that his colleague and friend of long standing, Professor Siegbert Prawer of Queen's College, Oxford, who was chosen by Pascal as his literary executor, will prepare these studies—which were already at an advanced stage—as a worthy posthumous monument to Pascal's breadth of enquiry and scholarship.

Owing to a prolonged and wearisome illness Pascal was unable to deliver in person, as he had been invited to, the 1977 Bithell Memorial Lecture in London. His text, *Brecht's Misgivings*, was nevertheless published by the Institute of German Studies; in it he confesses to a certain 'special relationship' with the great German playwright:

We were near-contemporaries, and though English and German circumstances and manners were not identical, they were close enough. The major social experiences, the intellectual choices, were similar, and in Brecht's responses I recognize the pattern of my own more hesitant ones. For this reason I thought that the present theme from Brecht's work, that has long occupied my mind as a literary, an ethical, and a personal problem, might be appropriate for this occasion.

The theme that prompted Pascal to perceive the articulation in the later Brecht of his own misgivings was that of the 'concept of goodness'. Brecht's 'obstinate clinging to his vision of simple goodness' conflicted with his 'dissatisfaction with the pragmatic, social ethic that he explicitly adhered to and his unease in a political society built upon it', and reflected Pascal's own doubts about the certainties of earlier beliefs and his nostalgia for an equitable society that was still no more than a Utopian dream. Pascal was realist enough to recognize that we are no nearer a just world than we were in the turbulent 1930s, but humane enough never to give up exploring ways of reaching it. This in turn was part and parcel of his warmth of feeling, a sympathy with his fellows that pervaded all he did. As a teacher and colleague he was accessible to the humblest, unstinting in praise, generous with wise advice, and full of understanding for the problems and difficulties of his fellows. He enjoyed a few pastimes—angling, carpentry, cricket, and other ball games—to which he brought the skill and gusto with which he cultivated personal relationships and pursued his researches. He will be remembered by many as a humble man who achieved eminence but was never spoiled by it.

A. V. SUBIOTTO

Note: I have drawn a considerable amount of factual material for this memoir from autobiographical sketches by Roy Pascal covering his years in Cambridge as well as the development of the German Department at the University of Birmingham.

PLATE XXIV

J. Russell & Sons

WALTER SIMON

ERNST JULIUS WALTER SIMON

1893–1981

ERNST JULIUS WALTER SIMON, Professor Emeritus of Chinese in the University of London, was born in Berlin on 10 June 1893. He attended the University of Berlin from 1911 to 1914, where his studies lay in the fields of Romance and Classical philology. He belonged to just that generation of young Europeans whose lives and careers were the first to be interrupted by the outbreak of the First World War, in which he served from 1914 to 1918. He was employed in military intelligence, as far as I can ascertain in the reading of enemy codes. In 1919 he returned to Berlin, and took his doctorate with a dissertation on the characteristics of the Judaeo-Spanish dialect of Salonika. This was published in the following year. In 1919, too, he passed the State Examination for Higher School Teaching in French, Latin, and Greek. He had pedagogic ambitions, and was attracted by the idea of teaching classical languages through conversation, as if they were modern tongues, but in the event he followed in the professional footsteps of his father, Heinrich Simon, and became a librarian. He entered the Higher Library Service at the University of Berlin in 1919, and in 1920 passed the Higher Library Examination. After a year's service at the University of Kiel, he returned, in 1922, to his old University of Berlin, where he remained until his dismissal in 1935.

It was not until after he had taken his doctorate that Simon turned his attention to Oriental studies, a discipline in which he was to build up, in Germany, a second career, parallel to that of librarian. He studied Sinology under the late Professor Otto Franke, but his linguistic interests and skills ranged far beyond China. He had a thorough knowledge of Japanese, Tibetan, and Manchu, could make use of Mongolian, and was at home in Russian as an ancillary language, an advantage enjoyed by few Sinologists of his own or the following generation. By his own admission, and Simon was the most modest of men, he was an extraordinarily gifted linguist. When, in 1935, he had to fill out a 'General Information' sheet for the Academic Assistance Council, one of the questions to be answered concerned the languages of which he had a speaking and a reading knowledge. To the second part of this enquiry he was able to reply, in good conscience: 'Almost all European languages, Chinese and Japanese.'

Simon began the study of Chinese in 1920. In 1926 he was admitted as *Privatdozent* at Berlin, authorized to teach in the field of Far Eastern linguistics. His teaching responsibilities were extended in 1929, and again in 1931, by which time he was permitted to cover the whole field of Sinological studies. In 1932 he became Professor, with the title of *Nichtbeamteter außerordentlicher Universitätsprofessor*: it was still the library service which provided him with his living. For a time, in 1931–2, during the hiatus between the retirement of Otto Franke and the arrival of Erich Haenisch, practically all the Sinological teaching at Berlin was in his hands. From 1930, too, he was a coeditor of the *Orientalische Literaturzeitung*, Germany's main vehicle for reviews of orientalist literature. Simon's library career flourished too during these years. In 1929 he was sent to England to study British libraries, and in 1930 he was relieved from part of his duties in order to be able to devote more time to academic research. The year 1932–3 saw Simon in Peking, as Exchange Librarian with the National Library there. It was as a result of this visit that he compiled the romanized index and the foreword to Li Teh-ch'i's *Union Catalogue of Manchu Books in the National Library of Peiping and the Library of the Palace Museum*. By 1935, when his career as a librarian was abruptly terminated in accordance with the discriminatory policies of the Nazi government, he was an established librarian, with the rank of *Bibliotheksrat*.

Simon left Germany early in 1936, under the stress of political and racial discrimination: there was no future left there for a Jewish scholar, even one of his eminence. While he was still in China, his wife had written to him to try to persuade him not to return, though in fact he did so. A former pupil of his, Professor Emeritus Wolfgang Franke, of the University of Hamburg (the son of Otto Franke), recalled to me many afternoon walks with his old teacher through the streets of Berlin, from the Sinologische Seminar to the Potsdamer Bahnhof, during which they had long conversations about the deteriorating political situation. This was before his visit to China. 'He was a German patriot, and still in 1931/2, in the face of the threat of the Nazis getting political power, much more optimistic than me. Unfortunately, later my view proved to be right.' It was possibly Simon's record of war service, and the international recognition which his academic work had won, which protected him for a short while, but in 1934 his *venia legendi*—the authorization to teach at university—was withdrawn, and in 1935 he was dismissed from his established library post. It was clearly time to leave Germany, and at the age of forty-three, married, and with two young sons, Simon had to take the difficult step of turning his back on the homeland which had deserted him, and on his career, and start again in a foreign environment.

Fortunately, Simon had made his mark in the world of international scholarship, and had won the respect of all those scholars whose opinion mattered, including those who, like Bernhard Karlgren, did not always agree with him professionally. Towards the end of 1935 he visited London, and began discussions with the Academic Assistance Council, later the Society for the Protection of Science and Learning, whose business affairs were conducted by its Secretary, Mr Walter Adams. Prospects were none too good for the out-of-work foreign scholar. Money was, as usual, tight, and Simon's fate was shared by many others whose skills the Nazis were shortsightedly prepared to dispense with.

Simon came to England with the highest references. The names of those who supplied the Academic Assistance Council with testimonials to his scholarly qualifications and his exemplary character read like a roll-call of contemporary Sinology. Hardly a name which counted is missing, and the record includes, to their credit, those of some of his recent German colleagues. It is well worth recalling the names of those who did their best to help a colleague who had fallen on evil days, and whose testimonials have survived. From Germany itself there were his old teacher, Otto Franke, his senior at Berlin, Erich Haenisch, and Paul Kahle of Bonn; from France, Jean Przyluski, Henri Maspero (who himself did not survive the holocaust from which Simon escaped), and Paul Pelliot; from the Netherlands, J. J. L. Duyvendak; from Sweden, Bernhard Karlgren; and from Britain, Lionel Giles and Arthur Waley. Simon had his well-wishers at the School of Oriental Studies (as it then was), his future academic home, also, notably the then Director, Sir E. Denison Ross. Yet, with all this, it was difficult at first for him to find a niche. Every one of his referees wrote of him in the most glowing terms, both as a man and a scholar, but none could offer any practical assistance. There were vague suggestions—what about Toronto, or the USA? Or a library post somewhere in China? Was anything to be hoped for from Jerusalem? If anything was going to be done to help Simon, that help would come only from England, yet here too it seemed, at first, as if it would not be possible for him to rehabilitate himself. The trouble was that the Academic Assistance Council was reluctant to make a grant unless there was some assurance that such help would definitely lead to his re-establishment in a university or similar career, while the School, the only potential refuge, had no money it could commit in the long term, and could not, on the spur of the moment, establish a post for him. The most it could do was to offer some hourly paid lectures, and that was not enough.

The problem was solved when 'certain anonymous donors' offered the Council enough money to maintain Simon from early 1936, when it was expected that he would return to London, until the end of July 1938. With this prospect, the School could make its offer of academic hospitality effective. The offer was made and accepted in February 1936, and in August the Home Office agreed to vary his conditions of landing in the United Kingdom so as to allow him to stay until 31 July 1938, and take up employment. But well before that time, the situation resolved itself in Simon's favour, at least as far as his career prospects were concerned. In June 1937 he was appointed to a part-time lectureship for the session 1937–8. During the course of that session, the University first granted him recognition as a university teacher, and then appointed him to a Readership by title.

It was only in September 1939 that Simon was granted permanent residence for himself and his family, and the outbreak of war brought with it new doubts and difficulties. The possibility of internment occurred to him at once, and he must have communicated this worry to the Director of the School, Professor R. L. (later Sir Ralph) Turner, for on 2 September, Turner, a constant and helpful friend, wrote to reassure him: 'I trust you will not be subjected to internment. I have informed certain Government Departments that your presence at the School will be required.' So far, so good, and the only disability which complicated his daily life was the irksome restriction on travel which applied to enemy aliens who were left at liberty, and who had to seek police permission for any journey lasting more than twenty-four hours. It looked at first as if he might need to travel up and down to Cambridge, to which the School had partially removed for a short while, and this provoked a certain amount of time-wasting and unsettling correspondence.

With the collapse of France in the summer of 1940, and the prospect of invasion, the spectre of internment darkened Simon's life once more. The Society for the Protection of Science and Learning prepared to appeal against his internment, and Professor Turner furnished them with the argument that the services of the Reader in Chinese would certainly be needed if the War Office and other Departments required to have officers trained in Chinese. At the beginning of October, Simon received official notification that he had been classified as exempt from internment until further order, though, in the correspondence which I have seen, there is a laconic note which reads: 'Not to teach Chinese to officers'—a self-contradictory compromise.

In the spring of 1941 Simon was detached to the Friends' Ambulance Unit Training Camp at Manor Park, Birmingham, where he spent a couple of months teaching Chinese. His teaching materials already included his forthcoming *Chinese Sentence Series*. Teaching, formal and informal, went on for most of the day and, sometimes, the evening too. As Simon wrote to his Head of Department at the School, Professor Eve Edwards:

> I teach group B from 2–3, and Mr. Hsiao takes them from 3–4. Then both of us can leave (and often do), if we do not stay (or return) for tea, which is at 5 o'clock. Supper is at 8, and Mr. Hsiao whose enthusiasm is boundless, has just now made up his mind to help students again in the evening, and the only comment I can make about this is that we must be thankful for the curfew at 10.30 which is imposed here at Birmingham. I have no doubt that, but for the curfew, he would go on until midnight. In any case, he will assure you, if you touch upon this subject, that he is doing very little.

So, one can be quite sure, would Simon himself.

Even into these short crash-courses of a professional, practical nature, Simon characteristically introduced a leaven of 'culture'. Saturday mornings were given over to revision and general talks, and in the same letter to Professor Edwards he wrote:

> I have prepared something on Mencius for tomorrow. And I think it is good for the students to know that Chinese, while enabling them to say 'I walk towards the blackboard', or 'I get up from my chair', has also been the vehicle of sublime thoughts, expressed in an incomparable way. What Mencius said about the 'True King' will, I hope, be of special interest to the students of this camp.

This chance quotation from a wartime letter to a colleague confirms what others have said about the breadth and humanity of Simon's teaching. As a beginner, Wolfgang Franke followed Simon's seminars in Berlin on *Liao-chai chih-i* and *Chuang-tzu* and his class on the reading of Japanese for Sinologists, an introduction to *Kambun*.

> Text-reading [he wrote to me], was the basis, but Simon understood well how to explain the contents and make reading interesting for the students. I greatly enjoyed his seminars and learned a lot from Simon, in particular in comparison with the rather dull, purely philological readings offered later by Haenisch, whose approach to texts I could not appreciate at all.

When in 1934 Simon was forbidden to teach at Berlin, his students protested to the university authorities, but to no avail, something which must have demanded a certain degree of civil courage, given the political conditions in Germany at the time. Quite independently, Dr Katherine Whitaker, a lifelong friend and colleague of Simon's at the School, and holder of a readership after him, told me how his London students would sometimes ask for extra classes, outside the agreed curriculum, recognizing his unusual scholarship and ability to communicate his knowledge.

Simon's status as an enemy alien irked him throughout the war years. He had applied for naturalization in mid-1941, with Professor Turner as one of his sponsors, but without success. In January 1943 he sent Turner a long letter on the subject, in which, with characteristic self-effacement matched with realism, he dwelt more upon the disadvantages which the School might experience through his remaining a German national, than upon his own bruised feelings, though he did not hide the personal side of the matter.

On the 15th January [he wrote] I had been teaching at the School for seven years exactly. And ever since I came, I felt that through my foreign nationality I was in an awkward position as far as my relations to 'modern China' were concerned. At the time when I emigrated to this country, I might have claimed that I was known in China as being distinctly sinophile and as one of the Western Chinese scholars who paid particular attention to modern Chinese publications, both academic and literary. I realised that through my immigration I would have to impose on myself great restraint in this respect and that I should have to make special efforts in order to avoid giving an ambiguous impression. While I proceeded with my teaching of modern Chinese, my publications were therefore devoted exclusively to non-modern subjects such as classical and Buddhistic Chinese and Tibetan. Through the war, which has brought practical teaching to the foreground, and even more through its latest phase, which has made China an ally of this country, this restraint has, however, no longer seemed possible. On the other hand the abandonment of this line has also given prominence to the discrepancy between my feelings towards China and the impossibility of putting them into full effect before becoming a naturalised British subject. As you know, I have pointed out the usefulness of the New Official Chinese Latin Script for the teaching of Chinese in the West. A Primer and a pamphlet have been published on this, a reader will be out in a few weeks, and a Chinese–English dictionary and an anthology will follow within this year, I hope. These publications may arouse a certain amount of interest in China, and it would certainly add to their interest if it could be said that not only was this script taught in our School, but that its propagator had also been awarded British citizenship.

In this self-revealing letter, Simon went on to explain that he was conscious of potential, and crippling, restrictions which might in the future be placed on his teaching. Somehow he must have surmised that officialdom had not fully trusted him, for he wrote:

It may seem as if I am not handicapped at all in my teaching at present in spite of my nationality. But I should like to point out that considerable difficulties exist at least potentially and may in fact crop up at any moment. I may assume that the School must desire their teachers to be able to teach without any limitations either as to the kind of material envisaged for teaching, or to the kind of students entrusted to them, or to the place where the teaching may proceed. No limitations are at present imposed apparently on my teaching of members of his Majesty's forces, but I think such limitations were imposed at some time in the past. [And he concluded:] There is, in fact not one of these plans, and in general not a single one of my present or future activities at the School (including those which are connected with research work and postgraduate training) which is or would not be impeded by my nationality, and none on the other hand which could not be turned to much greater effect by the award of British citizenship.

The Director evidently accepted the cogency of this argument, for he supported Simon's case in a letter to the Home Office, but the application was refused in accordance with wartime policy on the granting of naturalization, and it was not till some time after the end of the war that Simon finally achieved his ambition of obtaining British nationality.

The 'New Official Chinese Latin Script' in which Simon was now publishing was the transcription system known as *Gwoyeu Romatzyh*, or GR for short. This system had been developed during Kuo Min Tang days by the eminent Chinese scholar, the late Y. R. Chao (a Corresponding Member of the School and, until his death in 1982, a Corresponding Fellow of the British Academy), but, associated as it was with the republican government of Chiang Kai-shek, it could not survive the communist assumption of power in 1949, and its place was ultimately taken by the current official system for transcribing Chinese known as *pinyin*. In the nature of things, no transcription system for Chinese can be both scientifically accurate and easy to use. But GR had one unique characteristic which enhanced its usefulness for pedagogical purposes, and at the same time made it easier to read, write, and type. It dispensed not only with aspirates, as *pinyin* does, but with superscript tone marks, whether accents or figures, as well, and represented the four tones of standard Chinese by means of systematic spelling devices. Thus, at the mechanical level, it became possible, for the first time, to convey the whole phonological content of a Chinese word on a single line of type. More importantly perhaps even than this, the student became accustomed to think of tone as an inherent feature of the word, not as an afterthought applied to an ideal (and hence non-existent) toneless prototype. Right from the beginning, the student perceived the Chinese sound-system in Chinese, rather than European, terms. To accomplish such a revolutionary step in the representation of Chinese by means of the letters of the English alphabet meant adopting some strange conventions. Certain spelling devices, such as the insertion of the letter *r*, the doubling of certain vowels and consonants, the substitution of one vowel for another, were used, not for their anticipated phonetic effect, but quite artificially, to denote difference of tone. Even though standard Chinese consists, essentially, only of monosyllables, which are themselves limited to consonant plus vowel, or vowel alone, and admit of no closed syllables except those ending in -*n* and -*ng*, the varied structure of the Chinese word made it impossible to restrict the system to four spelling stages, each indicating one of the four tones. The system was much more intricate. Thus, Wade-Giles *hên*$^{1-4}$ came out as *hen, hern, heen, henn*, while *huang*$^{1-4}$ became *huang, hwang, hoang, huanq*. The principle behind the conventions, and the various conventions themselves, took some getting used to, but once the principle was understood, the details soon fell into place, so skilfully was the system devised. Simon was a great believer in the value of mnemonics, and he worked out a system of mnemonics, in which the consonants of the keywords corresponded, through values given in a substitution-table, with the number of the radical. The meaning of the radical was also associated with that of the keyword. The concept itself is a venerable one. In a learned footnote in his *Beginner's Chinese–English Dictionary*, Simon traced the principle of letter-figure substitution back to one Stanislaus Mink von Wenusheim, who publicized it in 1684. But whether this somewhat strained and artificial word-game ever actually helped any student gain a comprehensive knowledge of the Chinese radicals must be a matter of doubt. Some of the associations were rather far-fetched: thus radical 146, which means 'west', had, as its mnemonic, '*trip* (to the West)', and *t, r*, and *p* had, respectively, the numerical values 1, 4, and 6. On the other hand, no user of Chao's GR, and I am sure not Simon himself, can have remained unconscious of the mimetic and mnemonic association which seems to obtain between certain of the spelling conventions and their realization in speech. The doubled vowel used for the third tone in many words, or the added final *h*, the doubled final *n*, or the change of *ng* to *nq* representing the falling fourth tone, somehow seemed to display their mimicry once one had grasped how the scheme worked.

In spite of representations made early in the war by the School, government refused to admit that its reserves of officers expert in Chinese and Japanese was anything but adequate for all fore-seeable situations. Japan's entry into the war in December 1941 finally shattered this complacent illusion. A scheme for the award of scholarships in oriental languages to boys still at school was worked out, and approved by the Board of Education in February 1942. A selection board was appointed, under Professor Turner, which considered over 700 applications. More than 150 candi-dates were interviewed and 74 scholarships were awarded, 16 of them in Chinese. (In passing, we may recall that, once having woken up to the disastrous lack of trained linguists, officialdom did not do things by halves. While thirty scholarships were awarded to boys selected to study Japanese at the School, a separate Japanese language-training unit was set up at Bedford, as part of an inter-services intelligence school, and here, over the next few years, a series of six-month crash courses was run, at first under the late Captain Tuck, RN, and then under one of his first pupils, the late Lieut. E. B. Ceadel, who afterwards became University Librarian at Cambridge.)

The Director of the School, and some of his senior colleagues, had been instrumental in bringing this scholarship scheme into being, but the tasks of working out a syllabus of instruction, organizing the courses, compiling teaching material, and actually doing the teaching, fell, as far as Chinese was concerned, largely upon Simon's shoulders. This first exercise in large-scale language training at the School was followed by other courses for the services and government departments, in both standard Chinese and Cantonese, which continued after the end of the war, and if in no other way than this, Simon amply repaid his adoptive country for its hospitality by his contribution to its war-effort.

In 1947 the University of London established a second Chair of Chinese, to which Simon was appointed with effect from October of that year. Three years later, the School appointed him Acting Head of the Department of the Far East, and in 1952 he succeeded Professor Edwards as Head. During the immediate post-war years several possibilities of moving on from London presented themselves to him. In 1946 and 1947 he was offered the Chair of Sinology at the University of Berlin, which was situated in the Soviet sector of the city, but he declined. Refusal of this offer may not have taken much consideration: there is no mention of the circumstances in his correspondence with the School which I have seen, and knowledge of the offer comes from a private communication. He was, though, certainly interested in the Chair of Chinese at Oxford, which was advertised in the middle of 1946, though it is not clear whether he allowed his candidature to run the full course. What is quite certain is that he could have been the successor to Gustav Haloun at Cambridge. Approaches were made to him by that University, and he was much tempted to entertain them. But his natural loyalty, reinforced by his consciousness of the value placed upon his continued presence at the School by its Director and Governing Body, persuaded him to close his ears to the siren voices from the Cam. It was not an easy choice, for he felt attracted to Cambridge. As he wrote to the Director:

The talk I had with you confirmed the conclusion I had arrived at independently when thinking this matter over very carefully for more than one month, viz. that I should remain where I am. What you have written about the temptations of Cambridge is only too true. I feel a spell cast around me whenever I am in Cambridge and walk around the colleges, but I have come to the conclusion that this spell—not to mention other temptations—must be resisted and that in these last few years of my career I can serve sinological studies in this country best by remaining in London. I feel fortunate indeed that this decision of mine should agree with what you Sir, and, as you assure me, my colleagues wish me to do. I shall be glad to remain at the School, which to serve I have considered an honour ever since it first offered me academic hospitality.

What the Director of the School had written was, in part: 'I cannot disguise from you my conviction that your acceptance would be disastrous for the Far East Department and a severe blow to the School as a whole.' It would not have been in Simon's character to resist so urgent an appeal from the institution which had first sheltered him.

From September 1948 to August 1949, Simon was granted study leave from the School for the purpose of buying books and renewing contacts in the East. In China he was indeed able to meet several of his old friends from his Exchange Librarian days, but in some ways China itself was a disappointment. The republican government was disintegrating, and its decline was marked by its failure to deal honestly with the public, a failure which had been only too characteristic of the war years and after. In a long letter to Professor Edwards, Simon described, with distaste, how the authorities were manipulating the currency so as to fleece the general public, Chinese and foreigners alike, and line their own pockets. Prices were being allowed to rise while the rates of exchange for foreign currency were maintained, and there was barefaced swindling over the manipulation of the deadline for the exchange of foreign assets. This cost the holders of foreign currency enormous amounts of money.

I saw X. cashing big packages of Gold Yuan on a Monday morning realising that this (one week's ration only!) will cost the War Office thousands of pounds and nobody profiting from it except the 'Sung Dynasty' in control of the Central Bank of China. In the middle of October when inflation was well on the way I was told by a lady on the Council of YWCA that they changed all their reserves in Gold and in American Dollars on the 30th September as they were told to do, and the next day there came the promulgation of the extension of the period of surrender of these values. This extension was the signal for breaking away from the GY in the North because the people then saw that the Government were dishonest in their practices. I wonder whether China realises to what an extent she has forfeited the sympathies of foreigners by the GY fraud.

In spite of his dislike of spending money in an unorthodox way, Simon was forced to take steps to protect the School's funds, and he paid for many of his book purchases with cheques on Hongkong.

After the dishonest financial policy which I have just described I have no moral qualms either (nobody in fact has!) and even some satisfaction in the idea that this money remains in the sterling area and that it will buy us many more books instead of having simply come to nothing if changed at the official rate.

It was pleasant to meet old friends in China, and useful to make new contacts in Japan, but from the School's point of view the skill with which Simon fulfilled his major task—the purchase of books for its Library—was undoubtedly more significant. In Hongkong he was able to buy most of the important books which had been published during the last two decades by China's two biggest publishing houses, the Shanghai Commercial Press and the Chung Hwa Book Co., both of which had moved their head offices from Shanghai to British territory. At the Apollo Book Store he made substantial purchases of modern literature. There were many bargains to be had in Peking, where books were still cheap.

The old book is cheap in Peking because there are still large stocks of it there and few people who have money to buy. We shall get a good number of Tsongshu's both of works of different authors and collected works of one author. Furthermore I bought all important encyclopaedias which we have not got (except Ming prints) and also bought books on the ancient script which was another serious deficiency in our Library. New gazetteers have also been included, furthermore important modern reference books, a complete series of the Harvard Yenching Indexes, modern periodicals as from 1939. Of single items I mention only the *Ming Shyrluh*.

He also bought Manchu books, and Tibetan and Mongolian blockprints, some already irreplaceable, as the blocks from which they were printed had been used by Japanese soldiers as firewood. In Japan he bought Japanological works and 'a fairly complete collection of Japanese Sinological contributions'. It was not a unique purchasing trip, for Haloun, too, was able to go to China and buy on behalf of the Cambridge University Library, but it was of great importance for the School, which could now face the imminent expansion in Far Eastern studies confident that it had a working and reference library of unparalleled completeness in Europe, and that it would be relatively unaffected by China's approaching isolationism.

The post-war years brought distracting obligations of a different kind, which occupied the attention of the senior staff of the School until well into the 1950s. The Report of the Scarbrough Commission, completed in 1946 and published in 1947, recommended an unprecedented expansion in the provision for the study, at university level, of Oriental, Slavonic, East European, and African languages and cultures. The lion's share of this expansion, as far as Asia and Africa were concerned, was taken up by the School, and Simon was one of those who, having shouldered the burden of the war years, now had to turn his attention to the problem of planning and carrying out the reorganization of Far Eastern studies on a scale never before attempted. As Sir Cyril Philips, subsequently Director of the School, has written:

In defining and applying these plans, especially in recruiting and training young scholars to open up fresh fields of study while simultaneously maintaining the normal routine of university teaching and administration, the whole attention and energy of the senior members of staff was absorbed often at the expense of their own research, and in several instances of their health. The School's debt to a small circle of dedicated heads of departments, not least to Professor Eve Edwards,

Professor John Firth, Professor Walter Simon, and Professor Ida Ward, who, along with the Director carried the burden of the day, was immeasurable.

And indeed, the Department of the Far East at the School of Oriental and African Studies, as it exists today, over twenty years after Simon's retirement, is essentially his creation, even if its shape has been modified in detail and it has sustained some unrepaired losses. In January 1937 Simon was told, in an interview with the then Secretary of the School, G. W. Rossetti, that the staff of the Department would consist in the session 1937-8 of the Professor, the Assistant Lecturer, and himself. In the wake of the implementation of the Scarbrough Commission's recommendations, the Department came to comprise twenty-six established posts. Naturally enough, most appointments were made in the main fields in which research and teaching took place, that is, modern and classical Chinese, and Japanese. But Simon's vision stretched further, and he was able to utilize the opportunities afforded by Scarbrough to promote the study of the 'peripheral' areas of China, that is, Korea, Mongolia, and Tibet. For the first time in the history of the School there was academic coverage of the entire area which the Department was supposed to embrace, and this regardless of whether or not there was likely to be much demand for teaching.

Rapid expansion had, of course, its latent dangers, which are now being realized. War experience had opened the eyes of many young men of scholarly bent, who might otherwise not have encountered the East, to the possibility of applying familiar methods to what were then still exotic fields of study, and their return to civilian life coincided with the comparative wealth of opportunities afforded by the new order of things. Simon, like other heads of departments, could draw on a whole generation of young, prepared talent. But this 'Scarbrough generation' is now approaching retirement in a very different economic climate from that of the imaginative, if austere, post-war years, and the fate of departments like the one Simon once led must to some degree lie in the balance.

Simon's academic research took several directions. His earliest interest was in problems connected with the reconstruction of early stages of the Chinese language. The first tentative steps towards the recovery of the sound-system of what was to be known as Ancient Chinese, the Chinese of about AD 600, had been taken as long ago as the second half of the nineteenth century by men like Edkins and Schaank. More systematic progress was made by

Pelliot and Maspero, who drew up provisional schemes for the interpretation of the Ancient Chinese sound-system. But it was the Swedish scholar, Bernhard Karlgren, who made the subject his own. His systematic recovery of the Ancient Chinese sound-system excited all Sinologists of his generation, and was followed by his reconstruction of the Chinese language as it was a thousand years earlier still—Karlgren's Archaic Chinese. Karlgren's epoch-making studies began to appear during the war years, and in 1926, in *Philology and Ancient China* he accomplished the difficult task of popularizing his remote field of research, explaining the problem itself and what was to be gained from its solution, the methods by which it was being solved, and his results to date. Simon's first publications in the same field consisted of a review which appeared in 1924, of Karlgren's *Analytic Dictionary of Chinese* (Paris, 1923), and two independent articles: 'Die Spaltung der chinesischen Tieftonreihe' (*Asia Major*, Leipzig, 1927) and 'Zur Rekonstruktion der altchinesischen Endkonsonanten' (*Mitteilungen des Seminars für Orientalische Sprachen*, 1927–8). In the latter article, as Simon recalled in a review, published in the *Bulletin of the School of Oriental Studies* in 1938 of two later publications by Karlgren, he had accepted the completeness and coherence of the Swedish sinologist's system of reconstruction. In this, he said:

hardly any sound value may be replaced by another without upsetting the whole system. No matter whether one believes, as does the originator probably himself, in the reality of the reconstruction, or whether one considers its sound values rather as values of probability or in part merely as convenient symbols, one has made general use of these reconstructions and cannot be too grateful for the extraordinary trouble which Professor Karlgren has taken in them.

Here is the true voice of the sceptical Simon whom one remembers. Having gratefully acknowledged Karlgren's monumental scheme of reconstruction, he set about refining it, especially with respect to the principles for the recovery of the finals. The difference of opinion between the two eminent Sinologists led to a certain amount of controversy—as Simon wrote, Karlgren 'had at first at least in part, strongly objected to my reconstructions'.

Simon argued that his reconstructions were to some extent vouched for by the Tibetan–Chinese word equations which he had established in his paper 'Tibetisch–Chinesische Wortgleichungen. Ein Versuch' (*MSOS*, 1929, and separately, 1930). This paper, and his *Addenda* to the Reprint of H. A. Jäschke's *Tibetan Grammar*, compiled jointly with A. H. Francke, which also came out in 1929, were his first public excursions into what was

to prove a lifelong interest, and the hobby of his years of retirement—the study of problems of Tibetan philology and linguistics.

No doubt in consequence of his training and experience as a
librarian, Simon compiled several articles of a bibliographical
nature, in which he summarized and reviewed current trends in,
particularly, pedagogical publications. His article 'Yen-wen dui-
dschau und Kokuyaku Kanbun' (*MSOS*, 1930 and 1931) was
a useful synthesis of, and guide to, editions of classical Chinese
texts with accompanying modern Chinese, or Japanese, translations. In 1932 and 1934 he was reviewing recent handbooks of
the colloquial language of North China: the second part of this
double article dealt with seventeen Russian textbooks which had
appeared in Harbin between 1930 and 1932, as well as with more
accessible works in German and English. A fourth line of research
opened in 1933 when Simon made his own contribution to the
study of modern Chinese grammar with an article entitled 'Zur
Bildung der antithetischen Doppelfrage im Neuhochchinesischen'
(*Sinica*), and in the same year came his first publication in the field
of Manchu studies—the contribution to Li's catalogue mentioned
above. In 1934 he returned to Chinese grammar with an analysis
of the meaning of the final particle *i* 矣 (*MSOS*). Classical Chinese
lacked, as it still does, a comprehensive grammar, and the study of
individual particles proved, both before and after the Second
World War, one of the most fruitful ways in which self-contained,
but systematically linked, attacks could be made upon aspects of
that daunting problem. This line of research was resumed after the
war, in what was the major work of Simon's later years—a four-
part article entitled 'The Functions and Meanings of Erl 而'
which appeared in *Asia Major* (by now a British, and no longer
a German journal, and edited for several years by Simon himself)
in 1952-4.

During the war, Simon's attention was devoted almost entirely
to yet another task, the preparation and publication of practical
teaching and reference material. Between 1942 and 1947 there
appeared, one after another, *Chinese Sentence Series*; *Chinese National
Language (Gwoyeu) Reader and Guide to Conversation*; *1200 Chinese Basic
Characters*; *How to Study and Write Chinese Characters*; *Structure Drill
through Speech Patterns. No. 1. Structure Drill in Chinese* (with T. C.
Chao); and, finally, *A Beginner's Chinese-English Dictionary of the
National Language (Gwoyeu)*. Most of these ran into second editions,
though all have been overtaken by time. Simon's books are no
longer used, for example, at the School where they were developed, but this is a natural process, whose inevitability Simon

himself no doubt accepted with understanding. Fashions in teaching soon change, and those courses which replaced Simon's at SOAS have themselves been replaced. New ideas and new needs in language teaching, a new romanization system accompanied by a script reform in China, the development of the Chinese language under the stress of political revolution, the recent emergence of China from its self-imposed isolation, and the opening up of a Chinese book trade in London, have all combined to alter perspectives. Simon's *Dictionary*, probably the most durable of his wartime products, can still be used, though it has been overtaken by more up-to-date and comprehensive works like the *Pin-yin Chinese–English Dictionary*, but one no longer turns to it as a first resource, as one did thirty years ago.

In the post-war years Simon's researches moved away from pure Sinology. He did, admittedly, contribute an introduction and the romanized Japanese versions to his colleague, Mrs Liu's, *Fifty Chinese Stories*, in 1960, but this was a practical textbook, used for class teaching, not a product of research. His publications began to reflect more and more his preoccupation with Tibetan. There were forays into other fields, the most notable being *Manchu Books in London. A Union Catalogue*, which he produced jointly with Mr Howard Nelson in 1977, but the trend towards Tibetan is unmistakeably apparent in the numerous articles, mostly quite short, which he continued to contribute to *Asia Major* and *BSOAS*.

There was, then, no single underlying theme in Simon's work, no single goal towards which it all tended. Things would surely have been rather different had it not been for his exile and the distractions of wartime duties. Time, too, has taken its toll of much of what he published, though individual items still retain their brilliance, and some their utility. I would dare to suggest that it is for a different achievement that he will be remembered, and here I take my cue from the perceptive remark with which Herbert Franke, then Professor of Chinese at Munich, introduced his contribution to the *Festschrift* for Simon's old Professor, Erich Haenisch, in 1961. 'Die Bedeutung eines Gelehrten im Rahmen der Entwicklung seiner Wissenschaft darf nicht nur an seinen Veröffentlichungen gemessen werden. Entscheidend für das Fach ist oft das Wirken für die Anerkennung und Durchsetzung einer wissenschaftlichen Disziplin an den Universitäten.'

It is no exaggeration to evaluate Simon, along with Gustav Haloun, as one of the founders of modern, professional British Sinology. To do so is not to denigrate his predecessors at the three great universities, Cambridge, Oxford, and London, which have been the traditional (though by now not the only) homes of Chinese scholarship, nor to undervalue the contribution to Sinology made by his contemporaries. But it suggests that Simon's achievement was of a different order altogether. Right up to the time of the Second World War, British Sinology had remained, broadly speaking, the preserve of distinguished amateurs, the province of men who, after retiring from active life, and often brilliant careers, in the East, as government servants or missionaries, occupied their latter years in the pursuit of what remained exotic studies, outside the mainstream of university life. There was no academic tradition, in the sense of a continuing line of masters and pupils, constituting vigorous university departments, and enjoying the financial and psychological back-up expected by the older disciplines. Brilliant scholars there were indeed—men like James Legge, Thomas Wade, Herbert Giles, A. C. Moule, and, amongst Simon's contemporaries, the incomparable Arthur Waley. But for one reason or another, personal disinclination or the absence of a supportive climate of opinion, they did not, and could not, found schools. To have done this was Simon's merit.

Simon's tenure of the Chair of Chinese marked a new beginning in that he was, right from the start, a professional scholar, who brought to the study of Chinese in this country the painstaking and systematic methods of German classical philology, and raised the status of his adopted discipline to something like that of older-established fields of study. He, and Haloun, whose tenure of the Chair at Cambridge was disappointingly brief, were, in spite of the personal disaster of lost homeland and shattered ideals, ultimately fortunate in their time. The years of their greatest vigour and creativity coincided with a period of unprecedented expansion in their discipline, and, holding Chairs at two major universities, they could make the most of the opportunities which were presented to them. Government favoured expansion, and provided the funds and fostered the climate of opinion in which it was possible, with some assurance of continuity in policy, to plan for growth, and recruit young scholars and teachers to whom hopes, if not assurance, of careers in the universities could be held out. In Simon's case, some of these young recruits to professional scholarship had even passed through his hands as senior schoolboys. He and Haloun supplied their own, and each other's, universities with lecturers and future professors, and trained up scholars who today occupy Chairs of Sinology across the English-speaking world. To have set authoritative standards of scholarship and won international recognition for a youthful discipline is no mean claim to remembrance.

Simon retired from the Chair of Chinese in 1960, and in June of that year the University conferred upon him the title of Professor Emeritus, in appreciation and recognition of his distinguished service to itself and his subject. A few days later the School elected him one of its complement of twenty-five Honorary Fellows. Retirement freed him for writing and for taking up visiting appointments. He was Visiting Professor at the University of Toronto in 1961-2, at the Australian National University, Canberra, in 1962, and at Tokyo, Canberra, and Melbourne in 1970. In 1956 he was elected to the British Academy and at the beginning of 1961 his services were publicly recognized when he was appointed CBE. He was also elected an Honorary Research Fellow of the Toyo Bunko, Tokyo. In 1963, part 1 of volume x of *Asia Major*, still edited by his old friend Bruno Schindler, carried a congratulatory address in Latin to him, accompanied by his portrait and a list of the names of his well-wishers, followed by a bibliography of his publications to date, while part 2 carried a congratulatory address in Chinese, composed and written by Mr Lee Yim, a member of his old department at the School, and an authority on oracle-bones. This was in celebration of his seventieth birthday. Ten years later, the School celebrated his eightieth birthday with an issue of its *Bulletin*, part 2 of volume xxxvi, which was inscribed 'In Honour of Walter Simon'. A specially bound copy was presented to him at a little gathering at the School on 26 June, a few days after his birthday. His last public honour was the award of the Triennial Gold Medal of the Royal Asiatic Society, which he received in 1977. From the previous year he had been an Honorary Vice-President of the Society.

These were the official signs of recognition of a distinguished career, which had included, apart from his university duties, such other isolated or continuing activities as representing the School at the International Congress of Orientalists held at Istanbul in 1951; acting as member and chairman of the Editorial Board, and ultimately as editor (1964-75) of the revived *Asia Major*; the Presidency of the Philological Society (1967-70); and Trusteeship of the Institute of Tibetan Studies at Tring. At the personal level he enjoyed the respect, trust, and affection of everyone who came close to him. Arthur Waley knew him as 'a man of exceptional personal charm'. Otto Franke, too, was sensible of his attractive personality, finding him a man of high-minded character (*von vornehmer Gesinnung*) and absolute reliability. Those of us who belonged to a later generation may have found it less easy to penetrate his reserve, and to establish so direct a contact with him: one was always conscious of the gap in years and wisdom, and the distance in experience, which all his affability could not quite bridge over. There were definite stages of increasing intimacy: the invitation to drop the title of Professor, the use of the Christian name, and, perhaps most moving, the telling of a Jewish joke in German. One could not call Simon withdrawn, but he did give the impression of being rather a private man. Added to that, especially in his later years, his style of conversation became rather indirect. It was not always easy to pick up the thread of his discourse, which seemed on occasions to be no more than the momentary articulation of a continuing stream of thought. Simon was essentially a moral man, considered and deliberate in his actions, which must have been governed by a consistent feeling of responsibility for their outcome. He will indeed be remembered as a man of innate nobility of character.

Walter Simon died on 22 February 1981 at the age of eighty-seven, leaving a widow, Kate, née Jungmann, and two sons.

C. R. BAWDEN

PLATE XXV

STEFAN STRELCYN

STEFAN STRELCYN

1918–1981

I

STEFAN STRELCYN was born at Warsaw on 28 June 1918, the son of Szaja Strelcyn and Cywia, née Frank. He died at Manchester on 19 May 1981, suddenly and at the height of his scholarly achievements. Between those dates lies a career as *éthiopisant* and Semitist which has brought genuine enrichment to our knowledge and understanding of Ethiopian manuscripts, of magical, medical, and botanical texts and lore, as well as of sundry other aspects of Semitic studies.

At Warsaw Strelcyn attended the Gimnazjum Ascola and the Technical Engineering School, but at the age of twenty, in 1938, he left both engineering and Poland; the former because his interests had turned towards oriental studies, and the latter because he could no longer put up with the atmosphere of anti-Semitism so pervasive in Polish life and politics—irrespective of the ideological hue of the regime. He went to Belgium where he enrolled in the Université Libre de Bruxelles and devoted himself to the study of oriental archaeology and philology, including Egyptian and Coptic. Though the latter subsequently ceased to be at the centre of his interests, the smattering (no doubt it was a good deal more in reality) that he admitted having retained proved to be a useful adjunct to his later Ethiopian specialization.

These studies were interrupted by the events of 1940 when he enlisted in the Polish Forces in France until the defeat of the French brought all open fighting to a close. However, Strelcyn was never a defeatist and from 1941 he was a member of the French resistance movement. He was, fortunately, able at the same time to pursue his studies at the ancient university of Montpellier where he specialized in general linguistics and in the history of art (1940–2). Earlier, in 1940, he had married his fellow-Pole Maria Kirzner, his lifelong close companion who was associated with him in all the struggles, vicissitudes, and joys of his career. Later on, in the 1950s and 1960s, she held senior positions in the Polish civil service. She survives him together with the two sons of the marriage, the elder a mathematician in France and the younger a geologist in this country.

In 1944 his courageous activities in the French *résistance* came to a halt when he was deported to Eutritzsch near Leipzig. It was his impeccable French (a language to which he was devoted throughout his life and of which he was such a notable practitioner) that stood him in such good stead then, for the Germans never suspected him of being a Pole. After the war he was awarded the Croix de Guerre.

In 1945 he resumed his studies, now at the Sorbonne, the École Nationale des Langues Orientales Vivantes, and the École Pratique des Hautes Études—a period extending up to 1950. His energies and interest had become increasingly focused upon classical Ethiopic (Gəʿəz), Amharic, the modern official language, and Ethiopian studies in general. He came under the influence of Marcel Cohen to whom he remained utterly devoted. His closest colleagues, all disciples of Marcel Cohen, were Joseph Tubiana, Roger Schneider, and Maxime Rodinson who have all contributed so signally to Ethiopian and general oriental studies and also continued their ties of intimate friendship with Strelcyn. Tubiana has written a moving tribute to his late friend which I was allowed to see before its publication in the *Journal of Semitic Studies* (spring 1982) and from whose perusal I benefited in the writing of this memoir.

At the behest of Marcel Cohen, Strelcyn turned his attention to two main tasks: the completion of the catalogue of Ethiopic manuscripts in the Bibliothèque Nationale of Paris (a work of which Sylvain Grébaut had published several parts but which had not been concluded by him) and an edition of Ethiopian magical prayers. Neither enterprise was published during Strelcyn's sojourn at Paris. In 1949–50 he served as *attaché de recherches* at the Centre National de la Recherche Scientifique (CNRS) and was thus able to make much headway with the two projects commissioned by his *maître*. Marcel Cohen was an exacting teacher, a caring supervisor who, together with his solicitous wife, allowed his closest disciples into his hospitable home, and also exerted a strong influence, perhaps not entirely free of a somewhat imperious element, upon those under his tutelage. Cohen himself had always seemed to me more than a little naïve in his communist attachment, but Strelcyn was a passionate soul underneath his well-modulated exterior and deeply devoted to the amelioration of society and of the individual's lot within it. He fell foul of the French authorities and in the autumn of 1950 he was expelled from France and despatched to a Poland in which he had not lived for twelve years.

His reception at Warsaw was highly gratifying, a consummation to which his scholarly stature and the manner of his departure from France probably contributed in equal measure. He was soon installed as Associate Professor of Semitic Studies (1950-4) and head of the eponymous department. From 1954 to 1969 he served his university as a full professor. It was thanks to Strelcyn's initiative that in 1962 the Centre of African Studies was founded, under his direction, at the University of Warsaw; and Poland became an internationally recognized nucleus of oriental and African research, sustained by the excellence of Strelcyn's own publications (about which see anon) and by the contributions of the students he had trained.

When he attended the international congress of orientalists at Cambridge, in 1954, his recently published massive catalogue of the Paris Griaule collection and some fine articles, mainly in *GLECS* and the *Rassegna di Studi Etiopici*, had preceded him and provided him with an enviable introduction to his professional colleagues assembled in England. It was at that time that I first met Stefan Strelcyn in person; and having just reviewed his *Erstlingswerk* in enthusiastic terms I was naturally pleased to welcome a new face among the then small band of *éthiopisants*. We got on well from our first meeting, although at that time he was still a little edgy and defensive and had not yet developed the urbane personality his colleagues came to know so well later on. It was his first visit to Britain and to this side of the Iron Curtain since his return to Warsaw, and the scars of his expulsion from France had not yet healed.

The next important stage in Strelcyn's career (and, as it happens, also in the development of our friendship) was his research journey to Ethiopia in 1957-8. This was his first glimpse of the promised land, and he was not disappointed. When I arrived at Addis Ababa, early in 1958, it was with genuine surprise and pleasure that I found Strelcyn ensconced there. He had taken lodgings in a little French pension, while I was established in a somewhat run-down 'native' hostelry. I had little difficulty in persuading him, 'the representative of a socialist country', to move to the more authentic and humbler surroundings occupied by myself. Here we spent many happy weeks together in pursuit of our different purposes and exchanging information and impressions. He had made magnificent use of the opportunities offered, but he suffered a little from the absence in those years of any official representation of his country in Ethiopia. By comparison my passage was infinitely smoother. His conscience and his convictions forbade him at that time to seek any contact with the Palace; I offered to arrange an audience of the Emperor but he felt he had to decline. It was at a chance meeting, after an Easter church service, that I had an opportunity of presenting him informally to Emperor Haile Sellassie who made an indelible impression on Strelcyn. In later years he remained steadfastly faithful to the monarch and to his memory. Earlier on I had taken him with me to show him northern Ethiopia and Eritrea where I had served in the British Military Administration during the war. These travels consolidated our friendship and revealed Strelcyn's character and knowledge to best advantage.

In the following year, in 1959, Enrico Cerulli, the greatest of *éthiopisants*, convened the first international conference of Ethiopian studies at the Accademia dei Lincei at Rome. Strelcyn was able to attend, but it should be recalled that these relatively frequent journeys abroad entailed a great many problems of finance, organization, and indeed politics. Only someone in the strong academic and general position then held by Strelcyn was able to arrange and to maintain such virtually annual international contacts in the Western world. At Rome he occupied a fairly central stance; his scholarship was now generally recognized and acknowledged; Cerulli thought exceptionally highly of him, and Strelcyn was the only scholar to read two papers to the conference, on Ethiopian plant names and on Ethiopian magic, the twin subjects then absorbing his interests, to which he had made such important contributions. I myself was fortunate in having Strelcyn in the chair for my own paper. Rome also meant a reunion with Marcel Cohen, Tubiana, and Rodinson as well as the definitive confirmation, the decisive accolade, of his entry among the foremost names in the world of Ethiopian scholarship.

In 1961 the British Council facilitated a visit by him to Manchester where C. F. Beckingham and myself were then serving in chairs of Islamic Studies and Semitic languages, respectively. He delivered several lectures in French and participated in teaching and in the discussion of research projects. When, in 1963, I was able to go to Warsaw on a reciprocal visit, I saw him for the first and only time in his native ambience. I came to realize the pivotal position he held in Polish oriental studies. He showed me with pride the impressive rebuilding of Warsaw and the excellent department of Semitic, Ethiopian, and African studies he had established. His colleagues and students spoke with admiration and some awe of the central and influential position he occupied in Poland, a situation which was not without advantage to them. Not all of them were mindful of these benefits when, in the later 1960s, Strelcyn fell on evil days.

When I first arrived at his Warsaw department his colleagues and students were lined up outside the building and gave a splendid rendering of *gaudeamus igitur*—in classical Ethiopic. This was based on a bibliographical curiosum (Strelcyn was always a great collector of these) of which I had been quite unaware until then. In 1899 the young Enno Littmann, later to become one of the outstanding German orientalists, had privately printed, at the Straub Press at Munich, seventy-five copies of his translation into Ethiopic (Gǝʿǝz) of a number of German songs, including *yǝʾǝzeke nǝtfässaḥ* (*gaudeamus igitur*), *namsa namsa laʿlä kwǝllu* ('Deutschland, Deutschland über alles'), as well as birthday odes to Professors Nöldeke and Praetorius. This memoir may possibly contain the first published reference to this literary oddity.

In the summer of 1963 he returned to Manchester to attend the second international conference of Ethiopian studies. He was particularly gratified to see honorary degrees conferred upon his teacher Marcel Cohen and on Enrico Cerulli and H. J. Polotsky. The paper which he read to the congress marked a fresh departure in his scholarly concerns, although it arose from his preoccupation with early medical and botanical texts: henceforth the exploration of the earliest recorded phases of Amharic moved close to the centre of his interests (see presently).

1965 found him on his first visit to Israel attending the international conference of Semitists at Jerusalem. He combined this purpose with the first of several *sondages* in the Faitlovitch Library at Tel Aviv (foreshadowing a later interest, in the footsteps of Stephen Wright, in Ethiopian 'incunabula') and with the checking of some Hebrew manuscripts in several Israeli libraries. Since 1953 he had been preparing, jointly with F. Kupfer, a catalogue of Hebrew manuscripts in the Jewish Historical Institute at Warsaw, but this work of more than a thousand entries has never been published—for political reasons. This restriction and curtailment of objective (and entirely non-political) scholarship had by now begun to cause him a good deal of worry and anguish. The fetters and shackles, the restraints upon the mind, were becoming increasingly irksome to one who wished to be a loyal participant in the socialist experiment but found it hard to accept some of the concomitant phenomena. Yet he remained discreet and circumspect in the expression of such criticisms, even in conversation with his closest friends. He had experienced exile and expulsion before!

His first contact with Israel was not without problems either. Strelcyn was never an observant or a practising Jew, but he wished Israel well. The chauvinistic and discordant noises,

484 PROCEEDINGS OF THE BRITISH ACADEMY

emanating from Mr Begin in opposition, were as uncongenial to him then as they later became with Begin installed in government. It was a poignant irony (to anticipate a little) that, when he was forced to leave Poland in 1969, the Polish authorities compelled him and others to apply for emigration to Israel, in order to castigate them as Zionist lackeys, although Strelcyn wanted to go to England to which he had an entry visa and the offer of an academic post.

To revert to the chronological sequence: the third international conference of Ethiopian studies took place at Addis Ababa in 1966. By now there had occurred a very considerable accretion to the practitioners of Ethiopian studies in many countries, but particularly in Ethiopia itself and in the United States. The position of eminence which Strelcyn occupied in this company was eloquently confirmed when Warsaw was elected, in preference to the United States, as the venue for the next congress. This, alas, was the last time he could represent his country from a position of strength and authority: restrictions on freedom in general, and academic freedom in particular, began to grow apace; and, as so often happens, anti-Semitism in Poland was no longer a private pastime but had once again become an aspect of official policy. A minor victim of this recidivism was the fourth Ethiopian congress scheduled to be held at Warsaw University.

It so happened that the international Haile Sellassie Prize for Ethiopian studies was awarded in 1967 to the Polish scholar Stefan Strelcyn. The Poles felt that even their new policy had to yield before so significant an event and they permitted him to travel to Addis Ababa and to accept the prize, medal and money, from the hands of Emperor Haile Sellassie. But that was the last flicker of light and concession to one who was now increasingly in the doldrums.

The long-drawn-out saga of chicanery and harassment, leading eventually to exile, need not be rehearsed here in detail. These stories are part of all regimes of oppression and appear to attract media coverage in the West on a curiously haphazard and selective basis. Open communication between Strelcyn and his friends in the free world was no longer possible, and messages, often in somewhat garbled forms, reached us by all sorts of channels. The pressure on Strelcyn and his family became very harsh, and the severance of all external contact added to the sense of isolation and abandonment. This is a time when friendship undergoes genuine tests, and the courageous are distinguished from the faint-hearted. Strelcyn was above all a proud man and he watched with dismay, but without remonstrances, the behaviour of some of his closest colleagues and collaborators.

Meanwhile his friends abroad mustered their resources; there were principally three centres of action: Beckingham at SOAS, London University (by now strategically placed as head of the Near and Middle East department and supported by the then Director of SOAS, Sir Cyril Philips), Tubiana at Paris, and Cerulli at Rome (now in turn President or Vice-President of the Lincei). In the end, London was ready first, and Strelcyn, his wife, and two sons, with little English and fewer physical means (though abundant inner resources), arrived here in November 1969. During the 1969–70 session he served as Visiting Lecturer in Semitic Studies at the School of Oriental and African Studies, but in 1970 James Barr, then Professor of Semitic languages in the University of Manchester, was able to offer him a lectureship, at first on a temporary but soon on a permanent basis, which led to a close professional and personal relationship between these two fine scholars. In 1973 Strelcyn was promoted to a readership in Semitic languages, and shortly before his death in 1981 Manchester University decided to confer upon him a personal professorship. Already in 1976 he had been elected to a Fellowship of the British Academy. He became a naturalized British citizen in 1975.

His colleagues abroad did not relax even after his safe arrival in Britain. Tubiana was soon by his side, and Cerulli organized for him an annual seminar which Strelcyn conducted at Rome during the Easter vacations. Cerulli and the Lincei were a source of constant spiritual and physical support to him. The trauma of Poland had been of massive dimensions, almost overwhelming a man of such delicate sensibility. Henceforth he would shun all public exposure and withdraw from all activities that were not scholarly in the most narrow sense. In 1966 he had been advising UNESCO on Somalia and in 1974 on Ethiopia, but the viciousness and extreme violence of the revolution in Ethiopia made him recoil from that regime in horror—another trauma added to that of Poland, another light extinguished.

II

His arrival in England, the last eleven and a half years of his life, ushers in a prodigious literary activity, so that the output of this period, at first under adverse conditions, equals that of all the preceding years of his career. His bibliography runs to some 130 items, books, articles, and reviews. His last years in particular, since he became joint editor of the *Journal of Semitic Studies* in 1976 (he had also been joint editor of the *Rocznik Orientalistyczny* from 1954 to 1968), produced some magisterial reviews which added very substantially to our knowledge of the relevant bibliography as well as the subject itself. I am thinking here in particular of the volumes published under the auspices of the Ethiopian Manuscripts Microfilming Library at Collegeville, Minn., of Hammerschmidt's Ethiopic manuscripts from Lake Tana, T. L. Kane's work on Amharic literature, and of my own edition and translation of Emperor Haile Sellassie's autobiography, to all of which he was able to add comments, observations, corrections, and general guidance of much importance and value. He was always a scrupulously fair reviewer; and in the very few cases where an aggrieved author felt impelled to engage in controversy he would either silence him by his exquisite courtesy or recoil from contamination with any display of bad manners.

His first book as well as his last one were catalogues of Ethiopian manuscripts: the first was a volume of some 300 pages dealing with the Griaule collection in the Bibliothèque Nationale at Paris, while the last one described, in 185 choice pages, the Ethiopian manuscripts acquired by the British Library (formerly part of the British Museum) since 1877. He was thus able to deal with the two finest collections of Ethiopian manuscript holdings in the world. During the 1970s he published two further books on this subject, the first about the Ethiopic manuscripts in the John Rylands University Library of Manchester (which I had begun but had had to abandon), and the second a massive tome dealing with the Ethiopian manuscript holdings of the Accademia dei Lincei (the Conti Rossini and Caetani collections). His masterly descriptions of the manuscripts of the British Library, John Rylands, and Conti Rossini were the culmination of long years spent in the pursuit of these studies, but the catalogue of the Bibliothèque Nationale was, in chronological terms, the work of a neophyte—yet it was an accomplished production that had, Athene-like, sprung fully mature from the head of its creator.

It must not be supposed that the writing of such catalogues of Ethiopic manuscripts is a mechanical or routine undertaking. In Strelcyn's hands they represented major contributions to palaeography, manuscript lore, language and literature, art and history. In a series of articles he also described the Ethiopian holdings of the Wellcome Institute of the History of Medicine in London and of the Bibliothèque Royale de Bruxelles. It may thus be said that

Strelcyn became the most accomplished connoisseur of Ethiopian manuscripts in our generation. His only friendly rival to this claim would be Dr Getatchew Haile who has been engaged for some time on the description of the thousands of manuscripts microfilmed in Ethiopia and processed at Collegeville, USA. Perhaps I may be permitted to quote at this point from my review of Strelcyn's 1978 British Library catalogue:

There is, however, one major inaccuracy on p. xiii which is wholly characteristic of the author of this catalogue. He deplores, rightly, the absence of any reliable guide to Ethiopian palaeography and the dating of MSS and then continues: 'The experience of the author of the present catalogue is also insufficient to atone for this lack of information.' In fact, however, the remarkable knowledge and instinct for reliable dating, displayed by Strelcyn in this and previous catalogues, belie the accuracy of his modest disclaimer. (*JRAS* 1979/1, p. 53.)

And this is, indeed, another reason why Ethiopian scholarship has suffered such an irreparable loss by Strelcyn's premature death: during the last year or two of his life he had been engaged on collecting material for a systematic study of Ethiopic palaeography, a subject for which his entire career had constituted an unrivalled preparation. This expertise is now lost, for those who are currently working in this field, even with the benefit of his unpublished notes, will need very many years of experience and habituation to equal his sovereign command of the subject. I may, perhaps, take this opportunity of counselling these epigones not to rush into print without the advice of Getatchew Haile.

Strelcyn's second book, which had also been started at Paris, was published at Warsaw in 1955 under the title *Prières magiques éthiopiennes*. It constituted a veritable encyclopaedia of magical lore and included a consideration of Eastern magic in general. Others had worked in this field before him, but his treatment was infinitely more detailed as well as more comprehensive and included lists of magical names, diseases, plants, animals, as well as an excellent study of the grammatical and syntactical peculiarities of this genre. The book was later on followed, over a long period, by a series of *Einzelstudien* in the form of articles in learned journals. The only sad feature of this very considerable opus was the inclusion, entirely irrelevant in that context, of extracts from A. B. Ranovitch's *Marxist Analysis of Hellenism*—no doubt a *de rigueur* (but profoundly depressing) sop to the powers that be. Tubiana, in his forthcoming obituary (*JSS*, spring 1982), says that 'Strelcyn me confiera plus tard qu'il ne l'avait pas inséré de son plein gré'.

Fortunately (at least for the present obituarist) most of Strelcyn's writings were composed in French (two of his last books were written in English as well as a few more recent articles and reviews), but his third book was in Polish. It is an extract translation of the *Kebra Nagast*, the Ethiopian national saga, together with an introduction and annotation by the learned translator. It was, in Strelcyn's own words, a popular presentation of Ethiopia's premier literary creation for the benefit of his fellow-countrymen, without any claims to originality. Regrettably, I am unable to read this book.

Strelcyn had for many years been the foremost (perhaps the only?) authority on Ethiopian traditional medicine and plants. His two volumes (Warsaw 1968 and Naples 1973, respectively), running together to close on 1,100 pages, are eloquent as well as impressive testimony to this interesting and unhackneyed specialization. Like his catalogues and writings on magic, these two books were in their turn buttressed by a series of supporting and complementing articles. Anyone anywhere in the world desirous of instruction on Ethiopian plants and the traditional pharmacopœia of that country would turn to him and would receive a prompt reply which was as meticulous in factual information as it was patient and courteous in manner.

Apart from his unfinished work on Ethiopic palaeography, there are two other areas (already referred to *en passant*) on which he had published preliminary articles but not yet the comprehensive books of synthesis that were planned: (*a*) materials for the study of early Amharic, a by-product to some extent of his work on medical and plant names in old manuscripts, were first presented to the 1963 Manchester Congress (*JSS*, spring 1964) and remained a subject of abiding interest to him; (*b*) the study and collection of all the earliest works printed in Ethiopia itself. Between 1974 and 1980 he published three considerable articles on these 'incunabula' (thus first termed, with deliberate inaccuracy, by Stephen Wright) running together to some 140 pages. In search of these rarities he would travel far and wide and spend many days in libraries poring over such curiosa.

During the last two or three days of his life I repeatedly sought his advice over the telephone on the subject of the *Hebrew Letters of Prester John* on which Charles Beckingham and I were then engaged. In fact, the Publications Officer of SOAS received a letter from him on this subject a day or two after his death. We have dedicated that book (OUP 1982) to the memory of Stefan Strelcyn.

III

In appearance Strelcyn was short and stocky, tending to a measure of portliness in his later years. His eyes were at once humorous and sad. He had a fine voice, and his French had a magnificent authenticity; his Italian was sonorous, while his English (a relatively recent acquisition) and his spoken Hebrew and Amharic were serviceable; on his Polish and his Russian my ignorance compels me to remain mute. When I visited Warsaw as his guest in 1963 he took me to concerts and theatres. Tubiana confirms that he was much attracted to the theatre and that 'il avait beaucoup pratiqué l'art de la diction'. His delivery in whatever language certainly possessed an element of care and deliberation.

He was at all times a man of great courtesy and gentleness; bad manners repelled him. Above all, he had innate dignity. He could at times be slightly ponderous, but he was never pompous. His sense of humour was well developed, and for many years an atmosphere of banter and gentle teasing prevailed between us, whether we met in London or Rome or Addis Ababa. When I scoffed at his excessive devotion to his teacher Marcel Cohen, he would reciprocate with pinpricks aimed at my admiration for my master, H. J. Polotsky; and we would indulge in mock arguments whether Polotsky or Cohen was the greater scholar. When we were unable to meet, we would speak over the telephone every week ever since he came to live in Britain.

Friendship and loyalty mattered to him deeply. His friendships, particularly for his junior colleagues, were of a very unselfish kind, and he would take great pains and endless trouble to assist them in their work and their careers. On the rare occasions when disappointment came he would be profoundly upset. Expulsion, exile, and failure by some to rise up to his human expectations had given him an understandably pessimistic outlook. His own experience of life had taught him the supreme value of loyalty, and no more dependable or loyal friend could be imagined. He was very hurt by colleagues (though he would never remonstrate with them) who were willing to accept invitations from the department, the university, and the country from which he had been extruded. Such spinelessness he would not forget; he called them invertebrates. Similarly, he thought it highly distasteful ('extrêmement dégoûtant') for people who had eagerly sought contact with Emperor Haile Sellassie in good days to disavow and to decry him when things changed in Ethiopia.

He was absolutely steadfast in all circumstances and could be relied on whatever tribulations life had in store for him or his friends. He was a man of the greatest integrity. When, not very long ago, I resigned from a committee which had to my mind become excessively politicized, he was invited to take my place. We had not discussed the matter, but without a moment's hesitation (so I learnt later) he replied to the invitation in one sentence: 'What makes you think that I am endowed with less of a conscience than the scholar whom you wish me to replace?'

Ever since he returned from his annual visit, almost a pilgrimage, to Rome and to Cerulli and the Lincei, in April 1981, he had complained of heart trouble. When talking to his colleagues at the Near Eastern Department of Manchester University, on 19 May 1981, he suddenly suffered a massive heart attack and was rushed to the adjacent hospital where he died shortly afterwards. His death brought forth quite remarkable testimonies of affection and respect from colleagues and pupils in many lands. And the University of Manchester, with its Acting Vice-Chancellor and his colleague Mervyn Richardson first and foremost, responded with characteristic generosity and tact.

His memory will be cherished wherever Ethiopian studies are cultivated.

EDWARD ULLENDORFF

Note: Cf. J. Tubiana in *JSS*, spring 1982. A full bibliography will appear in the same issue of the *JSS*. See also *The Times*, 23 May 1981.

PLATE XXVI

Elliott Fry

SIR KENNETH WHEARE

KENNETH CLINTON WHEARE

1907–1979

I

DESPITE his service as university administrator, constitutional adviser, and head of an Oxford college, it is as Gladstone Professor of Government and Public Administration that many will remember Sir Kenneth Wheare. It was as Gladstone Professor that he established his role as the leading authority on the constitution and government of Britain and the Commonwealth.

Kenneth Clinton Wheare was born at Warragul, Victoria, on 26 March 1907, the eldest son of Eustace Leonard and Kathleen Frances Wheare. He attended Scotch College, Melbourne, and later the University of Melbourne, taking first-class honours in Greek and Philosophy. In 1929 as the holder of a Rhodes scholarship, he entered Oriel College, Oxford (having, it is said, travelled by tramp steamer to the United Kingdom). Like many Rhodes scholars who followed him he read Philosophy, Politics, and Economics, the new Modern Greats combination, then only recently established. His inclination towards the politics side of the syllabus was due in some measure to the advice of one of his Melbourne Professors, Macmahon Ball. But it is possible that the philosopher W. D. Ross may have borne some responsibility for it. Years later[1] Wheare recalled the manner of his first meeting with Ross:

> He fixed the time for my tutorial at noon on Saturdays. As I was about to take my leave, he said, 'This, I imagine, will be a new experience for you, Wheare, to work on Saturday morning . . . I understand that nobody in Australia works on Saturday.' 'No, sir', I said, 'We all do.' 'Indeed', he said. But I felt that he did not entirely believe me.

To be disbelieved by an authority on the Right and the Good must have seemed an awkward preliminary to the career of a Rhodes scholar. But Wheare survived it. He went on:

> I was an enthusiastic, even dedicated student of philosophy, but unfortunately I was no good at it. His (Ross's) relief when I decided to specialise in what he described as 'the rather less rigorous' study of political science must have been considerable.

In 1932 Wheare gained a First in the Final Honour School and began work in the following year for the Beit Prize in Colonial

[1] British Academy Presidential Address 7 July 1971.

History on a topic that remained for him one of permanent interest. In 1931, the National Government had secured the enactment of the Statute of Westminster, the legislation that became the legal cornerstone of the Commonwealth of Nations—possibly the most important United Kingdom Act of Parliament of the twentieth century. Wheare's essay on the Statute won him the Beit prize and the essay was published by the Clarendon Press in 1934. In that year he was appointed as University Lecturer in Colonial History and to a research lecturership at Christ Church. It was also the year of his first marriage (to Helen Mary Allen).

During the four years of his Christ Church appointment Wheare continued to work on the topic that he had sketched out in his prize essay. The development and legal implications of Dominion status was in fact a subject that had at this period occupied the attention of a small distinguished group of scholars, some historians, some lawyers. W. K. Hancock was engaged on his wide-ranging survey of Commonwealth affairs. Professor Berriedale Keith had recently published his work on the sovereignty of the British Dominions. There was also at All Souls Richard Latham, in whose brief monograph 'The Law and the Commonwealth' lay the seeds of a revolution in constitutional thought. To these may be added the work that Wheare completed and published in 1938. *The Statute of Westminster and Dominion Status* went through five editions between 1938 and 1953. It was his first major work and has remained the standard authority on the legal and political effects of the legislation of 1931.

In 1939 John Maud (later to be Lord Redcliffe Maud) left University College to become Master of Birkbeck College. A tutorial Fellowship in Politics thus became vacant and Wheare was elected to it. In the following year he also took on two university offices, serving as a Pro-Proctor and (like his predecessor) as a university member of the City Council. The University enjoyed at that time the privilege of electing a body of councillors and aldermen to take part in the municipal government of Oxford. The system was not universally esteemed outside the University and was abolished in the local government reorganization of 1974. But for many years it provided a small group of councillors tied to neither of the two major parties, many of whom gave useful service to the council and its committees. Wheare himself was, for a time, chairman of the City Education Committee and was a councillor for seventeen years. It was a sensible form of corporate representation, now sadly lost.

In 1944 the academic study of politics in Oxford took a step forward when the single chair of Political Theory and Institutions was divided, with the creation of separate chairs for the study of Social and Political Theory (G. D. H. Cole being the first incumbent) and of Government. Wheare was elected to the Gladstone chair at the relatively early age of thirty-seven. Its remit was the study of government and public administration—though public administration has always been conceived in a broad and liberal spirit.

Wheare's second marriage (to Joan Randell) had taken place in the previous year and the following decade was an active period of research and travel in which he saw something of the practical mechanics of constitution-building. In the years between 1942 and 1948 there were significant developments in Commonwealth affairs. Australia and New Zealand adopted the relevant sections of the Statute of Westminster and the changed status of India, Pakistan, and Ceylon required new and complex British legislation. Wheare's advice was sought both by the British and by overseas governments. In 1946–7 he served as constitutional adviser to the National Convention of Newfoundland. The convention was elected to discuss the status of Newfoundland which had been under commission government since a financial crisis in 1933. Under Wheare's constitutional guidance the committee proposed confederation with the Dominion of Canada, an object that was achieved, after the holding of a referendum in Newfoundland, by the enactment in Britain of the British North America Act (No. 1) of 1949. Two years later Wheare was invited to assist the Conference on Central African Federation. That federal association was to prove an unsuccessful one, though its failure was one of politics rather than constitutional machinery.

Academically this was a remarkably productive period. In 1945, encouraged by Sir William Beveridge, a leading figure in the Federal Union movement, Wheare had published his *Federal Government*, probably the best known, or at least the most widely quoted, of his works. In 1948 there was a small volume on *Abraham Lincoln and the United States*. In 1951 the first edition of his introductory textbook *Modern Constitutions* appeared and in 1955 *Government by Committee*, an original approach to one of the major institutional devices of British government.

Few could have been better qualified to describe the anatomy and strategy of the committee world. If the Gladstone Professor did not collect committees, committees collected him. As well as advising on colonial and commonwealth matters he took on in 1947 the chairmanship of a departmental committee on Children and the Cinema (the committee that invented the 'X' certificate with ultimate consequences for both the cinema and children that Wheare afterwards regretted and deprecated). In 1948 he became a Rhodes Trustee, and in 1952 a member of the General Advisory Committee of the BBC. In 1956–7 he served on the Franks Committee on Tribunals and Enquiries. From 1959 to 1963 he was on the University Grants Committee. In Oxford, besides his local government committees, he held, in addition to his All Souls Fellowship, a Faculty Fellowship at Nuffield College from 1944 to 1957 and there was also the Hebdomadal Council on which he sat for twenty years.[1] The committee role was one in which a number of his characteristic qualities were displayed. It was said by one who knew him well that on Hebdomadal Council he was 'unobtrusively the most significant influence whilst noisier members came and went'. His interventions and phraseology would often be recalled when the substance of the issue had been forgotten. 'Over my dead body, Mr Vice-Chancellor,' he was once heard to say, of some proposal that displeased him, 'if I may take up a moderate position in this matter.'

In 1956 Wheare was elected to the Rectorship of Exeter College and relinquished his tenure of the Gladstone chair and his membership of the City Council. He was to be Rector of Exeter for the next sixteen years and to devote much of his time to its affairs. In 1956–7, however, he joined Sir Oliver (later Lord) Franks on the Committee to survey the machinery of administrative appeals and inquiries, that had been appointed in the wake of the Crichel Down affair and the agitation that emerged in the 1950s about the discretionary powers of ministers and departments. The Committee's terms of reference were to consider the working of tribunals other than the ordinary courts of law and also the procedures for holding public inquiries, particularly into the compulsory acquisition of land. The Committee sessions produced a notable collision between two different views of the administrative process. Much of the evidence given by government witnesses supported the existing arrangements (as it generally does). But the Committee set out a number of proposals designed to promote openness and impartiality in the tribunal and public inquiry mechanism and most of them were accepted and embodied in part in the 1959 Tribunals and Inquiries Act. It was one of the more successful departmental inquiries and something of a landmark in post-war English administrative law.

[1] He also, from 1974 to 1978, held the office of Clerk of the Market (for which he received from the University a salary of £8 per annum).

Shortly afterwards Wheare was again associated with Franks in the commission of inquiry set up by Oxford University into its own machinery of government. In 1964 Heads of Houses were still rotated into the Vice-Chancellorship of the University and in that year Wheare as Rector of Exeter took office as Vice-Chancellor. As a member of Hebdomadal Council he had been associated with the setting up of the Committee of Inquiry under Franks's chairmanship. Though a great deal of evidence (including the Vice-Chancellor's) was received, the report of the Committee did not lead to any radical reshaping of the University's affairs. The principal change was certainly assisted by Wheare's support. This was the creation of a consultative Conference of Colleges. The Commission had wanted something stronger—a senate or council with decision-making powers, but the University opted for a confederal rather than a federal solution. Wheare became the first chairman of the Conference of Colleges and presided over its emergence into a seemingly permanent quasi-decision-making body.

In 1966 Wheare received a knighthood and in the following year was elected to the Presidency of the British Academy (having been a member since 1952). During his presidency relations with the Royal Society were improved by the initiation of joint symposia, the first being held in December 1969 on the impact of the natural sciences on archaeology. Other developments were the move to Burlington House from Burlington Gardens and a considerable increase in the government grant to the Academy (an increase of 100 per cent from 1966–7 to 1971–2). The Academy's responsibilities in the field of the social sciences were also extended. Closer relations were established with the Social Sciences Research Council, and the annual Keynes and Radcliffe-Brown lectures were instituted in economics and social anthropology.

In 1972 Wheare resigned the Rectorship of Exeter College. For a decade he had been busy in the administration of the College and the University and had had little time to give to research. His retirement from these activities gave him an opportunity to return to writing and reviewing and to some of his earlier academic interests. In the year following his retirement from the Rectorship he delivered the Hamlyn Lectures. Miss Hamlyn, a lady of Devon and a patriot, had endowed an annual lecture series whose object was to be the

furthering among the Common People of the United Kingdom of Great Britain and Northern Ireland of the knowledge of comparative jurisprudence . . . to the intent that the Common People of the United

Kingdom may realise the privileges which in law and custom they enjoy in comparison with other European Peoples.

Wheare chose the title 'Maladministration and its Remedies' to illustrate Miss Hamlyn's thesis. In the previous year he had also delivered the British Academy lecture on a Master Mind taking as his subject Walter Bagehot. The opening words of the lecture are reminiscent of his style. A recent author, he said, seemed to disapprove of Bagehot on the ground that he was a banker and liked money. The author, moreover, found it suspicious that nobody had a word to say against him. 'But ill-nature abhors a vacuum and our author does his best to redress the balance.'

Wheare's manner of speech and writing both on public and private occasions was brisk, cheerful, and inventive. When he was installed as Chancellor of Liverpool University in 1972, he said:

> What is a Chancellor for? A figurehead. I am proud to be a figurehead of this ship. I shall hope like most figureheads—not all but most—to be pointing in the same direction as the ship is going.[1]

Dr T. C. Thomas, Vice-Chancellor of Liverpool until 1979, recalls a letter written after Wheare had delivered the University sermon in Oxford on 'The Sin of Pride'.

> I prayed for the University of Liverpool in the bidding prayer [he wrote]—the first time it has been done. It was strictly speaking irregular, but once you are in the pulpit they cannot stop you. It is too soon to expect any striking results, but in the long term they may appear.

II

Any assessment of the contribution of Sir Kenneth Wheare to the study of politics in the United Kingdom must conclude that it was both substantial and known to be so. In the post-war years he was one of the small group of academics who, through their writings and through the founding of the Political Studies Association and its journal, put the teaching of politics on a satisfactory professional basis (the others who come to mind are W. A. Robson, Sir Ivor Jennings, Sir Denis Brogan, W. J. M. Mackenzie, Sir Norman Chester, and Wilfrid Harrison). About some of the claims made for the discipline of political science Wheare had reservations. He thought, for example, that Robson went too far

---

[1] Shortly after this Wheare was enrolled as an Honorary Admiral of the Isle of Man Herring Fishery Fleet—an appointment that gave him much pleasure (and a box of kippers each year). Unfortunately no account is available of the duties of this office or of the manner in which they were discharged.

in describing political science as a master science or a key to the greater welfare, dignity, and happiness of mankind. The term itself he did not object to. But, he added: 'If I am told that what claims to be political science is no more than recent or current political and constitutional history I am prepared to postpone the argument and get on with my studies.'[1] International relations, too, he thought of as being like politics in general, a subject-matter fit to be studied by historians, lawyers, sociologists, or any other type of scholar, rather than as a separate academic discipline. He did not think of himself as very philosophically minded, but he thought it a good thing that politics in Oxford had been linked to the study of philosophy. He did not believe that philosophy was a mere service activity for political science (as Robson perhaps did).

Of his writings *Federal Government* is probably the most widely known of his works. What most undergraduates know about Federalism is that Wheare defined it. But this is not altogether true. In the first two chapters of *Federal Government* he attempts to identify a federal *principle*. 'By the federal principle', he writes, 'I mean the method of dividing powers so that the general and regional governments are each within a sphere co-ordinate and independent.'[2] Some writers have considered Wheare's approach to be both legalistic and rigid but it is neither. What he proposes is that the terms 'federal government' and 'federal constitution' should be used widely. The federal principle should be stated rigidly or precisely because it is convenient to have a name for a distinct and different principle of organization from that which has commonly been called the unitary principle. But he explains that many political constitutions that we treat as substantially federal (including the governments of Australia, Canada, and Switzerland) depart in important ways from the federal principle. The 'rigidity' of the federal principle is simply a preference for a clear and precise identification of an idea or concept. Some have preferred to treat the concept permissively, as being a matter of infinite degree, or (like chastity) less a mechanical arrangement than a state of mind; so that it is found broadly distributed in a wide range of circumstances. On such a view it can be said to occur wherever there are social, financial, or psychological signs or 'instrumentalities' of regional independence. But this is to leave no serious or clear use for the term 'federal'.

The facility for comparison and selection that appeared in *Federal Government* can be seen in the two small volumes originally

[1] 'The Teaching of Political Science', *Political Studies*, 3 (1955), 70.
[2] *Federal Government*, 4th edn. (1963), p. 10.

published in the Home University library, *Modern Constitutions* and *Legislatures*. *Modern Constitutions*, though an introductory work, stood almost alone when it appeared, in a field that had been greatly neglected. It is simply conceived and written, defining and describing various types of constitution, discussing their establishment and authority, and explaining the way in which they are amended or changed by formal and informal processes. It concludes with a discussion of constitutional usage and convention— a topic that Wheare had found important in his study of commonwealth government (and which is the subject of chapter 1 of *The Statute of Westminster and Dominion Status*). He accepts the view propounded in Dicey's *Law of the Constitution* that conventions are rules of behaviour regarded as obligatory by those engaged in the working of the constitution and not enforced (though they may in some circumstances be recognized) by courts of law. Wheare did not subscribe to the view of some writers that law and convention can be treated as fundamentally similar in character, though he notes the possibility that conventions may be as important as or more important than laws; or may nullify the effects of laws; or may be incorporated by legislation into constitutional laws. He dissents from Dicey's opinion that in the British Parliamentary system conventions are designed to secure the ultimate supremacy of the electorate as the sovereign power in the state, pointing out that the purpose and ambit of conventions is much wider than this. They may protect civil liberties, or regulate the relationships of two Houses of the legislature or fix the relative powers of the executive and legislative branches of government, or link the workings of political parties with that of the formal legal institutions of the political system.

The little companion volume *Legislatures* has many of the virtues of its predecessor. One of them is that it helps the student to resolve a dilemma that confronts him in beginning the study of political institutions. It is impossible to compare institutions in general without some fairly detailed knowledge of some particular governments or institutions. Yet the working of particular governments may only become significant against a background knowledge of institutions that work differently. You cannot—as Bagehot knew—see what the important characteristics of cabinet government are without knowing what they are not and what happens in a non-cabinet system. So the utility of a simply written comparative work that exhibits with examples the varieties of legislative behaviour is very great, since it gives the beginner a readable framework in which he can arrange his ideas about

British Parliamentary behaviour. It is also a specific against parochialism and the view that what is familiar cannot be arranged differently—a common enough view in the philosophy of British administration. Wheare tells us, for example, that the British House of Commons is uncommonly large. The physical arrangements made for our elected representatives, though lately improved, are by comparative standards spartan. Unlike some political systems ours has in the post-war years been slow to contemplate intermediate situations between cabinet autocracy and *gouvernement d'assemblée*. These questions, clearly posed in Wheare's small study in the early 1960s, have not become less important in the 1980s.

In *Government by Committee* published in the mid-1950s Wheare used his comparative technique within the British political system to cut a furrow that would expose the character of a particular type of behaviour—namely, that form of behaviour exemplified at various levels by committee work. The book (subtitled 'An Essay on the British Constitution') was an ambitious one and perhaps a narrower focus might have improved it, but it is ingeniously constructed and a joy to read. Committees are classified by function. There is negotiation, administration, legislation, scrutiny, and inquiry. Within each function there are strategies and tactics of committee-making. There are committees to pacify, committees to delay, committees to kill, and committees for form's sake. There are committee characters of various kinds, some of their ploys being reminiscent of Stephen Potter's gamesmen (*One-Upmanship* was published in 1952). A particular feature of the committee world, clearly painted, is the blending of the professional and non-professional—the collaboration of the expert with what Jeremy Bentham called the 'lay-gent', the common law's ordinary reasonable man, found at every level of British administration. The good layman, Wheare tells us:

must have all the virtues of the reasonable man and all the virtues of the unreasonable woman. Indeed some of the best laymen are women and unreasonable women at that. It is the quality . . . of being unable to see the sense of what is being done, of questioning the whole basis of organisation . . . It is against criticism of this kind that officials and experts should be required to justify their proposals and procedures in public administration.[1]

That intuition about the control of administration was perhaps vindicated in the 1960s when the debate on administrative reform

---

[1] *Government by Committee* (1955), p. 23.

terminated not in the creation of more specialized instruments of control but in the creation of a 'lay-gent' in the person of the ombudsman to investigate public complaints about the Civil Service. In *Maladministration and its Remedies*, his last published work, Wheare sets out the history of the adoption of the Parliamentary Commissioner system, compares it with the operations of the French administrative courts and discusses the complexity of the term 'maladministration'. His conclusion is that the Parliamentary Commissioner had been effective in strengthening the machinery of control over ministerial discretion, though he adds that the success of an ombudsman is likely to be greatest in the sort of political and constitutional community that needs him least, being more likely to make good government better than to make bad government good. There are also some reflections on the impact of recent changes on the traditional theory of individual ministerial responsibility. There are occasions, for example, he says, when it may be the duty of a civil servant to thrust responsibility on a minister ('one can see that the nastiest moment for a minister is when a civil servant says to him "Will you order me to do this? If so I will obey." That is individual ministerial responsibility with a vengeance.'). He is equally clear that the legislation of 1967 has made a difference in both theory and practice to that sense of ministerial responsibility in which civil servants remain anonymous and have their sins and successes attributed to ministers. The activities of the Parliamentary Commissioners can only work on the supposition that there is a separation of some acts of an administrator from those of his minister, a supposition that the traditional theory finds it hard to accommodate.

Bureaucracy and the British Constitution continued to occupy Wheare's thoughts and it was one of the major themes of a manuscript that he had almost completed at the time of his death. He had given it the title 'Towards a Working Theory of the British Constitution'. It was to be a study of the present-day theory of checks and balances within the British political system. Prominent amongst the external checks on government is, he suggests, the right to strike, which can be considered in effect as a part of the machinery of government (in a wide sense). The book would have been a venture of a more theoretical kind than any of Wheare's previous writings. A section of the manuscript deals with the role of beliefs and doctrines held by the public at large, some of which may be inconsistent with each other. Egalitarianism, for example, may be at odds with 'differentialism'.

('The same trade unionists who claim egalitarianism in the franchise, in pensions, in the National Health Service and in Social Security may be strongly in favour of differentials.') There is also a pervasive idea of fairness that finds a place in many statutory contexts. (Fair rents, fair hearings, fair dismissals, and fair employment practices.) But a threat to balanced government besides being posed by possibly unstable external forces is also to be found within the government machine in the bureaucracy itself, now increased in size and increasingly unionized. This last development has threatened the separation of the bureaucracy as servants of the Crown from political activity. (Many bureaucrats, of course, never have been servants of the Crown, but that only shows that our theory of state functions and public employees is an untidy one.)

Some modern developments, Wheare thought, reinforced the imbalance rather than remedying it. Devolution and decentralization of power, for example, created more governmental activity at more levels and bred more officials.

Most of these themes are briefly sketched. Fully developed they would have illuminated the non-Parliamentary parts of the constitution that Wheare came to see as having taken on as large a role as the central legislative machinery. He was prepared to dub the modern British system not Parliamentary or cabinet government but 'Parliamentary Bureaucracy'.

The other project on which Wheare had been working in the late 1970s was a biography of Sir George Cornewall Lewis, the Victorian statesman and author. Many people now remember Lewis as an author, if they remember him at all, only because Walter Bagehot made a joke about him. Lewis wrote a large number of books and articles on a large number of subjects including early Roman history, ancient astronomy, the law of extradition, and the government of dependencies. In 1849 he published *The Influence of Authority in Matters of Opinion*, about which Bagehot said that it was written to show that if you did not know anything about a subject you should ask somebody who did. Wheare's interest, however, was almost certainly drawn to Lewis by his two works on political science, *Remarks on the Use and Abuse of Some Political Terms* and the much longer and duller *Treatise on the Methods of Observation and Reasoning in Politics*. The first of these, Wheare thought, was a praiseworthy exercise in clarification and an attempt to do in part for political science what John Austin had done for jurisprudence. Wheare's judgement on Lewis was that 'he clarified and purified part of the vocabulary of political studies'. This, he added, 'is a small achievement, but it is not trivial nor negligible'.[1]

If one had to make a judgement about Wheare's own contribution to political science it would be that his writings on the structure and development of the Commonwealth will be thought of as his most distinctive and valuable work. In the forefront stands the classic study of the Statute of Westminster. The Statute and its interpretation are still a matter of severe disagreement and Wheare's book, remarkable for the clarity of its exposition of the complex issues involved, is still appealed to as an authority on the Statute. What its intentions were in many respects remained unclear after 1931. At the time of its passage Mr Winston Churchill said that it was the plainest Act of Parliament that he had ever read and that it was not obscure or cryptic. But Churchill was wrong and it has proved to be both. The general intent of the Statute was indeed clear—namely, to give legal effect to the political equality of status of the Dominions, recognized in the Balfour declaration of 1926 and echoed in the statutory preamble in 1931. It was intended, therefore, to release the Dominions from the paramountcy of the Imperial Parliament and to empower them to amend their own constitutions. But besides raising basic and as yet unanswered questions about the sovereignty of the United Kingdom Parliament, it has given rise to difficult internal questions for the constitutions of the Commonwealth countries. The technique of Imperial abdication involved what in current terms might be called a patriation of constituent authority to the Parliaments of Australia, South Africa, Canada, New Zealand, Newfoundland, and the Irish Free State. But in the federal Dominions that power if unqualified would have arguably enabled their federal Parliaments to overturn the federal structure and so it was qualified. In the other dominions it was not. But both the qualifications and their absence have caused constitutional crises and litigation, first in Ireland, then in South Africa, and most recently in Canada. But all the major questions that have come into issue were foreseen by Wheare and are discussed in the various editions of *The Statute of Westminster and Dominion Status* published between 1938 and 1953.

Then there was the invention or exposition of the theory of constitutional 'autochthony'—one of the few (perhaps Cornewall Lewis-like) innovations in the vocabulary of post-war political science. It is to be found in Wheare's *Constitutional Structure of the*

---

[1] 'Sir George Cornewall Lewis as a Political Scientist', *Political Studies*, xx (1972), 407, at 420.

Commonwealth written in the late 1950s and published in 1960. This was not a revision or remodelling of his earlier work. It is written to an entirely different plan and discusses a wider range of topics. It is an examination, not of the original Dominion constitutions but of all the Commonwealth constitutions as they have developed in the post-war years. The method is, of course, selective, rather than comprehensive. Each chapter introduces and illustrates an idea or concept. There are chapters on the vocabulary of the Commonwealth, on its symbols, on the concept of membership, and on the modes of co-operation. Three of the central chapters are devoted to the ideas and implications of 'Equality of Status', of 'Autonomy', and of 'Autochthony'. 'Autochthony' puts a name to a pattern of behaviour that needed one. It differs from autonomy since that merely indicates the ability of a Commonwealth member country (as we must now clumsily call it) to change all of its laws without the intervention of the United Kingdom Parliament. But some members, Wheare pointed out, having tasted autonomy wanted a stronger brew. They wanted to say not merely that their institutions were no longer legally subordinate to those of the Imperial Parliament but that they were in some sense rooted in their own soil and had the force of law for that reason and not because they were given it by British legislation. Wheare traces the search for this ideal in Ireland, India, Pakistan, and Canada. He predicts that as Commonwealth countries gain independence and autonomy they will embody their constitutional instruments in a local document which they will claim owes its validity to no outside authority but to themselves. (In legal terms this will be false, but in most cases there will be no occasion or necessity for testing its falsity.)

We see here a genuine piece of constitutional metaphysics. Many questions about the Commonwealth and its headship and its forms of association indeed border on the metaphysical. But many of these formal, legal, or symbolic questions throw their shadows into the real world. Kenneth Wheare knew this and showed this. No one has more clearly explained and analysed the connections between formal structures and political reality in the government of the Commonwealth and the United Kingdom.

III

In 1979 Wheare was compelled to resign his office as Chancellor of Liverpool University when the illness against which he had struggled for some time seriously restricted his physical

capacities. He died on 7 September 1979. Throughout the difficulties of his illness his determination and cheerfulness stayed with
him. Those indeed were qualities that at any time would have
been brought to mind by any mention of his name in Oxford in the
post-war years. His colleagues would have added shrewdness and
a breadth of judgement that was direct but never immodest or self-
promoting. Those who were taught and examined by him would
have added generosity. His criticism could be sharply expressed
but he always wanted to let a viewpoint emerge or to find the
merits that would get the candidate through. Sir Norman
Chester, who knew him well, wrote of him that:

> He was a Politics man in the older sense of the term. He was familiar
> with the great writers in the field—both in theory and in institutions and
> concerned himself with the issues which had fascinated them. I suppose
> he was considered old fashioned. Certainly he would readily admit an
> inadequate knowledge of the socio-political forces in left-wing Pata-
> gonia or an inability to benefit from much of the fare provided for
> example by the *European Journal of Political Research*. . . . He believed that
> those who taught how political systems worked should be able to analyse
> any form of government.'[1]

Sir Edgar Williams in his annual private letter to Rhodes
scholars, written as Warden of Rhodes House in 1979, set down
some reminiscences of his public manner:

> As a speaker he was uniquely a creator of mood. When you came
> away chuckling still it would have been difficult to face a viva on exactly
> what he had said, how it had been phrased, but the tonic did not die with
> midnight. . . . He had a gift for parody, especially of his opponents'
> position, which he undermined so thoroughly that it was impossible to
> return to it, the foundations having been laughed away.

He added that:

> He seemed to have reached some curious decision by the time I got to
> know him well . . . that he would go straight from the role of the young
> professor, eschewing middle age, to the privileges, without the dis-
> advantages, of ripe old age. Behind this superficial whimsicality there
> was a very remarkable will. . . . People who threatened resignation were
> handed a pen across the table to put it in writing forthwith. . . . Physi-
> cally he seemed frail, but he was a man of the utmost resolution and
> when he held something to be wrong, wrong it remained and he would
> stand against it.

Sir Edgar concluded:

> He had a habit of backing into the limelight and quickly disappearing

[1] *Political Studies*, xxviii (1980), pp. i–ii.

again to get on with his work. He was an irreplaceable spirit, a wise and witty scholar who mocked the bogus and pricked the pretentious, and who found in the happiness of his family a safe refuge and a chaotic serenity.

That portrait would be recognized immediately by all who knew Kenneth Wheare, and especially by that large number of us who were guided and encouraged by him in the way of scholarship. He was immune to bluster or fashion and he cherished his privacy, the character of the public person being shaped by the instinct and humour of the man.

GEOFFREY MARSHALL

Note: I am much indebted to Lady Wheare and to a number of Sir Kenneth Wheare's friends and colleagues for assistance and information; and particularly to Sir Norman Chester and Sir Edgar Williams.

BIBLIOGRAPHY

1933   *The Statute of Westminster 1931*. Clarendon Press, 1933.

1938   *The Statute of Westminster and Dominion Status*. Oxford University Press, 1938. 5th edn. 1953.

1945   *Federal Government*. Oxford University Press, 1945. 4th edn. 1963.

1946   'The Machinery of Government' (inaugural lecture), *Public Administration*, xxiv (1946), 75.

1948   *Abraham Lincoln and the United States*. Hodder & Stoughton (English Universities Press), 1948.
        'The British Constitution in 1947', *Parliamentary Affairs*, i (summer, 1948), 8.
        'Recent Constitutional Developments in the British Commonwealth', *Journal of Comparative Legislation*, xxx (1948), 75.
        Review of L. S. Amery, *Thoughts on the Constitution*, *Public Administration*, xxvi (1948), 130.

1949   Review of Harvey Walker, *The Legislative Process*, ibid, xxvii (1949), 225.

1950   'Is the British Commonwealth Withering Away?', *American Political Science Review*, xliv (1950), 545.
        'The Impact of Federalism upon Parliamentary Government in the Commonwealth', *Parliamentary Affairs*, iv (1950-1), 163.
        Review of D. V. Cowen, *Parliamentary Sovereignty and the Entrenched Sections of the South Africa Act*, ibid., iv (1950-1), 484.

1951   *Modern Constitutions*. Oxford University Press, 1951.
        Review of Charles S. Hyneman, *Bureaucracy in a Democracy*, *Public Administration*, xxix (1951), 144.

1953   'The Nature and Structure of the Commonwealth', *American Political Science Review*, xlvii (1953), 1016.
        Review of Arthur Berriedale Keith, *The British Constitutional System* (2nd edn., ed. Gibbs), *Political Studies*, i (1953), 86.
        Review of L. S. Amery, *Thoughts on the Constitution*, *Parliamentary Affairs*, vii (1953-4), 348

1954   'The Teaching of International Relations: a Comment', *Political Studies*,
       ii (1954), 274.
       'A Vindication of the British Constitution' (broadcast), *Public Admini-
       stration*, xxxii (1954), 403.
       Errata on 'Civil Service Reform', ibid., xxxii. 323.
       Review of Louise Overacker, *The Australian Party System*, *Political Studies*,
       ii (1954), 181.
1955   *Government by Committee*. Oxford University Press, 1955.
       'The Teaching of Political Science', *Political Studies*, iii (1955), 70.
       Review of Lord Campion, *European Parliamentary Procedure*, ibid., iii
       (1955), 84.
       Review of V. Venkata Rao, *The Prime Minister*, *Public Administration*,
       xxxiii (1955), 108.
1056   Review of The Commission on Intergovernmental Relations, *A Report to
       the President for Transmittal to the Congress*, *American Political Science Review*, l
       (1956), 208.
       Review of ed. A. B. Lal, *The Indian Parliament*, *Public Administration*, xxxiv
       (1956), 437.
       Review of J. D. Miller, *Australian Government and Politics*, *Political Studies*,
       iv (1956), 106.
       Review of O. C. Williams, *The Clerical Organisation of the House of
       Commons, 1661–1850*, ibid., iv (1956), 100.
1958   Review of W. J. M. Mackenzie, *Central Administration in Britain*, ibid., vi
       (1958), 280.
1960   *Constitutional Structure of the Commonwealth*. Oxford University Press,
       1960.
       Booknote, 'Law Among States in Federacy', *American Political Science
       Review*, liv (1960), 795.
       Review of ed. R. N. Spann, *Public Administration in Australia*, *Public
       Administration*, xxxviii (1960), 187.
1961   Review of D. V. Cowen, *The Foundations of Freedom*, *Journal of Common-
       wealth Political Studies*, i (1961–2), 237.
1962   'The Redress of Grievances' (review article of Report by *Justice* on the
       Citizen and the Administration), *Public Administration*, xl (1962), 125.
1963   Review of *Parliaments* (study by the Inter-Parliamentary Union),
       Political Studies, xi (1963), 238.
1964   Review of ed. N. Mansergh, *Documents and Speeches on Commonwealth
       Affairs, 1952–62*, *Journal of the Parliaments of the Commonwealth*, xlv (1964),
       234.
1967   'The Universities in the News' (lecture). Cambridge University Press,
       1967.
       Review of works on the Commonwealth, *Political Studies*, xv (1967), 256.
1968   *Legislatures*. Oxford University Press, 1963. 2nd edn. 1968.
       Review of G. E. Caiden, *The Commonwealth Bureaucracy*, *Public Administra-
       tion*, xlvi (1968), 459.
       Review of Sir Robert Menzies, *Central Power in the Australian Common-
       wealth*, *Journal of the Parliaments of the Commonwealth*, xlix (1968), 49.
1970   Review of works on Federalism, *Political Studies*, xviii (1970), 573.
1972   'Sir George Cornewall Lewis as a Political Scientist', ibid. xx (1972),
       407.
1973   *Maladministration and its Remedies*. Stevens, 1973.

1973   Review of R. A. Chapman, *The Role of Commissions in Policy Making*, *Political Studies*, xxi (1973), 399.

1974   'Walter Bagehot (Lecture on a Master Mind)', *Proceedings of the British Academy*, lx (1974), 173.
        'Tribunals and Procedures' (review article), *Parliamentary Affairs*, xxviii (1974–5), 225.
        Review of ed. A. W. B. Simpson, *Oxford Essays in Jurisprudence*, 2nd ser., *Political Studies*, xxii (1974), 502.
        Review of R. N. Spann, *Public Administration in Australia*, 2nd edn., *Public Administration*, lii (1974), 235.

1975   'Crichel Down Re-visited', *Political Studies*, xxiii (1975), 268.
        Review of R. Gregory and P. Hutcheson, *The Parliamentary Ombudsman*, *Public Administration*, liii (1975), 446.

1976   'Law and Politics' (review article), *Parliamentary Affairs*, xxix (1976), 455.

1977   'The Constitutional Consequences of Mr. Wilson' (review article), ibid., xxx (1977), 337.

1978   'Australia's Constitutional Crisis' (review article on Gareth Evans (ed.)), *Labour and the Constitution 1972–1975: the Whitlam Years in Australian Government*, *The Parliamentarian*, lix (1978), 66.
        'Does it Really Exist? Some Reflections upon the Contemporary British Constitution' (review article), *Parliamentary Affairs*, xxxi (1978), 213.
        Review of Lord Hailsham, *The Dilemma of Democracy*, *The Parliamentarian*, lix (1978), 277.

1979   'Chairing the Rhodes Trust', *American Oxonian*, lxvi (1979), 236.
        'Law and Constitution' (review article), *Parliamentary Affairs*, xxxii (1979), 236.
        Review of L. F. Crisp, *Australian National Government*, *The Parliamentarian*, lx (1979), 61.

1981   Foreword to A. F. Madden and W. H. Morris-Jones, *Australia and Britain: Studies in a Changing Relationship*, Cass, 1981.